The Organization of Learning

LD   **Learning, Development, and**
&CC   **Conceptual Change**

Lila Gleitman, Susan Carey, Elissa Newport, and Elizabeth Spelke, editors

Names for Things: A study in Human Learning, John Macnamara, 1982

Conceptual Change in Childhood, Susan Carey, 1985

"Gavagai!" or the Future History of the Animal Language Controversy, David Premack, 1986

Systems That Learn: An Introduction to Learning Theory for Cognitive and Computer Scientists, Daniel N. Osherson, Scott Weinstein, and Michael Stob, 1986

From Simple Input to Complex Grammar, James L. Morgan, 1986

Categorization and Naming in Children: Problems of Induction, Ellen M. Markman, 1989

Concepts, Kinds and Cognitive Development, Frank C. Keil, 1989

The Organization of Learning, C. R. Gallistel, 1990

The Organization of Learning

C. R. Gallistel

A Bradford Book
The MIT Press
Cambridge, Massachusetts
London, England

First MIT Press paperback edition, 1993

This book was set in Palatino by the MIT Press. It was printed and bound in the United States of America.

Library of Congress Cataloging-in-Publication Data

Gallistel, C. R., 1941–
    The organization of learning.

    (Learning, development, and conceptual change)
    "A Bradford book."
    Includes index.
    1. Learning in animals. 2. Cognition in animals.
I. Title. II. Series.
QL785.G22   1989   153.1'5   88-26656
ISBN 0-262-07113-4   (HB),   0-262-57098-X (PB)

To A. F. and E. R.

Contents

Series Foreword   viii
Acknowledgments   ix

Chapter 1
A Computational-Representational Approach   1

Chapter 2
Representations   15

Chapter 3
Navigation   35

Chapter 4
Dead Reckoning   57

Chapter 5
The Cognitive Map   103

Chapter 6
The Geometric Module in the Rat   173

Chapter 7
Biological and Computational Foundations for the
Representation of Time   221

Chapter 8
Time of Occurrence   243

Chapter 9
Temporal Intervals   287

Chapter 10
Number   317

Chapter 11
Rate   351

Chapter 12
Classical Conditioning: Modern Results and Theory   385

Chapter 13
Classical Conditioning: A Representational Model   421

Chapter 14
Vector Spaces in the Nervous System   475

Chapter 15
The Unity of Remembered Experience   523

Chapter 16
The Search for the Engram   561

Chapter 17
Synthesis   581

References   597
Index   623

Series Foreword

This series in learning, development, and conceptual change will include state-of-the-art reference works, seminal book-length monographs, and texts on the development of concepts and mental structures. It will span learning in all domains of knowledge, from syntax to geometry to the social world, and will be concerned with all phases of development, from infancy through adulthood.

The series intends to engage such fundamental questions as

The nature and limits of learning and maturation: The influence of the environment, of initial structures, and of maturational changes in the nervous system on human development; learnability theory; the problem of induction; domain-specific constraints on development.

The nature of conceptual change: conceptual organization and conceptual change in child development, in the acquisition of expertise, and in the history of science.

Lila Gleitman
Susan Carey
Elissa Newport
Elizabeth Spelke

Acknowledgments

I wrote most of the initial draft of this book while on sabbatical leave as a Fellow at the Center for Advanced Study in the Behavioral Sciences. I am grateful for financial support from the Alfred P. Sloan Foundation while at the Center. I am also grateful to the staff there, particularly to Margaret O'Mara and Bruce Harley whose help in obtaining source material was invaluable. The first draft of the representational theory of classical conditioning was done during the month that I was at the Center for Interdisciplinary Research (ZiF) at the University of Bielefeld as a member of the workgroup on "Perception and Action." I am grateful for the support there and for the atmosphere, which was ideal for work that required prolonged periods of intense concentration. I am grateful also to Jürgen Engels, who refreshed my knowledge of matrix algebra. Many colleagues have read and commented critically on drafts of various parts of the manuscript and/or discussed the material with me at length. Heartfelt gratitude for comments and discussion goes to Ken Cheng, Russ Church, Tom Collett, Ruth Colwill, Nelson Donegan, Rochel Gelman, Paul Glimcher, Jim Gould, Dottie Jameson, George Mandler, Jack Nachmias, Frank Norman, David Olton, Harold Pashler, Ed Pugh, Paul Rozin, Roger Shepard, Peter Shizgal, Liz Spelke, Saul Sternberg, Meg Waraczynski, and Jeff Wine. If I have inadvertently left anyone off this list, I beg forgiveness. I have profited greatly from discussion with my colleagues at the University of Pennsylvania over the years, and I am grateful to them all for the contributions they have made to my education. I acknowledge support for my research from NSF Grant BNS-8619759, which helped defray some of the costs of preparing the manuscript for publication. I am grateful to Ken Cheng and Alan Spector for calling to my attention a number of typographical errors and inaccuracies in the text and figures, which have been corrected in this paperback edition.

The Organization of Learning

Chapter 1
A Computational-Representational Approach

On the featureless Tunisian desert, a long-legged, fast-moving ant leaves the protection of the humid nest on a foraging expedition. It moves across the desert in tortuous loops, running first this way, then that, but gradually progressing ever farther away from the life-sustaining humidity of the nest. Finally it finds the carcass of a scorpion, uses its strong pincers to gouge out a chunk nearly its own size, then turns to orient to within one or two degrees of the straight line between itself and the nest entrance, a 1–millimeter–wide hole, 40 meters distant. It runs a straight line for 43 meters, holding its course by maintaining its angle to the sun. Three meters past the point at which it should have encountered the entrance, the ant abruptly breaks into the search pattern by which it eventually locates it. A witness to this homeward journey finds it hard to resist the inference that the ant on its search for food possessed at every moment a representation of its position relative to the entrance to the nest, a spatial representation that enabled it to compute the solar angle and the distance of the homeward journey from wherever it happened to encounter food.

The naturalist normally breakfasts on his terrace punctually at 8 a.m. He has grown used to the buzz of bees around the marmalade. Under the press of work, he advances his breakfast to 7 a.m. and is surprised at first that there are no bees. He knows that they begin their shuttle between nectar sources and hive as soon as the sun rises, so why are they not there when he breakfasts an hour before his usual time? Within a few days, they are there at the new time. Intrigued, he postpones his breakfast to 9:00 and watches to see whether they come at 7:00, which in fact they do; they mostly show up between 6:30 and 7:00. If he puts marmalade out at 9:00 for a few days, the bees begin to show up between 8:30 and 9:00. He infers that bees represent the time of day at which nectar is available at a given source and time their visits to that source accordingly.

On another continent at a lower latitude, another naturalist has set up an artificial flower to study the strategy that hummingbirds use to monopolize the nectar sources. The naturalist shoos off every visitor but the hummingbird whose strategy he wishes to study. Each time the hummingbird visits the plastic source of sugar water and empties it, the naturalist waits 10 minutes before refilling it. At first the bird comes back only a few minutes after emptying it, but on these overly hasty visits it finds it empty. Soon it adjusts its intervisit interval to an average of a little more than 10 minutes. If, however, it once finds it empty, its next visit comes much sooner, because the only way it can monopolize this resource is by timing its visits to anticipate those of the other birds and bees. If the naturalist adopts a protocol whereby the amount of sugar water is doubled 20 minutes after the last emptying, then, after one or two tardy but more bountifully rewarded visits, the bird lengthens its average intervisit interval to more than 20 minutes. The naturalist suspects that birds represent interevent intervals and adjust their behavior accordingly.

Every day two naturalists go out to a pond where some ducks are overwintering and station themselves about 30 yards apart. Each carries a sack of bread chunks. Each day a randomly chosen one of the naturalists throws a chunk every 5 seconds; the other throws every 10 seconds. After a few days experience with this drill, the ducks divide themselves in proportion to the throwing rates; within 1 minute after the onset of throwing, there are twice as many ducks in front of the naturalist that throws at twice the rate of the other. One day, however, the slower thrower throws chunks twice as big. At first the ducks distribute themselves two to one in favor of the faster thrower, but within 5 minutes they are divided fifty-fifty between the two "foraging patches." This behavior is predicted by a model of an evolutionarily stable foraging strategy. The model assumes that ducks and other foraging animals can represent rates of return, the number of items per unit time multiplied by the average size of an item.

Yet another naturalist observes that night crawlers are among the important foods of the population of gulls that she is studying, but the night crawlers come out only after heavy rains. She observes that the gulls fly to the fields where they forage for night crawlers only on the mornings after heavy rains. She concludes that either gulls are born with a rather particular knowledge of the natural habits of night crawlers or they are capable of learning a conditional rate (of return), the rate of occurrence of some event conditional upon the occurrence of some other event.

These naturalists are witness to the myriad roles that the capacity to learn plays in the everyday behavior of animals. It would appear from these examples that animals learn the spatial and temporal relationships in their environments and use this knowledge to orient and time their behavior. One might expect that the experimental study of learning by psychologists would serve to clarify just what representations different animals can and cannot compute and something about the nature of the computations by which the animals derive these representations. By and large, one would be disappointed in this expectation because experimental psychologists do not generally view the phenomena of learning within a representational framework. It is my purpose to argue that they should.

My purpose is to sketch a new framework for the understanding of animal learning and the investigation of its cellular basis. In the framework here elaborated, quantities computed and stored by the nervous system represent aspects of the animal's environment and its relation to that environment. Thus I term this framework, a *computational-represen tational framework*. I use the term *representation* in its mathematical sense. The brain is said to represent an aspect of the environment when there is a functioning isomorphism between an aspect of the environment and a brain process that adapts the animal's behavior to it. Chapter 2 explains and illustrates the concept of a functioning isomorphism.

The representation of space and time play fundamental roles in the view to be elaborated. By the representation of space, I mean the representation of the geometric relationships among surfaces in the animal's environment and its momentary geometric relationship to them—the macroscopic shape of the environment and the animal's position within that shape. By the representation of time, I mean the representation of the times at which events have occurred (in a fixed temporal framework) and the representation of temporal intervals.

The evidence that animals represent space is drawn almost entirely from data on the courses they pursue in moving through their environment. Mobile organisms need to pursue courses adapted to the shapes of the spaces they live in. The ability to represent geometric relations among surfaces may be primitive in two senses. First, it evolved very early and is found in most mobile animals that possess a central nervous system. Second, it is a foundation upon which representations of other aspects of the environment are built.

There is neurophysiological evidence for the representation of high-level spatial relations by the nervous system of vertebrates. For example, the vertebrate nervous system maps the angular position of both visual and auditory stimulus sources onto the surface of the tectum in an orderly way (Knudsen 1982; Sparks and Nelson 1987). Neurons in the CA3 field of the hippocampus fire when the animal occupies a particular position in the environment, regardless of how it is oriented (Muller, Kubie, and Ranck 1987), while cells in the presubiculum fire when the rat's head is oriented in a particular compass direction regardless of where the rat is (Ranck 1984). Since the firing of neural elements depends upon the geometric relations between the animal and its environment, we must develop theories about how the animal represents space if we want to understand how the nervous system works. To do this, we need to know what it is about space that animals represent. The best way to get that information is from the study of how they determine their courses through their environment.

Navigation refers to the body of theory and practice that deals explicitly with the determination of courses. Chapters 3 through 6 are concerned with animal navigation. Navigation connotes the determination of marine courses that cover long distances, but I use it to refer to the determination of courses of any length anywhere because the principles appear to be the same regardless of the length of the course or the terrain traversed. In my usage, the toad determining its course around a small barrier between it and a mealworm is navigating just as much as is the migratory bird setting off from Nova Scotia en route to Argentina. While I believe we unconsciously apply principles of navigation in our routine daily movements, these principles have been given an explicit formulation only in marine and aeronautical navigation, and they are not well known. The section on animal navigation begins with a chapter on the principles of marine navigation.

Dead reckoning is a basic aspect of navigation whose role is little understood or appreciated by nonnavigators. The term is thought to be a corruption of *deduced reckoning* (from the abbreviation *ded. reckoning*). It refers to the process of updating one's estimate of one's position on the basis of knowledge of how fast one has been moving, in what direction, for how long. Chapter 4 reviews evidence that this process plays a fundamental role in the navigation of animals ranging from ants to humans. It also argues that the moment-to-moment representation of position in the dead reckoning subsystem (module) provides positional input to the process that constructs a map of the environment.

Dead reckoning is the process by which a navigator keeps track of his position when it is inconvenient or impossible to determine that position by observing recognizable points in the environment. *Piloting* refers to navigation done by reference to a map and the observation of points represented on that map (landmarks). The essence of piloting is orienting with respect to what cannot currently be observed by reference to what can currently be observed and to a map. The map, which represents the geometrical relationships between the observed and unobserved points, confers the ability to orient toward that which is not currently observed by reference to whatever is currently observed. Chapter 5 reviews evidence that animals from insects to humans routinely perform this feat, which leads to the conclusion that they possess the spatial representation upon which the feat depends: a map of their environment.

A map is a representation of geometrical relationships. If one concludes from the evidence of animal navigation that the animal makes and uses such a representation, it is natural to ask what sorts of geometrical relationships the map preserves. Ordinary maps preserve the relative positions of points, coded by, for example, Cartesian coordinates. Hence they preserve every kind of geometrical relation because geometrical relations such as "perpendicular to" or "collinear with" exist among points or point sets (lines and surfaces) by virtue of their relative positions. However, it is possible to have maps that do not preserve relative positions in the full sense of the term. These "weaker" maps preserve only certain classes of geometric relations. Their coordinates do not specify relative position as completely as do Cartesian coordinates. Chapter 6 reviews experiments designed to test what classes of geometric relations are preserved in the cognitive map a rat uses for navigation. They show that all classes are preserved. In short, the rat has a map in the ordinary sense of the term, a Euclidean (distance- and angle-preserving) representation of the relative positions of the points in its environment.

An unexpected byproduct of the experiments on the geometric power of a rat's representation of space was evidence that the computations by which a rat establishes its position and heading within a mapped space rely solely upon the shape of the perceived environment. These computations appear to make no use of the distinctive nongeometric properties of surfaces, such as whether a surface is black or white, smooth or rough, or smells of peppermint, although these properties of surfaces are clearly remembered and used for other behavioral purposes. The system for determining position and heading appears to be a module in Fodor's (1983) sense. It is impenetrable to (can make no use of) nongeometric data, even when those data are relevant to the task. Chapter 6 explains this impenetrability in terms of the kind of global computation upon which the determination of position and heading is presumed to depend. It gives reasons why that kind of computation is more suitable than other kinds and why it is unlikely to lead to difficulties under normal conditions.

In chapter 7, the focus switches to the representation of time. For more than fifty years, there have been experimental data showing that animals ranging from insects to humans are tuned to the times at which individual events occur and to the temporal intervals separating events, but the conclusion that they could represent time itself has been strongly resisted, perhaps because it is difficult to think of this representation as a stimulus trace. What is the stimulus of which a temporal representation is a trace?

In the last twenty years, the idea that organisms contain within them rhythmic biochemical processes that function as internal clocks has passed from the status of a controversial hypothesis to an accepted fact. That virtually all organisms, including bacteria, possess an endogenous twenty-four-hour clock is widely known. Less widely known is the evidence for rhythmic processes with much shorter periods—as short as a 1 thousandth of a second—and much longer periods—a year and longer. The existence of an array of internal rhythmic processes with vastly different periods provides a biological foundation for representing the time of occurrence of an event. Provided that the period of the slowest internal oscillation is as long as or longer than the lifetime of the organism, a record of the states of one's internal oscillations specifies the time of occurrence of an event. Chapter 7 reviews the evidence for these internal oscillations and explains how they are synchronized with external oscillations, the classic example being the synchronization of the internal twenty-four-hour rhythm (the circadian or approximately daily rhythm) with the environmental day-night cycle. It also reviews the various ways of representing the phase (momentary state) of an oscillation.

Chapter 7 continues with a discussion of the processes for generating a representation of a temporal interval. These fall into two categories: (1) subtracting the time of occurrence of the earlier event from the time of occurrence of the later event and (2) starting a rhythmic pulse generator when the first event occurs and counting the number of pulses it produces until the second event. It is argued that the former process is more plausible. It presents computational complications, however, in that phase vectors (specifying the phases of several different oscillations with different periods) do not obey the laws of vector algebra. The computations required to obtain temporal intervals from phase vectors are spelled out.

Chapter 8 reviews the evidence that animals routinely represent the time of day at which events occur and that they do so by recording the reading on their endogenous twenty-four-hour clock, that is, the momentary state (phase) of a physiological circadian rhythm. If the twenty-four-hour rhythm is the only endogenous rhythm whose phase is recorded, animals cannot distinguish the events of one day from those of the next. The little evidence there is bearing on the question suggests that bees cannot whereas birds can. Bees do not seem sensitive to periodic recurrences at two- or three-day intervals whereas birds do.

A record of time of occurrence consisting only of the phase of a twenty-four-hour oscillator does not specify a unique point in time. The representation is unique only up to a twenty-four-hour displacement along the temporal axis. If it is assumed that the representation of time of occurrence is based upon a preservation of the momentary states (phases) of endogenous oscillations, then the ability to recognize periodic recurrences at intervals longer than twenty-four-hours implies that the phases of endogenous oscillations with periods of many days are recorded.

The assumption that animals have a representation of the time of occurrence of an event within a fixed temporal framework is equivalent to the assumption that they have a representation of time unique up to a translation along the temporal axis greater than the lifetime of the organism. This in turn is equivalent to the assumption that among the endogenous rhythms whose phases are recorded to represent time of occurrence, there is at least one rhythm with a period longer than the life of the organism. There is no evidence to support this assumption. Its justification, if any, is aesthetic: it simplifies subsequent arguments to assume a representation of time within a fixed framework.

Chapter 9 reviews the experimental evidence on the representation of temporal intervals and a computational model of this process developed by Church and Gibbon (1982). Their model assumes that the representation of intervals derives from counting the pulses from a rhythmic pulse generator (a neurophysiological multivibrator). The count starts when one event occurs and terminates with the second event. I suggest a computationally equivalent model based on the assumption that the representation of temporal intervals is derived by subtracting the time of occurrence of the earlier event from that of the later.

Chapter 10 reviews the evidence that animals represent numerosity. It reviews the Meck and Church (1983) model of the process by which a representation of numerosity is obtained and shows that their model is formally equivalent to the counting model elaborated by Gelman and Gallistel (1978).

A representation of the numerosity of the items encountered in a given period of observation together with one of the duration of that interval makes it possible to compute a representation of the rate at which items were encountered. The ability to represent rate of morsel encounters (food density) is in turn crucial to rational decision making in foraging animals. Chapter 11 reviews evidence that foraging animals base their decisions about where to forage upon representations of the rate at which food is encountered.

Chapter 12 brings the book for the first time into contact with traditional treatments of animal learning. The data reviewed in the chapters on space, time and number have come predominantly from experiments done within a zoological tradition. In the zoological or naturalistic tradition, the problem of learning arose incidentally in connection with investigations of how animals solve biological problems. When it is discovered that a digger wasp repeatedly returns to her nearly invisible nest to provision it with live food for her larvae, the question arises, How is she able to locate the nest again? This leads to experiments showing that she does so on the basis of remembered geometric relations between the nest location and the locations of surrounding landmarks. Similarly, when it is observed that animals seek to monopolize certain periodically available food sources by showing up in anticipation of the next period of availability, the question arises, How are they able to time their behavior in this way? This leads to experiments showing that they represent the daily time of occurrence.

By contrast, the experiments in the psychological literature on animal learning grew out of philosophical convictions about the nature of the learning process itself. In particular, they grew out of the conviction that the process was one of associating stimulus traces, connecting the internal representations of stimuli that repeatedly occurred together in time and space. The experimental paradigms by which learning has been studied within this psychological tradition have involved pairing two stimuli and studying the development of a tendency to respond to one stimulus as if it predicted the occurrence of the other. The increasing strength of this tendency is taken to reflect the increasing strength of the associative connection between the two stimulus traces. The experimental paradigm and the associative process whose laws the experiments are intended to reveal are called classical conditioning.

Experimental results of the last twenty years have led to profound changes in the current conception of the associative process in classical conditioning, changes not widely appreciated by nonspecialists. In particular, it has been concluded that pairing is neither necessary nor sufficient for the development of an association. Pairing two stimuli is not sufficient for the formation of an association between their representations (traces) because the development of the association depends on what other associations already exist or are developing at the same time. Given appropriate strengths for these other associations, the increments to the associative bond may be 0 or even negative in the face of repeated temporal pairing of the stimuli to be associated. Pairing is not necessary because inhibitory associations develop when two stimuli are explicitly unpaired (when one predicts the nonoccurrence of the other). It has also been found necessary to introduce an internal trial clock into modern theories of conditioning, to permit the formation of associations of appropriate strength with continuously present background stimuli. Chapter 12 critically reviews these theoretical developments in the associative analysis of classical conditioning and the experimental findings that motivated them.

Chapter 13 gives a nonassociative analysis of the phenomena of classical conditioning. The starting point of the analysis is the assumption that classical conditioning phenomena reflect the development of an animal's representation of the rate or prevalence of one stimulus (the predicted stimulus, or, more conventionally, the US) conditional upon the presence or absence of another stimulus (the predicting stimulus, or the CS). Another central assumption is that this representation is a statistical one. The estimate of the rate of US occurrence predicted by the CS includes a representation of the statistical uncertainty associated with the rate estimates. The processes that translate rate estimates into behavior are assumed to be sensitive to the statistical uncertainty of those estimates. They do not generate behavior that anticipates the predicted stimulus when there is no statistically valid basis within the animal's experience for concluding that the predicted stimulus is more (or less) likely in the presence of the "predicting" stimulus than in its absence. The animal's response to the predicting stimulus gets stronger with repeated experience not because there is an increase in the strength of an underlying associative connection but rather because there is an increase in the statistical certainty that the rate of occurrence or prevalence of the predicted stimulus is higher (or lower) in the presence of the predicting stimulus.

Starting with these basic assumptions, chapter 13 develops a computational model of the process by which the system allocates rate predictions among the various possible predictors. This model rests on three simple principles. First is the *additivity principle:* the rates ascribed to various predictors must be such that the observed rates of occurrence when two or more predictors have been present simultaneously equals (within the limits of statistical uncertainty) the sum of the rates predicted by each predictor acting alone. Second is the principle of rate *inertia:* the rate of occurrence predicted by a given CS is assumed to be constant over all the intervals in which that CS has been present, unless the data give statistical reasons for rejecting the constancy assumption. This is called the inertia principle because it asserts that the value of a predicted rate is assumed constant unless acted on by a statistical force, a pattern of observations inconsistent with the assumed constancy of the rate. The third principle is *uncertainty minimization:* whenever more than one solution consistent with the additivity and inertia principles is possible, the system favors the solution that minimizes the number of predictors and hence the average uncertainty associated with the estimates of rates.

In chapter 14, the focus shifts to the nervous system. Representational theories of mind in psychology have not found favor at least in part because it has been thought that such theories were harder to reconcile with the facts of neurophysiology. However, all of the representations discussed in this book reduce to vectors of modest dimensionality— short strings of quantities, where each quantity represents a value on a spatial, temporal, or descriptive dimension. Chapter 14 reviews electrophysiological findings suggesting that vector representation is the preferred mode of representation in the nervous system. The nervous system represents the vectors that describe various aspects of the world by means of the position of the activity in a projection area whose anatomical dimensions correspond to dimensions of the stimulus description. For example, in the mapping of the angular position of a stimulus source onto the surface of the tectum, the anterior-posterior dimension of the tectal surface corresponds to the azimuthal dimension of angular position (the angular distance of the stimulus source to the left or right of the optic axis), while the dorsomedial-ventrolateral dimension corresponds to elevation (the angular distance of the source above or below the optic axis). A transient stimulus, such as the honk of a horn, generates activity in a localized region of the tectum. The anterior-posterior location of this activity represents the optic azimuth of the sound source and the dorsomedial-ventrolateral location represents its optic elevation.

The principle of using the dimensions of anatomical spaces to represent the dimensions of the abstract vector "spaces" that describe properties of the stimulus extends to nonspatial attributes of the stimulus. For example, a dimension of a subarea of the bat auditory cortex corresponds to (maps) the radial velocity of the stimulus source (the rate at which it is approaching or receding from the bat).

The most striking example of the brain's predilection for representing nonspatial stimulus attributes by vectors of modest dimensionality is in its "representation" of the surface color (the reflectance spectrum of a surface) by means of three bipolar dimensions. It is suggested that the mutual exclusivity of certain color judgments (red-green, yellow-blue) is the result of this spatial representation of the reflectance spectrum. Colors cannot be both red and green simultaneously because the central tendency of activity in a cortical mapping of reflectance spectra cannot simultaneously lie on both sides of an anatomical axis of the mapping, the axis that divides the spectra judged red from the spectra judged green, nor on both sides of the orthogonal axis that separates the spectra judged yellow from the spectra judged blue.

A computational-representational framework for the analysis of learning leads to a modular view of learning processes because the computations that underlie the construction of the representations must vary both as a function of the form of the representation and as a function of the sense data from which it is computed. The findings from cortical electrophysiology and functional anatomy reinforce this modular view of brain function. In recent years, cortical electrophysiologists have discovered repeated mappings of the retinal input onto the visual cortex, repeated mappings of the auditory input onto the auditory cortex, and repeated mappings of the somesthetic input onto the somesthetic cortex. The tuning characteristics of cortical neurons—what combinations of stimulus dimensions they are sensitive to—vary from one mapping to the next, which has led most electrophysiologists to conclude that each mapping gives a different description of the stimulus.

One might imagine that at some point the distinct representations of the same stimulus derived by distinct analytic modules converge to a unified representation of the stimulus in all its aspects and that it is this unified representation that gets stored. However, there is no electrophysiological evidence of this convergence, and the thrust of the preceding analysis of learning has been to carry the modularity of the stimulus analysis process through to the storage process. In this view, different properties of the stimulus—where it was versus what it smelled like or what its color was—end up stored in different information-gathering modules. This view forces one to consider the principles by which these separate stores of formally distinct stimulus descriptions are unified in the generation of action.

Chapter 15 addresses the problem of the unity of remembered experience. It suggests that representations of the place and time of an experienced attribute play a privileged role in the unification of the representations of diverse attributes. Every record of an attribute has incorporated in it a record of the time of the experience and the location of the distal stimulus. Higher-order records contain information computed from first-order records. For example, the records of conditional rates of occurrence are computed from records of individual CS and US events. Incorporated in a higher-order (propositional) record are place and time specifications reflecting the range of places and times in the event records from which the higher-order record was computed.

The spatiotemporal addresses incorporated into every record are used to link records that originated at the same or related places and times. The linking of records in this scheme is not limited to records that have coincident spatiotemporal addresses. A considerable advantage to the ex post facto linking of records is that the spatiotemporal relationship between the records to be linked need not be foreseen at the time the records are laid down. The system may use the spatiotemporal addresses of memories to search for records that are linked by a spatiotemporal relation whose importance has been realized after the fact.

Support for the hypothesis that a record of the location of a stimulus source in space plays a privileged role in relating one recorded stimulus property to another is found in modern work in cognitive psychology showing that space plays a privileged role in unifying separately perceived and remembered attributes of the same stimulus. Support for the temporal aspect of the suggestion is found in the fact that in response to concussions, electrical shocks and other gross disturbances of brain function, memory breaks down along a temporal dimension rather than along dimensions of content or significance. Access to the memories laid down during an interval of time ranging from minutes to forty years is lost, while access to memories formed outside this interval remains. The breakdown in so-called retrograde amnesia is to the retrieval process not to the storage process per se, because, commonly, access to the memories eventually returns. The idea that access to stored records is controlled by a temporal index renders this common clinical phenomenon comprehensible.

Chapter 16 considers the relevance of the representational analysis of learning to the problem of determining its physiological basis. It begins by distinguishing between the molecular storage mechanism and the neural circuits and physiological processes that compute the new values of stored variables, whether those variables are imagined to be the strengths of associative connections or the values of the dimensions in a vector that represents a stimulus or a spatiotemporal position. The associative connection—the physical embodiment of what has been learned—might lie entirely outside the circuit that computes its value from trial to trial. Current attempts to find the cellular basis of associative learning have not divided up the problem in this way, despite the fact that the computational complexity of modern associative theory would seem to require such a division. Because the process that determines changes in associative strengths must take the values of other associations into account and because it must be sensitive to temporal ratios, it is unclear how it could depend on the temporal pairing of chemical and electrical events at single sites in the nervous system. In the light of modern findings, the computations leading to changes in associative strengths appear to require a neural network for their realization.

Basic to the associative approach to learning is the assumption of computational universality, the assumption that there is an associative process and that knowledge of the formal and quantitative laws of association will permit us to recognize this process at the cellular and molecular levels of analysis. The computational-representational view rejects the assumption of computational universality. If the system computes representations of formally distinct properties of stimuli from formally distinct kinds of sense data, computational universality makes no sense. However, insofar as the resulting representations are all vector representations, it makes sense to assume that the physicochemical solution to the storage problem is universal. The problem of storing the values of vectors reduces to the problem of storing the values of the individual quantities of which they are composed. The fact that the vectors representing radically different aspects of the environment have been computed by radically different processes is neither here nor there so far as the storage problem is concerned.

From the perspective of the view of learning here elaborated, the ideal preparation for studying the cellular basis of information storage in the nervous system is one in which a neural pathway carrying the signal that specifies the value of a to-be-stored quantity terminates on a cell or cells in which the value of that quantity is preserved for subsequent readout. Preparations that appear promising from this perspective are discussed. The final chapter draws together the argument.

Chapter 2

Representations

Few other concepts generate such heated discussion among psychologists as the concept of representation. While the concept may be controversial and obscure within psychology, it has a long, uncontroversial, and clear use within mathematics. In this book, I use the term in its mathematical sense. The brain is said to represent an aspect of the environment when there is a functioning isomorphism between some aspect of the environment and a brain process that adapts the animal's behavior to it.

Isomorphisms

Isomorphisms are formal correspondences between distinct systems of mathematical study. The best known such isomorphism is the one discovered by Descartes and Fermat between geometry and algebra: the isomorphism that is the foundation of analytic geometry and calculus. Descartes discovered a procedure—the use of Cartesian coordinates—that mapped the entities studied by geometers—points, lines, curves, and surfaces—into the entities of algebra—numbers, vectors (strings of numbers), and equations. The discovery of the formal correspondence between, for example, a straight line in geometry and a "linear" equation in algebra (an equation of the form $y = ax + b$) enabled mathematicians to represent geometric problems algebraically and thereby bring algebraic methods of proof to bear on geometric problems. Conversely, it enabled them to represent algebraic problems geometrically and bring geometric methods of proof to bear on algebraic problems. The discovery of this isomorphism is arguably the most seminal discovery in the history of mathematics. Among the many things it eventually gave rise to was the strategy among mathematicians of looking for other useful isomorphisms, formal correspondences between a mathematical object that is not well understood and another more richly developed mathematical system. Demonstrating the existence of such a correspondence establishes an isomorphism (a parallelism of form). The exploitation of the correspondence to solve problems in the one domain using operations belonging to the other establishes a functioning isomorphism: an isomorphism in which the capacity of one system to represent another is put to use. Routine uses of isomorphisms between the system of number and various aspects of the real world are spelled out below.

An isomorphism exists when there is a procedure that maps entities, relations, and operations in the represented system into entities, relations, and operations in the representing system in such a way that two or more entities within the represented system are related in a given way *if and only if* (written *iff*) there is a corresponding relation between their representatives in the representing system. Under the Cartesian procedure for mapping points on a plane into pairs of numbers, two lines intersect *iff* there exists a common solution to their corresponding equations. Conversely, two lines are parallel if there is no common solution to their corresponding equations.

Examples from the Theory of Measurement

The concept of representation, in the mathematical sense of a functioning isomorphism, plays a central role in the theory of measurement. This theory is particularly appropriate for illustrating what is meant by representation in this book in that it makes clear the important fact that representations come in varying degrees of richness, depending on how extensive the isomorphism between the represented and the representing system is.

Numerical Representation of Mass

A measurement procedure establishes an isomorphism between a non-numerical system and the system of numbers (or numerically derived entities, like vectors). The procedure of weighing objects—placing them on a properly calibrated conventional scale and noting the reading—maps the system of masses into the system of positive numbers in such a way as to establish a rich isomorphism. The entities in the represented system are masses. The entities in the representing system are numbers. The weighing procedure assigns to every mass a corresponding number. Under this mapping of masses into numbers, the relation "heavier than" corresponds to the numerical relation ">." The relation "is the same weight as" corresponds to the numerical relation "=." The operation of "combining two masses" corresponds to the numerical operation "+." The operation of "replicating masses" (loading a gross of bricks) corresponds to the numerical operation of "x."

The representation established by the weighing procedure is a rich one because all of the elementary operations and relations of arithmetic may validly be employed with the resulting numbers. That is, the *iff* condition holds for expressions involving all of these operations. For example, two lead weights on one end of a symmetrical crane will balance a gross of bricks at the other *iff*: $L_1 + L_2 = 144 \times B$, where L_1 and L_2 are the numbers assigned by the weighing procedure to the pieces of lead, 144 is the number of bricks in a gross, and B is the number assigned by the weighing procedure to a brick. Note that this calculation employs the addition operation, the multiplication operation, and the equals relation. The fact that, for properly weighed masses, this is a valid calculation—a calculation whose results may be applied to the actual masses involved without tipping over the crane—is what establishes the richness and utility of the numerical representation of mass. The numerical representation of mass is rich because it makes valid use of all the arithmetic operators and relations.

Numerical Representation of Space

The numerical representation of mass is a simple case because there is a simple correspondence between basic operations involving masses and the elementary arithmetic operations. The relational operation of determining whether one mass balances or overbalances another corresponds to the arithmetic relational operator "≥." The operation of combining two masses corresponds to the combinatorial operator "+" in arithmetic, and so on. Often, however, an intuitively simple operation in the represented system corresponds to a complex operation in the numerical realm—one that is a combination of several elementary arithmetic operations. This is apparent when we apply the measurement theory framework to the vectorial representation of space.

A vector is a string of numbers. Conventionally, these are written separated by commas and enclosed by <>. One vector (one string of numbers) combines with another vector "of the same dimensionality" (another string of numbers, with the same number of numbers) to yield a third vector in accord with the rules of vector algebra. In the case of addition, these are very much like the rules of ordinary algebra. The sum of the vector <2,5> and the vector <1,3> is the vector <3,8>, that is, $\langle x_1, y_1 \rangle + \langle x_2, y_2 \rangle = \langle (x_1 + x_2), (y_1 + y_2) \rangle$.

The vectorial representation of two-dimensional space is mediated by a surveying procedure of some kind. The surveying procedure maps positions on the plane into two-dimensional vectors (number pairs—for example, the latitude and longitude of a point).

There is a simple correspondence between the operation of combining changes in position on the plane and the operation of vector addition. The changes in position are themselves vectors. (The vector that represents a change in position is equal to the new position vector minus the old position vector.) The correspondence between the operation of combining successive changes in position to yield an ultimate change in position and the operation of vector addition is indicated in table 2.1, which lays out the various numerical (or algebraic) representations of aspects of the real world.

The correspondence between operations in the spatial domain and their representations in the arithmetic domain, however, is not generally of the simple-to-simple, complex-to-complex form. Determining whether a given point is "in line with" two other points is a basic and intuitively simple operation in dealing with the arrangement of items in space. To do it, you sight from one of the two points to the other and see whether the third point falls on the line of sight. More formally, this elementary surveying operation determines whether three points satisfy a collinearity relation. Or in another kind of formal terminology, derived from computer science, the sighting operation is equivalent to applying a "collinearity operator" to the three points. The collinearity operator is a relational operator. It takes three points as its input (its argument) and "returns" the value 1 (= true) if the points are collinear or the value 0 (= false) if they are not.

Table 2.1.
Mappings and operational correspondences in various numerical representations

Numerical representation of mass

Represented system	Mapping/ correspondence	Representing system
Represented entities		Representing entities
Mass a		N_a
Mass b ——————————Weighing————>		N_b
Mass c		N_c
Comparative/relational procedures		Corresponding relational operators
Balancing ———————————————————>		$\geq$
Combinatorial procedures		Corresponding combinatorial operators
Combining masses ——————————————>		$+$

Isomorphisms

Mass a balances or overbalances mass b *iff* $N_a \geq N_b$

Mass a together with mass b balances or overbalances mass c
iff $N_a + N_b \geq N_c$

Numerical and vectorial representation of space

Represented system	Mapping/ correspondence	Representing system
Represented entities		Representing entities
Positions on a plane ——— Surveying ——————>		Cartesian Coordinates (2-D vectors)
Distances between——— Linear measurement——> pairs of points		Numbers
Angles between triplets———Angular measurement—> of points		Numbers
Comparative/relational procedures		Corresponding relational operators
Determining the collinearity——————————————> of points by sighting		Determining the vectors that satisfy the 2-point equation for a line
Determining the equivalence of distances between 2——————————————> pairs of points, using, e.g. a string segment,		$(x_2-x_1)^2 + (y_2-y_1)^2$ $=?$ $(x_4-x_3)^2 + (y_4-y_3)^2$
Combinatorial procedures		Corresponding combinatorial operators
Successive changes in——————————————> position combine to yield a net change in position		Vector addition

Isomorphisms

Two lines are parallel *iff* there is no vector that is a solution to both of the corresponding equations

Calendrical and numerical representation of time

Represented entities		Representing entities
Points in time——— Calendars & Clocks —>		Dates & times
Temporal intervals——— Timers ——————>		Numbers
Comparative/relational procedures		Corresponding relational operators
Later than? ——————————————>		Date & time >
Equal or longer?——————————————>		$\geq$
Combinatorial procedures		Corresponding combinatorial operators
Combining temporal intervals ——————>		+
Determination of temporal ——————————> interval between 2 points		Date-time -

Table 2.1 (continued)

Represented system	Mapping/ correspondence	Representing system

Isomorphisms

The interval from T_1 to T_2 is longer than the combined intervals from T_3 to T_4 and T_5 to T_6 iff $T_6 - T_5 + T_4 - T_3 \geq T_2 - T_1$.

Numerical representation of Poisson processes

Represented entities		Representing entities
Rates of random occurrence	—Observed #/Interval——>	Numbers (R_a, etc.)
"Width" of interevent histogram	—Sqrt(R_i)————>	Numbers [Sqrt(R_a), etc.]
Uncertainties———	$f_1(n_i)R_i \rightarrow f_u(n_i)R_i$ ——>	Numerical intervals ($L_1 \rightarrow L_u$, etc.)
Comparative/relational procedures		Corresponding relational operators
Selecting process that will— have greater yield	————————>	$R_i >? R_j$
Combinatorial procedures		Corresponding combinatorial operators
Combining 2 random— occurrence-generating processes (e.g., 2 radioactive samples)	————————>	$R_i + R_j$

Isomorphisms

Process a and process b operating concurrently have a high probability of producing a higher yield than process c iff $f_1(n_a)R_a + f_1(n_b)R_b > f_u(n_c)R_c$, the sum of the lower limits of the uncertainty intervals surrounding the estimates of the rates for process a and process b is greater than the upper limit of the uncertainty interval surrounding the estimate of the rate for process c

Note: The mapping procedures assign numbers or numerically derived representatives like vectors or date-times to entities in the represented system. The isomorphism depends on this mapping plus the indicated correspondences between operations in the represented system and arithmetic-computational operations.

The vectorial collinearity operator is complex in the sense that it is constructed out of a combination of elementary arithmetic operations. Given the coordinates for any two points, $<x_1,y_1>$, $<x_2,y_2>$, the collinearity operator forms the two-point equation of a line, which represents the line through the points using their coordinates as the parameters of the equation:

$$y = [(y_2 - y_1)/(x_2 - x_1)] x + [y_2 - x_2 (y_2 - y_1)/(x_2 - x_1)].$$

The expression "$[(y_2 - y_1)/(x_2 - x_1)]$" equals a and the expression

"$[y_2 - x_2(y_2 - y_1)/(x_2 - x_1)]$" equals b in the conventional equation for a line,

$$y = ax + b.$$

The representing system (commonly a computer) plugs into this equation the x-value of the third point and compares the resulting y-value to the y-value for the third point. If the two y-values are equal, the operator returns the value 1; if they are not, it returns the value 0. This complex collinearity-determining operation in the representing system (the computer) corresponds to the "elementary" sighting operation in the represented system (the spatial domain).

Table 2.1 gives another example of a simple relational operation in the spatial system that has a complex correspondent in the arithmetic system. The simplest of relational operations that applies to the distances between points is the operation of determining whether one distance is the same as another. This is often done by stretching a segment of string between the pair of points that define the first distance and then seeing whether that same segment is too short, too long, or exactly right when stretched between the other pair of points. The corresponding distance-comparing operation in the arithmetic domain uses the Pythagorean formula, which gives the distance between two points in terms of their coordinates (see table 2.1). Again, a complex formula (a combination of operations) in the representing system corresponds to a simple operation in the represented system. What is simple in the represented system need not be simple in the representing system, and vice-versa. The crucial consideration in determining whether a representation exists is whether a correspondence exists and is used, not whether simple corresponds to simple and complex to complex.

More than one measurement procedure may relate entities in the represented domain to entities in the representing domain. In addition to the surveying procedures that assign two-dimensional vectors to represent points in the plane, there are linear and angular measuring procedures. Linear measurement maps the distances between points into numbers. Angular measurement maps the angles formed by ordered triplets of points into numbers. The distances and angles whose numerical representation is determined by these measurement procedures may also be computed within the representing system from the vectors that represent the positions of the points. The validity of these computations depends on the validity of the isomorphism between the spatial domain and the arithmetic domain and on the validity of all the measurement procedures. The existence of different measurement procedures mapping different entities in the represented domain into computationally related entities in the representing domain permits the cross-validation or calibration of mapping procedures and the empirical validation of the isomorphism between vector algebra and geometry.

Numerical Representation of Time
Another form of representation that figures prominently in the chapters ahead is the representation of time, both temporal position and temporal intervals. The distinction between temporal positions and temporal intervals corresponds to the distinction between spatial positions and distances. A temporal interval is the distance between two points in time. To represent positions in space by vectors, we create a system of spatial coordinates that represents all points in space by reference to their distance along orthogonal directions away from an arbitrarily chosen point called the origin of the system of coordinates. Similarly, to represent position in time, we create a coordinate system, called a calendar-clock system, which represents moments by their distance along the single temporal dimension from the arbitrarily chosen point in time that is the origin of the calendar-clock system (often the time of some exceptionally significant event, like a birth).

Real calendars and clocks are key instruments in the measurement procedures that map temporal positions into calendar-clock numbers—for example, numbers of the form 05/14/1987 10:45.21, the form generated by the calendar-clock device on my microcomputer. Although time is unidimensional and can in principle be represented by a single number, calendar clock devices commonly represent single positions in time by a string of numbers. I will suggest that the same is true of the brain: it represents points in time by a set of several quantities, which I will term *temporal coordinates*. These temporal coordinates—the distinct numbers or quantities that compose a representation of a point in time— are different from spatial coordinates in one important way: distinct numbers in the string do not represent orthogonal dimensions. Thus the string of numbers that represents a position in time is not, strictly, a vector because it cannot validly be manipulated by the rules of vector algebra. Under the mapping of time into number strings performed by the calendar-clock on a typical microcomputer, there is no isomorphism between time and vector algebra; or, rather, there is only a very weak isomorphism. The only operation in vector algebra that can validly be applied to a calendar-clock number string is the identity operator: two moments in time are one and the same *iff* they have the same calendar-clock vector.

One may readily imagine a different mapping procedure that would establish an isomorphism between one-dimensional vector algebra (ordinary arithmetic) and the output of a calendar-clock device. The device could be constructed to read out the time elapsed in milliseconds since the moment of its installation. In this case, the extent of the isomorphism between points in time and the number system composed of the numbers generated by this calendar clock plus the operations of ordinary arithmetic would be much greater. The ordinary addition/subtraction operation, for example, could validly be employed to compute the temporal interval separating two points in time. Multiplication of points in time, however, would still not be valid. To perform this operation with a calendar-time number would be to generate nonsense, an invalid representation of the relations between points in time. It would not be true, for example, that the time represented by the number 16,000,000 was half as old as the time represented by the number 32,000,000. This defect in the numerical representation of time could be cured by making the calendar-clock device read the time in milliseconds since the the Big Bang. Time, like weight, does have a true 0. The assignment of the number 0 to a point in time need not inherently be arbitrary. If it is not arbitrary, then ratios between the temporal numbers may correspond to isomorphic relations among the times represented.

We have just considered enriching the isomorphism between points in time and ordinary arithmetic by changing the mapping procedure, which relates entities in the representing system to the things they represent. Alternatively we can create a richer isomorphism by changing the operations performed within the representing system. This is what has been done in the computer's temporal representation. The programmers have constructed a set of operations with calendar-clock numbers that enable one to work with them as if they were ordinary numbers. There is a calendar-clock ">" operation, which returns the value 1 (true) only if the first specified date and time is later than the second specified date and time. There is a calendar-clock addition-subtraction operation, which returns the time elapsed between two dates and times (in various user-specifiable forms: seconds, or hours and minutes, or months, days, hours, and minutes). The addition-subtraction operation can also return the date that is some specified amount of time later than another date, and so on. By setting up complex number processing routines in the computer, routines tailored to the peculiarities of calendar-clock numbers, programmers have created a system isomorphic to the system of time. The peculiarities in the operation of the calendar-clock system do not reflect formal peculiarities of time itself. Rather they reflect the peculiarities of the procedures by which we map points in time into numbers.

As with space, different measuring procedures map different aspects of time into different numbers. Calendar-clocks map points in time into numbers. Timers map temporal intervals into numbers; they measure temporal distances. As in the spatial system, these mappings are computationally interrelated, which is what permits their cross-validation.

Isomorphisms Defined between Systems, not Between Sets of Entities
The discussion of the numerical representation of points in time brings
out a point about the nature of representations that needs to be stressed
in any inquiry into the representational nature of brain processes: the
nature of a representation cannot be determined simply from a knowledge of the mapping between the represented entities and the representing entities. Isomorphisms exist between systems, not between sets of
entities. The statement that the number 10 is isomorphic to some particular mass is meaningless. It is the system of number that is isomorphic to
the system of masses. The system of number has numbers (the entities)
plus operators (such as <, =, +, x) and the system of masses has masses
plus operations with masses (combining them, balancing them). Sets of
entities that are related in some orderly way to external entities are
necessary to any representational system, but an orderly mapping is not
sufficient to establish a representation. The representing system must
perform operations on the entities generated by the mapping, and there
must be a correspondence between the operations the representing
system performs with the representatives and the relations or processes
in which the represented entities play roles—for example, the correspondence between numerical addition and combining two weights on a pan
of a balance.
   A rich, functioning isomorphism may exist even when the sensory
mapping from the external reality to its internal representation in brain
activity does not make it immediately clear what exploitable formal
correspondences there might be. Conversely a formally transparent
mapping is no guarantee that the brain itself exploits a formal correspondence obvious to the experimenter. The experimenter must know not
only what the mapping is but also what use is made of it. Until both are
known, the character of the representation cannot be ascertained.
   The practical importance of this point about the fundamental role of
operations on mappings is that it is often extremely difficult to know how
to determine by physiological observations what use the brain makes of
a given sensory mapping of the world. The best guide to the character of
the representations a brain makes is the behavior the brain generates.
Thus behavioral data play a more prominent role than physiological data
in this book, despite the fact that my agenda is a reductionist one: to
understand learning as a neuronal phenomenon. Since the property of
being a representation is a system property, we must study what the
system does. This is a necessary prelude to understanding what the
system does in terms of what its elements do.

Derived Representations: The Numerical Representation of Rate
Representations have a hierarchical structure in the sense that some

representations are computed from others. This becomes clear when we consider the numerical representation of rates of random occurrence. To represent the rate at which a radioactive source emits particles, we must first be able to represent how many particles have been emitted during our period of observation and the interval of time over which we have observed. To obtain the numerical representation of the rate of emission, we divide the number that represents how many particles we observed by the number that represents the duration of our observation interval. Thus, the measurement procedure for rate depends on the existence of a measurement procedure for numerosity (counting) and for temporal intervals (timing).[1]

The same point may be made with regard to the number that represents variation. When the average number of emissions is ten per second, in some percentage of 1-second intervals, fewer than ten emissions will be observed, while in other such intervals, more than ten will be observed. To obtain a numerical representation of the magnitude of this variation, we could use a measurement procedure in which we first make a histogram of the number of emissions observed in a large number of 1-second observation intervals. The creation of such a histogram would, of course, involve numerically or graphically representing how many emissions there were in each interval. We could then determine that deviation from the mean of all observations such that a certain percentage of the observations fell within it. This graph-based measurement procedure is an empirical mapping of variation into a number representing the magnitude of variation. More commonly, one does not derive the representation of the standard deviation of a Poisson process in this way; rather one takes the square root of the rate estimate. This exploits a correspondence between a number and its square root, on the one hand, and a Poisson rate of emission and its variance, on the other. The two relations are isomorphic because a Poisson process has the property that $\sigma^2 = \mu$; the variance is equal to the mean.

Not uncommonly, representations have a reflexive character as well in that the system may represent numerically properties of its representation. This is common in statistical representations, where many of the numbers represent the statistical uncertainty regarding the true value of an estimate. The standard error of an estimate is a number that represents the system's uncertainty regarding what the proper numerical represen-

---

1. I do not assert that a valid measurement procedure for rate must depend upon measuring numerosity and time. It may be possible to devise a procedure that does not depend on this by finding some physical variable that is a scalar function of rate and measuring that variable. In practice, however, the measurement of rate and most other "intensive" variables (such as density) is obtained by a computation performed with the results of "extensive" measurements.

tative is for a given aspect of external reality. Poisson rate processes, which figure prominently in the part of this book that deals with classical conditioning, have the property that uncertainty regarding the true value of a rate estimate based on n observations is determined solely by the value of n. Thus from a representation of the number of observations from which a rate estimate was computed, the system may compute a representation of the certainty regarding the true value of that representation. The theory of conditioning developed in a later chapter depends fundamentally on the assumption that the brain of an animal represents the uncertainty associated with its representations of rates of occurrence.

It is an interesting metaphysical question whether the numbers that represent statistical uncertainties should be regarded as representations of "external" reality or "internal" reality, that is, the reality of the represented system or the reality of the representing system. One is inclined to assume that there is a true rate of occurrence in the represented system (the "world") and that the uncertainty lies not in that system but in the system representing it. However, the uncertainty associated with a Poisson rate estimate based on five observed occurrences is intrinsic; it does not reflect any idiosyncrasy of the representing system; indeed, it does not reflect any property of the representing system. The uncertainty is inherent in the situation.

However one resolves the metaphysical question of where the numerically represented uncertainty is imagined to reside, it is important to realize that a representing system may represent its own properties. To take a banal example, a computer represents and performs computations on the size of its random access memory.

Nominal Representations
Nominal representations are the most impoverished form of numerical representation. The only numerical operation validly employed in a nominal representation is the "equals" or "identity" operator. The classic example of this kind of minimal numerical representation is the assignment of jersey numbers to athletes on a team. This assignment is a mapping from nonnumerical entities (players on a team) to numerical entities (the assigned numbers). It might be thought that this mapping is unconstrained, but that is not so. Two constraints are honored: the one-one constraint (every player gets one and only one number) and the uniqueness constraint (the same number is not given to more than one player on the same team). The constraints on the mapping from players to numbers make possible the valid use of the equals operator. The player who stole the ball and the player who scored the goal are the same player *iff* the number on the jersey of the thief equals the number on the jersey of the scorer. The numbers are assigned to permit this use of them. The

numbers serve as names but names that are superior to ordinary names in that two players on the same team cannot have the same numerical name. Because there is a systematic mapping from the players to numbers and because a numerical operation (=) is validly employed with the resulting numbers, this example satisfies the definition of a functioning isomorphism.

The term *nominal representation* is doubly appropriate. First, the numbers serve as names. Second, the use made of the numbers is so limited (the isomorphism between the number system and the player system is so impoverished) that most people view this representation as a degenerate case, a representation in name only, something that technically satisfies the definition of a numerical representation, but is not "really" such. This reaction reveals the fundamental role that operations play in our conception of a representation. If the only operation performed on the numbers is the identity operation (the check to see whether two numbers are the same), the use of numbers is representational only in the minimal sense of the term.

Similar intuitions do not govern the use of representation in the brain sciences and artificial intelligence. It is commonly said that some neuronal process represents some aspect of a stimulus or that the activity of a node in a connectionist network represents some aspect of an input when the only basis for the assertion is the demonstration of a mapping from different stimulus values to different sites of neuronal activity or from different properties of the input to different nodal activations. Often it is explicitly or implicitly assumed that the system applies an identity operator to the neuronal or nodal activation. The system reacts as if a particular stimulus value or input property is present *iff* the appropriate neuron or node is activated. It is seldom assumed that any more elaborate set of operations is performed with these "representations." It is not assumed that there are neuronal or computer operations or relations that correspond in their formal properties to operations or relations with or among input properties.

What distinguishes the use of the term *representation* in this book is the insistence that there is a rich formal correspondence between processes and relations in the environment and the operations the brain performs. Brain processes and relations recapitulate world processes and relations. The recapitulation is not fortuitous. To fit behavior to the environment, the brain creates models of the behavior-relevant aspects of the environment. The formal properties of the processes that realize these models reflect the formal properties of the corresponding external reality because these processes have been subject to evolution by natural selection. Selection has been based on the fidelity of these processes to the external reality. Evolution by natural selection creates rich functioning isomorphisms between brain processes and the environment, and learning is to be understood in terms of these isomorphisms.

Direct versus Indirect or Code-Mediated Isomorphisms

The isomorphisms between aspects of external reality and the brain processes that represent them may be direct, or they may be mediated by a code. An isomorphism is direct if the material or process embodying the representation has properties formally the same as those of the represented material or process. An isomorphism is indirect if there is no formal physical similarity between the representative and the represented. In such cases, the isomorphism is created only by way of an interpretive code or interpretive network. The representation of weight by line segments (as on a bar graph) is a direct isomorphism, while the representation of weight by numerical symbols written (or typed) on paper is not. The isomorphism between weights and line segments is direct because there is a formal correspondence between the physical properties of weights and lines. There is, for example, a natural ordering in both systems. For two unequal weights, one must be heavier than the other; similarly, for two unequal lines, one must be longer than the other. One does not need to know anything to perceive this ordering, which is manifest in any physical process in which these properties play a role. The heavier weight takes more energy to lift; the longer line extends beyond the shorter, and so on. By contrast, there is no physical ordering of the numerical symbols. To order them properly, one has to know the code for interpreting them. Insofar as these symbols enter into any physical processes, their ordering is not manifest therein; it does not take longer to write or erase the symbol "7" than to write or erase the symbol "2," and so on.

If the use of written symbols in the example seems inappropriate, the representation of magnitude by a digital computer serves equally as well to illustrate the concept of an indirect isomorphism. The computer represents magnitudes by patterns of "on" and "off" ("0" and "1") states in a bank of flip-flops (switches) called a register. There is no natural physical ordering of these patterns. The pattern 0101 is not, physically speaking, greater than (or less than) the pattern 0011. The ability of the register to represent magnitudes depends upon the network of AND gates that "read" (interpret) it. The proper ordering of the patterns (which patterns represent bigger magnitudes and which smaller) depends upon the structure of this interpretive network of AND gates. The network of AND gates does not yield a natural physical ordering any more than do the states of the register.

Analogue computers depend upon direct isomorphisms, while digital computers depend upon indirect isomorphisms. Analogue computers exploit the fact that the mathematical laws governing different domains of physical processes (electrical, hydraulic, mechanical, thermal, and others) show very great overlap. Ohms law that current is equal to voltage divided by electrical resistance corresponds to the law that hydraulic flow equals hydraulic pressure divided by hydraulic resistance and to the mechanical law that speed equals force divided by viscous resistance, and so on. This makes it possible to solve hydraulic, mechanical, or thermal problems by setting up the equivalent electrical circuits, that is, by representing them electrically. In an analogue computer, it is possible to find internal magnitudes (voltages or currents) that correspond in their physical behavior to the magnitudes that the computer is representing. A voltage in the computer may fluctuate in accord with, for example, wind velocity. When the same problem is dealt with by a digital computer, it is not possible to find such magnitudes, because the digital isomorphism is indirect. The patterns of on and off states in a given register may fluctuate in accord with wind velocity, but the isomorphism between contents of the register and the wind velocity will be appreciated only by someone who knows the interpretive code for that register.

Analogue computers have interpretive codes just as much as do digital computers. These codes establish which magnitudes in the computer represent which external magnitudes. But the isomorphisms upon which the valid operation of an analogue computer depends are manifest in the absence of the interpretive code. Indeed, the interpretive code may be deduced once the isomorphism is recognized. Recognizing the isomorphism is much more difficult in the case of the digital computer.

The claim that brain processes in learning are isomorphic to the aspects of reality that they represent is neutral with respect to whether this isomorphism is direct or indirect. For the sake of progress in behavioral neuroscience, one hopes that the isomorphism is direct. If it is not, it will be harder to establish which brain processes are isomorphic to which aspects of reality and how.

Relation to the Gestalt Theory of Isomorphism

The notion of an isomorphism between physiological processes and nonphysiological processes was fundamental to Gestalt psychology. However, in Gestalt theory the isomorphism was between the formal characteristics of conscious experience (or of the resulting behavior) and the formal characteristics of the underlying physiological processes (see Koffka 1935 for lengthy discussion). Köhler (1920) formulated the general principle as follows: "Any actual consciousness is in every case not only blindly coupled to its corresponding psychophysical processes, but is akin to it in essential structural properties." (p. 193) Secondly, the physiologically oriented Gestalt psychologists (Wertheimer, Koffka and Köhler) were committed to the idea that the isomorphism between conscious experience (percepts) and the underlying physiological state was direct. The most straightforward and best-known manifestation of the Gestalt psychologists' belief in the isomorphism between percepts and molar physiological states was the attempt by Köhler and Wallach (1944) to demonstrate an isomorphism between figural after-effects and changes in the electrical field on the cortex. By contrast, I argue for isomorphisms between the environment and brain processes (not consciousness and brain processes), and I have no commitment to the claim that the isomorphism is direct.

Definition of Computation

The claim that the brain computes is also controversial. For example, Harth (1986) writes, "It is an assumption that appears not too farfetched that some brain functions are *computable*, given enough information about neural properties and connections. But to assert that the brain or any part of it *computes* carries as much meaning as saying that a telescope computes the trajectories of the light rays passing through it."

I use the term *computation* to designate the processes that map one representation or set of representations into another. For example, the processes in the brain that map representations of number of occurrences and representations of observation intervals into representations of conditional rates of occurrence are called *computational processes*. I describe them as computational because their formal description is identical to a formal description of the corresponding mathematical operations. By the same token, I would describe the physical process by which two voltages in an analogue computer combine to determine a third voltage division *iff* this combinatorial operation had the same formal properties as division and the combinatorial operation in the computer functioned as the representative of a corresponding division-like operation among represented entities. (Recall that processes with the formal characteristics of division occur in the determination of current by voltage and resistance, the determination of velocity by force and viscous resistance, and so on.)

This use of the term *computation* makes it clear why one would not say that the telescope computes the trajectory of the rays passing through. The physical processes involved are not used to represent anything. There is no functioning isomorphism between what occurs in the telescope and anything extrinsic to it. There are latent isomorphisms between the optical processes in a telescope and other processes. If these isomorphisms were exploited to represent problems optically, we would describe these same processes as computational operations. One may create a high pass or low pass spatial frequency filter by placing appropriately shaped opaque spots or slits in the focal plane of the telescope's lens. Under such circumstances, it becomes more appropriate to refer to the optical processes in the telescope as computational processes. Now, these processes are used to transform one image into another. The transformation is formally equivalent to a mathematical operation (subtraction of the Fourier transformations of the original image and the filter followed by Fourier synthesis).

If the image transformation in the telescope represents another formally similar transformation to which images are subject (for example the low pass filtering that occurs in older forms of xerography), this use of the telescope optics would fully satisfy my definition of a computation. When the parallelism of form between what happens in the telescope and what happens in a photocopier is used to anticipate what will happen in the xerographic process, the isomorphism between the telescope and xerography is no longer latent; it is functional. If this use occurred within a biological system and the ability to anticipate what would happen in a xerographic process were important for reproductive success, this functionality would be selected for. It's presence would be no accident. The essence of my argument is that the parallelisms of form between processes in the brain and processes in the world are not latent; they are functional. They are used to adapt the animal's behavior to its environment; hence they enhance its reproductive success. Natural selection has been fine tuning the functioning of these isomorphisms for eons.

Summary

It should now be clear what it means to say that quantities computed by the nervous system represent aspects of the animal's environment. The substance of the claim is that there is an orderly mapping from entities in the environment to entities in the nervous system. The entities in the nervous system are the representatives of the entities in the external world. Thus, for example, the firing rate of a neuron might represent the velocity of the animal along the north-south axis, while the firing rate of another neuron might represent its velocity along the east-west axis. In this example, the velocities along the orthogonal axes are the entities in the environment, and the firing rates of the neurons are the entities in the nervous system. The "mapping" from the velocities to the firing rates refers to the sensory-perceptual processes that transform the sensory signals from various optical and/or kinesthetic receptors into signals that represent orthogonal velocities. In neurophysiological terms, this mapping refers to the neural circuitry that performs this transformation.

The neurophysiological entities produced by the mapping enter into neurophysiological processes that correspond in their formal characteristics to external processes. The formal properties of the external process and its corresponding internal process can be described by mathematical formulas, hence these processes are termed *computational processes*. For example, the manner in which velocity and time combine to produce a distance traversed is described by the integration operation in calculus, distance traversed being the integral of velocity with respect to time. In the kind of theory proposed here, the velocity signals in the nervous system feed into neural processes whose input-output characteristics are also described by integration with respect to time: the neural signal emerging from the process is the integral with respect to time of the neural signal coming into the process. The external process and the internal process have the same formal characteristics, the same mathematical description.

The mappings from the environmental entities to the neural entities and the neurophysiological processes in which the neural entities play a role together constitute a neural system isomorphic to an environmental system. This neural system contains many different variables—rates of neuronal firing, enduring accumulations of intracellular substances, and so on—which are the result of the sensory-perceptual processes that map from the environment to the nervous system. These neural variables play the role played by numbers in a mathematical representation of the environment. Neural processes interrelate these neural variables. These neural processes play the role of the mathematical operations—the procedures that apply to numbers or vectors.

Distinct systems of neural variables and neural processes model distinct aspects of the environment, which is another way of saying that distinct constituents of the nervous system form neural subsystems (or modules) that model (are isomorphic to) distinct aspects of the environment. The existence of subsystems within the nervous system whose operations are isomorphic to (have the same mathematical description as) selected aspects of the behavioral environment is not an accident. Each such subsystem plays a fundamental role in the genesis of behavior adapted to the corresponding aspect of the environment. The subsystem isomorphic to the geometry of the environment plays a fundamental role in planning the trajectories of the animal's movements from one subgoal to the next. The subsystem isomorphic to the temporal relationships among events is the subsystem that times the occurrence of these trajectories once goals have been decided on. The subsystem isomorphic to the probabilities of events plays a fundamental role in deciding among alternative subgoals once motivational processes have specified the current overall goals of behavior, and so on. In other words, each subsystem serves to adapt the animal's behavior to the aspect of the environment modeled by that module. Therefore these subsystems are functioning isomorphisms.

The neural modules accumulate information about the world over time. This accumulation of information about the world is what one calls learning.

Chapter 3
Navigation

Navigation is the process of determining and maintaining a course or trajectory from one place to another. Processes for estimating one's position with respect to the known world are fundamental to it. The known world is composed of the surfaces whose locations relative to one another are represented on a map. There are two fundamental processes for estimating one's position and orientation. One is carried on more or less continuously; the other is episodic. The continuous process is dead reckoning. The episodic process is the fixing of one's position using sightings on objects with a known position (charted objects).

Dead Reckoning

Dead reckoning is the process of determining the change in one's position by integrating one's velocity (directed speed) with respect to time. In the first great period of European marine exploration, when techniques for fixing one's position at sea by astronomical observation were rudimentary and extremely inaccurate, dead reckoning was the principal means by which a ship's position was estimated throughout a voyage. Hence, dead reckoning was a principal determinant of the (often erroneous) map positions assigned to newly discovered lands. It remains a fundamental aspect of modern navigation in its explicit, formalized aspect. In its implicit, unformalized aspect, it probably accompanies virtually every change of position a sailor or an animal makes.

The principal reason for keeping a ship's log is to assist in the reckoning. Every half-hour, entries are made. A reasonably complete one would record the heading of the ship by the compass (the point on the compass to which the steersman has been holding the ship), which sails were set and how they were trimmed, an estimate of the force and direction of the wind, an estimate of the prevailing ocean current's direction (set) and speed (drift), an estimate of the ship's actual course (course over the ground), estimates of the ship's speed through the water and its speed over the ground, and any observation that might give a clue as to the ship's position to someone familiar with "these waters"—birds sighted, the feel and appearance of the sea, and so on.

The crucial entries are for course and speed over the ground. These are used in the periodic calculation (reckoning) of the ship's new position. The other entries are used for recalibration and second guessing. For example, when a ship is sailing at an angle to the wind, the wind pushes it sideways, which is one of the reasons why the ship does not actually go in the direction in which it is pointed (why its course over the ground is different from the course steered). The person making the entry in the log has to estimate the ratio between the leeway (sideways movement) in a given amount of time and the forward movement in order to estimate the angular deviation of the course over the ground from the course steered (figure 3.1). When the navigator learns where in fact the ship ended up after steering a given course with the wind at a given force and angle with respect to the ship, he has the opportunity to verify or correct the estimate of leeway used in the reckoning. By constantly recalibrating his estimation parameters, the navigator becomes more accurate in subsequent estimates. The entries on wind force and direction, sail set and trim, and so forth also enable someone who did not originally make the entries on estimated course and speed over the ground to revise those estimates (second guessing).

At least once a day—and much more often when sailing close to shore at night or in a fog—the captain or the navigator uses the estimates of the course over the ground and the speed over the ground to calculate (reckon) the ship's present position and course made good. The course made good is the angular deviation from true north of the line connecting the last calculated position (latitude and longitude) with the newly calculated position (figure 3.1). The navigator calculates the new noon-day position of the ship by calculating its position at each intervening half hour. The calculation of each new position—the position at each "bell"—uses the formula distance = speed x time to calculate the distance progressed over the ground from the estimate of the speed over the ground and the half-hour interval of time separating the entries. The changes in latitude and longitude are then calculated trigonometrically

$$\Delta\text{latitude} = \cos (\text{COURSE}) \times \text{distance}$$

and

$$\Delta\text{longitude} = \sin (\text{COURSE}) \times \text{distance},$$

where COURSE is the angular deviation from true north of the estimated course over the ground (figure 3.1).

If the intervals at which the new position is calculated are made shorter and shorter, this calculation approaches closer and closer to the opera-

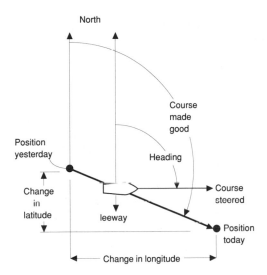

Figure 3.1
The "course made good" (heavy line) is the course steered plus the leeway due to wind and current. The course is decomposed into its orthogonal components, the change in latitude, and the change in longitude.

tion of integrating velocity with respect to time. Velocity, unlike speed, has a direction. A velocity on the plane is a two-dimensional vector; one dimension gives the speed along, for example, the north-south axis, while the other dimension gives the speed along the orthogonal (east-west) axis. The integral of speed with respect to time is distance; hence the integral of the velocity vector with respect to time is the distance moved along the orthogonal axes, the change in latitude and longitude over the interval of integration.

Large, modern ships carry dead reckoning equipment that performs this operation automatically and continuously. The ship's speed through the water is measured by a small propeller (screw) towed astern. The faster the screw turns, the faster the ship is going through the water. The signal from the screw (the speed signal) is converted to a velocity vector (longitudinal speed signal and latitudinal speed signal) by a computer, which gets the necessary course signal from the ship's compass. (The computation is given above; Δlatitude/Δtime = north-south speed; Δlongitude/Δtime = east-west speed.) The longitudinal and latitudinal speed signals are integrated to yield signals indicating the momentary longitude and latitude of the ship. These signals control a pen that plots the ship's course on a chart. The pen lifts from the paper at regular intervals to mark the time at which the ship was estimated to be at each point along its estimated course. Chapter 4 reviews the evidence that an animal carries a similar system in its nervous system—a neural circuit that provides it with a continuous estimate of its position by integrating its velocity vector with respect to time.

Dead reckoning is simpler when one is sailing along a line of latitude, which is why most ships "sailed the parallels" prior to the latter part of the eighteenth century, even though in doing so they knowingly went considerable distances out of their way. The ship sailed north or south to the latitude of its destination and then east or west "along the parallel" (the latitude line on the map). Doing this removes most of the trigonometry from the dead reckoning because one does not have to decompose the distance covered over the ground into its latitudinal and longitudinal components. The distance covered is entirely latitudinal when sailing due north or south and entirely longitudinal when sailing due east or west. Also, the trade winds tend to blow along the latitude lines, and midocean currents parallel the latitude, so a ship sailing along a parallel is generally sailing with the wind and current, which minimizes its leeway, making its course over the ground more nearly the same as its course through the water.

Finally, it is easy to determine approximate latitude from astronomical observation. With the season taken into account, the height (elevation) of the sun at midday is inversely related to one's latitude, and at night the elevation of Polaris is one's latitude. It is difficult (before 1700 well nigh impossible) to determine longitude from astronomical observation, because one has to know the time of day at some reference location (for example, Greenwich, England) with great precision to judge from the height of the sun how far one is to the east or west of that point. In sailing along a parallel, one can hold one's latitude approximately constant by astronomical observation and use the dead reckoning solely to estimate one's longitude, which was the general practice prior to the late eighteenth century.

The fact that dead reckoning computations for unrestricted courses are sufficiently complex to have imposed restrictions on the courses human navigators followed would seem an intuitive argument against the hypothesis that the nervous system of infrahuman animals like the ant routinely and accurately perform such computations. I raise this point specifically to argue against such intuitions, which I believe have been an obstacle to the acceptance of computational-representational theories of brain function. Symbolic manipulations that seem complex, hard to learn, and difficult to carry out by human beings often have simple physical realizations. Integrating a variable with respect to time sounds like an impressive operation, yet a bucket receiving a flow of water integrates that flow with respect to time. The filling of a bucket strikes most people as a simple physical operation. A symbolic (mathematical) presentation of the trigonometric and integrative operations involved in dead reckoning computations makes them sound forbidding, but the dead reckoning device on a ship is not complex. The trigonometric decomposition operations it performs are easily simulated with plausible neural circuits.[1]

The second point to stress is that experienced mariners do a great deal of unconscious, seat-of-the pants dead reckoning, a mental tracking of where they are that does not rest on any written record or any explicit computation. This is partly illustrated by the story of Columbus's dual reckoning. Columbus kept one reckoning for himself and one for the crew. The one given to the crew gave the distance they had progressed away from known land as about 10 percent less than what Columbus thought it actually was—to reduce their fearfulness and hence their inclination to mutiny. Interestingly, Columbus thought he could plausibly fool the crew by only about 10 percent. To an experienced seaman, this is not surprising. To become an experienced seaman is to acquire a tolerably accurate knowledge of how far a given ship may be expected to progress in a day's sail under given wind conditions. It was essentially this seat-of-the-pants knowledge that Columbus relied on in keeping his log. The irony is that the estimates Columbus gave the crew were nearer the truth than his private estimates because he was overestimating the ship's speed by about 10 percent.

The accuracy sometimes achieved in seat-of-the-pants dead reckoning is illustrated by Joshua Slocum's account of sailing alone around the world in the second half of the 1890s. Slocum was an extremely experienced seaman, but he sailed without a clock; hence he could not readily determine his longitude from astronomical observations and did not do so for long stretches of time. Furthermore he was often not at the helm of his ship, which had the remarkable property of holding a fairly constant course with no one at the helm, enabling him to sleep for hours at a time in his cabin and to spend many hours there reading when he was awake. On clearing the Straits of Magellan, Slocum set sail for the small island of Juan Fernandez, sitting by itself to the north northwest 500 miles off the coast of Chile. He made it "right ahead" after a fifteen-day sail of over 1500 miles. He took his leisure there and then set off on his most spectacular single leg. Sailing north from Juan Fernandez for 500 miles, he passed the small island of San Felix, the sighting of which gave him his last sure knowledge of his position before crossing the immense tract of

1. It must be admitted that the neurophysiological basis for perfect integration over long temporal intervals is a mystery, a mystery that may be closely linked to the physiological nature of information storage. See chapter 16.

open water that lay before him. He sailed on in a northwesterly direction to a latitude of 12° south, the latitude of the Marquesas, then turned west to "run down the longitude" before strong winter trade winds. Forty-three days after leaving Juan Fernandez, having covered a distance of about 4500 miles through the water since his last sight of land, Slocum reckoned that he had arrived at the longitude of the Marquesas, and he took difficult astronomical sightings to confirm this reckoning. He reckoned he was a few hours' sail (10–30 miles) from the Marquesas, and that afternoon he sighted Nukahiva, the southernmost of the island group. Without landing, he bore on toward his destination, the island of Apia in Samoa, where Robert Louis Stevenson's widow lived. He reached this destination when he was seventy-three days out, having covered 8500-9000 miles since last touching land, mostly by intuitive dead reckoning.

Slocum eloquently describes what it feels like to navigate long distances in this way:

> I sailed with a free wind day after day, marking the position of my ship on the chart with considerable precision; but this was done by intuition, I think, more than by slavish calculations. For one whole month my vessel held her course true; I had not, the while, so much as a light in the binnacle. [I never looked at the compass at night.] The Southern Cross I saw every night abeam. The sun every morning came up astern; every evening it went down ahead. I wished for no other compass to guide me, for these were true....Slowly but surely the mark of my little ship's course on the track-chart reached out on the ocean and across it, while at her utmost speed she marked with her keel still slowly the sea that carried her. [Slocum 1900, pp. 145, 147]

This quotation gives an intuitive feel for the methods by which small migratory birds accomplish journeys covering comparable distances over open water. They, like Slocum, mark their progress on a chart in the head (a cognitive map) by means of dead reckoning computations, using the sun and the stars for compass. I will argue that every mobile animal continuously keeps by dead reckoning a record of its momentary position on a representation of the macroscopic shape of its experienced environment and that, like Slocum, it only occasionally troubles to verify this estimated position by sightings on objects with a known position on its cognitive map.

The Slocum example gives an erroneous impression, however, of the accuracy that is routinely to be expected from dead reckoning computations, intuitive or explicit. A better indication of the accuracy to be expected is given by the fact that in the mid eighteenth century the British Commission for the Discovery of Longitude at Sea offered a reward of 10,000 pounds to anyone who could devise a method for reliably determining the longitude at sea to within 60 miles (= 1° of longitude at 30° of latitude) after a voyage to the West Indies and back, 15,000 pounds for a 40-mile limit of accuracy (= 40 minutes of longitude), and 20,000 pounds for a 30 mile limit. The Commission had in mind a method based on astronomical sightings in combination with a knowledge of the time at home (Greenwich Time), but the accuracy they hoped for from such sightings implies that after such a voyage (4000 miles one way), the dead reckoning estimate of longitude was commonly in error by substantially more than 60 miles. (Columbus was in error by 300 miles.) Slocum himself confessed that his experience was extraordinary and that any navigator would "tell you that from one day to another a ship may lose or gain more than five miles in her sailing-account" (Slocum, p. 147). As we will see in the next chapter, the typical nautical error of 5 to 10 percent in the reckoning is the error made by a desert ant in its dead reckoning.

Piloting

In the open water, knowledge of position is based mostly on dead reckoning. Sightings are infrequent, and when they occur, they are sightings on heavenly bodies since these are the only objects visible from a ship on the open sea with a knowable position relative to the earth. Fortunately, modest errors in the estimate of one's position, inevitable when the estimate is based on dead reckoning, are not dangerous far from land. Close to shore, however, in what are called pilot waters, modest errors in the knowledge of one's position are often fatal. The entrance to many harbors is less than half a mile wide and flanked by rocks a few feet beneath the surface. To quote Bowditch (1977), the Moses of American navigators: "piloting is used to mean the art of safely conducting a vessel on waters the hazards of which make necessary frequent or continuous positioning with respect to charted features." In short, piloting is the process of steering around unobserved obstacles and toward unobserved goals by reference to observed features of the land and to a map that records the geometric relationship between what you perceive and what you wish to avoid or find.

Crucial to piloting is the determination of one's position and one's heading. Position is represented by the coordinates of one's location in the system of coordinates established by or anchored to the map (chart). Heading is one's orientation on the map, which is the angular distance between grid north and egocentric north.

Definitions

Systems of coordinates.   The representation of the metric spatial relations between three or more points on a plane requires a system of coordinates or coordinate framework, by reference to which the positions of points are specified. When the representation is by means of a drawing on paper, the sheet provides the coordinate framework. When the representation is by means of numerical or physical vectors (strings of numbers or strings of quantities), the framework is established by the assignment of vectors to the first three points. This assignment corresponds to plotting the first three points. These initial decisions about which representing entities shall correspond to which represented entities dictate the assignment for all the other points (the positions where they must be placed on the paper or the vectors they must be assigned in the computer). Roughly, the first two decisions dictate the displacement and scale of the mapping—for example, where the Mediterranean appears on the sheet (displacement) and how much of the paper it occupies (scale). The third decision dictates the orientation of the mapping—whether Italy, Libya, Israel, or Gibraltar is at the top of the sheet. Displacement, scale and orientation exhaust the degrees of freedom allowable if the map (the representation) is to be isomorphic to the geometry of the shape (system of points) being mapped.

The system of coordinates established by assigning representatives to the first three points constitutes the "grid," which is anchored to the mapped system of points by the mapping. A fixed point in the mapping is a point whose coordinates (representation) are invariant within the system of coordinates. Usually the only nonfixed point represented continuously on a marine chart is the ship's position. All other points are fixed. The system of coordinates is said to be anchored to its fixed points. The fixed points define the macroscopic shape of the mapped environment.

"Grid" is in quotation marks because the system of coordinates does not have to be rectangular (Cartesian). It can, for example, be polar; in this case the value of one dimension of the vector specifies the angular distance of some point from "north" and the other specifies the distance of the point from the origin of the coordinate system.

The coordinates do not have to be orthogonal. In an orthogonal system, it is possible for an object to move in such a way that only one of its coordinates changes. When you move due north (move along a meridian), latitude changes but not longitude; when you move due east (along a parallel) longitude changes but not latitude. In a polar system of coordinates, moving along a circle centered on the origin changes angle but not distance, while moving along a radius changes distance but not angle. In a nonorthogonal system, in which the axes do not intersect at right angles, any movement changes both coordinates. Nonorthogonal systems of coordinates, while computationally inconvenient, can represent the geometry of a system of points just as completely as do orthogonal systems.

Various kinds of north.   "North" is in quotation marks because it refers to an arbitrarily chosen direction in a system of coordinates, a choice based on convenience or convention. For example, grid north refers to the top of the map being used, regardless of how the mapmaker has chosen to orient the representation of the world on that map. "Egocentric north" refers to the direction in which one's nose is pointing, which is a fixed direction in a system of coordinates anchored to the head but not in a system of coordinates anchored to the world or in one anchored to some other part of the body, such as the thorax. Different norths arise because the fixed points in one system of coordinates are moving points in another. Navigation can be thought of as the process of relating one's egocentric system of coordinates to a system in which points anchored to the earth are fixed points. Thus determining one's heading means determining the angular distance between grid north and egocentric north, which is the rotation of the egocentric system of coordinates with respect to the geocentric.

"True north" is the direction in which the northern end of the earth's axis of rotation points. "Local magnetic north" is the direction of the earth's magnetic field in a given locale; it varies from locale to locale and year to year but is generally aligned to within a few degrees of true north.

Methods for Determining Heading
In marine navigation, heading is most commonly determined by reference to a compass needle. It is an unsettled question whether any eukaryotic organism has a magnetic compass sense. Many published studies seem to offer convincing evidence of a magnetic compass sense in many different species (Dyer and Gould 1983; Quinn 1982), but experiments on the magnetic sense are bedeviled by unexplained failures to replicate (see special section of Animal Learning and Behavior 1987, vol. 15, pp. 107-134). There is unequivocal evidence that some bacteria can orient by the earth's magnetic field (Blakemore and Frankel 1981; Frankel, 1984), so it would be odd if no multicellular animal could. Nonetheless, it has proved difficult to develop reliably reproducible experimental demonstrations of this capacity.

If position has already been determined, heading may be determined from the position of any observable charted point. The determination is simplest when an observable charted point falls on the "lubber line," the line down the middle of the ship from its stern through its bow to infinity. (The direction in which the lubber line points might be called "shipcentric north.") One's "heading" is the angular deviation from grid north of the line from one's position to the position of a charted point on the lubber line (figure 3.2A). If there is no charted point to be seen on the lubber line, a charted point visible anywhere else will do. For a point off the lubber line, one's heading is the difference between the compass bearing (or azimuth) of the sighted point and its bearing. The "compass bearing" or "azimuth" is the angular distance from grid north to the line from the observer's position through the position of the point sighted, while the "bearing" is the angular deviation of this same line from egocentric (or shipcentric) north (figure 3.2B).

In animals that move within view of heavenly bodies, heading is commonly obtained by reference to them. As indicated in one of the passages from Slocum already quoted, this is also a common marine practice. The ability to determine heading by reference to the sun, and/

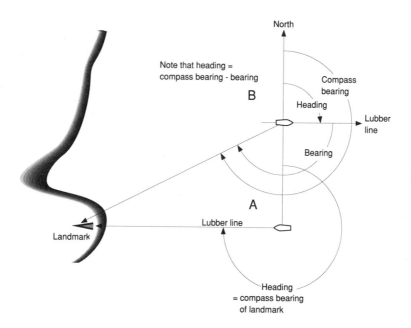

Figure 3.2
The determination of heading from the sighting of a charted object (object of known position). A. If the object is on the lubber line (dead ahead, at egocentric or shipcentric north), the heading is equal to the compass bearing of the landmark. B. If the object is off the lubber line, the heading is the difference between the compass bearing (azimuth) of the object (its bearing in a system of coordinates anchored to the earth) and its bearing (in a system of coordinates anchored to the ship).

or the moon, and/or the stars has been demonstrated in many organisms, including many insects. The widespread animal ability to determine heading from astronomical sightings is astonishing because these bodies are not fixed points in a system of coordinates anchored to points on the earth. They move in complex ways with respect to the earth, and these movements vary with the seasons (see figure 4.9). To get its heading from sightings on these bodies, the animal must know (represent) how these bodies move. In the case of the sun and the moon, it must also know (represent) the local time, the time indicated by a cyclical process in phase with the sun's locally perceived movement—for example, the time indicated by an entrained endogenous circadian oscillation (see chapters 5 and 7).

At any moment in time, the sun (or any other single heavenly body) may be regarded as a light atop a very high steeple; it is directly over some point on the earth's surface, which is called the "geographical position" of the sun. If the navigator knows the momentary geographical position of the sun, the sun may be used in the same way the sight point is used in figure 3.2B. The navigator's heading is the compass bearing of the sun's geographical position minus the bearing of the sun's geographical position. The problem is to know the sun's geographical position at the moment you happen to want to know your heading. Mariners carry with them "ephemeris tables," which specify the sun's geographical position at short intervals throughout the year, along with an equation for interpolating between the intervals specified. They also carry with them the highest-quality clock they can afford.

The mariner's ephemeris table is produced by astronomical observatories set up for the purpose, the most famous and historically influential of which is the observatory at Greenwich, England (whence the Greenwich Meridian and Greenwich Mean Time). Animals make their own ephemeris tables or functions, revising them with the seasons. Making one's own ephemeris table involves observing the sun's azimuth at each of several different times and recording both the azimuth and the time of observation (as given by one's endogenous circadian clock; see chapter 7). There must be enough time and azimuth observations to make a tolerable plot of the sun's azimuth as a function of the reading on one's circadian clock.

For animals living above the Tropic of Cancer, every point on the solar azimuth-time function varies with the seasons, except the point at midday, when the azimuth of the sun is always (very nearly) due south. For animals below the Tropic of Capricorn, the sun is always due north at midday; for animals in the tropics, it is due south at noon part of the year and due north the other part.

The azimuth of the sun at local noon is its azimuth at the moment it attains its maximum elevation (its "culmination"). The azimuth at culmination may be determined without knowledge of the time or date. Furthermore, the azimuths of all heavenly bodies at their culminations lie on the same meridian (north-south line). This astronomical invariant makes it reasonable to conjecture that animals generally align their cognitive maps with this direction (the axis of the earth's rotation), just as we do in conventional maps. Animals, including insects, demonstrably make ephemeris tables; that is, they demonstrably plot the course of the sun with respect to local terrain, as a function of local time. The local direction of the earth's axis is apparent in any ephemeris table, because it is the one and only direction in which the sun is always to be found at the same time each day and it is aligned with the center of rotation of the night sky.

To talk of plotting the azimuth of the sun as a function of the reading on the circadian clock may not give the best feel for what may occur within the nervous systems of the many animals that show "sun-compass" navigation. One might conjecture that the form of the solar azimuth-time function is innately given in the nervous system, with time and azimuth observations being used to compute the best-fitting parameters of this function. It is assumed to be understood from the discussion of representations and their physical realization (chapter 2) that to say the form of the equation is innately given is a shorthand way of saying that the development of a physiological process with isomorphic dynamics is programmed by the genes. To say the best-fitting parameters are computed from time and azimuth observations is to say that multiple simultaneous inputs from the eyes and the endogenous circadian oscillator affect the parameters of the dynamic process in such a way as to mold it to a closer mimicry of the sun's azimuthal motion (see the experiments on calibrating the ephemeris function in the next chapter).

An ephemeris table and a representation of local time are needed to determine heading from a sighting on an isolated heavenly body like the sun or the moon, but neither is necessary to determine heading from a look at the stars because the stars form a system of points. This system has a shape, in fact many local shapes. The local shapes salient in human perception are called constellations. The local shapes (star clusters) form a global shape called the celestial sphere. There are two points on the celestial sphere that lie on the extension of the earth's axis of rotation: the north celestial pole and the south celestial pole. In the current epoch, the north celestial pole nearly coincides with a bright and famous star, Polaris. No such star marks the south celestial pole. Within the span of written history, there was no such star in the northern half of the celestial sphere either. The precession of the earth's axis shifts the point of its

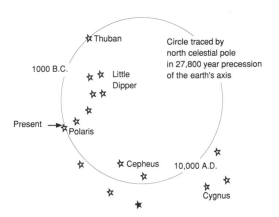

Figure 3.3
The earth wobbles on its axis (a phenomenon called the precession of the axis), which means that the intersection of the axis with the celestial sphere varies from epoch to epoch.

intersection with the celestial sphere very substantially, in a cycle lasting 27,800 years. In the time of Homer, the earth's axis pointed beyond the outer lip of the Little Dipper, whereas now it points to Polaris at the tip of the Little Dipper's handle (figure 3.3).

If you look attentively at the starry night sky off and on over a period of hours, you not only learn its shape (learn to recognize the constellations and their geometric relations to one another) you come to identify its center of rotation. As the night wears on, the stars change their position relative to the terrain that surrounds your point of observation. Stars that lie above Polaris move to the west during the night, while stars that lie below Polaris move to the east (figure 3.4). One point, however, does not move; its azimuth and elevation are constant. That point is the "celestial pole." Polaris is the only heavenly body with a fixed geographical position; it is always directly above the North Pole. Thus, one's heading may be determined from the azimuth of Polaris without reference to time (and one's latitude may determined from its elevation).

The fact that there is a bright star at the north celestial pole is a great aid to the precision with which one may easily determine one's heading at night under clear skies in the Northern Hemisphere, but the visibility of Polaris is in no way essential to the use of the stars to determine heading without a representation of local time. A look at any recognizable part of the celestial sphere—any part that contains a recognizable star cluster—suffices to determine one's approximate heading without reference to a representation of local time. This is because the macroscopic shape of the celestial sphere, the arrangement of the stars, is fixed (it varies percepti-

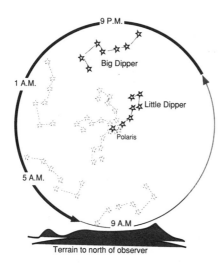

Figure 3.4
The stars make one complete rotation around the celestial poles every twenty-four hours, but only the portion of this cycle that occurs at night (heavy arc) is observable. The observable portion varies with the season. This figure shows the positions of the Big and Little Dippers at various hours during a spring night. The last shown position (9 A.M.) would not be visible because it occurs after sunrise. In the fall, however, this is the position soon after nightfall. When the stars are above Polaris, their azimuth (projection down to the horizon) moves to the west (left) with time, while when they are below Polaris, it moves to the east (right) with time. The Big and Little Dippers are circumpolar constellations because, for an observer at midnorthern latitudes, the part of the celestial sphere they occupy is visible at night all year. Stars closer to the equator of the celestial sphere are below the horizon during part or all of the night, depending on the season, that is, on where the earth is in its orbit.

bly only on a time scale measured in thousands of years). Since the arrangement is fixed, one may estimate the position of an unobservable point from a sighting of any recognizable part. The best-known example of this is the rule familiar to most people for finding Polaris by following the line defined by the outer lip of the Big Dipper for a distance that you come to know if you do it often. This enables you to orient by reference to the celestial north pole, even when you cannot see Polaris, provided you can see the Big Dipper. By the same token, a navigator in the Southern Hemisphere knows about where the southern celestial pole is though there is nothing to be seen there.

The ability to determine the position of an unmarked point on the celestial sphere by reference to whatever constellations happen to be visible is another illustration of the general principle that one can use a map, a representation of relative positions of perceptible and imperceptible points, to orient toward or away from what one cannot presently perceive by reference to what one can. The center of rotation of the star pattern is defined kinematically—by the manner in which the pattern changes position with respect to the earth in the course of the night. Migratory birds, when they are nestlings, learn the geometric relation between this kinematically defined point in the night sky and the statically defined points (the star clusters) by observing the night sky over periods long enough to perceive its rotation (chapter 5). They use their representation of the location of the center of rotation to maintain their heading while migrating at night.

Fixing Position by Sightings

Lines, arcs, and circles of position.   Fixing one's position is the process of determining the correct mapping of one's position into a system of coordinates anchored to points on the earth. In marine navigation, this is done by means of sightings on objects whose coordinates are known, objects represented on the map (charted objects, for short). These sightings establish lines, arcs, and circles of position. A line, arc, or circle of position is composed of the infinitely numerous set of points that satisfy the geometric relationship revealed by a sighting. If one sees that two charted objects are in line with one another ("in range"), then one's position lies on the line passing through their charted positions. The sighting reveals a collinearity relation between the positions of the objects and the navigator's position. The line of position is composed of the infinite set of points satisfying that relationship.

Suppose instead the navigator sights two charted points 74° apart. His position must lie on one of two arcs passing through those points (figure 3.5). The arcs are segments of "equiangular circles." Two points and an angle of separation define two circles; both have the same diameter, both pass through the two defining points, and their centers lie equidistantly on opposite sides of the perpendicular bisector of the line between the defining points. If the observed angle between the two sighted points is greater than 90°, the equiangular arcs are the larger of the two arcs into which the defining points divide each circle. If the defining angle is less than 90°, the equiangular arcs are the smaller arcs, and they form a lens. Every point on an equiangular arc occupies a position from which the two sighted points have the observed angular separation (figure 3.5). That is, the arcs of position are composed of the infinite set of chart positions that satisfy the geometric relation revealed by the sighting of the angular separation between the two charted positions.

A line of position is determined either by the sighting of two known points in range or by the compass bearing of a known point—the angular deviation of the line of sight from grid north (figure 3.6). Arcs of position are determined by a sighting of the angular separation of two

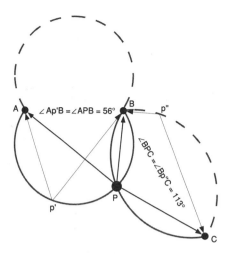

Figure 3.5
Sighting the angular separation of two charted points (*A* and *B* or *B* and *C*) determines two
arcs of position, one on the observer's side of the line between the positions (solid arcs) and
one on the other side (dashed arcs). These arcs are composed of all the points from which
the two observed points would have the observed angular separation, as indicated by the
sightings that would be made from alternative positions *p'* and *p''*. The intersection of the
arcs from two such sightings with a common point (*B*) fixes one's position (*P*).

known points. Circles of position are determined by the sighting of a
known point together with information that gives the navigator's distance from that point. The circle of position has the position of the charted
point as its center and the sighted distance as its radius.

The distance between an object and the observer is often difficult to
determine precisely. If the height of the object above the water is given on
the map, distance may be determined by trigonometric calculation from
its apparent height, the angular separation between the top of the object
and the water line (figure 3.7). The visual determination of distance
almost always relies on some kind of triangulation, because there is no
good means of measuring distance by sight alone without recourse to
triangulation.

Stationary fixes.   A stationary fix is obtained from intersecting lines
and/or arcs of position. When arcs of position are involved, the arcs used
must be restricted in some way so that one knows which of the two points
of intersection (between two pairs of arcs or between a pair of arcs and
a line) is the correct one. The most common fixes are from the intersection
of two compass bearing lines ("cross bearings" in figure 3.6), which is the
method favored by the bee in some of the experiments to be reviewed in
chapter 5. For arcs of position, the most common fix is the three-point fix,

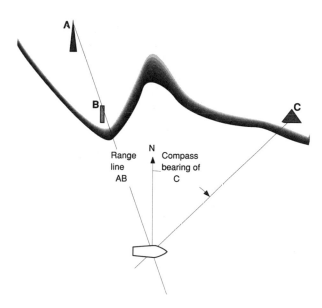

Figure 3.6
A cross-fix is the intersection of two lines of position, in this case, a range line and a bearing line.

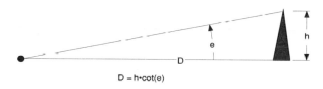

$$D = h \cdot \cot(e)$$

Figure 3.7
Triangulation is the principal means for visually determining the distance between oneself and a landmark. In this example, the distance is calculated from the known height of the tower (as noted on the chart or in a pilot's manual) and its "apparent size" (vertical angle as seen from the observer's position, which is equal to the elevation, e, of its summit).

which uses the arcs of position defined by sighting the angular separations between three points, one point being common to both observed angles. In a three-point fix, one of the two points of intersection between the pairs of arcs of position is coincident with the common point in the two angle sightings; hence it cannot be the navigator's position (figure 3.5). The navigator's position is the other intersection.

Running fixes.   A running fix combines two sightings of a single charted object, taken at different times and different observer positions, with the dead reckoning estimate of the distance between the first and second position of the observer. The bearings from the two fixes plus the knowledge of the distance between the positions from which the fixes were made enables the navigator to solve trigonometrically or graphically for the distance between the navigator and the object at the time of each sighting. The distance from the object defines a circle of position centered on the object. The bearing of the sighting gives a line of position through the object. The intersection between the line of position and the circle of position gives the fix (figure 3.8).[2]

The determination of one's position by a running fix is closely related to the parallax principle in the perception of distance. In its qualitative form, the parallax principle says that the farther an object is from an observer, the less its bearing changes for a given movement of the observer. In its quantitative form, it gives the formula for calculating the distance (D) of the object from the observer in terms of: the bearing of the object before the movement (α_1), the bearing of the object at the end of the movement (α_2), and the distance moved (d):

$$D = d\ [\sin(\alpha_1)/\sin(a_2 - a_1)].$$

The principle can also be given in its dynamic form—the distance between the object and the observer in terms of the observer's speed (s), the bearing (α) of the object and the angular speed of the bearing (α'):

$$D = s\ [\sin(\alpha)/\alpha'].$$

Because animals, like navigators, may estimate their speed with reasonable accuracy, moving helps them improve their knowledge of their position by informing them how far they are from whatever landmarks they are using to get their fix. This principle may help to explain why newly released homing pigeons that start off poorly oriented toward home soon improve their homeward orientation (chapter 5).

---

2. Usually, compass information rules out one of the intersections between the line and the circle; the compass bearing of one of the intersections from the ship will be wrong.

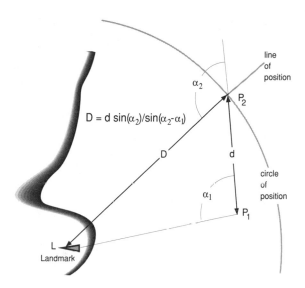

line
of
position

α_2

P_2

$D = d \sin(\alpha_2)/\sin(\alpha_2 - \alpha_1)$

D   d

circle
of
position

α_1

P_1

L
Landmark

Figure 3.8
A running fix uses the estimated distance (d) that the ship has moved as part of the information required to obtain by triangulation its distance (D) from a landmark. The distance
thus obtained defines a circle of position around the landmark. The bearing (α_2) of the
landmark establishes a line of position (P_2L). One's position (P_2) is the intersection.

Global Determination of Position and Heading

There is another approach to the determination of position and heading.
It is not used in marine navigation but may be important in the routine,
unconscious global fixing of position and heading that I believe, on the
basis of data to be reviewed in chapter 6, is done repeatedly when
humans and other animals move around. The methods for taking a fix in
marine navigation depend on the identification of individual sighting
points. Manuals caution the navigator to pick sharply defined and
unequivocally identifiable objects to sight on. By contrast, the global
method does not require the identification of individual points; it relies
on the overall configuration of points.

If we grant that most of the time an animal knows approximately
where it is on its cognitive map, then the process of taking a fix and determining its heading may be reconceptualized as a problem in image
alignment. By virtue of its knowledge of its approximate position on its
cognitive map, the animal may form an image composed of the points on
the map that should be perceptible from its estimated position. I will call
this map-derived image the anticipated image of the environment. The
animal also has an image of the environment derived from its current
perceptions, which I will call the current image. We may imagine both of

these images represented in an egocentric system of coordinates (figure 3.9). If the animal's estimate of its position and heading are in error, the two images will not be congruent. The anticipated image will be slid away (translated) and misoriented (rotated) with respect to the current image. The greater the error in the estimated position, the greater the translation required to make the centroid of the anticipated image coincident with the centroid of the current image. (The "centroid" of an image is the technical term for what one would intuitively call its center.) The greater the error in the estimated heading, the greater the rotation required to make the principal axis (long axis) of the anticipated image coincide with the principal axis of the current image. To correct its estimates of its position and heading on the basis of its present perception of its environment, the animal must adjust those estimates by the translation and rotation required to make the centroid and principal axis of the anticipated image coincide with the centroid and principal axis of the current image. I term fixes based on these kinds of computations "global fixes."

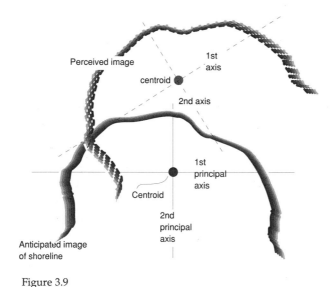

Figure 3.9
A global fix may be obtained by comparing the centroid and principal axes of an anticipated image with the centroid and principal axes of the actually perceived image. The anticipated image derives from one's cognitive map and one's dead reckoning estimate of one's position on that map. The correction to be applied to the dead reckoning estimate in order to get one's true position is equal to the vector difference between the centroids. The correction to one's estimated heading is the angular difference between the principal axes. Shepard (1975) has studied the psychophysics of this kind of image alignment in humans.

The computations of the centroid and principal axis of an image are closely related to the computations of the statistical descriptors of a scatter plot. In fact, it helps to forget that the points composing an image define a shape and think of them simply as the points in a scatter plot. The x and y coordinates of the centroid of an array of points are, respectively, the mean of the x coordinates of the points and the mean of the y coordinates. The first principal axis is the line of mutual regression. The line for the regression of y on x minimizes the mean square y deviations; the line for the regression of x on y minimizes the mean square x deviations. The mutual regression line minimizes the mean square deviations measured along an axis perpendicular to the regression line; that is, it minimizes the dispersion seen by an observer looking along the regression line. The second principal axis of an image is the line orthogonal to the first axis passing through the centroid. The squared deviations of the points from the first principal axis measured along (parallel to) this second principal axis are minimized in the computation of the principal axes of a shape.

Superimposing the centroids and aligning the principal axes of two images with approximately the same shape does not guarantee their proper alignment. The registration thus produced is unique only up to a 180° rotation about the centroid. If the animal is badly disoriented, it could get the anticipated image out of alignment with the current image by 180°. If, as is usually the case, the images are asymmetrical, the misalignment may be detected by checking for approximate correspondence of points or by computing a higher order moment of the distribution. If, however, the images are symmetric about both principal axes (as are rectangles, for example), there is no way based on shape alone that can detect a 180° misalignment of the anticipated and current images. Chapter 6 reviews experimental findings that this kind of 180° misorientation occurs routinely when rats are disoriented with respect to the larger world and required to establish their heading in a rectangular enclosure. The misorientation occurs even when the rectangular enclosure contains extremely prominent nongeometric features asymmetrically arranged, such as one white wall in an otherwise black enclosure and a strong peppermint odor at one end contrasting with a strong anise odor at the other. These misorientations in the face of prominently asymmetrical nongeometric features (reflectances, smells) suggest that in getting their heading in a mapped environment, rats rely on the principal axes established by the shape of that environment.

Celestial Fixing of Position
The ability to fix one's position by sighting on the sun and other heavenly bodies rests on the same considerations as does the ability to determine

heading from such sightings, except that now a precise knowledge of the time and a precise ephemeris table is essential even for stellar sightings. The ephemeris table gives the geographic positions of heavenly bodies in a coordinate framework anchored to the terrain surrounding the point of observation, as a function of the time at the point of observation. This tabular representation of the geographical positions of the heavenly bodies as functions of the time at the observatory enables one to use sightings on these bodies to obtain lines and circles of position provided one knows the precise time of day back at the observatory. At 30° of latitude, each 4-second error in one's knowledge of the time of day at the observatory results in a 1-mile error in the longitude of a line of position determined from a celestial sighting. The marine chronometer, which was developed in the eighteenth century in response to the fortune in prize money offered by the Commission for the Determination of Longitude at Sea, enabled mariners to carry with them the time at the observatory in Greenwich so that they could accurately determine their position at sea from celestial sightings. ("Accurate" in this context means "to within a few miles.")

The details of celestial fixes are not further described because the experimental evidence suggests that animals do not make or use such fixes (chapter 5) and it is a priori unlikely that they could. Celestial position fixing on the scale of movement of most animals requires a precision of time keeping and angular measurement that would not seem possible. Before the advent of quartz-crystal time keeping, even a rather good timepiece lost or gained a minute or two in a day (accuracy to one part in a thousand). These small temporal inaccuracies produce errors of 15 to 30 miles in celestial fixes. An error of 1° in the measurement of the sun's azimuth or elevation puts the navigator off by 100 kilometers. For comparison, a foraging ant whose estimate of its position is wrong by 100 meters is in mortal peril.

Animals get their direction from the heavens, not their position; they get their position from dead reckoning and point sights or global sights on the mapped terrain. The following three chapters review the experimental evidence for these claims.

Chapter 4

Dead Reckoning

The computation of their change in position by integrating their velocity with respect to time plays a fundamental role in adapting the behavior of mobile animals to the geometry of their environment. This chapter begins by reviewing experimental demonstrations of the phenomenon in operation in different contexts—the foraging ant returning to its nest, geese pulled in carts using dead reckoning to return home, a mother gerbil using the integration of angular velocity signals from the semicircular canals to correct for active and passive rotations in the course of a search for displaced pups.

After this initial look at the experimental evidence for dead reckoning in animals ranging from insects to mammals, we consider two computational models of the process. One model assumes that displacement is computed in a system of Cartesian (rectangular) coordinates; the other assumes that the computation is carried out in polar coordinates. Although the polar model is intuitively more appealing, it is computationally less attractive.

Crucial to any model of the computation of displacement is some means of keeping track of the direction of displacement. While inertial means can and are used to assess changes in the direction of displacement over short stretches, this approach is inherently unsatisfactory for keeping track of the direction of displacement during prolonged and tortuous trajectories when animals rely heavily on the sun as a point of directional reference. Their reliance on the sun is surprising because its direction varies as a function of time. We review experiments showing that ants, bees, and pigeons use an internal time sense to compute the change in the sun's azimuth (compass direction) during the course of the day and night. We also review studies in the bee showing that its computations depend on an empirically calibrated ephemeris, a representation of the sun's azimuth as a function of the time of day, which is constantly revised on the basis of the bee's experience of the relation between the sun and various landmarks.

The experimental demonstrations of time-compensated sun-compass orienting in the pigeon reveal another phenomenon on which the chapter focuses: animals commonly move under dead reckoning control even when the terrain is familiar and readily perceptible. In animal navigation, there is an interplay between dead reckoning and piloting that closely parallels the interplay between these processes in marine navigation. The position that is constantly recomputed by dead reckoning is the animal's position on a geocentric cognitive map. From time to time, the animal verifies its position by comparing its perception of the environment with what its map indicates it should perceive. In marine parlance, the animal periodically takes a fix on its position to correct its reckoning. Between fixes, animals rely on dead reckoning for moment-to-moment knowledge of where they are.

This thesis about the interplay between dead reckoning and piloting is supported by experimental studies of the transition between the two in the ant, which, like the mariner, looks for home only when its reckoning indicates it is in the vicinity. When its reckoning is seriously in error, the ant runs past its nest, oblivious to the landmarks it uses to pilot its way to the nest entrance. The same phenomenon is manifest in the maze running of the rat—to comic effect.

Dead reckoning generates the simplest of all spatial representations: the representation of the geometric relation between two positions on the earth's surface, the position where the reckoning commenced and the animal's current position. In the major period of European marine exploration, the captain's reckoning of the ship's position relative to its departure position played a fundamental role in bringing remote lands onto the same map as European lands. The reckoned longitude of the ship when new lands were discovered determined the longitude at which they were subsequently plotted on maps. The distortions in these early maps are testimony to how imperfect the mariner's reckoning often was. I argue that dead reckoning plays the same role in animals' construction of the map of their environment. Animals possess sensory-perceptual mechanisms that allow them to establish the positions of things in egocentric coordinates, coordinates anchored to the animal's position and heading at the time of observation. Dead reckoning relates the animal's position and heading during one observation to its position and heading at another, which is what makes it possible to compute a nonegocentric representation of the relative positions of objects and surfaces perceived at different times from different vantage points. Evidence for the use of dead reckoning in map construction comes from studies of rats locating themselves in familiar mazes by purely kinesthetic means and from experimental studies of the ability of a congenitally blind child to build a representation of the spatial relations among the various positions she is led to.

Experiments

Dead Reckoning in the Ant
When an ant or bee sets out from its nest searching for food, it pursues a tortuous path. The desert ant Cataglyphis bicolor may end up 100 meters from its nest after a journey many times that length. When the forager finds food, something deeply interesting happens: it turns and heads directly for home, moving at a rapid 15 meters per minute over the hard, almost featureless desert ground, until it is within a few meters of home, when it shows signs of looking for familiar landmarks. It does not retrace its winding outward path, as it would if it were following a chemical trace laid down on the way out; it goes home by the beeline (as does the foraging bee or wasp). We know that it is not following a beacon—a substance (for example, a volatile chemical) or a disturbance (for example, light or sound) that spreads out more or less radially from its source. Beacons can be used to home on their source if the direction from which they emanate may be determined by some sensory process. Beacon homing requires no representational capacity beyond the nominal; the animal need only distinguish the emanations from the source it seeks from emanations from other sources. However, there is no stimulus emanating from the nest or its environs that the ant can use to home on. How does it know where to head and how far to go?

There are two possibilities: either it sets and maintains its homeward course by piloting, in which case it must have a map of the terrain around its nest extending out 100 meters (covering the area of six football fields), or it continuously computes its position (displacement vector) relative to the nest over the hour or more of its twisting search and uses its displacement vector and current heading to calculate the turn that will put it on the course for home. We may feel some astonishment at the contemplation of either alternative. However, in the case of the foraging bee and the foraging wasp, there is evidence that both alternatives are available to the organism: at least some species have maps covering many square kilometers, and they all compute their displacement vector with some accuracy during long, winding journeys. The desert ant, however, has been shown to use its computed displacement to set its course for home, to hold that course by maintaining its orientation to the sun (and failing that, the wind), and to measure how far it has gone along its route home, so it knows when to switch on the piloting mechanism that will bring it to the 1 square centimeter of desert ground containing the opening to its nest.

That the foraging desert ant does not have a comprehensive map of the territory around its nest—and that the nest gives off no beacon the ant can detect at any distance—is shown by trapping foragers as they emerge from the nest and releasing them at randomly chosen locations 2–5 meters away (Wehner and Flatt 1972). When displaced as little as 3 meters from the nest, the ants show no evidence of knowing which way to head. They search for the nest in all directions. Only 57 percent reach the nest in less than 5 minutes. The mean time of 2.18 minutes needed by those 57 percent exceeds by a factor of ten the time required by a homeward-bound ant to cover the same distance. In short, the ants do not know where they are unless they themselves get there, which suggests that they know where they are by dead reckoning.

This assumption is verified by an experiment in which a feeding station is set up 20 or 40 meters from the ants' nest, located in a particularly featureless desert plane. On this plane, one area looks much like another, which puts a premium on dead reckoning. It also makes it possible to displace ants to other portions of the plane without their recognizing the change in terrain. On the plane about 600 meters distant from the nest and feeding station, Wehner and Srinivasan (1981) painted a gridwork of lines at 1 meter intervals. Foragers were captured as they departed the feeding station toward home and carried to the grid, where they were released at a fictive (nonexistent) feeding station and allowed to find their way to a fictive nest. The experimenter traced the ant's path on a data sheet that was a scale replica of the painted grid, making a cross-mark on the trace every 10 seconds, at the beep of a timer.

Figure 4.1A shows one such record. The fictive feeding station at which the ant was released is indicated by the small open square labeled S. The position of the fictive nest—where the nest would have been if the grid were superimposed on the territory from which the ant had been removed—is indicated by the open circle labeled N*. The tracing of the ant's path shows that it pursued with little wavering the direct route toward the place where home should have been. The regular intervals separating the 10-second cross marks show that it held a steady velocity. The ant's linear march terminated in a sharp turn at the filled circle labeled O. This turn marks the beginning of a search pattern. The point where the ant began its search was within 1° of the line connecting the fictive feeding station to the fictive nest and less than half a meter beyond the distance at which the ant should have encountered the nest.

Just how typical this result is may be seen in figure 4.1B, where the imaginary locations of the fictive station and the fictive nest are again indicated by an open square (at bottom) and an open circle (near top). The turning points for ten ants are indicated by the filled circles clustered at and just beyond the open circle. The slightly smaller filled circles, which appear in clusters over the stretch between the fictive feeding station and the fictive nest, indicate the positions of the ants at the 10-second cross marks. After a straight run of about 20 meters, all ten ants initiated their

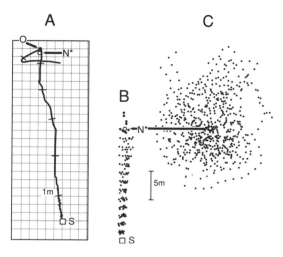

Figure 4.1
Homing in desert ants displaced to an unknown territory. *A.* Homing path of an individual ant (thick line). The cross-bars were made every 10 seconds. *S* = fictive feeding station,
where ant starts; *N** = fictive nest; *O* = the sharp turn with which the ant initiates its search
for the nest entrance (point of turn marked by filled circle). *B.* Superimposed plots of the
positions of ten ants at 10-second interval following their release at the fictive feeding
station. The larger dots clustered around the fictive nest mark the turns with which they
commenced their searches. *C.* Superimposed plots of the positions of the ten ants every
10 seconds during the 15 minutes after they started their searches. The open circle in the
middle of the cluster indicates the position of the fictive nest. (Redrawn from Wehner and
Srinivasan 1981, p. 318, by permission of author and publisher.)

search when they were less than 3 meters (and generally much closer)
from the place where the nest should have been. All remained close to the
beeline between food and home throughout their homeward run, and all
had made about the same progress at any moment after their release
(hence the clustering of the points). The ants are little machines, homing
by dead reckoning over ground they never covered before.

The homing performances charted in figure 4.1 testify to the precision
of the ant's mechanisms for computing its displacement, but they do not
reveal just how impressive the performance of this mechanism is. The
measure of the ant's powers of dead reckoning comes from the study of
the search pattern an ant carries out when it fails to find the fictive nest.
The search goes on for as long as the ant can survive under the desert sun,
which in summer is on the order of 2 1/2 hours. In this time, the ant walks
more than a kilometer, in convoluted, ever-widening loops that eventually carry it up to 50 meters from the place where it began its search.

The search has two important properties: it remains centered on the ant's original estimate of the nest's location, and the density with which a given square meter is searched (the frequency with which it is traversed) is higher the closer it is to the point where the search originated. Both of these properties are evident in figure 4.1C, where the small, filled circles represent an ant's position every 10 seconds for the first 15 minutes of its search (records from ten ants superimposed). The open circle representing the fictive nest lies in the center of this galaxy of points; the farther out from this center one goes, the less dense the points become.

The ant does not spiral steadily outward from the start of the search, as one might imagine it would. Rather it moves in tortuous loops. The loops get larger as the search progresses, but they repeatedly bring the ant back to within 1 or 2 meters of the start of its search, as indicated in figure 4.2. The repeated returns to the site where the ant's dead reckoning originally indicated the nest should be are accomplished by dead reckoning, not by piloting. This means that even after pursuing the extraordinarily winding paths indicated in figure 4.2 for the better part of an hour, the ant's reckoning of where it now is relative to where it started is sufficiently accurate to enable it to return to within a meter or two of its starting point.

Specific examples of these returns to the starting point are shown in figure 4.2. Panel A traces an ant's journey for the first 21 minutes of its search. Notice that its path repeatedly passes within a meter or two of the starting point, which is indicated by a small, open circle at the center of the tangle. At the end of 21 minutes, when this plot terminates, the ant is within a meter of its starting point (filled circle at the origin of the coordinate system). Panel B, where the coordinate frame has the same origin but a grosser scale, shows the ant's search over the subsequent 39 minutes. Now it ranges ever farther from the starting point, but it still returns to that point from time to time, so that it continues to search the area immediately around the starting point more densely than any other area. At the end of the hour, the ant was within 3 meters of the starting point (filled circle to upper right of origin). During this hour, the 12-milligram ant had walked half a kilometer at a steady rate of about 8 meters per minute carrying an 8-milligram piece of food.

Proof that the search is conducted by dead reckoning comes from displacing the ant again after it has searched some while. The displacement this time is about 10 meters, so that when the ant is released, it is on the periphery of the area it was searching (figure 4.3). If the ant took fixes on the landmarks surrounding the start of its initial search and subsequently piloted its way back to the start, it should react to this second displacement in one of two ways. One possibility is that the ant's search after the displacement would continue to be centered on the initial start-

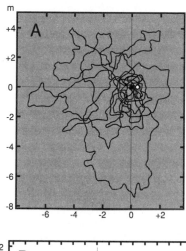

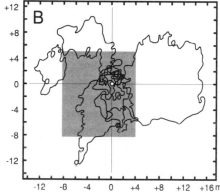

Figure 4.2
Ant's search path during first hour of search. *A*. The first 21 minutes. The open circle indicates the origin of the search. The filled circle at the origin of the coordinate frame indicates the ant's position at the end of 21 minutes. *B*. The next 39 minutes. The scale has been reduced by a factor of three, but the origin is the same. The open circle at the origin is the point where the tracing in *A* leaves off. The filled circle up and to the right of the origin indicates the ant's position at the conclusion of this tracing, 1 hour after the onset of the search. The gray area is the area shown in *A*. (Redrawn from Wehner and Srinivasan 1981, p. 320, by permission of author and publisher.)

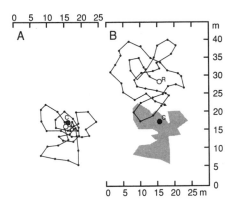

Figure 4.3
A search path before and after a mid-search displacement. The scale is in meters.
A. Before displacement. The search originated at the open circle. The ant was captured at
C, 4 minutes into its search. The small filled circles along the path indicate 15 second
intervals. B. Search path during the 8 minutes following its release at R. The gray area in
the lower part of the panel is the area covered by the search in panel A, with C indicating
the point of capture. Note that the center of the post-displacement search is displaced
relative to the center of the predisplacement search by the same vector as the displacement
from C to R. (Redrawn from Wehner and Srinivasan 1981, p. 322, by permission of author
and publisher.)

ing point. In this case, it would pilot its way back to that start from its
second release point, which is only 10 meters or so away, well within the
range from which the ant returns in the course of uninterrupted searches.
Alternatively, the ant might reset its search mechanism, take fixes on the
landmarks surrounding the new release point, and begin a search
centered there. The new search should begin with the tight loops characteristic of the beginning of a search rather than continuing with the wider
loops characteristic of the later stages of a search.

Neither of these outcomes is observed; the new search is not centered
on the old starting point. Regardless of how far the ant is from the starting
point of its search at the time it is displaced again, the center of the new
search is the point obtained by imaginarily shifting the original starting
point by the ant's second experimental displacement. With reference to
figure 4.3, the vector from C (the capture point) to R (the release point) is
the same as the vector from the center of the search prior to capture to the
center of the search after displacement. Also, the search path following
the displacement shows the wider loops characteristic of the later stages
of a search. In short, the ant behaves as it would if the search were entirely
controlled by dead reckoning, proceeding after the displacement as if
nothing had happened.

To appreciate fully the ant's dead reckoning, one must bear in mind
that the course tracings seen in figures 4.2 and 4.3 are reduced by a fac-

tor of about 100:1. They do not show the many very short changes in course that the ants in fact make. The turns are not made slowly; frame-by-frame analysis of movies made of these ants shows that their turning velocity attains rates of 4000 degrees per second—a complete rotation in less than a tenth of a second. In sum, the foraging ant computes its position relative to a starting position with a distance error on the order of 10 percent and an angular error on the order of 1° over violently twisting and turning courses that cover linear distances of as much as a kilometer. The precision and sophistication of dead reckoning in the ant suggests that this ability may be well developed in a wide range of mobile animals and play an important role in controlling their movements through their environment.

Dead Reckoning during Passive Transport in Geese
Ursula von St. Paul (1982) has demonstrated homing by dead reckoning in experiments in which tame wild goslings (and some adult domestic geese) were led or transported via indirect routes to unfamiliar release sites up to 1.5 kilometers away from their home pens and left to find their way home on foot (none of the subjects could fly). The goslings were being raised by human foster mothers, on whom they were imprinted. The adult domestic geese, also imprinted on human foster mothers when young, were now mothers themselves, with goslings left behind in the home area. Thus, homing motivation was high for all subjects. The goslings had been taught during daily exercise sessions that whenever their foster mother disappeared, she was to be found back in the home pen, and the adult mothers had young back in the home pen.

In her first experiments, von St. Paul either led the geese to the release site (the active condition) by a detour, or took them there by a similarly indirect route in a cage on wheels, which afforded a view of the passing terrain (the passive condition). The geese had never visited these release sites before. Whether they arrived at the site by their own efforts or were wheeled there in a cart, the abandoned geese generally set off in the direction of the home pen rather than back along the indirect route by which they had arrived at the release site (figure 4.4).

Variations on this basic experiment showed that the geese derived their homeward orientation by dead reckoning, rather than by calculating displacement from the bearings of known landmarks. The fact that the birds had never been to these sites before does not prove that there were no landmarks perceptible from these sites that were also perceptible from the home area (a crucial consideration when asking whether they could have been using a map to pilot their way home). Pigeons can orient toward home when released hundreds of miles from any area they

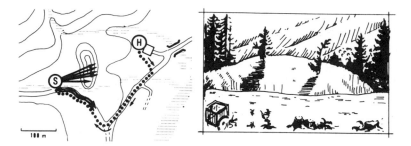

Figure 4.4
Left. Departure bearings (heavy arrows) from one release site (*S*) at Grünau. The release
site was in a forest clearing, which was reached via the road. Seven domestic geese
were transported one by one in an uncovered cage from *H* to *S* during the months of
April to June. Five geese chose the shortest return by climbing the mountain and
arrived home quickly. Two geese started on the path of arrival and got lost for hours.
At that season, the starting area was covered with thistles, which the geese were
hesitant to cross. *H* = home; dotted line = outward journey. *Right.* View toward home
from the release site. The geese traversed the steep slope that rises at the far side of the
clearing, zigzagging like mountaineers. (Reproduced from von Saint Paul 1982, p. 304,
by permission of author and publisher.)

have ever visited, after being transported there under conditions designed to prevent dead reckoning (Emlen 1975; see chapter 5 for further
discussion). This implies that the pigeons have access to widely perceptible stimuli whose approximate source positions may be estimated from
a very long way off. These sources, whatever they may be, must be
perceptible from the home loft and the release site. Thus, that an animal
has never been to a given site before is no guarantee that it cannot orient
homeward from that site by a piloting procedure, using directional
stimuli from sources whose positions are represented on the cognitive
map. The sources may be remote from both the release site and the home
site and yet give the animal the information it needs about its displacement. In this experiment, however, such stimuli were apparently not the
source of the requisite information because when the birds were wheeled
to the release site in a covered cage—without the velocity information
provided by optic flow—they were disoriented, and they generally
refused to leave the site.

Variations involving multileg prerelease journeys, with the cage covered during some legs and uncovered during others, indicated that the
geese computed their displacement only so long as the necessary visual
stimuli were present. They took no account of their displacements during the covered legs, when the stimuli needed to continue the moment to
moment computation of their displacement were no longer available.
When released, they oriented as if they were at the point where their

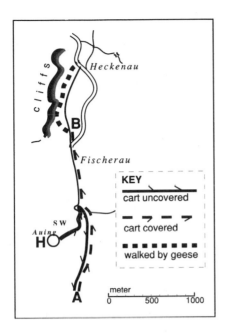

Figure 4.5
Example of one two-leg experiment. Two domestic geese were transported in the open
cage from *H* to *A*. At *A*, the cage was covered completely and the geese were further
transported to *B*, where they were released. The two geese walked together and stopped
at the indicated spot. The course they took was appropriate for the uncovered leg of the
cart-trip. Had they been released at *A*, this course would have carried them near home.
(Based on von Saint Paul 1982, p. 304.)

continued computation of displacement had been prevented by covering
the cage.

In the experiment of this type shown in figure 4.5, the birds were
wheeled away from the home site (H) in an uncovered cage, heading
roughly northeast. After about 600 meters, the experimenter made a
hairpin turn and wheeled the birds about a kilometer due south to point
A in figure 4.5. There the cage was covered, and then the birds were
wheeled due north 2 kilometers to point B, where they were released. The
birds took the indicated course to the north of the release site and,
initially, also somewhat to the west (further westward progress was
blocked by cliffs). Their trail on the map stops where the birds stopped.
They took a route that would have brought them approximately home
from point A but was inappropriate to point B, where they were actually
released. Like the ant, they had calculated not only which way they
should go to get home but also how far. They stopped after covering
about the distance from A to H, although A was reached by a circuitous

route covering much more ground than the straight-line distance from H to A. In the most elaborate experiments of this kind, the birds were wheeled back and forth on complicated routes, with the cover being put on and taken off several different times during the course of the prerelease trip. Upon release, the geese oriented as predicted from the vector sum of the uncovered segments of the prerelease journey.

Semi-inertial Dead Reckoning in the Gerbil

If a pup is removed from the nest of a gerbil and placed in a shallow cup somewhere in a circular arena 1.3 meters in diameter, the mother goes in search of it (Mittelstaedt and Mittelstaedt 1980). Like the foraging ant, she moves here and there in the arena, searching for her pup. The beacon effects of whatever odor she may be able to pick up from it are clearly weak. When she locates the pup, she picks it up, turns, and scurries directly back to the point she set out from. If the experimenter has moved her nest a little bit away, the mother returns to the point where it was, heedless of the noise and smell from the displaced nest nearby. Only when she has reached the point that was the origin of her journey does she search around and eventually find the displaced nest. This is the first of many examples that we will encounter in which beacon homing does not occur even under favorable circumstances. One might suppose that the mother gerbil would home in on her nest by following the sounds and odors emanating from it, but she does not. She moves by dead reckoning to a position defined by its geometric relation to other positions.

Inertial dead reckoning, like dead reckoning in general, involves the integration of angular and/or linear velocity to obtain angular and/or linear displacement. In the inertial case, the velocity signal derives from the integration of acceleration. The integration of acceleration with respect to time gives velocity as a function of time. The integration of velocity with respect to time gives position as a function of time. Inertial navigation represents the ultimate in self-reliance; it can be done without environmental input. The semicircular canals in the middle ear have long been recognized as sensory organs specialized for the detection of angular acceleration. The utricle and saccule, on the other hand, are specialized for the detection of linear acceleration. The question naturally arises whether the signals from these organs can serve as inputs to the dead reckoning process. The response of the mother gerbil to rotations and displacements shows the extent to which she does or does not take these into account in computing the direction of her homeward path.

If the pup is displaced to a cup located in the center of the arena on its own support and the experimenter quickly rotates the arena while the mother is on the cup picking up the pup, so that the nest is no longer where it was, the mother homes to where the nest was, not to where it now is. On the other hand, if the experimenter rotates the cup while the mother is on it, she takes account of this passive rotation and orients correctly toward the nest. She corrects for passive rotation unless the experimenter rotates the cup subliminally, by accelerating it smoothly to a rotary velocity of no more than 0.24° per second and decelerating it just as smoothly. When rotated very gently like this, the gerbil does not correct for the change in her heading: on her homeward scurry, she misses the nest by the angle through which she was rotated. It appears she keeps track of her heading during her foray by double integrating her angular acceleration.

The first stage of this integration is performed mechanically in the semicircular canals. Within the normal operating range, the neural signal from the canals is proportional to angular velocity rather than angular acceleration. This holds true only for velocities greater than those used in the gentler of the two cup rotations. The angular acceleration and deceleration for the gentler rotation were chosen from knowledge of the low frequency cut off in the capacity of the semi-circular canals to respond to angular accelerations (Precht 1978). The second stage of the integration—from angular velocity to angular position—is carried out within the central nervous system.

In order to set her course back to the nest, however, what the mother must have is not simply the double integral of her angular acceleration; she must take the accompanying linear displacements into account. She does not get the translatory velocity by integrating her linear acceleration. If the cup with the gerbil on it is shifted sideways rather than rotated, she does not correct for the passive linear displacement; she runs back on a course parallel to the course she should have taken. If the arena, cup and all, is linearly displaced, she homes correctly—as she should if she takes no account of linear acceleration. Evidently she does not derive her estimate of linear velocity from the vestibular system or any other acceleration-dependent detector of velocity.

It is probable that the gerbil's estimate of her displacement is based on the combination of a vestibular signal for angular velocity and a kinesthetic (reafferent) or efference copy signal for linear velocity (that is, either on the kinesthetic sensations that accompany locomotion or on the motor command that specifies the rate of forward locomotion; see Gallistel 1980). This points up the inherently multimodal nature of spatial and navigational computations. The sense of position transcends sensory modalities.

Another important point to be taken from this experiment is that when an animal is equipped with an acceleration-based sensory system for detecting angular velocity and with the capacity to integrate this signal to obtain its orientation, one has to take extreme measures to destroy completely the animal's sense of its orientation within a larger extraexperimental environment. Unless an experimenter has taken strong countermeasures, it is likely that an animal knows its rough geocentric heading, even when it is in an experimental space that the experimenter correctly imagines to be isolated from external sensory influences. When the animal cannot perceive a directional stimulus originating outside the experimental space, it may nonetheless know its approximate geocentric heading while it is inside that space, and this knowledge may have important effects on its performance. This point is important in the interpretation of a number of maze studies with rats.

Computational Models of Dead Reckoning

Computational models are psychological theories of a neurobehavioral process formulated in mathematical terms. Such a model constitutes an hypothesis about the computations that underlie an observed performance and the order in which they are performed. These models are psychological because they specify processes imagined to be going on in the nervous system in terms of their formal properties rather than in terms of their physiological embodiment. The models are formulated in terms of the operation of, for example, trigonometric decomposition rather than in terms of the neural circuitry that performs this decomposition. In explicating these models, however, I will indicate roughly the kind of circuitry that would be required, so that one can more readily imagine what such a model might look like at the neurophysiological level of analysis.

The flow diagrams that present these models may be regarded as charts for what to look for at successive stages of the neural processing of the stimuli that govern the behavior. Often more than one such flow diagram can be constructed to explain the same behavioral facts. It is wrong, however, to imagine that there is an infinity of quite unrelated models. Most models are minor variants of one another, as is obvious when they are completely laid out in flow diagram form. It is also wrong to assume that it is easy to generate a truly satisfactory and entirely explicit computational model for some behaviorally significant process like dead reckoning. It is also wrong, I would argue, to imagine that it is possible to understand complex processes in the nervous system at the physiological level of analysis without the guidance of one of these charts of what to look for at successive stages of processing. Often what one finds at one stage enables one to decide which general kind of computationally equivalent model one is dealing with, which in turn suggests what to look for at the next stage. Finally, there are often purely computational considerations that render one kind of model more likely than another.

The flow diagrams presented are intended to render mathematical models intelligible as a series of operations performed on signals (or, in the first stage, on stimuli that act on receptors). The arrows in these diagrams represent the signals. Mathematically, these signals are variables. Boxes and circles represent mathematical operations performed with these variables. Boxes represent unary operations like raising to a power, taking the cosine of, integrating with respect to time, and so on. Circles represent combinatorial operations like summing, subtracting, multiplying and dividing.

Physiologically, the boxes represent processes that transform one neural signal into another. A box with a square root symbol in it represents a hypothetical neurophysiological process in which the output signal is proportionate to the square root of the input signal. The circles represent circuits that combine two or more signals to generate a new signal—circuits that perform integration in the neurophysiological rather than mathematical sense of the term. The quasi-neurophysiological interpretation of the flow diagram will be given in the first diagram presented but omitted from later diagrams, on the assumption that by then the reader will understand how one translates from computational language into neurophysiological language.

The Cartesian Model
A decision that must be made at the outset of constructing a computational model of dead reckoning is whether the computations are to be carried out within Cartesian or polar coordinates. Does the animal represent its position relative to the nest on a rectangular grid or as a certain distance and angle away from the nest? The polar model is perhaps more intuitively appealing because to set a homeward course, an animal needs to compute the heading it should adopt and the distance it should run. These behaviorally relevant quantities are more or less directly given if the representation of current position is in polar coordinates with the nest at the origin. If the current position is in Cartesian coordinates, a further computation is required to derive the bearing and distance of the nest from the representation of the animal's current position and heading. However, it turns out that there are computational reasons for regarding the Cartesian model as more plausible.

A Cartesian model of dead reckoning was first spelled out by Mittelstaedt (1962). The first stage of the Cartesian computation involves decomposing the animal's solar heading (α) into its sine and cosine components. The sine component would be a neural signal that was strongest when the sun was directly lateral to the animal on one side and weakest when it was directly lateral on the other. Most likely, one would have the usual complementary push-pull arrangement in which one circuit is maximally excited when the sun is directly to the right while the complementary circuit is maximally excited when the sun is directly to the left, and the two circuits mutually inhibit one another. The cosine component would be a signal that was maximal when the sun was directly ahead and minimal when it was directly behind. Again, a push-pull arrangement of mutually inhibitory circuits would seem most plausible neurophysiologically—one peaking when the sun is dead ahead, one when it is dead behind.

The neural signals for the sine and cosine of the animal's solar heading depend on which portions of the retina the sun's image falls on. The other angular input to the computation, by contrast, has a purely internal origin. It comes from the ephemeris process, the process tied to the animal's entrained circadian oscillator in such a way that its output signals the solar azimuth. (In the model, the solar azimuth, σ, is assumed to be measured clockwise from due north.)

It is assumed that the representations of α, σ and all other angular quantities are in sine-cosine form rather than in circular measure. Circular measure represents an angle with a single number (quantity), for example 265° or 3.2 radians. Circular measures of angular position are discontinuous at the full circle point (360° or 2π radians), where their value drops from its maximum to zero. The sine-cosine representation expresses an angle in terms of two numbers (quantities), one being the sine of the angle and the other the cosine. These two quantities rise and fall continuously no matter where one is on the circle. There is no discontinuity at the full-circle point.

The sine-cosine representation of the ephemeris angle (σ) combines with the sine-cosine representation of the solar heading (α) to produce the sine-cosine representation of the sum of these two angles, which is the the animal's heading (η). The summation circle indicating the operation of combining the sine-cosine representations of angles to obtain the sine-cosine representation of their sum has the angle symbol in it, because more than simple addition is involved, as is apparent from the trigonometric identities,

$$\cos(\alpha + \beta) = \cos\alpha \, \cos\beta - \sin\alpha \, \sin\beta$$
$$\sin(\alpha + \beta) = \sin\alpha \, \cos\beta + \cos\alpha \, \sin\beta,$$

which give the cosine and sine of the sum of two angles in terms of the cosines and sines of the constituent angles. The circle with an angle in it represents this combinatorial process.

The sine and cosine components of the heading then combine multiplicatively with the third input, a signal indicating the animal's forward speed. This signal may have many origins, but one important source for such a signal is likely to be internal. There is reason to think that higher brain centers send a speed signal to the neural circuitry that coordinates stepping. This speed signal determines the rate of forward locomotion by determining the period of the stepping oscillators that control the rhythmic stepping of each individual leg (see Gallistel 1980, chap. 5). A copy of this speed command signal (an efference copy—Gallistel 1980, chap. 7) may serve as the speed signal in the dead reckoning computation, just as the rate at which the ship's screw is turning often serves in this capacity in shipboard systems. The two signals resulting from this stage of multiplicative signal combination give the animal's speed along the north-south (longitudinal) and east-west (latitudinal) axes.

The integration of these orthogonal velocity components with respect to time gives quantities that represent the animal's north-south (y) and east-west (x) displacements from the origin (the nest, N). One cannot readily suggest a neurophysiological embodiment for the integration process, because it requires precisely those formal characteristics that make the physiological basis of memory one of the unsolved mysteries of neural function. The integration process must be such that the value of the output changes so long as a signal is present at the input but remains perfectly stable whenever there is no input signal. In remaining stable in the absence of a nonzero input, the output preserves the animal's representation of where it is relative to its nest.

The bottom half of the flow diagram in figure 4.6 shows the computations required to derive from the Cartesian representation of displacement the distance (D) to the nest and the sine-cosine representation of the nest's bearing (θ), the quantities required to determine the distance the animal must walk to reach the nest and the turn it must make to put itself on the right course. It turns to the right if the sine component of θ is positive, to the left if it is negative. The magnitude of the turn is $\cos^{-1}\theta$.

In computing θ (the nest's bearing) from β (its compass bearing), one has to subtract out both σ (the solar azimuth) and α (the animal's solar heading). Subtracting an angle is, of course, the same as adding the negative of that angle. In the sine-cosine representation of angles, the negative of the angle represented by $<\sin X, \cos X>$ is represented by $<-\sin X, \cos X>$, which explains the minus signs that appear in front of the sine components of σ and α above and below the angle–summation circle at the bottom of the flow diagram.

The Polar Model

In the Cartesian model, the animal computes its speed along two perpendicular axes of the coordinate system for representing position, then integrates to get its displacement along those axes. In the polar model, the

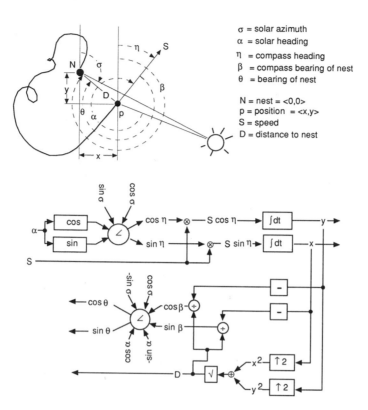

Figure 4.6
Computational model of dead reckoning in Cartesian coordinates. The upper diagram indicates the variables (top = north). The upper half of the computational flow diagram shows the computations of the Cartesian position coordinates <x,y> in a coordinate framework with the nest (N) at the origin. The x coordinate gives the distance east-west of the nest; the y coordinate the north-south distance. The inputs to the computation are α, the angle of the lubber line measured clockwise from the sun (the solar heading), S the forward speed, and σ, the signal from the internal solar ephemeris function, giving the sun's azimuth as a function of the time of day. The bottom half of the flow diagram shows the computation of the nest's distance (D) and the sine-cosine representation of its bearing (θ). The egocentric direction of the turn the ant must make to head to the nest is given by the sign of the sine of the nest's bearing ($+$ = right, $-$ = left), while the inverse of the cosine ($\cos^{-1}\theta$) gives the magnitude of the required turn.

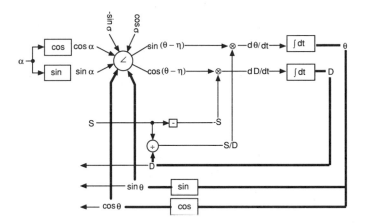

Figure 4.7
Computational model of dead reckoning in polar coordinates. For the definition of the quantities (variables), see diagram at top of figure 4.6. Note the feedback loops (heavy arrows), whose error-amplifying properties make this model computationally unattractive.

computation resolves the animal's forward speed into a component that is the angular velocity of the nest's bearing and a component that is the radial velocity (the rate of change in the distance from the nest), then integrates to get angular and radial displacement (figure 4.7).[1]

The key insight in constructing the polar model comes from a study of the trigonometry of the situation, which reveals that the angular velocity of the nest's bearing ($d\theta/dt$) is equal to the animal's forward speed scaled by the reciprocal of its radial distance from the nest and multiplied by the sine of the difference between the nest's bearing and the animal's compass heading:

$$d\theta/dt = (S/D) \sin(\theta - \eta)$$

The radial component of the animal's forward speed is given by:

$$dD/dt = -S \cos(\theta - \eta).$$

Finally, the animal's compass heading in terms of the two input angles is:

$$\eta = \sigma - \alpha.$$

In the flow diagram (figure 4.7), the first stage of the computation subtracts the ephemeris signal (solar azimuth) from the sum of the solar

1. This model was worked out by Ben Backus in a graduate seminar.

heading and nest bearing signals to get the angle $\theta - \eta$. The cosine of this angle combines multiplicatively with the inverse of the speed signal to give the radial velocity (dD/dt), which is integrated with respect to time to determine the distance (D) from the nest. The operation of inverting a signal (also called the unary minus operation), symbolized by the little box with a minus sign in the path for the speed signal, corresponds to inserting an inhibitory interneuron in a pathway.

To get the nest's bearing, the speed signal is divided by the signal giving the radial distance. This scales the impact of the speed signal by the reciprocal of the distance from the nest. The farther the animal is from the nest, the less effect a given forward speed will have on the nest's bearing (the parallax principle). The scaled speed signal (S/D) combines multiplicatively with the sine of the difference between θ and η to produce a signal that represents the rate at which the bearing of the nest is changing. This is integrated to get the current bearing of the nest.

The flow diagram for the polar model makes clear why this is not a satisfactory computational model. This model, unlike the Cartesian model, has feedback loops (heavy arrows); and embedded in these loops are operations that integrate signals with respect to time. The quantities θ and D enter into the initial stages of the computation, but the values of these quantities are derived by integrating signals that depend on the results of these initial computations. Feedback loops that contain integration with respect to time are ill advised from a computational standpoint because they amplify the inevitable errors in the signals being integrated. Signals always differ by some amount from what their true value should be. The integral of a signal contains the integral of this error plus some additional error due to the imperfections in any physically realized integration operation. When the integral is itself used in the computations that generate the signal that gets integrated, as in the polar model, then the errors get compounded by reintegration. Thus, on computational grounds, the polar model is less satisfactory than the Cartesian model. Insofar as evolution by natural selection favors computational solutions that minimize error, selection will favor the Cartesian model over the polar model.

The Maintenance of Compass Orientation

Navigation by dead reckoning requires that the animal determine its compass heading (its heading in a system of coordinates anchored to the earth's surface) and its translatory velocity. How do insects determine their moment-to-moment compass heading? The basic answer appears to be: in all the ways the marine navigator traditionally does. The navigator determines compass heading from the sun and other astronomical bodies, from the prevailing wind, from large-scale features of the terrain, and from the pointing of magnetized ferric needles. Insects apparently use all four methods. As Dyer and Gould (1983) emphasize, the determination of orientation, like other fundamental behavioral processes, is mediated by a variety of different mechanisms arranged in a precedence hierarchy so that another mechanism takes over when circumstances do not favor the operation of one higher in the precedence hierarchy.

Sun-Compass Orientation
Ants, bees, and many other organisms often hold a fixed orientation in an earth-anchored coordinate system by using the sun and other heavenly bodies as points or patterns of angular reference. The first demonstration that ants marching home across the desert floor maintained their compass orientation by reference to the sun was simplicity itself. Santchi (1913) found an ant marching with the sun on its left, obstructed its direct view of the sun, and put a mirror to its right, angled so the ant saw the reflection of the sun in the mirror. The ant turned around and marched the other way. When Santchi angled the mirror in various ways, the ant adjusted the line of its march so as to maintain its angle relative to the azimuthal angle of the sun's image.

What is startling about the discovery that the ant maintains a straight path on the earth's surface by sighting the sun is that the sun is a moving reference point. (The bee and even the marine slug *Aplysia* seem to do the same; Hamilton and Russell 1982.) If the animal holds constant its angle relative to the sun, it follows a curving path on the earth's surface. To hold a constant compass bearing by sighting the sun, it must continuously adjust its angle to the sun to offset the change in the sun's azimuthal angle.

The changes in the sun's azimuthal angle go on when the insects are out of sight of the sun, either because they are confined to their nest by inclement weather or because the sun is obscured by clouds. But the ant extrapolates these changes: when it resumes its travels after hours out of sight of the sun, it steers the same geocentric course it followed before. When the straight-line journeys of ants are interrupted by imprisonment in light-tight boxes for as long as 18 hours, the geocentric course they follow upon release does not deviate on the average from the course they pursued prior to imprisonment (figure 4.8). The data in figure 4.8 and similar data for bees and other animals that orient by the sun show that these organisms remember their compass bearing over intervals of many hours (indeed, over days) and that they extrapolate the changes in the sun's azimuthal position over such intervals.

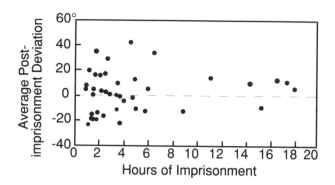

Figure 4.8
The average postimprisonment deviation of an ant's course from its preimprisonment course, as a function of the number of hours imprisonment in a light-tight box. The average azimuthal velocity of the sun is 15° per hour, so in steering the same compass course after its release that it steered before its imprisonment, say, 10 hours earlier, the ant changes its solar heading by 150°. (Redrawn from Jander 1957, p. 232, by permission of author and publisher.)

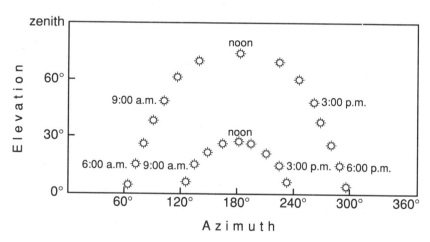

Figure 4.9
Sun's course in summer and winter. It always moves at 15° per hour along a route from east to west, but the rate at which its azimuth changes (horizontal displacement differs dramatically according to the time of day, the latitude, and the season. The upper curve is the sun's course on the summer solstice at 40° north latitude. The rate of movement along the azimuth at dawn is about 10° per hour; by noon it reaches 47° per hour. The lower curve is the sun's course at the same latitude on the winter solstice. (Redrawn from Dyer and Gould 1983, p. 588, by permission of the author and publisher.)

Calibrating the ephemeris function. The rate of change of the sun's azimuthal angle is not constant. It varies during the course of the day in a pattern that depends on the season and on the observer's latitude (figure 4.9). A mechanism that adjusts all bearing angles by 15° per hour of time elapsed since the taking of the bearing will not work well. The organism must extrapolate the movement of the sun on the basis of its most recent observations.

Gould (1980) trained bees to a food source and then imprisoned them for 2 hours, either at 11:00 solar time, when the rate of change in the sun's azimuthal angle was 33° per hour and increasing, or at 12:00, just as the sun's azimuthal velocity reached its peak of 47° per hour and began its deceleration. In both cases, he moved the hives to a new site before releasing the bees, so they could not rely on local landmarks in addition to the sun. At this new site, he set up feeding stations, both at the correct compass angle relative to the nest and at angles to either side of this. He monitored which stations the marked foragers arrived at, thereby estimating the change in the sun's azimuth computed by the bees for the 2 hours they were out of sight of the sun (figure 4.10).

When released, the bees pursued a solar heading indicating that they had extrapolated the sun's position from estimates of its angular velocity based on sightings taken over a period of approximately 40 minutes prior to imprisonment. Bees imprisoned at 11:00 were extrapolating for the period from 11:00–1:00, using an estimate of angular velocity based on measurements taken during the period 10:20–11:00, when the average velocity was appreciably lower; as a result, they systematically underestimated the change in the sun's azimuthal angle. Bees imprisoned at 12:00 extrapolated for the period 12:00–2:00, during which the average velocity decreased appreciably, using data from 11:20–12:00, the period when average velocity attained its peak; as a result, they systematically overestimated the change.

In a subsequent study, Gould (1984) made 30° step changes in the angle between a feeding station and the sun and found that the foragers took about 40 minutes (about ten round trips) to correct fully for the change in the apparent position of the sun. The amount by which they corrected was a linear function of the time since the change, indicating the averaging of successive sightings over a period of about 40 minutes.

Gould's experiments show that in calibrating their solar ephemeris function, bees average the data from repeated sightings of the sun. The sightings are separated by intervals during which the bees are in the hive, out of sight of the sun and the external landscape. The ability to average over separate sightings implies that the bees can reorient themselves to the same external terrain from one occasion to the next because a sighting is the measurement of the azimuthal angle of the sun, which is defined

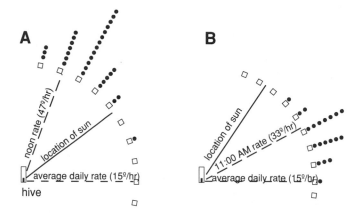

Figure 4.10
To test how bees deal with changes in the rate at which the sun's azimuth moves, foragers trained to use a food source at one site were trapped within their hive at solar noon (A), when the azimuth of the sun was moving at the rate of 47° per hour, and released at a new site two hours later. They were then captured as they arrived at an array of feeding stations positioned in such a way as to indicate how far the foragers judged the sun to have moved while they were in the hive. Squares indicate the location of the feeding stations; each dot represents one forager. Predicted directions are shown for three hypotheses: that the bees knew or could accurately calculate the sun's movement, which was 66°; that they estimated the sun's azimuth by assuming that the sun continued to move at 47° per hour, the same rate as when they had last seen it; or that they simply used the daily average rate of azimuth change, which is 15° per hour. When imprisoned at the time when the sun's azimuthal speed was greatest, the bees clearly overestimated the sun's movement (A). When the hive was closed at 11:00 a.m. (B) with the sun's azimuth moving at 35° per hour and opened two hours later, the bees underestimated its movement. In both cases, the foragers behaved as though their estimates of the sun's azimuth when the hive was reopened were based on the rate at which the azimuth was moving about 20 minutes before the hive was closed. Further experiments suggest that the bees estimate the sun's azimuthal speed by a process that takes a running average over a 40-minute wide interval. (Redrawn from Dyer and Gould, 1983, p. 589, by permission of author and publisher.)

with respect to a fixed direction on the surface of the earth, that is, with respect to the terrain surrounding the point from which the sighting is taken. The ability to calibrate a solar ephemeris function, which Gould's experiments demonstrate, implies the ability to orient oneself reproducibly with respect to the local terrain, which in turn implies a cognitive map of the terrain, a magnetic compass, or both. The next chapter reviews experiments demonstrating the terrain map. There is also evidence that bees have a magnetic compass sense (see Dyer and Gould 1983 for review), although it should be borne in mind that demonstrations of magnetic orientation have been plagued by problems of replication.

Effect of shifting the internal clock on sun-compass navigation. Another way to demonstrate the existence of an internal ephemeris function that gives the sun's azimuthal position as a function of the time indicated by an animal's endogenous circadian clock is to put the endogenous clock out of phase with the local day-night cycle (a so-called clock-shifting experiment). Renner (1959, 1960) did this by training bees in an open field in Long Island to fly to a feeding station northwest of their hive (compass bearing = 315°). One night, he packed up the hive and flew it to California, where he set it in a similar open field near the University of California at Davis. He placed feeding stations at 45° intervals around the hive in California, at a radius equal to the distance from hive to station on Long Island. The time difference between Long Island and Davis is a little more than three hours, which means that the azimuthal angle of the sun at Davis is on average about 45° behind its azimuthal angle on Long Island.

The bees from Long Island were jet lagged when their hive was opened at Davis; their endogenous clocks were roughly 3 hours ahead of the day-night cycle at Davis. When a bee whose internal clock is 3 hours ahead of local time tries to use the sun to set a northwesterly course, it will in fact set a westerly course; it will orient approximately to 315° − 45° − 270° instead of to 315°. This is what the bees did at Davis, proving that their ability to steer by the sun depends on an endogenous ephemeris function linked to their endogenous circadian rhythm. These experiments also indicate that bees can find a previously experienced feeding site by dead reckoning. To do so, they must represent the site's position relative to their hive—that is, they must have a cognitive map. Without the map, the dead reckoning system would not know what course to hold and how far to go.

Emlen and Keeton (reported in Emlen 1975) clock shifted homing pigeons by keeping them indoors on a light-dark cycle 6 hours ahead of the outdoor cycle. The bird's internal clock indicated it was 3 P.M. when it was in fact only 9 A.M. On a sunny day, the clock-shifted birds were driven away from the loft in Ithaca, New York, in closed cages to release sites at the cardinal points of the compass. Since the azimuthal position of the sun changes by about 90° in the course of 6 hours, a bird that holds its course by looking to the sun should be off by 90° when its internal representation of the time is off by 6 hours. In figure 4.11A, the azimuthal position of the sun given by the ephemeris function of a bird that represents the time as 3 P.M. is shown by the small, dotted circles to the southwest (lower left) of each circle. The dashed angles originating at these small sun circles and pointing out toward the goal are the angles the bird would steer with respect to the sun in order to get home if it really were 3 P.M. The solid angles originating at the actual position of the sun

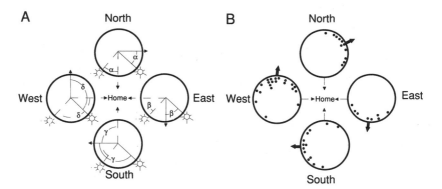

Figure 4.11
Predicted and observed compass bearings of clock-shifted homing pigeons released to the
north, east, south or west of home. *A*. Predicted compass bearings: The dashed sun
indicates the azimuthal position of the sun at 9 A.M. true local time given by the ephemeris
function of a pigeon whose circadian clock has been advanced by one quarter of a day
relative to the local day-night cycle, so that it is 3 P.M. on the internal clock. The dashed
angles indicate the solar headings birds must adopt at the time of day indicated by their
internal clock to put themselves on a course for home from that release site. The solid
angles indicate the compass course they will in fact pursue, given that the sun is actually
at its 9 A.M. azimuth (solid sun). *B*. Observed departure bearings. Each dot represents the
compass bearing of a pigeon at the time it flew out of sight after its release at the site
represented by the circle. The solid arrows indicate the mean of the observed departure
bearings. The dashed arrows indicate the compass bearing of the pigeons' home loft. Note
that the mean departure bearing at each site is about 90° counterclockwise from the true
course home, as predicted by the shift in the pigeon's internal clock and the consequent
error in the signal from the pigeon's ephemeris function. (Based on Emlen 1975, pp. 158,
159.)

to the southwest (lower right) of each large circle and pointing off at angles 90° counterclockwise from the goal are the courses the birds will in fact steer, given that it is really 9 A.M. The observed departure bearings appear in panel B. Each dot represents the compass bearing of a bird at the time it was lost to the sight of an observer standing at the release site. The solid arrows pointing outward from the center of each cluster of dots represent the mean bearing vectors (the average departure directions), which correspond closely to the predictions.

Stellar Orientation: The Role of Early Learning
The calibration of the solar ephemeris function by sightings of the sun's position relative to the local terrain at different readings of the internal clock is an example of what Rozin and Kalat (1971) have termed an adaptive specialization in learning. The learning mechanism plays a genetically assigned role in a complex behavior pattern. The computational principles in this kind of learning are more or less peculiar to it because they reflect the special demands that evolution has placed on this mechanism. Migratory birds maintain their orientation at night in part by reference to the stars. This, too, requires learning, but of a different sort from the learning required by the sun-compass mechanism.

Orienting by the stars presents problems and opportunities that do not arise when orienting by the sun. Every star has a different ephemeris function: the azimuth of a star at the north celestial pole does not change with the time of night, the azimuth of a star above the celestial pole moves from east to west, and the azimuth of a star below the pole moves from west to east (figure 3.4). If animals oriented to stars by means of internal ephemeris functions, they would need a different function for every star (indeed, a marine ephemeris has separate tables for the twenty-seven or so stars most commonly used in marine navigation). However, the orientation of many migratory birds with respect to the stars is unperturbed by clock shifting (Emlen 1975), indicating that they do not rely on an ephemeris function. When one works with birds like mallards, which migrate day and night, orienting by the sun during the day and the stars at night, one finds that clock shifting alters their daytime orientation but not their nighttime orientation (Matthews 1962).

How, then, do birds get a compass direction from the stars? They do it by exploiting the fact that the stars form a fixed pattern. The pattern moves with respect to an observer on earth, but within this moving pattern, there is a point that does not move, the celestial pole, the center of rotation of the night sky. The bearing of the celestial pole may be estimated from a view of any recognizable portion of the star pattern. To orient by the stars, birds must learn the static pattern they form and the unique point in the pattern defined by the pattern's rotation. In short, the birds must form a cognitive map of the stars.

A stellar map is an instructive example of what it means to have a purely geometric representation. A star seen in isolation is impossible to identify; it is simply a point of light with no distinctive intrinsic properties that enable it to be recognized. A star is recognized not by virtue of its intrinsic properties but by virtue of its geometric relations to other stars, its position in the pattern. Ordinarily, to know what it is you are seeing, you must see a configuration of stars, a constellation.

Because of the very slow proper motions of the stars (their motions relative to one another), the shape of the night sky changes over what are short intervals from an evolutionary perspective. In 100,000 years, the Big Dipper will be unrecognizable as such. Because of the precession of the earth's axis of rotation, the location of the center of rotation of the night sky changes even more rapidly. Hence, if generation after generation of a given species is to orient the nighttime portions of their migratory flight by reference to the stars, each generation must learn for itself what the night sky looks like and where its center of rotation is.

Songbirds learn the pattern of the night sky and its center of rotation as nestlings, at a time of life when they never leave the nest and hence have no immediate need of the information.

Emlen (1967) put indigo buntings in a planetarium in cages contrived so that he could measure the direction in which the birds attempted to take off. He blocked out different constellations one at a time and found that no one constellation was crucial. The birds attempted to take off in the direction appropriate to their autumnal migratory condition no matter which constellation was missing. But when he removed the entire circumpolar sky—everything within about 35° of the center of rotation— the buntings' orientation deteriorated. He also found that different individual buntings knew different constellations or combinations of constellations. Blocking out one combination would disorient some birds but not others. When another combination was blocked, some of the previously disoriented birds regained their orientation, while others lost theirs.

The finding that the birds relied primarily on the stars within 35° of the stellar pole is not surprising in the light of other experiments showing that buntings learn the configuration of the night sky and its center of rotation in the spring of their natal year, while they are unfledged nestlings. The circumpolar stars do not pass beneath the horizon for an observer in temperate latitudes, hence they are seen on spring nights as well as in the fall (see figure 3.4). Stars farther from the stellar pole pass beneath the horizon. Most of the ones seen on a spring night will not be seen on an autumn night. If what you learn about the stars in the spring is for use in the fall, you should focus on the circumpolar stars.

Emlen (1969a, 1972) demonstrated that indigo buntings learn the constellations and the center of rotation of the night sky while fledglings—and only while fledglings. He raised some of them in a planetarium, where he made the night sky rotate around Betelguese, on Orion's shoulder. When the fall came, the now-mature birds were shown a stationary sky; they oriented as they would if they were trying to take off toward the south southeast (their normal fall migration direction) and Betelguese were the pole star. Other buntings were denied a view of the night sky during their fledgling period. Subsequently, these birds never oriented consistently with respect to the night sky, regardless of their migratory condition. By the time the knowledge of the stars was of use to them, they could no longer master it.

For a bunting to take a compass orientation from the stars, it must learn their configuration and the center of their rotation. But this learning does not determine the orientation it will adopt, although one might imagine that it would. The stars visible in the more equatorial regions of the sky change between spring and fall, as do the positions of the circumpolar constellations. One might suppose that the spring sky was associated with northerly habitats and caused the bunting to wend its way back to those habitats when the spring stars reappeared in the equatorial sky and the Big Dipper was found once again to be upside down above Polaris. It is not, however, the appearance of the sky that determines whether the bunting orients to the south southeast (its autumnal migratory direction) or to the north northeast (its vernal migratory direction). Which of these two orientations it adopts depends on its physiological condition, particularly its hormonal condition.

In terms of the analysis of behavior-production mechanisms given by Gallistel (1980), the heading a migratory bird adopts with respect to the stars depends on which hormonally potentiated high-level motor unit is making use of the bird's learned representation of the constellations and of its ability to calculate from a view of one part of the learned pattern the bearing of another part, the center of rotation. Emlen (1969b) demonstrated the motivational dependence of the orientation adopted by manipulating the light-dark cycle in an indoor aviary so as to bring two groups of male indigo buntings into different migratory conditions simultaneously. One group was in the condition for a spring migration, while the other was in the condition for a fall migration. When he exposed both to the same stationary planetarium sky, the group in the spring condition oriented north northeast while the group in the fall condition oriented south southeast. Martin and Meier (1973) reversed the polarity of the migratory orientation of caged sparrows by appropriate hormone treatment, demonstrating that the motivational condition of the birds was embodied in their hormonal state.

The learning of stellar configurations by migratory songbirds illustrates a number of assumptions central to a representational approach to learning in general. First, there is no necessary connection between the behavioral context in which information is acquired (the context in which learning occurs) and that in which the animal makes behavioral use of the information (the context in which what was learned becomes manifest in what is done). The birds learn what they need to know about the stars at a time when they cannot fly. As far as anyone knows, this information is of no behavioral use to the nestbound fledgling during the learning period; it certainly is not used to control in-flight orientation. Later, when the bird has acquired feathers and needs to fly south to survive, it is difficult for it to learn what it needs to know, despite the heightened utility of the information. These findings undermine the utilitarian assumption that reinforcement is central to learning, that the immediate beneficial consequences of particular behaviors stamp into the nervous system the circuit changes that increase the likelihood of future performance of the same behavior (Hull 1943; Huston 1982). The learning of the stellar configuration cannot be conceptualized as "selection by consequences" (Skinner 1981). At the time of learning, there are no consequences, and by the time the animal is equipped to benefit from what it has learned, it is no longer capable of learning it.

The learning we confront in this example clearly involves, and essentially so, the operation of specialized computational mechanisms, working in intimate interaction with specialized storage systems. An understanding of the laws of this learning cannot be separated from an understanding of the computational mechanisms by which the information is acquired. The center of rotation of the sky cannot be derived from a single look. The fledgling bird must store the image of the sky it perceives at one time and the orientation of this image with respect to local terrain, just as the bee must store the azimuth of the sun in a coordinate system anchored to the local terrain. It must integrate the stored image with the image it gets when it looks again minutes, hours, or even days later, just as the bee calibrates its ephemeris function by integrating repeated sightings of the sun.

In making this argument, I assume that the extraction of the center of rotation of the night sky can be done only by a computation performed on at least two successive images, taken at different times of night, with a known orientation to the earth's surface. If this assumption is correct, this computation is only possible given a means for storing the image of the night sky. Otherwise it .would not be possible to integrate the information in the first stellar image with the information in the second stellar image in order to calculate the center of rotation.

A related lesson is that the learning mechanism is inherently hierarchical in the following sense. Some of the information that eventually gets coded and stored somewhere in the nervous system for subsequent use is obtained by computations performed on information laid down in intermediate stores (lower-level records). The information about the center of rotation has this second order character. It is possible for the system to compute and store this information only on the assumption that it can store the compass bearings of several different stars seen in a single look at the sky. This first-order learning capacity is a prerequisite for the higher-order capacity whereby the machinery computes and stores the center of rotation. The center of rotation is not given in the record obtained from a single look. It emerges only when two or more such records are operated on by the computational machinery. Later (chapter 13), I will argue that the learning involved in classical conditioning is similarly hierarchical. The first-order learning involves the recording of the times of occurrence of events. The second-order learning involves the computation of a prediction function from a series of such records. The computation of the prediction function presupposes a record of the times of occurrence of the events.

Another lesson is that specialized computational machinery is involved in the readout of the stored information into behavior. When the pole star is obscured by clouds or when, as in most historical epochs (and currently in the southern hemisphere), there is no perceptible star at the center of rotation of the sky, the readout machinery must compute the bearing of the unseen center of rotation from the positions of the stars the bird now sees. This computation makes it possible for the bird bound for the south southeast to adjust its orientation so as to keep this calculated point behind and slightly to its left.

Another lesson is that what is learned does not determine the use made of that information, contrary to incentive theories of learning. Incentive theories assume that information is acted on only if it becomes associated with a record of some beneficial or pleasurable experience. Hence, what is learned determines the direction of behavior. This idea goes back at least to Aristotle. Such an analysis is not applicable to the use that the bunting makes of the information it has acquired about the stars. By adjusting hormonally mediated motivational states, which do not, so far as we know, depend in any way on the night sky's appearance, one can induce two buntings with the same learning history to adopt opposing orientations with respect to the same sky. The bunting in a spring condition orients northward even under an autumn sky, and a bunting in an autumnal state orients southward under a spring sky. What the birds have learned about the sky makes it possible for them to orient themselves with respect to it, but it does not determine which orientation they will adopt. What is learned makes it possible for behavior to have a direction, but it does not determine what that direction will be.

In summary, the learning that underlies a migratory bird's ability to hold a compass heading by reference to the circumpolar constellations illustrates the assumptions that a representational theory makes about learning in general:

1.   Learning is intimately connected to computational machinery that extracts information with a particular formal structure from particular sensory inputs, independent of the immediate utility the information may have and independent of the uses to which it may subsequently be put by diverse readout mechanisms.

2.   Information acquired in different situations can have fundamentally different formal structures; the structures of the circuits that extract and store the different kinds of information will reflect these differences.

3.   The task in the analysis of learning is to figure out what is being extracted and stored—what it is about the external world that is represented by the stored code—and how this information is extracted—what kinds of computations are performed.

4.   A subsidiary and separable task is to figure out how the information extracted and stored by the different kinds of circuits is integrated by behavioral readout mechanisms and put to behavioral use. This should be treated as a separate question because different units of behavior (readout mechanisms) may be expected to use the same stored information in different ways.

Dead Reckoning and the Cognitive Map

In marine navigation, dead reckoning is done in connection with a map. The positions computed are expressed in a coordinate framework anchored to observed points on the earth's surface. Also, there is a subtle interplay between dead reckoning and piloting, which involves the use of a map in orienting. For example, in a running fix, one estimates one's position on a map by deriving the distance and bearing of a charted landmark, using dead reckoning to get the length of one side of an imaginary triangle and sightings on the landmark to get two compass bearings. From the two bearing angles and the length of the side they enclose, one calculates the length of the side of the triangle that corresponds to one's current distance from the landmark (see figure 3.8). Similarly in animal navigation, the positions computed by dead reckoning are expressed in a coordinate system anchored to observed points on the earth, and there is a constant interplay between processes like piloting, which requires a map, and dead reckoning, which is in principle sufficient unto itself, but which in fact is generally performed in the context of a map. Indeed, dead reckoning probably plays an important role in the construction of the map.

The Distinction between Setting and Holding a Course
An important aspect of the interplay between the map and dead reckoning is revealed by the Emlen and Keeton experiment on the homing of clock-shifted pigeons (figure 4.11). When pigeons were clock shifted by 6 hours and released 25 miles from home, in one or another of the four cardinal directions, the birds released at different sites set off in different directions. The average direction in which the birds departed from each release site was about 90° counterclockwise from the homeward direction. The fact that the birds released at different sites departed in directions that were related to the correct homeward direction by the same angular error implies that at each release site they correctly determined the approximate homeward direction. The process by which they set their course, which is a piloting process and requires a map, was functioning appropriately. What functioned in a systematically erroneous way because of the shifting of the internal clock was the course holding process, which is an aspect of the dead reckoning system.

A marine analogy may help to make this important distinction clear. When a sailor has been blown out of his way by a storm (analogous to the experimental displacement of the pigeons by Emlen and Keeton), the first thing he does when the storm has cleared is take a fix on his position. He establishes where he now is on his map by sighting on something that has a known position. When he has established where he is on the map, he calculates the compass bearing from his position to the position of his next port. This calculation is possible because his map shows his present position relative to the position of the port. In other words, setting the course is an exercise in piloting and, therefore, it makes reference to a map. Suppose the mariner sees from the map that he will reach his port by heading due east (compass bearing = 90°). However, in the storm some iron in the hold has shifted nearer the magnetic compass by which he steers so that when the magnetic compass indicates 90°, the heading of the ship is actually 0°—90° counterclockwise from the indicated heading, an error analogous to the sun-compass error produced by shifting the pigeon's endogenous clock ahead by a quarter of a day. The mariner will sail due north, not because he incorrectly estimated his position, or because he incorrectly calculated the compass bearing from his position to his port but because his magnetic compass, which he uses to hold his heading at the calculated value, is off by 90°.

The most interesting aspect of this example—and of the pigeon's performance, which it is meant to explicate—is that the mariner will be misoriented with respect to the very landmarks from which he correctly estimated his position relative to his port. Suppose, for example, that the mariner obtained his latitude by a sighting on Polaris. In sailing off on what is supposed to be a due east heading, he will in fact, because of the error in his magnetic compass, be sailing directly toward Polaris. One would expect that before long the mariner would notice that something was drastically wrong with his magnetic compass; he is pointed at Polaris while his magnetic compass indicates that the ship is heading due east. Thereafter he will either ignore the magnetic compass or recalibrate it by noting which direction it points when the ship sails at various angles with respect to Polaris.[2] One might expect the pigeons in the Emlen and Keeton experiment to react similarly, and in fact they did. Most of them made it home rather quickly, so they must have soon noticed—probably from the perception of the landmarks from which they first got their position—that they were not progressing in the expected direction. Then they either ignored their sun-compass or recalibrated it.

The tendency of birds to calculate their position from one set of inputs but hold their heading by another may be characteristic of animal navigation. The strength of this tendency is suggested by experiments in which clock-shifted pigeons are released on sunny days within a few kilometers of the home loft, in territory they have flown over many times, sometimes within direct sight of the home loft. Even under these conditions, which strongly favor holding a course with respect to landmarks rather than with respect to the sun, clock-shifted birds often set off on the wrong course (Graue 1963; Matthews 1968; Schmidt-Koenig 1972, p. 281). This may indicate that they do not make use of visual cues even to determine their displacement from the home loft. On the other hand, it may indicate that even when they estimate their displacement by the visual sighting of familiar terrain, they do not then hold their course by reference to that terrain but by reference to the sun. They may look at the familiar terrain and judge that they are southwest of the loft, then look to the sun in order to orient themselves on the appropriate northeasterly course. Presumably, when they have flown a while on the sun-determined orientation, new positional estimates indicate that they are not

2. The process of calibrating a magnetic compass by using charted landmarks to put the ship on known compass headings and writing down the readings of the magnetic compass is called "boxing the compass." Ships commonly box the compass before they get out of sight of the charted landmarks that enable them to do so.

going in the desired direction, at which point corrective mechanisms come into play.

The bizarre tendency of clock-shifted homing pigeons to fly off in the wrong direction when they are within sight of their loft is an indication that when an animal is moving, it holds its course and computes its position mostly by dead reckoning, even when it is moving through thoroughly familiar terrain—filled with charted landmarks. Only now and then does the animal verify its dead reckoning by reference to this charted terrain. In other words, there is a precise analogy between common marine practice and the way animals navigate.

The Transition from Dead Reckoning to Piloting

When the reckoning of the distance covered indicates that landmarks in the vicinity of the goal should now be sighted, piloting begins to take over. The information picked up from the sighting of familiar landmarks is used to correct the calculated position. This is as true for the desert ant as it is for the mariner. In an experiment by Burkhalter (1972), ants were captured as they started home from the feeding station 20 meters from their nest and displaced forward or backward along the line between the feeding station and the nest. In the backward direction, the direction away from the nest, they were displaced for distances of 5 to 25 meters; in the forward direction, toward the nest, for distances of 5 to 20 meters.

The distances these ants walked in a straight line before making the turn that indicated the beginning of the effort to pilot into the nest entrance were compared to the distances walked by the ants displaced into completely unfamiliar territory, where they had to go entirely by dead reckoning. The ants going by dead reckoning alone first turned to search when they had walked (on the average) a distance equal to 1.1 times the distance they should have walked. That is, by dead reckoning alone they overshot the true distance by an average of 10 percent. In figure 4.12A, the data for the ants displaced backward from the nest for varying distances are shown (thick lines) alongside the line that represents a 10 percent overshoot (thin lines ending in arrow heads). Below this is a bar graph of the percentage of ants that eventually found the nest. For displacements backward by 5 to 10 meters (displacements that increased the true distance home by 25 to 50 percent), almost all the ants continued straight ahead well beyond the 10 percent overshoot point, where they would have turned to search if they were still proceeding on dead reckoning alone, indicating that they were drawn onward by sightings on familiar landmarks, sightings from which they learned that they were not as close to home as they calculated. Figure 4.13B shows the results when ants were displaced toward the nest, so that the true distance was less than they represented it to be. These ants stopped their

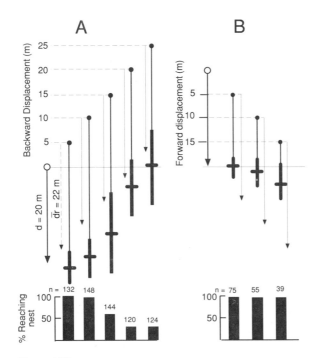

Figure 4.12
The effect of familiar landmarks on the length of an ant's homeward run after radial
displacement from its nest. A. Mean straight-line march of ants displaced backward from
the feeding station (farther from the nest) by 5–25 meters at the start of the homeward run
(line graph) and the percent eventually reaching home (bar graph). The heavy line at the
left of the line graph gives the route from the feeding station (open circle) to the nest (arrow
head); d = the true distance from the feeding station to the nest. The distance the ants would
run in the absence of an, familiar landmarks was determined by displacing another group
to unfamiliar territory, and this distance $\bar{dr}$ = mean dead reckoning distance = 22 meters)
is indicated by the thin arrows, which are displaced backward by an amount equal to the
displacement of the ants in each condition in this experiment. The distances run by the ants
displaced a given amount backward are indicated by lines terminating in heavy segments,
which indicate the mean (cross-bars) minus and plus one standard deviation. The number
of runs at each displacement is indicated below each line, above the bar for the percentage
of ants that found the nest. Note that the ants displaced 5, 10 and 15 meters backwards were
drawn on by the sight of familiar landmarks (running straight ahead longer than they
would have by dead reckoning alone), but the ants displaced 20 and 25 meters backward
did not see anything like what they expected to see when their dead reckoning indicated
they should be nearing home. They stopped and began to search for the nest when their
dead reckoning said they should be there. B. Same experiment, with ants displaced toward
home, so that they arrived there sooner than the dead-reckoning indicated they should.
Note that the sight of familiar landmarks cut short the runs. However, when these
landmarks appeared much sooner than expected by dead reckoning (15 meters forward
displacement), there was a strong tendency to overshoot the nest. (Based on Burkhalter
1972, pp. 305, 307.)

straight run well before they would have done were they going by dead reckoning alone, indicating that sightings of familiar landmarks informed them that they were closer than they had calculated.

Compass Bearings and Dead Reckoning in the Maze Running of the Rat
My hypothesis: first, when animals move, dead reckoning computations continuously generate an estimate of their position and heading on a cognitive map of the environment through which they move; second, the planning of movements is carried out on the basis of their representation of their position and heading on the map; third, the dead reckoning system's computation of distance and direction travelled is part of what enables animals to construct their map in the first place. This hypothesis may shed light on some long-standing and often replicated aspects of rats' performance in familiar mazes.

Carr and Watson (1908) trained rats in a Hampton Court maze (figure 4.13) until they ran it rapidly and without entering any blind alleys. Some of the rats were surgically blinded. Carr and Watson then ran a series of trials in which they introduced the rats at randomly chosen points in the maze and watched their performance, recording the times they took to reach the goal and any entries into cul-de-sacs. They observed that, for a little while, the rats wandered to and fro around the point where they had been placed, in a manner that suggested to Watson and Carr "uncertainty, perplexity, and lack of confidence." The authors continue:

> Finally, a change of behavior is observable. The suggestion of perplexity and uncertainty is gone, the rat starts off with a sudden burst of increased speed and every movement thereafter is characterized by the precision and regularity which mark the functioning of an automatic habit . . .This change of conduct has been termed 'getting the cue'. . . This change from random to controlled activity is striking and characteristic, but extremely difficult of description except in anthropomorphic terms. (p. 29)

Few who have watched a rat getting its bearings in a familiar maze would deny the aptness of this description. Carr and Watson go on to ask what the cue is that the rat gets. What could a surgically blinded rat be picking up as it wanders to and fro that would enable it ultimately to set off with confidence from a randomly chosen point in a complex maze? In the course of their review of the possibilities, they note:

> The alleys may be of the same length and be entered by the same direction of turn, but present possible differences in their stimulating effect because they extend in different directions. It is difficult to conceive why and how this can be so, and the possibility is suggested

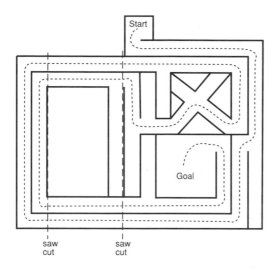

Figure 4.13
The Hampton Court maze used by Carr and Watson (1908). The saw cuts (coarsely dashed lines) made it possible to remove and reinsert the section between them. The finely dashed line indicates the correct route through the intact maze. (Redrawn from Carr and Watson 1908, p. 28.)

only because of certain observed facts. The successful functioning of an automatic habit depends upon the rat's orientation in relation to cardinal positions [that is, on the rat's compass heading, the direction in which it points in a coordinate framework anchored to the earth]. Change the [compass] direction of the path and the automatic act is disturbed to some extent. The same act accomplished in two different directions is thus different in some way to the animal. (p. 31)

Nine years later, Carr (1917) reported at some length the experimental observations that led to the just-quoted passage, without offering any more suggestions how this could be so. He was trying to determine what sorts of manipulations disrupted the performance of rats in a complex maze. The maze was indoors and completely enclosed by thick curtains. Between experimental sessions, the rats were kept in a rack of cages at the other end of a large room. At the beginning of a session, they were carried across the room and inside the heavy curtains surrounding the maze. The curtains were intended to block perception of the world outside the experimental enclosure. Carr found that rotating the entire apparatus, enclosure and all, so that it was oriented to a different point of the compass produced more disruption than did most of the other manipulations he tried (Carr 1917, p. 270). This was baffling, because it was unclear what the sensory basis for this disturbance could be. How could the rat know, while inside the heavy curtains of the enclosure, that it was oriented north and south instead of east and west?

Rotating the rats' home cages, which were at some remove from the experimental maze outside the canvas, also produced some disruption. When the rats were brought to the maze from home cages that had been rotated out of their normal orientation within the room, the rats appeared disoriented within the maze. It was not clear how or why a change in the compass orientation of the home cage should have an effect on performance in the remote maze, from which the rats could not see their home cages. This was the more puzzling in that variations in the route taken by the experimenter in carrying rats from the home cage to the maze had no effect on the rats' performance in the maze. Rotating the rats with respect to their environment while carrying them through it did not bother them, but rotating their home cage out of its normal orientation in the room did.

The experimental discoveries of the last half-century regarding the widespread animal ability to maintain a sense of position and heading by dead reckoning, including inertial dead reckoning, make Carr's observations less puzzling than they were at the time. When an animal is carried through a curtain that excludes sensory input from the world outside the enclosure, the animal does not lose its representation of its compass heading, its heading in a coordinate framework anchored to that world. The integration of angular velocity signals while inside the enclosure maintains the animal's representation of its heading with respect to the world outside the enclosure. The map of the environment outside the enclosure establishes the coordinate framework within which the dead reckoning system represents the changes in the animal's position and heading. The preservation of the representation of their compass heading by the dead reckoning system enabled Carr's rats to map the maze in the same coordinate framework that they used to map the world outside the maze. When they were brought through the curtain after the maze and its curtained enclosure had been rotated, they had a disorienting experience, an experience somewhat analogous to the one you would have if the inside of your office building were rotated with respect to its outside while you were away on vacation. The experience of walking through a door in a normally oriented exterior to find an interior rotated 90° with respect to its representation on our everyday map would no doubt disorient us too.

It seems likely that the coordinate framework of the rats' map of their environment was anchored to the home cages, where they spent the majority of their time. This would explain why rotating the rack of cages disoriented them when they were in the maze at the other end of the room, out of sensory contact with the home cages. If their home cage is a fixed point on their map of their environment, then rotating that cage by 90° is equivalent to rotating the world by 90°.

Getting the cue.   If we grant that in learning the maze the rat acquires a representation of the distances and compass bearings of the maze paths and if we grant that whenever the rat moves it accumulates by dead reckoning quantities that reflect the distances and angles through which it has moved (see Douglas 1966; Zoladek, and Roberts 1978), then the problem of what the cue was that a blind rat acquired in moving back and forth in the vicinity of wherever Carr placed it becomes less of a mystery. As the rat feels its way down a path, it uses the output of its dead reckoning system to construct a representation of the segments through which it moves—a representation of their lengths and orientations. If we assume the rat has circuitry that tries to find a congruence between the fragmentary representation that it is now building and some part of the complete representation of the maze, which it has acquired previously, then the rat "gets the cue" at the moment when this circuitry finds a satisfactory congruence.

Dead reckoning in the control of maze behavior.   The Carr and Watson experiment gave evidence that we might now interpret to indicate that rats represent the distances to be traversed in each arm of the maze, as well as the compass orientation of the arms. When the rats were thoroughly accustomed to running the maze in a given orientation and did so rapidly and without error, Carr and Watson removed a segment of the maze between the saw cuts indicated in figure 4.13—thereby shortening many of the pathways the rats had to traverse. On the first several trials following the removal of this segment, the rats ran headlong into the walls at the ends of the shortened pathways, often hitting the wall so hard their body flattened up against the wall and they appeared stunned for some while afterwards. They sometimes ran hard into one or more walls on several successive trials and in several different paths before they began to move in a more cautious and exploratory fashion. The rats with normal vision ran into the walls as much as did the blind rats.

When the rats had adjusted to the new shorter maze and were again running rapidly, the experimenters reinserted the previously removed section. The maze was so constructed that several cul-de-sacs in the lengthened maze were at positions corresponding to the correct path in the shortened maze. When the maze was lengthened, the rats generally turned into these cul-de-sacs and ran full tilt into the walls at their ends. Apparently the hard knocks taken during the adjustment to the initial shortening had not discouraged the rats from reverting to a reliance on dead reckoning while moving at speed through the maze. One is led to suspect that the determination of changes in displacement from the bearings of landmarks is sufficiently slow that it is of little use when the animal moves rapidly. The rat is like the homing pigeon in that it does not rely on the bearings of landmarks to hold its course.

I do not suggest the rat does not see the looming wall as it runs toward it. It may rely in part on that very looming to estimate its velocity. I suggest the rat does not take position fixes from what it sees as it runs. For its sense of where it is and what lies immediately ahead and to its left and right, the rat relies on its map and its dead reckoning. That is why it runs full tilt into walls that are not where they are supposed to be. When the rat runs a map-determined course under dead reckoning, the only effective behavioral control exerted by visual input may be through the dead reckoning system, which computes moment to moment changes in the rat's position on its map from velocity signals based in part on visual input. (For further experiments demonstrating the importance of map-directed dead reckoning movements in rodents see Grünwald 1969.)

When running in a lengthened path without cul-de-sacs turning off it, the rats ran at speed for approximately the previous length of the path and then attempted to turn, often striking the wall. On later trials, they slowed down when they reached the point where they had been accustomed to turn and proceeded from there in a slow, exploratory manner. In time, however, they came to run the maze as rapidly as ever.

Carr and Watson concluded that kinesthetic stimuli are very important when a rat runs a familiar maze. They did not consider, however, how kinesthetic stimuli might be used—for example, in the computations of how far the rat has come at any moment and its current compass heading. For these computations to be of use in determining where and in what direction it should next turn, the rat must have a map of the space through which it moves.

The early maze literature contains many examples of the "automatic, unthinking, reflex-like" running of a rat in a maze with which it is thoroughly familiar. When previously correct arms now end in empty space, the rat runs off the end of the arm (Dennis 1932). When the rat has learned to run for a small food reward at the end of an alley, and a large pile of food is placed in the middle of the alley, the rat runs right over the large pile for more than 20 trials (Stoltz and Lott 1964). These results contributed to the popularity of conditioned reflex explanations of complex spatial behavior. They may with more justice be taken as evidence of the role that dead reckoning of one's position on a map plays in the control of maze running.

There is one other important finding from the early work by Watson (1907) and Carr (1917) and others (for example, Honzik 1936) on the capacity of rats to run complex mazes when surgically deprived of one or more major sensory modalities. The essence of the findings is that the elimination of any one sensory modality had little or no effect on ease of learning or on asymptotic performance. Blind rats learn almost as readily and do as well as sighted rats; so do anosmic rats; and so do deaf rats. When, however, these sensory deficits are combined, their effects are much larger than the sum of their individual effects.

Carr and Watson concluded that under most circumstances, the running was controlled primarily by kinesthetic input—the one channel they could not experimentally eliminate—and that the other sensory channels had only nonlinear "tonic" effects. They imagined that when these tonic effects were reduced below a critical level by the elimination of two or more sensory channels, the kinesthetic cues were no longer so successful at eliciting the proper responses. One of the lessons that has since been learned from the study of homing in other animals is that animals rely on several different cues for each component of the navigational task: getting bearings, estimating the course required, holding that course, and estimating the distance so far covered. The importance of remaining oriented and aware of one's position is such that most animals have a number of redundant mechanisms and procedures for carrying out this vital function. Only when several are blocked do they become disoriented.

The sense of position and orientation is multimodally derived. It transcends the conventional sensory modalities. It does not depend exclusively on the information derived from any single one of them. Information from all available sources is integrated into a representation of the space the animal lives in and its current position and heading within that space.

Dead Reckoning in Humans

Thompson (see Lee and Thompson 1982) showed subjects a mark on the ground at distances ranging from 3 to 21 meters. After looking at the mark for 5 seconds, the subjects closed their eyes and walked until they thought they were standing on it. In some versions of the experiment, there were up to four obstacles in the direct path to the mark, around which the subjects had to walk. Out to a range of 9 meters, the subjects were as accurate at walking to the mark with their eyes closed as they were when they walked with their eyes open (but without looking at their feet to verify their final position on the mark). Their accuracy was unaffected by the presence of the obstacles; they wound their way around the obstacles they could no longer see, steering by dead reckoning to where they represented the mark to be.

To show that the subjects were updating their position in the represented space moment by moment, Thompson had subjects look at a target 10 meters away, then walk toward it with their eyes closed, carrying a block of wood in their hand. While they were somewhere en route, Thompson signaled them to stop and to throw the block at the target from where they stood, keeping their eyes closed. They threw almost as accurately under these conditions as they did when they were free to look at the target. The Thompson experiment shows that adults can use the spatial representation they pick up visually in a short study to direct locomotion around obstacles, locomotion that is carried out by dead reckoning, under nonvisual control.

Experiments by Landau, Spelke, and Gleitman (1984) show that the requisite spatial representation is acquired at an early age by a congenitally blind child in the course of her initial movements around a previously unfamiliar space. The child uses this representation to set her courses by dead reckoning alone. These experiments give a particularly clear demonstration of the use of dead reckoning in the construction of a map.

Landau and Gleitman (1985) studied the acquisition of spatial and visual language in a congenitally blind child. Early in these studies, Landau was impressed with the child's ability to move through the

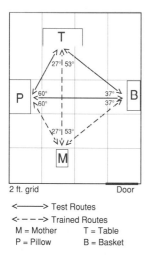

2 ft. grid   Door

<----> Test Routes
<- - - -> Trained Routes
M = Mother   T = Table
P = Pillow   B = Basket

Figure 4.14
The experimental room for the experiment with a congenitally blind 31-month-old child. The trained routes were those over which the experimenter led the child back and forth from M. The test routes were those she was asked to take on her own. (Redrawn from Landau et al. 1984, p. 230, by permission of author and publisher.)

familiar spaces in her home. These observations led to a series of laboratory tests of the child's ability to represent the spatial relationship between objects encountered for the first time in moving around a novel space and to use that representation to set novel courses—courses not taken during the acquisition of the relevant spatial relationships.

When the child was 31 months old, she and her mother were brought into the 8 by 10 foot laboratory playroom shown in figure 4.14. The mother was seated in the chair at M. From there, the experimenter conducted the child to some pillows and back (following the dashed line between M and P) and then to a table and back (dashed line between M and T) and then to a basket and back (dotted line between M and B). The child was then led again to the table and asked to go from there to the basket ("Find the basket"), from there to the pillows, from the pillows to

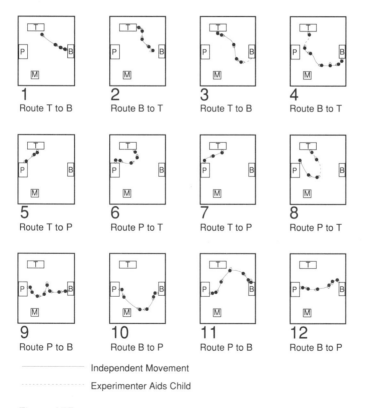

Figure 4.15
Tracings of the routes taken by the child on test trials (made from videotapes). Dots mark her position at 3-second intervals. Arrowheads indicate frontal direction. (Redrawn from Landau et al., p. 232, by permission of author and publisher.)

the basket, and so on, for each of the trajectories not taken during the acquisition phase (solid lines). Figure 4.15 plots (from videotapes) the routes the child took. A variety of statistical analyses confirm what is evident from inspection: the child had acquired sufficient command of the spatial relations among the objects in the room to be able to set a course from one to the other, even though the courses required were not ones she had been led along during the acquisition of the requisite spatial information.

Subsequent experiments showed that the courses the child took were approximately correct in angle and distance, that she was not using echolocation, and that she could not orient herself toward an object unless she had in fact been led to it (that is, she was not locating objects by a beacon of any kind). It was also shown that the deviations evident in the courses portrayed in figure 4.15 were in appreciable measure attributable to difficulty in holding the course rather than insufficient knowledge of the spatial relations among the objects. The deviations were just as great when the child was moving to a readily localizable auditory source.

In holding its course, the child was presumably entirely dependent on dead reckoning, calculating changes in her position from vestibular, kinesthetic, and efference copy signals. In setting the courses, she may have used the landmarks to help align herself with the various goals. It was shown, however, that she could also set a course when there was no landmark to use as an aid to alignment. In other words, dead reckoning alone sufficed to establish points in space to which she could return by novel routes—just as dead reckoning alone establishes points in space to which the ant returns when searching for its nest.

These results emphasize the central importance of dead reckoning in the formation and use of spatial representations. The information about the distances and angles between objects that constitutes the cognitive map of behavioral space comes in no small measure from the moment-to-moment computation of these quantities by the dead reckoning system, which operates whenever an organism moves about.

Chapter 5

The Cognitive Map

A cognitive map is a record in the central nervous system of macroscopic geometric relations among surfaces in the environment used to plan movements through the environment. A central question is what kinds of geometric relations the map encodes. A map in the ordinary acceptation encodes relative metric positions. The relative metric position of a point is given by its coordinates (its position vector). Each coordinate of a point (each dimension of the position vector) specifies the distance of the point from an axis or origin of the system of coordinates. The infinite sets of points that compose higher-order geometric entities such as lines, curves, and surfaces are represented by defining functions. The defining function for a line or surface specifies the vector for every point belonging to the set of points that compose the line or surface. For example, the function $y = ax + b$ specifies the vector for every point belonging to a given line. Any point whose x and y values satisfy the equation belongs to the line; any point whose x and y values do not satisfy the equation does not belong. The values of the parameters a and b determine which line is specified. Thus, this pair of values represents the line; they constitute a parameter vector (*vector* being used here in the loose sense). In a page-description language like Postscript™, curves of arbitrary complexity are represented by a series of six-dimensional vectors, where, roughly speaking, each vector specifies a Bezier spline between inflection points. A set of such vectors is the parameter vector that specifies the Bezier curve.

The representation of the geometric relations among points and sets of points by means of metric position vectors and parameter vectors preserves all the geometric relations among the mapped entities, in the sense that any such relation is in principle recoverable from the position vectors that represent the points and the parameter vectors that represent the point sets. Whether a given point does or does not fall on a given line is not explicitly given in the representations of the point and the line, but it may be recovered by testing whether the coordinates of the point satisfy the function that defines the line. Similarly, whether a point lies inside or outside a closed Bezier curve is recovered by the application of a suitable operator; the distance of a mapped point from a mapped line may be recovered by computation; and so on. Given a representation of the relative metric positions of points, any geometric relation among any selection of points may be verified or falsified by the application of a suitable operator to their specifying vectors.

It is often argued that while animals do record some geometric relations between behaviorally important points in their environment, what they record does not constitute a map in the usual sense, which I take to mean a record of the relative metric positions of points. The following example illustrates what it might mean to say that an animal has recorded a geometric relation among points in its environment but does not have a map in the usual sense. The digger wasp digs a small hole in more or less open ground to serve as a nest for her eggs. Before laying her eggs, she flies off in search of live food for the larvae that will hatch from her eggs. She stings various caterpillars, spiders, and other prey into immobility and returns to her nest, into which she stuffs the immobilized prey. In returning, she locates her nest by virtue of its geometric relations to surrounding landmarks (Tinbergen and Kruyt 1938). The wasp makes a survey flight upon leaving her nest. One might imagine (counterfactually, I will argue) that during this survey flight, she makes the equivalent of a series of pairs of snapshots of horizon segments that lie on opposite sides of the nest. One pair would record the retinal images of the horizon segments to the north and south, another pair the images of the horizon segments to the east and west, and so on. However, the angular relations between the pairs would not be preserved—the fact that one pair was a north-south pair while the other an east-west pair. From looking at the wasp's records, one could not tell how far it had turned between making the first and second pair of snapshots.

Despite the absence of angle or distance data, two or more such pairs of snapshots define the location of the nest by virtue of its geometric relation to the surrounding terrain. Each pair of retinal images of opposing segments of the horizon surrounding the nest defines a range line, a line of position along which the nest must lie (see figure 3.6 and accompanying discussion). Two such pairs uniquely define the nest's position; it lies at the intersection of the two range lines. Gallistel (1985) describes a procedure for using several pairs of horizon images to home on the nest (see also Levitt et al. 1987). The important point for present purposes is that the metric relations in the surrounding terrain cannot be recovered from records of this kind. This is an example of what it might mean to say that an animal has a record of certain geometric relations among points in its environment but does not have a map.

Another way to think about the example is that the map imputed to the wasp is a weaker map because it preserves only some geometric relations. (*Preserves* is used in the sense of "permit the recovery of", rather than "directly express.") It preserves the fact that the nest falls on the straight line defined by a pair of snapshots (more formally, it preserves selected collinearity relations). It also preserves the fact that the lines defined by three or more pairs intersect at the same point (a concurrence relation). But it does not preserve the relative metric positions of horizon segments that are not members of the same pair. One cannot recover from these records the magnitude of the turn that must be made to look from a segment in one pair to a segment in another pair because angular distance is a metric relation, nor can one recover the linear distance from the nest to any of the terrain features that determine the appearance of a horizon segment. One image may record the silhouette of a discarded tin can 1 meter from the nest, while the image on the opposing side records the silhouette of a mountain 50 kilometers away. The record kept by the wasp would differ from an everyday map in that only a limited set of geometric relations could in principle be recovered from it, whereas in an everyday map, any geometric relation is recoverable.

The attraction of thinking of different possible maps in terms of their strength, defined as the range of geometric relations among the mapped points that could in principle be recovered from the mapping, is that modern geometry has formalized this notion of strength. The different branches of geometry—metric geometry, affine geometry, projective geometry, and topology—are defined by the classes of geometric relations that are the object of study, and there is a hierarchical inclusion relation among these classes. All the relations studied in topology exist within projective geometry but not vice-versa. All the projective relations are in turn included within the class of relations found in affine geometry but not vice-versa, and all the affine relations are included within the class of relations that constitute metric geometry but not vice-versa. The strength of a geometric representation designates the level of this inclusion hierarchy, with maps in the ordinary sense of the term (metric maps) constituting the highest level of the hierarchy, the level that includes all the geometric relations.

The thesis I will argue is that the intuitive belief that the cognitive maps of "lower" animals are weaker than our own is not well founded. They may be impoverished relative to our own (have less on them) but they are not weaker in their formal characteristics. There is experimental evidence that even insect maps are metric maps. In the next chapter, the question of map strength is addressed in formally motivated experiments on the rat's cognitive map. By the time these more rigorous tests of the strength of a cognitive map are reviewed, I would hope that the less formally motivated experiments and naturalistic observations to be reviewed in this chapter establish beyond a reasonable doubt that even insects make metric maps.

Distance and angle are fundamental to a metric map. The making of a record that permits the recovery of angular and linear distance relations requires the equivalent of surveying procedures that map the surface of the earth into the digital representations of position and elevation that underlie modern computer-drawn maps of the earth's surface. These mapping procedures must generate quantities in the nervous system proportionate to linear and angular distances in the world.

The Construction of the Map

I suggest that the surveying procedures by which animals construct their cognitive map of their environment may be broken down into two inter-related sets of processes, which together permit the construction of geocentric metric maps. One set of processes constructs a metric representation in egocentric coordinates of the relative positions of currently perceptible points, lines, and surfaces—a representation of the geometry of what is perceived from one's current vantage point. The other process, dead reckoning, provides a representation in geocentric coordinates of the vantage points and the angles of view (headings). Combining geocentric representations of vantage points and angles of view with egocentric representations of the segment of the world perceived from each vantage point yields a representation of the shape of the behaviorally relevant environment in a system of coordinates anchored to the earth, a geocentric cognitive map.

The computations that combine geocentric dead reckoning with egocentric percepts to yield a geocentric map are sketched in figure 5.1. Those with little patience for mathematics may wish to take the hypothesis at the verbal level and skip to the next section, which begins the presentation of the experimental evidence for it.

In figure 5.1, the origin of the geocentric system (the coordinates used by the dead reckoning system) is at $\mathbf{n} = <0,0>$ and the geocentric reference direction (the direction from which heading is measured) is indicated by N (for "north"). The present position of the animal, as indicated by the dead reckoning system, is $\mathbf{o} = <x_o, y_o> = <6,4>$; that is, it reckons itself to be 6 units to the east of its nest and 4 units to the north. The vector $\mathbf{o}$ is the positional output of the dead reckoning system. The compass heading of the animal, also derived from the dead reckoning system (see figure 4.7), is η. In this example, η is 30° (measured clockwise from north).

The animal's sensory-perceptual system generates a representation of a point perceived to be at egocentric coordinates $p = <7,3>$, 7 units to the animal's right and 3 units to its front (figure 5.1B).[1] The egocentric representation, p, of the perceived point is combined with the geocentric representation of the animal's position, o, by means of the formula, $p = Rp + o$, where R is the rotation matrix. The rotation matrix is determined by the sine-cosine representation of the animal's compass heading η, as indicated on the figure. Multiplying the egocentric representation of the point by the rotation matrix generates a new vector (the product Rp), which is what the egocentric representation of the point would be if the observer were headed due north. Adding this to the vector that represents the animal's geocentric position gives the vector that represents the geocentric position of the perceived point.

In figure 5.1B, it is also assumed that the animal's sensory-perceptual system generates a representation of the line and its position relative to the observer. The egocentric representation of this line is symbolized by Λ. I have assumed that the line is represented by what is called the normal equation of a line, which represents a line in terms of three parameters rather than the more familiar two parameters of the gradient equation ($y = ax + b$). The normal representation of a line in the x-y plane is a function of the form: $x \cos \alpha + y \sin \alpha - d$. Thus, the line is encoded by means of a triplet of numbers (a triplet of quantities): $\cos\alpha$, $\sin\alpha$, d. This triplet is not a vector in the strict sense because it cannot be validly manipulated by the rules of vector algebra. There is a different set of rules for operating on this triplet. It is a vector in the loose sense of a string of numbers or quantities, each of which has a different representational significance. More generally, higher level geometric entities like lines, curves, and surfaces are represented by vectors in this loose sense, sets of ordered quantities, each quantity specifying a parameter of the function that defines the surface, curve, or line.

The angle α in the normal equation for a line is the direction angle of the vector that points from the origin of the coordinate system directly toward the line, hence perpendicular to it; "normal" in the term *normal equation* or *normal representation* of the line is used in the sense of "perpendicular." I call this the direction angle of the line because it represents the direction of the line as seen from the origin of the system of coordinates, the direction in which one must look to be looking right at the line. As with other specifications of circular or cyclical position, this angle is assumed to be represented by its sine and cosine. The third

---

1. For simplicity, the analysis is confined to a two-dimensional cognitive map. The vector p may be thought of as the egocentric representation of the position of a pole. Similarly, Λ may be thought of as the egocentric representation of a wall.

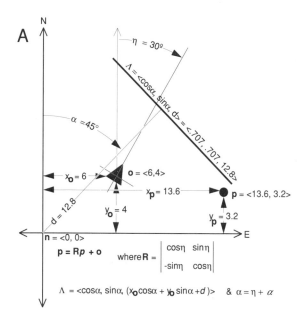

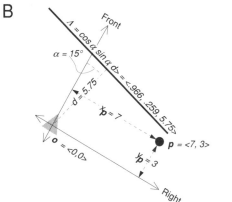

Figure 5.1

The computations required to convert an egocentric perception of a point and a line to a geocentric representation by combining the egocentric perceptual coordinates with the geocentric coordinates for the animal's position, which come from the dead-reckoning system. Unitalicized variables are geocentric; italicized are egocentric. *A*. The geocentric system of coordinates (N = north; E = east). **p** = the geocentric position vector of the point; **o** = the geocentric position vector of the observer (animal); **n** = the geocentric position vector of the nest (origin of the geocentric coordinate system). Λ = the normal representation of the line in the geocentric system; α = the direction angle of the line; d = the distance of the line from the origin; η = the heading of the animal. **R** = the rotation matrix defined by η. The equation at the bottom indicates how to obtain the geocentric rep-

parameter, *d*, is the length of the perpendicular from the origin to the line, that is, the distance of the line from the origin of the coordinate system. In the egocentric system, *d* is the distance of the line from the observer and *cos* α and *sin* α together specify the angle of the line with respect to the observer.

The computations required to derive the geocentric representation of the line (represented by the unitalicized Λ) from its egocentric representation are indicated on figure 5.1A. The cosine and sine parameters of the geocentric representation are the cosine and sine of the sum of the egocentric direction angle, α, and η, the animal's compass heading. The distance parameter in the geocentric representation depends upon the animal's distance from the geocentric origin, as well as on the geocentric direction angle (α). The formula for d, the distance parameter in the geocentric system, in terms of α, the angle of the geocentric normal to the line, and *d*, the distance parameter in the egocentric system, is given on the figure.

I include the representation of a line in this illustration to emphasize that it is extremely unlikely that the nervous system represents the world point by point. The nervous system is most concerned not with the representation of individual points but with the representation of higher-order geometric entities, above all surfaces. It no doubt has some process for representing the conformation and position of these surfaces economically. Those familiar with drafting and illustration programs for microcomputers will know that shapes of remarkable complexity are coded in small files. For example, the Postscript™ encoding of the Hampton Court Maze in figure 4.13 takes only 1.4 kilobytes of disk memory; whereas the bit-mapped file for the same image occupies 300 kilobytes. Whatever method the nervous system uses to obtain an economical egocentric representation of the conformation and location of surfaces, it will be able to convert from egocentric to geocentric coordinates by combining the egocentric representation with the geocentric representation of the vantage point, which is generated within the dead reckoning system. The computations in figure 5.1 show what such coordinate-transformation computations look like.

resentation of the point by multiplying the egocentric vector *p* times the rotation matrix **R** and adding the animal's geocentric position vector **o**. The equations for Λ and α give the geocentric representation of the line in terms of its egocentric representation, the animal's heading, η, and the coordinates of the animal's geocentric position, x_o and y_o. *B*. The egocentric system of coordinates. Λ = the normal representation of the line in the egocentric framework; α = the direction angle of the line in the egocentric framework; *d* = the distance of the line in the egocentric framework; *p* = the egocentric coordinates of the point; *o* = the coordinates of the observer in the egocentric system.

Evidence That Animals Perceive Angular and Linear Distance

The hypothesis about how animals construct geocentric metric maps presupposes that they have sensory-perceptual processes capable of generating an egocentric perception of the angular and linear distances of stimulus sources. There is experimental evidence that sensory-perceptual processes of this degree of sophistication are commonly found in arthropods, including "primitive" arthropods like the sand scorpion. The sand scorpion is a primitive arthropod in the sense that it is thought to have undergone relatively modest evolutionary modifications in its descent from an evolutionarily remote arthropod species ancestral to many modern arthropod species, most of which have undergone greater modification, as, for example, the social bees and ants.

Estimation of Egocentric Distance and Angle in the Sand Scorpion
As darkness settles over the Mojave Desert, the sand scorpion emerges from its burrow and sits waiting for something to move. If you touch the sand near it, it turns to orient toward the point touched (figure 5.2A), then darts toward it. The farther away the touch, the longer the scorpion's dart, up to a distance of about 15 centimeters (figure 5.2B). When the touch is farther out than 15 centimeters, the scorpion stops after about 15 centimeters and waits for another touch (in navigational terms, it stops to get another fix on the bearing and range of the target).

   What is surprising about this is that the scorpion has poor vision and poor hearing—the two traditional distance senses. It cannot hear or see the target. A fluttering moth elicits the directed attack only if it is held so that its wings strike the sand. If it is held just above the sand within a few centimeters of the scorpion, it elicits no reaction. Moreover, the scorpion

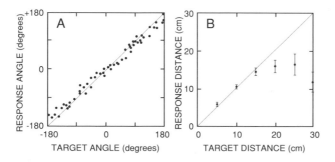

Figure 5.2
A. The bearing of the scorpion's movement (response angle) in response to a probe touched to the sand, as a function of the bearing of the point touched (target angle). *B.* The distance the scorpion moves as a function of the egocentric distance of the point touched. (Redrawn from Brownell 1984, p. 88, by permission of author and publisher.)

shows directed attack when the source of the disturbance is the desert burrowing cockroach, a root-eating insect that tunnels just below the sand's surface, where it seems unlikely to be heard, seen, or smelled. So how does this primitive arthropod estimate the angle and distance of the disturbance?

It turns out that sand is a better short-range transmitter of mechanical disturbance than one might expect and that the scorpion computes the angle and distance of the source from minute differences in the timing of the arrival of transmitted disturbances at its eight legs. One may demonstrate this by testing the animal with an experimentally constructed air gap, which blocks propagation of the disturbance (Brownell 1984). When the scorpion is on the other side of the air gap, it shows no reaction. When it straddles the gap, so that some of its legs pick up the propagated disturbance and some do not (figure 5.3A), it turns in the direction of the source but very inaccurately (figure 5.3B). Experiments in which the intensity and timing of the vibrations experienced by different legs are independently varied show that the computation of the angle rests on a comparison of the relative timing of the nervous signals generated in all eight legs. When the signals from half the legs are nullified by the air gap, the computation no longer gives an accurate indication of the target's bearing.

How the scorpion derives the distance to the target has not been experimentally verified, but a plausible model has been formulated. A mechanical disturbance of the sand generates two kinds of propagating waves: a fast-traveling compressional wave (like a sound wave) and a slower-traveling Rayleigh wave (a wave like the those that propagate on

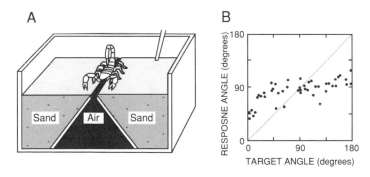

Figure 5.3
Air gap experiment. *A*. The scorpion straddles an air gap so that its left legs (on the probed side of the gap) experience the vibrations but its right legs do not. *B*. Regardless of where the sand is probed, the scorpion orients roughly perpendicularly to the air gap, indicating that sensory input from all eight legs is required to judge target direction accurately. (Based on Brownell 1984, p. 89.)

the surface of a body of water, involving only up-down motion on the part of the particles near the surface of the medium). The estimation of target bearing has been shown to depend only on the slowly traveling Rayleigh wave (which yields larger differences in arrival time at the legs). The Rayleigh wave is picked up by a specialized sensory structure called the slit sensillium, located in the equivalent of the scorpion's ankle joint. It is tuned to vertical displacements of the substrate. Electrophysiological recording shows that a different sensory structure, the hairs on the scorpion's "feet" (tarsi), pick up the fast-traveling compressional wave. The difference in arrival time between the fast-traveling compressional wave and the slow-traveling Rayleigh wave is proportional to the distance of the source from the receiver. It seems likely that the scorpion's estimate of distance is computed from this difference.

Thus, the scorpion's nervous system extracts distance information at least in part from minute differences in the arrival time of mechanically propagating waves. The same principle is used by surface-feeding fish to direct their attacks on bugs fallen into the water (Hoin-Radovsky, Bleckman, and Schwartz 1984) and is brought to a peak of perfection by the barn owl (Payne 1971; Knudsen 1984; Konishi 1986), the bat, and the whale (Busnel and Fish 1980).

Parallax Estimation of Distance

In the locust.   The locust can jump more than 18 times its body length— the equivalent on a human scale of a standing broad jump of better than 100 feet. The locust looks before it leaps; it estimates the distance of the object onto which it is going to jump. One of the mechanisms by which it does so is a mechanism that computes distance from motion parallax (Collett 1978; Sobel, 1989; Wallace 1959). Before it jumps, the locust moves its head from side to side, without changing the orientation of the optic axis. Since the orientation of the optic axis is preserved during this side to side motion, the distance, D, of the object is:

$$D = s / \tan(\alpha),$$

where s is the lateral displacement of the eyes from the point where the object lies straight in front of the locust and α is the corresponding change in visual angle. Wallace (1959) showed that the locust derives its estimate of the distance to be jumped from a parallax computation. He moved the target laterally in synchrony with the locust's lateral head movements. When the object moved in phase with the head, the change in its visual angle was reduced and the locust jumped long of the mark; when it moved in antiphase, the change in visual angle was augmented and the locust jumped short. Sobel (1989) reproduced the function relating take-off velocity to the distance to be jumped by substituting variation in the lateral movement of the target for variation in its distance, suggesting that at least under these restricted experimental circumstances, the locust's estimate of the distance to be jumped derived entirely from motion parallax during peering.

In the wasp and bee. Parallax estimation of distance (or distance triangulation) is a general-purpose procedure. It may be used by any organism endowed with a directional distance sense to estimate arbitrarily great distances. There is reason to suspect that it is used by bees and wasps to obtain information about the distance of landmarks around their nests and feeding sites. When they leave these sites—particularly when they leave for the first time after some sort of disturbance—they back away from the site in a stereotyped zig-zag flight pattern well calculated to yield parallax distance information over a large range of distances. If there is a lower limit on the accuracy with which one can make angular measurements, which there always is, then the greater the distance to be estimated in distance triangulation (the greater the height of the triangle), the larger the lateral displacement one must make (the larger the base). Thus, a general-purpose distance survey should involve ever increasing lateral displacements, which is what is seen in the backward-looking departure flight (figure 5.4). It has been shown that bees represent the distances of the landmarks surrounding a food source and use the nearer landmarks preferentially in relocating the source (Cheng et al. 1987), and that bees derive distance information from parallax motion while in flight (Cartwright and Collett 1979; Kirchner and Srinivasan 1989; Srinivasan et al 1989).

In the gerbil. Ellard, Goodale, and Timney (1984) videotaped gerbils jumping a gap between a take-off platform and a landing platform. As

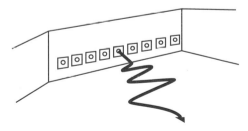

Figure 5.4
The wasp's flight path on departing from a nest hole. The wasp flies backward so that it looks at the nest hole and the landmarks behind it as it makes this zigzag. (Redrawn from Wehner 1981, by permission of author and publisher.)

the width of the gap varied from 10 to 35 centimeters, so did the length of the gerbils' jump (figure 5.5A) and the proportion of trials on which the gerbils made large vertical head bobs (figure 5.5B). In the locust experiments, the landing platform was moved in phase or counterphase with the animal's head movements, thereby diminishing or augmenting target parallax during the head movements, which augmented or diminished the length of the ensuing jump. In other words, there was an experimental demonstration that parallax was used to estimate distance. In the gerbil case (like the wasp case), the evidence is purely correlational. It is clear from the jumping data that the gerbil makes precise estimates of the distance to be jumped and calibrates its jump accordingly. It is

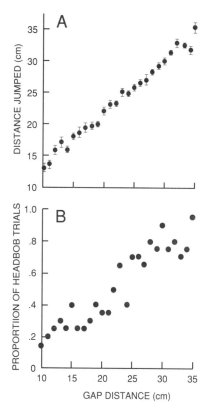

Figure 5.5
Head bobbing and distance estimation in the gerbil. *A.* The distance of the gerbil's jump (as measured from videotapes) as a function of the width of the gap. *B.* The proportion of trials on which the gerbil made vertical bobbing movements of the head, as a function of the distance it had to jump. (Redrawn from Ellard et al. 1984, pp. 33, 35, by permission of the author and publisher.)

obvious that parallax is not the gerbil's only source of distance information. The fact that its tendency to bob its head increases as the width of the gap increases shows that another cue or cues must indicate that the distance is longer and hence that parallax input will be helpful in improving the estimate. Also, accurate jumps occurred on trials without head bobs, although there was a significant correlation between the incidence of large amplitude bobs and the precision of the jumps. One of the other cues is the amount of loom in the visual image resulting from the forward darting motion with which the gerbil approaches the take-off point. Loom is the expansion of the visual image of an object as one approaches it. The closer one is to the object, the greater is the loom for a given forward movement. There was an inverse correlation between the magnitude of the last forward dart before the jump and the incidence of prejump head bobs. When prejump darts were restricted by shortening the take-off platform, the incidence of head bobs increased significantly. Thus, the incidence of head bobbing was positively correlated with the distance to be jumped and with the accuracy of the jump, and it was sensitive to variations in other available distance cues, increasing when these were diminished.

These correlational data not only support the hypothesis that the head bobs are a specialized behavior designed to obtain distance from parallax, they also suggest that distance is derived from looming, a special case of parallax. Images of objects loom because the edges of an object do not lie directly on the line of approach; hence, the general parallax formula applies to the edges of an object centered on the line of advance.

This brief survey shows that the nervous system of the locust is capable of making the trigonometric computations required to extract an estimate of the distance between itself and a planned landing site. The demonstrations of this capacity in the wasp and the gerbil are not as conclusive, but the correlational case is strong. Since there is no reason to assume that the nervous system of the locust is appreciably more sophisticated than that of these and other advanced arthropods and mammals, there is reason to assume that this is a widespread ability. In the scorpion, locust, and gerbil examples, the representations of source distance and source angle extracted by the nervous system may be transient. There is no evidence in these experiments that the information is incorporated into an enduring map of the environment. In the wasp example, however, the hypothesis is that the data derived from parallax estimates of the distance between the nest and various landmarks are incorporated into the cognitive map that enables the wasp to return to the nest. Experimental evidence for the existence of such a map in wasps and bees is given below, including evidence that these insects record and make use of the distance between landmarks and sought-for points (Cheng et al. 1987).

The scorpion experiments and locust experiments show the presence in insects of neural circuitry and behaviors that reflect the basic physics of distance estimation using different kinds of propagating waves. Mechanically propagating waves travel slowly enough so that differences in their time of arrival may be used to estimate the source angle and (in some circumstances) source distance. The ability of mammals and birds to compute source angle and source distance from differences in the arrival times (or phases) of sound signals has been thoroughly established by psychophysical experiments, and electrophysiological investigations of the neural mechanism are well underway (see chapter 14). The scorpion experiments show that sense organs specialized for this task— and presumably specialized neural circuitry—have already made their appearance in lower arthropods.

Electromagnetically propagating waves travel too rapidly for information about source angle and distance to be extracted from differences in arrival time. However, the vastly shorter wavelengths of perceptible electromagnetic energy permit much greater precision in the determination of the angle of arrival, which makes possible the direct apprehension of the bearing of the source and trigonometric estimation of source distance from changes in its bearing.

Visual mechanisms for estimating source distance and bearing differ from auditory mechanisms for estimating the same spatial parameters in ways that reflect the basic differences in the inherent physics of the problem. The structure of the physical world dictates basic aspects of the structure and functioning of biological mechanisms whose purpose is to adapt the animal to those aspects of its environment. There is no reason to think that this principle stops being valid when we penetrate beyond the sense organs—whose structure and functioning have obviously been so shaped—to the neural machinery that operates on the signals arising from those sense organs.

Integration of Two Distance Estimates in Chameleon Route Choices
In a representational approach to the phenomena of learning, the laws of learning are closely tied to the the sensory and perceptual mechanisms by which information of a particular kind is extracted from sensory data because the approach assumes that learning is the ongoing storage and integration of the information about the world extracted by sensory-perceptual mechanisms. It assumes, for example, that spatial learning requires the integration of many different distance and angle estimates made at different times and from different perspectives to form a coherent representation of the spatial relations among those parts of the

animal's environment that are of recurring relevance to its behavioral output. It assumes that if the nervous system of even the scorpion can solve the nontrivial computational problems inherent in the extraction of distance estimates from differences in the arrival times of mechanically propagating disturbances, then it is not farfetched to imagine that the nervous system also solves the computational task of integrating separate distance and angle estimates into an enduring overall representation of the disposition of the surfaces within the animal's behavioral space. It assumes that the study of the formal structure of these representations and the computational procedures by which they are elaborated is what the study of learning ought to be about. The next example concerns the integration of temporally discrete estimates of distance to form a representation that permits the animal to make decisions regarding the most appropriate route for it to take.

Chameleons live in trees and clamber around the branches of these natural mazes, routinely dealing with the kind of detour problems that experimental psychologists pose to the rat. If a young chameleon is confronted with the vertical wire maze shown in figure 5.6A, it makes for the top. At each choice point, it takes either the direct route by spanning across the gap, or the long way around. Which it does depends on both the size of the gap and the distance it must go to get around the gap. Collett and Harkness (1982) determined the frequency with which the

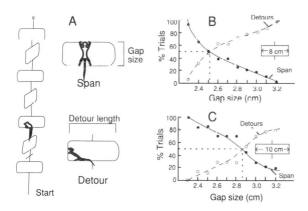

Figure 5.6
The integration of two distance estimates in the route choice of the chameleon. A. The vertical maze. The segments varied in the size of the gap to be spanned and the length of the detour that the chameleon could take in lieu of spanning the gap. B. Span choices versus detour choices, as a function of gap size, when the detour was 8 centimeters. C. Span choices versus detour choices, as a function of gap size, when the detour was 10 centimeters. (Redrawn from Collett and Harkness 1982, p. 119, by permission of author and publisher.)

chameleon either spanned the gap or went around it as a function of the size of the gap in two mazes with different detour lengths. When the detour was 8 centimeters long the chameleon's propensity to take the detour rose steeply with increasing gap size, reaching the 50 percent level at a gap of 2.5 centimeters (figure 5.6B). When the detour was increased to 10 centimeters, the propensity to take it rose more slowly and did not reach the 50 percent level until the gap was lengthened to 2.9 centimeters (figure 5.6C).

The chameleon has turret-like eyes with narrow fields of view, so it is unlikely that they can simultaneously assess the distance across the gap and around the detour. Simultaneous assessment of these two quite different distances is rendered even more unlikely by evidence that, for near distances, the chameleon relies upon accommodation—the extent to which it must adjust the focal length of its lens to bring an edge into focus. When it looks through spectacles while estimating the distance to its prey, it undershoots or overshoots by an amount predicted by the power of the lenses (Collett and Harkness 1982). When distance is estimated by optical focusing, only one estimate can be made at a time. On the other hand, the chameleon's eyes move independently of one another, so it is conceivable that one eye focuses on the gap while the other focuses on the detour. In all events, the choice between spanning the gap or taking the detour depends on the integration of separately derived estimates of the two distances.

It would be interesting to continue these studies to determine how elaborate and enduring an integration of spatial information the chameleon achieves. When it lives in a maze like this, some of whose branches lead eventually to the top and some of whose branches do not, and where there are cross-over opportunities at a considerable remove from a given choice point, does the chameleon come to exhibit spatial foresight? Does it choose an arm because it leads to a point not now in view, which previous experience has shown to lead onto the point the chameleon is headed for? We will see that cats and rats clearly make choices based on a memory for parts of their route that are not now visible. Evidence for place finding in both the fish and the desert tortoise makes it plausible to assume that the chameleon has this ability in common with most other vertebrates.

Nonegocentric Estimates of Distance in the Toad
In the examples of distance and angle computation so far reviewed, the distances and angles were egocentric, that is, they were the distances and angles of some object or set of objects from the animal. Lower vertebrates also estimate the distances and angles between two external objects, as shown by Lock and Collett (1979) experiments on detour taking in the

toad. When a toad sights prey that is too far away for it to strike at, it hops toward it. The journey toward the prey is made in straight segments of one to three hops, covering about 10-40 centimeters each, and taking 1-2 seconds to complete (see figure 5.7 top). There are pauses on the order of 5 seconds between segments. The orientation and distance covered in each segment is calculated by the toad during the pauses and not altered while it is underway. Moving the prey or even removing it altogether

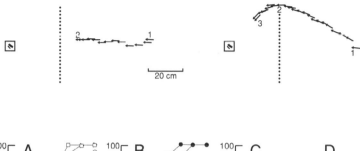

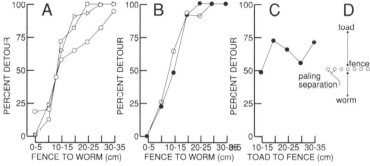

Figure 5.7
Toad's behavior when a picket fence is interposed between it and its prey. If distance between fence and worm is greater than 10-15 centimeters toad detours around fence; if this distance is shorter toad approaches worm directly. *Top*, shows examples of a toad (Bufo marinus) approaching directly or detouring. Position of toad's head and midline are marked by an arrow every 0.2 second. Numerals indicate brief pauses between walks. *Bottom, A.* Relation between percentage of trials in which toad detours and fence-to-worm distance with toad starting a constant 30 centimeters from fence for three different paling separations: 2 centimeters (open triangles), 4 centimeters (open squares) and 6 centimeters (open circles). Toad's choice depends on the distance between fence and worm but not on paling separation. *B.* Relation between detour percentage and toad-to-fence distance with toad starting either farther than 25 centimeters (open circles) or nearer than 15 centimeters (filled circles) from fence. Paling separation 4 centimeters. The toad's choice depends on fence-to-worm distance but not on toad-to-fence distance. *C.* Relation between detour percentage and toad-to-fence distance when worm is kept at a constant 10-15 centimeters from fence. The detour percentage does not depend on toad-to-fence distance. *D.* Schematic representation of the measurements. (Redrawn from Collett and Harkness 1982, p. 122, by permission of author and publisher.)

while the toad is moving has no effect. The distance the toad covers in one segment and the angular direction of that segment are linearly related to the position of the prey at the commencement of the segment. If there is a chasm between the toad and its prey, it leaps across it, clambers down into and back out of it, or turns away. The option it chooses is jointly determined by the width and depth of the chasm. Thus, the toad, like the chameleon, bases its behavior on integrated estimates of more than one environmental distance. If the toad opts for leaping across the chasm, the length of its leap is a linear function of the width of the chasm, so the toad, like the locust and the gerbil, looks before it leaps.

So far, the examples of distance estimation in the behavior of the toad have all involved egocentric distances. However, if there is a picket fence barrier between the toad and its prey, the toad either goes to the barrier and strikes at the prey through the gaps between the palings, or it goes around the fence. Which it does depends upon the distance between the fence and the prey, not on the egocentric distances from the toad to the fence and from the toad to the prey (figure 5.7, A-C).

The chameleon and toad experiments show that lower vertebrates not only extract individual distance estimates, they integrate two or more such estimates in determining their behavior. The toad experiments further show that the distance estimates that determine behavior need not be egocentric distances, the distance from the animal to a stimulus source. They can be the distance between two stimulus sources.

None of the experiments so far reviewed speaks directly to the question of whether these animals construct an enduring map of their environment. It is possible that the toad and chameleon discard the information about metric relations in their behavioral environment as soon as they have executed the behaviors that depend upon this information. What these experiments do establish is a prerequisite for the construction of a metric map: sensory-perceptual circuitry capable of computing the metric relations to be preserved on the map. We turn now to experiments demonstrating the existence of a cognitive map.

Piloting

If you can detect a directional energy field emanating from the point in the environment you wish to approach, then you can set a course for that point by orienting yourself properly with respect to the energy field, a process I have termed beacon homing. Commonly, however, there either is no such energy field (there is no detectable beacon emanating from the point one needs to approach) or, if there is, the animal ignores it in favor of another approach based on piloting. The piloting approach involves orienting toward the to-be-approached (or away from the to-be-avoided) point by adopting an appropriate orientation with respect to other stimuli with a known geometric relation to the goal. To orient toward a goal by a piloting method rather than by a beacon method, the animal must have a cognitive map—a record of the geometric relation between the goal and the parts of the environment with reference to which the animal sets its course. In the following review, I give a number of examples in which animals rely on a piloting method even when a beacon method is a clear option. I argue that orienting toward points in the environment by virtue of the position the point occupies in the larger environmental framework is the rule rather than the exception and, thus, that cognitive maps are ubiquitous.

In considering apparent instances of map-based orienting, there is often a concern that there may be some beacon present that is not apparent to the observer. Perhaps the animal detects something emanating from the source that humans cannot detect or do not notice. We are particularly inclined to worry about this possibility when a lower animal is involved, since we freely grant them many specialized sensory abilities but are reluctant to grant them the kind of representational capacity implied by the term *metric cognitive map*. For this reason, it is instructive to begin our consideration of the evidence for cognitive maps in animals with a case in which the point the animal returns to has no distinctive features of its own, no intrinsic features that permit it to be recognized independent of its relation to other points.

Hoverfly homing provides a clear instance of position determination by means of a spatial representation, because the "home" to which the hoverfly returns cannot by its very nature have any distinctive characteristics of its own. The male hoverfly hovers in mid-air for minutes at a time within a circumscribed station area, darting away from its station from time to time to chase passing flies and then returning. The hoverfly's station is a region in the air. Gertrude Stein's quip (made at the expense of Oakland, California) applies quite literally: there is no there there. The station has no intrinsic distinctive features; it is specifiable only by its relation to landmarks. To return to its station, the fly must encode sufficient information about the landmarks to enable it to establish on a subsequent occasion a correspondence between what it now sees and what it saw in the past. (Henceforth the establishment of such a correspondence will be called recognition.) The information stored by the fly must also capture something about the geometrical relation between the station and the landmarks.

Collett and Land (1975) filmed hoverfly homing with a view to determining its underlying principles. Their results establish a number of important points. The first is that the fly recognizes the landmark or landmarks regardless of the part of the retina that views the landmark.

The fly's orientation upon its return to its station often differs greatly from its orientation prior to its departure. On one series of six returns, the terminal orientations were: 129°, 165°, 345°, 96°, and 143°. This variation in terminal orientations does not reflect variation in which of several possible landmarks is used on successive occasions, since it occurs even when the fly determines its hovering position relative to a single isolated landmark provided by the experimenters. The variations in terminal headings establish that the fly can recognize the landmark regardless of the portion of the retina that views it.

Experiments in which the experimenters moved the landmark established that the hoverfly returned to its station by taking fixes on the landmark rather than by dead reckoning. In these experiments, the fly was observed to approach its station from many different angles, implying that landmarks can be recognized from more or less arbitrary viewing angles. The landmark recognition system can recognize not only the original projection of the landmark onto the retina but any other projection of the same landmark(s).

Collett and Land's experiments with moving landmarks establish three differences between the mechanism that the hoverfly uses in resuming its station and the mechanism it uses to hold its station once it is on it. First, the fix-taking mechanism does not operate continuously. It is active only at certain times, for example, on the return from a foray. (Recall that marine fix taking is also episodic.) Second, the fix-taking mechanism does not depend on image motion (as the optomotor position-holding mechanism does) but upon the static properties of the image—its size and shape relative to the memory image. Third, the position-holding mechanism operates globally and does not assign special status to any segment of the image, while the fix-taking mechanism assigns a special significance to the segment or segments of the image on which the fixes are taken.

Collett and Land's experiments show that the hoverfly uses information gained from fixes on the landmark to control the later stages of its approach to its hovering station. This implies that the fix-taking system not only recognizes whether the current image of the landmark does or does not correspond to the record of an earlier image (that is, to the memory image), it also determines, from the disparity between the current image and the memory image, the direction (and perhaps the distance) the fly must move to improve the correspondence. The fly uses the disparity between the memory image and the current image to calculate some aspects of the spatial relation between its current position and its station.

Collett and Land argue that while their results imply that insects have recourse to memory images to reestablish a position relative to a landmark or landmarks, this does not mean they have or use maps in the usual sense. They argue instead for a model in which when "the fly is displaced from its home it can find its way back by obeying relatively simple rules which make the fly move in such a way that the retinal image is transformed to what it is when the fly is at home." (Collett and Land 1975, p. 79). However, in subsequent elaboration of this kind of model in connection with experiments on the bee's use of landmarks to relocate a food source, it emerges that the bee at least is using a metric spatial representation (Cartwright and Collett 1983).

The Local Map in the Honey Bee
Cartwright and Collett (1983) trained individual honey bees to fly from their hive through the gap in a curtain into a matte white featureless room with a visually textured floor (without which bees cannot fly well). The room contained an inconspicuous feeder and one or more upright cylindrical black landmarks. The position of the landmarks and feeder within the room varied from one trial to the next, but their positions relative to one another remained fixed. However, when there was more than one landmark, the compass bearing of the configuration of landmarks and feeder (its orientation within the room) did not vary during training. To find the food, the bee had to use the landmark(s). On test trials, the landmark or landmarks were present, but the feeder was not. The bees flew around where the feeder should have been. From videotapes, Cartwright and Collett were able to enter a digital representation of the bee's convoluted flight path into a computer, which yielded statistical estimates of the center of the bee's search.

The first finding was that bees could not be trained to use the landmarks unless the food source itself was visible. When the feeder was a small, nearly invisible glass capillary tube poking through the floor, bees did not learn to find it. They did learn when the source was a small plastic cup made conspicuous by a metal washer. The bee looking for a food source, unlike the fly looking for a hovering station, requires that there be a perceptible there there. Nonetheless, it locates this intrinsically identifiable source by virtue of its relation to the surrounding (and much larger) landmarks.

Use of compass bearings. When the food source had been at a fixed distance from a single cylindrical landmark, the bee's search area on test trials with the source absent was centered on the point where the food should have been (figure 5.8). The area covered by the bee's search was not an annulus surrounding the landmark, as it would be if the bee relied solely on the remembered image of the landmark to position itself relative to it. A cylinder looks the same no matter what (azimuthal) angle

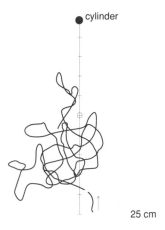

● cylinder

25 cm

Figure 5.8
The first few seconds of a bee's search flight after the bee was trained to forage at a food source 50 centimeters from a cylindrical landmark. The food source was absent during the test. Its position during training is indicated by the open circle on the straight line drawn through the landmark. Scale bars on the line are at 10-centimeter intervals. Landmark indicated by the filled circle and the bee's path (viewed from above) by the twisty line. The center of the search is in the correct compass direction and at approximately the correct distance from the landmark. (Redrawn from Cartwright and Collet 1983, p. 523, by permission of author and publisher.)

it is viewed from. If one is the right distance from it, its image subtends the correct angle no matter what point of the compass one views it from. If the position searched were determined only by the appearance of the landmark, then the search would necessarily spread out in a ring around the landmark. The fact that the bee searches only in one compass direction from the landmark proves that its use of that landmark depends on a geocentric map with metric information. The compass bearing of a landmark from a certain observation point is a geocentric angular distance relation—the angle of a landmark as measured relative to a fixed direction on the earth's surface.

Use of apparent size.   The fact that the bee searches for the food at approximately the correct distance from the landmark implies that something about its use of the remembered appearance of the landmark enables it to reconstruct behaviorally the distance of the observation point from the remembered landmark. Whether the map itself represents this distance remains to be shown. A principal means for establishing a distance between oneself and a landmark is by a triangulation based on the known size of the landmark (in linear measure) and its apparent size, that is, the visual angle it subtends from one's observation point (see figure 3.7).

Cartwright and Collett showed that the distance of the center of the bee's search from the landmark depended on the apparent size of the landmark. When they made the cylinder bigger, the bee searched farther away; when they made it smaller, the bee searched closer. Selectively varying either the diameter or the height showed that the bee was taking account of both.

This result establishes that the process by which the bee behaviorally reconstructs the distance of the observation point from the remembered landmark relies in part on the apparent size of the landmark, but it does not prove that the bee's map records the true size of the landmark. If the true size of the object shown in a snapshot is known, then one may adopt any distance one chooses with respect to that object by moving to a point at which the object has an appropriate apparent size. In the Cartwright and Collett experiment, however, it is possible that all that the bee was doing was moving until the image of the landmark had the remembered apparent size. Such a mechanism does not require a record of the true size of the object from which the image originates. Subsequent experiments, however, have shown that bees rely preferentially on landmarks closer to the feeder when the apparent sizes of landmarks at different distances have been equated by making the more distant landmarks bigger (Cheng et al. 1987). Thus, the local map represents angular and linear distances.

Additional landmarks.   Adding landmarks to the configuration focused the search (figure 5.9), as is to be expected when positioning is based on triangulation. When there was more than one landmark, changes in the sizes of the landmarks had negligible effects on the position of the bee's

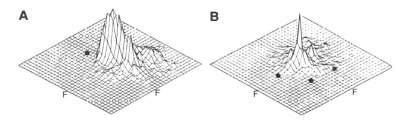

Figure 5.9
A. Distribution of a single bee's flight time when trained to a food source 50 centimeters from a single cylindrical landmark and tested with the same-sized landmark (4-centimeter diameter and 40 centimeters high). The coordinates of the food source during training are marked by *F*s on the *x* and *y* axes. Filled circles indicates position of the landmark. Height of plot gives relative time spent in each cell of the grid. Lines on the grid are 8.7 centimeters apart. *B.* Distribution of the bee's flight time when trained and tested with 3 landmarks in a triangular array (filled circles on grid). Note increased precision of source localization. (Reproduced from Cartwright and Collett 1983, p. 524, by permission of author and publisher.)

search. Cartwright and Collett interpret this to mean that positioning by crossed compass bearings takes precedence over positioning by apparent size, but this way of phrasing the matter is misleading. It implies two distinct mechanisms, but positioning by apparent size and compass bearing is a special case of positioning by crossed compass bearings. Both are a form of triangulation and both may be carried out by the same mechanism. If we assume that the positioning system relies on the compass bearings of contours, taking into account all contours represented in its memory image, then any reasonable weighting function for assessing the importance of discrepancies between observed and expected contour bearings will yield the result that the positions of widely spaced landmarks will have a much greater effect on the position taken up than will the apparent size of these landmarks. An error-weighting function in a procedure that fixes position by crossed compass bearings should have the property that many small discrepancies in bearing get much less weight than large discrepancies. As may be seen in figure 5.10, adjusting one's position so as to make the compass bearings of the contours of one enlarged landmark precisely right means trading six small errors for two perfect matches plus four large errors. A reasonable error-weighting function should reject this trade. It should favor the solution involving six small errors, because small errors are the inevitable consequence of an angle-measuring system with limited resolution, which is what the bee and every other organism has.

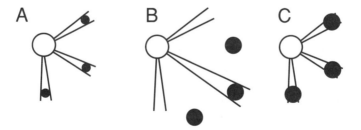

Figure 5.10
How bees resolve the conflict between landmark bearings and sizes when tested with landmarks that are too big. *A.* During training the bee learns where edges of landmarks lie on its retina (shown by open circle). When landmarks are enlarged, the bee can either fly to where the edges of just one of the landmarks are aligned correctly (*B*) or to where the edges all have wrong positions but the centers of all the landmarks have correct bearings (*C*). The bee chooses solution *C* as the better compromise; thus, the center of the search is not affected by the change in landmark size when there is more than one landmark. By comparing *B* and *C*, it is evident why an appropriately designed error-minimizing algorithm in the triangulation procedure will produce the observed result. (Redrawn from Cartwright and Collet 1983, p. 530, by permission of author and publisher.)

In another experiment by Cartwright and Collett, where the bee was allowed to choose between two configurations that varied in how well they fit the training configuration, bee preference was a systematic function of the relative goodness of fit, so the positioning system does compute an error function. Thus there is every reason to suppose that the bee finds the food source by the method of crossed bearings, using the remembered compass bearings of the contours of the terrain in the immediate vicinity of the source. When there is only one such local landmark, then this mechanism will find a position determined by the apparent size of the landmark. When there is more than one landmark, their apparent sizes will have little effect.

Importance of compass bearings. Evidence that compass bearings were being employed—even with multi-landmark configurations, where the location of the food could be derived from angular separation alone—came from experiments in which the orientation of the configuration was changed. When the configuration of landmarks was rotated through modest angles (< 45°), so that the compass bearings of the landmarks at the "correct" source position were not grossly discrepant from their correct compass bearings, the bees searched at the position from which the images of the landmarks had the correct angular separation. However, when confronted with a 90° rotation of the configuration, the bees no longer searched at the correct point relative to the landmarks. They rejected the landmark identifications and searched randomly. The differences between the compass bearings were acceptable (that is, the angular separations of the different parts of the configuration were congruent with the bee's record, when viewed from the correct position relative to those landmarks), but at the position that yielded these acceptable angular separations, the compass bearings themselves were unacceptably discrepant from those required by the stored spatial information.

The role of compass bearings in the bee's use of landmarks is strikingly similar to their role in marine piloting. Pilot manuals for a given coast contain sketches of headlands and other salient features of the terrain in the vicinity of harbor entrances. Associated with these sketches are compass bearings. The sketches are usually artist's tracings of the most salient contours, made from photographs taken from the mouth of the harbor. The chief purpose of the compass bearings associated with the sketched landmarks is to enable the pilot to steer the vessel into the correct position with respect to those landmarks. Once the pilot has paired a perceived landmark with a sketch in the manual, he takes the compass bearing of the landmark and compares it with the compass bearing recorded in the manual. This enables him to steer relative to the landmarks.

A subsidiary purpose of the compass bearings associated with the memory image of a landmark is to assist in establishing the proper correspondence between current perception and the memory image. Pairing the drawings in the manual with what one sees is not as straightforward as it sounds. It is common to conclude that such and such bump poking out from behind a cloud is such and such landmark in the manual, only to conclude subsequently that it is not. If you know from dead reckoning roughly where you are, then you can and often do reject possible pairings of current percept and manual sketch because the bearings are grossly wrong. You reason as follows: "Given that we're roughly here, Mount So-and-So must lie somewhere to the southwest of us, and that bump doesn't, so that bump cannot be Mount So-and-So." One of the results from Cartwright and Collett's computer modelling of the bee's navigation procedure is that compass bearings play this role there, too. One of the most serious problems they encountered in modeling the bee's navigational use of terrain images is that of false pairings between features of the memory image and features of the current image. Using compass-oriented memory images (rather than retinally localized images) reduces the number of these false pairings.

Affine transformations.   One of the demonstrations that the bee's navigation depends on for the storage of metric information about the geometric relation between the location of the food source and the location of the landmarks comes from experiments that Cartwright and Collett (1983) conducted for other reasons. The bees in this experiment were trained with the food source at the center of a square configuration of four cylinders and then allowed to choose between the square configuration and a rectangular configuration, produced by compressing the square along an axis parallel to one of its sides. This compression is an affine transformation of the landmark configuration, which may be defined as any combination of uniform compressions or expansions of a figure along one or more axes. An affine transformation alters the metric properties and only the metric properties of a configuration. It leaves unaltered every geometric relation definable in the absence of the axioms required to establish the metric properties of space (the congruence of line segments and all that follows therefrom). Affine geometry, which is the first (least extensive) weakening of metric geometry, is the study of geometric relations that are invariant under affine transformation.

If the bee's stored representation of the spatial relation between the food source and the landmarks did not preserve metric relations, then an affine transformation of the configuration could not affect the bee's preference between configurations. A rectangle is distinguishable from a square only by virtue of metric relations. In affine geometry, there is no distinction between squares and rectangles; the distinction exists only in metric geometry. If the bee's map does not preserve metric relations, it has no basis for preferring the original square configuration to the rectangular configuration. Cartwright and Collett found that the more the rectangular alternative departed from the square configuration on which the bees had been trained, the more the bees preferred the original square. Since the bees reacted to a purely metric change in the configuration, they must have preserved a record of some metric relations.

This conclusion from the affine transformation experiment does not depend on a model of how the bee positions itself relative to the landmarks. Even if the model elaborated by Cartwright and Collett in their computer model of bee navigation should prove to be incorrect, it nonetheless follows from the results of the transformation experiments that the bee's navigational performance depends on the preservation of some metric information about the relation between the position of the food source and the position of the landmarks.

Contour correspondence versus point-by-point correspondence.   Given that the bee positions itself by comparing a compass-oriented memory image with what it now sees, the question arises, What is it about the two images that must correspond? The simplest correspondence is point-by-point correspondence: the bee might compare the darkness of each pixel (picture element) in the memory image with the darkness signaled by each omatidium (that is, with the darkness of each pixel in the currently perceived image). However, anyone familiar with the ubiquity of contour extraction mechanisms in the early stages of most visual systems might imagine that the comparison is between contours in the memory image and contours in the current image. To distinguish between these alternatives, bees were trained with a solid black square and then tested with a square outline made of black dowels. With the outline, the bee searched at the same place as it did with the filled square. It did appear to notice the change, however; it was more likely to fly and search with the original than it was with the frame. One should keep in mind that the frame not only preserves the original contours of the square, it introduces a new set of contours as well, and these may prove distracting.

From the results with the outline figure, it is clear that the bee does more than a point-by-point comparison because such a comparison would find negligible resemblance between the filled-in square and the square outline. Beusekom (1948) reached a similar conclusion from experiments with the digger wasp in which he successfully substituted an open plastic triangle in place of the triangular array of pine cones and sticks the wasp had been trained on. He concluded that the wasp oriented by the gross form of the contours in the local terrain rather than by point-by-point matches because the wasps accepted substitutions that utterly destroyed point-by-point matches.

Except in testing whether the bees were doing point-by-point or contour matching, Cartwright and Collett (1983) used same-shaped landmarks in training and testing trials. Gould (1987) used one shape in training and then presented the bees with a choice between a configuration made of landmarks with that shape and the same configuration made of landmarks of equal area but different shape. The bees strongly preferred the configuration made of landmarks of the same shape. He also showed that they preferred a configuration made of landmarks with the same color as the training color. Finally, in elegantly designed parametric experiments, he measured the angular resolution of the memory images used in fixing a food source, revealing a horizontal resolution of about 3° and a vertical resolution of about 5–6°. This resolution is substantially less than the 1° resolution demonstrated by optomotor tests (Wehner 1981), indicating that the remembered "sketch" does not include all the detail that the bee's optical system is capable of resolving. On the other hand, this resolution is considerably better than the 8–10° limit of resolution that Gould (1986b, 1985) has shown for the bee's memory of the pattern of the food source itself. In other words, the bee makes a higher-resolution map of the terrain surrounding a food source than it does of the pattern of the food source itself.

Does the bee parse the contours?   The pilot's manual parses the contours to be seen in the vicinity of the harbor into sketches of distinct objects or features of the terrain. There is no clear evidence that the bee does this. If the bee really has a distinct mechanism for orienting by apparent size, then it must parse the contours into groups of contours associated with particular objects or features of the terrain. But positioning by apparent size may be a special case of the general principle of positioning by the compass bearings of contours, in which case there is no need to assume any grouping (parsing) of the contours—that is, any recognition of distinct objects or features defined by some constellation of contours.

From the computer simulations that Cartwright and Collett did, however, does come the suggestion that one simple kind of parsing may be necessary for their kind of model to work. They found that the introduction of contours from distant landmarks (hence contours whose bearings did not change much with changes in the bee's position) seriously degraded the performance of their models. Every landmark is a source of information—insofar as changes in its bearing aid the bee to position itself—and of confusion—in that additional landmarks increase the problem of false pairings between contours in memory and current contours, which is one of the more serious problems models of this kind face. Since the bearings of distant landmarks do not change measurably as the bee moves about within a small search area, contours from distant objects add confusion but not useful information. It seems likely that distant contours are filtered out of the memory image, and possibly also of the current image, prior to the correspondence-finding operation. The property that makes these contours useless—their failure to change their bearings in response to translatory movements of the bee—may serve as the basis for their removal.

However, distant contours from large scale features of the terrain play an important role in the bee's macroscopic navigation, the navigation that gets it from the hive to a food source, tens, hundreds or even thousands of meters away.

The Large-Scale Map in the Honey Bee
The experiments reviewed demonstrate that the bee can reproducibly orient itself with respect to landmarks surrounding a food source, giving greater weight to segments of the terrain image that originate from nearby sources. However, for this ability to find a food source by virtue of its geometric relation to the local terrain to be of use, the bee must first get from the hive to the locale of the food. In doing this, bees orient with reference to the large-scale features of the terrain.

In chapter 4, we reviewed Gould's experiments demonstrating that bees recalibrate their ephemeris functions from sightings of the sun. The fact that bees average the data from repeated sightings of the sun, sightings separated by intervals in which the bee is in the hive out of sight of the sun and external landmarks, implies that they must be able to orient themselves reproducibly with respect to something other than the sun—something fixed in its relation to the earth's surface and recognizable from one sighting to the next. A sighting is a measure of the angle between two lines intersecting at the observer. A sighting of the sun is a measure of the angle between the sun's azimuthal position and something fixed in its relation to the earth. The orientation of the lines of flux for the earth's magnetic field is one earth-anchored reference that can be reestablished from one sighting to the next, provided the organism has a magnetic compass. There is evidence that bees do have magnetic compasses and do orient by them under some circumstances (Gould 1980).

Another reference the bees might use to form the other side of the angle to be measured are large-scale features of the terrain. These do not usually change their orientation with respect to the rest of the earth's surface. To combine data from different sightings, the bee must use the same features from one sighting to the next. This means that the bee must store a representation of the features it used during one sighting so that it may recognize them subsequently.

It would seem to follow that bees must represent the angles and distances of food sources not only with reference to the sun but also with reference to prominent features of the terrain surrounding the hive. That this is so was demonstrated in an experiment by Dyer and Gould (1981). Before considering their results, however, we must learn more about alternative experimental methods for assessing a bee's estimate of the angular relation between the sun's azimuth and the compass bearing of a food source.

In his second study of averaging, Gould (1984) did not estimate the bees' computation of the sun's angular position by recording which feeding station they arrived at. He relied instead on the fact that a bee's representation of the solar bearing of a food source and its distance from the hive is not used only for the bee's own guidance, it is made externally manifest in symbolic behavior—the dance through which one forager communicates its representation of the food's location to other foragers. The dance is in the form of a fat figure eight. The angle of the food source relative to the sun's current azimuth is represented by the angle that the central portion of the eight (the portion where the two loops join) forms with respect either to the pull of gravity, when, as is usually the case, the dance is on a vertical surface out of sight of the sun, or with respect to the sun itself, when the dance is on a horizontal surface and the sun or some sunlike contrivance of the experimenter is visible. The latter arrangement was the one Gould used. To estimate the experimentally induced changes in the forager's representation of the food's solar bearing, Gould watched the returned foragers dance on a horizontal surface, orienting to an artificial sun set up inside the hive. With this arrangement, Gould could "listen" to the angular instructions one bee gave to the other bees.

The Dyer and Gould (1981) experiment showing that bees may orient their flights by reference to prominent features of the terrain, as well as by reference to the sun's azimuth, grew out of their concern with the long-established fact that bees continue to forage on overcast and even very foggy days. It had been suggested that the ultraviolet polarization-sensitive visual channel found in bees enabled them to see through clouds, estimating the sun's azimuth from information contained in the pattern of skylight (Von Frisch, Lindauer, and Schmiedler 1960). While bees can orient with respect to the polarization patterns in clear patches of sky, clouds block ultraviolet more than they do other wavelengths of light, and they completely depolarize the skylight (Brines and Gould 1979). These purely physical findings led Dyer and Gould to conjecture that on cloudy days, bees orient by prominent large-scale features of the terrain around the hive rather than by the sun.

It had earlier been shown that even when the sun is visible, bees may use prominent features of the terrain as a guide to a previously visited food source rather than the sun. Von Frisch and Lindauer (1954) set up hives and feeding stations at substantial distances from them along prominent large-scale features of the terrain—roads or long lines of trees at the edges of fields. After foragers had spent a day flying to and from the stations, the experimenters moved both hives and stations during the night to other locales that had similar gross features but oriented at different compass angles. Thus, a hive and station would be moved from beside a north-south-oriented line of trees to beside an east-west-oriented line of trees. After setting the hive down in this new location, the experimenters set up a feeding station at the point where the bees should expect to find one if they oriented by the sun (and/or the earth's magnetic field)—that is, at a point with the same compass bearing relative to the hive. They also set up a station at the point where the bees should expect to find one if they ignored the sun's position (and/or the pointings of their compass needles) and oriented their search flight with respect to the line of trees. When dawn came, most of the foragers showed up at the station one would find in orienting by the prominent landmarks rather than by the sun. When the same experiment was done using locales where there were no prominent features of the terrain to orient by, most foragers showed up at the location that has the correct position relative to the sun's azimuth. This result demonstrates among other things that the precedence that experienced bees accord to one reference (the sun) over another (gross landmarks) is circumstance dependent. Whichever is easier to use is given precedence.

The most important implication of this experiment is that bees have a metric large-scale map, a representation of the approximate location of a food source in terms of the angle one must fly relative to large-scale features of the terrain around the nest and the distance one must cover.

Dyer and Gould (1981) replicated this result and then went on to show something even more startling: when the hive was displaced during the night and the next day dawned completely overcast, all of the foragers went to the station that was correct relative to the line of trees rather than the station that had the correct compass bearing. Most interestingly, when they returned to the nest and danced, they signaled to their fellow foragers the previous day's compass bearing—the bearing of the station they had not visited. More interestingly yet, when foragers recruited by this dance left the hive to find the station, they flew not to the station with the correct compass bearing (the station indicated by the dance) but rather to the station from which the initial foragers had returned. In other words, both the early and the later foragers based their estimate of the sun's position upon the (erroneous) assumption that the line of trees they now saw outside the hive was the same line they had seen the previous day, with, of course, the same compass orientation. Their dance—and the interpretation of that dance by their fellow foragers—was based on their having memorized the course of the sun relative to this prominent landmark, or alternatively, on their having memorized the data necessary to compute its position as a function of the time of day. In short, it was based on their ephemeris function, a learned relation between the time of day and the position of the sun with respect to the local terrain.

Just as interesting were the results obtained when the displaced hive was opened at the new location with the sun visible. The great majority of the foragers still went to the station whose position relative to the line of trees was correct rather than to the station whose compass bearing (hence, relation to the sun's azimuth) was correct. In other words, most of the emerging bees, finding a disagreement between the course suggested by the position of the sun and that suggested by the orientation of the line of trees, opted for the latter course, while a few opted for the former. The bees who returned from the station that they reached by paying attention to the line of trees rather than the sun nonetheless correctly signaled the station's true solar bearing in the dance they made on returning. In other words, the dance made on cloudy days rested on the remembered time-referenced relation between trees and sun, while the dance made on sunny days showed only the effect of the new sun sightings made on the first foraging flight—despite the fact that the heading on at least the outward portion of this flight was determined by reference to the trees, not the sun. The bees had recalibrated their ephemeris function.

The Dyer and Gould experiment shows that bees represent the daily change in the angular position of the sun relative to the terrain surrounding the hive. When the sun is not visible, they orient their flights by reference to this terrain. Bee communication, however, is more circumscribed than human communication. They have mechanisms for behaviorally symbolizing bearings and distances but not for behaviorally symbolizing the appearance of the terrain. They get around this limitation by mechanisms that represent the course of the sun relative to the local terrain, enabling them to refer to the current position of the sun in communicating the position of a food source when neither the sender nor the receiver of the communication has sighted the sun for hours or even days.

These results imply a large-scale map of the terrain that a bee forages in. Subsequent experiments by Gould (1986a) demonstrate this map unequivocally. Gould tested whether bees had a general map of the terrain in which they forage, as opposed to the kind of route-specific map suggested for bees (Wehner 1981) and for rats (Deutsch 1960; Lieblich and Arbib 1982). A route-specific map would consist of a series of sketches of landmarks lying on the route between various feeding sources and the bee's hive. The bee would get to and from the sources by a sequence of beacon-homings, flying until it was over the first landmark and then looking for the next one, and so on (see Deutsch 1960 for a model of this kind of cognitive map). Such a map is an example of one that is weaker than a metric map. All it preserves is collinearity information about selected sets of points (points lying on a line between the hive and the food source).

Gould worked with a hive in an open field flanked by woods (figure 5.11). By first setting up a feeding station close to the hive and then moving it away by modest distances along the path that entered the woods to the west of the hive and roughly paralleled the field boundary, Gould trained foragers to fly back and forth between the station at location A and the hive. All the foragers visiting the station at site A were either individually marked (with small plastic numbers on their back) or disposed of. Site A was chosen because it was an unlikely site for a bee

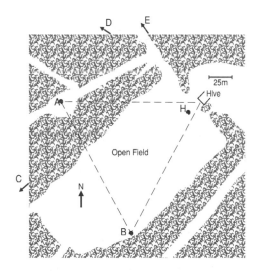

Figure 5.11
Honey bee displacement experiment. Bees from a hive (top right) were trained to either site *A* , *B*, or *C* (off the lower left of the map). On subsequent days, these foragers and others were captured and transported to a different site and released. As a control, some trained foragers were released at *H* as well. (Redrawn from an original supplied by J. L. Gould and used with his permission. For published version, see Gould 1986.)

to visit in the absence of the training received by the individually marked bees. It was in a small clearing, devoid of flowers, along the path.

Observation of the marked foragers arriving at and leaving the station showed that they generally came in from and left in the direction of the hive. In other words, there was good reason to think they were flying to and returning from the feeding station by a direct route. While they would have become familiar with the general terrain around the hive prior to their specific training, the training was such that the bees would generally have reached the feeding station in the woods by a direct route. They were unlikely ever to have reached that particular station by a highly indirect route that took them over the experimental release site.

Gould captured his marked foragers as they emerged from the hive, en route to the feeding station, and carried them in a dark box to site B, where he released them one by one. The release site was downhill from the woods that surrounded site A, so that the treetop horizon in the direction of site A was 24 to 28 meters above the elevation of the release site, preventing any view of Site A from Site B.

The compass bearing of the feeding station from the hive, where the emerging foragers were captured, was 270°. Its compass bearing from the release site was 330°. The compass bearing of the hive from the release site was 30°. If the released bees behaved like the ants in the Wehner and Srinivasan experiments and took no cognizance of the fact that they were not in the same locale as the one in which they had been captured, then they should depart on a course of 270°, the course they were setting out on when captured. If they were able to recognize their displacement from the hive (having visited site B in the period prior to their training to site A), but they knew only how to progress from one place to another along route-specific sequences of collinear landmarks, then their only option would be to return to the hive and resume their outward flight from there, in which case they should depart from the release site on a compass bearing of 30°. If they recognized their release site and had a record of the relative metric positions of site B and site A, then they would be able to orient with respect to the terrain surrounding site B in such a way as to put themselves on a course for the (unperceived) site A, despite the fact that they had never followed this course in getting to site A. In that case, the bees should depart from site B on a compass bearing of 330°, the direction of site A from site B, which is what they did (filled circles in figure 5.12A). All of the bees arrived at the feeding station and they did so in about the same amount of time (28.9 +/- 9.4 seconds) that it normally took them to cover the similar distance from the hive to the station (25.2 +/- 5.5 seconds), a time so short that, given the known flying speed of bees, they could not have returned to the hive in the course of getting from site B to site A.

The departure bearings of the bees released at site B were a function both of the positions of sites B and A and of the bee's intended course at the time of capture, as shown by the following control experiments. When, on one or more subsequent occasions, the same marked foragers were captured as they emerged from the hive, carried halfway to site B and then back to 15 meters in front of the hive, where they were released, they departed on the compass bearing of site A from the hive (open triangles in figure 5.12A). Thus, their departure bearings upon leaving the release site varied as a function of the release site in such a way as to orient them toward the feeding station for which they were bound when captured. In a second control, Gould captured unmarked foragers as they arrived back at the hive. These foragers, who had been bound for the hive from different points of the compass at the time of their capture, were carried to site B and released. They departed on the compass bearing of the hive (open squares in figure 5.12A). This shows that different courses are set from the same release site when the bees have different destinations. It also shows that these bees represented the geometric relation between site B and the hive, although they were returning from various other points of the compass. Finally, Gould caught unmarked foragers emerging from the hive bound for unknown and presumably diverse destinations. When these bees were released at site B, there was no consistency in the their departure bearings. They went off in all directions. The length of their mean departure vector (short arrow labeled "4" in the circle in figure 5.12A) was not significantly different from zero, the expected length of the mean of randomly varying departure vectors.

To test for possible asymmetric site effects, Gould repeated the experiment with a group of foragers trained to a station at site B and released at site A. The results were the same (figure 5.12B). When marked bees were captured on their way out, they oriented toward the feeding station from the release site; when unmarked bees were captured as they returned to the hive and released at site A, they oriented toward the hive; when marked bees were captured on their way out and released near the capture point, they oriented on the bearing of the station from the hive.

To get some idea of the range of the bee's foraging map, another group of foragers was trained to a station in a heavily wooded location 350 meters west southwest of the hive (site C), captured when outward bound, and released in a small clearing (site D) 350 meters west northwest of the hive. These bees departed on the correct bearing for C from site D (filled circles in figure 5.12C). When released at the hive instead of site C, they adjusted their departure direction accordingly (open triangles in figure 5.12C). When unmarked foragers coming into the hive

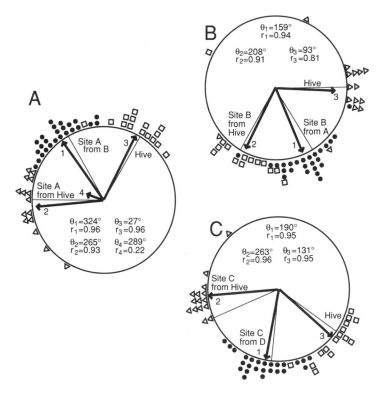

Figure 5.12
The vanishing bearings of bees trained at one site and subsequently transported to and released at another site are indicated by points plotted on the unit circle. A. Filled circles are the vanishing bearings of foragers trained to a station at site A, captured when outward bound from the hive and released at site B. The line labeled "Site A from B" gives the compass bearing of A from B. The vector labeled "1" is the mean vector for the filled circles. θ_1 is the angle of this vector and r_1 is its length, which is a measure of directional consistency (with a maximum value of 1). Open triangles are the vanishing bearings of outward-bound marked foragers released at H. Corresponding line and vector labeling follows the conventions just described in connection with the filled circles. Open squares are the vanishing bearings of unmarked foragers captured as they arrived at the hive, transported to site B and released. The short vector 4 is for unmarked foragers (hence foragers bound for sites other than site A) captured on their way out and released at B. Its length is not significantly greater than 0, indicating that there was no consistency in the vanishing bearings of these bees. B. The same experiment as in A, but with the training and release sites reversed. C. The same experiment using two different and more remote release sites. The training station was at site C; the release sites were D and H. (Redrawn from Gould 1986, by permission of author and publisher.)

from assorted (unknown) directions were transported to site D, they departed in the direction of the hive (open squares in figure 5.12C).

As a final control, to demonstrate that the capacity of these bees to orient themselves appropriately depended on their familiarity with the terrain surrounding their hive, Gould captured ten foragers visiting site C and released them at a site almost 41/2 kilometers away to the northwest of the hive, outside the normal foraging range of this species (Site E). The bees released at site E departed in random directions; none ever returned to the feeding station or the hive. By contrast, none of the bees released from closer in got lost.

The range of a bee's map depends on its foraging habits. Orchid bees in Central America forage on widely dispersed individual orchid blooms. Janzen (1971) removed twelve orchid bees from their hive and transported them in a jeep to arbitrarily chosen release sites between 14 and 23 kilometers distant from their hive in the rather featureless rain forests of Costa Rica. Seven of the twelve bees released at these distances returned to the hive on the day of their release. One bee made it home from 20 kilometers out in 65 minutes, an average speed of better than 5 meters per second along the "beeline" from the release site to the hive.

The ability to make it home from an arbitrary release site does not depend on the bee or wasp's being able to fly. Thorpe (1950) did similar experiments, involving displacements of many tens of meters to different points of the compass, with digger wasps that were walking home with prey too large to carry in flight.

These capture-and-release experiments provide strong evidence that bees and wasps make and use a large-scale metric map of the terrain over which they forage, but they do not fully convey the sophistication of the bee's use of its map. The full sophistication is suggested by an experiment in which Dyer and his collaborators (the fullest account is in Gould and Gould 1988) manipulated the dance of returning honey bee foragers so that it indicated a food source in the middle of a small lake. Other bees could not be recruited by this dance. If, on the other hand, the dance of the returning foragers indicated a site on the far shore of the lake, other bees were recruited by the dance. This implies that bees use their terrain map in evaluating the message contained in the dance of a returning forager. Instead of simply taking that dance as a set of flying instructions, they take it as the specification of a point on a terrain map that the foragers share. When the point specified is not in terrain where forage could be found, the message is ignored.

The Gould capture-and-release experiments with honey bees are among the best-controlled demonstrations that an animal has a large-scale cognitive map of its environment, which enables it to set a course for different destinations from an arbitrary release site within the mapped terrain. The entire honey bee is considerably smaller than the brain of a rat, and yet it has been a matter of enduring controversy whether a rat could be credited with a true map of its environment (for recent doubts, see Lieblich and Arbib 1982) because there are no experiments with the rat as compelling as Gould's experiments with the honey bee. Nonetheless, the well-documented capacity of insects in this regard may soften one's skepticism regarding the capacity of vertebrates to form large-scale metric maps. Evidence that they do will be reviewed shortly. One point, however, needs to be stressed before we turn our attention to vertebrates: Gould's behavioral measure of orientation (compass bearing) is a metric geometric relation. There is no such thing as compass bearing in nonmetric geometries because angular relations are not invariant under affine transformation (excepting the cross-ratio in a fan of four angles, which is invariant even under projective transformation). While it might in principle be possible to generate a metrically correct behavioral output from a nonmetric representation of the relevant geometric relations, it does not seem likely that this is what is in fact done. The simplest assumption is that metric piloting implies the use of a metric map.

Homing in Amphiprion: The Importance of the Relative Position of a Site
The *Amphiprion* are a genus of fish that are symbiotic with sea anemones. Unlike other marine creatures, they do not excite the contraction of the anemone's tentacles, so they find safety within those tentacles, where they spend most of their time. Each fish has a home anemone to which it returns. Since the different anemones within a tidal pool or restricted area of a reef often differ in ways that are obvious to the human observer and since the fish seldom ventures more than a few meters away from the protection of its anemone, one might imagine that an amphiprion would find its way back to its anemone by a visual beacon method. This does not appear to be the case. Instead the fish finds its way back by moving to a particular position in space. This is shown by displacement experiments (Mariscal 1972, p. 335ff). If one removes an amphiprion's anemone from its normal position and puts it down a foot or so away, the fish returns to the previous position of its anemone, searches, and hovers, and then finally discovers it in its new location. Even after discovering the anemone in its new location, the fish returns to the original location with diminishing frequency over several days. Even when the space is a generally featureless aquarium and the fish stays within the anemone's tentacles during the displacement, the fish nonetheless returns from its initial postdisplacement forays not to the new location of the anemone but rather to its previous location. In these aquarium experiments, the sought-for anemone is among the more prominent local features in the animal's experimentally limited behavioral space. Thus, even in a highly

visual vertebrate like the fish under conditions that favor beacon homing, the animal uses an overall sense of spatial position as the basis for
guiding its homeward movement. It moves toward a remembered
location in space, not toward a remembered set of goal features.

Puddle Jumping: The Use of a Map for Purposes Other Than Homing
Aronson (1951) observed that when gobies were stranded in small tide
pools by the receding tide, they jumped from one small pool to the next,
though the rim of the pool they jumped from prevented their seeing the
pool they jumped to. The fish jumped from pool to pool until they
reached the open sea. He subsequently did an experimental test of their
ability to orient appropriately in jumping from one artificial pool to the
next (Aronson 1971). He constructed an artificial series of tide pools
within a large outdoor tank. At the lowest level was a large main pool (*M*
in figure 5.13*A*). On a step a few inches above the main pool, separated
from it by a low ridge, was a small irregularly shaped pool (*C*). Behind
it and a few inches higher still were two more small pools (*A* and *B*). The
water level in the tank could be raised to flood over all the pools, allowing
the fish to swim anywhere in the tank, and it could be lowered so that the
pools were isolated from each other by the intervening low ridges.
    Twenty-seven gobies were collected from tide pools and kept in a
home pool separate from the experimental tank. On the first day, with the
"tide" out so that the pools were isolated from one another, each fish was
placed in one of the two highest pools, along with a conch shell for shelter,
and allowed to acclimatize itself for an hour. Then the conch shell shelter
was removed, and the water was disturbed during a 10-minute trial by
random pokings with a stick, care being taken not to give the pokes a
directional component. Each fish received three of these preliminary
trials, whose purpose was to determine how well the fish did when they
had not had any experience with the overall configuration of the pools,
experience that could give them the spatial information necessary to
orient their jumps appropriately.
    In these preliminary trials, the fish often jumped out of the pool they
were in, but the jumps were poorly oriented, so they landed on the
concrete and flopped around until they got back into a pool. The fish
reached the main pool on only 15 percent of these three preliminary trials;
nineteen out of twenty-seven did not reach it on any trial. At the end of
the preliminary trials, each of the twenty-one fish in the experimental
group was left in one of the small upper pools while the "tide" was
allowed to rise overnight, flooding the tank and uniting the pools. In the
morning, when the tide was made to recede, the fish was invariably
found swimming in the lower pool. With the tide out and the pools once
more isolated from each other, the fish was returned to one of the two

uppermost pools and given three escape trials just like the preliminary trials. Now the fish did much better; all twenty-one experimental fish reached the main pool on at least one of the three trials—often in two quick jumps made within a few seconds of the start of the trial—and all but two reached the main pool on each of the three trials. (The overall success rate for fish in the experimental group during this phase was 97 percent.) Figure 5.13B shows a goby leaping from pool C into the main pool.

Six additional fish served as controls. They got the three preliminary trials and three more subsequent trials, but they were returned to their home pool between the two sets of three trials and never got to swim around the tank when the pools were united by the high tide. These control fish did no better on the second set of three trials than they did on the first.

In a follow-up experiment, 40 days intervened between the single night at high tide and the test of the fish's ability to orient its escape jumps. The fish nonetheless did well. The fish too looks before it leaps, but it can look now and leap later, orienting its jumps by reference to an enduring record of the topography of the sea bottom.

Larger reef fish range over areas of hundreds of meters and they return to their territories when experimentally displaced over this range of distances (Bardach 1958), but records of their homing paths or time taken to home have never been obtained, and so the mechanism of this homing remains obscure. In the light of the following data on the tortoise, however, it is not unreasonable to imagine that this homing depends on large-scale knowledge of reef geometry.

Trips to Special Resources in the Desert Tortoise
Many animals move within a restricted space most of the time but occasionally venture far afield to obtain special resources. One example is the desert tortoise. Having more bone than most vertebrates, it needs more calcium. This need is acute in gravid females, which must supply the calcium for the development of the thick calcareous shells of the eggs. Tortoises excavate calcium mines in parts of the desert with a layer of calcium salts 2–6 centimeters below the soil surface, and they exploit these mines for years at a time. The mines commonly lie at some remove from the tortoise's normal foraging area. Figure 5.14 shows a tortoise departing from her visit to one such mine, headed back to her foraging area on the planes below the hill, trailing the thread-unreeling device from which the experimenters obtained a continuous record of her movements over several days. Figure 5.15 is that record.

Most of the time the tortoise foraged on the sparse vegetation growing within a radius of about 100 meters from her burrow, which was within

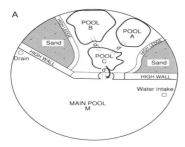

Figure 5.13
A. Map of the artificial tide pools used in recording goby jumps. Direct paths to the main pool (M) are labeled d. (Redrawn from Aronson 1971, p. 380, by permission of the author and the publisher.) B. Photo of goby making the jump indicated by the curved arrow at outlet from Pool C in A (ibid., p. 386, by permission of author and publisher).

25 meters of the edge of the vegetated area. While foraging, she did not venture more than 25 meters in the direction of the calcium mine, and she seldom moved more than 5 meters without stopping to browse, commonly altering her direction of movement after each stop. One day, however, she emerged from her burrow and set off on a straight walk of 175 meters to the calcium mine from which she is shown departing in figure 5.14. It appears from the photograph that the tortoise could not have seen the calcium pit at the time she set her course for it. It is hard to resist the conclusion that the course was set with reference to other landmarks and that this ability requires that the tortoise remember the spatial relation between these landmarks and the calcium mine. In other words, the tortoise at the outset of her journey was orienting toward a remembered position in space, a position that she could not then perceive but whose location relative to what she could perceive was coded in her nervous system.

The journey in figure 5.15 probably does not give a proper idea of the extent of the tortoise's spatial representation. (Darwin 1845, p. 383ff) observed that the Galapagos tortoise lumbers day and night for 3 days on 8-mile excursions from its arid lowland foraging fields to highland springs. The first mariners to land on the islands found the springs by following the paths worn by the tortoises.

Homing from Unfamiliar Release Sites
The pigeon. The study of homing in birds, particularly homing pigeons, has been an active and productive international enterprise since the pioneering work of Kramer (1951, 1961). These studies have not yet solved the central mystery, which was first clearly highlighted by Kramer (1952), when he distinguished sharply between the mechanisms by which birds hold their course once they have set it and the mechanisms by which they set the course. Considerable progress has been made on the first question. What has emerged is the conclusion already stated with regard to course holding in bees and ants: birds hold their course by most of the methods that human ingenuity has been able to imagine—the sun, the stars, the movement of the ground beneath them, the direction of the wind, the source of sounds (perhaps), and others (see Emlen 1975). What remains mysterious despite a great deal of experimental ingenuity is how they are able to set their course in the first place.

Two conclusions are apparent. First, it is clearly possible for an animal to know the approximate spatial relation between its home and stimulus sources located well outside any area it has ever visited or seen. When an animal is far from home in an area it has never visited and without visual access to anything it has previously seen, it may have access via other sensory modalities to landmarks with a known location relative to the

Figure 5.14
Tortoise equipped with a thread-trailing device, walking away from a calcium mine that was used from 1969 to 1980. The tortoise's burrow and normal foraging area are in the area of sparse vegetation visible beyond and beneath the crest of the low ridge toward which the tortoise is headed. (Reproduced from plate in Marlow 1982, p. 476, by permission of author and publisher.)

home site. Second, it is clear that birds use their spatial knowledge in subtler ways than one would at first imagine. The experimental results have repeatedly forced experimenters to search for hitherto unsuspected sensory capacities and to think and think again about the various navigational strategies that might conceivably be employed. A review of this extensive literature is beyond my present scope and purpose (see Emlen 1975; Gould 1983; Papi and Walraff 1982). Here I give only enough of a review to illustrate the use of spatial knowledge that extends beyond the area the bird has previously visited and the subtlety of the use made of this information.

A homing pigeon that has never flown more than a few kilometers from its loft can be transported hundreds of kilometers away in the trunk of a car and, within minutes of its release, it will set a course in the approximate direction of home and will arrive there in a time that indicates that it could not have deviated very far from the straight-line course between the release site and the home loft. In many cases, the birds cannot see any familiar sight when released. Under exceptionally clear conditions, a bird 2 kilometers up may be able to see for 100 kilometers in all directions, but pigeons rapidly set a course for home when released well outside that radius, under heavily overcast conditions—in short,

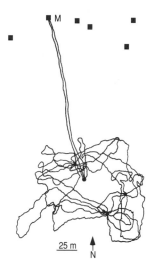

Figure 5.15
Daily pattern of movements of the tortoise shown in Figure 5.14 for several days before
and after taking the trip to the calcium mine. Each filled square is an active mine site. The
filled circle is the burrow in which she spent her nights. With the exception of the trip to
M, the movement pattern is typical of a foraging tortoise. (Redrawn from Marlow 1982, p.
477, by permission of author and publisher.)

under conditions where there is no possibility that they can see anything
from the release site that they have ever been able to see from their home
site (Keeton 1974). Even when fitted with frosted but translucent contact
lenses, which prevent form vision but permit localization of the sun's
position, birds released 130 kilometers from the home loft adopt a home
orientation nearly as well as do control birds. Many of these birds fly to
within a few kilometers of the home loft and then flutter down and wait
to be picked up. Some of them flutter down within as little as a 100 meters
of the loft (Schlichte and Schmidt-Koenig 1971; Schmidt-Koenig and
Schlichte 1972; Schmidt-Koenig and Walcott 1973).

These findings imply that the birds can estimate their position relative
to the home position from nonvisual stimuli that propagate over long
distances (for example, odors; see Papi 1982; Walraff 1983) or very low
frequency sound (Kreithern and Quine 1979; Quine and Kreithen 1981).
So far as anyone has been able to imagine, there are only two alternatives
to this conclusion: inertial dead reckoning and bicoordinate navigation.
Inertial dead reckoning is the calculation of one's displacement vector by
double integration of the acceleration vector. As we have seen, there is
clear evidence that vertebrates can do this for angular displacement, but
there has never been an experimental demonstration that they can do this

for any appreciable linear displacement. There is in any event extensive experimental evidence that this is not how pigeons determine their position when released at an unfamiliar site, or at least not the only way (see Emlen1975; Keeton 1974).

Bicoordinate navigation is navigation by reference to stimuli that are perceptible anywhere on the earth's surface and that vary in an orderly way with changes in latitude and longitude—stimuli, in other words, from which it is possible to compute one's latitude and longitude. The positions of the sun and stars provide one basis for bicoordinate navigation if one accurately knows the current time of day at the home location. However, extensive tests of the celestial bicoordinate navigation hypothesis have repeatedly failed to confirm it. The most damaging results come from clock-shifting experiments in which the bird's sense of local time is altered prior to its release by exposing it to artificial day-night cycles. Small changes in estimates of the time at the home site should lead to very large changes in homeward orientation if the birds are making celestial estimates of their longitudinal displacement. These errors are generally not seen (Emlen 1975). If, for example, the clock-shifted pigeons whose departure bearings are shown in figure 4.11 computed their release longitude from celestial observation, then they should orient as if they were thousands of kilometers to the west of home, which they clearly do not.

The other basis for bicoordinate navigation that has been entertained is the earth's magnetic field. Latitudinal displacement can be obtained from changes in the dip angle of the lines of magnetic force, which are parallel to the earth's surface at the equator and perpendicular at the poles, and also from the increase in the strength of the magnetic field toward the poles. It may even be possible to estimate longitudinal displacement from the magnetic field, at least in some areas, but the physical principles are not worth the extensive explanation they would require in view of the repeated failures to obtain any convincing evidence that birds can in fact extract displacement from magnetic input (see Emlen 1975). Even the claim that birds and other animals can obtain compass orientation from magnetic input has been among the more controversial and hard-to-substantiate claims (Griffin 1982).

In short, it is clear that birds do not rely exclusively—perhaps even primarily—on visual input in determining their displacement from home. The experimental evidence is heavily against the assumption that they can determine their displacement by any bicoordinate procedure yet conceived. It appears that they can estimate their displacement by reference to nonvisual stimuli that propagate over very long distances and whose angle of arrival can be determined in some way.

It is worth noting one feature of the data to bring out the subtlety of the birds' use of sensory information during homing. The initial courses homing birds set are far from random. When a large number of pigeons is released, their initial mean bearing is often close to the true bearing of the home site. However, there is commonly a very substantial dispersion about this mean (see figure 4.11 for example). The birds do not set a precise initial course for home. If they were to continue on their initial course, many birds would end up a long way from home. But in fact many of the initially poorly oriented birds arrive at the home loft in a time that indicates that they must have corrected their initial course before they had strayed far from the correct course. The importance of this common finding is that it implies that the birds' short-term estimate of the compass bearings of the stimulus sources they use to estimate their displacement from the home site may be extremely inaccurate.

It further suggests that as they go along, they improve their estimates of their position—probably by averaging over time their estimates of the angular position of the sources and by the parallax information, which they gain by virtue of their movement. In other words, they not only look at the average estimated compass bearing of each perceptible source over time, thereby steadily reducing the error surrounding the triangulation estimate of their position, they also do a trend analysis on these estimates. The trend analysis yields an estimate of the change in the angular position of each source per kilometer flown. This parallax information in turn permits them to put limits around their possible distances from the sources, which further improves their estimate of their position.

The bat.   Bats also home when displaced into areas they are unlikely ever to have visited. They do so even when the shelter to which they are homing no longer exists. Gunier and Elder (1971) collected Missouri cave bats (*Myotis grisescens*) from a barn about to be razed, banded them, and released one group 35 miles to the south southeast of the barn site and another group 75 miles to the northwest. The latter site was outside the cave region of Missouri, beyond the area in which bats of this species are generally found. About 25 percent of the bats from both releases were home by the next morning, including 38 percent of the females that were released 75 miles away, outside the species range.[2]

Another group of bats was captured on the day the razing began and released at the same two sites. Many of these came back to the site of the

2. It should not be concluded that the other 75 percent got lost. Internal features of the data from this study and many others make it likely that a large percentage of the bats that do not come home from such a release do not come because they decide to go elsewhere, where perhaps they will not be so rudely treated. Females that leave young behind when they are captured are much more likely to return than are males, for example.

barn when the structure was no longer there. The following spring, when the barn had been gone for months, many bats were observed circling the site at dawn and dusk, but none of the bats from this barn ever showed up at other barns in the vicinity (roosting in barns is rare for this species, or rather, it is a rare barn that they will roost in). Note once again that animals home to a point in space not by relying upon the intrinsic sensory qualities of that point (beacon homing) but rather by moving to a position in space, a position defined by its geometric relation to the surrounding terrain. The bat coming home from 75 kilometers out is similar in this regard to the amphiprion coming back to its anemone from a meter away.

Müller (1966) captured cave bats in Wisconsin in October and November, when most have gone into hibernation for the winter, and released them (by now wide awake) on warm nights up to 100 kilometers away, after marking them with paint. He caught them in a net rigged at the entrance to the cave or lead mine from which they were taken. Of the bats released 40 meters from the cave mouth, in territory they had flown over every summer night of their lives, only 91 percent returned. This is the kind of evidence that leads to the conclusion that some failures to come home are not failures of knowledge but failures of motivation. From 25 kilometers out, about 50 percent came home the night of the release. From 97 kilometers out, only 10 percent came home that night, but one of these hit the net at the entrance just three hours after its release, which calculates out at an average beeline flying speed of 32 kilometers per hour, close to the maximum flight speed of that species of bat (M. lucfugus). This bat must have been well oriented toward home within minutes of its release.

What is puzzling is that bats are all but blind. The species used in this experiment have no form of vision that would enable them to recognize anything at any appreciable distance on a dark fall night, and in fact, many bats made it home even after they had been blindfolded with a thick layer of collodion and lampblack, which rendered them unable to orient to a bright lamp. It has been estimated that bats do not get much in the way of form information out of the echos from their cries at ranges beyond 10 meters. To fly home at the rates observed, these bats must have stayed farther above the trees than that. The bats may have access to the same long-distance sensory information that enables pigeons to determine their displacement from the home position. How they hold their course once they have set it is more of a mystery than it is for the pigeon, but reference to a magnetic directional sense may reasonably be suspected. In any event, it is clear that the maps animals have often extend well beyond the territory they have visited, encompassing the locations of remote stimulus sources. The known locations of these remote sources

enable them to set a course for home when they are outside their usual
territory.

Avoiding Hard-to-Perceive Obstacles
Neuweiler and Möhres (1967) trained large winged bats (*Megaderma lyra*)
to fly from a roost beneath the ceiling in one room through a doorway into
another room, pluck a mealworm from a forceps, and fly back through
the doorway to the roost, where they ate the worm (figure 5.16). The
experimenters then strung wires in the doorway to create obstacles that
the bats had to learn to avoid. The 0.12-millimeter wires could be detected
only when the bat was very near them or when it struck them. Although
these bats have a wingspan of close to half a meter, they quickly learned
to fly through gaps 14 centimeters square between the wires, folding
their wings just as they came to the opening and reopening them on the
other side. When the wires were first installed, the bats flew into them,
indicating that they could not detect them when approaching at speed.
In time, however, the bats again approached the doorway at speed,
folded their wings, and sailed through a gap in the wires. Although the
gaps between the wires were identical, each bat had a favored few that
it preferred to go through on its way in and others that it favored when
coming back out. These favored openings changed from time to time
within a bat and differed widely between bats.

    When the frame containing the wires was shifted by 8 centimeters, so
that wires now obstructed the patches of space that had previously been
unobstructed, the bats again flew into them, indicating that they still
could not detect the wires during a fast approach and therefore that the
bats were negotiating the passage of the gaps between the wires by
means of a map that represented the position of the wires relative to more
readily perceptible objects. Given what we have so far learned, it is likely
that the bats got their initial sense of position and orientation from the
large-scale geometry of the room and controlled their trajectory while in
flight by dead reckoning, choosing a trajectory that would avoid the obstacles represented on their map of the doorway. Bats must routinely
make their way out of tortuous subterranean passages in the midsts of
hordes of their fellow bats, whose echoing cries make it hard to hear one's
own echo. It is not surprising that they have a well-developed capacity
to learn the geometry of the passageways through which they must fly
and an equally well developed capacity to fly by dead reckoning around
the smaller, less perceptible obstacles.

    The clearest demonstration that the bats avoided the wires by calculat-
ing their own momentary position relative to the remembered position
of the wires came from experiments in which a wire that narrowed the
passageway to less than the bats' wingspan was removed after the bats

had learned to avoid it. The bats often continued for some while to fly in such a way as to avoid the nonexistent wire. Sooner or later, however, they discovered that the wire was no longer there, and then they quit avoiding it. In this experiment, the door was obstructed with vertical wires at 2-centimeter intervals (too close for the 10-centimeter thick bat to squeeze through), except for a 42-centimeter wide opening—just wide enough to accommodate the bat's wingspan. The bats quickly learned to fly through this "wide" opening without incident. The experimenters then strung a new and extremely thin (120 micrometer) thread off center in this opening, leaving a 24-centimeter-wide opening to one side and an 18-centimeter-wide opening to the other. To avoid the eccentric thread, the bats had to bring their wings together as they approached the main opening and stay close to one or the other side of this main opening. The bats' success at avoiding the eccentric thread in the opening was monitored by a light beam and photocell, so positioned that when a wing hit the thread or passed through where the thread once had been, the beam was interrupted.

The bats initially flew into the eccentric tread, but in four days of training they learned to avoid it most of the time. Then the thread was removed. In figure 5.17 the performance of each of three bats is shown for two repetitions of the experiment. Sometimes the bats noticed the removal of the thread immediately, and sometimes they did not notice it for days. In the latter cases, they went on drawing their wings together and holding to one or another side of the main opening for as many as a hundred passages. Sooner or later, however, they noticed, and then they rapidly began to fly through the middle of the opening.

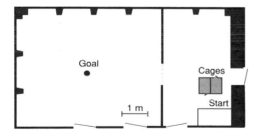

Figure 5.16
The experimental space for the bat wire-avoidance experiment. Between trials, the bats hung from a net strung just below the ceiling in the location labeled "Start." At the cluck of the experimenter's tongue, they flew through the doorway strung with wires, grabbed a mealworm on the wing (held in a pair of forceps by the experimenter at "Goal"), and returned to the starting net, where they consumed the mealworm. The bats were kept in the cages between experimental sessions. (Redrawn from Neuweiler and Möhres 1967, p. 149, by permission of author and publisher.)

One curious aspect of the results is that the bats sometimes stopped avoiding the thread going one way well before they stopped avoiding it coming the other way (M1, second test; M3, first test). This suggests that for each route that they regularly fly, they construct a detailed map of the terrain immediately surrounding that route, somewhat like the detailed route-specific maps that an automobile club supplies to tourists.

One might be tempted to suppose that this performance on the part of the bats was the running off of a rote motor program, without representation of the spatial position of the obstacle, but that was not the case. Each bat usually followed a stereotyped flight path, but all of the bats deviated widely from the normal path on occasion yet still negotiated the narrow passages successfully, pulling their wings together as they approached the door and holding to one side of the main opening. More important is the observation that when large objects such as the cage racks (see figure 5.16) were moved to a different location in the room, the bats became upset and reluctant to fly through the door, though these cages played no role during the experimental session—the bats did not fly and return from them. It would seem likely that they needed those large-scale, easily perceived features of the layout to establish their orientation, and they probably used dead reckoning to control their flight once they were oriented and underway.

The pattern we saw in connection with bird homing and rat maze running reappears here: the animal uses one procedure to establish where it is and to determine the route it needs to follow and then it shifts to another procedure in actually following that route. The animal first gets its position and its bearings from fixes on the large-scale geometry of its environment; then it runs a segment of its route by dead reckoning, updating its position from moment to moment by integrating reafferent or efference copy velocity signals. At the end of a segment, it takes a new fix on its position and its bearings to verify that it is where it now calculates itself to be.

Orienting toward Hidden Goals
The hypothesis is that the orientation of animals toward the goals they seek to approach or avoid is not governed by the intrinsic characteristics of those goals but rather by their geometric position, as represented on the animal's cognitive map. The intrinsic characteristics of a point determine whether it will be a point the animal seeks to approach or to avoid, but they do not provide the sensory input that controls the animal's orientation on its approach or avoidance course. The course is set by reference to the position the goal occupies on the map. This is most clearly brought out in experiments in which the goal is imperceptible until it is reached. Morris (1981) had rats swim for a platform in a pool

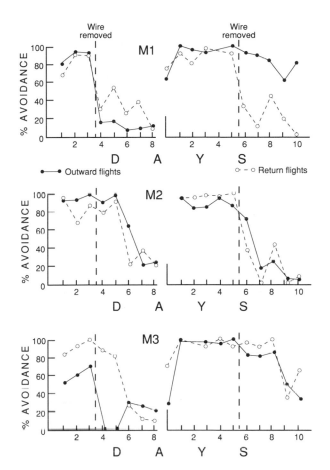

Figure 5.17
Percentage successful avoidance of the ultra thin wire. The vertical lines indicate the
removal of the wire. Notice that the bats frequently continued to avoid it for several days
after its removal. Notice also that they sometimes stopped avoiding it when going in one
direction well before they stopped avoiding it going the other way. (Redrawn from
Neuweiler and Möhres 1967, p. 164 by permission of author and publisher.)

filled with opaque water. For some of the rats, the platform projected above the surface in a fixed location, where it was clearly visible. For another group, the location of the platform varied randomly, so the rats had to find it by looking for it rather than by simply moving to a fixed location. For others, the platform was submerged and invisible but in a fixed location. For yet another group, the platform was submerged, and its location varied from trial to trial. There was no way these rats could orient toward the platform; they had to find it by random search.

The group that had to find the submerged brick by its coordinates alone learned nearly as rapidly as did the two groups for which the platform was immediately perceptible; they oriented toward the location of the platform as soon as they were dropped in the pool, no matter where in the pool they were dropped, and they got there nearly as fast as the rats that could see the goal. The groups that had to search for a randomly located submerged platform showed no evidence of being able to orient toward it when dropped in the pool. They appeared to find it only by a systematic search. The improvements in their latency to find it reflected improvements in the efficiency of their search pattern. From the outset, they took much longer to find the platform than did any of the other groups.

In a follow-up experiment, Morris showed that even when rats were always released into the pool at a single point during the time they were learning the location of the submerged platform, they oriented toward that location when subsequently released at a different compass point for the first time. The rat, like the hoverfly, can go to a spot that has no distinguishing sensory characteristics of its own, a spot that differs from other spots in the world only in terms of its spatial coordinates.

Multiple Goal Sites
So far the examples we have considered have mostly involved animals using a map to orient themselves toward one or two special sites—the home site or the site of the only feeding station that they are regularly visiting. Both insects and vertebrates can orient toward home or toward a feeding station from arbitrary release sites. But the great advantage of a map is that it enables one to orient from any mapped point toward any mapped point. The following studies show that a single map may contain thousands of different points toward which the animal may at one time or another direct its behavior.

It is probably wrong to believe that goal sites have any special status on the map itself. The animal may orient toward or away from any address if that address has something the animal wants or wants to avoid. It will be argued in subsequent chapters that the attributes that endow addresses with motivational significance are not themselves represented on the map. They are represented in other files, along with addresses that relate those motivationally significant attributes to positions on the animal's cognitive map.

Some birds feed principally upon seeds that are abundant only during a short season. These birds commonly store up seeds for future use by making innumerable seed caches during the period of high seed abundance and then visiting those caches when seeds are no longer available. Clark's nutcrackers inhabit the Sierra Nevada at high elevations and feed mostly on the nuts of the piñon pine, which are only generally available in the early fall before the first heavy snows. During this period of a few weeks, a single nutcracker may make as many 33,000 seed caches (Vander Wall and Balda 1981, 1977). To make a cache, it fills its pouch with seeds, selects some spot in the ground, and then jabs its bill deeply into the ground to make a small hole, into which it empties its seed pouch. It then rakes the earth back over the hole with swipes of its bill. In the course of the ensuing winter, the nutcracker lives mostly off these seed caches. They furnish it with such a secure and abundant supply of food that it can afford to begin breeding in the high alpine environment in March and April, before the food supply at lower altitudes is sufficient to permit many less provident birds there to breed.

The nutcracker must recover 2,500 to 3,000 caches in the course of the six months after the snow comes, in order to survive and breed successfully (Balda and Turek 1984). In the wild, its probability of digging at the site of a cache that still contains seeds is estimated at between 30 and 85 percent (Tomback 1978), with the lower figure coming from digs made in the summer, eight to ten months after the caches were made, when many of the caches have been plundered by rodents. These estimates are made by surveying for the characteristic holes made by the bird when it probes down through the snow or earth in search of a cache and counting how many of those holes have seed husks beside them. (The bird commonly husks and eats the seeds as soon as it removes them.) The question is, How does the bird know where in the field of snow to poke in search of one from among more than 20,000 caches, which it made months earlier when there was no snow?

There is an evolutionary argument why the bird must localize its caches by memorizing their positions at the time they are made, and this argument is supported by laboratory demonstrations that the birds in fact do this. The evolutionary argument rests on the observation that the nutcracker is not the only animal for which the nuts are a valuable food source. The numerous rodents covet the seeds as much as the nutcracker that hid them. If the seeds gave off any odor or other beacon cue that advertised their location, the rodents would presumably be as alert to that cue as the birds and better positioned to pick it up. Or suppose that the bird relied upon some burial rule of the kind, "Always make a cache 2 feet to the south of a tree." Any such rule is an invitation to parasitism—from rodents, from other birds, and, most obviously, from other nutcrackers, who presumably know the rule. If you know where the others hide their food, why hide your own?

There appears to be only one "evolutionarily stable strategy," that is, only one procedure that if adopted cannot readily be defeated by the evolution in some other animal of a procedure that exploits your procedure to your disadvantage. (Connoisseurs of the fictional deliberations of pirates with treasure to hide will recognize the logic of the situation.) Burying the food in essentially arbitrary locations and finding it by remembering its location is immune to counterstrategies. If you were not there when it was buried, you cannot know where exactly to look for it, which gives the burier an inherent advantage.

To exploit this advantage, the burier must have a good memory and must be able to locate things not by reference to small features of the environment in the immediate vicinity of the burial site but rather by reference to a large-scale spatial framework anchored to innumerable objects at a considerable remove from the burial site because the site is usually covered with snow between the time of burial and the time of retrieval. The local appearance of the site changes radically between October and February, but the general arrangement of large objects and terrain features does not. It is therefore advantageous to localize caches by their coordinates within this general framework rather than by the intrinsic characteristics of the site.

Laboratory studies show that the nutcracker possesses the requisite memory. Balda (1980) tested a semitame Eurasian nutcracker in a large outdoor aviary. The bird was given a supply of seeds and observed while it made caches, whose locations were recorded by the experimenter. The bird was then kept in isolation for 18 days and food deprived just before being allowed back into the aviary. On reentering the aviary, the bird came up with seeds in its beak on twelve of its first fifteen probes. In a subsequent trial, the bird was isolated for only 7 days between caching and recovery, but during this period the experimenter removed all the seeds from the caches and swept the ground clean of debris. A map was made of the cache locations before the seeds were removed. When the bird was allowed back into the aviary, it was scored as having "recovered" a (now-nonexistent) cache if the swipe of its bill through the earth covered an area in which it had buried seeds. The bird recovered ten of its twelve caches.

Its hit rate was difficult to estimate because it clearly became increasingly frustrated by its repeated failure to find seeds where it had made its caches. It often probed around repeatedly in the vicinity of a cache, and eventually jabbed its beak into the ground several times more or less at random toward the end of the session. After another trial like this, the bird stopped searching for caches altogether and, interestingly, stopped making caches within that aviary. The best estimate of the bird's hit rate on experimentally emptied seed caches, correcting for repeated probes, and disregarding the random probes at the end, was 65 percent.

Vander Wall (1982) did similar experiments with two wild Clark's nutcrackers that could be induced to make and retrieve caches in captivity. He included the interesting control of having the bird that made the caches and a bird that did not make them both attempt to retrieve them. When the experimenter did not smooth over the ground after the caches were made, so that telltale disturbances of the earth were still noticeable, the non-cachers were well above chance. They probed successfully about 10 percent of the time, indicating that the considerations entertained above in connection with the optimal strategy from an evolutionary point of view were not idle ones. If caches can be recognized without knowledge of where they were made, they will be—by other animals. The hit rate in the birds that made the caches was 64 and 77 percent, which indicates the advantage of knowing where the food is hidden and not having to search for telltale signs. When the experimenters smoothed over the ground, the noncachers' hit rate fell to 1-2 percent, and the cachers' rate to 34-52 percent. In Vander Wall's aviary, there were logs and large rocks on the ground. In one of his experiments, he displaced all such landmarks in half of the aviary by a common vector (that is, they were all moved the same distance in the same direction). In this half of the aviary, the birds probes were systematically in error by an amount approximately equal to the landmark displacement vector, demonstrating that the birds were localizing the food caches by virtue of the spatial relation they bore to the constellation of surrounding objects.

In similar experiments with chickadees, Sherry (1984) showed that when the experimenter systematically removes seeds only from caches of a certain type (with certain distinguishing features), the birds stop using caches of that type. Sherry also showed that there is little relation between the order in which the bird creates caches and the order in which it empties them. The visits to caches are not strongly clumped. The bird is not particularly likely to move from the cache it has just emptied to one nearby. Also, the birds are less likely to visit caches that they have already emptied than caches they have not yet emptied, and they are less likely to revisit a cache they have discovered to be empty but did not themselves empty. Finally, the chickadees preferentially visit caches that contain preferred seed types. They remember what they buried where.

In summary, the map that makes possible the survival and breeding of the nutcracker and other cache-making birds has not only the nest on it but also, in addition to the landmarks, the location of thousands of food caches. While the nutcracker is perhaps unusual in the number of remembered sites toward which it can orient, the presence of multiple remembered sites of possible behavioral orientation is probably the rule rather than the exception. The foraging orchid bee, for example, has, in addition to its hive, dozens of widely separated orchid blooms, each of which it visits (Janzen 1971). In some species of digger wasp, the female makes several different nests. Each nest is a 1 mm hole in the ground, in which she deposits eggs, and which she then carefully covers with inconspicuous pebbles. At the beginning of each day, she visits each of these nests in turn, deciding which one she will devote her provisioning efforts to that day (Beusekom 1948). The South American arrow poison frog returns to the place where she laid her eggs at the time the tadpoles hatch and carries each tadpole to its own small water reservoir in nearby plants. She later returns to those plants where she has deposited tadpoles and lays infertile eggs for them to consume (Myers and Daly 1983). I mention these diverse examples to indicate the widespread prevalence of the ability to orient behavior repeatedly to a number of different sites.

Choosing Routes on the Basis of Remembered Relative Distance
The chameleon and the toad assess the relative distances between two possible routes before choosing which to follow. In the demonstrations examined, however, it was not necessary to suppose that the representations of the relative distances persisted beyond the moment when the decision was taken. Those experiments left unresolved whether the animal could choose the shorter of two routes when their relative lengths were not perceptible at the time of choice, so that the choice relied upon an enduring representation of the relative lengths of the routes, a representation acquired in the course of the animal's earlier experience. Rats can make such a choice even when choosing the shorter route involves orienting away from the goal, while choosing the longer route involves orienting toward the goal. Blanchteau and Le Lorec (1972) used the modified T maze shown in figure 5.18. They first trained hungry rats to run down the final common segment from T to food at "Goal" (with the removable panel in place). Then they began starting the rats at "Start," with the removable panel gone. One group was free from the outset to choose either the route to the right, which started in the direction of the Goal (a direction made more salient by an appropriately mounted luminous panel) but was the long way around, or to the left, which started away from the goal and the luminous panel but was nonetheless the shorter route. By locking one or another of the one-way doors, the experimenters forced another group to take alternating routes on alternating trials. The rats in the forced-choice group were yoked to rats in the

free-choice group. When the yoked free-trial rat gave evidence over several trials of having settled on a preferred route, the corresponding rat in the forced-choice group was allowed to choose freely for ten trials.

On the first five-trial session, seven of eight rats in the free-choice condition chose the long route on almost every trial, the route that was oriented almost in the direction of the (unseen) goal. All but three shifted to taking the shorter route every time after having sampled the shorter route between two and five times. Two of the rats that did not switch to the short route never sampled it, and one sampled it only twice in twenty-seven trials. By contrast, seven of the eight forced-choice rats (the rats with forced exposure to the shorter route, as well as to the longer route) chose the shorter route as soon as they were given a choice, though the shorter route pointed away from the goal they were headed for.

The experimenters timed each trial and did an analysis to see whether taking the shorter route had led to more rapid reinforcement in the trials preceding a rat's fixation on that route. In the early trials that preceded a rat's fixation on a route, most of the rat's time was taken up by exploratory behavior, with the result that there were no differences on average between the time it took a rat to complete the long route and the time it took to complete the short route. The same was true for the rats in the forced-choice condition: from differences in the average amount of time it had taken a rat to cover the two routes during the forced trials, one could not predict what was in fact observed: that they chose the shorter route as soon as they were allowed to choose.

Blancheteau and Le Lorec conclude that the rat can choose a route that does not head toward the goal, in preference to the route that does, on the basis of a representation of the subsequent lengths of the route, lengths that are not perceptible at the time of the choice. (For further experiments demonstrating the insightful choice of alternate paths based on their relative lengths, see Deutsch 1960. For similar experiments with cats— with similar conclusions—see Poucet, Thinus-Blanc, and Chapuis 1983.)

Remembrance of Places Passed
In 1976, Olton and Samuelson published the first of a series of influential experiments using a new maze paradigm, the radial or multi-armed maze (figure 5.19). At the start of a trial, food is placed at the end of every arm. The rat is placed in the center. The trial terminates when the rat has taken all eight baits. The measure of the rat's success is the number of arms it enters in the process of taking all the baits, which reflects how good it is at remembering the arms it has not yet visited—the places passed. It turns out that rats are very good at remembering this and that what they usually rely on are the spatial locations of the arms they have not yet visited rather than their distinguishing nonspatial characteristics.

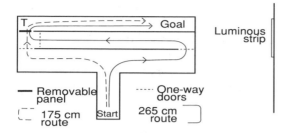

Figure 5.18
Route choice based on remembered relative distances of routes. (Redrawn from Blan-cheteau and Le Lorec 1972, p. 9, by permission of author and publisher.)

When there are eight arms, the rat's propensity to enter arms it has not yet visited rather than arms it has already visited is well above chance from the outset. After forty trials, rats choose a mean of 7.9 arms in their first eight choices, which is to say that most of the time they never make a mistake; they never revisit an arm they have already visited until they have visited all eight (Olton and Samuelson 1976). When there are seventeen arms, the rats at asymptote enter fifteen different arms in their first seventeen choices (Olton, Collison, and Werz 1977), which again means that not uncommonly a rat does not make a single error. Roberts (1979) created an eight-arm radial maze in which three secondary arms radiated from the ends of each of the eight primary arms, making twenty-four different food locations. After a few days experience, the rats entered a mean of 25.5 arms in collecting the twenty-four baits. In a second experiment, Roberts blocked one of the three arms radiating from the end of each primary arm during the first of every two trials, then unblocked them on the second trial, which was run after the rats had collected the 24 - 8 = 16 baits available on the first trial. In collecting the eight baits that were unavailable the first time around, the rats entered on average about twelve secondary arms. When the rat is removed after having chosen four arms and returned 4 hours later, it chooses the remaining four arms with about 90 percent accuracy (Beatty and Sha-valia 1980).

The rat does not detect which arms it has and has not visited by sniffing out the baits at the ends of the arms or by scent marking the arms it has traversed. If the arms are rebaited just after the rat has visited them, it nonetheless chooses all eight arms before making repeat visits. The rats do as well as ever when they are anosmic (Zoladek and Roberts 1978) or when the room is filled with a strong odor (Maki, Brokofsy, and Berg 1979). The most compelling demonstration that it is the position of visited and unvisited arms within the spatial framework of the room and not the sensory attributes of individual arms that is remembered comes from an experiment by Olton and Collison (1979). The rat was confined to the center of the maze halfway through each trial, while the experimenter rotated the arms, moving the visited and unvisited arms into different spatial locations. For one group of rats, the remaining four baits went with the arms. For the other group, the baits stayed in the same location, so that a bait remained at an unvisited point in space, resting on an arm the rat had traversed on one of its first four choices when that arm led to a different point in space. The group that had to find the remaining four baits on the basis of spatial position rather than on the basis of the arm they rested on were only slightly perturbed by the manipulation. The group that had to find the remaining four baits by choosing unvisited arms, some of which occupied previously visited positions, remained at chance over 30 days of testing.

The rats do not choose unvisited arms by adhering to a stereotyped sequence of choices. Olton and Samuelson (1976) showed that the sequence of choices varied greatly from trial to trial. When the rats are made to wait a while in the center between each choice, the sequence of choices from trial to trial becomes completely random, except that at any point in a sequence of choices the rat is more likely to enter an unvisited arm than it is an already visited one. After visiting sixteen of the seventeen arms in the larger radial maze, a rat's probability of choosing the one unvisited arm on its next entry is better than 50 percent (calculated from data in Olton et al. 1977). When the experimenter forces the rat to visit a randomly chosen sequence of arms during the initial part of a trial, the rat chooses the unvisited arms on the later (unconstrained)

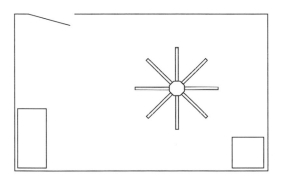

Figure 5.19
Schematic representation of the Olton radial maze. The maze is shown in a room with other large objects to emphasize the relevance of the large-scale extramaze room geometry, from which the animals derives its sense of position and orientation while in the maze in most kinds of radial maze experiments.

choices (Suzuki, Augerinos, and Black 1980; Beatty and Shavalia 1980; Roberts 1979).

A later, theoretically interesting variant on the basic paradigm is to bait only a constant subset of the arms at the outset of each trial. In time the rat seldom enters the arms that are never baited, but continues within each trial to avoid the initially baited arms it has already visited on that trial (Olton and Papas 1979).

The radial maze is not the only situation in which rodents show a highly developed ability to keep track of where they have been. Bättig and his coworkers (Fitzgerald et al. 1985; Uster, Bättig, and Nägeli 1976) use the hexagonal maze shown in figure 5.20 to study the exploratory behavior of rats. The rats are allowed to explore this maze repeatedly. It can be made into a variety of configurations by the insertion of blocks at various points. The rats usually do not receive a reward for anything they do in the maze and when they do, the food rewards have negligible effects on the pattern of the rats' patroling. In repeated exposure to this maze and the variants created by the insertion of blocks, the rats became proficient at exploring it efficiently. They seldom went through one segment again until they had visited all the others. Yet the routes by which they accomplished these efficient patrols were not the same from one patrol to the next. In other words, the rats were able to use their representation of the complex configuration of the maze to plan a route through it that would keep the amount of retracing and revisiting to a minimum, but they did not fix upon a single such route; they used a variety of these efficient routes, varying them from one patrol to the next.

Complex as the maze in figure 5.20 is, it is probably not nearly complex enough to do full justice to the rodent capacity to remember complex configurations. Kavanau (1969) attached a 512-choice-point vertical maze to the living quarters of some captive white-footed mice. Within two days, the mice could traverse it without error, although there was nothing to be found at the other end.

Results like these highlight the difficulties with theories that conceive of learning in terms of "selection by consequences" (Skinner 1981)—that is, theories in which the concept of reinforcement and the law of effect play a pivotal role. To see the difficulty these results pose for reinforcement theories, one need only consider the Hullian explanation of "spontaneous alteration." When a rat that has just visited—and been rewarded in—one arm of a T maze, it has a strong tendency to visit the other arm on the next trial (for reviews, see Dember and Fowler 1979; Douglas 1966). This is puzzling for any consequentialist approach to learning. Why should the rat avoid making the response that has just led to reward? The results obtained with the radial maze pose this question even more forcefully. It now appears that spontaneous alteration is a special case of what is observed in the radial maze. Rats tend to use a win-shift strategy rather than a win-stay strategy (Levine 1959; Olton, Walker, et al. 1977). Having found food in a particular place (and consumed what they found) they (quite rationally) try to go somewhere else to find more food. Hummingbirds do the same thing (Kamil 1978). However rational a win-shift strategy is, it is awkward to deal with from within a reinforcement framework. Hull's approach was to assume that performing a response gave rise to transient reactive inhibition so that the animal was less likely to perform that response again. The trouble with this explanation is that one sees the win-shift result even when the animal is directly placed at one of the baited locations. When later offered the opportunity to choose locations, the rat avoids the location into which it has previously been placed.

These results also pose difficulties for associative theories of learning and motivation. It is awkward, within an associative framework, to explain why the rat in the selectively baited radial maze both avoids those arms that are never baited (not associated with food) and avoids those arms from which it has most recently collected the bait (arms whose association with food has just been verified). The awkwardness gets still greater when one tries to deal with results like those obtained by Dashiell (1930). Dashiell had rats run to food through an open arena offering many different paths of equivalent length (figure 5.21). He found that experienced rats had a strong tendency to vary the path they took from trial to trial, yet in taking these paths, they seldom made errors; that is, they seldom turned in a direction that did not advance their approach to the goal. In this case, all paths are equally associated with food. They all terminate at the same place, and every time the rat takes a given path to

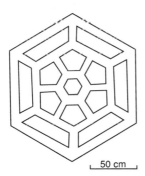

Figure 5.20
Hexagonal maze used to study exploratory behavior. (Based on FitzGerald et al. 1985, p. 452.)

that place, it finds food there. The most recently taken path is most recently associated with food, so it is hard to see how differences in the strengths of associations could explain the rat's tendency to avoid the most recently taken path in favor of paths whose association with food has less recently been confirmed.

Again we see the importance of adopting an approach to learning that distinguishes between the information acquired from experience and the use that may be made of that information in the control of subsequent behavior. The information that one has found and eaten food at a given place may lead to the avoidance of that place in the short run (within a sequence of visits) but the return to that place in the long run (in a new sequence of visits). Models of learning that make intelligible this sort of use of the information provided by experience need to assume that the animal can represent more about the structure of its past experience than is readily represented within the confines of traditional associative theories of information acquisition by animals.

For example, successful models need to assume that the animal can represent the temporal structure of that experience—how long it has been since it last found food at a given place. Theories of conditioning have usually assumed that animals do not do this. They assume that learning does not involve the representation of the temporal structure of experience. Most models of classical conditioning reject at the outset the assumption that when there is a new occurrence of the CS (conditioned stimulus) or the US (unconditioned stimulus), the animal is able to process this new event in a manner that takes account of the temporal distribution of several previous occurrences of the CS and the US. Most models of classical conditioning adopt as an essential constraint on theory building the "pathway independence assumption," which is the assumption that animals do not have access to the temporal structure of the experiences that produced a given spectrum of associations. The animal's current behavior—and what it learns from any new occurrences—must be based only on the current strength of its associations, without regard to the temporal structure of the events that produced those associative strengths.

When a machine has no records that allow it to determine how recently a place has been visited—that is, when the machine has no record of the temporal structure of events—then it is difficult to see how to program it to visit only those places where baits have previously been found but to avoid those places where bait has been taken during the present sequence of visits. On the other hand, if the machine has a record of the places and times at which food was encountered, then it is not difficult to see how one might design a readout mechanism that selected for visit

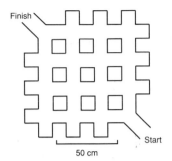

Figure 5.21
Maze used to study rat choice of routes when there are multiple routes of equivalent length. (Redrawn from Dashiell 1930.)

those places where food has commonly been found and crossed each such place off the visit list as it was visited. The essential point is that the design of such a readout mechanism presupposes the machine's capacity to represent the spatial and temporal structure of past experience.

Choosing a Route Between Remembered Places
We have seen several examples in lower vertebrates of the capacity to select routes based on an assessment of the relative distances involved. We have also seen that lower vertebrates use their representation of their behavioral space to approach many different goal positions within that space (in the case of the nutcracker, thousands of different cache sites). It would be surprising if the capacity to represent space in such a way as to be able to find many different points within that space and as to be able to choose routes through that space on the basis of their relative distances were not also well developed in primates. Experiments by Menzel (1973) with the chimpanzee demonstrate both of these capacities simultaneously

Menzel and his assistants worked with six juvenile chimpanzees that lived together in an enclosure 30 x 120 meters. At the start of a trial, they locked the chimpanzees in a small holding cage, picked up one, and carried it around the enclosure while they hid food at eighteen different randomly selected locations. The locations differed from trial to trial. Within any one trial, the experimenters avoided as much as possible using the same type of cover for more than a few of the hiding places. Some food was hidden in stumps, some in clumps of grass, some behind logs, and so on. The animal that had been shown the food was then returned to the group. the experimenters ascended an observation tower and released the entire group into the enclosure. The experimenter recorded on a map of the enclosure the location of each piece of food that was found, which animal found it, and when.

The results remind us of the enormous biological advantage that goes with knowing where things are (hence, with the capacity to represent relative position in space). In the course of sixteen trials, the animals between them found 217 of the 288 hidden pieces of food. The animal that had been shown the hiding places found 200 of those; the other five animals found 17.

In finding the food, the animal that had seen where it was hidden moved directly and rapidly from one hiding place to the next, even when the next hiding place was distant and obscured by visual barriers. There was no correlation between the pathway the animal took in collecting the foods and the pathway along which it was carried by the experimenter when watching the food being hidden. The pathways seemed to be chosen by a procedure that minimized the total distance covered in collecting all those foods whose locations the animal recalled (figure 5.22), just as the rat minimizes the distance it runs in patrolling a complex maze. In other words, the chimpanzees used their representation of the spatial locations of the foods to compute approximate solutions to the "traveling salesman" problem. This problem—to find the distance-minimizing route between a number of to-be-visited points—is much studied in linear programming. While I do not know of a formal proof of this, I presume that it would not be hard to show that it is in principle impossible to find solutions to this problem if the route-finding algorithm must work with a non-metric geometric representation, a representation that does not preserve the distances between points.

The number of possible different routes between N sites is $N!$, so with eighteen sites the calculation of the least-distance route was prohibitive even for the experimenters. They did not attempt to verify whether the solutions shown in figure 5.22 were in fact the best possible ones. In a subsequent experiment, they hid food in only four locations, two in the left third of the field and two on the right third (with the exact locations within those thirds randomly chosen from trial to trial). In twenty-eight such trials, the chimpanzee did not once visit the locations in the order in which it had been shown them. In all but two trials, the animal collected the food on one side first, then went to the locations on the other side (thereby approximately minimizing the distance it traveled). It often (the exact figure is not given) followed the shortest of the twenty-four possible routes between the four hiding places.

In the experiment with equal amounts of food at the two ends of the enclosure, the chimpanzee began with a location on the right twelve times and with a location on the left fourteen times. A further experiment demonstrated that the locations of the other sites to be visited were taken

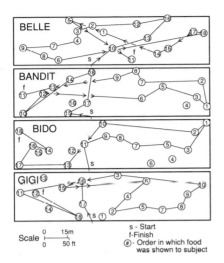

Figure 5.22
The routes taken by chimpanzees in collecting morsels of food that they observed being
hidden at different sites within their compound. The numbers inside the small circles that
mark the hiding places indicate the order in which the baits were hidden. This is not the
order in which they are retrieved. (Redrawn from Menzel 1973, p. 944, by permission of
author and publisher.)

into account in choosing the first site. Two pieces were hidden in one
third of the field while three were hidden in the opposite third. On thir-
teen of sixteen trials, the animal went first to the side that had the greater
number of hidden pieces of food.

The experimenters also hid a preferred food (fruit) in some sites and a
nonpreferred food (vegetables) in others. The animal visited the sites
with the preferred food first. (Recall that chickadees show similar behavior in visiting the caches of preferred and nonpreferred seeds.) In yet
another variant, the experimenters did not carry the chimpanzee around
with them; they had it watch from the holding place while they hid the
food. The results were basically the same.

The point has been made in connection with the behavior of a great
many species that animals commonly do not home on a point in space by
virtue of its intrinsic sensory qualities but rather by virtue of its coordinates. In this connection, it is worth quoting Menzel's observations on
the procedure by which the chimpanzees appeared to home on the
hiding place:

> If food was not located within 5 m of a distinctive landmark (such as
> a tree), the chimpanzees more often slowed down when they came
> within a few meters, and visually scanned the ground. In all of these

experiments the animals' most common error was to search a grass
clump, dead branch, or other features that looked (to us) almost
precisely like the correct hiding place, *and was within a few meters of
it*. I would speculate that, like human beings, the chimpanzees used
a hierarchy of visually perceived object-relations for determining an
exact location. In the cue-giving phase of the experiment, one
initially had the impression that they did not even attend to the
food. . . . Instead, they glanced once at the hiding place and then
looked up toward a tree or around the field, as if to first locate the
position of food relative to a local cue and then locate the position of
that local cue with respect to some landmark or the field in general.
(—p. 945, italics added.)

The chimpanzee is like the hoverfly, the wasp, and the bee in that when
it has a location that it wishes to return to, it looks around to fix its position
relative to the larger space. Also like the bee, the chimpanzee uses large-
scale features of the environment to set a course that brings it into the
vicinity of the sought-for place and then shifts its attention to more local
cues. (For earlier experiments similar to Menzel's, some of which involved delays of hours or days between the time when a primate
witnessed the hiding of the food and the time when it was allowed to
retrieve it, see Köhler 1925 and Yerkes and Yerkes 1928.)

Comparative Primatology in an Analogue of the Radial Maze
Tinkelpaugh (1932) did a series of experiments analogous to the Olton
radial maze experiments, but he used chimpanzees, monkeys, human
adults, and children. He arranged between three and sixteen pairs of
containers in a circle 20 feet in diameter, with an observation stool at its
center (figure 5.23). With one exception, the members of each pair of
containers were as nearly identical as possible, but there were marked
differences between the pairs. Some were wooden boxes painted gray;
some were unpainted wooden boxes of a different size; and some were
tin cups. In each setup, there was one pair whose members differed from
each other as well as from the other pairs—a pair of cigar boxes, "the
labels of which were as dissimilar as could be secured" (p. 220).
A subject in this experiment was brought in and seated on the stool. The
subject watched while the experimenter walked around the circle, hiding
a piece of fruit (or a lure for the adult humans and a penny for the
children) in a randomly chosen member of each pair. The subject was
then allowed to go to the pairs one by one, returning to the stool between
pairs. At each pair, the subject was allowed to look only under one
member. (The experimenter controlled the infrahuman subjects with a
leash while they were choosing, but they had previously been trained on

the routine and did not require much control.) On some trials, the chimpanzee subjects were required to visit the pairs in the reverse order from that in which they had seen them baited; on others, they were required to start in the middle of the baiting order.

The two chimpanzees were very good at this. When there were eight pairs, one chimp chose the correct member of each pair on 144 of 160 choices (90 percent), while the other chose it on 133 occasions (85 percent). With sixteen pairs, their percents correct dropped to 78 and 79, respectively. There was no effect of the order in which they were induced to choose. Each chimp was run for twenty trials with eight pairs, for eleven trials with twelve pairs, and for eighteen trials with twenty pairs. Since the containers to be baited were chosen randomly on each trial, the bait on one trial was frequently in a container that had not been baited on the preceding trial, and vice-versa. One might have expected massive interference (confusion between the trials), but an analysis for interference revealed only a slight effect. (Similarly minimal levels of intertrial interference are obtained with rats in radial mazes, even when a trial on one radial maze is interpolated midway in a trial on another radial maze—Roberts 1984.)

Chimpanzees were as good at this as adult humans and better than children. Five adults ranging in age between 26 and 50, run on a single trial with sixteen pairs, achieved scores ranging from 43 to 100 percent correct (mean = 75 percent). Four children aged 7 to 9 had scores ranging from 43 to 62 percent (mean = 54 percent). Monkeys were much poorer; they could do well above chance with three to six pairs, but were only marginally better than chance with eight.

To show that the chimps were not sniffing out the fruit, Tinkelpaugh baited the containers before the chimps came into the room and found that they then chose at chance. In another control, he baited one member of each pair before the chimp came into the room, then baited the other member while the chimp watched. The chimps chose the containers they saw baited. He also had one experimenter bait the containers and then leave the room. Another experimenter, who did not know which containers were baited, controlled the chimp during the choices. This "blind" procedure had no effect on the accuracy of the chimps' choices.

Tinkelpaugh concluded that the chimps chose the correct member of each pair by spatial position rather than by the distinctive sensory qualities of the correct container. The frequency of the chimps' choosing correctly between the distinctively different cigar boxes was no greater than the frequency of their choosing correctly between identical containers. When the subject was removed from the room after watching the placement of the baits and the experimenter then switched the containers in each pair, so that the baits remained in the positions the chimps had

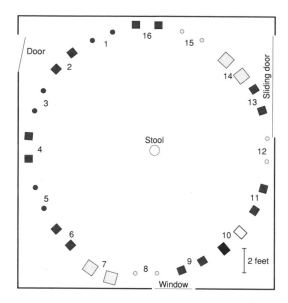

Figure 5.23
Plan of the multiple delayed choice set-up with sixteen pairs of containers. On a given trial, the subject watched while a randomly chosen container in each pair was baited. Subject was then removed from the room and later returned to it and allowed to choose one container from each pair. The containers were as follows: Pairs 1, 3, 5 = tin cans 4 inches tall by 4 inches in diameter, painted gray. Pairs 2, 4, 6, 9, 11, 13, 16 = wooden boxes 7 inches square by 4 inches deep, painted gray. Pairs 7 and 14 = unpainted wooden boxes 12 inches square by 6 inches deep. Pairs 8, 12, 15 = unpainted tin cups 3 inches tall by 3 inches in diameter. Pair 10 two cigar boxes chosen because there labels were as different from one another as possible. (Redrawn from Tinkelpaugh 1932, p. 221.)

seen baited but in the containers that it had seen not to be baited, the chimps, when they returned, chose as accurately as ever. This is further evidence that animals direct their behavior on the basis of the spatial position of their goal and not on the basis of its distinctive sensory characteristics. This is as true of the chimpanzee as it is of the amphiprion, the digger wasp, and the honey bee.

By contrast, when the circle of eight containers was rotated slightly to the right or left, so that the right member of one pair was where the left member of the neighboring pair had been, the chimps' percentage correct dropped significantly. On such trials, the chimps frequently chose from the position of the circle that they had seen baited, though that position was now occupied by a different kind of container. Yerkes and Yerkes (1928) earlier found that their four chimpanzees could readily learn to go to the position of the container they had seen baited, after delays of hours, but that when they were to choose on the basis of the colors of the

containers rather than their positions, they were at first "entirely incapable of adjustment."

In the course of Tinkelpaugh's experiment, the chimps gave clear
evidence that they, like rats and birds, keep track of where they have and
have not been during a sequence of visits:

> They [sometimes] appeared to skip a pair accidentally, particularly
> when the containers were close together as in the situation with 16
> pairs. After they had gone on around the circle making their choices,
> if I remained perfectly quiet, neither commanding them nor releas-
> ing them, both of these animals would commonly look about the
> circle, head directly to the pair they had skipped and choose one of
> its members. . . . Furthermore, if after a series of trials was over, the
> chimpanzees were given the opportunity, they would return to the
> pairs in which they had made errors and correct their choices. (p.
> 232)

The chimpanzees (and the monkeys) also gave clear evidence of what
is termed *metacognition*; they knew when they did not know:

> On these relatively rare occasions [when the chimps were reluctant
> to approach a given pair] Dwina [the female chimpanzee] com-
> monly, and Bill [the male] at times, would turn to me and, whining,
> seem to plead not to be forced to make that choice. On several
> occasions, following behavior such as this, Dwina has reluctantly
> gone forward, and then hesitated directly in front of the pair from
> which she was to choose. Finally, after much wavering, she has
> reached out, taken hold of one member of the pair of containers,
> tipped it over slowly, at the same time lowering her head to the floor
> so that she could peek under and see if the banana was there. If she
> had chosen correctly, she would give a guttural sound, seize the
> banana and, with evidence of glee, rush back to the center ready to
> make the succeeding choice. (p. 232)

Tinkelpaugh describes a monkey that would attack the experimenter
if forced to make a choice it did not want to make but went rapidly and
peacefully ahead with the business of making its subsequent choices if it
was allowed to skip the pair in question.

Conclusions

When the more advanced mobile organisms—arthropods and vertebrates, at least—move, they generally do so by reference to a cognitive
map of their environment. The map records the geometric relations
among the points, lines, and surfaces that define the macroscopic shape

of the animal's behavioral space. When a motivational system has identified a position on this map to be approached or avoided, the navigational system uses the map to orient the animal appropriately. The orientation is not generally based on the currently perceived character-istics of the goal position. Goals do not function as beacons with respect to which the animal orients, even when the goals make suitable beacons (as, for example, its anemone would for an amphiprion or a distinctive cigar box would for a chimpanzee). Because the system works in this way—by specifying to-be-approached or -avoided positions on the map—the trajectories of animals toward or away from their goals are determined by the remembered position of their goal within the macro-scopic shape of their environment, not by the current perception of goal characteristics. The currently perceived sensory characteristics of the goal position become important only at the last moment, when the animal calculates that it is at the correct position and begins to look for the expected goal characteristics. This surprising conclusion appears to be as true of primates as it is of fish and insects.

It is a corollary of this conclusion that an animal's cognitive map is intimately involved in the control of its every movement. As in marine navigation, the course to be followed is computed from the map and then put into execution. Finally, the moment-to-moment monitoring of the animal's position and heading on the map, knowledge of which is essential in using the map to determine future movements, is maintained by dead reckoning, with episodic fixes taken to verify and correct the reckoning. Thus, animals' responses to the spatial configuration of their environment are generally based not on immediate sensory input from that environment but rather on their map and their computed position on the map.

Chapter 6

The Geometric Module in the Rat*

The findings reviewed in preceding chapters suggest that the more advanced mobile animals represent the shape of the environment in which they move around and their moment-to–moment location within that shape. The construction of this representation and the monitoring of the animal's place within it may be a fundamental form of learning, distinct from other forms. Because the construction of this representation requires computations of a geometric, trigonometric, and integrative character, the pressure to perform these computations in as sophisticated and efficient a manner as possible may have led to the evolution of a learning organ specialized for this function. The structure of this organ may suit it to deal with multimodal sensory data containing information about geometric relations in the animal's behavioral space but not to deal with information about other attributes of the experienced world.

Probability distributions, feature spaces, and temporal sequences do not have a geometric formal structure. The information about these nonspatial aspects of the world may require for its assimilation other organs, whose structure was shaped by the demand for different sorts of computations. If this is so, then the organ that assimilates the shape of the animal's environment (and the animal's position within that shape) is a module in Fodor's (1983) sense; it deals only with a restricted range of the data potentially relevant to a task confronting an animal. This chapter gives experimental evidence for the existence in the rat of a module that determines the rat's heading within an experimental enclosure on the basis of the enclosure's shape alone, ignoring other task-relevant and salient features of the enclosure.

Shape is largely defined by the distances between and along surfaces (or lines) and by the angles they form, that is, by the uniquely metric relations. When a system cannot represent the uniquely metric relations among points in the world, it cannot represent shape in the sense in which we ordinarily understand it. The previously reviewed experi-

*This chapter is based on a published PhD thesis by Ken Cheng (1984,1986), done under my supervision.

ments, whose results suggested that animals represent the shape of their behavioral space, did not proceed from a formal analysis of the question. They strongly suggested that animals formed enduring representations of metric relations because it seemed difficult to explain the observed performances of the different kinds of animals without assuming that the mechanism generating the performance had quantities in it proportionate to distances and angles in the environment and that these quantities were subject to computational operations isomorphic to corresponding procedures in analytic geometry. The experiments were not, however, designed specifically to rule out alternative possibilities.

In some partially formalized theories of animals' spatial representations, the assumption that the cognitive map captures the metric properties of the behavioral space is explicitly rejected (e.g., Deutsch 1960; Lieblich and Arbib 1982). Less formalized cognitive map theories, which assume the capacity to organize sensory data within a three-dimensional framework in which distances and angles are represented at least implicitly (Tolman 1948; O'Keefe and Nadel 1978; Yonas and Pick 1975; Bower 1975; Gibson 1966), have rested on purely intuitive conceptions of the behavioral implications of such a representation or its lack.

Geometry is the study of spatial representations. It has been a focus of mathematical investigation for more than 2000 years, serving throughout most of that time as a model of what formal analysis was. In a domain as thoroughly formalized as spatial relations, the experimental analysis of animals' capacities ought not to proceed with no attention to the formal side of the subject. Cheng's and my original purpose was to bring formal considerations to bear on the design of an experiment to test the hypothesis that the spatially oriented behavior of an animal depends on a scheme for coding metric relations.

Our initial attempts along this line were discouraging. There are a forbidding number of different geometries, some with metric assumptions and some without.[1] It was not clear at first how to organize formal treatments of geometric concepts in a way that would lead to systematic experimental investigation. We eventually formulated two heuristic principles that yielded a strategy for applying formal geometric considerations to the formulation of experimentally testable questions regarding an animal's representation of the experimental space (Cheng and Gallistel 1984). The strategy rests on the quasi-hierarchical nature of the formal structure of geometry, the fact that it is impossible to code relative spatial positions in such a way as to permit the recovery of "stronger"

---

1. Metric assumptions are axioms that make it possible to define congruence of line segments and angles. In nonmetric geometries, it is impossible to define the conditions that determine whether two line segments or two angles are or are not congruent.

higher-order geometric properties without also permitting the recovery of "weaker," more primitive relations.

Principle 1. Animals may not represent all of the spatial relations, but those they do represent, they will not represent in such a way that the formal characteristics of a relation within their coding scheme are at odds with the formal characteristics of the corresponding relation in the external world.

This principle eliminates from consideration a variety of eccentric or special-purpose geometric systems whose assumptions are known to be at variance with the properties of the space we live in. It eliminates, for example, geometries that have nonstandard metrics, such as city-block metrics. In a geometry with a city-block metric, the distance between two points with coordinates $<x_1, y_1>$ and $<x_2, y_2>$ is not given by the formula:

$$\sqrt{(x_2 - x_1)^2 + (y_2 - y_1)^2}$$

but rather by the formula:

$$|x_2 - x_1| + |y_2 - y_1|.$$

The city-block metric is one of an infinite series of similar metrics called Minkowski metrics, each of which gives rise to a different geometry. Some of these geometries are useful in certain restricted contexts. For example, the city-block metric is useful for calculating travel distances in a grid city. The Minkowski geometries, however, treat distance in a way that is formally at variance with the way distance behaves in the world we know. Distance in Minkowski geometries is not isomorphic to distance in the real world.

The nonisomorphism between these geometries and our world gives them a variety of bizarre properties. For example, in city-block geometry, the number of distinct straight lines connecting two points varies depending on which two points one is considering. For some, there is only one such line. For others, there are many different straight lines between the same two points. Thus, in city-block geometry, straight lines do not behave properly, and there are bizarre consequences of this misbehavior. There are, for example, "bigons"—plane figures like a squares or a triangles, but with only two vertices. A bigon is the shape defined by two different straight lines connecting the same two points.[2]

The justification for Principle 1 rests on evolutionary considerations. It seems plausible to imagine that the computational demands of a certain powerful kind of coding scheme might be such as to preclude a given

2. For an informal discussion of other bizarre properties of this geometry, see M Gardner, Mathematical Games, *Sci. Amer.*, (November 1980): pp 18 - 30.

kind of animal's developing the requisite circuitry. An animal might plausibly evolve only a weaker coding capacity, which enabled it to code relative spatial position in such a way as to capture some behaviorally useful relations between surfaces, points and lines in its environment but not the full set of Euclidean relations. While it seems plausible to imagine a coding scheme too weak to capture all the geometric relations, it does not seem plausible to imagine a scheme that gets the relations it does capture fundamentally wrong. It is not clear how the circuitry that would generate a fundamentally erroneous coding of spatial relations could evolve. Any tendency to represent the facts about the animal's behavioral space in a formally erroneous manner ought to be selected against.

This principle does not mean that we assume that the circuitry involved in coding relative spatial position always codes correctly. There are surely circumstances under which it does not. Rather, this principle assumes a formal isomorphism between the properties of the representation and some subset of the properties of everyday space. If the representation includes quantities that correspond to distances in the external world, then it will handle these quantities in a manner consistent with that in which distances behave in the real world. If the representation includes entities that correspond to straight lines in the real world, then it will treat these entities in a manner consistent with real straight lines. It will not, for example, explicitly represent two distinct straight lines through the same two points. The practical effect of this first heuristic principle is to narrow our focus to mainstream geometry—the Euclidean geometry that formalizes the structure of space as we know it.

Euclidean geometry has a quasi-hierarchical structure. Certain relations in Euclidean geometry presuppose others, but not vice-versa. The distance relation presupposes the collinearity relation but not vice-versa. Therefore the distance relation is said to be stronger than the collinearity relation or higher in the hierarchy, while the collinearity relation is said to be weaker or more primitive. Our second principle specifies the restrictions this formal hierarchy places on the imaginable codes that a nervous system might employ to represent spatial relations:

Principle 2. An imaginable neural code cannot capture formally stronger relations while failing to capture the weaker, more primitive relations. The code for spatial position used by a nervous system may make it impossible to recover from the encoded positions some formally stronger geometric relations among them (such as distance and angle) while permitting the recovery of formally weaker relations (such as collinearity), but not vice-versa.

Principle 2 concerns the inherent power of the code employed by a nervous system to represent spatial position. It is not a principle about what the nervous system itself may or may not be able to get out of its own code. To illustrate this important point, imagine someone using Cartesian coordinates to describe the positions of points in a surveyed environment. Suppose they remember the Pythagorean formula for computing the distance between two points but not the formula for determining whether one point is on the line defined by two other points (see Table 1.1). Such a person is using a position code powerful enough to capture distance and also—and necessarily so—powerful enough to capture collinearity-noncollinearity, yet the person (the system using the code) has algorithms for extracting from the coded data the stronger distance relation but not algorithms for extracting the weaker collinearity relation.

Principle 2 is really the requirement for logical consistency in the formal description of the code by which the nervous system captures the spatial relations among points in behavioral space. It says that we can reject on analytic grounds any theory that claims that the code captures distances, angles, and other uniquely metric relations but does not capture the weaker relations formally presupposed by these relations. We can say that if the distances between points can be recovered from what is stored, then in principle other weaker spatial relations such as collinearity must also be recoverable, although the nervous system in which the information about position is stored may not itself be designed to recover some of these weaker relations from its own data stores. Although principle 2 is tautological, an appreciation of this tautology and the formal structure of geometry on which it rests is crucial to an understanding of the experimental strategy that Cheng pursued.

The Structure of Geometry

The quasi-hierarchical ordering of the different kinds of geometric relations is schematized in figure 6.1. This structure emerges from two different but complementary forms of analysis: transformational analysis and axiomatic analysis.

The program for using transformations to structure or categorize geometric relations was inaugurated by Felix Klein in a speech in Erlangen in 1872, where he laid out what came to be called the Erlangen program (Klein 1939; Modenov and Parkhomenko 1965). Klein proposed that the properties of a shape could be organized into categories on the basis of which transformations left which properties unchanged.

The transformations that generate these categories are nested. The less radical transformations, which define the highest category of geometric relations, are special cases of the more radical transformations, which isolate the lower, more basic or primitive relations. All of the properties

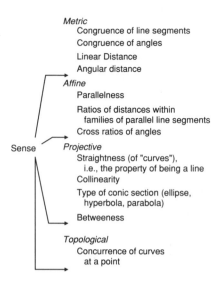

Figure 6.1
The hierarchy of spatial relations. The levels of the hierarchy are identified by italicized labels; classes of relations are unitalicized. A level includes all the classes of relations listed below it. Sense is independent of the other relations; it may be included or omitted at any level.

of shapes treated in the tradition that dates from Euclid are invariant under the displacement transformations of translation and rotation—sliding a shape laterally or vertically or rotating it (within some arbitrary observational framework). Looking at the question from the perspective of analytic geometry, the properties of a shape are unaffected by the choice of a coordinate frame because choosing a different coordinate frame is equivalent to rotating and/or translating the object within the original coordinate frame. Because all of the intrinsic properties of a shape are invariant under (unaltered by) displacement, mathematicians, physicists, and others who wish to compute a property of some shape choose whatever coordinate frame will prove computationally convenient, confident that this choice will not affect the validity of the conclusions they draw about the shape.

In analytic geometry, a shape is a set of points whose positions are coded by means of numerical coordinates. If the coordinates are Cartesian coordinates, a translation of the shape is accomplished by adding (or subtracting) a constant from the x coordinate of every point and another constant from the y coordinate. (In this discussion, I deal only with shapes in the plane. The generalization to three-dimensional shapes is straightforward.) The translation of a point is computed by the formula:

$$x' = x + m$$
$$y' = y + n,$$

where $<x', y'>$ are the coordinates of the point after the translation, $<x, y>$ are the coordinates before the translation, and m and n are parameters, whose values specify a translation. The translation of a shape consists of choosing values for m and n, thereby specifying the translation and computing the new coordinates for every point in the shape. As we saw in chapter 5, when the shape is defined by a function, the transformation may operate on the parameters of the function, which is computationally more economical. (See figure 5.1.)

The rotation of a point about the origin of a Cartesian coordinate frame is computed by the formula:

$$x' = ax + by$$
$$y' = -bx + ay,$$

where a and b are the cosine and sine of the angle of rotation. A rotation of a shape is the application of this formula to all the points that compose the shape.

Since a displacement transformation is a combination of a translation and a rotation, the general formula for the displacement of the points in a shape is:

$$x' = ax + by + m$$
$$y' = -bx + ay + n,$$

where m and n are parameters whose values are arbitrarily choosable and a and b are, respectively, the cosine and sine of the arbitrarily choosable angle of rotation.

From the geometric point of view, displacements are entirely benign; they alter nothing of geometric interest. They merely alter where in some larger framework we must look to find the shape and the orientation of that shape. Since the framework is arbitrary—it is chosen only to enable us to code shapes numerically—alterations of location and orientation within the framework are irrelevant. They alter the particular numbers that we happen to use to code the relative positions of the points that compose the shape, but they do not alter what is described by these numbers. Another way of stating this is to say that the numerical description of a shape by Cartesian coordinates is unique up to a displacement transformation.

Affine transformations, on the other hand, destroy much of what we ordinarily think of as shape. An affine transformation is any combination of uniform stretches or squashes along one or more axes. If we imagine that we draw our shape on a rubber sheet and then place that sheet in a stretching rack and stretch it out along one axis, that is an affine transformation. If we now stretch it out along any other axis (or squash it), the combined result of these two stretches (and/or squashes) is still an affine transformation.

Affine transformations can turn squares into rectangles, rectangles into parallelograms, ellipses into circles, equilateral triangles into right triangles, and so on. That is why they destroy much of what we ordinarily regard as the shape of an object (or the shape of a behavioral space). But they do not destroy everything. An affine transformation cannot make a circle into a square or a triangle into a rectangle. It cannot make a straight line into a curved line, or vice-versa; collinearity is a relation among points that is invariant under affine transformation. Nor can it render previously parallel lines no longer parallel; parallelism is a relation among lines (sets of points) that is unaffected by affine transformations. There are many others. For example, any set of points that formed an ellipse before the transformation will still do so afterward, though not the same ellipse, and likewise for hyperbolas and parabolas. Categories of conic sections are invariant under affine transformation.

Analytically the affine transformation of a point within a coordinate framework is accomplished by applying the formula:

$$x' = a_1 x + b_1 y + c_1,$$
$$y' = a_2 x + b_2 y + c_2.$$

This looks similar to the general formula for a displacement transformation. The difference is that in this, the more general transformation, the values for a_1, a_2, b_1, and b_2 are arbitrarily and independently choosable constants, whereas in a displacement transformation,

$$a_1 = b_2 = \cos \alpha$$

and

$$b_1 = -a_2 = \sin \alpha,$$

where α is the arbitrarily choosable angle of the rotation. In short, displacement transformations are special cases of affine transformation; any displacement transformation is an affine transformation, but not vice-versa.

The spatial relations that are altered by affine transformations are the uniquely metric relations, which depend for their definition on the specification of the distances and angles between points.

By considering still more general types of transformations, one can isolate other categories of geometric relations. In a topological transformation, one may stretch and compress the rubber sheet in arbitrarily complex ways, provided only that one does not tear it or bring two edges together. The relations among a collection of points that are invariant under this very general kind of (bicontinuous) transformation are the topological relations, which are generally taken to be the most primitive or basic of all geometric relations.

The important fact about this categorizing of geometric relations on the basis of the classes of transformations that do and do not alter them is that the categorization is inherently hierarchical because the transformations that yield it are nested. Topological relations survive the most general kind of transformations (topological transformations). Affine relations survive affine transformations. Affine transformations are special cases of topological transformations. Hence topological relations are included within the class of affine relations. Metric relations survive displacement transformations. Displacement transformations are special cases of affine transformations; hence affine relations are included within the class of metric relations. The uniquely metric relations are those that survive displacement transformations but not affine transformations.

The hierarchical categorization of geometric relations one gets by considering which relations survive which degree of transformation is not dependent on an arbitrary selection of transformations. One does not get a different hierarchy by selecting some other set of transformations. There is no transformation that changes the collinearity relations in a shape but not the angles and distances between the points. Also the same hierarchical structure may derived from axiomatic analysis. Roughly, axiomatic analysis is the study of what kinds of relations come in together as one enriches the structure of a formal system by adding axioms and which relations depend on which axioms. (For axiomatic analyses of Euclidean geometry, see Forder 1927; Hilbert 1921) Axioms that make it possible to specify an equidistance relation between points (hence, the congruence of line segments) also make it possible to specify angular relations. Thus, angular and distance relations come in together. It is possible to have sets of axioms rich enough to allow the definition of a collinearity relation but not rich enough to allow the definition of an equidistance relation. The reverse is not true; there is no set of axioms that permits the definition of an equidistance relation but does not permit the definition of a collinearity relation. The ability to determine whether the distance between one pair of points is the same as the distance between another pair depends on the full set of axioms required to generate the standard theorems of Euclidean geometry, whereas the ability to specify collinearity depends only on a subset of those axioms.

The importance of this conclusion for our experimental strategy is this: If the formal structure of a coding system is rich enough to enable that system to capture the uniquely metric relations, which are invariant under displacement transformation but not under affine transformation, then the structure is also rich enough to capture every other type of geometric relation (except sense). It follows that if one wants to know what categories of geometric relations the neural code is capable of capturing, one should begin by testing whether the code can capture the uniquely metric relations.

There is one property of a shape that is not categorized by the sequence of ever more general transformations: sense, or the distinction between right and left. From the geometric standpoint, the mazes A and B in figure 6.2 are identical; maze B is maze A rotated 180° and rotation is a transformation that leaves shapes congruent—that is, geometrically identical. If a rat recognized which maze it was in solely on the basis of the maze's shape, there is no way the rat could show behavior in maze B that differed from its behavior in maze A. Maze C is another matter. Every metric relation in C is the same as in A and B, but C does not have the same shape. In C the rat turns right in going from the longer to the shorter arm, whereas in A and B it turns left. Maze C is a reflection of maze A. Reflection preserves metric relations but alters the right-left relations. One might think, therefore, that sense is the most exotic or powerful of geometric relations, standing at the top of the hierarchy in figure 6.1, but this is not so because there are transformations that change the metric relations but do not destroy sense relations. Affine transformations do just this. Even topological transformations do not alter sense. Sense stands outside the hierarchy; it is an independent geometric property. One can alter the sense of a shape without altering any of the other geometric relations and one can alter any of the others without altering sense. Full congruence—geometric identity—depends on the sameness of all the metric relations plus the sense relation. If all of these relations are the same within two shapes, they are geometrically identical. If any is altered, they are not congruent.

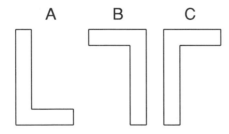

Figure 6.2
The sense relation in maze geometry. *A* and *B* are geometrically identical mazes, but *C* is not, even though every metric relation in *C* is the same as in *A* and *B*.

The Geometric Power of the Rat's Spatial Code

The experimental approach that Cheng eventually adopted was suggested by Klein's transformational approach to the categorization of geometric relations and by an experiment done by Suzuki, Augerinos, and Black (1980). The Suzuki et al. experiment was not suggested by formal geometric analysis or interpreted within the conceptual background provided by the Erlangen program. Nonetheless the transformational analysis of geometric relations provides an appropriate background for the presentation of this important and elegant experiment.

Suzuki et al used an eight-arm radial maze, set up in the center of a circular chamber formed by heavy black curtains. At the ends of seven of the eight arms, they hung multimodally prominent stimulus objects: a white board with a light bulb on it, a string of Christmas tree lights, a fan with tinsel, which made a clicking sound, a toy bird, a wooden box, a wooden pyramid, and others. As in other radial maze experiments, all the arms were baited with food at the start of a trial. During the course of a trial, the choice of an arm was correct if the arm chosen was not one the rat had already visited on that trial (and eaten the bait). Doors from the central platform to each arm allowed the experimenters to control which arms the rat could enter. The experimenter controlled the first three choices on a trial by opening one door at a time. After the third forced choice, all the doors were kept closed for 2.5 minutes to allow time for the transformation of the maze. Then the doors were opened, and the rat was allowed to make five choices. When the rats had become accustomed to the 2.5-minute confinement and were making four or five correct choices in the five free ones they got on each trial, they encountered transformations of the experimental space. The transformations were made by the experimenter during the 2.5-minute period between the forced and free choices.

For one transformation (which I will call the identity transformation), the walls, stimuli, arms, and other features were moved around but returned to their original positions by the beginning of the free choices. This controlled for the rats' reaction to the commotion made by the moving operation. A lid placed on the framework for the doors prevented the rats' seeing the transformations. In a second transformation (a rotation), the walls, ceiling, and stimuli were rotated 180° and the food baits went with the stimulus objects. This condition tests whether the rats orient by the experimentally provided stimulus objects and only by those objects. If they do not rely on anything else for their orientation within the experimental space, then their behavior cannot be affected by the rotation because this transformation changes none of the geometric relations within the experimental space. It is a displacement transformation.

The third transformation was a transposition, which altered all of the geometric relations within the experimental space. The stimulus objects were randomly interchanged, with the baits again going with the objects. If we imagine the radial maze drawn on a rubber sheet, one can see that this kind of rearrangement of the stimuli (and the remaining baits) can be accomplished only by tearing the sheet. The transposition also alters the sense relation—the cyclical order of the stimulus objects and the baits. Thus, it alters every geometric relation. If the animal relies on geometric relations of any kind in keeping track of the positions of the remaining baits, then its behavior should be perturbed by the transposition transformation but not by the other two transformations. On the other hand, if the rat pays no attention to spatial relations but relies simply on the association between certain stimulus objects and the unvisited locations, then its behavior should not be perturbed by the transposition transformation. The untaken baits are under the same objects after the transformation as before.

The two control transformations—the identity transform and the rotation transform—had no effect on the accuracy of the rats' choice of still-baited arms, whereas the transposition reduced their accuracy to chance levels. Clearly the rats relied on some geometric relations within the experimental space to determine their sense of the position of the still baited arms.

Suzuki et al. went to some efforts in their training procedure to discourage the rats from orienting with respect to any framework other than the experimentally provided space. The walls, ceiling, and enclosure of the radially symmetric experimental chamber were rotated randomly and independently of each other between trials. The stimulus objects and the maze were also rotated with respect to these surfaces and with respect to the earth's surface. Finally, the arms were interchanged with each other, and the center platform was interchanged between trials. In view of the experiments by Carr and Watson (1908) reviewed in the preceding chapter and in view of the results of some analyses done by Cheng in the course of his experiments, one must bear in mind that rats generally preserve some sense of their geocentric heading. Rotations of the experimental space are important components of the training procedure in experiments in which one wants to test the determinants of a rat's sense of spatial orientation. They discourage reliance on the omnipresent sense of geocentric heading. They force the rat to take its heading from the experimental space—an apparatocentric heading.

The X-maze Experiment
The Suzuki et al. experiment proves that rats code and use some kind of geometric relation in keeping track of the positions of the remaining baits

in a radial maze. The question addressed in Cheng's and my first experiment was, Which geometric relations? From the formal considerations already discussed, it was obvious that one should start testing first for the most powerful kinds of geometric relations, the uniquely metric ones, because these relations presuppose all the others, except sense. We therefore used affine transformations to test for reliance on the uniquely metric relations and reflection transformations to test for the use of the sense relation. We reasoned that if the rat represented the relative positions of things in space with a code that could not capture the uniquely metric relations, then the rat's ability to find those positions could not be affected by an affine transformation, which alters uniquely metric relations but not more primitive ones. If the spatial code does not capture some class of geometric relations, such as the uniquely metric relations, then there is no way that the animal's behavior can depend on those relations. A change in those relations could not affect behavior—provided one could be confident that the change was not accompanied by any other detectable change, geometric or otherwise.

The proviso is not an easy one to satisfy. Geometric transformations may bring in their train changes in other nonspatial sensory properties of the space. Changing a rectangle into a parallelogram, for example, changes how tight the corners feel when you back into them. However, the fact that affine transformations may be thought of as uniform squashes and stretches suggested to Cheng an ingenious way of performing an affine transformation that would alter nothing else about the experimental space. Cheng's idea was to use a rectangle with distinctive stimuli and baits in the corners and to effect an affine transformation by moving all the stimulus panels and the baits one corner clockwise or one corner counterclockwise. This is equivalent to squashing the rectangle down to a square along its long axis, then stretching it out back into a rectangle again along the orthogonal axis (figure 6.3). One ends up with the same rectangle, except the stimulus panels are in different corners separated from each other by different distances and angles. Nothing has changed physically (the panels have not changed, the enclosure has not changed, and so on), so the risk of bringing some nongeometric change in the train of this geometric alteration is minimized.

Initial conception of the experiment. We took it for granted that the rats would orient themselves in space by means of the stimulus panels, if we made them distinctive enough. We saw our experiment as a straightforward adaptation of the Suzuki et al. experiment in which rats clearly oriented with regard to an array of stimulus objects. Neither the fact that Suzuki et al. used objects rather than distinctive surface markings nor the fact that their asymmetric array of seven objects provided unambiguous

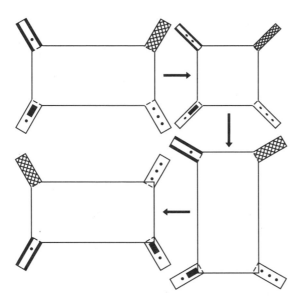

Figure 6.3
Moving all of the corner panels one corner counterclockwise has the effect of a sequence
of two affine transformations. In the first, the box is compressed longitudinally by a factor
of two. In the second, it is elongated along the orthogonal axis by a factor of two. The third
transformation is a counterclockwise rotation, made here to facilitate comparison between
the initial configuration and the configuration that results from the affine transformations.
The result is the same as is achieved by displacing all the panels one corner counterclockwise.

orientation information quite apart from the individual identities of the
objects struck us as important initially. In retrospect, these details were
probably essential to the results they got.

   We used a maze in the form of an elongated X, located inside the
rectangular enclosure, with large and exceedingly prominent stimulus
panels in the corners, looming above the ends of the arms (see figure
6.4). To increase the statistical power of the choice data, we adopted the
differential baiting procedure of Hulse and O'Leary (1982). We placed
eighteen food pellets under one stimulus panel (the same panel on every
trial), six under the diagonally opposite panel, three under the panel in
a neighboring corner and none under the panel diagonally opposite it.
Which panels had which baits under them varied from rat to rat. For any
one rat, the association of bait sizes with panels was the same on every
trial in this experiment. The fact that the second largest bait happened
always to be associated with the panel diagonally opposite the largest
bait was an unintended consequence of our counterbalancing procedure.
Only later did we appreciate its significance.

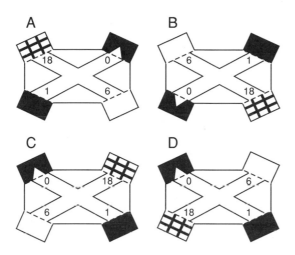

Figure 6.4
A. The original configuration of corner panels and bait magnitudes (numbers) for one rat.
B. The result of the rotation transformation. C. The result of the reflection (sense-altering) transformation. D. The result of an affine transformation. (Redrawn from Cheng 1984, p. 62, by permission of author.)

We trained the rats until their tendency to choose the arms in the order of their bait magnitudes had reached asymptote. During this training, we took precautions similar to those taken by Suzuki et al. to induce the rats to rely for their orientation only on the stimuli within the experimental enclosure and not on a sense of their geocentric heading (compass sense in the nonmagnetic meaning). The experimental enclosure was inside a black sound-attenuating chamber. There was a lid on the enclosure, and the experimenter observed the rat through a one-way mirror. The enclosure was rotated into randomly chosen orientations between trials. The rats were kept in cages near the sound-attenuating chamber. During an experimental session, they were in complete darkness. They were placed into the center of the X maze in randomly chosen orientations. All of the light in the experimental enclosure came through the illuminated stimulus panels in the corners.

When the rats' tendency to choose arms in the order of the bait magnitudes had reached asymptote, they began to encounter transformations on some trials. The transformation trials were interspersed among control trials, identical in all respects to the training trials. The transformations were of three kinds: rotations, affine transformations, and reflections. In a rotation, diagonally opposing stimulus panels (and baits) were interchanged. (This can also be thought of as shifting the panels and baits by two corners—see figure 6.4B). Provided that the rat is not attending to some unintended feature of the experimental space (for example, a knothole in one of the arms), the rotation changes nothing and should have no effect on performance. As in the Suzuki et al. experiment, this transformation tests whether one has experimental control of the cues the rat orients by.

For the affine transformation, the panels and the baits were shifted one corner counterclockwise (figure 6.4D). The distances and angles separating the panels (and the different bait magnitudes) were altered, but their cyclical order was preserved. For the reflection transformation, the stimuli and baits at the two ends of each long wall were interchanged (figure 6.4C). The distances and angles between the panels (and the different bait magnitudes) were unaltered, but their cyclical order was altered.

The affine and reflection transformations reduced the rats' performance to chance levels, while the rotation transformation had no significant effect (figure 6.5). This was true for each individual rat, as well as for the group as a whole. Since the rotation had no effect, we concluded (erroneously) that we had experimental control of the stimuli by which the rats oriented. Since the affine and reflection transformations destroyed the rats' ability to choose arms on the basis of the bait magnitudes, we concluded (correctly) that the rats relied on uniquely metric relationships and the sense relations in coding the positions of the baits.

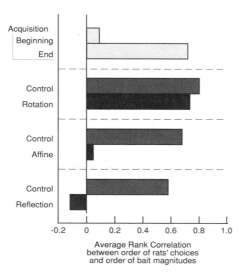

Figure 6.5
The effect of transformations on the correlation between order of arm choice and order of bait magnitudes. (Redrawn from Cheng 1984, p. 86, by permission of author.)

In other words, the code for spatial position in the rat is powerful enough to capture the full range of basic (foundational) Euclidean geometric relations, and the rat relies on some of the metric relations in determining the location of goals within the experimental space.

Retrospective conception of the experiment.   In this first experiment, we took it for granted that the rats got themselves oriented within our experimental space by attending to the highly salient stimulus features, which differentiated one corner panel from another and loomed directly over the baits the rats were seeking. We assumed that affine and reflection transformations disoriented the rats, either by altering the distances and angles between particular panels or their cyclical order. It emerged in subsequent experiments, however, that rats do not orient themselves by means of the global geometric relations between the nongeometric features of surfaces—their patterns of reflectance, their textures, their smells, and so on. Under our conditions at least, rats orient only by the overall shape of the environment, ignoring the distinctive features of surfaces. They ignore the distinctive features of surfaces even when these features would enable them to find the unique correct orientation within symmetrically shaped spaces, such as the rectangular space we used, where shape alone does not define a unique correct orientation. This later discovery forced us to reconceptualize the experiment, further analyze the data from it in accord with this new conception, and conduct some follow-up experiments to test the new conception.

   If one assumes, as we now do, that rats can only make indirect use of factors other than overall shape in orienting within an experimental space and that primary orientation is determined by shape alone without regard to any distinctive features that differentiate one surface from another, then both the affine transformation and the reflection transformation test the hypothesis that the rat's sense of shape rests on both the uniquely metric relations and sense. Both transformations involve moving the baits into corners that have the wrong relation to the macroscopic shape of the experimental box. The wrongness of the relation depends for its definition on both metric and sense relations. In figure 6.4A, the eighteen-pellet bait is in a corner that has a longer wall to the right and a shorter wall to the left. The same is true for the six-pellet bait. That is, the two largest baits are in corners that have the same relation to the shape of the box. This relation to the shape of the box differentiates these two corners from the other two corners, those containing one and no pellets. Both of these latter corners have a longer wall on the left and a shorter wall on the right. The affine transformation (figure 6.4D) and the reflection transformation (panel C)—but not the rotation transformation (panel B)—carried the baits into corners that had the wrong relation to the shape of the box. They also carried the panels into corners with the wrong relation. What may have disrupted the rats' performance was not the change in the geometric relations among the panels (or among the baits) but the fact that each panel (and each bait) was now in a corner with the wrong relation to the shape of the box.

What makes the eighteen- and six-pellet corners the same and differentiates them from the one- and no-pellet corners is a combination of a metric relation (longer-shorter) and a sense relation (right-left). In any representation of the shape of the experimental space in which either type of relation is not preserved, there is no way to distinguish among the four corners on geometric grounds alone. In affine geometry, there is no distinction between a rectangle and a square. Similarly, in a representation that does not preserve sense, there is no distinction between the two diagonals of a rectangle. In our original conception, the affine transformation tested the hypothesis that the rats relied on a uniquely metric relation of some kind, while the reflection transformation tested the separate and independent hypothesis that they also made use of a sense relation. If, however, one assumes that the rats relied entirely on general environmental shape, ignoring the geometric relations among the locations of particular panels and particular bait magnitudes, then each transformation tested the hypothesis that the rat's coding of environmental shape captures both sense and metric relations. Each transformation tested the single hypothesis that the rat has a fully Euclidean coding of environmental shape.

One implication of this reconceptualization is that in their initial choice on each trial, the rats might fail to distinguish the location of the eighteen-pellet bait from the location of the six-pellet bait. If the rat's orientation in space were determined by congruence between remembered shape and the shape it now perceives—with no account taken of anything but shape—then for an axially symmetrical shape like the rectangle, there are two equally good congruences. Imagine two identical rectangles drawn on two different transparencies. Let one be the animal's current perception of the environment's shape and the other its remembered shape (shape on the map). Suppose further that the rat has a food list—a nonspatial representation of the foods it has found—and that each item on this list has associated with it an address. The address gives the coordinates of the point where food was found, a coding of the food's position within the spatial framework anchored to the remembered shape of the environment. Because the rectangular environment has axial symmetry, there are two equally good alignments between any two representations of it. Suppose when the rat is reintroduced to this environment, its navigation system establishes its position and heading by means of a global fix (see figure 3.9 and accompanying discussion). In trying to establish congruence between the currently perceived shape and the remembered shape, the navigation system would hit on an "erroneous" congruence half the time. The erroneous congruence is the congruence such that the remembered address for the eighteen-pellet bait corresponds not to the correct location but to the diagonally opposite, geometrically indistinguishable location, where the six-pellet bait is. This location is the rotational equivalent of the correct location. The correct location can be made to coincide with this location by a rotation, which changes none of the geometric relations in the environment. (This is a more formal way of saying that diagonally opposite corners have the same relation to the macroscopic shape of the environment.) In short, if the congruence between remembered space and currently perceived space were based on shape alone, then the rat would be misoriented by 180° at the beginning of half the trials. On those trials, it finds the six-pellet bait where it expects to find the eighteen-pellet bait.

When the results of later experiments led us to believe that the rat's initial orientation within a space was based on shape alone, Cheng reexamined the data from the training phase of this first experiment to see if the rats in fact failed to distinguish the eighteen-pellet arm from the six-pellet arm. Figure 6.6 shows for each of the four rats the percentage that each arm was entered first, during the last six days of the training phase, when the accuracy of the rats' choices was asymptotic. Every rat chose almost unerringly to enter first a geometrically correct arm, an arm on the diagonal that contained the two largest baits ($p < .001$ in each case). By contrast, no rat chose the eighteen-pellet arm in preference to the six-pellet arm ($p > .10$ in each case). This might be taken to mean only that the marginal utility of additional pellets decreases rapidly above six, so the rat does not regard it as worth its while to differentiate between six and eighteen pellets, but we do not think so, for the following reason. Our procedure was modeled on that of Hulse and O'Leary (1982), who used these same differences in bait magnitudes. The Hulse and O'Leary rats did differentiate on their first choices between the eighteen-pellet arm and the six-pellet arm, by a ratio of at least 3.5:1.

This analysis explained why the asymptotic performance in the training phase of our experiment was substantially lower than the asymptotic performance observed in the Hulse and O'Leary experiment. In the latter, there is no reason to suppose that the rats' orientation while on the X maze did not depend on compass orientation—that is, on their sense of their geocentric heading. By contrast, we took pains to render it difficult for the rats to maintain their compass orientation and to discourage their reliance on it if and when they did succeed in maintaining it. When an experimental space has a fixed geocentric orientation (as was true in the Hulse and O'Leary experiment) and when rats succeed in

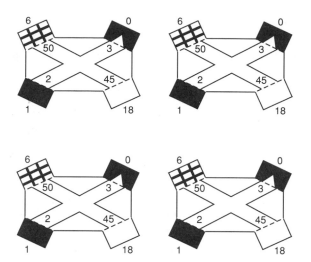

Figure 6.6
The percentage of first choices of each arm for each rat during the period of asymptotic performance prior to the introduction of transformation trials. The rats distinguished the large-bait diagonal from the small-bait diagonal but did not distinguish the eighteen-pellet end from the six-pellet end. (Redrawn from Cheng 1984, p. 93, by permission of author.)

maintaining their sense of their geocentric heading during the running of the experiment (which they often do), then their performance will not be affected by symmetries in the shape of the experimental apparatus . The effects of these symmetries become apparent only in experiments in which the rats have not been able to retain their geocentric heading or have been induced to ignore it by constantly changing the compass orientation of the experimental space.

Margules and Gallistel (1988) showed that when experiments like Cheng's are run under conditions where the rats are not disoriented with respect to the space outside the box, they do not make rotational confusions. These same rats, when subsequently disoriented with respect to the space outside the box, do make the rotational errors observed by Cheng. This explains why the rats in Hulse and O'Leary's experiment clearly differentiated between the eighteen-pellet and six-pellet arms in their first choices and consequently attained considerably higher asymptotic choice accuracy than was achieved by the rats in the Cheng and Gallistel experiment. The Hulse and O'Leary rats were not disoriented with respect to the space outside the experimental setup.

The two ends of the diagonal containing the smallest baits are just as indistinguishable on purely geometric grounds as are the two ends of the diagonal with the two largest baits. However, Cheng's analysis showed that the rats reliably chose the arm with one-pellet prior to choosing the arm with none. If we discount an explanation in terms of greater marginal utilities, this suggests that the rats may have used the confirmation or disconfirmation of their expectations on their initial choice either to stay with or recompute the congruence that established their initial sense of orientation within the experimental space. The reader may have had the experience of emerging from a subway station or movie theater in a grid city like Manhattan 180° misoriented. One walks with this unwitting misorientation until one fails to find some expected building or street at the spot one takes oneself to have arrived at. There follows a hard-to-describe sense of something rotating inside one's head to produce the proper alignment between the perceived city and one's cognitive map. It is conceivable that the same thing happens to the rat when it fails to find the eighteen-pellets on trials on which it inadvertently chooses the six-pellet arm first because it is misoriented with respect to the rectangle by 180°.

The hypothesis that the failure to find something in a given location (or finding something there that should be at another location) may induce a recomputation of the congruence between the environmental shape one now perceives and the map implies that nongeometric information is not altogether excluded from the process of finding an acceptable congruence, that is, from the process of establishing the rat's heading within a remembered environmental shape. Nongeometric information may be excluded from the congruence computation itself, but it may help to determine whether the computed congruence is acceptable. It may induce the system to try to find another geometric congruence as good as or better than one that has led to erroneous anticipations. Cheng designed two follow-up experiments to test this post hoc hypothesis regarding the role of nongeometric information in determining the rat's sense of orientation.

Food in only one arm.   Cheng reasoned that when there was only one food location and it was always the same, the rats might learn to check the distinguishing nongeometric features of the panel just behind that location before venturing down an arm. He trained six new rats on the X maze, with food always in the same arm (a different arm for different rats). As in the previous experiment, he took pains to interfere with the rats' sense of their geocentric heading and to discourage their reliance on it. Under these conditions, he found it surprisingly difficult to get the rats to choose the correct arm with high frequency. All of the rats rapidly learned to choose it at least 50 percent of the time—the level attainable by relying on geometry alone, that is, by choosing the correct diagonal but not differentiating between the ends of that diagonal. Only four of six rats learned to choose the correct arm 75 percent of the time. Although this is a statistically significant preference, this would be a weak and easily met criterion for rats run under conditions where compass orientation enabled them to choose the correct arm (Olton and Papas 1979).

It might be thought that the rats that met this criterion had learned to ignore their sense of the food's location within the rectangular experimental space and attend only to the distinctive and highly salient characteristics of the panel at the food's position. By contrast, we hypothesized a three-stage procedure in which the rat established an initial congruence, looked to see whether the panel at the supposed location of the food had the right characteristics, and recomputed the alignment between its map and the environment when it did not. To differentiate between these explanations, Cheng ran transformation trials with the four rats that met the 75 percent criterion. If the rats had learned to find the food by using the panel behind it as a beacon, ignoring its position within the rectangular space, then it should not matter in which corner that panel was found. Thus, performance should not be affected by either an affine or a sense transformation. On the other hand, if nongeometric feature mismatches serve only to induce recomputation of purely geometric congruences, then both of these transformations should severely disturb performance. They make it impossible to achieve a geometric congruence that correctly predicts which panel will be observed in which corner.

In all four rats, performance fell to chance on the transformation trials. The ability to use panel features in choosing an arm clearly depended on an interaction between those features and the rat's sense of the overall shape of the space. One example of such an interaction would be a procedure wherein the rat recomputes congruence on finding a local feature mismatch.

Choosing by feature associations alone.   From an associative perspective, the results of these first two experiments are astonishing. The transformation trials, of which each rat experienced a great many, could be viewed as procedures for inducing rats to ignore their spatial representation and choose on the basis of the unfailing association between the food (or the largest amount of food) and the highly salient and distinctive features of the panels that loomed behind the rewards. The panels were an unfailing guide to the rewards the rat sought, whereas position within the environmental shape was an unreliable guide. Nonetheless, the rats persistently relied on this latter guide and were disoriented when they had to ignore position and choose on the basis of panel features alone. We were the more surprised by this result in that it has repeatedly been demonstrated, with both the T maze and the radial maze, that rats readily learn to choose arms on the basis of nongeometric features (e.g., whiteness-blackness) rather than on the basis of position in space (Jarrard 1983; Olton and Feustle 1981). The third experiment was designed to determine whether under our conditions rats could learn to choose on the basis of panel features alone, without regard to position.

Four new rats were trained on the X maze, with the food always before the same panel (a different panel for each rat) but with the assignment of the four panels to the four corners randomly determined on each trial. In this experiment, the maze had the same orientation within the room on all trials, but the rat could not see the room and was transported in the dark to the maze and placed in it with different orientations from trial to trial. In short, it was still difficult for the rat to maintain a sense of compass orientation, but reliance on this sense was not otherwise discouraged. By the end of five weeks and 120 trials of training, only one of the four rats was choosing the correct arm significantly above the 25 percent chance level; it chose the correct arm 56 percent of the time during the last two weeks (last forty-eight trials).

Clearly under our experimental conditions, rats could use distinctive characteristics of the panels to accept or reject a geometric congruence defining the location of food, but it was extremely difficult for them to ignore relative position and attend only to the nonpositional characteristics of the panels behind the food, despite the fact that these characteristics were very distinctive and prominent. We can think of two reasons why this is difficult under our conditions but not under some others. In most if not all of the experiments where rats have learned to choose arms by their nongeometric sensory characteristics rather than by their position in a space defined by several widely separated 3 dimensional objects one or both of the following were true:

1.   No effective precautions were taken to destroy the rat's compass orientation. One may imagine that when conditions are such as to make it difficult for the animal to maintain its orientation with respect to the larger spatial framework within which the maze is found, then establishing its orientation within the maze has priority over other operations (and this orientation is established entirely by congruence).

2.   The distinctive features were features of the arm in which the food was found rather than of a panel that was very close to but disconnected from the arm itself. One might imagine that the ability to choose an arm on the basis of its nonpositional characteristics depended on the sought-for food's having some particular relation to that arm, such as being found in it.

It remains for future experiments to determine whether either or both of these possibilities is correct.

Working Memory Experiments
The experiments just reported all involved the use of what is called reference memory, a memory for aspects of the experimental environment that endure from trial to trial. For a variety of reasons, reference memory is commonly distinguished from working memory, the retention of information acquired in the course of a single trial and useful during only that trial (Honig 1978; Olton, Becker, and Handelmann 1979). The operational distinction between reference memory and working memory is highlighted by the radial maze paradigm employed by Olton et al. (1979). Their maze had seventeen arms, eight of which were always baited at the start of a trial and nine of which were never baited. Reference memory refers to the memory for the eight arms that were always baited. Working memory refers to the memory for which of those eight arms has already been visited during any one trial. The question arises whether the findings indicating that the rat has an overwhelming preference for orienting itself by reference to the overall shape of a space depend in any way on using paradigms involving reference memory rather than working memory. The following experiments addressed that question. They also further addressed the question of cue salience; the panels used as corner landmarks in these experiments were as visually distinctive as we could make them, and they differed in texture and smell as well.

Cheng's working memory paradigm involved showing rats the location of food buried in pine chips that covered the bottom of a rectangular experimental space, allowing them to eat some of it, removing them, reburying the food, and then releasing them back into the space to dig out the food. In this paradigm, the rat's digging gave a clear, easily scored indication of where it believed the food to be.

Since the experimental space was again rectangular, shape alone did not yield a unique orientation. If, when they were returned to the box, the rats were to orient by its shape alone, they would be 180° misoriented half the time. To enable them to disambiguate their orientation, Cheng put panels differing in texture, visual appearance and smell in the corners. One panel was made of dark, smooth Masonite, had a stripe down its center, a single light shining out of a pinhole, and, below the pinhole, a larger hole, behind which was a wad of cotton impregnated with a drop of anise at the beginning of each day's running. Another panel was made of shiny aluminum, had no lights shining out of it, and no experimenter-supplied odor. Another panel was rough and had a cotton wad impregnated with peppermint.

To keep the delay between their initial exposure to the food and their reintroduction to the space to a minimum and to obviate the possibility of a rat's leaving some telltale sign to mark the location of the food, Cheng used two identical boxes, with the food buried at the same location in both. The rat was shown the location of the food in one, removed from it, and returned 75 seconds later to the other, where it could dig for food at the same location. Our intent was that the rat never realize there were in fact two different boxes. The results suggest that this intent was realized.

On the floor of the rectangles, beneath the pine chips, there was a 9 x 9 gridwork of lines. The location at which the food was buried on a trial was chosen at random from among eighty of the eighty-one intersections in this grid, the intersection at the exact center of the box not being used. The rat's chances of finding the buried food by random digging were low, and in fact, in the 1 minute they were in the box at the beginning of each trial prior to being shown where the food was buried, the rats almost never succeeded in finding it. When the rat was shown the location of the food—by the experimenter's reaching in and digging a little bit at that location—the dish contained seven bits of cereal. The rat was allowed to eat three bits before being removed. The dish buried at the same location in the replica space to which the rat was returned after 75 seconds contained four pellets. When the rat found this dish, it was allowed to eat these "remaining" pellets. If the rat did not find the dish within 2 minutes, the experimenter uncovered it. The experimenter recorded the point on the grid where the rat first dug after being returned to the replica environment.

It was the rats' unexpected behavior in this experiment that first alerted Cheng to the possibility that the rats were not orienting by the landmarks we had provided but were relying on environmental shape alone. The rats in this experiment soon learned to dig at the correct location at well above chance levels, but they never attained a high hit rate for the surprising reason that they frequently dug at the rotational equivalent of the correct location, the location that cannot be distinguished from the correct location on the basis of environmental shape alone. Figure 6.7A plots for each of the three rats the percentage of the last sixty trials on which they dug at the correct location (C), the rotational equivalent of the correct location (R), and elsewhere (E). For the sake of presentation, the figure represents the correct location at a single position in the rectangle, but the actual position of the correct location (and therefore the position of the rotationally equivalent location) ranged all over the box from trial to trial. From the purely geometric point of view, the correct location and its rotational equivalent are indistinguishable, so digs at either position should be scored as correct. If the data are scored by a criterion of "correct up to a rotation," the rats' asymptotic percentage of correct digs ranged

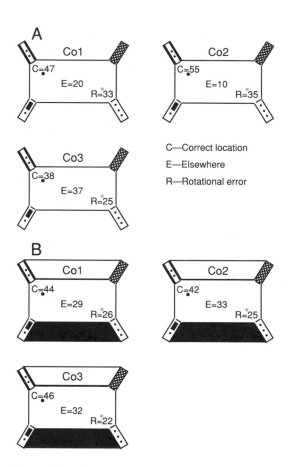

C—Correct location
E—Elsewhere
R—Rotational error

Figure 6.7
A. The percentage of trials on which individual rats first dug at the correct location, made a rotational error, or dug elsewhere, in the experiment without the Styrofoam wall. *B.* Results from the subsequent experiment, with the Styrofoam wall added to one side of the box. (Redrawn from Cheng 1984, pp. 145, 155, by permission of author.)

from 63 to 90 percent. If one scores on absolute correctness, however, the figures drop to 38 to 55 percent. While all three rats chose the correct location slightly more often than its rotational equivalent, this difference was not statistically significant in any of them. On the other hand, both the probability of digging at the correct location and the probability of digging at its rotational equivalent were well above chance levels (p < .001 in all cases).

These results were sufficiently startling to raise again the question whether we made the potentially disambiguating nongeometric properties of the surfaces in this environment sufficiently salient. In a follow-up experiment, Cheng covered one long wall of the rectangle with a sheet of white Styrofoam. Now, in addition to the four distinctive panels in the corners, one smelling of anise and one of peppermint, one 4-foot wall of the enclosure was white, while the other three walls were black. The white wall had the texture of Styrofoam, while the others had the texture of plywood. When the rat faced the Styrofoam side of the box, the highly reflective white wall subtended a visual angle of 120° or more. When it turned around to face the opposite wall, that dark black wall subtended a similar visual angle. Cheng continued running the three rats in this augmented environment for another seventy-two trials. Making one of the long walls white Styrofoam did not alter the results. The rats continued to dig almost as often at the rotationally equivalent position as they did at the correct position (figure 6.7B).

Evidence for the coding of metric relations and sense.   The rotational confusions observed in these experiments are another proof that the rat's coding of relative spatial position captures both the uniquely metric relations and the sense relations and that the rat relies on these relations in orienting itself within a coded space. If the rat took no account of one or the other of these kinds of relations in establishing a correspondence between the space it perceived when returned to the replica and the space it remembered from 75 seconds earlier, then there would be at least four positions in the space that were geometrically indistinguishable from the correct position. Only the combination of a sense relation (left-right) and a uniquely metric relation (longer-shorter) renders one pair of diagonally opposite corners in a rectangle geometrically distinct from the other pair. In the absence of either type of relation, the four corners of a rectangle are indistinguishable. (Remember that in the absence of the uniquely metric relations, a rectangle is indistinguishable from a square and a square is congruent with itself after any rotation that is an integer multiple of 90°.) More generally, in the absence of either one of these relations, any one point in a rectangle (except the center) is geometrically indistinguishable from three other points (the rotationally and reflectionally equivalent points), whereas if both sense and distance are defined, then each point is indistinguishable from only one other point (the rotationally equivalent point). Cheng analyzed the data to see if there was any tendency to dig in the other two locations—the ones that would be indistinguishable from the correct location if the rat took no account of either sense or relative distance. There was no such tendency. Only the rotationally equivalent location was confused with the correct location.

Importance of compass sense. In this experiment, as in the earlier ones, Cheng made it difficult for the rats to maintain their compass sense and discouraged their reliance on it. One of the measures taken was to rotate the replica box by a randomly chosen amount during the 75 seconds before the rat was returned to it. On his data sheets, Cheng categorized these rotations by their extent: less than 60°, between 60° and 120°, and greater than 120°. He later analyzed the digging data for the influence of other factors. Whether a trial was the first or second of the day had no effect on the accuracy of a rat's digging (so interference effects were not strong). The quadrant in which the food happened to be located had no effect, nor did it matter whether the food was close to a wall or a corner. But the extent of the rotation of the box frequently did matter. Figure 6.8 shows the data from one of the rats in the first digging experiment, broken down by the extent of the rotation done during the delay. When

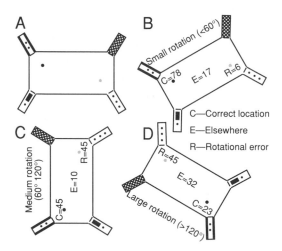

Figure 6.8
The percentage of trials on which rat "Col" in the experiment without the Styrofoam wall dug at the correct location, made a rotational error, or dug elsewhere, as a function of the extent to which the experimental box had been rotated during the 75 second intratrial delay. (Redrawn from Cheng 1984, p. 150, by permission of author.)

the rotation was less than 60°, the rat was much more likely to dig at the correct location than at its rotational equivalent, whereas for larger rotations, it was as likely or even more likely to dig at the rotational equivalent. These differences were statistically significant in this rat ($p < .01$) though not in the other two rats. In the continuation of the experiment, after the insertion of the white Styrofoam wall, both of the other rats began to show a similar effect of the degree of rotation of the replica. (Chi- square tests for the significance of these tendencies yielded ps of $<.01$ and $< .06$.).

Thus, despite the precautions taken to prevent the rats from maintaining or making use of a sense of their orientation with respect to the extraexperimental space, they nonetheless did to some extent maintain it and make use of it. This result underscores two important and related points. First, symmetry within an experimentally contrived space will give rise to a purely geometric orientational ambiguity only if the rat loses its sense of orientation with respect to the extraexperimental space. If the rat has some sense of the orientation of the experimental space within the extraexperimental framework, then it need not confuse locations with their rotational equivalents even though it orients entirely on the basis of the shape of experienced space. The geometric equivalence of rotationally equivalent points in a symmetrical shape holds only so long as that shape constitutes the entire frame of reference (see Margules and Gallistel 1988). If an animal has any sense of orientation with respect to a larger frame of reference, then the geometric properties of the experimental space are no longer invariant under rotation. If there is some larger framework—one anchored to external aspects of the world—then rotating a shape embedded within that framework alters purely geometric properties of that shape: its orientation in the larger framework. Only when the shape itself becomes the whole world—the only world to which the animal can be oriented—is it true that all of its purely geometric properties are invariant under displacement transformations. Put another way, if an animal knows its compass headings, then rotating the experimental maze alters the compass bearings of points in that maze (the geocentric bearing of one point from another point).

Second, because animals can maintain some sense of orientation by double integration of their angular acceleration, it is difficult to destroy completely their knowledge of their compass heading. A sense of orientation is profoundly important to an animal, and most of them are good at maintaining at least a crude sense of compass orientation under adverse circumstances. The surprising ability of diverse animals to reckon their compass heading was first called to our attention by Carr and Watson's discovery that rats were sensitive to the compass orientation of their maze, even though it was inside an axially symmetric canvas enclosure. It was again called to our attention by Cartwright and Collett's discovery that bees maintain their compass orientation while inside a matte white experimental chamber.

Perhaps the most surprising point these data make is that it is easier to detect the influence of compass orientation than it is to detect any use, for orienting purposes, of the salient visual, tactile, and olfactory information provided by the landmarks in the enclosure. The rat relies more on its compass heading, derived either from integrating angular velocity signals and/or a magnetic sense, than it does on the fact that one corner of the enclosure smells of anise, another of peppermint, and one long wall is black while the wall opposite it is bright white. Any single one of these nongeometric features of the enclosure's surfaces suffices to remove the orientational ambiguity arising from the axial symmetry of the enclosure's shape, yet the rats do not make use of this information for this purpose. In effect, the rat's brain will not use information about the nongeometric properties of surfaces in the solution of what, from its standpoint, is apparently the inherently geometric problem of establishing where the rat is and which way it is pointing.

Affine transformations. The extraordinary extent to which the rat ignored the nongeometric features of the surfaces in reestablishing its orientation in the experimental environment was unexpected. We again wondered whether it was possible to overcome this exclusive reliance on environmental shape by making the contingencies strongly favor reliance on something else. To test this, Cheng ran another group of three rats in a version of the digging experiment that strongly discouraged reliance on Euclidean shape and encouraged reliance either on some weaker affine property of the environment or on the association between panel features and the sought-for location.

For the rats in this experiment, there were only four possible locations for the food (as contrasted with eighty). The food was always buried in a corner immediately in front of one of the panels. On some trials it was buried immediately in front of the smooth Masonite panel that smelled of anise, on others in front of the shiny aluminum panel that had no odor (at least none supplied by the experimenter), on still others in front of the rough panel that smelled of peppermint, and so on—the burial site being randomly selected anew on each trial from among the four possibilities. When the rat had been shown where the food was on a given trial and allowed to eat three of the cereal bits, it was removed for 75 seconds and then returned to the replica box, an affine transformation of the original in which all the panels had been shifted around one corner. The food also was shifted, so it remained under the panel it was under when the rat first found it. The affine transformation carried the food (and the panel associated with it) into a corner with a different relation to the shape of the box, so reliance on the position of the food within the shape defined by the box was strongly discouraged. The food was never in the Euclidean location in which it had just been found, but it was always under the same panel as the one under which it had just been found.

From the human perspective, the best way for the rats to proceed under these conditions would be to associate the food with the panel beneath which the food was found and then look around (or sniff or feel around) for that panel when returned to the box. This the rats did not do. Instead they fell back on an affine relation, a geometric relation that was not nearly as good a guide to the correct location of the food as were the distinctive nongeometric characteristics of the panel surface in front of which the food was buried. In figure 6.9, for the sake of presentation, the correct location is shown in one corner. In fact, each corner served as the correct location on 25 percent of the trials. Whatever was the correct corner on a given trial, one could categorize the other three corners as "the corner reached from the correct corner by going along the longer wall," "the corner reached by going along the shorter wall," and "the diagonally opposite corner." These categories were used to derive the percentages written in the corresponding corners of the rectangles in figure 6.9. The percentage digs at locations other than corners are given in the center of each rectangle. Note that the rats learned to dig almost always at a corner, but they showed no significant tendency (even after 80 trials) to dig at the correct one of these four corners.

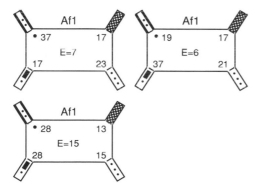

Figure 6.9
The percentage of trials on which each rat in the affine-transformation condition of the digging experiment dug first at each corner. The filled circle represents the correct corner, which varied from trial to trial. The other corners are defined relative to this correct corner (see text). (Redrawn from Cheng 1984, p. 139, by permission of author.)

Corner is a weaker geometric relation than difference in length. A set of points forms a corner if every point may be assigned to one of two subsets of collinear points with one point (the point of intersection) belonging to both subsets. This relation survives any affine transformation; hence corner is an affine relation but not a (uniquely) metric relation. What does not survive arbitrary affine transformation is the relation wherein one subset of the points belongs to a longer line segment than the other subset. We saw in earlier experiments that rats would rely on this longer-shorter relation when it helped establish the location of the food. In the present experiment, where a choice of the corner with the correct longer-shorter shape was always wrong, the rats fell back on the weaker corner relation. What they did not do, despite the encouragement provided by the design of this experiment, was to rely on the nongeometric features of the panels. As a result, they were only about 25 percent accurate. The rats were less accurate in this experiment, where only four locations were possible burial sites, than in the preceding experiment, where there were eighty possibilities.

Proof of the Detectability of the Nongeometric Stimuli
The results reported so far are so at variance with one's intuitive expectations (and with what a simple associative account of learning would lead one to expect) that one is driven to ask whether for some reason our rats in this setting could not or did not notice or could not or did not record in some memory the nongeometric sensory information provided by the panels (and, in some cases, by the white Styrofoam wall). As in the experiments with the X maze, we wanted to show that there were circumstances under which these panel and wall features could be shown to aid the rat in determining a correct location. To that end, Cheng used the same apparatus employed in all the working memory experiments but reverted to a reference memory paradigm in which the food was always in the same single location directly beneath the same panel. The details of the task were also varied to show that the findings regarding the primacy of geometric relations in the determination of a spatial location do not depend on minor details of the experimental tasks.

This experiment used the boxes employed in the working memory experiments, complete with pinechip bedding, but the food was no longer buried in the bedding. Instead a bottle full of cereal bits was placed upside down on its cap in each of the four corners, immediately in front of one of the distinctive corner panels. For three of these bottles, a snap-on center cap was in place, so that when the bottles were knocked over by the rat, no cereal spilled out. The fourth bottle had no snap-on cap, although this was not apparent until it was knocked over. When it was knocked over, cereal spilled out. The rat's task was to learn which bottle to knock over. The correct bottle was the same from trial to trial, standing always in the same corner in front of the same panel. If the rat regarded only the shape of the corner, it would be wrong 50 percent of the time. Taking the nongeometric characteristics of the panel (and/or wall) surfaces into account would enable it to achieve 100 percent accuracy. Cheng trained the rats first with the Styrofoam wall in place. When they were successful, he removed the Styrofoam to verify that they could do it on the basis of panel characteristics alone.

When they were again successful, he removed the panels in the correct corner and the diagonally opposite corner. Removing these two panels tested the hypothesis that the rats were taking into account the features of only the panels in the two geometrically correct corners, although taking any panel into account would uniquely specify the correct location. It also verified that the rats in fact relied on the panel in the correct corner to achieve better than 50 percent correct performance.

Figure 6.10A shows the rats' asymptotic percentage choices of each bottle under the initial conditions, with the white Styrofoam wall in place. Figure 6.10B shows their asymptotic percentage choices after the Styrofoam wall was removed, so that the panels alone served to disambiguate the geometrically equivalent bottle positions. In both conditions, the rats made some use of the nongeometric clues to the proper position, choosing the correct bottle significantly more often than the bottle in the rotationally equivalent location. Figure 6.11 shows that when the panels in the correct corner and its rotational equivalent were removed, the rats no longer differentiated between the two corners, proving that the successful differentiation of these two corners evident in figure 6.10B depended on the presence of the panels. In other words, the rats could notice and remember the nongeometric characteristics of the panel surfaces and could use these characteristics as an aid to the determination of the correct location.

The Irrelevance of Global Congruence in Nongeometric Features
From the data in figure 6.11, it appears that while nongeometric features of surfaces may signal that a computed alignment between perceived and remembered spaces is incorrect, these properties of the surfaces still do not enter into the alignment computation itself. If the nongeometric features of the panel surfaces entered into the computation of overall congruence, then panels remote from the correct corner should disambiguate just as effectively as panels in the correct corners, but figure 6.11 shows that they do not.

The final experiment tested the hypothesis that the rat is oblivious to a global incongruence of nongeometric features, provided it finds the features it expects in a corner that is geometrically acceptable. In this

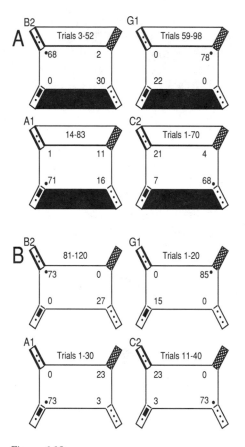

Figure 6.10
A. The percentage of first bottle-tips at each corner for each rat at asymptote in the environment with the white Styrofoam wall and the corner panels. The filled circles represent the correct bottle. B. Results from the subsequent bottle-tip experiment, without the white Styrofoam wall. (Redrawn from Cheng 1984, pp. 170, 179, by permission of author.)

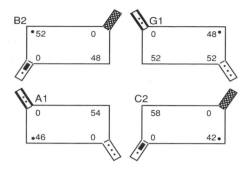

Figure 6.11
The percentage of first bottle-tips at each corner for each rat after the removal of the corner panels in the correct corner and its rotational equivalent. (Redrawn from Cheng 1984, p. 179, by permission of author.)

experiment, the four panels were put back in place and the four rats used in the just-recounted experiments were retrained until they were again choosing the one correct corner at least 75 percent of the time over a stretch of at least thirty trials. One of the four rats failed to reach this level of proficiency. The three that did were then given forty trials in a setup in which the panel in the correct corner was interchanged with the panel in the rotationally equivalent corner (with the correct bottle going with its panel). This is a transposition transformation. It destroys even the topological relations among the four panels. If the features that render these panels distinctive are taken into account in searching for a congru ence between perceived and remembered spaces, then the rats' perform-ance should be disturbed by this change because such a congruence is no longer possible. On the other hand, this transformation carries the correct panel into a corner that has the same geometric relation to the experimen-tal box as the corner it was previously in. If all the rat does is check to see that the corner it intends to choose has the right panel in it, then its performance will not be disturbed by this transformation.

As may be seen in figure 6.12, the diagonal transposition of two panels had no significant effect on the performance of the three rats that were reliably using the panel characteristics as an aid in choosing the correct corner.

Computational Reasons for Impenetrability

Cheng's findings support the thesis that there is an organ (neural system) in the rat brain dedicated to the computational task of finding a congru-ence between the Euclidean shape of the space the animal now perceives

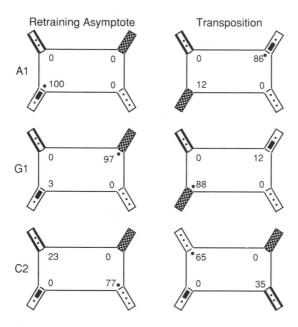

Figure 6.12
The effect of interchanging the panel in the correct corner with the panel in the diagonally opposite corner ("transposition"). A. Choice percentages before transposition. B. Choice percentages after transposition. None of the differences is statistically significant. (Redrawn from Cheng 1984, p. 189, by permission of author.)

and the remembered shape of the environment. They also imply that this congruence computation plays a fundamental role in enabling the rat to direct its movements so as to bring itself to the remembered position of the goals it seeks. They further support the thesis that this organ constitutes a module in Fodor's (1983) sense; it works only with certain kinds of information, even under circumstances where other kinds of readily perceptible data are highly relevant to successful performance. Fodor termed this property of a module impenetrability. Cheng's data provide a clear example of impenetrability. The organ that computes congruence between perceived shape and remembered shape appears to be impenetrable to information about aspects of surfaces other than their relative positions. The congruence computation takes no account of the smells emanating from surfaces, their reflectance or luminance characteristics, their texture, and so on. It takes no account of the nongeometric properties of surfaces, even when the relative positions of the perceptible surfaces do not suffice to establish unambiguously the correct congruence.

The notion of impenetrability is controversial. It strikes many people at first as extremely implausible. It contradicts the common conception of the brain as a unified general-purpose problem-solving organ, capable of taking any sense data into consideration in the solution of any problem. It argues instead for a conception of the brain as an integrated collection of special-purpose organs, each dedicated to the solution of a particular kind of computational problem. In order to make more plausible the idea that the congruence-finding process or algorithm in the brain might be impenetrable to any data except those about relative position, it helps to consider formal, computer-based attempts to deal with this same problem. In the process, we will see that Cheng's findings have implications regarding the type of algorithm (computational process) employed by the brain to solve this problem.

Computerized image alignment (or image registration, or template matching) algorithms may be divided into two fundamentally different types: local correspondence algorithms and global parameter-matching algorithms. Local correspondence algorithms are those that vary the assignment of local correspondences between points (or features = point sets) in the two images (or shapes), searching for the correspondence that minimizes some error function or maximizes some matching function. The most common example of an algorithm of this type is one in which the computer displaces one image relative to the other, looking for the displacement that maximizes the spatial cross-correlation function (for examples of this type of approach, see Cabot 1981; Pratt 1974; O'Gorman and Sanderson 1984; Goshtasby, Gage, and Bartholic 1984). If we let one image be represented by the function $f(x,y)$ and the other by the function $g(x,y)$, then this algorithm searches for the values of the translation-defining parameters, m and n, that maximize the cross correlation between $f(x,y)$ and $g(x+m,y+n)$. When this algorithm tries new values for m and n (that is, a different displacement of the image represented by g), it implicitly assumes that points assigned the same coordinates are corresponding points; it assumes that the point $<x-m, y-n>$ in the g image corresponds to the point $<x, y>$ in the f image. It uses the cross-correlation of the two images at this translation to evaluate the goodness of fit produced by this particular set of pointwise correspondences between the two images. (For an example of a correspondence algorithm based on features and the relation between features, rather than on points, see Cheng and Huang 1982.)

In the given example of a local correspondence algorithm, it is assumed that the two images differ only by a translation. In principle, the same approach can be applied when they differ by both a translation and a rotation, but in practice the computation becomes impracticably large because the computer has to try all possible translations at each possible rotation. A local-correspondence algorithm is greatly facilitated when there is some basis for narrowing the range of local correspondences to be evaluated. For example, if some points in both images have unique and reproducible intensity values—that is, if there is an intensity that holds for one and only one point in each image and those two points are corresponding points—then the computational problem is radically reduced. In a local correspondence algorithm, information that picks out corresponding points on some basis other than their relative position within the images is immensely valuable because it radically reduces the number of correspondences that must be evaluated.

In ordinary images, one seldom finds points with unique and reproducible intensity values, so a priori reductions in the number of possibilities that must be evaluated are rarely possible. One might imagine, however, that the richness of the sensory data differentiating points in the experienced world of an animal makes local correspondence algorithms biologically attractive. That is, the brain might try to pair points or surfaces in the currently perceived space and the remembered space on the basis of their smells, feels, brightnesses, and so on. Cheng's data imply that the brain does not use a local correspondence algorithm. He found the opposite of what one would expect if the brain were establishing global correspondence (congruence) by trying out various local correspondences and calculating which assignment of these correspondences maximized the overall correspondence.

Cheng's data imply that the rat's brain uses the other kind of algorithm for bringing two images or shapes into registration: a global parameter-matching algorithm. These algorithms compute descriptive parameters for the shapes to be aligned and determine from a comparison of these parameters the displacement required to make the shapes maximally congruent. (For examples of this kind of approach, see Lucas 1983; Hu 1962.) The parameters most commonly computed are the low-order shift-invariant central moments, in mechanical terminology, or, in geometric terminology, the principal axes. The principal axes of a shape are the axes of rotation that minimize the angular momentum (for a fixed angular velocity). Two shapes are brought into maximal congruence by the displacement that makes their centroid and their principal axes coincide.

If the rat's brain employs an algorithm like this, then it is apparent why the algorithm is impenetrable to nongeometric data—that is, to data about anything other than the relative position of the points that compose the shape. The (shift-invariant) principal axes are determined by the relative positions of the points within a shape and by nothing else. These algorithms do not make use of data about nonpositional attributes of the points that compose a shape because they do not operate by trying out various patterns (or mappings) of local correspondences between points or small regions of the two images to be aligned. While it is possible to allow nonpositional information, such as mass or intensity, as weighting factors in a calculation like the principal axis calculation, it defeats the purpose of the calculation to do so in cases like these in which the function of the calculation is to maximize the congruence of the shapes. In short, one reason for impenetrability is that the computation used to solve a certain type of problem might by its nature admit only data with a certain kind of formal structure. The computation of a principal axis admits only data with the formal structure of positional information.

The algorithms for maximizing the congruence between two shapes by computing shape parameters are not search algorithms; they are computational formulas that yield the principal axes of a shape when given the coordinates of the points that compose the shape. There is no trial and error, no iterative recomputation and reevaluation in these procedures. This makes them attractive from a computational point of view; they do not explode (become impracticably large). The other interesting point about these algorithms is that unlike search and cross-correlation algorithms, these are inherently confounded by shape symmetries because symmetries yield nonunique solutions to the equations for shape parameters. For symmetrical shapes, there are multiple principal axes. For radially symmetrical shapes, there is an infinity of such axes because any diameter of a circle (or sphere) is a principal axis.

Evolutionary Reasons for Impenetrability

Computational analysis of neural and psychological functioning is not yet common, so arguments for impenetrability based on computational considerations may have an air of unreality. When such arguments lead to conclusions that seem nonsensical from a biological perspective, they should be viewed with skepticism. That, however, would not appear to be the case in the present instance. The case of the nutcracker, reviewed in the preceding chapter, shows why the procedures by which the nervous systems of animals establish correspondences between the regions they now find themselves in and regions they have had previous experience of should not rely on the correspondences between nonpositional features of surfaces. The nutcracker makes its caches in the fall but retrieves them in the winter when snow covers the ground. The change in seasons—and the passage of time in general—brings with it manifold changes in the nonpositional attributes of many, if not all, environmental surfaces. Any attempt to utilize distinctive, nonpositional attributes of surfaces would have to include a weighting scheme that allowed one to trade off changes along seemingly incommensurable dimensions. How much should one weight a change in the reflectance characteristics of a surface relative to a change in its smell? (This is a computational consideration surfacing in the midst of an evolutionary argument.) What does not change—barring a rare catastrophe like the eruption of Mount St. Helena—is the macroscopic shape of an animal's environment. A tree may fall or a boulder may tumble down, but if the animal's behavioral space extends over several hectares, as is probably generally the case, then none of these minor events alters the overall shape of its environment. In relying on overall shape alone, the nervous system finesses the problem of finding the optimal weights for mediating the trade-offs between changes occurring along incommensurable sensory dimensions.

It might be objected that symmetries will defeat orientations based on shape alone, as shown by Cheng's results. This objection overlooks the likelihood that animals take their orientation ultimately from the shape of the full environment with which they have become familiar—the relative positions of surfaces tens, hundreds, or thousands of meters apart. Once they have established their geocentric orientation—their orientation with respect to this large domain—they retain a sense of their geocentric heading even when they penetrate into smaller, possibly symmetrical spaces, where they are temporarily cut off from direct sensory access to the larger world. On a scale of tens, hundreds, or thousands of meters, there are no symmetrical behavioral spaces, so animals that get their ultimate orientation from spaces of these magnitudes should seldom, if ever, be confounded by symmetries. In short, the shape of the animal's large-scale environment is a sure guide to location, whereas the distinctive nonpositional attributes of surfaces are not. It makes biological sense that animals should orient themselves on the basis of the macroscopic shape alone.

Definition of Geometric and Nongeometric Properties

The essential nature of the distinction between geometric and nongeometric properties of surfaces, points, and lines has been implied but not explicitly stated. A geometric property of a surface, line, or point is a property it possesses by virtue of its position relative to other surfaces, lines, and points within the same space. A nongeometric property is any property that cannot be described by relative position alone. Any property whose description requires language that does not ordinarily appear in a textbook on geometry is nongeometric. Black and white (relative reflectance) are not concepts that ordinarily appear in a geometry textbook, nor are luminance versus nonluminance, differences in smell, differences in texture, and so on. This means that a white triangle (or a circular patch of luminance, for another example) on an otherwise black surface is not a geometric property of the surface, although geometric relations figure in the description of this property. A geometric property of a point is a property it has by virtue of its relative position alone.

This definition says nothing about the physical interpretation to be assigned the abstract concept of a surface. What is it about the physical world that leads an animal to perceive a surface? It seems likely that phase transitions—the loci of changes from liquid to gaseous to solid forms of materials—are an important aspect of material reality for most animals and that the perception of surfaces is, in appreciable measure at least, the perception of the loci of these transitions in material phase.

The definition of a geometric property gets gray around the edges. Differences in texture, for example, are differences in the microscopic shape of surfaces. A rough surface to a human is a mountain range to a mite. Even if we set that aside as a quibble, we are not off the hook. The panels in the corners differed not only in smell, luminance, and texture, but also in their small scale-geometry. Some had 3/8-inch holes in them, behind which the cotton wads were placed, and some did not. Why were not these purely geometric differences taken into account by the rats? This question leads to another thesis, also suggested by computational considerations.

Multiple Scales of Representation

It seems likely that animals use several different scales of spatial representation in mapping the world. We first encountered suggestions of this in the experimental studies of bee navigation. From their modeling of the process by which bees use landmarks to position themselves over food sources, Cartwright and Collett (1983) concluded that the bee filters out the contours deriving from distant objects (tens of meters at most). But later we saw that bees rely for compass bearings on landmarks like treelines, which are defined on a scale of hundreds of meters. In a similar vein, it seems likely that a desert gopher mouse knows the shape of its burrow with some accuracy. The burrow is on the order of a meter long. The mouse has a home range of about 3.4 hectares (8 acres or 16 football fields; Frank and Johnston, personal communication, March 7, 1985). It does not seem reasonable to suppose that the mouse represents the shape of those 8 acres at the same scale as it represents the shape of its burrow.

General-purpose human mappings are made at several different scales. The finest-scale high-detail maps readily available in the United States are the Geological Survey 7.5 minute quadrangle maps, done at a scale of about 5 1/4 inches to the mile. In rural areas, they show every house. No one contemplating a drive across the country would do it using these maps. A map of the U.S. at that scale would cover more than a quarter mile when unfolded. On the other hand, the scale is not sufficiently fine for the purpose of fixing residential lot boundaries, so surveyors use still finer-scale maps.

The visual system maps the visual image onto the cortex with about ten different resolutions (ten different spatial frequency domains; see Watson and Robson 1981). Marr (1982) shows how neural images of the retinal image made within different spatial frequency ranges may be computationally useful. I suggest that the brain maps the shape of behavioral space at several different scales and that a congruence computation is carried out within only one such mapping. Aspects of environmental shape too small to be resolved at the scale at which a congruence computation is done will not affect the outcome. The holes in the stimulus panels were two orders of magnitude smaller than the overall dimensions of the box, so they would not be resolvable on a mapping scaled to capture the shape of the box itself.

The thesis that animals code the shape of their environment at several different scales is motivated primarily by computational considerations. It is clear that animals know the small-scale structure of some parts of their behavioral space while also knowing the large-scale structure of that space. It does not seem reasonable to suppose that they can or would represent the whole space at the scale they would need to capture the important aspects of some parts of that space, such as their burrow. However, this thesis helps explain otherwise puzzling observations. A corollary of the thesis is that different parts of the behavioral space will be represented with different degrees of fidelity. No one makes maps of the mid-Atlantic at quadrangle scale. Similarly, it seems unlikely that the gopher mouse ever maps many parts of its home territory at the scale at which it maps its burrow and its immediate environs. It seems likely that animals make the higher-scale maps only for those parts of their behavioral space that require it—for example, parts that lie along familiar routes through that space. This hypothesis explains the otherwise puzzling observation that the bats sometimes stopped avoiding the nonexistent wire in the doorway when going in one direction through the doorway well before they stopped avoiding it when going in the other. This suggests that they used different maps of the same area when coming and going. If animals commonly go out by one route and come back by another—which was the case with the bats—and if they make fine scale maps of the territory immediately around their habitual routes— and the bats did have habitual routes requiring precise representation of the positions of the wires—then we can understand why the bat would have two different fine-scale maps of slightly different parts of the same doorway: one for use on the way in and one for use on the way out.

Place versus Response Revisited

The question whether the movements of animals through familiar spaces is mediated by elaborate chained-reflex movement programs (motor habits) or by a knowledge of spatial relations (cognitive maps) was a topic of considerable theoretical interest to psychologists in the middle decades of the present century, and interest in this question has continued to the present time (O'Keefe and Nadel 1978). The place versus response question was a focus of experimental controversy within this broader theoretical debate. Like many other experimental controversies in psychology, it was never clearly resolved. The upshot is commonly stated in secondary sources to be that the response theory is correct under some circumstances and the place theory under others.

Cheng (1984) has pointed out that his results shed a new light on this controversy. He has shown, first, that the interpreters of these experiments were not sufficiently clear in their conceptualization of what a place was and, second, that they took no account of the possibility that the definition of place depended on environmental shape alone and not on any other feature of the surfaces or objects in that environment. If one interprets the "place theory" to mean that animals move to a point defined by its position relative to the surfaces that define the space rather than by the program of movements that brings it to that point from some other known point, then, in the light of Cheng's analysis and data, it is likely that the place theory is always the correct one. Cheng showed that many of the results taken at the time as support for a response theory are in fact support for a place theory as place theory has just been defined.

Cheng's analysis points up how mischievous—from the standpoint of his own ideas—were some features of Tolman's best-known experiment, the experiment with the sunburst maze (Tolman, Ritchie, and Kalish 1946a). A rat was first taught to run to a goal via a circuitous route. This route was then blocked, and the rat was offered a choice among several different routes radiating out from the starting point. To mark the goal, Tolman et al. hung a light bulb over it. What was mischievous about this was that—to some extent in the minds of the original authors and even more so in the minds of subsequent workers and authors of secondary texts—the light bulb or some equivalent thereof was thought to be what made a place a place. The goal was at the place where the light bulb was, and the question was whether the rat could orient toward that place (toward the light bulb) or whether it would run off the motor program it might have learned, in which case it would not start off in the direction of the light bulb. From the standpoint of Cheng's conclusions, the light bulb or any other small place marker, no matter how salient, has nothing to do with the definition of a place. A place is a place by virtue of the geometric relations it bears to the surfaces in the animal's behavioral space, not by virtue of its intrinsic sensory characteristics. In fact, insofar as animals treat light bulbs as sun substitutes (and they generally do), a light bulb is a terrible place marker.

Cheng's analysis clarifies why so many seemingly minor details had such a big experimental impact. For example, one of Tolman's demonstrations of place learning came from training rats in a cross-shaped maze, with food in the arm on, say, the right (Tolman, Ritchie, and Kalish 1946b). The rats started in the lower arm at first, so that they had to turn right to get the food. Later they were started from the upper arm, and they immediately turned left rather than right, reaching the same place by a different set of movements. Later the same authors did a seemingly similar study, but this time they used a T maze rather than a cross-shaped maze (Tolman, Ritchie, and Kalish 1947). When it came time to test for response versus place learning, they rotated the maze 180° and tested whether the rat now turned left instead of right. Their intuitive conception of what constituted a place suggested to them that the rat should turn left toward the same place just as readily in this experiment as in their earlier experiment. In fact, the results were not nearly so favorable to the place theory. The response-learning group, which had to learn to turn right after as well as before the rotation, did better, while the place learning group, which had to turn right before the rotation and left afterward, did more poorly than in the earlier experiment.

Once it is realized that place is defined by geometric relations alone, it is apparent why the experiment with the cross-shaped maze should favor results consistent with Tolman et al.'s conception of a place response, while the experiment with the T maze should yield results more consistent with their conception of a "response" response. The T maze version of the experiment puts the definition of place with respect to the maze itself in conflict with the definition of place with respect to the larger framework, whereas the cross-shaped maze experiment does not. Rotating the T maze changes some of the geometric relations in the animal's behavioral space (all those relations involving both points in the maze and points outside the maze) while not altering others (all those relations involving only points in the maze or only points outside the maze). What the rats do when confronted by this alteration cannot be predicted unless one knows just which points the animal happens to attend when it makes its choice. One can predict, however, that isolating the maze as much as possible from the larger framework so that it is more difficult for the animal to sense the change in the geometric relation between the maze and the rest of the world will greatly favor the animal's choosing arms on the basis of the shape of the maze rather than on the basis of the shape of the rest of the world, which was in fact what was observed in those experiments whose results were generally taken to favor a response interpretation.

Scharlock (1955), for example, surrounded the T maze with heavy curtains in the form of a square, so that a rotation of the maze in any multiple of 90° was indistinguishable from the original geometric relation between the maze and its surroundings. To define a place in this larger environment, Scharlock followed the Tolman et al. lead and hung light bulbs. Scharlock explicitly defined a place response as moving toward "certain features of the extramaze environment." This way of defining place has carried down to the present day in the tendency to define place responding as responding based on extramaze stimuli (e.g., Olton et al. 1979). Scharlock rotated the maze 180° from trial to trial. One group of rats had to learn always to turn right—in Scharlock's conception of this experiment. In Cheng's conception of the experiment, this group had to learn to go to the same place within the framework established by the shape of the maze—the only shape they had ready perceptual access to. The other group—the place learning group—had to learn always to turn toward the light bulb, in Scharlock's conception of the experiment. In Cheng's conception, this group had to learn to ignore the spatial framework established by the asymmetrical maze itself and attend only to the framework established by the symmetrical curtained enclosure plus the light bulb. At the scale appropriate for establishing a congruence between perceived and remembered space in this experiment, the light bulb was probably a single point; hence it, unlike the maze itself, would make little contribution to a computation of the shape parameters of the space as a whole or to any evaluation of overall congruence. Not surprisingly, the response group learned more readily than the place group. In Cheng's analysis, this result simply verifies the predominance of global shape in the definition of place. The 200-watt light, despite its salience, makes a negligible contribution to defining the global shape of the experimental environment, while the asymmetrical T maze makes a large contribution. Thus the rat chooses a place as defined in a coordinate system anchored to the maze.

Whereas light bulbs carry only the weight of single points in the evaluation of a congruence between perceived and remembered spaces (or in the computation of shape parameters), large objects should make a much greater contribution to these computations, hence a much greater contribution to the psychologically appropriate definition of a place. We have already seen a suggestion of this in the experiments involving bats' avoiding wires in a doorway. When the rack of bat cages was moved to a different position in the starting room, the bats seemed disoriented and reluctant to fly through the doorway, even though the cages played no role in the experimental sessions themselves. Ritchie (1947) made a similar observation in the course of one of his experiments. He was running rats in a T maze in the center of a square room, using a 200-watt light as an extramaze orientation point for the rats. The T maze was rotated 180° between trials and the rats were trained always to go to one place in the room, that is, enter the arm which pointed either toward or away from the light bulb. When the rats had learned this, Ritchie moved the light bulb to the other side of the room, but the rats continued to choose the same arm as before, to Ritchie's surprise. The rack of cages in which the rats were housed between experimental sessions was always in one corner of the room. When Ritchie moved that rack to the rotationally equivalent location in the other corner of the room, the majority of the rats immediately began to choose the other arm of the T maze. In short, the large rack of cages at some distance from the experimental apparatus had much more weight in the rats' global congruence calculations than did the light bulb, despite the unusual brightness of the bulb and its undoubted salience for the rats.

The Distinction between Landmarks and Signs

The repeated failure of the rats in Cheng's experiments to use nongeometric attributes of surfaces in determining what places in the currently perceived environment corresponded to places in a previously perceived environment must not be taken to indicate that place—and therefore the shape of the environment—is the only basis on which a rat will choose where to go in looking for food. There have been many T maze experiments in which the positions of a black and a white arm (or black and white cards in the Lashley jumping stand) were interchanged on a random schedule, and the rat learned to choose the baited arm (or card) regardless of its position (for a review of the literature on brightness discrimination in the rat, see Munn 1950). The nonpositional properties of an arm will also serve as a basis for rats' choices in the radial maze paradigm. Olton and Feustle (1981) used a four-armed maze, in which the rats could be confined to the center after each choice. The arms were differentiated one from the other in a variety of ways (painted patterns, grooves down the center, texture of the surfaces, etc.). After each choice, the positions of these arms were randomly permuted, so that the rats could not choose correctly on the basis of position. Rats learned to choose arms on the basis of their intrinsic nonpositional properties almost as readily as when they could choose on the basis of position (see also Jarrard 1983).

There are several differences between Cheng's paradigms and those in which rats learn to choose arms on some basis other than position. First, although Cheng differentiated his corner landmarks in many and salient ways and although these landmarks were very close to the places where food was found, it is important to bear in mind that in all cases, the panels formed part of the continuous surface that enclosed the experimental space. They were not separate objects, on which, under which, in which, behind which, or next to which the food was found. By contrast, paradigms in which rats orient by nonpositional properties of objects almost always involve distinct objects, in relation to which the food may be sought. In the T maze and radial maze experiments, the food was in an arm with a particular color. In experiments with the Lashley jumping stand, it was behind a door with certain properties, and so on. Another difference is that Cheng intentionally made it difficult for the rat to establish its sense of spatial position except by reference to the enclosure. This was seldom the case in experiments where rats learned to choose on the basis of nonpositional properties. The importance of this may be that choice based on other features occurs only when the animal has a secure sense of position. In any event, there is no doubt that animals including the rat can and do orient their locomotion toward objects selected on bases other than their position in the behavioral space. What Cheng's thesis appears to establish is the need to distinguish between landmarks—features of the terrain used in establishing one's position and heading in a mapped space—and signs—indicating the location of a goal whose location varies over time.

Cheng's thesis further indicates that rats do not generally use nongeometric signs to establish their heading in a familiar space and that when they do use such signs, they use them indirectly. They use them as an indication that they are misoriented, but not in computing the correct orientation. Remembered locations are relocated by way of a calculated congruence between the cognitive map and currently perceived space. The congruence calculation is impenetrable to anything except information about the relative positions of surfaces. It works with shape alone.

Summary

When care is taken that rats are geocentrically disoriented, they misorient themselves within an axially symmetric rectangular enclosure on 50 percent of the trials. Their misorientation is manifest in their going to the place that is the rotational equivalent of their goal—the place their goal would occupy if the floor of the environment were rotated 180°. The nature of this disorientation is strong evidence that the rats have a representation of the shape of the environment that includes the uniquely metric relations and sense. If their representation of the shape of the environment did not capture either of these two classes of relations, they would confuse a place with three other places, the places their goal would occupy if the rectangle were compressed into the shape of a square and then rotated by any integer multiple of 90°. However, there is no tendency to confuse their goal place with any place other than the rotationally equivalent place. Because a rectangle is congruent with itself when rotated 180°, there is no way to distinguish a place from its rotational equivalent in a computation that relies on environmental shape alone. Thus, rotational confusions are to be expected if the system takes its heading solely on the basis of the shape of the environment.

Rotational confusions occur even when multimodally salient sensory features of the enclosure distinguish one end from the other. There was no nongeometric attribute of a surface that Cheng and I could discover— not maximal differences in the reflectances of major surfaces, or strong odors, or distinctive surface textures (feels), or distinctive patterns of pinhole lights—that would reduce the tendency to make rotational confusions. The rats would use the distinctive features of corner panels to choose between two corners that were indistinguishable on geometric ground alone, but they would not use these features in taking their heading within the enclosure.

These findings lead me to suggest that the cognitive map represents only the (Euclidean) shape of the environment and that the rat gets its heading and position on its map by finding the rotation and translation required to produce a congruence (shape match) between the currently perceived shape of the environment and a corresponding region of its map. The sensory attributes peculiar to a place may be stored separately, with a spatial address (set of coordinates) identifying their position in the environment.

Chapter 7

Biological and Computational Foundations for the Representation of Time

Space is one fundamental behavioral matrix; time is the other. Animals ranging from insects to humans record the time of occurrence of an event or observation. They also extract elapsed intervals. This capacity is the foundation of the capacity to represent the temporal structure of experience. A representation of the temporal structure of experience makes it possible for an animal to predicate its behavior on what may be predicted to occur, that is, to adapt its behavior to the temporal structure of the events in its behavioral space.

Biological Rhythms

Living systems contain self-sustaining biochemical and biophysical oscillations that play an important role in the control of animal behavior. Anticipations of this now-well-established fact may be traced back some centuries, but it is only in the last two decades that a large body of compelling experimental evidence has been marshaled in support of this idea and that biologists have come to appreciate the general importance of endogenous oscillations in the timing of biological processes. In the first half of the seventeenth century, William Harvey observed that pieces of isolated heart muscle continued to contract rhythmically. By the end of the nineteenth century, it had been established that this rhythm was determined by processes within the muscle tissue itself. The rhythmic contractions were not driven by any external rhythmic stimulus, nor did they involve self-excitation; that is, the next contraction was not stimulated by the effects of the preceding contraction. The experiments establishing this were known to Sherrington and probably to other neurobiologists of his time, yet Sherrington and most others (Brown 1914, being a notable exception) viewed the function of the central nervous system (CNS) entirely in terms of the conduction of the excitation elicited by stimuli acting on specialized receptors. They did not imagine that self-sustaining oscillatory excitation and inhibition processes in the CNS played a fundamental role in the patterning of motor output (see Gallistel 1980). Von Holst (1939) was the first to explore systematically the role that endogenous oscillators played in the genesis of locomotory motor patterns. His work did not gain attention outside Germany until the 1960s, when neurobiologists began to appreciate the ubiquity and complexity of endogenously generated and patterned rhythmic neural discharges. (For recent reviews of the cellular mechanisms underlying short-term rhythmic electrical activity, see Connor 1985; Roberts and Roberts 1983.)

Von Holst worked with oscillations whose periods ranged from fractions of a second to a few seconds, but endogenous oscillations with periods many orders of magnitude longer also play a fundamental role in the timing of physiological and behavioral processes. Experimental demonstrations of the fact that daily rhythms of activity are commonly controlled by endogenous circadian oscillators (self-sustaining oscillations with a period of approximately 24 hours) begin with the work of Bünning (1936), Darwin (1881), Richter (1922) and Szymanski (1920). In the thirties, the possibly endogenous nature of tidal, lunar and annual variations in behavior began to be appreciated (Stein-Beling 1935). However, the behavioral importance of long-period endogenous oscillators was not widely recognized until several years after the publication of Bünning's (1958) influential monograph *Die Physiologische Uhr* (*The physiological clock;* Bünning 1973). As recently as 1969, Ornstein, in his monograph on the experience of time in animals and humans, dismissed this work as of no clear relevance. In the last two decades, the study of endogenous long-period oscillations and their role in the control of behavior has become an industry. There are numerous reviews, covering aspects of the phenomena ranging from the behavioral down to the molecular, in organisms ranging from man to the unicellular (e.g., Aschoff 1981; Jacklet 1985; Turek 1985).

The idea that animals can represent time has been resisted at least in part because it was difficult to imagine a plausible physiological basis for this representational capacity (Adams 1977). Now, however, we know that multicellular organisms are Gepetto's workshops, stocked with endogenous oscillators whose periods range from seconds or less, to minutes, to hours, to days, to weeks, to a year (see Aschoff 1981 and Farner 1985 for reviews of the experimental literature demonstrating endogenous oscillations at each of these periods). When a system contains within itself oscillations with widely different periods, it can represent the time at which something occurred by recording the momentary states (phases) of these oscillatory processes. The endogenous oscillators provide a physiological foundation for the capacity to represent time. They are the internal clock.

If the recorded readings on internal clocks are used to anticipate recurrences at the same phases in subsequent cycles, the internal cycle must remain synchronized to an external cycle. No physically realizable oscillation is perfectly periodic, and no two physical oscillations have exactly the same period. If external oscillations, such as the day-night cycle, the tidal cycle, and the lunar cycle had no effect on physiological oscillations with roughly corresponding periods, then the two oscillations—the external and the internal—would not be synchronized. From the phase (position in the cycle) of the internal oscillation, one could not predict the phase of the external oscillation. Hence the internal oscillation would be of no use in coordinating the organism's activity with the periodically recurring events in the external world. However, endogenous oscillations respond to certain periodically recurring extrinsic events in such a way as to maintain a fixed phase relationship between the two cyclical processes, that is, in such a way that a given phase in the endogenous oscillation always coincides with a given phase (or set of phases) in the extrinsic oscillation. The process by which the influence of one oscillation on another holds that other oscillation in a fixed or pre-ferred phase relationship is called entrainment. Endogenous self-sus-taining oscillations enable animals to synchronize their activity with cycles in the environment (and with their conspecifics) because these oscillations are entrained by timing signals from extrinsic oscillations or from other oscillators within the same organism.

Figure 7.1 gives an example of the entrainment of the daily activity rhythm in the cockroach. Movements of the roach were picked up by a sensitive detector. Each detected movement caused a brief downward deviation in the pen on a slowly running event recorder (a blip). The continuous record of movements was cut into 24-hour segments, which were mounted one immediately beneath the next to produce the display. On this display one can visualize the recurring daily variations in the roach's overall activity and follow their changing relation to the earth's day-night cycle. The light-dark cycle in the experimental enclosure is given by the bar at the top of the display. In the records for the first twenty days, there is an abrupt onset of activity shortly after the lights go out. A burst of dusk-onset activity is extremely common in animals that are most active at night. There are recurring bouts of activity during the remainder of the night, but very little activity during the day (lights-on) period.

One might suppose that these variations in activity are exogenous—that the darkness elicits activity and the light suppresses it. Experiment demonstrates that this supposition is false. On day 20, the experimenter painted over the roach's eyes, so that it could no longer detect light. The roach continued to show a pronounced daily variation in its activity, but the onset of activity no longer maintained a fixed phase relationship to the light-dark cycle. The daily variation in the blinded roach's activity was controlled by an endogenous oscillator with a period of about $23\frac{1}{2}$ hours. Because the period of the endogenous oscillation was shorter than that of the extrinsic oscillation (the period of the light-dark cycle) and because the extrinsic oscillation could no longer entrain the endogenous one, the roach's activity began 30 minutes sooner each day. This phase-drift produces the steady day-by-day shift to the left seen between days 20 and 50 in figure 7.1. A drift line has been drawn in on the figure to high-light the drift in dusk-onset activity. This line has an x/y slope of $+.5/24$, a half-hour phase advance per 24-hour day. After 24 days, the onset of activity coincided with the onset rather than the offset of the lights. The internally determined "subjective" dusk now coincided with objective dawn.

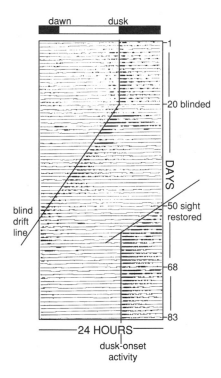

Figure 7.1
Record of the locomotor activity of a roach. The bar at top shows the (artificial) day-night cycle. At day 20, the eyes of the roach were covered with nail polish. Its internal clock was no longer entrained and free ran with a period of 23 hours, 30 minutes, with a consequent steady leftward phase drift of 30 minutes per day. On day 50, sight was restored. The entraining influence of the day-night cycle accelerated the internal clock (note change in slope of drift line) until it came into phase with the day-night cycle, then held it there (phase locking). (Modified from Roberts 1965, by permission of author and publisher.)

The phase-drift seen in the middle portion (days 20–50) of figure 7.1 is indicative of a free-running oscillation, the oscillation seen when an endogenous oscillator is not subject to an entraining influence. At day 50, the experimenter peeled the nail polish off the roach's eyes so that it could again see. Now we see clearly that the onset of the roach's activity at dusk is not a response to the extinguishing of the lights. For the first 8 days following the restoration of its sight, the roach's activity begins some while after the lights go off. The onset of activity is controlled by an endogenous oscillator (clock), which is running behind the extrinsic light-dark cycle. The roach's activity does not begin at lights out because the endogenous oscillator has not reached the activity-initiating point in its cycle when the lights go off. However, now that the roach can again see, the endogenous oscillator is again subject to the entraining influence of the light-dark cycle, as may be seen from the drift line for the period immediately after day 50. The drift in the onset of activity is faster now than the free-running drift. The transitions from dark to light and light to dark are not eliciting and suppressing activity, but, when they fall, as they now do, a few hours too late with respect to the endogenous cycle, they transiently accelerate the endogenous oscillator. They set the roach's internal clock ahead about a half hour each day, so that the drift line during entrainment has an x/y slope of $1/24$, or 1 hour per day. These daily phase advances eventually bring the internal clock into the proper phase relationship with the extrinsic cycle. On day 58, the endogenous oscillation catches up with the extrinsic one and locks into the proper phase relationship. From there on, the endogenously timed onset of activity coincides with the exogenously timed lights out, which makes it look as though the extinguishing of the lights initiates activity. At this point, the endogenous oscillation is said to be entrained to the extrinsic cycle.

The principle underlying entrainment mechanisms is that the direction or sign of the receiving oscillator's response to a timing signal depends on its phase at the moment the timing signal arrives. The response of a marcher to the beat of the drum illustrates the principle. If the marcher hears the timing signal after his foot has struck the ground, he slows his step, so that his next footfall coincides more nearly with the timing signal. If he hears the timing signal (drumbeat) before his foot has struck the ground, he accelerates his next step, which again makes the next footfall coincide more closely with the drumbeat. The marcher's response to the timing signal—whether decelerating or accelerating his step—depends on where in his stepping cycle he hears the drum—before or after the fall of his foot. Phase means position within a cycle; thus, the marcher's response is phase dependent.

The mechanism that entrains the endogenous circadian cycle to the extrinsic day-night cycle operates by the same principle, as is shown in figure 7.2, which plots the activity patterns of a hamster, using a common variant on the method used in figure 7.1. Again, there is a slow-running event recorder, which makes a blip on the time line every time the hamster does something, in this case, every time it makes a running wheel go around. The record is cut into 24-hour segments, which are mounted one below the other, as before. The 24-hour display is then photographed at a 1-1 scale and the photographic reproduction is mounted alongside the original, but one line up from it, to produce the 48-hour "double-day" display seen in figure 7.2. In a double-day display, the first line shows days 1 and 2, the second days 2 and 3, the third days 3 and 4, and so on. Double-day displays make it easier to follow the drift in a daily bout of activity when the bout extends across the 24-hour line where the records are cut. In such cases, the beginning of a bout appears on the right of one segment (the end of one day) while the rest of the bout appears on the left of the next segment below (the beginning of the next day). The artificial breaking up of a continuous bout of activity into what appear to be two bouts is confusing. By mounting a reproduction of the 24-hour display to the right and one line up, the experimenter makes the continuation of a bout of activity (in the reproduction) continuous with its onset (in the original). In looking at this display, one must bear in mind that the display is now 48 hours wide and that each daily record is shown twice: first in the right half of a line and then again in the left half of the line below.

The hamster in figure 7.2 was in constant darkness. The sharp onset of its running wheel activity at approximately daily intervals was controlled by an endogenous oscillation, running 11 minutes per day fast (its period was 23.8 hours). This produces the steady, slow, leftward drift of activity onset as one scans down the display. When Pittendrigh had established the free-running period of the circadian oscillator in this animal, he introduced timing signals at various phases of the endogenous cycle. The timing signal was a 15-minute light pulse. Each dot on the right side of the display indicates the delivery of a light pulse. These dots tend to obscure the response of the oscillator, but remember that the record is duplicated; to see the unobscured response of the oscillation to each light pulse, look at the drift in activity onset on the left side of the display.

The first such pulse was delivered early in the hamster's nightly activity bout, that is, early in the subjective night, the phase of the endogenous oscillation that coincides with the dark phase of the extrinsic cycle under natural (entrained) conditions. When delivered early in the subjective night the timing signal produced a phase delay of about one-nineteenth of a cycle. That is, in the next 24-hour period, the onset of

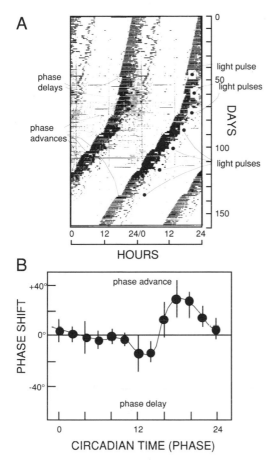

Figure 7.2
Derivation of the phase-response curve for the internal clock of a hamster. *A.* Activity
record in double-day form. During the first 40 days, the animal free ran in constant
darkness (note steady small phase drift). Thereafter, it received a series of 15 minute pulses
of bright light delivered at various points in its internal cycle (dots). The first few pulses,
delivered soon after the onset of activity, retard the internal clock (shift subsequent days'
activity onsets to the right). Later pulses, delivered during the inactive phase, accelerate the
internal clock (shift activity onsets to the left). *B.* The magnitude of the phase advances and
delays as a function of the phase of the internal clock at the time the pulse was delivered.
(Based on figure in Pittendrigh 1980.)

activity occurred about 1 hour and 15 minutes later than it would had the light pulse not been given (the rightward notch in the onset of activity). In the days following the phase shift produced by the light pulse, the endogenous oscillator continued to drift at the same rate as before the phase shift; only its phase was altered. The stability in the free-running period of the hamster's endogenous circadian oscillator made it possible for Pittendrigh to measure the effects of timing signals with some precision.

The second light pulse was delivered somewhat later in the hamster's subjective night. It, too, produced a phase delay of about one-nineteenth of a cycle (or $19° = 1.25hrs/23.8hrs \times 360°$). By contrast, the third pulse, delivered still later in the subjective night, produced a small phase advance—the onset of the next bout of activity occurred slightly sooner than it would have without the timing signal (the leftward displacement of activity onset seen opposite the third dot). Pulses delivered still later produced large phase advances (larger leftward shifts in activity onset).

The hamster's circadian oscillator is like the marcher: when the timing signal arrives at certain phases of its cycle, it slows down; when it arrives at others, it speeds up. Just as this pattern of responding to the timing signal holds the marcher more or less in step with the drummer, so this response of the circadian oscillator holds it in a fixed phase relationship to the extrinsic day-night cycle. The data from a number of experiments like this are shown in figure 7.2B. The curve through the data in figure 7.2B is called the phase-response curve because it plots the oscillator's response to the timing signal as a function of the phase of the oscillator when the timing signal arrives. To a first approximation, the phase-response curve may be thought of as the rule the system follows for resetting its internal clock when it gets a timing signal from the external world. This rule is phase dependent; the system sets its internal clock either somewhat ahead or somewhat back depending on what the clock is reading when the timing signal is received. The phase-response curve for an entrainable oscillation determines the phase relationship it will assume with respect to the periodic entraining signal

The timing signal that holds an oscillation in some fixed phase relationship to another oscillation need not have the same period as the oscillation it entrains. Endogenous oscillations with very different periods may nonetheless maintain a more or less fixed phase relationship through an exchange of timing signals. Many rodents have an ultradian (faster than daily) activity rhythm with a period of 1.5-3 hours. There is a similar rhythm in the behavioral and physiological functioning of other mammals, including humans. This rhythm is most apparent in human sleep patterns (Webb and Dube 1981). In some rodents (such as voles), this rhythm has a fixed phase relationship to the circadian rhythm (figure

7.3), which is maintained even when the circadian oscillation is free-running (figure 7.4). Thus, endogenous oscillations with different periods may maintain a fixed relationship, just as do the hands on a clock. On a clock, the period of the second hand is 1 minute, the period of the minute hand 1 hour, and the period of the hour hand 12 hours, but the phase relationship among these cycles is fixed. The second hand completes its circle just as the minute hand indicates the minute, and the minute hand completes its circle just as the hour hand indicates the hour.

The ultradian activity rhythm in rodents has not been conclusively shown to depend on a distinct endogenous oscillator. Another possibility is that each bout of activity is triggered when the circadian oscillator arrives at a different phase in its cycle. However, a variety of findings suggest that the ultradian rhythm depends on a separate oscillator (Daan and Aschoff 1981). First among these is the fact that in some rodents the rhythm is not phase locked to the circadian rhythm (Cowcroft 1954). If the shorter rhythm were produced by trigger points (trigger phases) spaced 2.4 hours apart in the circadian oscillation, this rhythm would always be phase locked to the circadian rhythm, but if there is a separate oscillator, it may or may not be phase locked to the circadian oscillator,

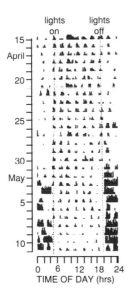

Figure 7.3
Records of vole wheel running in the presence of an entraining day-night cycle. Note the pronounced ultradian rhythm (rhythm with a period much shorter than 24 hours) and the fact that this rhythm is phase locked to the day-night cycle (the short and repeated bouts of activity occur at the same time each day). (Reproduced from Erkinano 1969, by permission of author and publisher.)

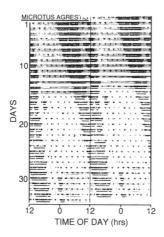

MICROTUS AGRESTI...

DAYS

TIME OF DAY (hrs)

Figure 7.4.
Activity records of free-running voles (not entrained by a day-night cycle). Note that the ultradian rhythm in their behavior is still prominent and that it is synchronized to the
circadian rhythm; that is, the little bursts of activity appear in the same positions from day
to day in the circadian cycle of variation in the overall level of activity. (Reproduced from
Lehmann 1976, by permission of author and publisher.)

depending on whether it receives an effective timing signal from the circadian oscillation. Even in voles, where the shorter rhythm is clearly
phase locked to the longer rhythm, one sees occasionally some drift in the
phase relationship between the ultradian and circadian cycles (see, for
example, Aschoff 1984, p. 456). These drifts are most readily explained by
the assumption that there are two distinct oscillators.

   Another set of findings strongly suggesting separate oscillators is that
the period of the short-term rhythm is systematically affected by nutritional factors that have no effect on the period of the circadian oscillation.
Factors that increase the amount of food the vole must consume, such as
lactation or increases in the cellulose (nonnutritive) content of its diet,
shorten the period of the ultradian oscillation but not the period of the
circadian oscillation (Daan and Aschoff 1981). This is readily explained
if we assume that the ultradian rhythm is driven by its own endogenous
oscillator. It is difficult to explain if we assume that it is driven by
different trigger phases of the circadian oscillator.

   The effect of nutritional factors on the ultradian rhythm might lead one
to suppose that it is driven by the filling and emptying of the stomach or
by some other metabolic cycle in which the ingestion of food plays a
pivotal role, but this is not the case. The rhythm persists even when the
vole has no access to food or water (Daan and Slopsema 1978). The same
is true in the rat (unpublished observations by the author).

The fact that nutritional factors shorten or lengthen the period of the ultradian activity rhythm illustrates another fundamental form of sensory control over endogenous oscillations. Most endogenous oscillations are influenced by extrinsic inputs in two ways. Transient extrinsic inputs may serve as timing signals that shift the phase of the oscillator to a different part of its cycle, as we have already seen. In addition, tonic (slowly changing) extrinsic inputs may modulate the period of an endogenous oscillation. For example, the free-running period of most circadian oscillators is lengthened by increasing the steady level of environmental illumination (figure 7.5). The nervous input to the heart functions in this way too. The nerve signal does not drive the heartbeat, but it does control the rate of beating. A change in the rate of firing of the vagus nerve changes the rate at which the heart beats, but the heart is not beating in response to any periodic firing of the nerve; it will beat in the absence of any neural input. Signals that govern the period of an oscillator determine where the weight on the pendulum of the endogenous metronome is set.

Recording Moments in Time

Mechanisms or processes that make possible the recording of moments in time and the determination of temporal intervals come in two basic forms: oscillatory processes and nonoscillatory decay or accumulation processes.

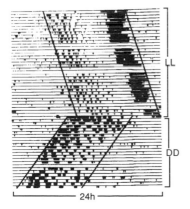

Figure 7.5
The effect of ambient light on the period of the free-running circadian activity rhythm of a cockroach. Under high ambient light (*LL*), the period of the internal clock is longer than 24 hours, and the phase of activity onset drifts rightward. In darkness (*DD*), the internal clock completes a cycle in less than 24 hours, and the phase of activity onset drifts leftward. (Reproduced from Lohmann 1967, by permission of author and publisher.)

Methods Based on Oscillatory Processes

Oscillatory processes are processes that repeat themselves at regular intervals. The duration of the interval is called the period of the oscillation. Oscillations are commonly produced through the interaction of two or more physical variables. The values of these variables at a given moment describe or specify the state of the process at that moment, otherwise called its phase. Consider a vibrating guitar string: The relevant variables in the physical description of this oscillation are the momentary position of the string (above or below its resting or zero position) and its velocity (how fast it is moving upward or downward). To specify the momentary state of the vibration, one must specify both of these quantities. The description of the process may be thought of graphically as the coordinates of a point in a two-dimensional Cartesian framework (figure 7.6A). One axis of the framework (the y-axis in figure 7.6A) gives the string's distance above (+) or below (–) its resting position. The other axis (the x-axis in figure 7.6A) gives the upward (+) or downward (–) velocity of the string. When the point specifying the phase or momentary state of the vibration is at the top of the circle in figure 7.6, at coordinates <0,1>, the string has reached its uppermost displacement (arbitrarily designated a displacement of one unit in figure 7.6), and its upward velocity has completely dissipated, so that at this moment it has 0 velocity. When the string passes downward through its resting position, it attains its maximum downward velocity (again arbitrarily scaled to -1); hence the point is at <–1,0> on the graph at this moment.

As the string vibrates, the point on the graph of its displacement and velocity traces out a trajectory. The trajectory is a closed curve because after a while the trajectory meets itself. This occurs when the displacement and velocity of the vibrating string have the same values at the present moment as they did at some earlier moment. Among such closed trajectories are some to which others tend to converge. The closed curves to which other closed curves tend to converge are called limit-cycle curves. The oscillations they describe are called limit-cycle oscillations. For example, the trajectory of the string in the first cycle of vibration after the string is plucked and released is a closed curve, but it is not a limit cycle because the subsequent back-and-forth motions of the string do not repeat this first motion. The string rapidly settles into a harmonic vibration, in which the back-and-forth motion does repeat itself from one cycle to the next. (I ignore the gradual damping out of the oscillation seen in real guitar strings.) The trajectory for this regular vibration is the limit-cycle oscillation to which the non-limit-cycle initial or transient trajectory converges.

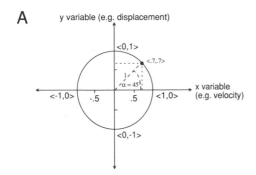

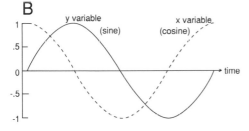

Figure 7.6.
The graphic representation of the variables in an oscillatory process. *A.* The phase-plane representation has the value of one state variable along one axis and the value of another along the other. A point in this representation defines a momentary state of the system in that the coordinates of the point give the values of the two state variables at that moment. Harmonic oscillations describe circular trajectories in the phase plane. Thus, the state of the oscillation may also be described by an angle (the so-called phase angle), which for the point shown is 45°. The Cartesian coordinates of the point are equal to the cosine and sine of the phase angle because the axes have been scaled to make the radius of the circle equal to 1. *B.* The sine-cosine representation of angle as a function of time plots the values of the state variables as functions of time. When the maximum and minimum values of the variables are set equal to one, then these functions are the sine (*y*-variable) and cosine (*x*-variable) functions. By recording the momentary values of these variables, a system specifies a momentary state of the oscillator (a reading of the clock). This yields a specification of time unique up to a translation by an integer number of periods along the temporal axis.

The portrayal of the oscillatory process in figure 7.6A is called the phase-plane representation because each point in this Cartesian plane is a potential description of some momentary state (phase) of the process. The two axes of the framework are called the state variables because they are the variables whose values describe the state of the process. Because the plot of the value of one of these variables as a function of the value of the other generally yields a circle or circle-like trajectory in the phase plane, it is also natural to consider representing the state of the oscillation by polar coordinates rather than Cartesian coordinates. There is a simple relation between these two representations. If we scale our measures of the state variables appropriately, we may make the radius of the limit cycle equal to 1. Then the state of the oscillation is given by the angular coordinate of the polar representation (a in figure 7.6A). This value is called the phase angle of the oscillation. Since we have made the radius of the polar system equal to 1, the x and y coordinates in the Cartesian representation of the state of the oscillation are equal to the cosine and sine, respectively, of the phase angle (see figure 7.6). The artifice of scaling the state variables in such a way as to make the radius of the limit cycle equal to 1 brings out the fact that the Cartesian coordinates are proportionate to the cosine and sine of the angle coordinate in a polar representation (the phase angle). The advantage of the sine-cosine representation of phase over the angle representation is that the Cartesian (sine-cosine) representation is everywhere continuous, whereas the angular representation is discontinuous at the end of each cycle, when the phase angle drops discontinuously from 360° (or 2π, etc.) to 0.

The phase-plane graph of an oscillatory process does not show how the values of the variables change with time; it just shows how these interdependent values relate to one another at any point in the cycle. When we plot the state variables as functions of time, we get the sine-cosine graph in figure 7.6B, assuming we are dealing with a harmonic oscillation, like that of a guitar string. If the oscillation is not harmonic, the plots of the state variables as functions of time do not have so symmetrical and aesthetically pleasing a form, but they have qualitatively the same form, which is all that matters. One variable rises to a peak as the other falls to near zero; then as the other continues its fall past zero toward negative values (or toward the lowest value it attains during the cycle), the first variable begins to decline. As the first variable approaches zero, the second attains its minimum and begins to increase; it continues this increase while the other drops to its minimum and then begins to increase again. The physical variables underlying any limit-cycle oscillation exhibit this general pattern of variation over time.

The manner in which the variables underlying a limit-cycle oscillation vary with time makes it possible to specify any moment (any phase) within a period of oscillation by recording the values of the two variables at that time, or, to say the same thing in a different way, by recording the coordinates for the momentary position of the point on the limit-cycle trajectory. If the passage of time is marked by an oscillatory process, then moments in time are specified by two interrelated quantities that describe the state of the oscillatory process at that moment (the phase of the process).

This manner of recording moments in time works only over the period of a single oscillation. The values of the sine and cosine components of the circadian oscillation distinguish between moments within a day, but they do not distinguish between a moment on day 1 and the corresponding moment on day 2, and so on. If time is specified by the sine and cosine components of an oscillatory process, then the specification is unique only up to a displacement along the time axis equal to an integer multiple of the period of the oscillation. This means that a memory for moments in time based on the recorded values of the components of an oscillatory process does not distinguish between corresponding moments in different periods of the longest oscillation contributing to the record. In principle, one cannot derive from such a record temporal intervals longer than the period of the slowest oscillation. For many animals, this may not matter. The bee may live for the day and do so without cost. Since in summer it lives only about three weeks, it is not clear that it has any need to distinguish the events of one day from those of another, so we may not be surprised to find that a bee cannot recognize that something happens only every other day.

Longer lived animals do distinguish the events of one day from the events of another. A bird recognizes that something happens only every other day. This may mean simply that the bird's coding of moments in time includes values derived from oscillators with periods of, say, a month and/or a year. Circannual oscillations—endogenous oscillations with a period of approximately a year—have been demonstrated in a variety of longer-lived animals (Gwinner 1981; Farner 1985). It is an interesting question whether any of these animals distinguishes the events of one year from the events of another. The question is not whether memory reaches back further than a year; it is whether the code by which the nervous system records the time at which an event occurred permits it to distinguish the events of one year from the events of another. Whenever we have evidence that an animal distinguishes the events that occurred in one cycle from those that occurred at the same phase in another cycle (such as the same time on another day), we must assume that its temporal record includes coordinates that come from a yet slower oscillation, whose period embraces several complete cycles of the faster oscillation. If all one notes is the time of day at which something happens, not the day of the week, then the mnemonic system does not distinguish between the successive occurrence of three different events at the same time on different days and their simultaneous occurrence on a single day.

In principle, only one oscillatory process is needed to supply recorded time coordinates (quantities that specify a moment in time), provided that the period of that oscillation extends over the full interval within which the system needs to distinguish between moments. In practice, however, the mechanism that must read the record will almost certainly not be able to distinguish reliably between recorded quantities that are nearly the same. The quantitative resolution in the process that records the momentary magnitudes of the state variables must have a limit. This means that the system will not be able to distinguish moments separated by seconds if it records moments in time by storing the values that describe the momentary state of a circannual oscillation. One is led to assume that to span an appreciable interval and yet retain the ability to discriminate small differences in recorded times of occurrence, a time-recording system based on oscillators would need to refer to several different oscillations, whose periods spanned several orders of magnitude. To be useful, these oscillations would have to exchange timing signals so as to maintain their phase relationships at least to some extent, that is, at least for oscillators with adjacent periods. Thus, a versatile time-recording system based on oscillators would need to record the momentary values of the state variables in each of several different phase-locked oscillations, just as we record the second, minute, hour, day, month, and year using clocks that are phase locked to the daily cycles and calendars that include leap years to keep the days and months phase locked to the years.

There is evidence that the timing of some innately programmed organismic behaviors is controlled by multiple oscillations in the manner envisaged. The best evidence comes from observations of the reproductive behavior of organisms that reproduce for only a very brief interval each year. In these organisms, the synchronized release of sperm and eggs is crucial. For example, the swarming of the eptokous segments and the release of gametes by the marine Palolo worm *Eunice viridis*, which is found on some beaches in the South Pacific, occurs mostly during one 2-hour period just after midnight during the last quarter of the harvest moon in late October or early November (Caspers 1961; Hauenschild, Fischer, and Hoffman 1960). It is likely that this act of mass reproduction is synchronized by the combined operation of circannual, circalunar, and circatidal or circadian oscillations within each of the thousands of individual organisms.

Methods Based on Decay or Accumulation Processes
A moment in time may also be committed to memory by recording the value for a quantity that decays or accumulates monotonically. Radioactive decay, for example, enables us to determine the times at which various organic and inorganic compounds formed. Unlike methods based on recording the states of oscillatory processes, this method has the advantage that it does not confound different moments in time—moments that correspond to recurring phases of a cyclical process. On the other hand, one of the reasons for recording the times of occurrence of events is because so many behaviorally important events do recur periodically. A disadvantage of a method based on noncyclical decay or accumulation processes is that it does not lead readily to the representation of periodicity in experience. Another disadvantage is that the method must either work for only a very short interval or it must have very poor resolution. If something is to serve to differentiate moments in time over a long interval, it must decay or accumulate slowly, which means that it will not serve to differentiate closely spaced times of occurrence. Carbon 14 dating is useful for specifying the century in which a camp fire was built but not which year.

The most attractive system is a mixed one in which the slowest oscillation in the system provides an input to a counter. In such a system, an oscillatory process provides the input to a linear accumulation process (the counting process). This mixed method permits the system to distinguish temporal intervals with arbitrary precision over arbitrarily long periods. Modern man certainly uses such a system in keeping track of time, but this may be an emergent property of symbolic culture. Whether any other organism does this remains to be determined. Such a mechanism is an attractive candidate for explaining the ability of rats and pigeons to estimate short intervals (see chapter 9).

Determining Temporal Intervals

By Computation from Recorded Times of Occurrence
One way to obtain records that represent time intervals as opposed to times of occurrence is to compute them from differences in times of occurrence. The requisite computation is most simply envisioned if one imagines that the system relies on a linear accumulation process for the specification of time, as it would if it possessed a mechanism that counted each cycle of an oscillator (in digital circuit terms, a counter fed by a multivibrator). In this scheme, a time of occurrence is represented by a single coordinate (the count at the time of occurrence), the interval between two occurrences is the simple difference in the temporal coordinates of the occurrences, and the coordinate for the predicted time of next occurrence

is obtained by adding an interval (derived from the difference between earlier times of occurrence) to the last recorded coordinate. This scheme cannot explain the animal's predicting food at the same time the next day after a single training day (see chapter 8), a prediction that follows naturally from models that assume that time of occurrence is specified at least in part by the phase of a circadian oscillator.

Also, if we imagine that there is a simple physiological quantity (such as the amount of some intracellular substance) on whose linear increase the internal sense of time is based, then for this quantity to remain within reasonable magnitudes in the course of the life of an organism, it would have to increase very slowly, which would mean that the system could not readily resolve differences in recorded times of occurrence on the order of hours, much less seconds. One might imagine that to achieve higher temporal resolution the system employed a chain of accumulators analogous to the chain of flip-flops in a binary counter. At the front of this chain would be a rapidly increasing accumulator, which incremented the next, more slowly increasing accumulator each time it reached its limit and reset itself. This mechanism is equivalent to the use of a set of phase-locked oscillators of ever increasing periods. Each flip-flop in a binary counter is an oscillator with a period equal to twice the period of the flip-flop in front of it in the chain, which is why binary counters can also serve as frequency dividers. In short, when one introduces multiple accumulators with accumulator resetting, one has a multiple phase-locked oscillator model. In such a model, the states of the various oscillators represent the count. This representation is unique only up to the period of the last oscillator in the chain, the oscillator with the longest period.

If we assume that times of occurrence are in fact specified by recording sine-cosine representations of the phases of several different physiological oscillations, then the computations of next predicted time are slightly more complex than they are if we assume that time is measured by a linear accumulation process. There is a special combinatorial operation for adding and subtracting the sine-cosine representations of angles to obtain the sine-cosine representation of their sum or difference:

$$\sin (\alpha \pm \beta) = \sin\alpha \ \cos\beta \pm \cos\alpha \ \sin\beta$$
$$\cos (\alpha \pm \beta) = \cos\alpha \ \cos\beta \mp \sin\alpha \ \sin\beta$$

The combinatorial operation described by these formulas makes it possible to compute the sine-cosine representation of a temporal interval from the sine-cosine representations of two times of occurrence. It also makes it possible to obtain a predicted time of occurrence for event 2, given event 1, if there is a known temporal interval separating these two classes of events. The sine-cosine representation of the predicted time of occurrence is the sine-cosine representation of the time of occurrence of event 1 "plus" the sine-cosine representation of the temporal interval that characteristically separates the two events, where "plus" is to be interpreted in accord with the above formulas.

The addition and subtraction operations with the sine-cosine representations of times of occurrence and temporal intervals are equivalent to adding and subtracting phase angles, the angles that represent the phases of the various oscillations being used to represent time. As with other oscillatory representations of time, the representation is unique only over an interval shorter than the period of the slowest oscillation. When the intervals involved exceed the period of the slowest oscillation, then different moments in time have the same representation. The nth time around the circle cannot be distinguished from the first time around.

By Entrainment?

The discussion of how to compute time intervals is motivated by evidence that vertebrates, at least, can learn to anticipate the recurrence of something at a wide range of short intervals—intervals measured in seconds to tens of minutes. It is implicitly assumed that these recurrence intervals do not correspond to the periods on any endogenous oscillation; hence, these anticipations cannot be based simply on a record of the phase of an internal oscillation at the time an event occurred. Alternatively, one might imagine that the system anticipates recurrences with arbitrary periodicities not by computations based on recorded times of occurrence but rather by having the recurring events entrain endogenous oscillations whose periods correspond to the period of recurrence. This explanation has been advanced to account for the ability of the rat to anticipate feeding periods that recur at 25- or 26-hour intervals (chapter 8). While the idea may be tenable for periods close to the natural periods of selected endogenous oscillations (and the phenomenon is only observed for such periods in the rat), it is hard to see how to carry it through for the general case. The problem is that the first time something occurs, there is no knowing what the interval to the next occurrence may be. If successive occurrences are to interact by means of endogenous oscillations whose periods happen to correspond to the interval between recurrences, then the first occurrence of anything would have to set in motion a large number of endogenous oscillations, each with a different period. These endogenous oscillations would have no behavioral consequences until there was another recurrence of the event or observation. This recurrence would suppress all the endogenous oscillations except for the one whose period happened to correspond to the interval between the repeated occurrences. Thenceforth, the return of that oscillation to its initial state would elicit anticipatory behavioral activity.

The trouble with this idea is that the oscillations set in motion by the

occurrence of one thing would have to be kept distinct from the oscillations set in motion by the occurrence of each other thing. In short order,
there would have to be an extraordinary number of event-labeled oscillations going on simultaneously and independently, most of which will
never prove to be of any consequence because they will fail to correspond
to the interval of recurrence in the event whose label they bear. A
computational solution, in which the anticipation of a temporal interval
rests on the ability to compute or measure differences between times of
occurrence, seems clearly preferable.

The point of greatest importance is that the ability to detect and make
behavioral use of temporal intervals of arbitrary duration is distinct from
the ability to record the time at which something happens. One must
distinguish between what Church (see Gibbon and Allan 1984, p. 469)
has called periodic clocks and interval clocks. Stein (1951) also insisted on
this distinction, for which she suggested the the terms *Zeitsinn* (time
sense) and *Zeitgedächtnis* (time memory). The terms *phase sense* and
interval sense would be more appropriate. *Phase sense* refers to the ability
to anticipate events that recur at a fixed time of day (a fixed phase of the
day-night cycle), while *interval sense* refers to the ability to respond to
something that comes a fixed amount of time after an event that occurs
at varying points in the day-night cycle. Church attributes behaviors
based on circadian phase sense—or on the learned phase of occurrence
in some other endogenous oscillation—to periodic clocks. He explains
behaviors based on an interval sense in terms of interval clocks.

The distinction between phase sense and interval sense is fundamental. The bee clearly has a well developed circadian phase sense. So far as
I know, an interval-sense has not been demonstrated in the bee. Beling's,
Wahl's, and Kolterman's experiments (to be reviewed in chapter 8)
indicate that the bee does not learn ultradian (1-5 hour feeding intervals)
or infradian (48 hour) intervals. On the other hand, many vertebrates
clearly learn both the time of day at which an observation is made and the
temporal interval separating two events that recur with a fixed interval
between them (see Chapter 9).

Church assumes that phase sense and interval sense are mediated by
different timing mechanisms, phase sense being mediated by endogenous
oscillators that run all the time and interval sense by interval timers that
may be started, stopped and reset by the occurrence of events. Distinct
time-keeping mechanisms need not be postulated. Behavior based on
elapsed intervals could derive from computations performed on recorded phases of occurrence. In either case, however, new computational
considerations come into play when one considers behavior based on
learned time intervals, which may commence with the occurrence of a
temporally arbitrary time signal, a signal to which no endogenous

oscillation is phase locked. That is why it is important to distinguish clearly between the representation of time of occurrence and the representation of temporal intervals.

Chapter 8
Time of Occurrence

It has been sixty years since the first experimental demonstrations that insects record the time of day (circadian phase) at which they obtain food at a source, along with the color, odor, form, and location of the source. They use the recorded time to schedule their subsequent visits (Beling 1929). However, the suggestion that the recording of the circadian phase of occurrence may be a fundamental and extremely widespread form of learning has only begun to gain some currency (Enright 1975). This chapter reviews the experimental evidence that diverse animals routinely record the time of day at which something happens and use this record to schedule behavior on subsequent days.

In the Honey Bee

The experimental investigation of the capacity of bees to remember the time of day at which food was to be found in a certain place—or in a flower with a certain smell or color—grew out of field observations that when bees found nectar or sugar water at a particular place at a particular time of day, they reappeared at that place at the same time the next day. Forel (1910) observed that bees came to forage on sweets at his patio breakfast table at his customary breakfast time, whether the breakfast was laid or no. The evolutionary significance of this capacity was appreciated by Buttel-Reepen (1915), who observed that bees sought nectar from buckwheat flowers only up to 10:00 a.m., when nectar production ceases in this species of flower. At later hours, the same bees visit other nearby flowers, which produce nectar at other times of the day (Kleber 1935). Beling (1929), a student of von Frisch, began the systematic experimental investigation of the phenomenon. Her work was closely followed up by Wahl (1932). This work made use of the methods developed by von Frisch for the study of bee behavior, most notably setting up feeding stations at selected points within 20 to 50 meters of a hive and numbering the bees that visited these stations so that the times of reappearance of identified bees could be recorded.

Typically the experimenter let one bee discover the source and recruit others by dancing in the hive. When a troop had been recruited and numbered, the concentration of the sugar water given the bees was reduced to the point where the already recruited bees continued to come regularly but were not sufficiently excited to dance much in the hive. Thus, the troop of numbered experimental bees did not tend to recruit too many new bees. The new bees that did arrive were caught and killed, as were any numbered bees that did not show sufficiently regular visiting behavior during the periods of food availability (training periods).

In the experiment shown in figure 8.1, there were five successive training days on which sugar water was available to a troop of recruited bees from 8:00 to 20:00. The bees in the troop were only those that had visited the table regularly every 5 to 15 minutes throughout each training day. On test days, no sugar water was available at the feeding station. The specially designed feeding beakers were there, but they contained no sugar water. The data come from these test days. Panel A records the arrivals of numbered bees at the feeding table during each half-hour

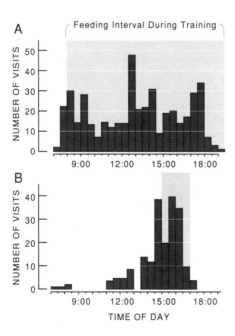

Figure 8.1
Number of bee visits to the feeding station on test days, when the beaker was empty. *A.* After a training with continuously stocked beaker. *B.* After training with a beaker that had been stocked only during the period indicated by the light gray background. (From Wahl 1932, pp. 532, 535.)

period between 7:00 and 20:00 of the test day following the five training days on which there was sugar water between 8:00 and 20:00. The bees' visits to the barren feeding station on this test day are spread through the day, with wide fluctuations in frequency from one half-hour to the next, fluctuations not seen on the training days. These fluctuations probably reflect a have-another-look-every-now-and-then behavioral strategy on the part of bees confronted with a barren food source that has proved reliable on several preceding days. Following the test day whose data are shown in figure 8.1A, there were ten more training days, but on these days the sugar water was present only between 15:00 and 17:00. This sequence of training days was followed by another test day during which the feeding beakers were never stocked with sugar water. Panel B records the arrivals during that test day. Notice that practically no bees arrived before 12:00 (in contrast to the control day in panel A). After 12:00 there is a steady increase in the frequency of arrivals, despite the fact that there is no sugar water (nor was there any at these times during the preceding ten training days). The frequency of arrivals attains a peak in the half-hour just before the period when the sugar water had become available on the preceding ten training days.

The tendency of the arrivals to anticipate the onset of food availability is characteristic of experiments of this kind, in animals ranging from insects to mammals, provided there is no strong penalty for anticipation (that is, for food-seeking activity prior to the availability of food). The amount by which anticipatory behavioral activity precedes the onset of food availability is too great to be explained by the assumption that the internal clock is running fast. Rather, this early onset reflects the use the animal makes of its representation of the time of occurrence of food. It times its behavior to anticipate the appearance of the food—to be the "early bird."

The memory for the time at which food is to be found is linked to the memory for the location of the food and to the memories for other sensory characteristics of the source. The bee may simultaneously retain several different mnemonic constellations, each specifying sources at different locations, with different sensory characteristic, providing food at different times. In one of Wahl's experiments, he trained with food available at one table from 9:00 to 10:30 and at the other from 15:30 to 17:00, then tested, as usual, with a day during which food was not provided at either location. The results are shown in figure 8.2. The bars in the figure give the number of bees in each half-hour that visited each location. The filled portions of these bars give the number of visits on which the bee landed and entered the (barren) beaker. The other visits were simple fly-bys. The onset of arrivals at the feeding stations again anticipates the beginning of the previous periods of food availability.

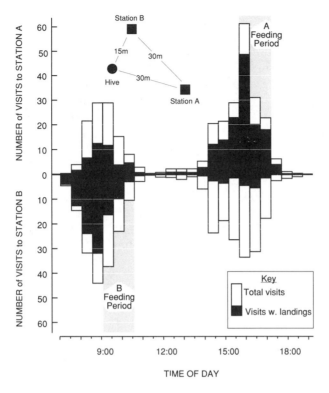

Figure 8.2
Numbers and types of visits to two feeding stations whose beakers had been stocked at different times of day during the training period. The bars indicate the total visits, including fly-bys only and land-and-enter visits; the filled portion of each bar gives the proportion of land-and-enter visits. Note the changes in the proportion of these visits at the two sites.as a function of the time of day. (Data from Wahl 1932, pp. 544, 546, 547.)

Two features of the data in figure 8.2 are of considerable theoretical importance. They bear on the distinction between a time-dependent memory and a memory for time. There has been some tendency in the recent literature to interpret the time memory in bees as a variant of state-dependent learning, that is, as if the behavioral expression of what the bee has previously learned about food sources is dependent on the bee's being in the same circadian state that it was in at the time it acquired this information (Koltermann 1974), just as the expression of behaviors learned in a drugged state may require reinstatement of the drugged state (John 1967). The time-dependent memory hypothesis may be contrasted with the hypothesis that the time of day at which something occurs is as much a part of what is learned as is the location, color, and other features of the goal object and that this representation of the time of day at which something has occurred enables the bee to make diverse appropriate adjustments in the timing and other characteristics of its behavior. The essential distinction between the two ideas is this. A state-dependent memory is available to influence behavior only while the animal is in that state, in the present case, while it is in a certain phase of its circadian cycle (usually assumed to be the same phase in which it acquired the phase-dependent memory). A memory for the time at which something occurred is available to influence behavior at any time, although its influence will appear in different ways at different times because the same information has different practical import under different circumstances.

The data in figure 8.2 favor the latter interpretation—the hypothesis that the bee's behavior is based on a remembered time of occurrence. During the last several days preceding the test days, the bees rarely visited station A during the morning feeding period or B during the afternoon feeding period. However, when they found station B barren during the morning feeding period of the test day, they then flew to the vicinity of station A. And, in the afternoon, finding station A barren, they flew to station B. Thus, the bees' going to the stations is not dependent on the phase of the circadian cycle at which they have been fed at those stations, although one might have supposed so from their behavior on training days.

The bees' behavior at the two stations varied depending on the time of day, in a manner suggestive of a behavioral strategy. At the station where food should have been available, the bees were more likely to land on and enter the (barren) feeding beaker, whereas at the other station, they usually confined their visit to a quick fly over, without landing. (The beakers were constructed in such a way that a bee could not tell whether the beaker contained sugar water except by landing and crawling into it.) During the morning, landings occurred on substantially more than 50 percent of the visits to Station B but on substantially less than 50 percent of the visits to Station A. In the afternoon, this pattern was reversed; the visits to B were mostly fly-bys while the bees landed and investigated at A.

The fly-by visits were probably checks for other bee activity at those sites. Bees use the presence or absence of other bees at a potential feeding site as one of the cues determining whether they will land there (von Frisch 1919). It seems likely that the bees were checking for activity at the other site, although it was the wrong time of day. In any event, it is clear that their memory for the location of the other source can find behavioral expression at the "wrong" time of day. It is also clear that the time of day adaptively determines not only whether a visit will be made but also the kind of behavior exhibited during that visit.

Bees make sophisticated use of the remembered information about the time at which another sensory-perceptual property of their environment is recorded in memory, as shown by experiments in which Wahl (1933) varied the concentration of the sugar water in the course of each training day. He kept it at 20 percent during most of each day but raised it to 60 percent during one or more daily high-concentration periods. Again, the bees' memory was probed by a test day during which the feeding beakers were barren. Some of the results are given in figure 8.3. In assessing the import of these data, it is important to bear in mind that 20 percent sugar water was a satisfactory reward for these bees. During training, Wahl deleted from the troop of numbered experimental bees all those that did not come regularly during the 20 percent concentration periods, as well as during the 60 percent periods. Thus, the intense peaks of bee arrivals in the half-hour immediately preceding the onsets of what had been the high-concentration period(s) do not reflect any similar pattern of visits during the training periods. Rather it reflects the fact that while the bees visited the source regularly all day long during the training days, they had nonetheless noted the differences in concentration at different times of day. When they found the beaker barren on the test day, they programmed their subsequent "lets-look-again" visits on the basis of their representation of the previous period of maximum concentration.

Koltermann (1971) showed that bees also recorded the time at which food was obtained from a source of a particular odor or a particular color. Kolterman worked with one bee at a time, to eliminate the possible effects of communications among the bees (either in the hive or because one bee chooses to land on the beaker when it sees one or more other bees there). Kolterman controlled the bee's experience on the basis of the number of its visits rather than on a predetermined temporal period. Each bee visited the food source every 5 minutes all day long, taking about 1.5 minutes to fill its crop on each visit and emptying the crop while back in the hive between visits to the station. When Kolterman wished a bee to experience a certain color or a certain odor at a particular food source at a particular time of day, he presented that color to the bee on three successive visits, beginning at the specified time.

In Kolterman's experiments, there was a single feeding station, with food available there at all times. What varied was the color of the cardboard on which the feeding beaker sat or the odor given off by a piece of filter paper placed beneath the beaker. The training of a bee took place on a single day. For example, in training bees to recognize nine different periods when the odor of geraniol (geranium extract) was present at a food source, Kolterman put geraniol-soaked filter paper under the feeding beaker at 9:15. At about 9:30, after three visits by the bee, he removed it. The bee continued to visit the feeding source during the

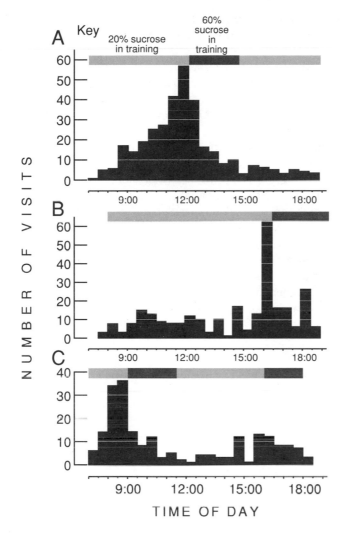

Figure 8.3
Number of bee visits to the feeding station on test days after training in which the beaker
had been stocked with a higher-concentration sugar water during the indicated parts of
the day. A. High-concentration period had been from 12:00 to 14:30. B. High-concentration
period had been from 16:30 to 19:30. C. Following training with two high-concentration
periods, one from 9:00 to 11:30 and a second from 16:00 to 18:00. (From data in Wahl 1933,
pp. 711, 713, 714.)

ensuing odor-free 45 minutes. At 10:15 Kolterman again put the geraniol-soaked paper under the beaker, removing it at about 10:30 after a further three visits by the bee. The geraniol was again placed under the beaker at 11:15, and so on, with the ninth and final three-visit placement of the geraniol filter paper occurring between 17:15 and 17:30.

The next day, there was again sugar water available at the source—except during 5-minute test periods, which occurred every 30 minutes, beginning at 8:50. During these short test periods, there were two barren beakers at the feeding station, one with geraniol under it and one with filter paper soaked in extract of thyme. Preliminary experiments had shown that naive bees had no preference between these two odors and were equally trainable to both. Kolterman tabulated the number of times during this period that the trained bee landed on and entered each beaker. When the bee expected food in a beaker, it would repeatedly land and enter, reappear, fly around, land again, and so on. Counting the number of landings gave a measure of what Kolterman called *Suchinten-sität*—the intensity of food-seeking behavior.

The results, from an experiment employing 285 individually trained and tested bees are given in figure 8.4. The bees almost never landed on

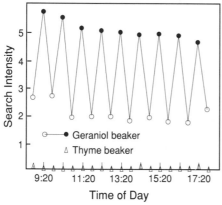

• Times that coincide with previous day's experience

○ Times that don't coincide with previous day's experience

Figure 8.4
Search intensity (average number of landings on empty beaker per visit to the station) at each of two empty test beakers following a single day's training, during which a geraniol odor had been present for three visits beginning at quarter past each hour, and absent during visits at other times (visits occurred roughly every 5 minutes all day long). Circles that coincide with the times when geraniol was previously experienced are filled. Circles that do not coincide are open. (Redrawn from Kolterman 1971, p. 58, by permission of author and publisher.)

the control beaker with the odor of thyme; the landings on this beaker never averaged more than 0.3 per 5-minute test period, and in most periods there were no landings here (open triangles on the abscissa in figure 8.4). By contrast, the bees landed with great frequency on the geraniol beaker during each short test period. Again we see that the phenomenon does not lend itself to conceptualization in terms of state-dependent learning. The memory for the odor associated with food was expressed in preference behavior regardless of the time of day. The bees always landed on the geraniol beaker in preference to the thyme beaker. The remarkable finding is that there was a statistically highly significant ($p < .001$) elevation of the intensity of the bees' food seeking during each of the nine different periods when food had occurred together with the geraniol odor. Geraniol heightened the expectation of food at those times of day when geraniol had been connected with food. Each point in figure 8.4 differs significantly from the preceding point, and since there are 19 points in all, the experiment demonstrates that bees can distinguish nineteen different times of day after a single day's training.

Kolterman (1971) further showed that the bee could connect different odors to different times of day. He put geraniol under the beaker for five visits at 9:00 and thyme extract under it for five visits at 15:00. The next day, during 5-minute test periods, which occurred every 1 1/2 hours, the bees encountered two barren beakers: one smelling of geraniol, the other of thyme. Between test periods, there was only a single beaker, and it was always stocked. During a test period, a landing on either beaker was counted as a choice of that beaker. Figure 8.5 plots the percentage choice of each beaker as a function of the time of day of the test period. Figure 8.6 gives the results from a similar experiment with color. In that experiment, blue-green cardboard was placed under the beaker for five visits in midmorning and violet cardboard for five visits in midafternoon. As in the odor experiment, the bee confronted two barren beakers during the 5-minute test periods run the next day, one on each color of cardboard. In these experiments, the memory for the time of an odor or color experience finds expression in choice behavior because different odors (colors) were experienced at different times.

In the light of the results showing that memory for place, concentration, odor, and color of food sources are all linked to a memory for the time of day at which the bee has observed these attributes, one may reasonably propose that the bee always records the time at which it makes a recorded observation. Put another way, all representations in bee memory appear to be linked to temporal coordinates, coordinates that represent the time of day at which the records of color, smell, and location were made.

attention to all three facts

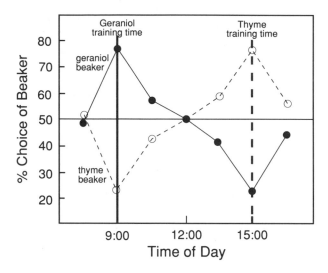

Figure 8.5
Percentage choice of (barren) geraniol-smelling and thyme-smelling beakers, as a function
of time of day, in bees that had experienced geraniol odor at 9:00 and thyme odor at 15:00
on preceding training day. (Redrawn from Koltermann 1971, p. 62, by permission of author
and publisher.)

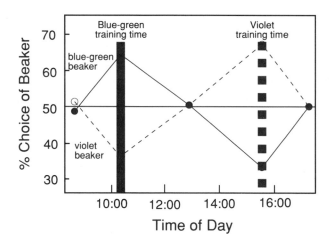

Figure 8.6
Percentage choice of (barren) beakers on blue-green or violet paper, as a function of time
of day, in bees that had experienced blue-green at 10:00 and violet at 15:00 on preceding
training day. (Redrawn from Koltermann 1971, p. 64, by permission of author and publisher.)

Time of Day, Not Periodicity (Phase, not Phase Intervals)
In the experiments of Beling (1929) and Wahl (1932, 1933) the training
schedules had strong 24-hour periodicity, even when the bees were
trained to several different times simultaneously. The training always
extended over several days, and the bees were always fed at the same
time(s) each day. One could imagine that what the bees were learning or
reacting to was this 24-hour periodicity. One version of this hypothesis
would be that feedings recurring at 24-hour intervals entrain internal
oscillation with a 24-hour period and the bees seek food whenever an
entrained internal oscillation reaches a fixed trigger point, a position in
the oscillatory cycle at which the oscillatory process activates food-
seeking behavior. Most of the sugar water gathered by a bee is given up
at the hive, but some of it is ingested. One might imagine that the
metabolic processes governing the assimilation of the ingested amounts
had a 24-hour period so that the bee in effect became hungry again 24
hours after it last ate. It would be hard to make this account deal with the
cases in which there were several different feeding times in each training
day. Also Wahl showed that interpolating feedings at the hive had no
effect on the bees' timing of their reappearance at a feedings site.

    Kolterman's experiments clearly demonstrate that it is the time of day
at which the training experience occurred rather than the periodicity of
training experiences that is important. He trained his bees in a single day.
In one of his experiments, the bees experienced geraniol on three successive visits over a 15-minute period beginning at 10:00 and then again for
another three visits at 11:00. The only periodicity in this feeding schedule
is the 1-hour periodicity. Since the training was done on a single day,
there was no 24-hour period in the training schedule. Figure 8.7 shows
that on the 5-minute test periods given the next day, the bees' behavior
reflected the phases of the circadian cycle at which they had experienced
the geraniol but not the 1-hour periodicity in the training schedule;
search intensity did not show periodic peaks at 1-hour intervals.

Noncircadian Intervals
Beling (1929) trained bees with a $3\frac{1}{2}$-hour feeding period every 19 hours
for 10 days and then tested to see whether there would be a peak in their
food-seeking 19 hours after the last feeding. There was none. There was,
however, a small but significant increase in food seeking at the feeding
station 24 hours after the last of these ten feedings. Wahl (1932) provided
sugar water on a 48-hour schedule for 16 days (eight feedings). He found
no indication of an adjustment to this every-other-day schedule. The
bees' visits to the feeding site approximately coincided with the time of
day at which the feedings had occurred, but in the 4-day test period that

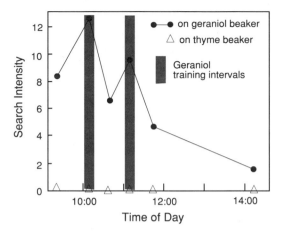

Figure 8.7
Search intensity (average number of landings on empty beaker per visit to the station), as a function of time of day, in bees that had experienced geraniol for 15 minutes at 10:00 and again at 11:00 on the preceding training day. On the test day, two (barren) beakers were presented simultaneously, one on filter paper soaked in geraniol, one on filter paper soaked in thyme extract. (Redrawn from Kolterman 1971, p. 57, by permission of author and publisher.)

followed the end of the training the bees came just as frequently on the first and third test days as on the second and fourth. In short, so far as the bee is concerned, all of the evidence is consistent with the assumption that the temporal information recorded by a bee is the phase of one or more of its endogenous circadian oscillators. It represents the times of day at which things occur, but it does not compute elapsed intervals (differences between times of occurrence), at least not over intervals measured in tens of hours or in days.

Dependence on Internal Circadian Oscillations
Beling and Wahl addressed the question of what specified time of day for the bee. Their experiments strongly implicated endogenous circadian oscillations, although they were understandably cautious in advancing this interpretation because the existence of such processes was not widely conceded at the time. Both experimenters showed that the bees reappeared at a feeding site 24 hours after the last of several daily feedings even when the experiment was run indoors in constant light, with noncyclical variations in the temperature both inside and outside the hive. (In these experiments, the feeding site was located only 30 centimeters from the hive.) Wahl (1932) went so far as to replicate the

experiment in a salt mine, where the bees would be isolated from daily fluctuations in cosmic rays. Wahl (1932) also replicated the experiment with a troop of bees raised since hatching under constant light in a constant-temperature incubator. These bees never experienced a 24-hour cycle of any kind, yet they sought food 24 hours after its last occurrence.

Beling and Wahl were not familiar with the technique of phase shifting: manipulating either the light-dark cycle or the animal's longitude so as to alter the phase relationship between an endogenous circadian oscillation and the external cycle to which it is ordinarily entrained. We have already seen the use of this technique to prove that bees and pigeons refer to an internal time sense in setting a compass course by the sun. These same experiments have been used to prove that the bee's ability to remember the time of day at which something occurs and to refer to this memory in the timing of its subsequent behavior rests on readings it makes on its internal clock. These phase-shifting experiments were first done in the form of longitudinal displacement experiments by Renner (1960). Renner first worked with bees inside a small experimental chamber, where they were isolated from the external day-night cycle. They were trained to collect sugar water between 20:15 and 22:15 French Daylight Time and then flown overnight to New York while inside the experimental chamber. When the hive was opened in New York, the bees appeared at the feeding site 24 hours after the last feeding in Paris—that is, at 15:00 Eastern Daylight Time. No bees appeared at 20:15-22:15 Eastern Daylight Time (the locally correct time). This result proves that the bees' temporal indicator is not any external variable whose momentary value at some point on the earth's surface depends on the daily rotation of the earth.

In the first experiments, the bees were isolated from the external day-night cycle. It remains possible that when external indications of local time of day are available (such as the altitude of the sun), the bee makes use of them. To test this, Renner trained bees in an open field on Long Island and flew them overnight to a similar field near the University of Davis in California. (This experiment figured in the discussion of sun-compass navigation in chapter 4.) The bees appeared at the feeding sites around the hive in California approximately 24 hours after the feeding time in Long Island, even though the sun in California at that time was inappropriately positioned in the sky (as were other variables whose values depend on the rotation of the earth). There was no peak in visits at the locally correct time of day, when the external variables dependent on the rotation of the earth took on the values in California that they had during the daily period of food availability on Long Island.

In the course of three days of testing, the bees' time of appearance at the feeding sites drifted toward the locally correct time, as the experience of day and night at Davis entrained the bees' endogenous oscillation(s). The bees were not fed while in California. The drift was due to the local entrainment of their endogenous clock, not to new learning.

In the Long Island-to-Davis experiment, Renner (1959) actually observed two peaks in the frequencies of arrival of trained bees at the feeding sites in California. Neither peak coincided initially with the correct local time, but Renner argued nonetheless that one of the peaks indicated a complex interaction between the bees' endogenous time sense and some reliance on exogenous indicators of time, such as the altitude of the sun. However, in response to abrupt and substantial phase shifts in the timing signal, animals often show signs that several different endogenous circadian oscillations go transiently out of their normal phase relationships to each other. Different internal circadian oscillations are entrained at different rates by the phase-shifted timing signal, so during this entrainment period, the phase relationship among the internal oscillations is transiently perturbed. An alternative explanation of the double peak in the arrival frequencies of the translocated bees is that the bees have more than one internal clock. Ordinarily these clocks agree, but when there is a sudden phase shift in the external cycle to which they are daily adjusted, the different internal oscillations take varying amounts of time to come back into the proper phase relationship to the external cycle. During this period of adjustment, the bee may experience conflicting or inconsistent internal time signals.

Experiments with CO_2 narcosis by Medugorac and Lindauer (1967) reveal the presence of two decouplable clocks determining the visiting times of time-trained bees. When the bees are subject to 2 hours of complete narcosis with 100 percent CO_2, those that survive and recover function (about 60 percent of the sample) show two peaks in their subsequent visits to the feeding stations, one at the correct time and one 2 hours late. This result is obtained even under constant illumination and even when the trained bees are inserted into another hive stocked with bees trained to a different time under a different light-dark cycle.

The sine-cosine model for the internal representation of time of day given in figure 7.6B requires recording the momentary values (magnitudes) of two different physiological variables that oscillate 90° out of phase with one another. Both oscillations must, of course, be entrained by the external day-night cycle. A sudden, large phase shift in the external cycle might disrupt the phase relationship between them. The current values of the two physiological variables are jointly required to specify unambiguously the time of day. A disruption of the phase relationship in their oscillations might yield the two peaks that Renner observed.

Computations with Times of Occurrence
Most non-representational approaches to the phenomena of animal learning implicitly or explicitly assume an unvarying connection between what has been learned—conceived of as a structural alteration of the nervous system produced by experience—and the behavioral expression of that learning. Representational approaches make a much sharper or more consequential distinction between what has been learned and the effects that the existence of this representation may have on diverse behaviors. Representational approaches assume that these effects will be as diverse as are the computational mechanisms brought to bear on the represented information by different behavioral readout systems. The difference between the two approaches may be illustrated by considering two different explanations of an important aspect of the bee data that has not yet been sufficiently emphasized: it takes several days of training in periodic feeding before bees show a strong anticipatory effect.

A characteristic nonrepresentational explanation of this finding is that it takes several repetitions for the association between food and a particular time of day to get strengthened to the point where it is clearly expressed in behavior. A contrasting representational-computational explanation is that bees compute from their representations of times of occurrence on successive days the statistical likelihood that these times are clustered around one circadian phase. On this hypothesis, the bees' tendency to make anticipatory visits is monotonically proportionate to the likelihood that there is clustering in the times of occurrence. This explanation assumes that the recorded times of occurrence are treated by the bee in a manner analogous to that in which human experimenters treat experimentally recorded departure bearings (for example, figure 5.12). A single point on a circle—a single recorded time of occurrence or a single recorded departure bearing—gives no justification for concluding that times of occurrence are clustered (or that departure bearings are reliably oriented). Only when there are several clustered points on the circle (several observed times of occurrence at or near a single phase) is there any evidentiary justification for assuming a concentration around a single mean phase of occurrence.

The second explanation seems at first a good deal more complex. One's first reaction is that it should be rejected on grounds of parsimony. Why opt for a complex computational explanation when a simple noncomputational explanations seems adequate? The answer comes from a consideration of the diverse behavioral consequences of a single learning experience. These considerations may eliminate or reverse the seeming difference in parsimony between the nonrepresentational and the representational explanations. The nonrepresentational explanation is more parsimonious so long as one uses only a single behavioral test in evaluating what has been learned and/or ignores some of the details in the behavior observed.

The first relevant observation is that the bees' visits to the feeding source, when they do become linked to the time of day, do so in an anticipatory manner. The tendency to appear at the food source reaches its maximum not in the middle of the experienced feeding period, as would be predicted by an explanation based on the strengthening of temporal associations, but rather in the period just before the experienced onset of food availability, at a time of day that has reliably been associated with the absence of food. The increase in the frequency of visits to the source begins as much as 1 to 2 hours prior to the time of day at which food has been experienced, much too long to be accounted for by the assumption that the internal clock runs fast. We know from the precision of the behavioral dependence on time shown in, for example, figure 8.4 that the bee's clock is accurate to within an error of no more than 5 or 10 minutes a day. The frequency with which a given time has been associated with feeding after, say, ten days of restricted food availability must increase from the onset to the midpoint of the feeding interval, but the bees' tendency to visit a (barren) test beaker declines steeply during this period (see figures 8.2 and 8.3). In short, the details of the behavioral expression of what has been learned, even when that expression is tested only in a single way, are not explained by the nonrepresentational account. They are explained if one assumes that the bee uses its representation of the time at which food becomes available to schedule a visit that gets the bee there before its best estimate of first availability. Observations by Gill, Mack, and Russell (1982) on hummingbird foraging reveal why the bee should use its representation in this way. Bees compete with hummingbirds for the nectar in many plants. If the hummingbird gets there first, it empties the flower.

When one expands the behavioral analysis in anticipation experiments still further, differentiating between fly-by visits and land-and-investigate visits, the advantages of the representational account again become apparent. As was pointed out in connection with the data in figure 8.2, the relative proportions of the two kinds of visits to two different sources show systematic time dependencies.

The scheduling of visits is not the only behavior in which one may see an expression of what the bee has learned about a time of occurrence. When we shift attention to other behavioral expressions of this representational capacity, we find clear expressions of knowledge of time of occurrence after a single day's training, involving only three to five visits. Kolterman did not use anticipatory activity to test for the expression of what had been learned; he used two other behavioral indexes. One index was the bee's preference between a source with the sensory characteristics experienced at a given feeding time and a source with different sensory characteristics. The time-dependent preferences he saw were highly significant after a single day's training (figures 8.5 and 8.6). Since the bee must choose one source or the other in this paradigm, there is no point in its requiring multiple days' experiences before committing itself. Thus, it is not surprising from a computational point of view that one gets a strong time-dependency effect from one day's training in a preference test but not in an anticipation test.

The other measure that Kolterman used was search intensity—the number of times that a bee landed on and entered an empty beaker in the course of an interpolated 5-minute test with a barren beaker. In the anticipation experiments, the beakers were barren throughout the test day, and the experimenter counted inspection visits. In Kolterman's experiments, the beakers were barren only during the short test periods, and he tabulated the intensity of the bee's attempts to find the expected food. This measure of search intensity is plotted in figures 8.4 and 8.7. Here too one sees highly significant time-dependencies after a single day's training, in which the odor was experienced only three times during each distinct period of odor presence.

In trying to account for the variations in the apparent rate of learning as a function of the behavioral context in which learning is tested, nonrepresentational theorists are driven to make a variety of ad hoc parametric assumptions. The problem is to explain seemingly large differences in the rate of learning in consequence of seemingly minor variations in the behavioral test of learning. The concept of rate of learning (or associability), which is central to nonrepresentational theories of learning, has no counterpart in the present representational interpretation. The present interpretation assumes that each observation of a behaviorally important aspect of external reality gives rise to a separate representation (and thus to a distinct set of enduring changes somewhere in the CNS). Associative theory assumes that renewed observations strengthen the structural changes wrought by earlier similar observations, while the present interpretation assumes that each observation forges its own changes. Learning curves, which are taken by associative theory to indicate the growing strength of an underlying associative bond, are here assumed to reflect computational mechanisms that operate on the representations of times of occurrence to derive statistical properties of the animal's overall temporal experience. Different behaviors depend to different degrees on the computable statistical parameters, and these differences are usually seen to be adaptive (functionally appropriate).

Daily Habits

Animals live in a world with many periodically recurring phenomena of behavioral relevance. Much of this periodicity is in the behavior of the other animals with which they interact. Kestrels, a small Eurasian falcon, for example, often feed predominantly on voles and other small rodents. As we have already seen (figure 7.3), there is a pronounced ultradian rhythm in vole activity, reflected in the rates at which voles are taken in traps in the course of a day (Rijnstrop, Daan, and Dijkstra 1981). One might imagine that it is to a kestrel's advantage to be able to time its hunting activity to coincide with experienced peaks in the frequency of vole sightings, and indeed daily peaks in kestrel flight-hunting activity often correspond with peaks in the frequency with which voles are taken in traps (Rijnstrop et al. 1981). The amount of vole activity is only one of several hunting-relevant factors that vary systematically as a function of time during the day. Others include the winds, the temperature, and the availability of other kinds of prey. Each bird's experience of these factors and which factors are most important to it may be expected to vary. One might expect therefore that each bird would develop daily habits, which are modified on the basis of its experience. If it is successful hunting in a given area at a given time on one day, it should tend to hunt there again at that time next day, and if it is unsuccessful it should avoid hunting there at that time. Rijnstrop et al. (1981) have shown that both of these assumptions are true. Different kestrels have different daily habits, and these habits are modified to adapt them to the timing of the bird's experienced successes and failures at different hunting sites. When a bird has been successful at a given site at a given time of day, it tends to hunt again at that site at that time the next day. When it has been unsuccessful, the probability of its hunting at that site at that time is diminished. When the experimenter intervenes to increase the prey found at a certain site at a certain time, modifications of the bird's daily hunting habits rapidly follow. For both the birds and the bees, the capacity to represent the time of day at which something has occurred and to time the next day's behavior correspondingly is a foundation for successful adaptation to the temporal structure of the behavior-relevant processes that surround them.

Anticipation of Daily Feedings

Since the pioneering work of Richter (1922) and Bolles (Bolles and de Lorge 1962; Bolles and Stokes 1965; Bolles and Moot 1973), it has repeatedly been shown that the lever pressing and running wheel activity of the rat anticipates one or two regularly recurring daily feeding times and that the ability to do this depends—in the rat, as in the bird and the bee—

on endogenous circadian oscillations (see, for recent examples, Aschoff, Goetz, and Honmah 1983; Boulos, Rossenwasser, and Terman 1980; Coleman, Harper, Clarke, and Armstrong 1982; Edmonds and Adler 1977b; Gibbs 1979; Stewart, Rosenwasser, and Adler 1985). The divergent approaches to the same phenomenon by investigators in different traditions (the animal learning tradition, the biological rhythms tradition, and the zoological-ethological tradition) are evident in this literature. Bolles and his collaborators interpreted the phenomenon in terms of an increase in incentive motivation based on the use of time of day as a predictive cue (Bolles and Moot 1973). They did not cite the zoological literature on memory for the time of day in insects in support of this argument—it strongly supports the same conclusion—but they developed compelling evidence for this conclusion with regard to the rat's behavior. Subsequently researchers working in the biological rhythms tradition have interpreted the phenomenon in terms of entrainment. In so doing, they have had to ignore some of the findings by Bolles and Moot (1973), findings that can be reconciled with an entrainment model with difficulty, if at all.

The findings regarding the anticipation of daily feeding times by the rat parallel those with bees and birds in essential respects. If the rat is fed only at a certain time of day, its activity (visits to the food cup, running in a running wheel, pacing back and forth in its cage, and so on) increases in anticipation of the feeding time. The anticipatory increase in activity is based on a representation of the time of day at which feeding occurs, not on a representation of the interval between feedings. If the feeding interval departs appreciably from the circadian interval, if, for example, the interval between successive feedings is 19 hours or 29 hours, the rat never shows anticipatory activity at the appropriate intervals (Bolles and de Lorge 1962), even when it is born and raised in an environment where the feedings occur at these intervals, with the period of the light-dark cycle set correspondingly (Bolles and Stokes 1965). Thus, the rat, like the bee and the bird, learns the phase of an endogenous circadian oscillation at which feeding occurs.

The culminating paper in the study of anticipatory running activity by Bolles and his collaborators (Bolles and Moot 1973) described the results of feeding rats two 1-hour meals each day, with a 6-hour interval from the onset of the first meal to the onset of the second. There was a 12:12 light-dark cycle. For one group of rats, the meals occurred during the night, at 21:00 and 3:00, "subjective time." Subjective time, the time of day as specified by an animal's endogenous circadian oscillations, is estimated by taking "subjective midnight" (when the reading on the internal clock goes from 24:00 to 00:00) to be the midpoint of the lights-out period in the entraining light-dark cycle. Then, 6:00 is subjective dawn and 18:00 subjective dusk. Since the rat is nocturnally active, 21:00 and 3:00 are more or less normal eating times for it. For the other group of rats, the meals occurred at 9:00 and 15:00 subjective time. These are not normal eating times for the rat; under unrestricted conditions, it eats very little during its subjective morning and afternoon.

Several of the Bolles and Moot findings are of considerable importance in the evaluation of different models for the anticipatory eating phenomenon. First, both groups anticipated both meals (figure 8.8), even though the meals were temporally grouped—6 hours apart, with an 18-hour interval from the onset of the second meal of a day to the first meal of the next day . This finding—which again corresponds to findings with bees (compare figure 8.8 and figure 8.7)—cannot readily be reconciled with entrainment interpretations of anticipatory activity.

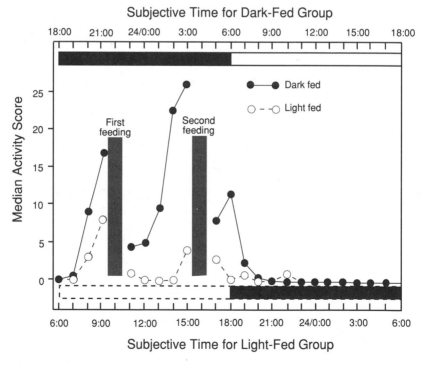

Figure 8.8
Median hourly wheel-running activity in rats fed twice a day at 10:00 and 16:00 our time, corresponding to 21:00 and 3:00 subjective time for the dark-fed group, and 9:00 and 15:00 subjective time for the light-fed group. The half-black-half-white bars give the light dark cycles for the two groups. (Redrawn from Bolles and Moot 1973, p. 512, by permission of author and publisher.)

Second, the magnitude of the anticipatory activity and how far prior to the onset of feeding it began varied with the subjective phase for which the meals were programmed. The rats that anticipated meals during their subjective day, when they are not ordinarily inclined to eat, showed less anticipatory activity and the onset of the activity preceded meal onset by a shorter interval (figure 8.8). Rats also eat less during such meals (Boulos et al. 1980).

Third, feeding intervals programmed for the rats' subjective day strongly suppressed dusk-onset running (see data for light-fed group in figure 8.8). Under unrestricted feeding conditions, running is seen throughout much of the rat's subjective night, with an abrupt onset at subjective dusk. With restricted feeding during the subjective (and objective) day, there was often no running activity, even at lights off (subjective and objective dusk).

Fourth, on test days when the anticipated feedings were omitted, there was a decline in activity soon after the end of what should have been the first feeding period, a rise to a new peak in anticipation of the second period, and a fall following the end of what should have been the second period. The declines in activity following the failure of each anticipation indicate that the anticipatory activity did not depend on growing hunger (or on any other variable that increases monotonically with the interval since the last feeding).

Finally, the anticipatory activity rapidly disappeared when the rats were returned to unrestricted feeding, but renewed deprivation (after ten days on unrestricted feeding) led to the immediate reappearance of correctly timed anticipatory peaks in both groups of rats (figure 8.9). On the first day of renewed deprivation, the rats correctly anticipated the time of onset of the first and second feeding intervals, though they had not experienced feeding at these times for a 10-day period, during which their behavior had ceased to show the anticipatory peaks.

The interpretation of anticipatory circadian activity peaks in terms of entrainment began with the work of Edmonds and Adler (1977a, b), who showed that anticipatory activity peaks for one and two meals a day were present even under free-running conditions, that is, when there was no environmental light-dark cycle, and even when one meal was delivered at 24-hour intervals while the other was delivered at 25-hour intervals. They suggested that the anticipatory activity was timed by an endogenous circadian oscillation that became entrained by the periodically recurring feedings. The essentials of the extensive work that has followed these seminal papers are all to be seen in figure 8.10, a double-day display of the running activity of a rat in a chamber under constant illumination. In the upper part of the record (days 11 to 85), there were two feedings a day: one at 12:00 our time (indicated by N) and one at 24:00 (indicated

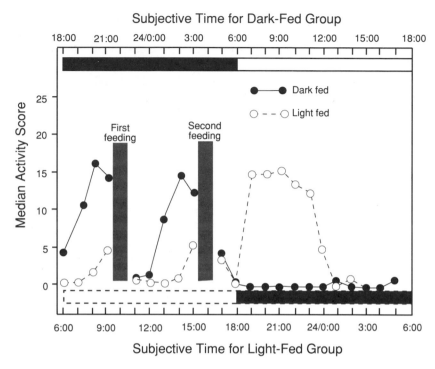

Figure 8.9
Reinstatement of correctly timed anticipatory activity on the first day of renewed deprivation, following 10 days' unrestricted access to food. The anticipatory activity peaks had
disappeared from the daily activity of these rats during the period of unrestricted access.
(Redrawn from Bolles and Moot 1973, p.512, by permission of author and publisher.)

by *M*). Initially these feedings lasted 2 hours (day 0, which is not shown,
to day 21), but they were eventually reduced to 1 hour (day 22 onward).
At day 85, the *M* feeding was switched to a 25-hour period. From this
point onward, the (until now vertical) line indicating the onset of the *M*
feeding slants to the right and downward with a slope of 1 hour per day
(48 hours in 48 days).

It is apparent in figure 8.10 that the scheduled feedings do not act as
timing signals for the circadian oscillator controlling the rat's night-
phase running. Throughout the record, even during the period when the
rat received one feeding every 12 hours, there is a free-running activity
rhythm whose period is about 24 hours, 37 minutes, so that the onset of
running at subjective dusk slants downward to the right across the
display with an x/y slope of 48 hours in 77 days. The phase drift in
subjective dusk has been estimated by eye by the present author and
drawn in as a hairline.

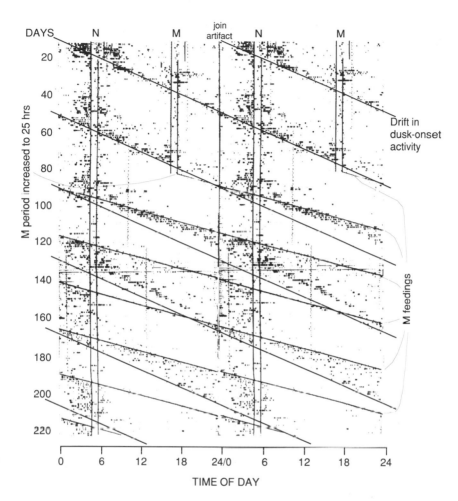

Figure 8.10
Double-day plot of running wheel activity from a rat in a constantly illuminated chamber
with two periods of food access (N and M) per day. The solid lines sharply slanted to the
right from day 85 onward mark the onset of the M feeding when it was on a 25-hour
schedule. The lines that slant somewhat less sharply to the right were drawn in by me to
indicate the onset of activity at subjective dusk This onset is used to determine the period
and phase of the animal's endogenous circadian clock. (Modified from Edmonds and
Adler 1977b, p. 925, by permission of author and publisher.)

In many rats, the suppressing effect of anticipatory activity on the running that normally begins abruptly at subjective dusk (Bolles and Moot's third finding) is so strong that the continuation of the free-running activity is not as apparent as it is in figure 8.10. However, when feeding is no longer restricted, free-running dusk-onset activity returns in these animals. One can do an analysis of the phase of this onset (that is, at what time does it occur with respect to the external daily cycle?) to see whether this phase is predicted by the phase of the prior feeding schedule or by extrapolating from the phase drift in subjective dusk prior to the imposition of the feeding schedule. Even in rats where free-running dusk-onset activity is not apparent during restricted feeding, the phase of this activity when it reappears is predicted by extrapolation from the pre-restriction phase drift (figure 8.11), not by the phase of the feeding schedule (Boulos et al. 1980; Aschoff et al. 1983). This means that the oscillation that triggers dusk-onset running runs free throughout the period of restricted feeding, with little or no entraining (phase-shifting) effect from the feedings.

One explanation for the occurrence of anticipatory prefeeding activity under free-running conditions is that it depends on the ability to note the time on the internal clock (the capacity revealed by studies of bee foraging). Under free-running conditions, a 24-hour feeding will be experienced at progressively earlier subjective times each day. In figure 8.10, the rat's circadian oscillator ran with a 24-hour, 37-minute period, while the N feeding occurred with a 24-hour period. Therefore the rat's subjective hour was 61.56 objective minutes long (one-twentyfourth of a 24-hour, 37-minute period) and the N feeding was experienced 36 subjective minutes earlier each day. By the rat's internal clock, the N feeding occurred at subjective dusk (subjective 18:00) on day 60, a bit before subjective dusk on day 61 (17:24), well before subjective dusk the next day (16:48), and so on. By day 70, the N feeding fell at subjective noon, when the rat is least active and least disposed to show anticipatory activity.

The reciprocal suppression phenomena discovered by Bolles and Moot, in an environment with an entraining light-dark cycle, are also seen in experiments where the circadian oscillator is running free. On days 10 to 20, 45 to 60, and 80 to 95 in figure 8.10, the N feeding was anticipated at or within 6 hours after subjective dusk and the rat showed pronounced anticipatory activity. (Look in the regions to the left of the vertical line that marks the onset of the N feeding.) On days 30 to 40, 65 to 75, and 105 to 115, when the N feeding was anticipated during the subjective day, there is little anticipatory activity to be seen to the left of the N feeding. The reciprocal effect is also seen. Around day 120, the N and the M feedings were both anticipated at subjective dawn (12 hours

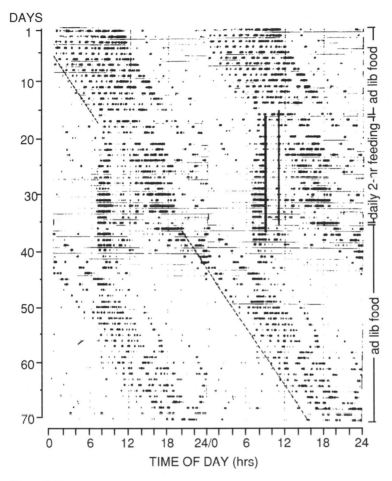

Figure 8.11

When the onset of activity at subjective dusk reappears after the termination of a restricted feeding schedule, its phase is predicted by extrapolation from the prerestriction phase drift, not by the phase of the feeding period. Double-day plot of running wheel activity of a rat kept in constant dim illumination. Onset and offset of feeding period are indicated by vertical lines drawn in on the right half of the plot only. The dashed line slanting downward to right indicates phase drift in dusk-onset activity. Note that this activity is absent when the scheduled feeding fell in the first few hours before subjective dusk. Note also the fluctuation in the amount and extent of anticipatory activity as a function of whether the scheduled feeding falls during subjective night or subjective day. (Redrawn from Honmah et al. 1983, p. 906, by permission of author and publisher.)

after subjective dusk) and there was no onset of activity at subjective dusk. (Note the white space to right of the drift hairline in this region.) On days 150 to 160, both feedings were anticipated during the 12 hours preceding subjective dusk and dusk-onset activity is markedly attenuated and delayed (region to right of drift hairline).

Bolles and Moot (1973) showed that anticipatory running disappeared within a few days after a return to continuous feeding but reappeared when food deprivation was reintroduced. Its reappearance preceded the first feeding of the reestablished regimen, showing that the renewed anticipation was based on a persisting memory for the time of day at which feeding had occurred. Subsequent experiments in which the endogenous circadian oscillator has been phase shifted or allowed to run free before the period of renewed food deprivation show that the renewed anticipatory behavior depends on a reading of this internal light-entrainable clock (Coleman et al. 1982; Rosenwasser, Pelchat, and Adler 1984). Figure 8.12 shows the running records from a rat run with a stable light-dark cycle (the Bolles and Moot conditions). During the baseline period at the top of the record, food was ad lib. From day 15 to day 42, food was available only during a 2-hour interval near the middle of the light-on phase, and the rat developed clear anticipatory running, which disappeared when ad lib food was restored but reappeared during a 4-day period of total food deprivation instituted 35 days after the return to ad lib food (days 77 to 81).

Figure 8.13 gives a double-day plot of the activity of another rat subject to a similar sequence of conditions, except that the lights-on, lights-off cycle was shifted by 10 hours on day 65, the day that ad lib food was restored. The rat's "nocturnal" activity is like the cockroach's; it is initiated by the reading on the internal clock rather than by the perception of environmental darkness. Thus, on the first few days after the shift in the light-dark cycle, the rat's activity occurs during the middle of the light-on phase. Like all other circadian oscillations, however, the rat's internal clock is entrained by the light-dark cycle. Over the 7 days following the shift in the light-dark cycle, the rat's daily period of activity drifted rapidly toward the right, so that by the end of a week, its activity again fell during the dark phase. At this point, the period of total food deprivation began and "anticipatory" running reappeared during the middle of the rat's normally inactive phase. Whatever times this activity shifted along with the internal clock.

The crucial data, showing that it is the activity clock itself that times this learned anticipatory activity, are shown in figure 8.14. At the end of the period of restricted food access, this rat was shifted to a continuous light regime so that its internal clock could run free (day 40). In the presence of the constant illumination, the internal clock ran with a period of about

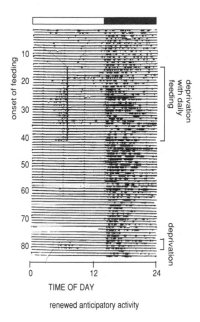

TIME OF DAY

renewed anticipatory activity

Figure 8.12
Single-day plot of rat running wheel activity, showing the reinstatement of anticipatory running by renewed food deprivation. Food was available ad lib except where indicated. Note that renewed food deprivation elicited daily bouts of running activity that straddled the daily time at which food had previously become available. The black bar at the top of the plot indicates the 10-hour daily period of lights off. (Modified from Rosenwasser et al. 1984, p. 26, by permission of author and publisher.)

$24\frac{1}{3}$ hours, drifting to the right with a slope of 48 minutes per 24-hour day. A drift line with this slope has been drawn in on the right side of the double-day plot to mark the phase of the animal's internal light-entrainable clock at which the feeding period had begun. On days 74 to 80, and again on 105 to 109 and 115 to 119, there were periods of total food deprivation, during which "anticipatory" running reappeared at the phase of the internal clock at which feeding had occurred much earlier when the internal clock was entrained to a day-night cycle.

Rosenwasser et al. (1984) conclude from these records that "animals in all groups appeared to 'learn' the circadian phase of food availability during the feeding schedule, to 'remember' the phase of food access over many days of intervening ad lib feeding, and to 'expect' to be fed at the appropriate time, relative to the photically entrainable rhythm, when subsequently subjected to complete deprivation."

Rosenwasser et al. (1984) put scare quotes around learn, remember, and expect in part because they feared to venture into the terrain of

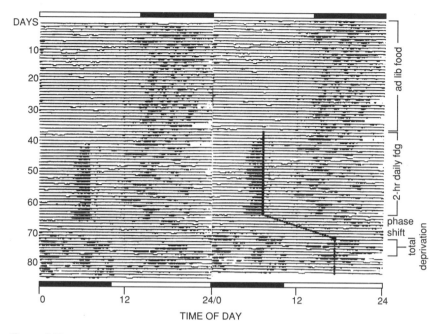

Figure 8.13
Double-day plot of rat running wheel activity, showing the reinstatement of anticipatory running by renewed food deprivation after a 10 hour phase-shift in the light-entrained endogenous circadian oscillation. During the restricted feeding regime, food became available at 10:00, somewhat past the midpoint of the daily lights-on phase of the light-dark cycle. The dark phase of cycle indicated by bars at top. The vertical line indicating the onset of food availability is drawn in only on the second (right) half of the double-day plot. At the end of the restricted feeding regime, the phase of the light-dark cycle was shifted 10 hours rightward. The dark phase of new cycle is indicated by the bars at the bottom. The dotted extension of the vertical line is drawn with the slope of the drift in the rat's photic oscillator in response to this shift in the entraining signal (compare the similar drift after day 50 in Figure 7.1). A period of renewed and total food deprivation began when the endogenous oscillation came into the proper phase relationship to the light-dark cycle. Note that the anticipatory running elicited by the renewed deprivation has undergone the same shift as has the photically entrained oscillation (it straddles the dotted extension of the feeding-onset line). (Modified from Rosenwasser et al. 1984, p. 27, by permission of author and publisher.)

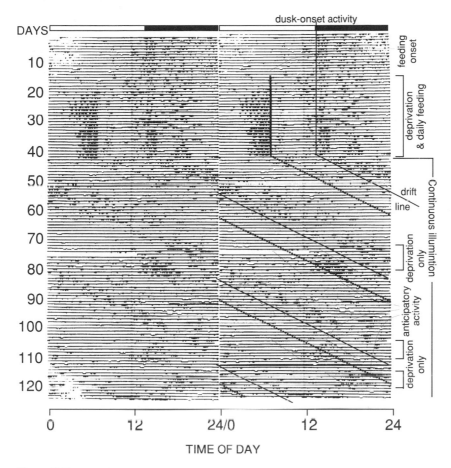

Figure 8.14
Double-day plot of rat running wheel activity, showing the reinstatement of anticipatory running by renewed food deprivation after long periods of constant illumination during which the photically entrained circadian oscillator ran free. The light-dark cycle indicated by the bars at top was present until the end of restricted feeding regime, where the rat had access to food from 10:00 to 12:00 every day (vertical line on right half of plot). Thereafter, the rat was in constant illumination. The activity onset at subjective dusk (hairlines) shows a phase drift of 48 minutes per 24-hour day, the slope of the extension of the feeding-onset line. Renewed total deprivation elicited bouts of anticipatory running that occurred at the same phase of the free running cycle as in the earlier restricted feeding reigime (at subjective 10:00). (Modified from Rosenwasser et al. 1984, p. 28, by permission of author and publisher.)

learning theory and in part because they favor an explanation in terms of a food-entrainable oscillator. Edmonds and Adler (1977a) gave an entrainment interpretation of their data, and subsequent authors in the biological rhythms tradition have followed their lead (Aschoff et al. 1983; Calhoun et al. 1982; Honmah, Goetz, and Aschoff 1983). They assumed that although the feedings did not function as timing signals capable of entraining the endogenous circadian oscillator that determined the free-running activity cycle (the so-called photic circadian oscillator), the feedings nonetheless entrained other endogenous circadian oscillations, which gave rise to the anticipatory feeding activity.

It is surprising that this explanation has gained so much currency in the circadian rhythm literature because it presupposes decidedly odd entrainment properties on the part of these special feeding-entrained oscillations, properties that make them unlike any other circadian oscillator ever studied. The data from the experiment with concurrent feeding schedules (figure 8.10), which were reported by Edmonds and Adler (1977a) in the paper in which they introduced the hypothesis of a food-entrainable oscillator, are, I believe, impossible to reconcile with such a hypothesis. In the lower portion of figure 8.10, the free-running rat (in a constantly illuminated chamber) had access to food on two concurrent schedules. On one (the N schedule), a 2-hour feeding period began every 24 hours; on the other, a 2-hour feeding period began every 25 hours. The rat ran in anticipation of both feedings. Because the M and N feedings were indistinguishable, this scheduling of feedings approximated an aperiodic schedule of timing signals. One may doubt that any entrainment at all could have occurred. One must ask whether it is possible to demonstrate the entrainment of circadian activity by light pulses (which are known to be potent entraining signals for the rat) using such a schedule. I have not been able to find a demonstration that it is possible to get any entrainment with this kind of timing signal. Yet for the Edmonds and Adler food-entrainable oscillator hypothesis to explain the double anticipation, one must maintain that one oscillator (or group of oscillators) became entrained to the N feedings while another became entrained to the M feedings.

Intuitively, entrainment is closely analogous to the regular resetting of an internal clock in accord with some time signal. The presentation of identical signals on concurrent schedules with different periods gives rise to irregular sequences of timing signals, so the internal clocks get set at irregular intervals and do not become entrained. More formally, I believe it is impossible to devise a phase-response curve that would make it possible for oscillators to become entrained to either one of two identical timing signals, one delivered on a 24-hour schedule and the other on a 25-hour schedule. In short, it is not clear that the Edmonds and Adler data can be reconciled with the model they suggested.

The hypothesis of a food-entrainable circadian oscillator has also led to more or less contradictory assumptions regarding the entrainment relationship between this oscillator and the circadian oscillator entrained by the light-dark cycle (the photic oscillator). On the one hand, the phase drift of the free-running photic oscillator is unaffected by the presence of a supposedly entrained food oscillator (figure 8.11), indicating no coupling between these two circadian oscillators. On the other hand, when the entraining feeding schedule is discontinued on the same day as the entraining light-dark schedule, the circadian oscillation that was supposedly entrained to the feeding schedule remains phase locked to the free-running photic oscillator for more than sixty days (figure 8.14), which implies very tight coupling between the two oscillations. It also implies, as Rosenwasser et al. (1984) note, that the oscillation entrained by the feeding schedule can be stably coupled to the photic oscillation at an arbitrary phase relationship. The oscillation supposed to be entrained by feeding maintains a fixed phase-relationship to the photic oscillation when the feeding cycle is discontinued regardless of the phase relationship between the light-dark cycle and the feeding cycle at the time of discontinuation. In summary, the entrainment characteristics of the putative food-entrainable circadian oscillator have no empirical precedents, and it is difficult or impossible to give a satisfactory formal description of what these characteristics would have to be.

The alternative to the hypothesis of a food-entrainable oscillator takes the Rosenwasser et al. summary of their findings at face value. It assumes that the rats learn the internally indicated time of day (the phase of an endogenous light-entrainable circadian oscillation) at which food becomes available and use this representation of feeding time to govern their activity on subsequent days. The next section gives a computational model of this process and shows how it accounts for the well-established characteristics of the activity that anticipates daily feeding periods.

A Computational Model for Anticipatory Circadian Activity

There are several plausible computational models built around the same basic idea, with little in the present data that would permit one to choose among them. The idea is embodied in three basic assumptions:

1. The animal records the subjective time at which a behaviorally significant event occurs. That is, quantities derived from the state of the animal's endogenous circadian oscillations at the moment of event onset are incorporated in the memory of the event itself.

2. An animal does not show anticipatory activity unless its records from several preceding days show a significant clustering of onsets within a circumscribed phase interval (circumscribed period of the subjective day).

3. When the onsets in recent days do cluster in a circumscribed interval of subjective time, the timing of the animal's anticipatory activity is determined primarily by the most recently recorded onset time, with earlier recorded onsets being accorded progressively less weight in the estimation of the currently most likely time of onset.

When the feeding schedule has approximately the same period as the endogenous circadian clock, there will be a clustering of onsets within a circumscribed interval of subjective time in the course of several days, and the animal will show anticipatory activity. When the feeding schedule has a period appreciably different from that of the subjective clock, successive feeding onsets occur at such widely separated subjective times from one day to the next that there is never a significant clustering of feeding onsets within a circumscribed interval of subjective time; hence, the animal does not show anticipatory activity (Bolles and Moot result with rats), or shows it only very weakly and only at 24 subjective hours after the last recorded onset (the result that both Beling and Wahl got with bees).

More specifically, let us assume that the animal shows anticipatory activity only when the probability of the observed degree of phase clustering in its last four observations is less than 0.25 (one chance in four). One computationally simple way it could assess this probability is to compute the square of the resultant phase vector divided by the number of times of occurrence entering into the calculation. Recall that the sine-cosine representation of the phase of an oscillation may be regarded as the Cartesian coordinates of a vector of length 1—the hand on the internal clock (see figure 7.6). The square of the resultant phase vector is computed simply by summing separately the cosine and sine coordinates of the recorded onset times, squaring both sums, and adding them together. Dividing the resulting quantity by the number of observations that entered into its computation yields a quantity whose critical values are almost independent of the number of observations (Batschelet 1981, p. 56). For a sample drawn from a random population of phase vectors, the chances that the square of their resultant divided by the number of observations will exceed 1.5 are about one in four regardless of how many observations there are.

Suppose now that the rat is free running, with the period of its clock equal to 24.5 hours, and that it is exposed to a feeding schedule with a 20.5-hour period, three hours shorter than the period of the subjective clock. Let the first feeding occur at subjective 18:00. The next feeding will occur at 14:05, 20 subjective hours and 5 subjective minutes later (subjective elapsed time is only 98 percent of the 20.5 real hours that elapse between feedings). The third feeding will occur at 10:10 and the fourth at 6:15. Thus the first four feedings are dispersed over a 12-hour phase interval. The probability of four randomly scheduled daily feedings' falling by chance within an arbitrary (post hoc) half-day phase interval is approximately 0.4 (the square of the resultant phase vector divided by the N is .99), so the observed clustering does not satisfy the < 0.25 probability criterion that clustering must meet to elicit anticipatory activity.

We see by this example that the well-established failure of animals to show anticipatory feeding when feeding schedules depart from the period of the endogenous oscillator by more than about 3 or 4 hours follows from the assumption that the animal does not show anticipatory activity unless there is significant clustering in the most recently recorded subjective times of occurrence. The fact that it takes several days for anticipatory activity to emerge when a circadian feeding schedule is imposed is evidence that this assumption is justified. It is evidence that animals require significant clustering in the recorded phases before they will show anticipatory activity. It takes repeated observations to make a cluster. Just how many depends on the significance level the animal uses in its test for clustering. Thus this parameter of a computational model could be estimated from the number of days it takes for anticipatory feeding to emerge as a function of how dispersed in subjective time the feedings are. From this and the free-running period of the rat's clock, one should be able to calculate the periods of the feeding schedule that would just fail to elicit anticipatory feeding.

The failure to see anticipatory activity when the period of the feeding schedule departs substantially from 24 hours has been one of the principal arguments in favor of the food-entrainable oscillator hypothesis. We see, however, that it follows from the assumption in the present model that the animal will not show anticipatory activity unless there is a statistically significant clustering in the recorded subjective times of occurrence. When the period of the feeding schedule is only 1 or 2 hours shorter than the period of the animal's clock, one does see anticipatory feeding because now there is significant clustering of the subjective times of occurrence in the course of several days. However, the amount of time by which this activity anticipates the onset of food availability should be reduced under these circumstances, as in fact it is. When the period of the feeding schedule is longer than that of the animal's clock by an hour or two, anticipatory feeding is also seen, and now the anticipation time is longer than normal (Aschoff et al. 1983). Again, this is predicted by the present model.

Aschoff (1984) has cited the shrinkings and lengthenings of the anticipatory interval as important evidence in favor of an entrainment model.
The entrainment model assumes that the animal has a feeding clock that
runs at the same rate as its other endogenous clocks but gets reset to the
"correct" time at each feeding. In the entrainment model, the rat shows
anticipatory activity whenever its feeding clock reaches a fixed time , let
us say 9:30. The rat resets its feeding clock to, say, 12:00, at the onset of
food availability. If the animal is on a 23-hour feeding schedule and it is
fed at 12:00 one day, it will be fed at 11:00 the next day. Suppose the rat's
putative feeding clock runs 30 minutes a day slow (a period of 24.5
hours). By assumption, this clock was set to subjective 12:00 at the onset
of the previous day's feeding. The next day, 9:30 subjective time coincides with 9:57 real time. Feeding onset occurs at 11:00 (real time), so the
animal will anticipate its onset by only about an hour (11:00-9:57) rather
than by $2\frac{1}{2}$ hours (12:00-9:30). On the entrainment model the animal is
assumed to advance its subjective feeding clock to 12:00 at each feeding
onset. This is what keeps the feeding clock entrained to the feeding
schedule. Thus, the same shortening of the anticipation time must be seen
every day. The shortening of the anticipation time is the phase lag that
develops in one day between the feeding cycle and the animal's feeding
clock. Similarly, the increased anticipatory interval seen when the period
of the feeding cycle is longer than the period of the animal's clock is the
phase lead that develops each day.
    The present model also explains the shortening and lengthening of
anticipatory intervals as consequences of the daily phase lags and phase
leads between the internal clock and the external schedule. The difference between the present model and the entrainment model is in what
gets reset. In the entrainment model, the feeding clock gets reset. In the
present model, the animal's estimate of feeding time is altered each day.
Suppose feeding occurs at subjective 12:00 one day and that the rat then
expects it at the same time the next day. On a 23-hour feeding schedule,
it will in fact come at subjective 11:00 (assuming for the sake of simplicity
that the period of the rat's clock is exactly 24 hours). The rat will reset its
expectations to, say, 11:15 (weighting the most recent occurrence, 11:00,
more than the earlier occurrence, 12:00), but the next feeding will be
observed at 10:00, necessitating a bigger correction in the best estimate
than was required the first time. In a few days, the length of the anticipation interval will stabilize at a value jointly determined by the difference
between the two periods (the period of the schedule and the period of the
subjective clock), as in the entrainment explanation, and the extent to
which the animal weights earlier times of occurrence in computing its
current estimate of the next time of occurrence; the more it weights earlier
observations, the greater the lag or lead. Thus the computational model

predicts a slope greater than one for the function relating the amount of shortening or lengthening in the anticipation interval to the difference between the schedule period and the period of the internal clock. Aschoff et al. (1983, p. 97) determined this function. Their data show about a 1.3 hour change in the length of the anticipation interval for each 1 hour change in the schedule period. This slope of greater than 1 is predicted by the present model but not by the entrainment model.

The greatest attraction of the present model is the ease with which it explains multiple anticipation peaks when there is more than one feeding per day and the ease with which it explains the immediate reinstatement of appropriately timed anticipatory activity when feeding sched ules are reinstated. Multiple feedings, even concurrent feeding schedules with unequal periods, pose no problems for the present model (other than the need to develop a statistical procedure for detecting clusters in circular data), whereas they pose seemingly insoluble problems for entrainment models. The present model also explains the reinstatement data. Lifting the feeding schedule so that food becomes continuously available is not the same as extinction because the animal does not get any data that contradict those it got under the feeding schedule. It is not that the onsets of food availability now occur at a different time of day. Rather, because there was no food offset, there cannot be an onset. When there is again an offset—when food deprivation is reinstated—the rat looks to the most recently recorded times of food onset to time its anticipatory activity; hence, it immediately shows anticipatory activity that is appropriately timed within the temporal framework provided by its internal photically entrainable clock. When this internal clock is entrained to the external 24-hour day-night cycle, then the activity is appropriately timed within the external temporal framework as well.

Time of Training Effects

Recall that bees gave evidence of routinely recording the time of day at which they experienced a noteworthy sensory input. As with rats, their tendency to show anticipatory visits to a feeding place developed only over several days. It has just been argued that this is for statistical reasons and not because there is an association between time and feeding that needs strengthening. When other behavioral measures are employed, one sees strong evidence that the time of an experience has been recorded even when there is but a single day's training. The same may be expected to be true of the rat. As one moves away from paradigms in which a rational behavioral strategy would require statistically significant evidence of a regular time of food onset to paradigms in which the payoff matrix is such as to warrant a negligible significance criterion, one should see evidence that the rat remembers the time of day at which an experience occurred, even when that experience has occurred only once.

If at 12:00 a rat is shocked for stepping through a doorway from a safe white chamber to a dangerous black chamber in a passive avoidance box, it is more reluctant to step through that doorway when tested at 12:00 on subsequent days than when tested at any other time of day (Holloway, and Wansley 1973). If it is shocked at 18:00, its reluctance the next day is greatest at 18:00, and so on. The effect depends on the circadian phase of testing relative to the circadian phase of training, not on circadian phase per se. The same result is obtained in active avoidance tasks, where the rat must do something in order not to get shocked rather than refrain from doing something. The readiness with which the rat performs the avoidance response is greatest when it is tested at the time of day at which it was trained (Holloway and Sturgis 1976). The same result is obtained with appetitive tasks. If, at varying times of day, rats are placed in the start compartment of a maze and allowed to run to another compartment for a drink, the next day a rat runs most readily when it is tested at the time it was trained (Wansley and Holloway 1975). In the rat, as in the bee, the tendency to act on acquired information is linked to the time of day at which that information was acquired.

The analogy between these time-of-training effects in the rat and similar effects in the bee and the bird is a close one. Koltermann (1971), for example, showed that the behavioral expression of the bee's experience of color and odor was linked to the times of day at which these experiences were acquired. However, the insect results are not usually cited in the rat time-of-training literature. More surprisingly, the results on time-linked reactions to scheduled feedings—in the bee, the bird, and the rat—are also not cited. This is true despite the fact that the time-of-training effects appear to share a so-far unexplained oddity with the food anticipation effects: there is an intermediate elevation in the animal's inclination to act at a 9-12 hour phase interval after the circadian phase of training (the subjective time of day at which training occurred). Figure 8.15A plots data from rats on restricted feeding schedules, with a feeding period of 2 to 4 hours (depending on the rat) every 24 hours, under free-running (constant illumination) conditions. The figure plots the rat's normalized activity as a function of the number of hours preceding and following the onset of food. Beginning a couple of hours before the onset of food availability, there is a sharp rise in activity—the anticipatory activity we are already familiar with. Surprisingly, a second but lower peak in activity occurs 9 to 10 hours later. Figure 8.15B plots a rat's hesitancy to step through the door into the shock chamber as a function of the number of hours since it experienced shock for doing so. The hesitancy is maximal 24 hours later, but there is a clear intermediate peak in

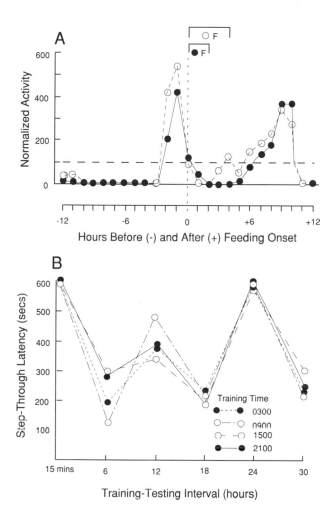

Figure 8.15
Comparison of data on the intermediate (9-12) hour peaks seen in restricted-feeding and
time-of-training experiments. A. Running wheel activity in free-running rats (percentage
of hourly activity averaged over the whole day), as a function of time before and after the
onset of the 2- to 4-hour feeding period, which occurred once every 24 hours. Note that in
addition to the anticipatory peak, there is another lower peak, which is phase locked to the
feeding time but occurs 9 to 10 hours later in the rats' subjective day. (Redrawn from
Aschoff et al. 1983, p. 97, by permission of author and publisher.) B. The step-through
latency of rats in a two-chamber passive avoidance box, as a function of the time elapsed
since a single training trial, on which they were shocked for stepping from the safe to the
dangerous chamber. There were four main groups, each given a training trial at a different
time of day, as indicated in the key. Each point is for a different sub-group, that is, a given
rat was tested only at a single training-test interval. Note the intermediate peak in the rats'
hesitancy to step through (at the 12-hour training-test interval). (Redrawn from Holloway
and Wansley 1973, p. 5, by permission of author and publisher.)

hesitancy at the 12-hour point. This intermediate effect at roughly half a cycle away from the training phase is clearly seen in all the time-of-training experiments in the rat, regardless of the time of training. I know no explanation for it, either in the time-of-training literature or in the restricted feeding literature. Whether the intermediate peaks seen in panels A and B of figure 8.15 are in fact connected remains to be determined. The fact that the intermediate peak is at 9 to10 hours in the feeding data and at 12 hours in the shock-avoidance data probably reflects that each point in figure 8.14B is from a different group and there was no group tested at the 9-hour interval, whereas the activity of the rats on restricted feeding was monitored continuously. When more groups are added to a time-of-training experiment, so that there are data points at 3-hour instead of 6-hour spacings, the rise to the intermediate peak is seen to occur 9 hours after training (figure 8.16).

One of the most interesting time-of-training experiments also illustrates the difference between representational and nonrepresentational accounts of these results. Hunsicker and Melgren (1977) put naive rats into the safe, white compartment of a passive avoidance box and allowed them to step through into the dangerous black compartment and drink sugared milk there for 5 minutes, without being shocked. One group did

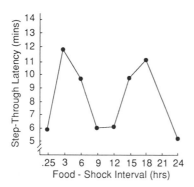

Figure 8.16
Rat's step-through latency 24 hours after a single shock trial in a two-chamber passive avoidance box, as a function of the interval between the termination of a 5-minute, no-shock feeding experience in the chamber and a subsequent shock experience. Note that the rats were least hesitant at the 0.25- and 24-hour intervals, when the time of day of the feeding experience approximately corresponded to the time of day of the shock experience. Note, however, that there is another period of markedly reduced hesitancy at 9-12 hours, when the time of day of the feeding experience differed from that of the shock experience by about half a day. These data are averaged across two groups of rats trained at different times of day because time of training had no effect. The effect depends on time of testing relative to time of training, not on time of training. (Redrawn from Hunsicker and Melgren 1977, p. 15, by permission of author and publisher.)

this between 8:00 and 11:00, while another group did it between 14:00 and 17:00. At different intervals thereafter (0.25, 3, 6, 9, 12, 15, 18, and 24 hours later), subgroups of these two original groups were returned to the safe, white chamber and given a strong shock shortly after they stepped through into the black compartment, which they all did in less than 3 seconds. Twenty-four hours after this punishment, the rats were placed in the white compartment for the third time, and their latency to step through into the black compartment was measured. The results are given in figure 8.16. There was no effect of the difference in the time of day at which the two major groups received their initial sugared milk training. All the effects depended not on time of day per se (whether objective or subjective) but rather on the time of testing relative to the time of training.

The single punishment trial made all the rats very hesitant to enter the black compartment, no matter when they were tested. The lowest average step-through latency in figure 8.16 is about 5 minutes, whereas before the shock (but after the sugared milk), every rat stepped through in less than 3 seconds. However, just how ready the rats were to venture into the black box varied depending on the relation between the time of day at testing and the time of day at which they had got the sugared milk. The rat's hesitancy to step into the black compartment was always measured at the same time of day as the time at which it had experienced the shock. What varied from group to group was whether or not the rat had, on an earlier occasion, experienced sugared milk (and no shock) at about that same or at some other time of day. For the 0.25-hour group and the 24-hour group, the conflicting experiences had occurred at about the same time of day. For the other groups they had occurred at different times. The 3-hour group and the 18-hour group were most reluctant (took the longest to step through). These rats were asked, in effect, to venture into the black compartment at a time of day when they had been shocked there but had never gotten anything good there. The .25-hour and the 24-hour group were least reluctant. These two groups were asked to hazard the black chamber at a time of day when they had received conflicting experiences there: one good and one bad. In the 0.25-hour group, these experiences had occurred on the same day. In the 24-hour group, these experiences had occurred at the same time on two successive days. In the 9- and 12-hour groups, the conflicting experiences had occurred about a half-circadian cycle apart. As noted above, the similarity of the data for the 9- and 12-hour groups to the data for the 0.25- and 24-hour groups is not readily explained by any theory yet advanced.

Setting aside the puzzling intermediate peak (or, in this case, valley), the representational explanation here advocated is suggested by the manner in which the situation was summarized. The explanation assumes that the mnemonic representation of any sensory experience incorporates a representation of the time of day (circadian phase) at which the experience occurred. Indeed, the representational account takes these time-of-training effects as further evidence for the general validity of this claim. This account further assumes that the temporal component of a memory commonly plays an important role in the animal's subsequent behavioral timing. Many interpretive mechanisms, which read representations out into behavior, are designed on the assumption that the time of day at which something occurs may predict the time of day at which it next occurs. On the representational account, time of day is always taken into account—by the 3- and 18-hour groups just as much as by the 0.25- and 24-hour groups. The first groups hesitate more because they know that at this time of day (the time at which they are being tested), the only thing that has happened to them is bad. The good thing happened at another time of day. The lesser hesitancy of the latter groups reflects their knowledge that both the good and the bad happened at about this time.

The nonrepresentational account offered by Hunsicker and Mellgren, which closely follows that offered by Holloway and his collaborators, is that the memories undergo periodic fluctuations in their retrievability. They propose a state-dependent or stimulus-generalization hypothesis in which "the state of the organism [the phase of some endogenous oscillation] becomes an essential part of the conditioning and shifts away from the state influence retention performance via the decreased availability of relevant cues" (p. 16). The difficulties with state-dependency interpretations of these time-of-training effects have already been discussed in connection with Kolterman's similar results with bees. It must be emphasized that the effects of the shock experience are strongly evident in the rats' behavior no matter what time of day they are tested. Instead of stepping through within the first few seconds, they wait many minutes. The best summary is to say that the relationship between the circadian phase of testing and the circadian phase of the positive training has some effect on when they finally overcome their hesitancy.

One could interpret the Hunsicker and Mellgren hypothesis to be that subjective time was one of the stimuli associated with both the shock and the food and that the rats' tendency to step through was a function of how closely the subjective time at testing corresponded to the subjective times associated with these two experiences. In that case, the nonrepresentational account becomes indistinguishable from the representational account because it concedes its essential assumptions: rats represent the subjective time at which something occurs and their subsequent behavior depends on the extent to which the current subjective time corresponds to the remembered subjective time. Under this interpretation of their hypothesis, there is no reason to speak of fluctuations in retrievability because all aspects of the remembered experience enter into the determination of behavior at all times of day.

In summary, the evidence implies that in the rat, as in the bee, the memory of any experience incorporates a representation of the subjective time of day at which the experience occurred—that is, of the state of an endogenous circadian oscillation—and that behavioral outputs based on this memory frequently reflect the extent to which current subjective time corresponds to remembered subjective time. In the rat, this is demonstrated in both the anticipatory activity seen in restricted feeding experiments and in the tendency for the behavior observed in a variety of standard learning tasks to depend on the relation between the time of training and the time of testing.

Precision of the Recorded Circadian Phase

It is of considerable theoretical interest to know how precisely an animal can note the phase of an internal circadian oscillation. The size of the anticipatory interval provides no useful indication of this precision because it varies a great deal depending on the observed behavioral output. Visits to the food cup also anticipate the appearance of the food (as do visits to the drinking spout, even though water is continuously available), but the rise in the frequency of these visits occurs much closer to the onset of food availability than does the rise in running wheel activity (Aschoff et al. 1983). The length of the anticipatory interval clearly reflects the use the animal makes of the recorded temporal information and not the accuracy of the record itself.

Experiments by Horter (1977) show that the rat's record of the time of day at which food becomes available is accurate to within a few minutes. Horter had rats press a lever for food, then limited the period of food availability and shocked the rats for lever presses outside this period. The period of food availability began at a different time of day for each of his seven subjects. For some, it was during the light phase of the 12:12 light-dark cycle; for others, during the dark phase. The onset of food availability never occurred sooner than 1 hour after a change in illumination, so changes in illumination never directly signaled food availability. Horter began with a 12-hour period of food availability and narrowed the period by hourly decrements whenever an individual satisfied a stringent criterion for the confinement of its presses to the period of food availability. In this way, Horter obtained rats that seldom pressed the lever during the entire period when food was not available (the total number of such presses in one day was usually fewer than 10 and often fewer than 5). But his rats began pressing very soon after food became available and pressed at a high rate throughout this period. The ultimate duration of the daily period of food availability varied from rat to rat, mostly as a function of where in the rat's circadian cycle this period fell. As one might expect, the ultimate period was longer when it fell during the inactive phase. The ultimate durations ranged from 1 to 6 hours.

Horter collected data on the time of occurrence of the last lever press prior to the onset of food availability and the first press after the (unsignaled) onset—the data that would serve to pin down exactly how accurately the rat can represent the time of day. Unfortunately, although he refers to these data at several points in his report, he never gives them. It is nonetheless clear from the data he does give that the rat represents the time of day to an accuracy of appreciably less than 10 minutes. In many of his published plots, the number of lever presses are shown in 10-minute bins. Often there were no lever presses in any of the bins immediately preceding the first 10 minutes of food availability and eighty or more presses within that first 10 minutes. In view of the large numbers of presses in the first 10 minutes, the rat must have made the first one within no more than 3 or 4 minutes after the onset of food availability. The rats were able to maintain this degree of accuracy in the first day under constant illumination, so what is involved is the accuracy with which the rat can represent the momentary phase of its endogenous circadian oscillator (the time on its clock), not the accuracy with which it can represent an interval since lights out or lights on.

If we adopt (conservatively) an estimate of ± 3 minutes as the average uncertainty in the rat's record of the reading on its internal clock, then these readings are made and stored with an accuracy of about 1 part in 500. Until well into the previous century, few humans had routine access to an external time-keeping device that permitted them to note the time of day with comparable accuracy. If we imagine that the record of the time of day is based only on the quantities that define the state of a circadian oscillation (the state variables), then this result means that these state variables can be read with extraordinary precision; in other words, the high temporal resolution implies high resolution in the quantification of the state variables. Alternatively, we might imagine that the high resolution is obtained by monitoring not only the state variables in a circadian oscillation but also the state variables in ultradian oscillations phase-locked to the circadian oscillation.

Do Animals Record the Phases of Infradian Oscillations?

The suggestion that the high resolution in an animal's record of the time of day may mean the record incorporates phase information from ultradian as well as circadian endogenous oscillations raises the question whether the record of time of occurrence also incorporates phase information from oscillations with periods much longer than twenty-four hours. In the model of anticipatory activity advanced above it was implicitly assumed that they did because it was assumed that the rat weighted records from more recent days more heavily than records from less recent days. To distinguish the record of yesterday from the record of the day before, the animal would need to record the phase of an infradian oscillation.

There is astonishingly little experimental work on whether animals can adapt their behavior to anticipate events that recur only every so many days or weeks. The only experimental study I have found of the question whether birds can represent intervals measured in days is an unpublished experiment by Caubisens and Edmonds. In the fall, on a wooded part of the State University of New York's Purchase campus, they set up a feeding station in the woods, which was visited by a mixed flock of chickadees, titmice, and nuthatches, many of which were banded for individual identification. Initially the feeders were kept filled with sunflower seeds throughout the day. From late October to early January, however, the experimenter came to the feeders each morning at 8:00 and filled them only once, with seeds from a white feed bag she carried. After filling the feeder, the experimenter remained near it for the next hour to record the visits of the numbered birds. She also visited the feeder for another randomly chosen hour each day to check whether her presence at the feeder induced the birds to come. Finally, from early January onward, the experimenter stocked the feeding station only every second day, although she continued to come every day from 8:00 to 9:00, carrying the bag of seeds each time.

In the late fall and early winter phase of the experiment, the birds soon learned to appear there at 8:00. They were much more likely to be found there then than at the randomly chosen other observation hour, although the experimenter came to the station for both of the hours. Most interestingly, within two weeks after the initiation of the every-other-day routine, the birds appeared at the station only every other day (figure 8.17), despite the fact that the experimenter came to the station every day with her bag of seeds. The birds' appearance at the station anticipated the experimenter's usual time of appearance. When the experimenter came early, they were not yet there; when she came late, they were waiting for her—but only on feeding days. Given the simplicity of this experiment and the clear-cut nature of the results obtained, it is surprising that it is so difficult to find published experiments of this kind. Given the suggestive field observations on gulls (Sibly and McCleery 1983), which appear to recognize that garbage dumping does not occur every seventh day, more experiments exploring the capacity of birds to represent intervals measured in days are clearly called for. Laboratory studies with individ-

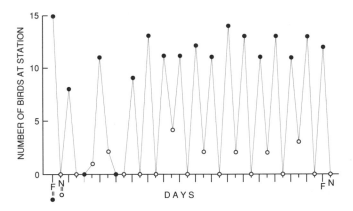

Figure 8.17
Number of banded birds observed at feeding station on successive feeding (*F*) and nonfeeding (*N*) days. Feeding only every other day was begun January 6. These data are for the period from February 12 to March 19. The experimenter went to the station every day, carrying a bag of seeds, but emptied it into the feeder only on feeding days. The birds' arrival at the station on feeding days anticipated the arrival of the experimenter. (From unpublished manuscript by M. Denise Caubisens, kindly supplied by Susan Edmonds, who supervised this work.)

ual birds under free-running conditions would be particularly informative.

Conclusion

A substantial body of experimental work demonstrates that animals ranging from bees to rats routinely record the time of day at which they have a noteworthy experience and make use of this record to time their subsequent behavior. In chapter 15, I argue that recording the time of occurrence of a to-be-remembered experience is obligatory because this record, together with the equally obligatory record of place, constitute the spatiotemporal addresses by which one memory is linked to another.

Chapter 9

Temporal Intervals

When learning is studied within the zoological tradition, it is tacitly assumed that the learning is tailored to a particular behavioral function. On the other hand, experimental psychologists took over from empiricist philosophy of mind the assumption that learning is a general process, not tailored to the particular material to be learned or shaped by natural selection to serve different roles in different species. The findings regarding the adaptations of bees and vertebrates to events that recur with a daily period conform more to the expectations of the zoological tradition. The animals readily learn to anticipate events that recur with the 24-hour period that dominates their environment, but they do not learn to anticipate events that recur with periods several hours less or greater. It appears that the period is a biological given; what the animals learn is not the elapsed interval between feedings or the period of the feeding cycle but rather the phase of the 24-hour cycle at which feeding occurs. The nervous system structures the learning in this way, which is why the animals do not learn cycles that do not have a 24-hour period. It also appears that there are species differences in the learning of infradian periods. Birds can apparently learn periods measured in days, while bees apparently cannot.

These findings raise the following types of questions:

1. What other periods can animals represent? The Caubisen and Edmonds experiment in which a feeder was stocked every other day suggests that they can represent a feeding cycle with a 48-hour period. Are the periods a bird can learn only multiples (and submultiples) of the circadian period? Alternatively, is the performance Caubisen and Edmonds observed based on a representation of the interval that elapses between one stocking of the feeder and the next? That is, do the birds represent the restocking process not as a periodic or cyclical process but rather as a regenerative one in which each restocking starts anew the process that will generate another restocking after a certain interval has elapsed?

2. Can animals represent elapsed intervals, as opposed to periods and phases? Operant experiments with fixed interval schedules of reinforcement suggest that they can represent elapsed intervals measured in seconds and minutes (Gibbon 1977; Killeen 1975).

3. By what experimental procedures can one distinguish the learning of a period from the learning of an elapsed interval? By definition, a period is the period of a cyclical process, which also has a phase, while an elapsed interval is the interval elapsed from a point in time marked by a particular event. Elapsed-interval processes do not have a phase (a constant position in time).

4. Under what naturally occurring conditions and for what biological purposes is it useful for a given kind of animal to represent a periodic process whose period is of a given order of magnitude?

5. Under what naturally occurring conditions and for what purposes is it useful for a given kind of animal to be able to represent an elapsed interval of a given order of magnitude?

The answers to questions 4 and 5, which are questions about the natural history of animals, may suggest suitable choices of subjects and the design of appropriate experimental paradigms. This chapter is concerned with the representation of temporal intervals measured in seconds and minutes, so we begin by reviewing some naturalistic studies that indicate some of the circumstances under which different kinds of animals might need such a representation in the wild.

Natural Conditions Requiring the Representation of Elapsed Intervals

Replenishment Intervals
Gill (1988) has studied the role that the representation of elapsed intervals plays in the behavioral strategy of the long-tailed hermit hummingbird in the Costa Rican jungle. Like the bees studied by Janzen (1971), these birds "trapline," that is, they regularly visit widely separated sources of nectar. (Plants in tropical habitats tend to grow as isolates, while in temperate habitats, they tend to grow in clumps.) Traplining involves no uncertainty about prey locations. The main foraging decision is when to revisit. In traplining species, the scheduling of their visits to their food sources is their principal means of controlling the resource. Since the blooms whose nectar the bird needs to sustain life are widely dispersed in the jungle, it cannot hover around the resource and drive off other harvesters. For the trapliner, being the early bird is often the difference between success and failure.

The hummingbird's problem is to schedule its revisits in such a way that it obtains the maximum amount of energy per visit. Blooms regenerate their nectar over time after each visit. The longer the hummingbird postpones its next visit, the larger its potential harvest—but also the greater the probability that another harvester will have gotten there first. There is no predicting the optimum interval in advance. Different flowers regenerate nectar at widely differing rates, and the probability of another harvester's stealing the harvest depends on the extent to which there are competitors in the area.

Male long-tailed hummingbirds assemble on leks, where they spend much of the morning trying to attract females by their displays. The males leave the lek every so often to feed for 5-10 minutes. These visits to one or more blooms on its trapline often require the bird to fly 0.5 kilometer from the lek and return. A 6-gram hummingbird, which is among the smallest homeotherms, expends energy at an enormous rate, both in hovering and in defending its body temperature. It must never go for very long without feeding. Each male on the lek feeds in a different direction from the lek, so the males on the lek do not generally compete for food sites. However, at any one time there are a number of males that are not on the lek, poaching from the blooms on the traplines of males on the lek. The amount of time a male can spend on the lek (hence its probability of successful mating) is directly proportional to the efficiency of its feeding excursions (the ratio of energy gained to energy lost). The efficiency of its excursions is closely tied to how well it adjusts the timing of its visits. Visits that are either too early or too late seriously degrade efficiency. The hummingbird's ability to forage efficiently depends on its ability to represent time intervals precisely and to extract subtle features of temporal structure from its observations.

The problem the bird confronts is inherently one of representing elapsed intervals rather than periods because the environmental variation to which it must adapt is aperiodic. Flowers do not fill and empty themselves cyclically. They fill themselves at a more or less steady rate (the rate, however, depends on the time of day), and they are emptied by various foragers. When only one forager is exploiting a given flower, the time elapsed since the last visit determines the short-term probability of collecting a large reward; the longer the interval, the greater the expected reward. When more than one forager is visiting a bloom, the problem is more complex because the longer a forager waits, the greater the probability that the bloom will recently have been emptied by a competitor. The bird must adopt a strategy that tends to get it to the bloom when sufficient time has elapsed since the last known emptying to allow a reasonable reward to accumulate but not enough to make it likely that a competitor will have beaten the bird to the accumulated reward. Clearly such a strategy must depend on the ability to represent elapsed intervals precisely and to make sophisticated use of such a representation. Hence,

these hummingbirds should make good subjects in experiments designed to assess the capacity of a bird to represent elapsed intervals. Their
ability may be no better than that of many other animals, but they may
employ this representational capacity in a behavioral strategy that
allows us to gauge the precision of the representation.

Naturalistic considerations also suggest that the behavioral output
likely to reflect most sensitively the bird's ability to represent elapsed
intervals is the timing of visits to the source—not the timing of bill
insertions. Historically at least, there has been a tendency for experimental psychologists to assume that the behavior selected for study in a
learning experiment is arbitrary, that key pecking is as good an index of
underlying learning as any other. From a zoological standpoint, this is
not a plausible assumption. There is no reason to suppose that if a
hummingbird of this species were kept always in front of an artificial
flower, which was refilled periodically, the timing of its bill insertions
(the presumed analogue of key pecks) would necessarily reflect the same
sensitivity to elapsed intervals as would the timing of its visits to that
flower when it was free to pursue other biologically essential behaviors
in the meanwhile, such as displaying on the lek. It is possible that both
behaviors reflect equally precisely the same underlying representation
of elapsed interval, but to any evolutionary biologist, such an assumption ought not to be regarded as so obviously justified that it requires no
experimental support.

The discussion illustrates the use of naturalistic considerations to
guide the choice of animal subjects and the design of suitable behavioral
paradigms. This species of hummingbird is an extraordinarily favorable
subject for the experimental study of the capacity of higher animals to
represent elapsed intervals measured in minutes. Just as nutcrackers
must experience considerable selection pressure on their ability to record
a great many different cache locations, so the long-tailed hermit hummingbird must experience considerable selection pressure on its ability
to represent elapsed intervals and/or to make sophisticated and precise
use of such a representation.

Gill (1988) has begun the experimental study of this behavior, working
in the field with artificial flowers, stocked at experimenter-chosen times
with sugar water. In one set of field experiments, he refilled the artificial
flower on periodic schedules and showed that the birds did not adapt to
variations in the refill period. For example, when the flower was refilled
every 20 minutes with 100 microliters of artificial nectar, the bird continued to return with a median intervisit interval of 7 minutes throughout
the day, with the result that the majority of its visits went unrewarded.
The bird was visiting the artificial flower sufficiently often to detect a

cycle with a period of 20 minutes. A cycle may be detected from discrete-time samples provided the frequency of the samples is at least twice the frequency of the cycle (the sampling theorem). When Gill varied the refill period from 20 to 40 minutes over four successive days in the sequence 20,40,40,20, there was no significant effect on the median revisit interval. By contrast, when he varied the size of the refill from 100 to 20 microliters on four successive days in the sequence 100,20,20,100, there was a significant effect; the revisit interval was longer for the smaller reward. (This is probably a manifestation of the general tendency of foraging animals to match their relative rates of visiting different food sources to the relative rates of return expected from them.)

When Gill switched to elapsed-interval schedules, he found that the hummingbird's behavior was sensitive to elapsed intervals. When the flower was refilled with 100 microliters 10 minutes after the last empty-ing all day long for 3 days, the bird increased its modal intervisit interval from 6 minutes to 12 minutes, with a consequent significant increase in the percentage of successful visits. Gill also experimented with ramp schedules in which the flower was filled with 100 microliters when 10 minutes had elapsed since the last successful visit and an additional 100 microliters was added after a further 5 minutes, so that the bird harvested nothing if less than 10 minutes had elapsed since its last successful visit, 100 microliters if the elapsed interval was greater than 10 but less than 15 minutes, and 200 microliters if the elapsed interval was greater than 15 minutes. The birds appeared to adapt quickly to the experience of obtaining a larger reward after a longer interval by lengthening their intervisit intervals. However, controls for the time of day and the effect on intervisit interval of increases in reward size uncorrelated with intervisit interval were not adequate to rule out alternative interpreta-tions. Whenever, by accident or design, a bird found an empty flower after a relatively long intervisit interval, the next visit was made after a much shorter interval, suggesting that the bird's behavioral strategy depended on the details of its recent record of intervisit intervals and their outcomes. Gill's field experiments provide a naturalistic context for one's appreciation of the more tightly controlled laboratory experiments of Church and his collaborators.

In schedules where pigeons must postpone their key pecks to obtain a larger reward, they learn with difficulty and seldom attain a high level of "self-control" even when the required postponement is only on the order of seconds (Ainslie 1974; Mazur and Logue 1978; Rachlin and Green 1972). With DRL schedules (differential reinforcement of low rates), extending the postreinforcement interval (during which pecks postpone reward) to as little as 15 seconds prevents the bird's mastering the schedule (Richelle and Lejeune 1984). By contrast, the hummingbird quickly learns to postpone its visits to the artificial flower by several minutes to get a higher reward. These divergent findings may have as much to do with differences in the behavior being used to assess the animal's representation of the temporal interval—key pecks versus visits—as with differences in the representational capacity of the two species of bird. There is all the more reason to think this in that the same bird that cannot learn a DRL 15-second schedule shows postreinforcement pauses of longer than a minute when run on a schedule with a fixed interval of 120 seconds from one reward to the next arming of the feeder (Richelle and Lejeune 1984). This illustrates the importance of choosing a behavioral paradigm on the basis of a knowledge of the natural history of the animal.

Gill's field observations and experiments illustrate why the capacity to represent the temporal structure of its experience over intervals on the order of minutes could be highly advantageous to at least some birds. Kamil (1978) has shown that the nectar-feeding amakihi in Hawaii avoids visiting the flowers it has recently visited. This requires both the capacity to represent the locations of the flowers it has visited and the interval elapsed since the last visit. Under a variety of foraging situations, this must be the rule: it does not pay to return too quickly to the place where you have most recently been successful. What will vary from species to species (and food type to food type) is what constitutes too quickly. In short, approximations to fixed interval schedules of reinforcement are readily found in nature, which is part of the reason that the capacity to represent a wide range of temporal intervals confers a selective advantage.

Scheduling Family Get-Togethers
Field observations on the nursing of hares (Broekhuizen and Maaskamp 1980; Rongstad and Tester 1971) illustrate the often surprising ways in which the capacity to represent precisely both time and place forms the foundations of animal behavior. Like all other mammals, doe hares nurse their young. They do not, however, stay with them during the nursing period. They leave their young on the day (actually, on the night) of their birth, spending that day and all subsequent days as much as several hundred meters away from their litter. In the hour after sunset on each night, the doe returns to the place where she left her litter and nurses them all simultaneously for about 5 minutes, then disappears again until the following night. The precise time of her first return is apparently chosen by the mother, but it almost always occurs within 10 to 70 minutes after sunset. Whatever the precise time of her first return, that time

becomes the appointed time of nursing and the place of birth the appointed place. During the first few days of life, the leverets (babies) do not disperse far from the place of birth, but each succeeding day they disperse farther, each in its own direction. By the second week, each leveret in a litter is likely to be separated by several tens of meters from any other littermate, but every dusk, at the appointed time, the littermates assemble at the place of their birth a few minutes before the doe arrives to nurse them. The assembly at the nursing place and the dispersal immediately following nursing are so tightly scheduled that radio position fixes taken every 15 minutes frequently miss it. Most remarkably, the time of assembly differs from family to family in the same locale (figure 9.1).

The appropriate laboratory studies of this phenomenon have not been done, but the field observations suggest several hypotheses. It is likely that the phenomenon represents the combined influence of phase timing and interval timing. That is, the programming of the assembly behavior in the doe and her leverets depends both on a record of the circadian phase at which assemblies occur (the subjective time of day) and on a record of the interval elapsed since some temporally well-defined event that reliably occurs at approximately that subjective time, most probably sunset. It is not clear how the assembly behavior could be based purely on circadian phase because the assembly occurs at about the same interval after sunset throughout the summer, which means that it occurs at different phases of the 24-hour cycle. In the course of the long breeding

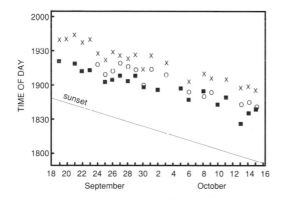

Figure 9.1
The starting time of nursing for three different litters. The two litters indicated by x's and o's were nursed in the same pasture; the litter indicated by filled squares was nursed about 800 meters away from the others. Rongstad and Tester (1971, p. 341) give similar data for the American snowshoe hare. (Redrawn from Broekhuizen and Maaskamp 1980, p. 494, by permission of author and publisher.)

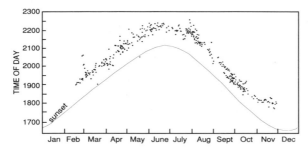

Figure 9.2
The start of nursing in the field for litters of wild hares over the course of the breeding season in Holland. Each dot gives the start of an observed nursing. Ambient light when nursing started varied from dusk to full darkness, depending on the season. (Redrawn from Broekhizen and Maaskamp 1980, by permission of author and the publisher.)

season in the Netherlands, the time of nursing varies from around 19:00 to as late as 22:00 and then back to as early as 16:00 (figure 9.2).

The assembly cannot be based on a measure of the ambient light intensity at the time of assembly because this varies substantially during the 3- to 8-week period over which the members of a single litter may continue to assemble with their mother. The midsummer twilight is prolonged at high latitudes. In June the nursing may be observed with the naked eye, whereas later or earlier in the summer a searchlight is required. The temporally well-defined event most reliably detectable under varying conditions of cloud cover would seem to be the extinction of the sun's last rays, so it is reasonable to conjecture that the timing of the assembly depends on the doe and her leverets' having a common representation of the interval that must elapse from this event to their assembly.

This would appear to be a good preparation for laboratory or semi-naturalistic studies of the capacity of a mammal to represent elapsed temporal intervals in the 10-70 minute range. The timing of assembly even under field conditions appears to be more precise than would be suggested by laboratory data on the fixed interval scallop in the rat (Ferster and Skinner 1957; Richelle and Lejeune 1984), by data on the rat's anticipatory behavior following a stimulus that signals food availability at some interval after the onset of the signal (Terman et al. 1984), or by data on trace conditioning in classical conditioning paradigms (Balsam 1984). This may not mean that the rabbit represents elapsed intervals more precisely but rather that this particular behavioral pattern makes precise use of the representation, whereas the experimental paradigms used by the cited authors may tap into behavioral mechanisms that do not put a premium on precision.

The Representation of Experimental Cycles with Short Periods

The ability of animals to represent the circadian phase (subjective time of day) at which events occur rests on an innate representation of the day-night cycle (the circadian clock). Experiments with feeding schedules several hours shorter or longer than 24 hours have repeatedly failed to demonstrate behavioral adaptation to cycles with these periods because these cycles do not match the innately represented cycle. On the other hand, the Caubisen and Edmonds experiment with a 48-hour feeding schedule suggests that birds may learn cycles much longer than 24 hours. Alternatively, the performance they observed may indicate the bird's ability to measure elapsed intervals of 2 or more days duration. Stein (1951) investigated whether birds would adapt to cyclical feeding schedules with periods measured in minutes rather than hours or days. She worked with sparrows, canaries, and finches in cages that gave automated recordings of the number of hops a bird made per minute. In other words, she measured activity, which is what experiments on the anticipation of circadian feeding schedules have also measured. She set up hoppers that opened at regular experimenter-chosen intervals, allowing the birds to feed for 30 seconds. When the intervals between openings were between 4 and 10 minutes, the birds' hopping showed crescendos whose peaks anticipated each opening.

When Stein disabled the hopper at the end of a training session, the birds showed several successive appropriately timed peaks. If, for example, the hopper had been opened every 10 minutes, there was a peak at 10 minutes after the final opening, followed by a sharp dip (even though the hopper had not opened), followed by a second peak at 20 minutes, and so on, for three to five cycles (figure 9.3). This suggests that the birds represented the hopper openings as a periodic or cyclical process.

When Stein tried intervals of 3 minutes or less, she found that "the excitement from the expectation of food [grew] too strong and extend[ed] over the entire training interval, so that no clear peak [was] seen" (p. 400). A switch to operant techniques would in all likelihood have shown that these birds distinguish intervals shorter than 4 minutes. In other words, the problem was not a failure of representational capacity at these short intervals but rather insensitivity in the behavioral index of the representation of temporal structure. Stein found that when she extended the period between openings of the hopper to 30 or 40 minutes, it took much longer for the birds to develop an anticipatory peak in their hopping activity. She suggests that the birds may not be able to represent periods much beyond 30 minutes. This conclusion, if true, is of considerable interest. Its verification will require much more extensive experimenta-

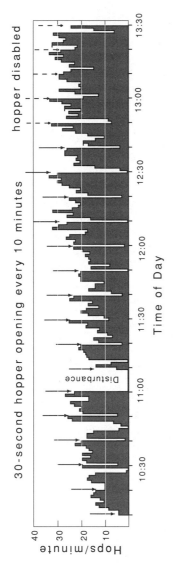

Figure 9.3
Hops per minute of a finch, in a cage with a hopper that opened for 30 seconds every 10 minutes, beginning at 10:10 and stopping with the opening at 12:40. Note that activity continues to peak every 10 minutes for four cycles after the last opening of the hopper ("hopper disabled"). The disturbance that interfered with the recording between 11:00 and 11:10 is not specified, but it may have been an air raid warning, since the subjects fell victim to an air attack in the course of these experiments, which were conducted in 1943. (Redrawn from Stein 1951, p. 399, by permission of author and publisher.)

tion. The design of these experiments should give consideration to the bird's natural history, to determine what behaviors might be most likely to reflect the representation of longer periods. Perhaps reluctance to visit a previously emptied food source might be a better index for these longer intervals than is anticipatory hopping in front of a single food source or pecking at a key.

Stein's experiment is an example of what is called a fixed-time (FT) schedule in operant conditioning because the timing of reward delivery is fixed by the program, independent of the animal's behavior. Killeen (1975) reviews data from many different FT schedules, focussing on the temporal patterning of behavior within an interval. Unfortunately, Killeen did not report what his subjects did when food stopped being delivered on schedule. Did they show periodic peaks of behavior for several cycles like Stein's birds, or did their performance look like the extinction performance of pigeons trained on fixed-interval schedules?

A fixed-interval (FI) schedule is one in which the reward becomes available at a fixed interval after the harvesting of the last available reward. With this schedule, unlike with an FT schedule, the timing of reward delivery depends on the animal's behavior because the timer for the next reward does not start until the animal has harvested the previous reward. FI schedules produce what is called an FI scallop—a pause in responding following a reward followed by an accelerating rate of pressing that may or may not attain asymptotically high rates prior to the delivery of the next reward (Catania and Reynolds 1968; Hawkes and Shimp 1974; Killeen 1975). The scallop is scaled to the interval: the longer the interval the longer the delay before responding begins and the slower the acceleration (Gibbon 1977).

At least some pigeons show clear FI scallops when the interval between reinforcements is in the 45 to 110 minute range, with a time out following each reinforcement (Ferster and Skinner 1957, pp. 190–91, 261–264). However, the pigeon's behavior during extinction when the food fails to become available on schedule provides an instructive contrast to the behavior of Stein's birds, illustrating the difference between the representation of a periodic process and the representation of an elapsed interval. During extinction following an FI schedule of reinforcement, the pigeon does not show periodic FI scallops. When the first reinforcement fails to appear, the pigeon goes on pressing at a very high rate for an interval three or four times longer than the fixed interval, pauses for an unpredictable amount of time, resumes pressing with another burst much longer than the fixed interval, and so on (see, for example, Ferster and Skinner 1957, p. 199). In other words, it would appear that when a process is periodic and the period is short (on the order of minutes), birds may be able to represent it as such, and when it is aperiodic but with a predictable interval between the harvesting of one reward and the availability of the next, birds may represent the interval that elapses from harvest to next availability. It is possible that the upper limit on the periods that a given species of bird may represent is different from the upper limit on the elapsed interval. However, as yet, neither limit has been carefully determined.

Stein reports that birds rapidly adjusted to a change in the period of the cyclical hopper openings. The experimental record of an adjustment from a period of 4 minutes to one of 5 minutes is shown in figure 9.4. The transition portion of this adjustment is particularly interesting (lower panel of figure 9.4). There was apparently a disturbance of some kind at the end of the training with the 4 minute period. The hopper opening that begins the training on a 5 minute period (first F in lower panel) falls at the time predicted from the preceding 4-minute cycle, but the bird appears somewhat confused, with its peak hopping occurring after the hopper is opened. Its next peak in hopping occurs 4 minutes later, anticipating the next hopper opening, which comes 5 minutes after the previous one, so that at this point the bird's expectations are in phase with the event. The interesting question is whether the bird will maintain the phase of the 4-minute cycle during the time when it maintains the period of this cycle or will it rephase its anticipations on a cycle-by-cycle basis. The moments at which the hopper should open if the phase of the 4-minute cycle is maintained are indicated by the dashed lines labeled p (for phase) in the lower panel of figure 9.4, while the moments at which it should open if the phase of the representation of the 4-minute cycle is fully adjusted each time the hopper opens are indicated by the solid arrows labeled i (for interval). It is clear that the bird adjusts the phase of its representation of the 4-minute cycle more or less completely each time the hopper opens because the peak of its anticipatory behavior reliably occurs 4 minutes after the preceding opening throughout the transition period. On the next few cycles after those shown in the insert, the bird shifted to anticipatory peaks that occurred at 5-minute intervals.

If the transition behavior shown in the lower panel of figure 9.4 should prove to be reproducible, it would suggest that the bird's representation of cyclical processes with short periods is based on concatenated elapsed intervals. The bird may represent the interval that elapses between one hopper opening and the next and when one hopper opening fails, it may represent the next one as due 4 minutes after the previous opening should have occurred. When a hopper opening occurs a minute late (delayed by 25 percent of a 4-minute cycle, which is analogous to a 6-hour circadian phase shift), the timing is immediately reset. If the bird represented the feeding cycle as truly cyclical rather than as a concatenation of elapsed intervals, its estimate of the phase of the rhythm, like its estimate

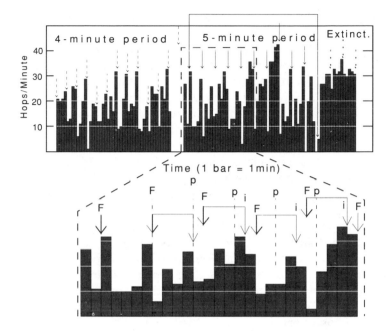

Figure 9.4
Hops per minute of a finch, in a cage with a hopper that opened for 30 seconds every 4 minutes from 10:52 to 11:44, and every 5 minutes from then until 12:34, at which time the hopper was disabled ("Extinct"). The lower panel gives a magnified view of the transition period: F = hopper opening; p = expected time of hopper opening if one assumes a 4-minute opening cycle with an opening at the first F; i = expected time of hopper opening if the phase of a 4-minute opening cycle is rezeroed at each opening of the hopper. (Upper panel redrawn from Stein 1951, p. 399, by permission of author and publisher.)

of its period, should be based on an average taken over several cycles. In that case, one would see phase-shift inertia at the transition to a different cycle, which is what one sees in the circadian clock when it is out of phase with an experienced day-night cycle (see, for example, figure 7.1). There is no evidence of phase-shift inertia in figure 9.4. Thus, Stein's findings are consistent with the hypothesis that birds represent cyclical feeding schedules with short periods as concatenations of elapsed intervals rather than as inherently cyclical processes.

Meck, Komeily-Zadeh, and Church (1984) have investigated the response to a change in elapsed interval and shown that it occurs in two discrete steps. The first step is to an interval that is the geometric mean of the previous interval and the new interval; the second is to the new interval. It would be interesting to see if the same discrete stepwise change occurs when one changes the period of an FT schedule. If so, this would strengthen the hypothesis that the animal represents ultradian FT schedules as concatenated elapsed intervals.

Stein contrasted the birds' learning of short temporal intervals or periods with their capacity to learn the time of day at which something occurred, a representation that clearly treats the feeding schedule as a cyclical process, not a concatenation of elapsed intervals. In the time-of-day experiments, the hopper was open most of the time, but it was closed from, for example, 9:00-13:00 each day of training. After a few days of this experience, the birds' hopping reached a peak shortly before the hopper was due to reopen. When the hopper was closed an hour earlier or later than usual, the hopping nonetheless peaked at the usual opening time, demonstrating that it was the time of day that determined the birds' anticipatory hopping crescendo, not the duration of the interval since the closing of the hopper or any other factor such as hunger, whose intensity would depend on that interval. The birds also showed anticipatory hopping peaks in constant-illumination chambers, demonstrating that the ability to anticipate the daily feeding time depends in birds, as it does in bees, on an internal clock, an innate representation of the daily cycle. Like rats, the birds also readily learned to anticipate the beginning of each of two daily feeding intervals.

Stein tried to teach the birds a 26-hour rhythm, with results similar to those Wahl obtained with bees. After extensive training, there was no sign of anticipatory activity at the 26-hour interval, but the birds did show an anticipatory peak each day at the time the hopper had opened the preceding day. In other words, as field observations would lead one to expect, a single occurrence suffices to imprint in the memory of a bird the time of day of that occurrence, that is, the phase of its endogenous circadian oscillation, but no matter how many times one repeats a 26-hour interoccurrence interval, the bird does not learn to anticipate the next recurrence. On the other hand, they can readily learn to anticipate the recurrences of events that happen on a cycle whose period is measured in minutes, and they can readily learn to anticipate non-periodic events, whose occurrence may be predicted from elapsed intervals measured in minutes.

Remembering and Comparing Elapsed Intervals

In recent years, there have been a number of important experiments and analytic reviews establishing the characteristics of the processes by which animals represent the temporal structure of operant schedules of reward. Influential early papers are those by Killeen (1975) and Gibbon (1977). The latter brought a new level of mathematical sophistication to the theoretical analysis of these data. In the 1980s, investigators at Brown and Columbia, most notably Church, Gibbon, Meck, and Roberts have collaborated on a series of experimental investigations aimed at constructing and validating a computational model of the process by which elapsed intervals are estimated, remembered, and compared. They have successfully used a variety of experimental paradigms, some of astonishing complexity. What follows is based primarily on summaries of this work in two recent reviews (Gibbon, Church, and Meck 1984; Church 1984).

Experimental Procedures

The peak procedure.   In this procedure, perhaps the simplest of their paradigms, a signal (light or noise) comes on at the beginning of a trial. After a fixed latency (the reward latency), the food dispenser is armed on some percentage of the trials, so that a response (key peck or lever press) yields a reward. Whether a trial is to have a reward is randomly determined. On trials without a reward, the signal persists for a long while after the reward latency; then the lever withdraws and/or the house lights go out, signaling the end of the trial. The procedure is a discrete-trials version of the FI schedule, with the additional wrinkle that the reward occurs only on some trials. Also the elapsed interval begins with the onset of a trial (when the house lights come on) rather than with the harvesting of a reward.

The data come from the unrewarded trials, on which the animal's rate of responding rises to a peak that coincides approximately with the latency at which the reward should occur and then declines. The latency at which responding peaks commonly differs from the reward latency by a multiplicative factor, whose value varies from animal to animal but is constant within an animal. For example, in figure 9.5, the rat's peak response rate occurred at 24 seconds when there was a 20-second reward latency and at 48 seconds when there was a 40-second reward latency. In both cases, the peak, which is taken to indicate when the rat expects the food, occurs at an elapsed interval equal to the correct interval multiplied by 1.2. It is this finding (and numerous similar ones in other tasks) that leads to the term *scalar timing theory* (Gibbon 1977). The model developed by Gibbon and his collaborators postulates that the remembered duration of an elapsed interval is its experienced duration multiplied by a scalar factor, which varies from animal to animal. For the rat in figure 9.5, the value of this scalar factor was 1.2, which means that the elapsed intervals it stored in memory were 20 percent longer than the intervals it experienced.

The curves for rate of responding as a function of elapsed interval from experiments using different reward latencies are superimposable (that is, congruent) if the abscissa is scaled in terms of the ratio between the elapsed interval and the interval at which responding peaks (figure 9.6C). Scaling the abscissa in this way brings out the fact that the rat's rate of responding at 96 seconds into a trial after training with a 40-second reward latency is the same as its responding at 48 seconds into a trial after training with a 20-second reward latency, because the ratio of 96 to 48 is the same as the ratio of 48 to 24. It brings out the fact that the rat's rate of responding is determined by the ratio between the remembered reward latency and its measure of the interval so far elapsed in the current trial. The fact that response rate as a function of elapsed interval after training with different reward latencies may be predicted from the ratio between the elapsed interval and the interval at which peak responding occurs has been found in many other experiments. It leads naturally to the assumption in the computational model that responding is based on the ratio between the currently elapsed subjective interval and the remembered interval rather than, for example, on the difference between these two subjective quantities.

In other words, the nervous system compares two intervals by forming their ratio rather than by, for example, taking the arithmetic difference between them. If responding were based on the difference between the two subjective durations rather than on their ratio, then the curves for rate of responding at different elapsed intervals would be superimposable if every curve were simply slid along the time axis until its peak coincided with zero. This is equivalent to subtracting the peak interval out, so that each point along the abscissa corresponds to a difference between the elapsed interval on a trial and the peak interval (that is, the remembered interval at which reward is expected). It is obvious from

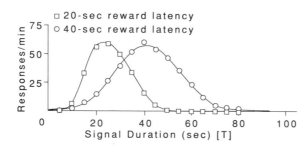

Figure 9.5
The response rate of a rat as a function of the duration of the signal in two different peak-procedure experiments, one with a reward latency of 20 seconds (*squares*) and one with a reward latency of 40 seconds (*circles*). The curves through the data points were calculated from the computational model of Gibbon and Church. (Data were gathered by Seth Roberts. The figure is redrawn from Gibbon et al. 1984, by permission of author and publisher.)

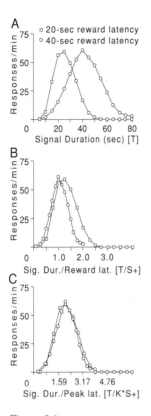

Figure 9.6
The effect of various transformations on the superimposability of the two data sets in Figure 9.5. A. Reproduction of the data sets with the points connected by line segments (rather than with the theoretical curve of Fig. 9.5). The curves are not superimposable by a simple translation along the time axis. B. The abscissa is now the ratio between the duration of the signal (T) and the reward latency (S_+). The curves are still not superimposable. C. The abscissa is now the ratio between the duration of the signal (T) and the estimated value of the remembered reward latency ($K*S_+$). Now the data are superimposable. This result implies that responding is based on the ratio between currently elapsed duration and the remembered reward duration and that the standard deviation in the distribution of criterion values is proportional to the mean. (Redrawn from Gibbon et al. 1984, p. 65, by permission of author and publisher.)

inspection of the two curves (figure 9.6A) that they cannot be rendered superimposable by sliding them along the abscissa until both peaks coincide with zero. Hence, we may conclude that the animal's rate of responding is not based on the arithmetic difference between its measure of the currently elapsed interval and the interval at which it expects reward to occur.

Note that the superimposability of the curves is obtained only if one normalizes with respect to the remembered reward latency (figure 9.6C) not the actual reward latency (figure 9.6B). What determines the rat's rate of responding is the memory it has of the latency at which previous rewards have occurred, not the originally experienced latencies of those rewards.

The generalization procedure. In this experimental paradigm, a stimulus whose duration is to be judged comes on for a variable duration. It goes off just as a lever extends into the box, enabling the rat to give a response. If the stimulus was on for the "correct" duration (the rewarded duration), a response yields food. Following other durations, a response does not yield food. The rat's probability of responding as a function of the duration of the preresponse signal shows a peak at approximately the rewarded duration. The scalar properties are again evident. Remembered duration departs from experienced duration by an animal-specific scalar constant, and response probability is determined by the ratio between the signal's duration and the remembered duration of rewarded signals.

The bisection procedure. In this paradigm, the animal again hears or sees a preresponse signal of varying duration, but now two levers come into the box when the signal ends. A press on one is rewarded if the signal was the shortest in the range of signals being used; a response on the other is rewarded if the signal was the longest; and neither lever pays off if the signal was of intermediate duration. The data are the probabilities of responding on the "long" lever as a function of the duration of the preresponse signal. This experiment provides further evidence that responding is based on duration ratios because it turns out that the point of indifference, the intermediate signal duration at which the "long" lever is chosen on half the trials, is the logarithmic midpoint between the shortest and longest intervals, the interval such that the ratio between the longest interval and it is the same as the ratio between it and the shortest interval. If responding were based on differences in the subjective temporal quantities rather than on the ratio between these quantities, the point of indifference between a 2-second and an 8-second signal would be at 5 seconds, the equidifference point [(5 – 2) = (8 – 5)], but, in fact, it occurs at 4 seconds, the equiratio point [4/2 = 8/4].

The time-left procedure. A fourth paradigm in which both pigeons and rats show surprisingly orderly behavior is quite complex. Gibbon and Church (1981) call it the time-left task. It requires the animal to judge from moment to moment which of two response options will pay off in the shorter amount of time. At the start of each trial, one option is likely to pay off sooner than the other, but as the trial goes on, the time considerations shift in favor of the other option.

In the pigeon version of this task, each trial begins with the illumination of two response keys: one red, the other white. Continued responding on the red key yields a reward at, say, $T + 30$ seconds. The 30-second interval is the so-called standard interval (S), and T is randomly determined from trial to trial, by choosing with equal likelihood from among six alternative times ranging from one-sixth of S (= 5 seconds) to eleven-sixths (= 55 seconds). If the pigeon confines its pecks to the red key, it finds out that the T for a given trial has timed out when one of its pecks turns the key green. At that moment, the bird loses the option of responding on the white key (the key goes blank). It has committed itself willy-nilly to finishing the trial with the red-then-green key. It gets its reward 30 seconds later (S seconds later) for pecking on this key.

Turning now to the white key; continued responding on this key yields a reward at $60 - T$ seconds. The 60-second interval is the so-called comparison interval (C). In most of the experiments, it is twice the standard interval. If the pigeon confines its pecks to the white key, it finds out that T has timed out when one of its pecks extinguishes the red key, leaving the white key as its only response option for the remainder of the trial. The pigeon has now committed itself willy-nilly to finishing with this key, and it must wait $60 - T$ seconds (that is, $C - T$ seconds) before a peck will be rewarded. Which terminal sequence the pigeon ends up in (whether it must finish out on the red-green key or finish out on the white key) depends on which key it happens to peck first after T has timed out.

In this task, the rational thing to do is to peck the red key for the first 30 seconds because if T has timed out, pecking the red key will put the pigeon on the road to getting its reward in only 30 more seconds, whereas pecking the white key will put it on the road to getting a reward after $60 - T$ seconds, which is longer than 30 seconds so long as $T < 30$. However, when more than 30 seconds has elapsed since the start of the trial, the rational response is to switch to pecking on the white key because now it will yield a reward in a shorter time. To behave in an approximately rational manner, the bird must compute the difference between the remembered duration corresponding to C and the time elapsed since the onset of the trial. It should shift from the red key to the white key when the ratio between this difference and the remembered duration corresponding to S is less than some critical value. (Full rationality would require that this critical value be 1, but the animal may have some biases that make its performance suboptimal.)

Surprisingly, both pigeons and rats show an approximation to rational responding under these conditions. Their probability of responding on the white key starts out low and rises during the course of a trial, while their probability of responding on the red key starts out high and sinks. Most important, the point of indifference—the latency at which the probability of responding on the white key equals the probability of responding on the red key—is a linear function of the $C - S$ difference. This result implies that subjective time is a linear function of objective time rather than, for example, a logarithmic function of objective time.

Computing with Interruptions
In the time-left task, the numerator of the ratio on which responding was based was the arithmetic difference between the elapsed interval and the comparison interval. In other tasks, the numerator used in the underlying ratio comparison may be the arithmetic sum of two subjective intervals. Roberts and Church (1978) taught rats to respond on an FI 60 schedule of reinforcement: the reward dispenser is rearmed 60 seconds after the last reward was dispensed. When the rat's performance exhibited the usual FI scallop, Roberts and Church introduced on some trials a 15-second break at some point in the interreward interval. During the break, a noise came on, and the lever withdrew from the box. For some of the rats, the reward clock continued to run during this break; for others, it stopped and resumed after the break. The question was how the rats would initially react to this break and whether they could learn to react differently. Would they ignore the interruption in computing the elapsed interval or count the interruption interval as part of the elapsed interval, and could they learn to treat the interruption interval either way (how flexible a temporal accountant is the rat). The rats initially ignored the interruption. Their response pattern at any moment after the break was what one would expect at that point 15 seconds earlier in an uninterrupted inter-reward interval. However, the group for which the reward clock did not stop learned eventually to count the break as part of the elapsed interval.

Simultaneous Comparisons of Different Elapsed Intervals to Different Remembered Intervals
Meck and Church (1984) have shown that rats can simultaneously and continuously update two temporal ratios with different denominators

and different numerators. They trained rats on a peak procedure in which the reward, if it occurred at all on a given trial, always occurred 50 seconds after the onset of a light. On some trials, there were also 1-second noise bursts. The first burst came on with the light, and there was a burst every 10 seconds thereafter, except at 50 seconds, when the reward would occur if one were scheduled for that trial. Thus the occurrence of a burst signaled that there could not be a reward for at least another 10 seconds. On trials without the noise bursts, one observed the pattern of responding portrayed in figure 9.7A. On trials with noise bursts, one observed the pattern portrayed in figure 9.7B. Superimposed on the behavior controlled by the timing of the duration of the light signal (the bell-shaped overall response rate) are sharp scallops at 10-second intervals. These scallops are not simply reactions to each separate tone burst. While timing the duration of the light, the rats were concurrently timing the interval elapsed since the last tone burst, as shown in two ways. First, notice that although there was no tone burst at 50 seconds, the two points in figure 9.7B that fall at 50 seconds show a sharp dip in anticipation of the recurrence of another noise—the burst 10 seconds after the preceding one. Similarly, on some trials with noise bursts, a randomly chosen burst was omitted. There was, nonetheless, a dip in responding just after the burst should have occurred.

The ability of the Gibbon and Church computational theory of animal interval timing to account for the results obtained in all of these experiments—and in several others not reviewed—is impressive. They have also been able to show with pharmacological treatments that there are distinct functional components of the system determining the values of some of the basic parameters in the computational model. Methamphetamine, for example, increases λ, the rate at which the internal subjective clock runs. So long as the internal clock by which intervals are measured runs at the same rate during testing as it does during training, its rate has no effect on the data. If the internal clock is running too fast, the remembered durations of intervals will be too long, but so will the current elapsed durations used for comparison with these remembered durations. The two errors will offset each other to yield correctly timed performance or, more precisely, to yield performance whose externally measured timing is the same regardless of the rate at which the internal clock runs.

In fact, the judgments of rats running in timing tasks while drugged with methamphetamine do not differ systematically from their judgments when not drugged, provided they are both trained and tested in one state or the other. The only way to show an effect of amphetamine on the rate at which the internal clock runs is to train the animal with the clock running at one rate and test it with it running at a different rate,

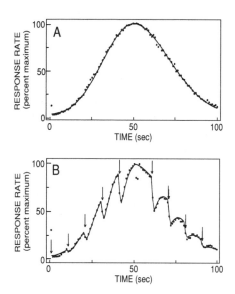

Figure 9.7
Evidence that rats can concurrently track two different elapsing intervals, comparing
each to a different remembered interval. A. Average normalized response rates of rats as
a function of trial duration in a 50-second peak procedure experiment on those trials when
only the onset of a steady light at the beginning of the trial signaled the time to reward.
The curve through the data points is calculated from the Gibbon and Church computational model. B. Data from trials on which there was also a 1-second burst of noise every
10 seconds (arrows) except at 50 seconds, the reward latency. The curve through the data
is calculated from the computational model. (Redrawn from Meck and Church 1984, pp.
18, 19, by permission of author and publisher.)

which is what Meck (1983) did. In one version of his experiment, he
trained the rats while they were dosed with methamphetamine and
tested them when they were drug free. Their behaviorally expressed
judgment of duration shifted to the right (toward longer intervals) in
testing, relative to the same judgment during training. This is expected
on the assumption that their clock was running too fast during training,
so they remember intervals as being longer than they really are. In the
reverse version, the rats were trained drug free and tested under methamphetamine. Now their judgments during testing were shorter than those
during training.

The results with methamphetamine are to be contrasted with the
results with vasopressin, which affects the multiplicative constant relating remembered duration to experienced duration. Remember that the
value of this parameter is evident in the data obtained when testing and
training conditions match. The further the value of this parameter

departs from 1.0, the more the animal misses the correct time when trying to match a current elapsed duration to a remembered duration. Vasopressin decreases the value of this parameter of the computational model, so that rats trained with this drug give shorter time judgments than do rats trained undrugged. With vasopressin, it does not matter what the animal's pharmacological state is during testing; only its state during training matters.

The Computational Model

Church (1984) distinguishes three levels of analysis: the formal or computational level, where one specifies what sorts of computations are made; the psychological level, where one gives an abstract description of the components that implement these computations; and the physiological level, where one specifies what physiological variables affect which parameters in the computational model and which neural structures and processes embody the components of the psychological model. There has been work at all of these levels, but most of it has aimed at validating the computational model. Here, I put along side the psychological model proposed by Gibbon and Church a different model, one that reflects my commitment to the hypothesis that the ability to record times of occurrence is the foundation of all time dependencies in behavior. The psychological model that Gibbon and Church proposed requires that the system know that it has been presented with an event that makes it appropriate to start an internal timer and later that it has been presented with an event that makes it appropriate to stop the timer. I favor a model in which times of occurrences (stimulus onsets and offsets) are invariably recorded and computational analyses are continually applied to these recorded times in an unceasing search for temporal structure. This computational model for the search for temporal structure is elaborated in chapter 13 as an alternative to the theory of classical conditioning.

The model for the representation and use of elapsed intervals that I offer here is computationally identical to Gibbon and Church's model. Hence there is no way of distinguishing between them by purely behavioral experiments. It may be possible to distinguish them by various physiological manipulations, but, for the moment, the chief value in presenting two psychological models for the same computational model is to illustrate the independence of the computational and psychological levels of analysis.

The quantities in the computational model, using the Gibbon and Church notation, are:

1. λ, the scalar parameter that relates the subjective (internal) measure of an elapsed interval to the objective (external) measure.

2. M_T, the subjective measure of the interval so far elapsed since the subjective onset of an event:

$$M_T = \lambda \, (\tau - d_{on}),$$

where τ is the objective interval elapsed since t_{on}, the externally defined time of onset, and d_{on} is the delay between the external onset and the subjective onset of the timing operation, T_{on}.

4. d_{off} is the delay between the objective termination of the event and the termination of the subjective timing operation.

5. M_{S+}, the subjectively measured interval, the experienced duration of an event or latency:

$$M_{S+} = \lambda \, (T_{off} - T_{on}),$$

and

$$T_{off} = t_{off} + d_{off}$$
$$T_{on} = t_{on} + d_{on},$$

so

$$M_{S+} = \lambda \, [(t_{off} + d_{off}) - (t_{on} + d_{on})].$$

Empirically, it has been found that $d_{off} < d_{on}$, the latency to start the internal timing operation is longer than the latency to stop it. This means that M_{S+}, the subjective measure of the completed interval, is a linear function of the objective interval, t_d:

$$M_{S+} = \lambda \, (t_d - D),$$

where $D = d_{on} - d_{off}$.

6. M^*_{S+} is the remembered interval, which is a scalar function of the experienced interval:

$$M^*_{S+} = K^* M_{S+}.$$

The distinction between the experienced and remembered interval is counterintuitive. It implies that what is remembered is a systematic distortion of what was subjectively experienced. The evidence requiring the positing of this scalar distortion in the memory for the initial subjective experience was given in the preceding review of the experimental findings on which the computational model is based.

In the various behavioral tasks that test animals' interval timing mechanism, the animal is assumed to compare the currently elapsing interval, M_T, to the remembered interval, M^*_{S+}. The nature of the variance in the behavioral outputs seen in these experiments—the rate of pressing or the distribution of judged intervals around the correct interval—leads to the assumption that the animal's probability of giving a "yes" response (a response appropriate for an animal that estimates that the currently elapsed interval matches a specified remembered interval) is based on M_T/M^*_{s+}, the ratio between the currently elapsed interval and the remembered interval. The more nearly this ratio approximates one, the higher is the probability of the appropriate response. This rule applies in the simplest of the tasks, the peak procedure. Other tasks require slight variations in this decision rule, but in all of them the decision rests on a ratio between two subjective intervals. Gibbon (1977) was the first to call attention to the ubiquity of decision rules based on temporal ratios in the timing of animal behavior.

Alternative Functional Structures

Figure 9.8 gives two different psychological models for this computational theory. In the terminology of modern cognitive psychology, these are information-processing models. In the terminology of the German behavioral physiologists, these are models of the functional structure (*Wirkungsgefüge*). These models interpret the quantities in the computational theory in terms of the inputs and outputs of assumed components in a system. The components are specified in terms of their functional properties rather than in terms of their neurophysiological embodiment. In these diagrams, I have followed certain conventions. A box or circle represents an operation of some kind performed on the variables represented by the arrows terminating at the box or circle (for example, switching, integrating with respect to time, multiplying, adding a constant). The operation performed is indicated by a symbol and / or a graph inside the box or circle. A solid arrow represents a variable that is a function of time, a quantity that takes on different values at different moments. A dashed arrow represents a discrete variable, a quantity that has a single value, such as the time at which an event begins, or the record in memory of a reward latency. Memory files are represented as bins (boxes open at the top). When an arrow penetrates a box, it represents a signal that changes the operation in the box (for example, closes the switch) rather than a variable that is operated on. t stands for time as determined by some external process; T stands for time as determined by internal processes.

Figure 9.8A is the model given by Gibbon et al. (1984). I have retained their notation as much as possible, but to facilitate comparison with the alternative model, I have made the flow diagram more detailed and explicit than the one they present. In their model, the parameter λ is the number of pulses per second from a pacemaker. The pacemaker runs all the time, but the pulses from it are fed to an accumulator (integrator in the mathematical sense) in working memory only when a switch is closed. The onset of a to-be-timed interval closes the switch with latency d_{on}. The offset of the interval opens it with latency d_{off}. The output from the switch to the integrator is a pulse stream at rate λ when the switch is closed and nothing at other times. The quantity accumulated in working memory is M_T. It is the subjective measure of the time elapsed since the onset of a to-be-timed interval. When the reward occurs, it opens the switch that gates the pacemaker output to the accumulator, reads out the current value in the accumulator, and resets the accumulator to zero. The quantity read out from the accumulator is multiplied by a constant to determine the quantity recorded in the memory file that preserves the records of reward latencies.

The reference memory, that is the remembered interval used as the denominator of the comparison ratio on a given trial, is a sample from the population of remembered reward latencies, a different sample on each trial. The variance in the reference memory resulting from this sampling procedure is an important component of the total observed variance in the onset and offset of responding. The multiplicative constant, K^*, which relates the reference memory to the originally experienced interval, could apply only to the interval sampled from memory rather than to each experienced interval as it is stored in memory, or it could be an amalgam of two successive scalar distortions, one that applies to the intervals at storage and one that applies to an interval when it is sampled from memory. All the data allow one to say is that there is a scalar distortion operating in the pathway between the original subjective measures of the elapsed intervals and the remembered quantity used in the denominator of the comparison ratio on which responding on subsequent trials is based.

When a new trial starts, the system computes the moment-to-moment ratio between the current value in working memory (the currently experienced elapsed interval) and the comparison interval in reference memory. The decision process, which decides whether to put out a response, looks at this ratio and applies some criterion factor, b, which determines how close to 1.0 this ratio must be for the animal to respond. The value of b fluctuates from moment to moment. The distribution of b's values is assumed to be approximately normal, with a standard deviation proportional to its mean. The ratio-based decision and the proportionality of the standard deviation to the mean yield what Gibbon has termed the scalar variance property, a ubiquitous feature of data from animal timing studies.

Figure 9.8B gives an alternative functional structure for the same computational theory. The parameter λ is the scalar parameter relating subjective time, T (the output of an internal clock), to objective time. The clock is the clock that supplies the times stored in memory as occurrence times. Since the intervals in question in these studies are often measured in seconds, it is unreasonable to assume that the readings recorded from this clock could be based solely on the states of circadian and infradian oscillators. The precision required in the recorded times of occurrence implies that these records include coordinates derived from the states of ultradian oscillators as well, oscillators with periods measured in seconds and minutes. The occurrence of any abrupt change in any salient aspect of the environment is stored in memory along with its time of occurrence, which is a record of the momentary phases of the oscillators that constitute the subjective clock. The latency to read the clock at the onset of a sensory input is d_{on}, and the latency to read the clock at the offset of an input is d_{off}.

From the recorded subjective onset and "offset" (reward delivery times, the system computes the duration of a sample interval. In the diagram, a duration, ΔT_i, is computed on each trial from a random sample of a remembered onset time and the following offset time. The reference memory, $\overline{M}^*_{s*}$, is this sample interval multiplied by the distortion factor, K^*. When the animal experiences another onset of the same stimulus, it begins the on-line computation of the subjective elapsed interval, M_T, which is the difference between the most recently recorded onset, $T(on)_n$, and the momentary reading of the internal clock, T. As in the first model, the behavioral output depends on the ratio between the currently experienced duration and the reference memory. When this ratio is greater than 1-b but less than 1+b, the animal responds.

The scalar variance property is explained on this model as follows. Times of occurrence are represented by the phases of oscillators with different periods, with only rather weak phase coupling. The weak phase coupling between slower and faster oscillations means that an interval can be determined only with a precision equal to the precision of the phase readings on the fastest oscillator whose period exceeds the time interval to be determined. Because still faster oscillators are not strongly coupled (phase locked) to the slower oscillators, the phase readings from oscillators with periods shorter than the interval to be determined cannot be used to make the determination of that interval more precise. Thus there is a distinction between the resolution of the system and its precision. Its resolution—the minimum detectable difference in times of occurrence—is determined by the fastest oscillator, but its precision— the standard deviation of a series of measurements of the same interval— is determined by the precision with which readings can be made on the oscillator whose period is of the same order of magnitude as the interval being measured. As the interval increases, the period of the oscillator whose recorded phases are used to compute the interval also increases. If we assume that the precision with which the phase of an oscillator can

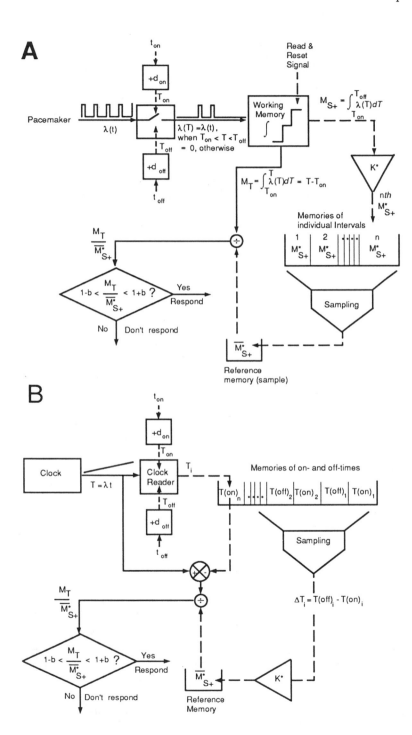

be read (the standard deviation in a series of readings of the same point) is a constant fraction of its period, we get the scalar variance property for the error in the measurement of temporal intervals.

Conclusions

The results obtained by Church, Gibbon, Meck, and Roberts show the power of a computational-representational approach to the phenomena of learning. They also justify the assumption that the nervous systems of warm-blooded animals are capable of carrying out temporal computations of considerable complexity. These computations utilize memory data concerning time, and they generate new, higher-order temporal memories, which derive from computations performed on data stored in a lower-order memory. Both of the functional structures portrayed in figure 9.8 exhibit this kind of hierarchical structure in memory. In the Gibbon and Church model, the contents of the file that records individual intervals derive from computations carried out using data from working memory, and the record of the average reward latency is computed from the records of individual reward latencies. In the alternative I propose, the record of the average reward latency derives from computations performed on data stored in occurrence memory.

The results in the literature on animals' memory for times of occurrence together with the results from the literature on animals' ability to compute temporal intervals justify the assumption that animals can store the times at which events happen and can carry out computations based on these stored data. There is a very large body of evidence to the effect that animals routinely respond on the basis of temporal ratios, the ratio between the interval elapsed since the most recent occurrence of an event (such as a CS onset) and a reference interval in memory. Thus the isomorphism between objective temporal intervals and the brain processes that adapt the animal's behavior to these temporal regularities is a rich one; it includes the operations of division and subtraction (in the time-left paradigm).

Figure 9.8

Two different functional structures for the computational model of animal timing proposed by Gibbon et al. (1984). Enclosed boxes and circles symbolize computational operations. Bins (boxes open at the top) symbolize data storage devices. Solid arrows symbolize variables that are functions of time. Broken lines symbolize discrete (single-valued) variables. Arrows that do not penetrate boxes or circles represent inputs operated on by the process in the box or circle. Arrows that penetrate boxes or circles represent signals that alter the operation of the process, causing a change of state. The letter notation for variables generally follows Gibbon et al. A. The functional structure proposed by Gibbon et al. B. An alternative based entirely on occurrence times.

The computations performed on times of occurrence appear to include the computation of elapsed intervals, which may involve the subtraction of one time of occurrence from another. To argue, as I do in chapter 13, that the phenomena of classical conditioning derive from a time-series analysis of the animal's experience with two or more stimuli presupposes that the animal has available to it in memory data giving the times of event occurrences and that the animal has the ability to do computations with temporal intervals and numbers of occurrences. The experimental results reviewed in this chapter make these assumptions plausible insofar as temporal intervals are concerned. In the next chapter, we turn to the question whether animals represent number and whether they can carry out an extremely basic computation involving number and temporal intervals: dividing the number of occurrences by the interval of observation to obtain a representation of rate of occurrence. The theory of classical conditioning proposed in chapter 13 takes rate of occurrence as its primitive.

Chapter 10
Number

The previous chapter reviewed the experimental evidence that animals represent temporal intervals. They map from intervals to representations of those intervals, and they perform complex operations on the representations generated by this mapping. For example, they may simultaneously track the ratio between two different remembered standard intervals and two different currently elapsing intervals. They track the value of the variable obtained by dividing the current value of the elapsing interval by the value of the remembered standard (see figure 9.8). Thus the results reviewed in the chapter 9 imply that the commonly employed laboratory animals represent elapsed temporal intervals in a rich sense of the term: the internal operations performed on the representations of temporal intervals include operations isomorphic to division and subtraction.

In this chapter, I review experiments demonstrating that the common laboratory animals also represent number. This means, at a minimum, that there is a one-one mapping from the numerosity of events to behavior-controlling entities—presumably entities located in the brain. Following Gelman and Gallistel (1978), I will call these behavior-controlling entities to which numerosities map *numerons*. This neologism is adopted to avoid confusion between what is represented (the numerosities) and the entities used as representatives (numbers or numerons). For *numeron*, one may substitute *mental number*, provided that one is clear that no internal monologue is thereby imputed to the animal. Numerons refer to the "inner marks" by which nonverbal organisms may "think unnamed numbers" (Koehler 1950). More formally, they refer to the entities on the representing side of a process that maps from numerosities (the represented variable) to number (the representing variable). The experiments demonstrating that common lab animals have at least a nominal representation of numerosity all involve demonstrations that numerosity may function as a discriminative stimulus.

Given that a one-one mapping from distinct numerosities to distinct behavior-controlling entities may be demonstrated, the question of how rich an animal's representation of number is turns on the question of the kinds of operations the brain performs with the numerons. Direct tests for the richness of an animal's numerical representation check for whether it can respond to the sum or difference of two numbers or their ratio. Recall that experiments by Church, Gibbon, Meck and Roberts have shown that rats and pigeons sum temporal intervals, take their difference, and take their ratio. Thus there is no question that the brains of pigeons and rats are capable of the relevant operations; the only question is whether they apply such operations to numerons. A number of experiments to be reviewed suggest that animal brains perform operations with numerons that are isomorphic to the arithmetic operations of addition and subtraction. Insofar as we are persuaded that animal brains add and subtract numerons, in that measure may we say that the animals have a rich representation of number, or, more colloquially, that they have a concept of number. However, if we allow that animals obtain their representations of numerosity by a counting process, then none of the demonstrations of animal arithmetic is compelling because the same results may be obtained by a suitable use of the counting process.

The most obvious situations in which operations isomorphic to the basic arithmetic operations need to be performed with numerons are in the computation of rates of return and other statistical properties of events. I have twice assumed that animals use numerons in statistical computations: in computing the mean phase vector for events that recur at approximately the same time each day (Chapter 8) and in computing the mean reward latency (Chapter 9). The computation of a mean involves summing a set of values and dividing the sum by the number that represents the numerosity of the set of summed values. The uses of numerons in these sorts of computations cannot be achieved through counting. Thus evidence that these sorts of computations are performed is the strongest evidence that animals have a rich representation of numerosity, one that combines numerons with each other and with other variables in operations isomorphic to addition, subtraction, multiplication, and division.

The best evidence for the richness of an animal's numerical representation may come from the extensive experimental demonstrations of animal sensitivity to differences in rates of reinforcement or prey density, which are reviewed in the next chapter. How compelling this evidence is depends on how convincingly we can reject other explanations of this sensitivity to rate, explanations that do not involve the computation of rate per se. To this end, the next chapter also reviews alternative accounts of the well-documented ability of animals to "integrate reinforcements over time" (Lea and Dow 1984), pointing out their inadequacies.

The adaptive value of the capacity to count has sometimes been regarded as something of a mystery (Davis and Memmott 1982; Church and Meck 1984). If animals count to estimate rate, there is no mystery. The adaptive value of being able to represent rate of return is obvious.

The Discrimination of Number

The earlier literature on numerosity as a discriminative stimulus has been reviewed by Davis and Memmott (1982). The highlights of this literature are two operant techniques for investigating the ability of pigeons and rats to discriminate the number of responses made since the last reward, when the program for delivering rewards depends on this number. These techniques yield data whose remarkable orderliness is reminiscent of the timing data generated by the Church et al. paradigms. In the first paradigm, developed by Mechner (1958), there are two levers, A and B. The rat must make some number, N, of responses on lever A before the food delivery system is enabled. When food delivery is enabled, the rat activates delivery in one of two ways. On some percentage, P, of the trials, it must make a press on lever B to activate delivery. On these trials, the optimal response sequence is N responses on lever A followed by one response on lever B. On the balance of the trials, food delivery is activated by the $N+1$th press on lever A. On these trials, the optimal sequence is to make $N+1$ responses on lever A. The rat is given no means of discriminating which kind of trial it is running. If it is the second kind of trial, the $N+1$th press on lever A will produce a reward, but if it is the first kind, neither the $N+1$th nor any subsequent press on lever A will yield reward; the rat must shift to lever B to collect its reward. Furthermore, if the rat shifts to lever B prematurely, it pays a penalty: the counter is reset to zero.

These rather complex contingencies yield two desirable results. First, on a percentage, P, of the trials, the rat is required to indicate when it judges it has made a sufficient number of responses by switching to lever B. One may measure its probability of switching both when it has made less than N and when it has made more than N responses. Second, by manipulating P one can manipulate the criterion of numerical sufficiency that the rat uses—in effect, how sure it has to be that it has pressed the requisite number of times before it ventures a press on lever B. When P is low, most of the rewards are collected simply by continuing to press on lever A, and the rat does not switch to lever B until it is quite certain that it has given more than the requisite number of presses on lever A. On the other hand, when P is 1, it is always a waste of time and energy to give more than N presses on lever A; hence the rat is more disposed to take a chance on a premature press on lever B in the hope of avoiding useless presses on lever A.

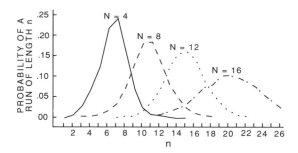

Figure 10.1
The probability of the rat's switching from lever A to lever B as a function of n, the number of consecutive responses on lever A, for various values of N, the number of consecutive responses required to arm the delivery of reward. (Redrawn from Mechner 1958, p. 113, by permission of author and publisher.)

Representative data from Mechner's experiment are shown in figure 10.1, which is based on the 50 percent of the trials when the rat had to switch to lever B to collect its reward. For that population of trials, it gives the rat's probability (relative frequency) of a run of length n on lever A prior to a press on lever B. It gives this function for different values of the required number of presses, N. Note that the most probable run length on lever A (the most frequent value of n) is consistently three presses more than the required number N, as shown in figure 10.2A, which plots the median value of n as a function of N. This means that the probability of switching from lever A to lever B is controlled not by the ratio between the number of presses the rat estimates it has made and the number it remembers to be required (as was the case in judgments of temporal intervals) but rather by the difference between these two quantities.

Note also that the dispersion about the $N+3$ value increases with the value of N, though not in proportion to the increase in N nor to the increase in the median n. These distributions are symmetrical and the distributions at different values of N are scaled replicas of one another, as illustrated in figure 10.2B, which treats these discrete probability distributions like probability density functions and normalizes them with respect to the mean n and the peak probability. In figure 10.2B, the distributions shown in figure 10.1 have been slid along the abscissa until their mean coincides with the ordinate, graphically setting all the means to zero. Then each distribution for an N greater than 4 is scaled upward by the factor required to make its peak match that of the distribution for $N=4$ and scaled down along the abscissa by the reciprocal factor, so that the area under the curve remains constant. (The integral of a probability density function or the sum of a discrete probability distribution function

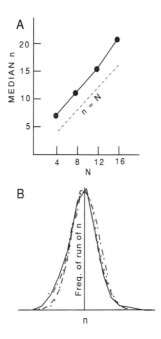

Figure 10.2
A. The median value of n from the distributions shown in Figure 10.1, as a function of the value of N, the required number of consecutive presses. (Redrawn from Mechner 1958, p. 115, by permission of author and publisher.) B. The probability distributions in figure 10.1 after normalization to set their peaks equal and their means equal to zero.

must be one.) This normalization renders the distributions approximately congruent, which is what one would expect if the probability of shift to lever B were a constant function of the rat's uncertainty regarding whether the number of presses it had made did or did not exceed the required number and the level of uncertainty for a given discrepancy between its count and the required number was greater for larger numbers. Human number estimation has this property: the larger is the numerosity of the set to be counted, the greater is the probability of an error of a given magnitude in one's count; hence, the less certain one is that the correct count does or does not exceed a specified value.

As one might expect, the rat's conservatism in this task is manipulable by the pay off matrix. When Mechner varied the value of P, the probability that on any given trial the rat would need to move to B to collect its reward, the value of n at which the rat was most likely to switch shrank toward N, the required number, below which a penalty was incurred. However, in his experiments, there was always a substantial penalty for a premature shift to lever B (the count was reset to zero); hence the value

of n at which the probability of that shift peaked was always greater than
N. Platt and Johnson (1971) manipulated the prematurity penalty in a
slightly modified version of Mechner's paradigm. The rat had to press a
lever N times before its entry into a photocell-monitored feeding area
would trigger the delivery of food. Premature entries could trigger one
of four penalties: no penalty (the response counter was not reset and
there was no time out); a 10-second time-out, during which the lever
retracted and the houselights went off but the response counter was not
reset; a resetting of the response counter, but no time-out; both a time-out
and a resetting of the response counter.

As might be expected, when there was no prematurity penalty, the rat
tended to break off pressing and go for the food before it had reached the
proper value, and this tendency got stronger the larger the value of N.
The penalty condition that produced the most precise match between the
required N and the value of n at which the probability of breaking off to
enter the feeding area peaked was the condition in which there was a 10-
second time-out after premature entries but no resetting of the counter
(figure 10.3). Under these conditions, the value of n at which the rat was
most likely to try the food area was almost exactly the required value N,
for N's from 4 to 24 (figure 10.4C).

The rats' behavior after premature entry into the feeding area was
adjusted to the nature of the penalty. If there was a reset penalty, the n for
the rats' subsequent run was the same function of N as the ns of the runs
following reinforcement (figure 10.4A and 10.4B), as it should be, since in
this condition any entry into the feeding area reset the response counter.
By contrast, when premature entry did not reset the counter, the length
of a run following such an entry did not vary as a function of the required
N (figure 10.4D). If in this condition some of the premature entries occur
because the rat, in effect, gambles that its count is erroneously low, one
might expect to see a negative correlation between the length of the run

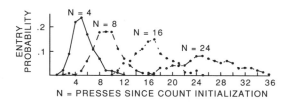

Figure 10.3
The probability of breaking off to enter the food delivery area as a function of n, the number
of presses made since the initialization of the response counter, for various values of N, the
required number of presses, under conditions where a premature entry triggers a 10-
second time-out but does not reset the response counter. (Redrawn from Platt and Johnson
1971, p. 401, by permission of author and publisher.)

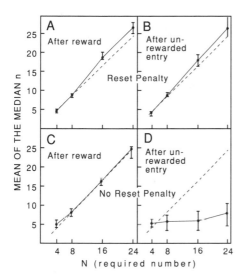

Figure 10.4
Mean of the median numbers of consecutive presses prior to an entry into the feeding area, as a function of N, the required number, under two different penalty conditions and as a function of whether the last entry yielded food. Each point gives the mean of the individual medians of the four rats run in a given condition. The bars give the range of the medians. The dashed line in each plot gives the locus of points such that $n = N$. A. Consecutive presses following the last food reward, in the condition in which a premature entry reset the response counter. B. Consecutive presses after a premature entry, which reset the counter. C. Consecutive presses following the last food reward, in the condition in which a premature entry produced a time-out but did not reset the response counter. D. Consecutive presses following a premature entry, which did not reset the response counter. (Redrawn from Platt and Johnson 1971, p. 403, by permission of author and publisher.)

preceding a premature entry and the length of the succeeding run. Significant negative correlations of this kind were found in both the no-reset conditions, particularly when the value of N was high. That is, when premature entries did not reset the counter and when the number of required presses was high, the more presses the rat made before prematurely trying the feeder, the fewer it then made before trying it again. This suggests that the rats subtracted their count of the first run from the required count to get the numeron appropriate for the subsequent run; however, it can also be explained by assuming that they merely continue their count after a premature entry.

In their initial studies, neither Mechner nor Platt and Johnson attempted to rule out the possibility that the rats based their responding on the temporal interval elapsed since the last reward rather than on a representation of the numerosity of the responses given. In a subsequent experiment, however, Mechner and Guevrekian (1962) varied the level of deprivation. Increasing deprivation significantly reduced the pause that the rats make before initiating a run of responses and also the rate at which they pressed during a run. The combined result was about a twofold reduction in the interval that elapsed from the initialization of the response counter to the completion of a run, but there was no significant increase in the number of presses made on lever A prior to switching to lever B, nor was there any change in the standard deviation of the distribution. This result rules out an interval-timing explanation. If the switch from lever A to lever B were based on the interval elapsed since the last reward, then the median number of responses before a shift to lever B would increase when the number of responses per unit time increased, but it did not.

In the Mechner paradigm, the animal makes a go-no go decision based on a count of the number of responses it has made. The experimenter does not control this number. In the paradigm developed by Rilling and McDiarmid (1965), the experimenter determines which of two numbers of responses the animal has just made, and the animal must then use that number as a discriminative stimulus in choosing which of two responses to make. The Rilling and McDiarmid apparatus confronts a pigeon with a row of three keys, which may be illuminated from behind. First the center key is illuminated. The pigeon must peck it until its light extinguishes and the two flanking keys light up. This happens after one of two experimenter-specified numbers of pecks at the center key. One of these numbers was fixed at 50. The other was varied in the course of the experiment. For the sake of illustration, assume that the value of this alternative number is 45. When the two flanking keys light up, the pigeon has made either 50 presses on the center key or 45. If it has made 50, then it is rewarded for pecking the key on the right flank; if 45, for pecking the left flank. When Rilling and McDiarmid varied the alternate number from 35 to 47, they found that the percentage choice of the correct key did not fall below 60 percent until the alternate number reached 47 (figure 10.5). The pigeons discriminated 40 pecks from 50 pecks about 90 percent of the time.

Rilling and McDiarmid did not attempt to determine whether their birds' discrimination was based on the number of responses they had made or on the interval that had elapsed while they made them. Rilling (1967) addressed this question. He contrasted a fixed-interval version of the paradigm with the fixed-number version. In the fixed-interval version, the flanking keys lit up in response to the first peck on the center key that came after one of two intervals had elapsed since termination of the last reinforcement (that is, since the closing of the grain hopper). The bird had to peck the right key if it was the longer interval that had just elapsed

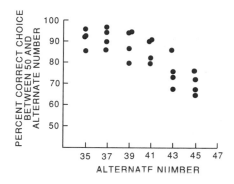

Figure 10.5
Scatter plot from four determinations of a pigeon's ability to discriminate between a run
of fifty key pecks and an alternative run whose number varied systematically in the range
from thirty-five to forty-seven. (Redrawn from Rilling and McDiarmid, p. 527, by permission of author and publisher.)

and the left key if it was the shorter. The longer interval was 45 seconds.
The shorter was adjusted to yield 80-90 percent correct discrimination. It
fell somewhere between 30 and 36 seconds, depending on the bird. Thus,
in the fixed-interval condition, the birds had to judge between an interval
of 45 seconds and one in the range of 30-36 seconds (depending on the
bird).

Rilling analyzed the distributions of elapsed intervals for the four
different trial outcomes in birds run in the fixed-number discrimination
and the distributions of numbers of responses for the four different
outcomes in birds run in the fixed-interval discrimination. Consider first
the birds run on the fixed number-discrimination. Suppose that the
number to be discriminated from 50 was 35. The four possible trial
outcomes were: (1) the number was 35 and the bird chose 35—a correct
"fewer" choice; (2) the number was 50 and the bird chose 35—an
erroneous "fewer" choice; (3) the number was 35 and the bird chose 50—
an erroneous "more" choice; (4) the number was 50 and the bird chose
50—a correct "more" choice.

Figure 10.6A shows that if the bird's choice of "fewer" and "more" is
based on an elapsed interval criterion rather than on a count of the
number of responses made, then the median elapsed intervals for these
four distributions must fall in the order just given. In particular, the
median elapsed interval for erroneous "fewer" choices must be greater
than the median elapsed interval for correct "fewer" choices, and the median elapsed interval for correct "more" choices must be greater than the
median elapsed interval for erroneous "more" choices.

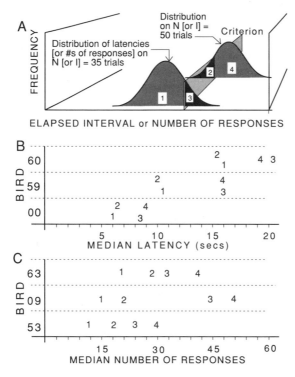

Figure 10.6
Theoretical and observed values of median latencies or median numbers of responses in birds required to make a choice based, respectively, on the number, N, of responses made on the center key or on the interval, I, elapsed during the run of responses. *A.* Schematic illustration showing how the median latencies for the four categories of trials must be ordered if the choice is based on a representation of the interval elapsed, or, mutatis mutandis, how the median numbers of responses must be ordered if the choice is based on a representation of the number of responses. In this illustration, it is assumed that the value of the constant term is 50 (responses or seconds) and the alternative term 35. For the fixed-number case, the categories of responses are: 1 = correct choices of the "fewer" key (the part of the $N=35$ distribution below the bird's hypothesized elapsed interval criterion); 2 = erroneous choices of the "fewer" key (the part of the $N=50$ distribution below the criterion); 3 = erroneous "more" choices (the part of the $N=35$ distribution above the criterion); 4 = correct "more" choices (the part of the $N=50$ distribution above the criterion). *B.* Median latencies for the different categories of responses from birds in the fixed-number task. The position of a category number along the abscissa gives the observed median latency of the responses in that category. The relative positions of these median latencies are not consistent with the hypothesis that the birds respond to the elapsed interval rather than to the number of responses made. The standard number of responses was 50; the values for the alternative number were: bird 00: 38; birds 59 and 60: 32. *C.* Median numbers of responses for birds in the fixed-interval task. The standard interval was 45 seconds; values of the alternative interval were: bird 63: 36 seconds; birds 09 and 58: 30 seconds. (Data from Rilling 1967, table 1.)

On the other hand, if the choice of a flanking key is based primarily on number of responses rather than interval elapsed, such an ordering need not be observed. Suppose that the birds routinely represent both time and number regardless of the task. Their choice in the fixed-number task is based primarily on their representation of number but reflects to some extent their representation of the elapsed interval, which tends to covary with the number of responses made. Under these conditions, they will tend to make erroneous "fewer" choices only on those trials in which they made 50 or more responses (the greater number) in an exceptionally short time, a time shorter than the time commonly taken to make 35 responses. Thus the median elapsed interval preceding erroneous "fewer" choices will be less than or approximately equal to the median elapsed interval preceding correct "fewer" choices. A similar argument gives the psychological conditions under which the median elapsed interval for an erroneous "more" choice may be longer than or approximately equal to the median elapsed interval for a correct "more" choice: the bird's representation of time elapsed outweighs its representation of number of responses made only when it has taken an exceptionally long time to make the fewer number of responses, an amount of time longer than that usually required to make the greater number.

Figure 10.6B shows that the median elapsed intervals for the four distributions in the fixed-number condition do not fall in the order they would have to fall in if the birds' choices were based primarily on elapsed interval. The pattern of median latencies suggests that temporal considerations override numerical considerations only on exceptionally short fixed-number 50 runs and exceptionally long fixed number 32-38 runs.

A similar analysis for the distributions of numbers of responses made in each category of trial in those birds responding in the fixed-interval condition shows that the median numbers of responses made fall in the order they would be expected to fall in if these birds' choices were based more on the number of responses they had made than on the interval elapsed (figure 10.6C). In a second experiment, Rilling manipulated the number of responses that these birds made on the center key during the fixed interval between the end of one trial and the next illumination of the flanking keys and showed that this had the predicted effect on their choices. When they were induced to make fewer responses, they were more likely to make the "shorter" choice. In other words, under Rilling's conditions, pigeons that had to time an interval in the 30 to 45 second range were inclined to rely instead on the number of responses they made during the interval, while birds that had to count responses in the 30-50 range did not rely very much on the interval elapsed during the count.

Rilling's finding is not consistent with the Davis and Memmott (1982) hypothesis that animals rely on counting only as a last resort. Nor is it consistent with the widespread assumption that if animals can count at all, they can count only very small numbers (the "one-two-three-many" hypothesis). Rilling's data imply that they rely on counting (or, in any event, on a procedure for measuring numerosity per se) in preference to timing, even when the counts are large. This in turn implies that measuring large, serially presented numerosities with reasonable accuracy is not difficult for a pigeon. The percentage error in its measurements of numerosities—even large numerosities—is no worse than the percentage error in its measurements of temporal intervals.

One other aspect of Rilling's data merits comment: the median latencies under fixed-number conditions, when the birds were discriminating a serially emitted numerosity of 32 to 38 from a serially emitted numerosity of 50 with better than 80 percent accuracy. The median latencies to complete the runs ranged from 6 to 20 seconds. For the speediest bird, none of the median latencies exceeded 10 seconds. This bird was estimating to an accuracy of roughly ± 20 percent the numerosity of a sequence of 30 to 60 of its pecks delivered at an average rate of 5 pecks per second. It would be interesting to compare the accuracy of its performance to human accuracy in counting responses made with comparable rapidity.

Counting Stimuli (Rather than Responses)
The older operant literature on counting (or the discrimination of numerosity) is important because it demonstrates that the standard laboratory animals can discriminate between large numerosities. It discourages the common belief that if animals can deal with numerosity at all, they can do so only for very small numerosities. More recent studies, all done with smaller numerosities, expand the earlier findings in a number of interesting ways. For example, the work so far reviewed focused on the animal's counting its own responses. The question arises whether animals can count other entities. Fernandes and Church (1982) showed, in a rigorously controlled experiment, that rats can discriminate the number of light flashes or tone beeps in a sequence of flashes or beeps and that there is immediate cross-modal transfer of this discrimination, as might be expected if the numerosity rather than the sensory quality of the stimulus sequence is the decisive attribute from the animal's standpoint.

Fernandes and Church presented rats with a sequence of either two or four sounds just prior to inserting two levers into the test chamber. If the sequence had two elements, the rats had to choose the right lever to get a food reward; if four, the left. The durations of the sounds and the intervals between them varied in an intricate design contrived so that neither the duration of a single sound, nor the duration of an interval between sounds, nor the duration of the sequence could reliably lead to correct discrimination. For all the sequences, the rats chose correctly 70 to 90 percent of the time. When light flashes were substituted for sound beeps, the discrimination transferred. In a follow-up experiment, Davis and Albert (1986) showed that rats could discriminate a sequence of three beeps from both sequences of two and sequences of four beeps.

An alternative approach to deconfounding duration and numerosity in stimulus sequences is to let them covary during training and then render one of the cues of no discriminative value during testing. Meck and Church (1983) adopted this approach. They taught rats to choose between two levers on the basis of the sound sequence they had just heard. The two training sequences consisted of cycles comprised of equal periods of white noise and silence. One sequence had two cycles and lasted 2 seconds. The rat heard a half-second of noise, a half-second of silence, a second half-second of noise, and a second half-second of silence. The final silent phase terminated with the emergence of the choice levers. The other sequence had eight cycles and lasted 8 seconds. When the discrimination reached asymptotic levels of accuracy, testing began.

On test trials, which were interpolated among continued training trials, the rats heard stimuli that were intermediate in duration and number of cycles. In the series of trials designed to test for responses to intermediate numerosities, the duration of all the stimuli was set to 4 seconds, the geometric midpoint between 2 and 8. It had previously been shown that the geometric midpoint is the crossover point when an animal is forced to choose a duration stimulus intermediate between two anchor points. With stimulus duration held constant at 4 seconds, the rat's choices following sequences of 2, 3, 4, 5, 6, and 8 cycles were determined. The period of one cycle was, of necessity, reduced to keep the duration of the alternating stimulus constant. In this test series, the rat's choice was a systematic function of the number of cycles in the stimulus, with the crossover number being 4 (filled circles in figure 10.7).

In the other test series (all rats got both series), the number of cycles was fixed at 4, and the duration of the stimulus was varied—2, 3, 4, 5, 6 or 8—seconds. Again, of necessity, cycle period covaried with stimulus duration. In this series, with number held constant, the rat's choices were a systematic function of stimulus duration.

The Meck and Church (1983) experiment establishes what was assumed in interpreting the Rilling (1967) experiment: under training conditions where number and duration covary, the animal represents both variables. Also, the results from the number-testing series in figure 10.7 imply that in comparing a test numerosity with the two anchor numer-

osities (2 and 8), the rat relied on the ratios between the test numerosities
and the anchor numerosities. This follows from the fact that the equipreference numerosity was 4 (the geometric or equiratio midpoint: 8/4 = 4/
2 = 2) rather than 5 (the linear or equi-interval midpoint: 8–5 = 5–2 = 3).
By contrast, when the rat had to compare a count of the responses it had
made to a remembered criterion count, it relied on the difference (see
figures 10.2A and 10.4A-C). This suggests that rats may compute either
the difference of two numerons or their ratio, depending on the task.
Another striking aspect of figure 10.7 is the similarity in the psychophysical functions for numerosity and duration.

Adding the Numerosities of Stimuli in Two Different Modalities
Church and Meck (1984) report an experiment in which sound sequences
and light sequences alternated from trial to trial during training. The rats
were taught to choose the right lever following a two-sound sequence or
a two-light sequence and the left lever following a sequence of four in
either modality. A sound burst or light flash lasted 1 second. In both
modalities, the interstimulus interval varied between 0.8 and 4.4 seconds, so that on some trials, a sequence of two stimuli lasted 2.8 seconds

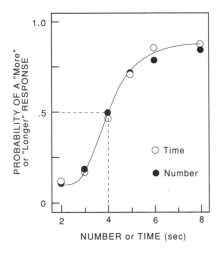

Figure 10.7
Probability of choosing the right lever (equivalent to a "more" or "longer" judgment) as
a function of either the number of cycles in the prechoice stimulus or its duration, with the
other variable (duration or number) fixed at its equipreference value. The curve through
the data is calculated from Gibbon's (1981) "sample known exactly with a similarity
decision rule" model for timing, with the Meck and Church modification to handle counting. (Redrawn from Meck and Church 1983, p. 323, by permission of author and publisher.)

and on some trials 6.4 seconds, while a sequence of four stimuli lasted either 6.4 or 17.2 seconds. On a single test day, half the trials were as during training (sequences of either lights or sounds), but half presented sounds and lights simultaneously. On some, there was a 1-second sound and simultaneously a 1-second light (thus, two stimuli). On other trials, there was a 1-second sound-light pair, followed by an interval of either 0.8 or 4.4 seconds, followed by another 1-second sound-light pair (thus, four stimuli, presented as simultaneous pairs at varying interpair intervals). On these test trials, there was never a reward. The purpose was simply to see what the rat would do when confronted with these never-before-encountered combination stimuli.

The results were very clear. On trials on which the rats experienced a single sound-light pair, they chose the "two" lever (the left lever), and on trials when they experienced two sound-light pairs, they chose the "four" lever. Their choices on the respective kinds of compound trials did not differ significantly from those they made when they got two or four stimuli unimodally. Given the novel experience of two sequential sound-flash pairs, the rats were as likely to choose the "four" lever as they were on trials on which they either heard four sounds or saw four flashes (the stimuli for which a "four" response had been rewarded during training).

There are two clear explanatory possibilities for these results. One is that the rats counted flashes and sound bursts without regard to modality or sequence. In response to the simultaneous sound and flash, they incremented a counter twice (even though during training they had always incremented the count in response to sequentially experienced stimuli) and, in response to the second sound and flash, they incremented the counter twice more, generating a count of four. Alternatively, the sound and flash may have incremented separate counters, with the tallies on the two counters being added when the choice levers appeared. If this interpretation is correct, the rat computes that one plus one equals two and two plus two equals four. This would mean that the rat has a concept of number because it maps from numerosities to numerons and performs with the numerons an operation isomorphic to the arithmetic operation of addition.

It is worth pausing to consider how odd this result is from the standpoint of associative theories of instrumental learning. The rat had always been rewarded for making a left response after hearing two sounds and likewise after seeing two flashes. Then it was given the two stimuli together. Both stimuli had always predicted reward on the left lever, and yet the rat pressed the right lever—with as high a probability as if it had just heard or seen one of the stimuli that had always predicted reward on that lever.

Numerosity Labeling and Addition in the Chimpanzee

The capacity of the chimpanzee to label the numerosities of small sets has been investigated by Matsuzawa (1985). He taught a 5-year-old female chimpanzee to choose a key with the correct arabic numeral when she was confronted with sets of objects varying in numerosity from 1 to 6. She was initially trained with sets composed only of red pencils, then tested for generalization to sets composed of other objects with other colors. Generalization was immediate. Once she had learned to pick "5" when shown a set of five red pencils (and "4" when shown a set of four, and so on), she would pick "5" when shown a set of five blue gloves, "4" when shown a set of four green toothbrushes, "3" when shown a set of three black bricks, and so on.

Subsequently she was required to identify the object, color and numerosity of a set to collect her reward. When shown a set of five black gloves, she had to press one key signifying glove, one signifying black, and one signifying 5. There were five kinds of objects, five possible colors, and five numerosities (1-5), making 125 different test displays. In her final run on this task, the chimp was given 604 test displays in 127 minutes (almost five problems per minute) and made only three errors.

It took longer to train the numerosity identifications than to train the object and color discriminations. From this, one might be tempted to conclude that the representation of numerosity is more difficult for a chimp than color or form. Such conclusions should be made with caution. The results might be taken to imply the opposite. Humans often have very little conscious access to processes that are basic to their representation of the world. For example, people are very poor at identifying retinal image size, even though the size of the retinal image is clearly an important determinant of the object percept. For another example, many introductory psychology students who have never had a course in calculus are astonished to discover that their retina computes the second derivative of the local distribution of light intensity. Similarly, estimations of numerosity may enter into many very basic mental processes in the chimpanzee, and yet the chimp may have only limited or no conscious access to those representations. Insofar as the ability to label explicitly a numerosity may depend on some kind of special access to representations of numerosity (here designated by the term *conscious access*), the chimp may have difficulty because the requisite access to the representation is difficult, not because the representation itself is formed with difficulty. It is not clear that a chimpanzee could readily be taught to label numerically the distances from itself to various objects in its environment, yet there is evidence in its spatial behavior that a representation of those distances exists in its brain and is used in some aspects of its behavior.

Rumbaugh, Savage-Rumbaugh, and Hegel (1987) had two adult male chimpanzees choose between two trays containing bits of semisweet chocolate, with the numbers of chocolate bits ranging from 1 to 9. The bits on each tray were distributed between two wells. The chimps got to eat the bits on whichever tray it chose, so its only incentive to choose the tray with more bits was that it thereby got to eat more chocolate. On many trials, the chimp could not correctly pick the tray with more bits unless it summed across (or counted across) the two wells in each tray. For example, the tray with the lesser number of bits might have 1 in one well and 4 in the other (total = 5), while the tray with the greater number might have 3 in both (total = 6). Choosing the tray with the most bits in any one well would lead the chimp astray on such a trial. In the course of several hundred trials, both chimpanzees came to pick the tray with the greater total number regardless of how the bits were distributed among the wells (for example, on trials involving the above choice, they chose the 3 + 3 = 6 tray over the 1 + 4 = 5 tray 90 percent of the time). The accuracy of their choices was a function of the ratio of the sums rather than of any other property of the two number pairs, such as, for example, the magnitude of the smallest number, whether the two pairs had a number in common or did not, and so on. By the end of testing, the chimpanzees almost never made a mistake when the sums differed by two or more (for example, 5 + 4 = 9 versus 5 + 2 = 7); the infrequent mistakes chiefly occurred with large sums differing by only 1 (for example, 5 + 2 = 7 versus 4 + 4 = 8).

The results of Rumbaugh et al. (1987) are interesting from two perspectives. They indicate that "summation skills" in the chimpanzee are "rapidly acquired, ... highly accurate, and generalize without substantial decrement to previously unencountered novel pairs of food quantities" (p. 113). Rumbaugh et al. draw this conclusion because they assume that chimps cannot count. They assume that the chimps have direct perceptual access to numerosity. If one assumes that they determine numerosity by a counting process, then instead of adding the results of two different counts, they may have obtained the sum by simply continuing the count from one set to the next. Second, they are the first demonstration so far encountered that animals can map simultaneously presented numerosities as well as sequentially presented numerosities. Recent experiments from Davis' laboratory demonstrate the same capacity in subprimate mammals.

Simultaneously Presented Numerosities

Two recent experiments from Davis's laboratory are of considerable significance in that they involve discriminations based on the numerosity or ordinal position of simultaneously presented objects. All the studies so far reviewed, with the exception of the Rumbaugh et al. and

Matsuzawa chimpanzee experiments, involved sequentially presented stimuli. Davis (1984) reports an experiment in which an assistant trained a raccoon to choose the Plexiglas box containing three items (sometimes grapes, sometimes toy bells) from among a set of five boxes, one containing only one grape (bell), one containing two, one three, one four, and one five. Only the box with three could be opened. When the raccoon attempted to open one of the other boxes, an error was recorded, and the experimenter scolded the raccoon and left it alone in the room for 1 minute. When the raccoon's first attempt was with the correct box, it not only got to eat the contents (or play with them for 5 minutes, in the case of the bells), it also got experimenter approval. For this highly socialized pet raccoon, the experimenter's approval and disapproval were more potent reinforcers than the grapes. On repeated tests at the end of training, the raccoon chose the correct box on seventeen to twenty out of of twenty-five trials—far above chance.

Davis and Bradford (1986) required rats to choose a tunnel on the basis of its ordinal position in a set of six tunnels arrayed along one wall of an experimental enclosure. The spacings of the tunnels varied widely from trial to trial, so they could not be chosen on the basis of their position in the room. Also, the correct serial position varied across rats (from the third to the fifth tunnel along the wall). The rats readily learned this task. One of the more interesting aspects of the results was that all of the rats required to learn to enter the fifth tunnel initially solved the task by running directly to the far end of the sequence of tunnels and working backward from there (in which case, the correct tunnel was the second one encountered). However, all but one subject eventually switched to running along the tunnels from the entry end of the chamber, so that the correct tunnel was the fifth one they came to.

The rats that had learned to choose either the fourth or the fifth tunnel were given further trials in which the sequence of tunnels now turned the corner at the far end of the chamber, so that some number of tunnels were along the left wall of the chamber, as during training, but some were along the back wall (how many were along which wall varied from trial to trial). The rats transferred above chance selection performance immediately to the sequences of tunnels that turned the corner.

Counting Different Kinds of Rewards
Capaldi and Miller (1988) have recently reported a series of elegantly controlled experiments demonstrating that rats can control their behavior in a runway on the basis of the numerosity of the preceding sequence of rewarded trials. Part of the interest of this sequence of experiments is that it involves counting events (rewarded trials) that were separated by 15 to 60 or more seconds, unlike the earlier operant studies, in which the

animals counted responses given at rates of 1 per second or higher. Another point of interest is their systematic testing of the assumptions in a formal analysis of counting given by Gelman and Gallistel (1978).

In nearly all of the Capaldi and Miller experiments, the rats were run each day on multiple presentations of two different sequences of runway trials, a sequence of three trials (*RRN*) and a sequence of four (*NRRN*), where *R* symbolizes a rewarded trial and *N* an unrewarded trial. Sequences, which lasted a couple of minutes on average, were separated by about 15 minutes. Because the different types of sequences were presented in an irregular order, the rat could not know on the first trial of a sequence whether it was to be rewarded or not. One would expect them to run equally fast on the first trial of a sequence, regardless of its type, and they did. In both types of sequence, the terminal trial, which followed two rewarded trials, was not rewarded. If the rat could count the number of rewarded trials they had experienced in a given sequence, they might be expected to slow down after receiving two such trials in succession, and indeed they did.

Because time since the first reward was confounded with the number of rewarded trials, Capaldi and Miller increased the intertrial interval and/or the amount of time the rats were confined to the goal box on each trial. Manipulating the various elapsed intervals in this way had no effect on the rats' tendency to slow down on the terminal trials, that is, on the fourth trial of an *NRRN* sequence and the third trial of an *RRN* sequence.

It might be objected that the rats were responding on the basis of the identity or nonidentity of the last two trials rather than on the numerosity of the set of consecutively rewarded trials. It could be argued that no count is implicit in this identity comparison because the occurrence of a trial identical to the preceding trial predicted nonreward on the next trial. An algorithm that detected the identity of any two sequential outcomes would work. To check on this, Capaldi and Miller ran a further experiment, employing the series *NRRRN* and *RRRN*. The rats trained this way slowed down after the third rewarded trial rather than the second. One could still argue that identity considerations were involved, but now it is not identity of outcome per se (as when only two identical trials occurred) but rather identity over three trials. In short, a measure of the numerosity of the set of identical trials would seem to be a necessary for the discrimination shown.

Next Capaldi and Miller turned to the interesting question of whether the rat could learn to delimit or not to delimit the kinds of rewards that it counted. In the first of the experiments addressed to this question, they introduced two new groups, each of which got two kinds of trial series in an unpredictable order as before. For the group "Different," the series were *RRN* and *R'RRN*, where *R'* was a reward (Kellogg's Sugar Smacks or Kellogg's Corn Pops) that differed from the reward received on the next two trials (Pops or Smacks). If this group were to learn to slow down on the terminal trial of both series, it would have to learn not to count the R' at the beginning of the second kind of series. The other group, a control, got the series RRN and $RRRN$. This group should not learn to slow down on the N trial of the RRN series because there should be no way for it to discriminate the N trial on an RRN series from the third R trial on an $RRRN$ series. The "Different" group learned to slow down on the terminal trial of both series, while the control group slowed down only on the terminal trial of $RRRN$ series.

The just reported results from the $R'RRN$ group imply that rats can learn to leave a reward out of their count if it differs from the other rewards. The question then becomes, Can they learn to include it? To answer this, Capaldi and Miller trained a group that got four different series of trials, as always in a randomized order, so that they could not know in advance what a given series was going to be. Letting P stand for Pops and S for Smacks, the series were: PSN, SPN, $NPSN$ and $NSPN$. If the rat cannot learn to "count across" the two different rewards (that is, ignore their difference for the purposes of counting them), then it should run equally rapidly on all trials because, given that one may be in any of the above four series, there is no predicting what will follow either a P or an S trial. The rats trained in this way learned to run slowly on the terminal N trials of all four series, indicating that they could use the occurrence of two successive rewarded trials to predict nonreward when the rewards being counted together differed. The difference between the rewards that was ignored in this experiment was the difference that was the basis for excluding one of the rewards from the count in the previous experiment. Thus rats may vary the criterion for inclusion in a to-be-counted set (shorthand for a set whose numerosity is to be assessed in some way).

In their last two experiments, Capaldi and Miller asked whether the rats' discrimination depended on the numerosity of the set of consecutive identical rewards, independent of the composition of that set, or whether the particular rewards that yielded the count of two were crucial to the discrimination. They trained rats with the series $R'RRN$ and RRN. When the rats reliably slowed down on the terminal trials of both sequences, the experimenters shifted them to series of $RR'R'N$ and $R'R'N$. Even on the first day of the shift, the rats continued to slow down on the terminal trial of both series, albeit some disruption was apparent (as is only to be expected, since the rats had to be tracking which rewards they were getting on each trial to solve the problem). Thus, having learned to slow down following a sequence of two R trials, the rats immediately also slowed down following a sequence of two R' trials. Capaldi and Miller finished this experiment with yet another shift—to $NRRN$ and RRN series—and the rats continued to slow down on the terminal trials in the face of this second shift. In short, they behaved as though their criterion for slowing down was two preceding trials with the same kind of reward, independent of what that reward was.

The conclusion that rats could base their behavior on the numerosity of the sequence of identical rewards, independent of the identity of those rewards, was confirmed in a final experiment employing four different kinds of rewards (Pops, Smacks, Cocoa Puffs, and Noyes pellets). Let the first two kinds be designated R and R' and the last two kinds r and r'. Rats were trained with the first two kinds of rewards. Every odd day of training, they got $R'RRN$ and RRN series. Every even day, they got $RR'R'N$ and $R'R'N$ series. Thus these rats were being trained to count consecutive identical rewards independent of reward identity. In the shift phase of the experiment R' was replaced with r' and R with r: they thus suddenly encountered two new kinds of reward. In the first phase, the rats learned to slow down on the terminal trials regardless of whether they experienced $R'RRN$ or RRN or $RR'R'N$ or $R'R'N$ and when r and r' were substituted for R and R', they continued this pattern.

Capaldi and Miller's conclusion that the rat can learn to respond to numerosity per se, transferring immediately to differently constituted sets with the same numerosity, is powerfully supported by an experiment by Meck and Church (1983). They trained rats to press the left lever when they heard a two-cycle sound stimulus (sound-on, sound-off, sound-on, sound-off, levers enter) and the right lever when they heard an eight-cycle stimulus (eight sound-on segments and eight sound-off segments). When rats thus trained are tested with stimulus cycles of intermediate numerosity, the indifference point is four cycles (four sound-on segments alternating with four sound-off segments)—see figure 10.7. Meck and Church tested the effect of test cycles in which the sound-on segments alternated with cutaneous segments (subpainful electric shocks to the feet). In other words, shock segments replaced the sound-off segments. When tested with a 4-cycle mixed stimulus (4 sound-on segments and 4 shock-on segments), the rats chose the right lever on 85 percent of the tests, a percentage not very different from the percentage choice of this lever when they heard an eight-cycle purely auditory stimulus, and much higher than the roughly 50 percent level of choice that would be expected if the rats took into account only the sound segments of the mixed stimulus. In other words, the rats treated four sounds plus four shocks as equivalent to eight sounds.

Capaldi and Miller (1988) concluded that the numerosity discriminations of the rats in their runway tests indicated that the rats were counting in the sense specified by the formal analysis of counting given by Gelman and Gallistel (1978).

The Mapping Process in the Representation of Numerosity

I have used *counting* as a shorthand for the mapping process by which the brain assigns numerons to numerosities because counting is the only commonly used procedure for measuring numerosity. The question arises whether there is any other process for measuring numerosity. In cases where some other variable (for example, weight or volume) is a scalar function of the numerosity of the to-be-counted set, one may measure the other variable to obtain an estimate of numerosity. However, these indirect approaches work only for special cases. They do not apply when the to-be-counted set is composed of different kinds of entities or to sets that are presented serially rather than simultaneously. The question is whether there is any generally applicable process for measuring numerosity, or at least some delimited domain of numerosities, other than the counting process.

In addressing this question, we need a formal analysis of counting, specifying the characteristics a process must possess if it is to be regarded as a counting process. We recognize a process as a counting process whether it involves a sequence of count words, a sequence of raised fingers, a sequence of indicated points on the body, a sequence of positions of the wheels in a mechanical or electromechanical counter, a sequence of state-transitions in a binary flip-flop counter, and so forth. Thus we clearly do not wish to tie the definition of counting to any particular symbolic or material realization of the process. In particular, we do not want to tie the definition to the common human device of using words as numerons. We need a formal analysis that specifies the characteristics that all acknowledged counting processes have in common— verbal and nonverbal processes, human and machine. Gelman and Gallistel (1978) offer such an analysis.

A counting process is a mapping process. It associates sets of differing numerosity with entities or states of the representing system that stand for distinct numerosities. In other words, it maps from distinct numerosities (in the domain of the mapping) to distinct numerons (in the range of the mapping). *Domain* and *range* are used here in the way they are used in the discussion of mathematical functions. The domain of a function is the set of possible arguments of the function. For example, the domain of the logarithm function is the real numbers greater than 0; negative numbers do not belong to the domain of the function that maps from numbers to their logarithms because there is no such thing as the logarithm of a negative number. The domain of a process that maps from sets to representations of their numerosity is the set of all sets to which the mapping procedure may be applied—the set of all countable sets. The range of a function is the set of values that the function may assume. For example, the range of the logarithm function is from minus infinity to plus infinity because the logarithm of 0 is minus infinity, and the logarithm of infinity is infinity. By contrast, the range of the squaring function is from 0 to plus infinity because the squares of negative numbers are positive. The range of the process that maps from sets to representations of their numerosities is the set of all possible numerons.

The domain of numerosity (the number of distinct numerosities that the process can map) is limited by the number of numerons in its range—that is, by the number of distinct entities or states of the system that may serve as numerical representatives. This is a formal statement of the obvious point that you can count only to ten on your fingers.

Given the availability of a set of numerons that constitute the range of the mapping, a counting process is defined by three formal principles:

1. In proceeding from item to item or event to event within a currently defined domain (a to-be-counted set), the process must assign one and only one numeron to each item or event—*the one-one principle*.

2. The order of assignment of numerons (entities or states in the range of the process) must be the same from one occasion to the next—*the stable-order principle*.

3. The final numeron assigned must apply to the set as a whole, rather than to the particular item or event to which it happens to be assigned. This is called *the cardinal principle* because the last numeron assigned represents the cardinality of the counted set.

Gelman and Gallistel (1978) give two other principles of counting, but these are not definitional; they do not limit the class of processes that may be regarded as counting processes. These further "principles" merely call our attention to the absence of certain constraints in the principles that define a counting process. The three defining principles say nothing about the order in which the items in a set must be assigned a numeron. Any order is acceptable, provided the one-one constraint is honored. The *order-irrelevance principle* calls our attention to the absence of this constraint in the defining principles, emphasizing that the validity of a counting process does not depend on which event or item is assigned which numeron.

The principles that define what is and is not a counting process do not say anything about the sets that may be counted, although technically one must stipulate that these sets be finite. With infinite sets, there is no last assignment, so counting does not yield a representation of the cardi-

nality of the set. Provided, however, that it is understood that the process
applies only to finite sets, the principles do not say that some finite sets
may be counted and others not, or that only homogeneous sets may be
counted, and so on. The *abstraction principle* underlines this lack of constraint, emphasizing that the characteristics of the items in a set are
irrelevant to its numerosity.

Application of the Formal Analysis to the Meck and Church Model
Meck and Church (1983) propose a model for the measurement of
numerosity based on the Gibbon (1981) model for the measurement of
temporal intervals. Their model is an instantiation of the counting
process defined by Gelman and Gallistel's formal analysis. The functional structure of the Meck and Church counting model is the same as
the functional structure of their timing model (see figure 9.9A), with one
exception. In the timing or "Run" mode, the switch between the pulse
generator and the integrator ("Working Memory") is closed by the onset
of a stimulus and opened by its offset. Thus the amount accumulated in
working memory is proportionate to the duration of the stimulus. By
contrast, when the same system functions in the counting or "Event"
mode, the switch is closed for a fixed and brief duration by the onset of
a stimulus belonging to the to-be-counted set. Each brief closing of the
switch gates a train of pulses to the integrator, which increments the
quantity stored in "Working Memory." When the last event has occurred, the quantity in "Working Memory" is taken to represent the
numerosity of the set of counted stimuli. Thus, when the switch functions
in what Meck and Church call the "Run" mode, the functional structure
portrayed in figure 9.8A measures durations; when the switch functions
in what they call the "Event" mode, the same functional structure counts
events.

The mechanism Meck and Church proposed maps from to-be-counted
events to states of the integrator; thus states of the integrator constitute
the numerons in this counting system. The mapping is one-one because
each event gates one and only one burst of pulses to the integrator; hence
each successively counted entity is paired with a successively higher
quantity in the integrator. The states of the integrator are run through in
an order that is always the same because the ordering relation for
quantity or magnitude (that is, for the successive states of the integrator)
is the same as the ordering relation for numerosity. The fact that adding
successive equal increments to a quantity produces an ordered set of
quantities just as adding successive ones produces an ordered set of
numbers is part of the reason that quantity or magnitude can be represented numerically, and vice-versa. Finally, the state of the integrator at
the end of the series of events is taken to represent a property of the series

(its numerosity), not a property of the final event itself. Thus the process envisioned by Meck and Church conforms to the principles that define a counting process.

The constraints whose absence Gelman and Gallistel emphasize with their order irrelevance and abstraction principles are also absent in the Meck and Church model. The model says nothing about conditions on the events or stimuli that may trigger a closure of the switch when the switch operates in the counting or "Event" mode. Hence it does not require that to-be-counted events or entities occur in any particular order or have any particular sensory characteristics. We have reviewed a number of experimental demonstrations that animal determinations of numerosity are similarly unconstrained. Capaldi and Miller (1988) showed that rats were indifferent to the order in which different kinds of rewards occurred (when they were trained to count across kinds of reward), and several different experiments have shown immediate transfer from the numerosity of a training set to the numerosity of a set of novel items (the abstraction principle).

Meck and Church (1983) and Meck, Church, and Gibbon (1985) give several lines of experimental evidence in support of their hypothesis that the system that measures time and the system that measures numerosity differ only in the mode of functioning of the switch that gates pulses to integrators. The striking similarity in the psychophysical functions for the discrimination of durations and the discrimination of numerosities is one line of evidence (figure 10.7). Amphetamine, which speeds up the timer by which the rat measures the durations of stimuli, increases its measure of numerosity by the same factor. In both cases, the effect can be interpreted as an effect of amphetamine on the average rate of pulse generation by the pacemaker. Increasing the pulse rate will increase the accumulation in the integrator at the end of a given duration or a given number of counts (event-linked increments in the integral). Third, the numerical and duration discriminations transferred from purely auditory stimuli to mixed auditory and cutaneous stimuli equally strongly.

Meck and Church's fourth and most persuasive line of evidence comes from an experiment that directly tests the hypothesis that decisions in the timing and counting tasks are based on the same quantitative variable, the value of the integral stored in "Working Memory." This quantity represents duration when the switch operates in the timing or "Run" mode and numerosity when the switch operates in the counting or "Event" mode. If in both tasks the behavioral decision (which lever to choose) depends on the outcome of a comparison between the current magnitude of this quantity and the memory for the quantities accumulated on previous trials, then one might expect to see immediate transfer from a judgment based on duration to one based on numerosity. A count that yielded the same accumulation as some already trained duration might be responded to as if it were that duration.

The basic idea behind this intricately designed experiment was to train rats to judge whether they had just heard the longer or the shorter of two familiar sound durations and then to test them with cyclical stimuli whose duration was very much longer than either of the training durations. However, the number of the cycles in these very long test stimuli was such that, according to pilot work, the quantities accumulated in the integrator from counting the cycles of the test stimuli would fall in the same range as the quantities accumulated in timing the durations of the steady (noncyclical) training stimuli. Meck and Church were proceeding on the assumption—justified by their earlier experiments—that rats routinely both time and count the stimuli they are exposed to, regardless of which variable is rewarded. Meck and Church gambled that when the accumulation generated by a counting operation approximated the accumulations that had been selectively rewarded during duration training, the rats would apply to these count accumulations the same decision rule they had learned to apply to the duration accumulations. In effect, they would base their behavior on the magnitude of the representative, independent of what that representative represented.

First Meck and Church taught the rat to press one lever when it heard a steady noise of 2 seconds' duration and the other lever when it heard a steady noise of 4 seconds' duration. Next they determined the duration discrimination function. They interspersed the training trials with test trials, on which the rat heard steady noise bursts of intermediate duration ($2 < d < 4$) and was not rewarded for either choice (there being no "correct" choice when the stimulus was intermediate between the trained values of 2 and 4). By means of these interspersed trials, they could measure the discrimination function, that is, the tendency to choose 4 as a function of the duration of the stimulus.

Finally, they interspersed counting trials. On these trials, the rats heard 1-second noise bursts alternating with 1-second silent segments. On any one trial, the discriminative test stimulus consisted of somewhere between ten and twenty cycles of this stimulus. Both the total duration of the test stimuli (20-40 seconds) and the summed durations of their sound-on or sound-off segments (10-20 seconds) greatly exceeded both training durations (2 versus 4 seconds). If, as pilot work had led Meck and Church to believe, the switch, when operating in the counting or "Event" mode, stays open for about 200 milliseconds for each counted event and if rats count stimulus sequences as a matter of course, then the accumulation from the counting of a sequence of ten sound bursts would match the accumulation from the timing of a single burst of 2 seconds' duration

(0.2 x 10 = 2) and the accumulation from the counting of twenty bursts would match the accumulation from the timing of a single 4-second burst (0.2 x 20 = 4). The accumulations from timing these cyclical test stimuli would be very much greater than the accumulations that were rewarded during duration training. But the accumulations from counting the number of bursts would fall in the same range as the accumulations rewarded during duration training. Thus the rats might be expected to apply the decision rule learned for durations to the quantities generated by their counts of the number of bursts, which in fact they did (figure 10.8).

The results in figure 10.8, which were replicated and extended by Meck et al. (1985), imply that the rat counts by making successive roughly equal increments in the magnitude of some physiological variable—the variable corresponding to the integral in the "Working Memory" of the Meck and Church model. In effect, the nervous system inverts the representational convention whereby numbers are used to represent linear magnitudes. Instead of using number to represent magnitude, the rat uses magnitude to represent number.

Subitizing?
Counting processes are among the simplest of representational processes, both from the standpoint of how readily they may be formalized

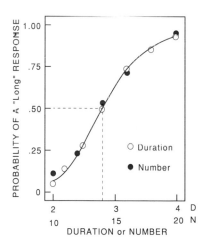

Figure 10.8
Probability of choosing the lever rewarded after the "long" (4-second) stimulus as a function of either the duration of a steady test stimulus or as a function of the number of cycles in a test stimulus consisting of alternating bursts of noise and silence. (Redrawn from Meck and Church 1983, p. 331, by permission of author and publisher.)

and from the standpoint of the simplicity of the devices required to give physical realization to them. Nonetheless there is evident in the literature on animal behavior and numerosity a deep reluctance to postulate counting processes in animals. The roots of this reluctance are probably to be found in the sway that empiricist theories of mind hold over theorists in experimental psychology. Since numerosity is an abstract property of a set—not a property directly given in the proximal stimuli— it must be a property that the mind apprehends with difficulty. Some such intuition presumably underlies the repeated reluctance of theorists to assume the obvious in the face of the extensive experimental evidence that animal behavior is sensitive to the numerosities of stimuli and events—both simultaneously and successively presented, independent of the spatial or temporal pattern in which they are perceived, and for numerosities extending at least as high as 50.

The only process for measuring numerosity that is both well understood and generally applicable is counting. Thus in the face of evidence that an animal bases some aspect of its behavior on a representation of numerosity, the obvious assumption would be that its brain determined numerosity by a counting process of some kind. Meck and Church (1983) provide a functional structure for such a process, showing that it can be realized by a minor modification of the mechanism responsible for measuring temporal intervals, and they provide experimental evidence for the existence of this mechanism. Despite the formal simplicity of the counting process, the ease with which it may be physically realized, and the existence of an experimentally supported model for a counting process in the rat, Rumbaugh et al. (1987), in explaining the ability of their chimpanzee subjects to choose the tray with the greater number of chocolates, assume that the chimpanzees subitize the number of chocolate bits in each well of the tray rather than count them. Regarding this subitizing process, they confess that "what the specifics of its operation are is currently unclear" (p. 114), but they nonetheless think it more likely that the chimpanzees subitize the "fiveness" of the set of chocolate bits in a well than that they arrive at their representation by a counting process.

Subitizing has come to mean a process by which a human or an animal perceives the numerosity of a set without the mediation of a counting process—a direct or unmediated perception of numerosity. There is some irony in this in that the coiners of the term, Kaufman et al. (1949), concluded that "there is no such phenomenon as the immediate cognition of number." Kaufman et al. used the term to refer to the (unknown) process that mediated the ability of adult human subjects to give rapid and accurate judgments of the numerosity of small arrays that were presented briefly (200 milliseconds) and simultaneously. What operationally differentiated this process from ordinary counting was that the increment in reaction time per item in the set was less than the 380 milliseconds per item characteristic of adult subvocal counting. The reduced slope in the reaction time function for simultaneously presented arrays of numerosity less than 6 is the operational definition of the subitizing process.

The operational definition of subitizing is consistent with the theoretical assumption that performance in the subitizing range reflects a special form of sophisticated counting, which adult humans in highly number-oriented societies have learned to use to deal with small, simultaneously presented arrays (see Gelman and Gallistel 1978, p. 219ff). In other words, it is consistent with the assumption that the underlying process is the opposite of the kind of process that the theoretical term *subitizing* has come to connote. The experimental data on subitizing are consistent with the view that the underlying process is a sophisticated, specialized strategy that is learned, appears late in human cognitive development, and has no counterpart in animal cognition. Gelman and Gallistel (1978) argue that the data on cognitive development in humans support the view that in humans, at least, counting is the developmentally primitive process for estimating even the smallest numerosities. Since counting has nothing inherently to do with the capacity to verbalize, there is no reason to assume that counting is not also the process by which infants differentiate numerosities (Starkey and Cooper 1980; Starkey, Gelman, and Spelke 1983).

The most thorough modern investigation of the phenomenon that operationally defines subitizing reached conclusions similar to those advanced by Gelman and Gallistel (1978). Mandler and Shebo (1982) concluded that subitizing is a learned strategy, which is effective only with arrays of four or fewer because only with such arrays is there a reasonable probability that the configuration of a randomly arrayed set will conform to some directly perceptible canonical pattern. The Mandler and Shebo (1982) data are important in a number of respects. First, they showed once more that even in practiced adult human subjects, the slope of the reaction time function for the accurate estimation of the numerosity of a simultaneously presented array is not flat over any range. Even in the range from one to four, there is an appreciable, statistically significant slope to this function, albeit a slope less than the 380 milliseconds per item characteristic of adult subvocal counting. In the secondary literature, it is sometimes stated or assumed that the slope of the reaction time function is flat in the subitizing range. In fact, however, from Kaufmann et al. (1949) onward, it has repeatedly been found that there is a significant slope to the reaction time function even in the range from one to two. It takes longer to perceive twoness than it does to perceive oneness, and longer yet to perceive threeness. These systematic increments in reaction time are consistent with the assumption that threeness, twoness, and oneness are distinguished through the mediation of a serial counting process, specially adapted to take advantage of the opportunities unique to small arrays.

Mandler and Shebo (1982) show further that the slope of the reaction time function for accurate responses is essentially constant above four. The increment in the time needed to distinguish fiveness from fourness or sixness from fiveness is within 10 percent of the increment needed to distinguish twentiness from nineteenness, which suggests that ordinary counting begins when the numerosity of the array is greater than four.

The slope of the reaction time function is critical in assessing the evidence for the direct perceptual apprehension of small numerosities because a formal characterization of a subitizing process has never been given and the functional structure of a subitizing mechanism has never been specified. The only empirical motivation for postulating the existence of a capacity to perceive threeness directly would be the discovery that threeness is appreciated just as rapidly as oneness. If threeness is distinguished from oneness by a counting process, it should take longer to obtain the representation of threeness. The counting process appears to be inescapably serial because there appears to be no way to distinguish the cardinal numeron from the other numerons employed if numerons are paired with items in parallel. One might imagine the numerons being paired with the items in a perceived array by a process analogous to an electrostatic process, which ensured that one and only one numeron stuck to every distinctly perceived object. However, in that case, there would be no basis for deciding which of the bound numerons should serve as the representative of the numerosity of the set. By contrast, when the numerons are serially applied, the last numeron applied is the representative of the numerosity of the set.

A flat reaction time function would be inconsistent with mediation by a serial counting process. The discovery of a flat reaction time for small numerosities would motivate the search for formal processes and/or mechanisms that could mediate the direct perception of (small) numerosities. However, the reaction time function is not flat over any range. And in very young children, where reaction time experiments are not feasible, it has been shown that the accuracy of twoness judgments increases when the duration of the display is increased, even when the shortest duration is 1 second, which is longer than is required to form a clear perception of the array (Gelman and Tucker 1975).

Klahr and Wallace (1973) argue that the increments in the reaction time function in the range from one to six are due to the retrieval of number names from a list searched seriatim. They argue that threeness is distinguished from twoness by a perceptual process that requires no longer to recognize threeness than it does twoness, but the name *three* appears after the name *two* on a list of number names that must be scanned seriatim once the perceptual process has done its work. In essence, they argue that the slope is an artifact of the requirement that the numerosity be identified verbally. However, Mandler and Shebo (1982) measured the reaction time to name the numerals 1, 2, 3, and so on and found no systematic increases. When confronted with the perceivable pattern 4 (the numeral itself), subjects took no longer to find the word *four* than they took to find *three* when confronted with 3.

Mandler and Shebo also ran a condition in which the patterns of dots at each numerosity were restricted to canonical patterns. All arrays of three dots were arranged in the form of an equilateral triangle, all arrays of four in the form of a square, and so on. Under these conditions, the slope of the reaction time function was flat from 1 to 4. Thus when small numerosities are presented in such a way that each numerosity forms a pattern perceptually distinct from the pattern formed by any other small numerosity, subjects rapidly learn to label correctly and with equal rapidity all these patterns, up to and including the pattern formed by arrays of four. This implies that the number names used in labeling small arrays are not, or at least need not be, retrieved by progression through a serially ordered list of names, which was what Klahr and Wallace (1973) assumed in order to account for the nonzero slope of the reaction time function for small arrays.

By constraining the perceptual pattern formed by an array of a given numerosity, Mandler and Shebo showed that it was indeed possible to obtain a flat reaction time function in the range from 1 to 4. The fact that when the perceptual forms of arrays are not so constrained, the reaction time function is not flat over this same range, is therefore evidence against the hypothesis that twoness and threeness may be percepts just like cowness and treeness.

There may be generally applicable processes for obtaining a representation of the numerosity of small sets that do not conform to the formal definition of counting processes. (By generally applicable, I mean processes that apply no matter how the items in the set are distributed in space and time.) However, it must be acknowledged that no one has yet described how such a process might work or how it could be physically realized. It must further be acknowledged that there are no behavioral data that motivate the search for such a process. The reaction time data and the data on exposure duration versus accuracy do not suggest a nonserial estimation process for small numerosities, either in adults or in three year olds. The only apparent motivation for the recurring postulation of such a process is a reluctance to impute counting processes to nonverbal organisms. This reluctance is surprising given the ease with which counting processes are formally described and mechanized. To build a machine that reliably recognizes cowness is beyond the reach of modern technology; to build a machine that counts to two is child's play. Nonetheless, many feel that it is more plausible to assume that animals and human infants derive their representations of small numerosities like two and three from some unspecified but supposedly simple, primitive, and nonserial perceptual process than it is to assume the mediation of a counting process. The preference for an unspecified nonserial perceptual process is the more remarkable when we recall the data showing that pigeons and rats discriminate serial numerosities in the range from 20 to 50 in a manner that appears to be quantitatively of a piece with their discriminations of small serial numerosities. Indeed the upper limit on animal serial numerosity estimates has yet to be established.

Until someone describes how a generally applicable nonserial perceptual process for esti.nating small numerosities might work or until there are experimental data implying the existence of such a process, one should probably assume that animal representations of numerosity derive from counting processes. Gelman and Gallistel (1978) have formally characterized such processes, and Meck and Church (1983) have described a mechanism for realizing such a process in an animal. Further, they have provided experimental data substantiating the central assumption in their model: that the counting mechanism is closely related to the mechanism that generates representations of temporal intervals.

Do Animals Add and Subtract Numerons?

There is an extensive body of experimental evidence that animals can discriminate the numerosities of sets. They discriminate on the basis of numerosity for both simultaneously and serially presented sets, whether those sets are homogeneous or heterogeneous and whether they are the training set or a novel set of stimuli. These discriminations have been demonstrated in a variety of animals with a variety of stimuli and a variety of experimental paradigms. The discriminative ability has been shown to extend up to fifty in the pigeon and up to twenty-five in the rat (no upper limit has been established in either case). To discriminate on the basis of numerosity is not, however, to have a concept of number, if by "having a concept of number" we mean that an animal is capable of manipulating numerons in accord with the relational and combinatorial operations of arithmetic.

Three findings might be taken as indicating that animals perform operations isomorphic to addition and subtraction with numerons (the neural representatives of numerosities). First, there are the data of Platt and Johnson (1971) for the case where premature entry of the rat into the feeding area did not trigger resetting of the counter. Under these conditions, there was a negative correlation between the number of responses the rat had made prior to its entry and the number it then made before trying the feeder again. This could be interpreted to indicate that the rats subtracted the numeron representing the responses they had made from the numeron representing the required number to obtain the numeron representing the responses they should now make. On the other hand, if we imagine that the rats obtained these numerons by a counting process, one could interpret this to mean that in this condition rats simply did not rezero their response counter after a premature entry. Second, there are the Church and Meck (1984) data. Rats had been taught to choose the right lever following either a sequence of two lights or of two sounds and the left lever following sequences of four of either kind of stimulus. When they were then given one light and one sound simultaneously, they chose the right ("two") lever and when given two light-sound pairs, they chose the left ("four") lever. This could be taken to indicate that they counted the lights, counted the sounds, and added the results to obtain the variable that determined their choice. On the other hand, one could imagine that they incremented a single counter twice in response to the first light-sound pair and twice more in response to the second pair. Finally Rumbaugh et al. (1987) showed that chimpanzees learn to choose trays of chocolates based on the total number of chocolates contained in two wells. If one assumes, as Rumbaugh et al. did, that chimpanzees cannot count—they apprehend by some process of direct perception the numerosities of the two sets of chocolates on a tray—then discriminations based on the sums of those sets imply a concept of number in an animal that cannot count. On the other hand, if one assumes that chimpanzees can count, they may simply have counted the chocolates on each tray, without regard to how they were grouped into wells.

   A compelling demonstration of operational competence with numbers comes from recently published work by Boysen and Berntson (1989). They taught a juvenile female chimpanzee the arabic numerals for numerosities one through five. When she had learned this, she was able without further training to check the oranges concealed in two or three different hiding places and then choose the arabic numeral that represented the total number of oranges. This performance might be mediated simply by counting over the two sets. However, when the sets of oranges were replaced with arabic numerals, she chose the arabic numeral that was the sum of the two numerals she saw. Her performance on the first session with numerals in place of sets was significantly above chance. This is strong evidence for the operational use of numerals in a subhuman primate.

The evidence for arithmetic operations with numerons in nonprimates that is the least susceptible to explanation in terms of counting comes from the tasks where the animal's behavior varies systematically as a function of the discrepancy between a current count and a target count. In the Mechner (1958) paradigm and Platt and Johnson's (1971) adaptation of it, the rat's probability of abandoning the lever to seek food peaked at a fixed difference between the target value (the required number of presses) and the current count (the number of presses since initialization of the counter). The size of this difference—the number by which the n at peak exceeded the required N—was a systematic function of the prematurity penalty (see figures 10.2A and 10.4A-C). This implies that the rat's decision to try the feeder was determined by a computation of the difference between a reference numeron in memory and the numeron from its current count of its presses. On the other hand, in the Meck and Church (1983) paradigm, where the rat has been trained to choose one lever after seeing or hearing one number of cycles and the other lever after seeing or hearing two to four times as many cycles, when the rat is presented with an intermediate number of cycles, it appears to choose on the basis of the ratio between the number of test cycles and the two reference numbers (figures 10.7 and 10.8). This implies the computation of the ratio of two numerons. It is not readily apparent how either of these comparisons could be based on appropriate uses of the counting process; hence these results are the best evidence we have—within the realm of purely numerical tasks—for the conclusion that animals can perform with numerons the same kinds of addition and division operations that they perform with the representatives of temporal intervals.

One need not look for evidence of a rich representation of number solely within the domain of pure number tasks. For some crucial tests of the richness of the operations into which numerons enter, we may have to turn to tasks in which a numeron must enter into a combinatorial operation with the representative of a magnitude rather than with another numeron. One such case occurs when an animal estimates the rate of occurrence of some event by counting occurrences and dividing the count by the duration of the observation interval to obtain an estimate of rate.

Chapter 11

Rate

It has long been known that under certain circumstances, when confronted with a choice between alternatives that have different expected rates for the occurrence of some to-be-anticipated-outcome, animals, human and otherwise, proportion their choices in accord with the relative expected rates (Bitterman 1965; Brunswik 1939; Estes 1964). If one choice pays off with probability .66 and the other with probability .33, the rat chooses the former twice as often as the latter, in accord with the ratio of the payoff rates (.66/.33 = 2).

I assisted at demonstrations of this phenomenon that reliably discomfited introductory psychology students at Yale in the 1960s. A rat was trained to run a T maze with feeders at the end of each branch. On a randomly chosen 75 percent of the trials, the feeder in the left branch was armed; on the other 25 percent, the feeder in the right branch was armed. If the rat chose the branch with the armed feeder, it got a pellet of food. If it chose the unarmed branch, the trial ended without its getting a pellet. Above each feeder was a shielded light bulb, which came on when the feeder was armed. The rat could not see the bulb, but the undergraduates could. They were given sheets of paper and asked to predict before each trial which light would come on. Thus they, like the rat, had to make a choice between two mutually exclusive probabilistic outcomes, where one outcome was three times as likely as the other. The demonstration was a great hit because the students cheered for the rat when it succeeded and groaned in sympathy when it failed. Also, they pitted their choices against his and against each other.

Under these noncorrection conditions, where the rat does not experience reward at all on a given trial when it chooses incorrectly, the rat learns to choose the higher rate of payoff on most of the trials, thereby nearly maximizing its rate of success. Since there is no way to know in advance which feeder is armed, the strategy that maximizes success is always to choose the more frequently armed side. The maximum possible rate of success is 75 percent, which may be attained only by choosing the left side on every trial. To choose the right side is to opt for the side that pays off only 25 percent of the time in preference to the side that pays off 75 percent of the time; hence, the greater the percentage of right choices, the further one's rate of success departs from the maximum attainable rate. The undergraduates, by contrast, almost never chose the high payoff side exclusively. In fact, as a group their percentage choice of that side was invariably within one or two points of 75 percent. They matched the relative frequency of their choices to the relative frequencies with which the sides were armed. They were greatly surprised to be shown when the demonstration was over that the rat's behavior was more intelligent than their own. We did not lessen their discomfiture by telling them that if the rat chose under the same conditions they did—under a correction procedure whereby on every trial it ended up knowing which side was the rewarded side—it too would match the relative frequencies of its initial side choices to the relative frequencies of the payoffs (Graf, Bullock, and Bitterman 1964; Sutherland and Mackintosh 1971, p. 406f).

This phenomenon—commonly called probability matching or probability learning—is by no means a laboratory artifact. Smith and Dawkins (1971) studied the hunting behavior of individual great tits that were allowed to feed in any of several patches. The patches differed in food abundance. The feeding bouts did not last long enough for any appreciable depletion of the food in a patch. One might have expected the tits always to choose to feed in the patch in which the food was most abundant, but they did not; the relative frequency with which they chose a patch was roughly proportionate to the relative abundance of food in that patch.

The seeming irrationality of this common pattern of behavior is a challenge to the biological theorist because it is virtually an axiom of evolutionary theory that the behavior of organisms should on balance tend to optimize the rate of exploitation of biologically critical resources like food. It was eventually realized that this behavior is not at all irrational when one considers the natural situation from a broad enough perspective. On the contrary, under natural circumstances, it may be the only evolutionarily stable strategy, the only pattern that does not tend to create conditions that select against that very behavioral pattern. Under the experimental conditions in which matching behavior is commonly observed, the observed animal is the only one attempting to exploit the resource that occurs at different rates in different places. This state of affairs is unlikely to persist for long under natural circumstances. Wherever there is food, other animals will gather. The more of them there are, the smaller is each one's share. The strategy of always choosing to forage in the area where previous experience suggests that food is to be found in greatest abundance is not evolutionarily stable. If such a pattern became the rule among animals, natural selection would favor those exceptional animals that went to the areas where food was less abundant but so were the competitors. It may be shown that under plausible assumptions, a strategy for choosing among patches of differing abundance that does not create a countervailing selection pressure is the strategy of matching the relative frequency of one's choices to the relative abundances in the options (Fretwell and Lucas 1970; Fretwell 1972).

The conditions under which animals might be expected to be selected on the basis of their ability to distribute their choices among options in accord with relative food densities are ones in which each animal has an approximately correct representation of the rate of food occurrence in each patch and is free to move from patch to patch. The distribution expected under these assumptions is called the ideal free distribution, because the animal's knowledge of the food densities is assumed to be "ideal" (that is, generally correct) and the animal is assumed to be free to go to any patch whenever it chooses. Since the ideal free distribution was first derived, there have been many experimental tests of the extent to which it describes the observed distribution under experimentally controlled circumstances. In most of these tests, a close approximation to the ideal free distribution has in fact been observed, even when some of the assumptions used in deriving it do not obtain.

Experiments with Groups

Ideal Free Fish
Godin and Keenleyside (1984) worked with "schools" of six cichlids, kept in a tank 56 x 87 centimeters, with a plastic feeding tube at each end. A line across the tank halfway between the ends divided the tank into two "patches" (the two end halves). A television camera mounted over the tank recorded the moment-to-moment positions of the fish for the 5 minutes preceding the onset of a feeding trial and then for 7 minutes of feeding. During feeding, fish larvae were dispensed through one tube at a rate of 10 per minute and via the other at one of three rates: 10 per minute, 5 per minute, or 2 per minute. Each of eight schools had one trial with each ratio of patch profitability (1:1, 2:1, 5:1), in a randomly varying order, with the more profitable end also varying randomly. Figure 11.1 shows the distribution of fish between the two patches at 15-second intervals throughout the 5-minute prefeeding control period and the subsequent 7 minutes of feeding. The onset of feeding is indicated by an arrow. The filled circles give the mean number of fish observed in the less profitable half of the tank. In the case of the 1:1 profitability ratio, the designation of a less profitable end is arbitrary. The vertical bars give the 95 percent confidence intervals. The open circles give the complemen-

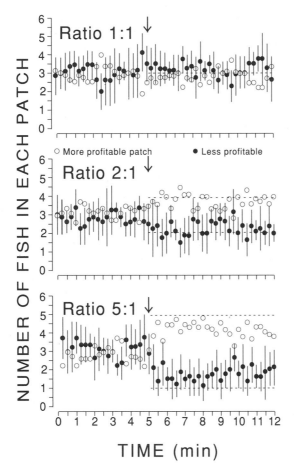

Figure 11.1

The mean number of fish observed at each end of the tank at 15 second intervals since trial onset, for each of three patch profitability ratios. The vertical bars about the solid dots give the 95 percent confidence intervals. The open circles are redundant because the number of fish at the more profitable end is equal to six minus the number at the less profitable end. The vertical arrows mark the onset of feeding, 5 minutes into a 12-minute trial. The finely dashed lines indicates the apportionment that accords with the ratio of the rates of food delivery. (Adapted from Godin and Keenleyside, p. 124, by permission of author and publisher.)

tary mean, the number of fish in the more profitable half (= 6 - the mean for the less profitable end). The finely dashed lines indicate the numbers that would be expected if the fish were distributed in proportion to the ratio of the provisioning rates.

What is remarkable about these data is the rapidity with which the fish apportion themselves among the two halves of the tank in a manner that roughly approximates the ratio of the provisioning rates. When the provisioning ratio was not unity, there was a significant differential distribution of the fish within the first 30 seconds of provisioning, and this distribution did not change significantly over the ensuing 7 minutes. Within the first 30 seconds, the school of six fish got five morsels at the end of the tank with the higher rate and two or one at the end with the lower rate, for a total of between seven and six morsels, or about one morsel per fish. Even if we assume that the apportionment of the fishes between the two ends did not really reach asymptote until the end of 1 minute, each fish would have gotten only two morsels total in that interval, if the rates at which individual fish acquired morsels were equal. However, these rates were far from equal; the rates at which individual fish fed differed by as much as a factor of 10. In short, the fish apportioned themselves among the two ends in rough accord with the relative rates of provisioning before many of them had acquired a single morsel and before almost any of them had acquired a morsel from both ends.

The apportionment of the fish between the two ends of the tank was not realized by the more aggressive or higher-ranking fish taking up stations at the better end and forcing lower-ranking fish to the other end; there was no significant correlation between the frequency with which a given fish attacked the others and its feeding rate or between rank within the school and feeding rate. The more successful feeders switched sides less often than the less successful fish, but almost all the fish (98 percent out of 144 observations) switched sides at least once in the course of a 7-minute feeding interval.

The rapidity of the adjustment would appear to rule out models that assume that the decision parameters within each individual fish are determined by the morsels it has actually obtained in each of the two patches (the individually experienced rate of reward). The rapidity of the adjustment implies that the parameters of a fish's decision processes are determined not by what it has got but rather by what it has observed. The probability of a fish's switching from one patch to the other is determined by relative rates at which it has observed morsels to appear in the two patches, whether it has garnered any of those morsels for itself or not.

The assumption that from any position in the tank a fish may observe a morsel appearing at either end of the tank and that its rate of switching between patches is determined by how many morsels it has observed per

unit time at each end of the tank might explain the fact that the apportionment of the fish between the two ends was significantly less than the ratio
of the provisioning rates, particularly at the more extreme ratio. Since
there were more fish in the end with the higher provisioning rate, the
chances that a morsel would be snapped up before a fish some distance
away noticed it would be higher at that end than at the other. Thus one
would expect the ratio of the observed rates of provisioning to be less
than the true ratio. One could test this explanation by running fish
individually and recording the amount of time a fish spent at each end.
The apportionment of times between the two ends in fish run individually might better match the provisioning ratios.

We will see that the assumption that the apportionment of an individual animal's time between two patches or two manipulanda depends on
the ratio of the observed number of rewards per unit time is the fundamental assumption in successful quantitative models of the process by
which animals apportion their time in concurrent reward schedules. A
concurrent reward schedule is one in which the animal is free to exploit
two different patches or two different manipulanda (levers or keys), and
the two alternatives are programmed to pay off in accord with two
different schedules of reinforcement. It is an operant conditioning analogue of the foraging experiment, but the experiment is run with one
subject at a time. It yields data that match those from these foraging
experiments, which expose groups of animals to differing concurrent
payoff schedules and record how the group apportions itself. The data
from the operant conditioning paradigms most closely analogous to this
foraging paradigm show that individual animals do apportion their time
in accord with the relative rates of observed provisioning. The operant
paradigm is best for studying the behavior of the individual animal, but
the foraging (group) paradigm is best for revealing the rapidity of the
adjustment and the natural context within which this pattern of adjustment makes biological sense.

Ideal Free Ducks
Harper (1982) did an experiment with a flock of thirty-three ducks
overwintering on a small lake. Each day for several successive days, two
experimenters, each carrying a sack of precut 2-gram bread morsels,
positioned themselves about 20 meters apart along the lake shore and
began throwing the bread out one morsel at a time at regular intervals.
The relative rates at which they threw were systematically varied. On
trials where the rates were not equal, the experimenter who threw at the
higher rate was chosen randomly and could not be predicted from trial
to trial. From the outset of the experimental trials, the ducks very rapidly

distributed themselves in front of the two experimenters in proportion to the relative rates of throwing (figure 11.2). A distribution proportionate to the rates of throwing was achieved in just a little over 1 minute, during which time only 12 to 18 pieces of bread were thrown by the two experimenters combined. As with the fish, the apportionment of the ducks was achieved before most ducks had obtained a single morsel and before any duck had obtained morsels from both patches.

The sophistication of the computations that animals make in the process of determining their relative tendency to switch from one patch to another is shown by the final experiment in Harper's (1982) series, the results of which bear strongly on the question of the richness of a bird's representation of number, time, and magnitude. In some trials of this final experiment, the food was thrown at the same frequency into both patches, but the morsels being thrown by one experimenter were twice as big. On these trials, the ducks initially distributed themselves in accord with the relative rates at which morsels were being thrown (that is, fifty-fifty), but discovered within the first 5 or 6 minutes that the morsels were larger in the one patch and adjusted their individual choice likelihoods accordingly (figure 11.3B). The distribution after 5 minutes accurately reflected the ratio of the net rates of provisioning, that is, the ratio between the products of morsel magnitude and morsel rate. This result

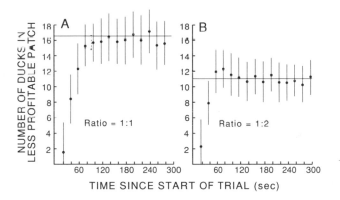

Figure 11.2
The mean numbers of ducks in front of the slower food thrower, as a function of the time since the onset of throwing. The horizontal lines indicate the number to be expected if the thirty-three ducks apportion themselves in accord with the relative rates of throwing. A. The slower thrower throws at the same rate as the faster thrower (once every 5 seconds). Points are means of twenty-nine trials. Solid vertical bars are standard deviations. A representative 95 percent confidence interval is indicated by the dashed vertical bar to the left of the mean (at 80 seconds). B. The slower thrower throws at half the rate of the faster (= once every 10 seconds). Points are means from twenty-four trials. (Adapted from Harper 1982, pp. 576, 577, by permission of author and publisher.)

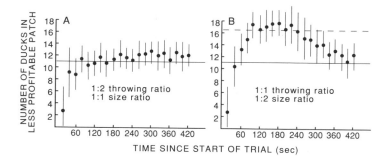

Figure 11.3.
The mean numbers of ducks in front of the thrower providing the least food per unit time, as a function of the time since the onset of throwing. The solid horizontal lines indicate the apportionment that accords with the relative rate of food provision. The dashed horizontal line in B indicates the apportionment that corresponds to the relative rates of throwing, not taking into account that one thrower is throwing chunks twice as big. Vertical bars are standard deviations. A. Data from eleven trials in which equal-sized pieces of bread (2 grams) were thrown, but the less profitable thrower threw half as often. B. Data from fourteen trials in which the throwers threw equally often, but the more profitable thrower threw 4-gram chunks instead of the usual 2-gram chunks. (Modified from Harper 1982, p. 582, by permission of author and publisher.)

suggests that birds accurately represent rates, that they accurately represent morsel magnitudes, and that they can multiply the representation of morsels per unit time by the representation of morsel magnitude to compute the internal variables that determine the relative likelihood of their choosing one foraging patch over the other.

A representational approach to animal learning assumes that the current behavior of the ducks is to be explained along the following lines. There is a mapping from the number of morsels thrown to a corresponding variable in the CNS of each duck. The magnitude of this internal variable increases in proportion as the number of morsels thrown by a given experimenter increases. This internal variable represents the number of morsels that experimenter has thrown. There is also a mapping from the times since the onset of throwing to a corresponding CNS measure of temporal interval. This internal variable represents the time that has elapsed since the onset of throwing. There is also a mapping from the magnitude of the items thrown to a corresponding CNS variable, which represents magnitude. Finally, these representational variables in the CNS combine with one another in neuronal signal-combining processes isomorphic to the division and multiplication by which one computes net quantity per unit time given the magnitude of a morsel and the number of morsels per unit time.

The challenge for nonrepresentational theories of animal learning and behavior is to propound a nonrepresentational model of the process by which a duck's past experience determines its present choice of patch. In a nonrepresentational model, one seeks a system that is altered by its past experiences in such a way that it chooses patches in proportion to their relative net rate of food abundance, from experiences that involve observations alone (in the absence of significant consumption), without the system's having any internal variable proportionate to the number of items thrown, any internal variable proportionate to the time since the onset of throwing, any internal variable proportionate to the magnitude of a morsel, or a fortiori any operations that appropriately combine these nonexistent representatives of number, time, and magnitude. Is it possible to propound a model of the internal causation of the duck's behavior that avoids postulating an isomorphism between a system of variables and operations inside the duck and the corresponding system of number, time and magnitude external to the duck? This is the question at the heart of the dispute between those committed to representational theories of mind and those committed to nonrepresentational theories—now sometimes called subsymbolic models (Smolensky 1986).

Operant Experiments with Individual Subjects

Choice as Time Allocation

Baum and Rachlin (1969) ran a fairly close analogue of the foraging experiments, using individually tested pigeons in an operant chamber with a food hopper at each end. There was a red light at one end, a green light at the other, and a white light in the middle. The floor for each half of the box rested on a microswitch that was activated when the pigeon stood at that end of the box. The hoppers at the two ends were provisioned by automatic provisioning equipment programmed on variable-interval (VI) schedules, schedules in which the delivery of food varies about some mean interdelivery interval. The program that scheduled deliveries to a given hopper ran regardless of whether the pigeon was standing before that hopper, but if a delivery was programmed while the pigeon was not in front of the hopper, the actual delivery was postponed until after the pigeon came into that half of the box and the so-called change-over delay had timed out. (A change-over delay is a programmed delay between a change from one side to the other and the delivery of the first reward on the new side. It is a common part of concurrent reward schedules because it discourages overly frequent shifts from side to side.) In principle, what the pigeon observed was dependent on what it did, as in most other operant experiments, but in practice the birds alternated sides with such frequency that the actual rates of food delivery were determined almost entirely by the automatic programs rather than by the interaction between the program and the pigeon's behavior.

Baum and Rachlin varied the ratios between the two VI schedules over a wide range, including ratios as high as 16:1 (VI 8 versus VI 0.5 minutes). They also tested one of the ratios (8:1) at two different overall rates (VI 8 versus VI 1 minute and VI 4 versus VI .5 minutes). The pigeons, both individually and as a group, proportioned the time they spent at each end to the relative rates of food delivery, over the full range of ratios tested. Figure 11.4 plots the logarithm of the ratio between the average amount of time the pigeons spent on the left and the average amount of time they spent on the right as a function of the logarithm of the ratio of the number of rewards they got at each end. The slope of the best fitting line in figure 11.4 is not significantly different from 1, meaning that, as a group, the relative amount of time pigeons spent at a given end was directly proportionate to the relative rate of food delivery. The fact that the best-fitting regression line lies below the diagonal means that the pigeons had a bias toward the right end, which combined multiplicatively with the ratio of the rates of return to determine how the pigeons allocated their time. In other words, the ratio of the time spent on the left to the time spent on the

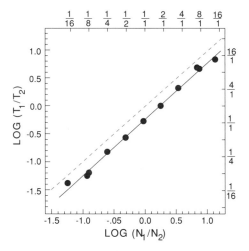

Figure 11.4
The ratio of the times spent on the left (T_1) and right (T_2) sides of the operant chamber, as a function of the ratio of the numbers of rewards received (log scale). Average of six pigeons. The data points would fall on the dashed line if there were no side bias. The solid line is the best fitting linear regression. Its slope does not deviate significantly from 1. Its offset from the dashed line indicates the multiplicative side bias. (Redrawn from Baum and Rachlin 1969, p. 868, by permission of author and publisher.)

right was equal to the ratio of the number of rewards received multiplied by a bias factor.

The experimental paradigm Baum and Rachlin used departed from the usual concurrent operant paradigm in that the only response the pigeon had to make was to stand at one end or the other. So long as it stood at one end, it received rewards at the average rate programmed for that end. They used this paradigm to test their hypothesis that "response duration or time spent responding can be just as basic a measure of behavior as response frequency," the usual operant measure of behavior (p. 861). Indeed, from a foraging perspective, it may well be a more basic measure in that when an animal forages, it is constantly engaged in foraging "responses"—whatever they may be. (Foraging behavior often cannot readily be analyzed into the discrete responses that are the foundation of the operant world view because this behavior consists mostly of moving around attentively scanning the terrain.) What matters to the foraging animal is not how many foraging responses it makes but rather how long it should forage in various locations. The Baum and Rachlin paradigm thus provides a bridge linking the study of foraging behavior to the study of response allocation on more conventional concurrent operant schedules. It suggests that we shift our focus from the relative rates of responding on those schedules (or the percentages of responses on a given manipulandum) to the amount of time allocated to responding on a given key.

The Matching Law

Herrnstein (1961), in a classic experiment that was a forerunner of the Baum and Rachlin experiment and numerous other "matching" experiments, ran pigeons on concurrent VI schedules under conventional operant conditions. The pigeon obtained its rewards by pecking one or the other of two keys, each programmed to pay off after varying amounts of time, with the mean interval between payoffs defining the schedule. In principle, a pigeon's rate of foraging success in this situation could depend heavily on how frequently it pecked a given key. This would be the case if the mean interpeck interval on a given key were roughly the same as, or longer than, the mean interval from one reward delivery to the next arming of the delivery system. In fact, however, the pigeon's mean interpeck interval on a key is much less than the mean programmed interval, so the rate of foraging success at a given key is determined by the schedule for that key, not by the pigeon's behavior. In other words, when a pigeon is at a key, it forages steadily on that key (pecks at it steadily); hence it collects whatever comes along as soon as it comes along. Even when there is another key, the pigeon moves back and forth between the two so often that a collectible reward seldom remains uncollected for any length of time on either key. Note that in moving back and forth between the more profitable and the less profitable key, the pigeon collects more food than it would if it confined its foraging to the more profitable key.

Herrnstein plotted the percentage responses that an animal made on a given key (key A) as a function of the percentage of the pigeon's foraging successes accounted for by that key, that is, as a function of the percentage total reward coming from that key (figure 11.5). This is basically the same plot that Baum and Rachlin made because the higher the percentage of reward coming from key A (Herrnstein's measure), the greater the relative rate of reward delivery at key A (Baum and Rachlin's measure), and the higher the percentage of responses on key A (Herrnstein's measure), the greater the amount of time spent at key A (Baum and Rachlin's measure). Herrnstein summarized his results with the formula:

$$\frac{R_1}{R_1 + R_2} = \frac{r_1}{r_1 + r_2}$$

where the Rs are the rates of occurrences of the two responses and the rs are the rates of reward. This formula is algebraically equivalent to:

$$\frac{R_1}{R_2} = \frac{r_1}{r_2}$$

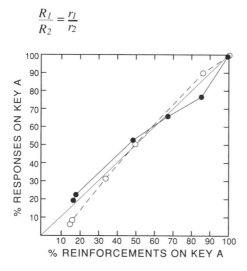

Figure 11.5
The relative frequency of responding on key A, as a function of the relative reinforcement on key A, for two pigeons. The thin, straight line on the diagonal represents perfect apportionment of responding on the basis of relative frequency of reinforcement. (Redrawn from Herrnstein 1961, by permission of author and publisher.)

that is, to the assertion that the ratio of the rates of responding matches the ratio of the rates of reward. This result, often replicated since, has come to be known as Herrnstein's matching law. The ideal free fish experiment and the ideal free duck experiment may be viewed as further replications of this result—but under group rather than individual testing conditions.

Matching on the Basis of the Product of Rate of Reward and Reward Magnitude
The last experiment in the series on ideal free ducks (see figure 11.3) suggested that the matching of the relative amounts of time spent foraging in two patches to the relative rates of reward occurrence in those patches was just a special case of a more general law, in which net food availability is the crucial variable. Net food availability is the product of the average magnitude of the observed morsels and the average rate at which these morsels appear. Neuringer's (1967) results in an operant paradigm confirm this conclusion.

Neuringer (1967) used a concurrent VI paradigm, modified in such a way as to make it a discrete choice paradigm. When the house lights came on to begin a trial, the pigeon was confronted with two lit keys. Pecking one of them committed the bird to that key for the duration of a trial because it caused the light to go out on the unpecked key, signaling that it was futile to peck it. The chosen key—the key initially pecked—remained lit, but 5 seconds had to elapse before pecking it had further consequences. There was no penalty for pecking it during this 5 seconds, and the pigeons generally did so.

The first peck on the chosen key after 5 seconds had elapsed either produced a reward—a timed access to the food hopper—or extinguished the house lights, ending the trial. Which outcome occurred on any given trial was determined by the VI program for the chosen key. The interval timer in the program ran at all times except during the intertrial blackouts and the timed accesses to the food hopper. The mean interval of the VI program (1 minute) was the same for both keys. What varied between keys was the duration of the access to the hopper on rewarded trials. One key (the standard key) always yielded access periods of 2 seconds' duration. The duration of the access to food yielded by the other key varied between blocks of thirty sessions. There was one block at each of seven values—6, 10, 4, 3, 2.5, 2, and 2.25 seconds, in that order.

Neuringer found that the pigeons' percentage choice of a key matched the relative total access to reinforcement for a key, where total access to reinforcement was defined as the number of obtained reinforcements on a key multiplied by the duration of each reinforcement (see figure 11.6.). The data in figure 11.6 are an operant counterpart to the data in figure 11.3B on the distribution of ideal free ducks when the two experimenters

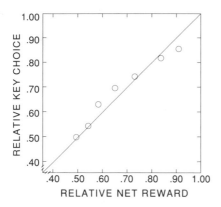

Figure 11.6
Pigeons' relative frequency of choosing one of two keys, as a function of the relative net reward obtained from that key. Relative net reward is the product of the number of rewards (number of accesses to the feeding hopper) and their magnitude (duration of access) divided by the total reward obtained in the apparatus (the total duration of food access while in the apparatus). The line on the diagonal represents a perfect correspondence between the relative net access to reward obtained by choosing a given key and the relative frequency of choosing that key. (Redrawn from Neuringer 1967, p. 421, by permission of author and publisher.)

threw at the same rate but one threw morsels twice as big. Both data sets suggest that birds compute the product of morsel magnitude (or access duration) and the number of morsels (accesses) per unit time. In any event, both ducks and pigeons clearly allot their time and choices among foraging patches or keys in fairly precise accord with the ratios of these products, that is, in accord with the ratios of the net rate of food return.

Other aspects of Neuringer's data call attention to the shortcomings of the Skinnerian analysis of the learning phenomenon, which singles out the rate of responding and the probability of response reinforcement as the significant variables in a learning situation. Data now to be reviewed suggest that the response is largely irrelevant, and so is the probability of its reinforcement. What the bird learns is not a response but rather a representation of food density—the amount of food observed per unit time. What determines its representation of food density is not the probability that a response will be rewarded but rather the amount of food it has observed. The behavior of the bird is relevant only insofar as variations in it cause variations in the amount of food observed in a given patch.

The irrelevance of response rate and probability of response reinforcement, at least under Neuringer's conditions, is shown by the fact that there was an inverse relationship between both the probability of reinforcement and the response rate, on the one hand, and the percentage choice of a given key, on the other. As the relative magnitude of the reward received from the standard key decreased (because the reward from the other key was increasing), the pigeon chose that key less often. As its choice of that key became less frequent, the likelihood increased that the VI reward programmer for that key had timed out and programmed a reward by the time the pigeon finally chose that key again. Hence, as shown in figure 11.7B, the decreasing preference for the standard key went hand in hand with an increase in the probability that a choice of that key would be reinforced, while the increasing preference for the variable key was accompanied by a decrease in the probability that this choice would be reinforced. When the ratio of the reward magnitudes was 1:5 (and likewise the ratio of choice frequencies), the probability that a choice of the standard key would be reinforced was

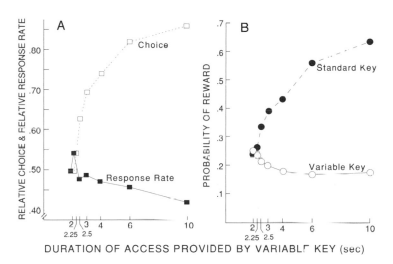

Figure 11.7
The effect of reward magnitude (access duration) at the variable key on the relative response rates, relative choice frequencies, and the resulting probabilities that a choice would be rewarded. A. As the duration of access to food provided by the variable key increases, the relative frequency of choosing that key increases (relative choice = percentage choice of that key), but the relative response rate (= response rate on variable key/sum of the two response rates) declines. The response rate is the rate of pecking the key during the delay between choice and access to food. B. As the duration of access to food at the variable key increases, the probability that the (increasingly frequent) choices of that key will be rewarded decreases, while the probability that the (increasingly rare) choices of the standard key will be rewarded increases. (Redrawn from Neuringer 1967, pp. 420, 422, by permission of author and publisher.)

greater than .6 while the probability that a choice of the preferred variable key would be reinforced was less than .2. In short, preference and probability of response reinforcement were inversely related.

Furthermore, the response rate on the variable key during the 5 second wait after a choice tended to go down as the reward magnitude increased, and the response rate on the standard key tended to go up as the reward it yielded grew relatively smaller, as if the pigeons were trying to increase the yield from that key by working harder on it. Thus the response strength, as measured by rate of pecking, underwent a modest decrease as a result of a manipulation that greatly increased the probability of the pigeon's choosing to make that response (figure 11.7A). In short, response rate and choice likelihood were also inversely related.

Concurrent Variable Ratios
The most dramatic demonstration that the crucial variable governing response allocations is relative observed food density and not the relative probability that a response will be reinforced comes from the study of response allocations under concurrent variable-ratio (VR) schedules. In a VI schedule, the reward programmer counts the seconds elapsed since the last reward and arms the feeder when a certain number of seconds has elapsed, a number that varies around the mean for the schedule. In a VR schedule, the reward programmer counts the pigeon's responses since the last reward and arms the feeder when a certain number of responses has been made (a number that varies around the mean for the schedule). Thus on a VR67 schedule, the bird is rewarded on average for every sixty-seventh peck, while on a VI67 schedule it is rewarded on average every 67 seconds.

Whereas concurrent VI schedules lead to response allocations whose ratio is inversely proportionate to the ratio of the mean payoff intervals, concurrent VR schedules lead the bird to allocate all of its responses to whichever key pays off more often. Given VR67 versus VR33, a bird pecks almost exclusively on the VR33 key (Herrnstein and Loveland 1975), that is, it "maximizes." By contrast, when it is given VI67 versus VI33, it pecks 67 percent of the time on the VI33 key and 33 percent of the time on the VI67 key.

When the VR schedules are equal, the resulting allocation of responses is indeterminate, that is, it varies greatly from one determination to the next; when concurrent VI schedules are equal, the responses are always divided approximately fifty-fifty between the two keys. Thus at first glance, pigeons would appear to behave in accord with different principles when confronted with concurrent VR schedules than when confronted with concurrent VI schedules, which is decidedly odd. However, Herrnstein and Loveland (1975) pointed out that the behavior on concurrent VR schedules is of a piece with the behavior on concurrent VI schedules, provided one assumes that in both cases it is the number of rewards observed per unit time that is the crucial variable, not the probability of response reinforcement. To understand why Herrnstein and Loveland (1975) concluded their article with the surprising assertion that "matching and maximizing are just two words describing one outcome," one has to abandon the idea that the probability of a response's being reinforced is the crucial variable in operant conditioning. One has to focus instead on the rate of observed reward occurrence on a given key per unit time in the chamber and the effects on this variable of the interaction between the type of schedule and the animal's behavior.

On a VR schedule, a decrease in responding on a given key produces a proportionate decrease in the number of rewards per unit time observed on that key, and an increase produces a proportionate increase. Therefore concurrent VR schedules set up positive feedback loops between the crucial driving variable—the rate of reward occurrence—and the resulting behavioral change—the amount of responding allocated to a key. The simplest case in which to see what is going on is the case in which the two VR schedules are equal. Despite the equal probabilities of response reinforcement, the birds often peck almost entirely at one key or the other. To see why, suppose that the bird initially responds about equally often at either key and that, due to the fluctuations to be expected from a random scheduling of response requirements, there is a run during which several more rewards are observed at key A than at key B. In response to this observation, the bird begins to favor key A. This results in a proportionate decrease in the number of rewards observed per unit time at key B and a proportionate increase in the number per unit time at key A—due not to random fluctuations but rather to the pigeon's favoring key A. This imbalance in the observed rates of reward at the two keys will sustain the unequal allocation of effort, which is the cause of the imbalance. Hence we see why the choice of keys when the VR schedules are equal should be indeterminate and often far from fifty-fifty. We also see why, when there is a genuine difference in the rates of payoff, the pigeon's response to this difference amplifies the difference in observed rates of reward occurrence until the pigeon spends all of its time at the key where reward occurs more often. We also see why the result is so different with VI schedules. With VI schedules, the rate of food occurrence at a given key is very nearly independent of the pigeon's response allocation; with VR schedules, it is proportionate to the bird's response allocation.

For those who are troubled by the idea that the probability of a response's being reinforced is irrelevant in operant conditioning, the following imagined dialogue between a pigeon and an experimenter may help. The experimenter asks the pigeon why it spends all its time at the one key, and the pigeon responds, "Because food never occurs at that other key." The startled experimenter says, "But that's only because you never peck there." To which the pigeon answers, "Don't be ridiculous! Why should my pecking determine whether food is or is not going to pop up there? The world isn't built that way. Food is either going to pop up or it isn't, independent of whether I happen to be pecking around there or not. What one has to do to beat the system in this pigeon's world is know how much food is to be expected at various places and apportion one's time accordingly. It doesn't make sense to waste time in front of a key where food seldom or never pops up." It would be hard to gainsay the pigeon's knowledge of the world since the operant situation is an unnatural one. In the world in which the pigeon lives, seeds do not fall from trees just because the pigeon pecks beneath them. Foraging behavior is designed to find what is there to be found, not to bring food into existence.

It should now be clear why Herrnstein and Loveland (1975) can claim that matching on concurrent VI schedules and maximizing on concurrent VR schedules are two manifestations of the same phenomenon: that animals apportion their foraging time in accord with the observed rates of food occurrence—the matching law. On a concurrent VR schedule with a 2:1 ratio of payoffs (say, VR67 versus VR33), the pigeon is matching when it spends all of its time pecking at the key with the greater payoff because 100 percent of the rewards occur at that key and that key gets 100 percent of the responses. The pigeon would not be matching—in the sense of matching that applies to VI schedules—if it spent only 67 percent of its time on the higher-payoff key and 33 percent on the lower-payoff key. The relative rates of reward occurrence would be 4:1, which would not match the 2:1 allocation of responses or time. If one alternative pays off twice as frequently as the other and one spends 67 percent of one's time with the higher payoff alternative and 33 percent with the lower, the relative frequencies of payoff per unit time at the task are (.67 x 2 = 1.34) versus (1 x .33 = .33), or 1.34/.33 = 4. In this calculation, we define frequency of payoff in the same way as it is defined in the VI case: the number of rewards per unit time.

When the probability of reinforcement is the same on both VRs, the pigeon is matching its response allocation to the relative frequencies of rewards no matter how it allocates its responses among the two keys. If it allocates 20 percent to one key and 80 percent to the other, then 20 percent of the rewards occur at the first key and 80 percent at the second, and so on, for any other allocation one cares to specify. Thus the key to understanding the pigeon's behavior is to focus on the relation between the frequency with which rewards are observed to occur at a given key and the frequency with which the pigeon chooses to peck at that key and to assume that causality flows from the former to the latter. Assume, in short, that the pigeon bases its allocation of foraging time at each key on representations of the frequencies (rates) with which rewards are observed to occur at that and other available keys.

A Computational Model

Myerson and Miezin (1980), building on an earlier mathematical analysis by Staddon (1977) and a suggestion by Pliskoff (1971), have elaborated Herrnstein's matching law into a computational model, which accurately predicts the asymptotic response allocations under three different kinds of concurrent schedules (VI-VI, VR-VR, and VI-VR). It also accounts for the form of the transitions in response allocation when the ratios between the schedule profitabilities change. Myerson and Miezen do not present their model in the same spirit in which Gibbon, Church, and Meck present their models of timing and counting behavior, that is, as a model of the functional structure for the underlying causative process. Rather they adopt a "Newtonian" or "black-box" stance. They cast the model in the form of a set of mathematically formulated inductions about the laws of behavior. However, I will treat their model as a model of the causative process in the brain of the animal.

The central assumptions of the model, thus conceived, are:

1.   For each alternative open to the animal, there is an internally computed relative preference variable, which I will call the animal's relative patch affinity. Relative patch affinity is equal to the observed food prevalence in a patch divided by the sum of the food prevalences observed across the available alternatives.

2.   The animal's tendency to switch to a given alternative is governed by a Poisson transition parameter, λ, whose value is proportionate to the animal's relative affinity for that alternative. The greater the relative affinity for an alternative, the more likely the animal is to switch to it.

3.   The sum of an animal's switching rates is a constant. Hence any increase in its rate of switching to one alternative is accompanied by a commensurate decrease in its tendency to switch to other alternatives. This constant overall rate of switching, which varies from animal to animal, may be regarded as the "flightiness" or "switchiness" constant. The higher the value of this constant, the more often the animal switches patches. (The experiments testing the ideal free

distribution have repeatedly shown that individuals vary considerably in how often they switch.)

4.   When there has recently been a change in the relative prevalences of food in the patches, so that the animal's current relative
affinities are not proportionate to the current relative prevalences,
then the greater the imbalance and the higher the rates of reward, the
more rapidly affinities change. (The differential equation for the
change in affinity is given below.)

In what follows, I assume that pecking a key is equivalent to spending
time in a patch (in effect, pecking at the key is what the pigeon happens
to do while waiting for food to appear) and that an animal's representation of the prevalence, p, of food in a given patch is proportionate to the
number of morsels of food observed in that patch per unit time and the
average size of a morsel. In other words, the second assumption is that
the animal computes an approximately veridical representation of observed food prevalence. In formal terms, for the usual experimental case
in which there are only two alternatives, the first assumption in the
reinterpreted Myerson and Miezen model is that:

$$A_1 = \frac{p_1}{p_1 + p_2} \qquad A_2 = \frac{p_2}{p_1 + p_2} \tag{11.1}$$

where A_1 is the affinity for the first alternative, A_2 the affinity for the
second alternative, p_1 the prevalence of reward in the first alternative,
and p_2 the prevalence in the second alternative. The second assumption
is:

$$\lambda_1 = cA_1$$
$$\lambda_2 = cA_2, \tag{11.2}$$

where λ_1 is the transition rate to patch 1 (from patch 2), λ_2 the transition
rate to patch 2 (from patch 1), and c the switchiness constant. Also,

$$c = \lambda_1 + \lambda_2, \tag{11.3}$$

the transition rates sum to a constant, which is the constant of proportionality that relates the underlying affinities to the observed rates of
switching. Finally, the rates of change in the relative reward affinities
when they do not correspond to the relative prevalences are:

$$dA_1/dt = k (p_1 A_2 - p_2 A_1)$$
$$dA_2/dt = k (p_2 A_1 - p_1 A_2). \tag{11.4}$$

In the natural foraging situation and the concurrent VI paradigm,
where the allocation of an animal's time among the alternatives has a
negligible effect on the observed food prevalence, it is easy to see that this

model yields a relative allocation of time that matches the relative prevalences of food: From equations 11.1 and 11.2, it follows that:

$$\frac{A_1}{A_2} = \frac{p_1}{p_2} = \frac{\lambda_1}{\lambda_2} = \frac{1/\lambda_2}{1/\lambda_1} \tag{11.5}$$

In a Poisson process, the expected duration of the interval before the occurrence of an event (in this case, a switch out of patch 1 to patch 2) is the reciprocal of the rate parameter. Hence, the quantity $(1/\lambda_2)$ is the mean duration of a stay in patch 1 because λ_2 is the likelihood per unit time that the animal will leave patch 1 by switching to patch 2. Similarly, $(1/\lambda_1)$ is the mean duration of a stay in patch 2—the expected interval before the animal switches out of patch 2 to patch 1. Thus equation 11.5 asserts that the ratio of the mean durations in the two patches will match the ratio of the food prevalences. Since the visits to the two patches alternate with one another, this means that the ratio of the total times allotted to the two patches will match the ratio of the food prevalences, which is the observed experimental result.

Turning our attention to the transitional behavior, suppose that the affinities have become adjusted to one set of prevalences, p_1 and p_2, so that $A_1 = p_1/(p_1 + p_2)$, and then the prevalences change to p'_1 and p'_2, creating a discrepancy, D, between the equilibrium affinity under the previous set of prevalences and the equilibrium affinity under the new prevalences:

$$D = \frac{p_1}{p_1 + p_2} - \frac{p'_1}{p'_1 + p'_2}$$

Solving the system of differential equations for A_1 as a function of the time, t, since the change in prevalences, yields:

$$A_1(t) = De^{-(p'1 + p'2)kt} + p'_1/(p'_1 + p'_2), \tag{11.6}$$

whence $\lambda_1(t) = c[De^{-(p'1 + p'2)kt} + p'_1/(p'_1 + p'_2)]$.

That is, the discrepancy, D, between the new and old affinity disappears with an exponential time course (as indicated by the first term on the right of equation 11.6), and the rate of its disappearance (the speed of the transition) is proportionate to the sum of the new prevalences, $(p'_1 + p'_2)$. When the discrepancy has disappeared, the asymptotic affinity, $A_1(\infty)$, equals $p'_1/(p'_1 + p'_2)$, the second term on the right side of equation 11.6.

That the rate of transition should be proportionate to the new prevalences is to be expected because the more food is observed per unit time, the less time it takes to accumulate the data required to recognize the new levels of prevalence. The statistical significance of a difference between two estimated Poisson rates of occurrence is a function solely of the number of observations. If, in a given period of observation, ten morsels have been observed in patch 1 and five in patch 2, then the probability that the rates of occurrence differ in the two patches is the same regardless of the period of observation. When the rates are higher, the time required to make the requisite number of observations is correspondingly shorter; hence the higher the new rates of occurrence, the sooner the transition to a new equilibrium should be complete, which is in fact what is observed (Myerson and Miezen 1980).

When the animal's allocation of its time among the patches has an appreciable effect on the observed prevalence of food in each patch, as is the case with concurrent VR schedules, then one must include in the system of equations an equation that describes the dependence of observed prevalence on the allocation of time. In the VR case, this equation is:

$$p_1 = r\phi_1 \frac{1/\lambda_2}{(1/\lambda_1) + (1/\lambda_2)} \tag{11.7}$$

$$= r\phi_1 \frac{\lambda_1}{\lambda_1 + \lambda_2}$$

$$= r\phi_1 A_1$$

where r is the rate of responding and ϕ_1 is the ratio of rewards to responses at key 1. This equation represents the fact that the food prevalence the animal observes at a given key depends on how it allocates its time, which in turn depends on its rate of switching from one patch to another, which in turn depends on its relative affinities. The expression $\{(1/\lambda_2)/[(1/\lambda_1) + (1/\lambda_2)]\}$ represents the proportion of the time that the animal spends in patch 1, that is, the proportion of its time that it devotes to pecking key 1. Equation 11.7 asserts that the observed food prevalence at key 1 is the rate of pecking the key times the rewards per peck times the amount of time spent pecking that key. Equation 11.7 embodies the counterintuitive conclusion of Herrnstein and Loveland, namely, that the psychologically crucial variable in schedules of reward is not the probability that a response will be rewarded but rather the amount of food that appears "at" a given key per unit time in the environment (not per unit time at that key). With a VR schedule, unlike a VI schedule, this crucial variable is tightly linked to the animal's behavior. The less time the animal spends at a given key, the less is the observed amount of food at that key per unit time in the environment. Thus with VR schedules, there is a feedback relationship between the animal's allocation of its time and the observed relative prevalences of food. Observed relative prevalence determines the λs, that is, the rates of switching from one patch to the other, but the rates of switching in turn determine the allocation of time between the patches, and this allocation determines the observed prevalence.

When the system of equations that includes 11.7 is solved for the animal's affinity for patch 1 as a function of time, one obtains:

$$A_1(t) = A_1(0) \frac{1+R}{1+Re^{-kr(\phi_1-\phi_2)t}},$$

(11.8)

where R is the inverse ratio of the initial affinities: $R = A_2(0)/A_1(0)$. Equation 11.8, unlike 11.6, has no time-independent term, no term that the affinity approaches when the time-dependent term becomes negligible. When the rewards per response (the ϕs) are unequal, there are only two possible values of $A_1(\infty)$: 1 and 0. The sign of the exponent for the exponential factor in the denominator of 11.8 determines whether the asymptotic affinity is 1 or 0. If $\phi_2 > \phi_1$, then $(\phi_1 - \phi_2)$ is negative; hence the exponent $-kr(\phi_1 - \phi_2)t$ is positive; hence the exponential factor goes to infinity as t goes to infinity, which means that $A_1(t)$ goes to 0. On the other hand, if $\phi_1 > \phi_2$, then the sign of the exponent is negative, the exponential factor goes to 0 as time increases, and $A_1(t) \rightarrow [A_1(0) + A_2(0)] = 1$. This mathematical result corresponds to the empirical finding that for concurrent unequal VR schedules, the birds eventually allocate all of their time (and pecking) to the key that pays off more frequently. If the ϕs are equal, time is irrelevant (the exponent is 0, which means that the exponential factor is equal to 1) and the affinity remains at whatever initial value happenstance has given it. This mathematical result corresponds to the empirical result that the distribution of responses between the two keys for concurrent equal VR schedules is unpredictable, varying greatly from one determination to the next.

Representational Implications

There is extensive empirical support for the claim that animals allocate their foraging time in proportion to the observed prevalence of food at various foraging sites. Such a strategy makes sense from an evolutionary standpoint in that the universal adoption of this strategy does not create a selection pressure favoring another strategy (hence the strategy is evolutionarily stable). Furthermore a model in which the rate at which an animal switches to a given patch is assumed to be proportionate to the observed prevalence of food at that patch accounts for the extensive data on the distributions of time and responses among alternatives in concurrent schedules of reward. Thus there are powerful empirical and theoretical reasons for assuming that animal behavior is finely tuned to relative food prevalence over a wide range of relative prevalences. The question is, What does such an assumption imply about animals' representational capacities?

Food prevalence is the product of the rate of food encounters or observations and the average amount of food per encounter or per observation. The rate of food encounters is in turn the number of encounters in a given interval divided by the duration of that interval, and the average amount of food per encounter is the total amount of food observed or encountered divided by the number of encounters or observations. If one assumes that animals are possessed of neural apparatus that can measure temporal intervals, count occurrences, estimate magnitudes, and perform operations isomorphic to division and multiplication on the resulting internal variables (the neural representatives of the temporal interval, the number of occurrences, and the magnitudes), then it is possible to elaborate a straightforward account of the internal processes that explain the observed proportionality between an animal's tendency to switch to a given patch and the relative prevalence of food in that patch. Such an account is a computational-representational account of the internal causative processes because at its heart are neural processes isomorphic to computational operations, and these processes involve neurophysiological variables proportionate to temporal intervals, numerosities, and magnitudes. Insofar as one accepts such an account of the internal causative process, one accepts the conclusion that the animals have a rich representation of number, as well as a rich representation of time and magnitude.

For historical and in some cases metaphysical reasons, however, there has traditionally been a great reluctance to impute the requisite representational-computational capacity to infrahuman animals. The question is whether it is possible to elaborate an explanation of the internal causation of their behavior that avoids the kinds of assumptions underlying representational-computational models. Lea and Dow (1984) review their own and others efforts to elaborate a nonrepresentational account of the ability of animals to "integrate reinforcements over time." They begin their discussion with some remarks that capture the traditional dismissal of representational accounts:

> You or I, faced with the problem of estimating the rate at which discrete events occur, would doubtless solve it by counting them, then dividing by the time that had elapsed…. We have no evidence that animals can use this solution. So far as we can tell, the capacities of even the largest-brained birds to discriminate between numbers are quite modest. [They do not cite Rilling and McDiarmid's work— see figure 10.5.] …. We have no evidence at all that animals can

manipulate numbers in the kind of way required for division. Besides, this solution ignores an additional, fundamental aspect of the problem: the density that is being estimated is liable to change.

Lea and Dow go on to point out that all the nonrepresentational solutions offered in the literature are essentially the same as regards their core idea, although the details surrounding the elaboration of this core idea vary greatly. Not surprisingly, this core idea is taken over from associative models of learning, where it is also the core idea. The idea is that the animal maintains a "current estimate of prey density" in each patch (more traditionally, an association of a certain strength between each patch and food). "Ordinarily, this estimate remains constant from moment to moment, but at certain points in time, the subject updates it." (This is the assumption, deeply embedded in associative theories, that life is organized into discrete trials—just as are experiments in classical conditioning.)

The mathematical form of this updating process is common to all nonrepresentational accounts that have been offered. Each update involves multiplying the old estimate (the previous value of the associative strength) by a weighting factor less than unity, call it w ($w < 1$), and then adding a "current capture quantity" multiplied by the complement of the weighting of the old estimate $(1 - w)$. The current capture quantity, C, usually has a value of 1 if prey has been captured on this "trial" and 0 if it has not, but its value can be made a function of, for example, the amount of food captured on this "trial." Thus the model is that the internal quantity on which time allocation depends is determined by an updating equation of the form:

$$E_n = wE_{n-1} + (1 - w)\, C, \tag{11.9}$$

where E_n is the strength of the estimate at the conclusion of trial n (after updating) and C, the current capture quantity, is understood to be a function of what happens on trial n—whether prey is captured and how much is captured. The expression for the change in E on a trial is:

$$\Delta E = (1 - w)(C - E),$$

which expresses the fact that the increment (or decrement) in E on a given trial is proportionate to the discrepancy between what happened on that trial (C) and a sort of running average of what has happened on recent trials (E). The value of w determines how recent is recent. (Lea and Dow call it the memory constant.) The closer is its value to 1, the greater is the number of trials over which experience is averaged to obtain the current value of E; hence, the less is the impact that any given outcome of the current trial will have on E.

Lea and Dow point out that this model is a variant of the linear operator model of Bush and Mosteller (1951), which is a model for the growth of associative strength (or probability of response) in learning experiments. In learning models, where E is taken to be the association between two stimuli (say, the patch and food) or between a stimulus and a response (say, the patch and the response of going to it), the constant $(1 - w)$ is the associability parameter—the parameter that determines how quickly the association develops. Note that the faster the animal learns, the shorter its memory; that is, the greater the value of $(1 - w)$, the smaller the value of w. Lea and Dow point out that the details of the models that have equation 11.9 as their core assumption vary with respect to the following issues:

1.   What aspect of the animal's experience E is designed to approximate? Is it the density of prey per response or the density of prey per unit time? If the latter, is it density per unit time in a patch or density per unit time foraging? The literature just reviewed implies that the empirically valid assumption here is that E should approximate the density per unit time foraging. This in turn dictates the assumption one has to make in response to the second issue.

2.   What is the event that triggers updating? Is it the occurrence of a response, the capture of prey, or the passage of a certain amount of time? If E is to approximate an estimate of the number of prey encountered per unit time spent foraging, as the behavioral data seem to require, then one has to abandon the common and more intuitively appealing idea that the updating is contingent on a response or on the occurrence of a reward (prey), in favor of the idea that updating is triggered by an internal trial clock. One must assume that updating occurs at regular intervals regardless of what does or does not happen to the animal. (This same assumption is made in the most influential modern model of classical conditioning, the Rescorla-Wagner model.) The need to posit an internal trial clock—and the attendant puzzles about what the interval for that clock should be assumed to be—may make one wonder about the commitment to trials inherent in associative models. Life in the learning laboratory is organized into trials—discrete temporal intervals marked by the onset and offset of stimuli—but it is not clear that nature can be thought of as so organized.

3.   What is the value of w and is it fixed or does it vary? This is a thorny problem for models in the form of equation 11.9 with periodic event-independent updating because the value of w together with the update frequency determines how rapidly the value of E decays with time. The temporal decay of E between events limits its useful-

ness as an approximation to the rate of event occurrence. The assumptions required to yield an index of rate that does not gyrate require that the animal be slow to learn, that is, slow to adjust to new rates, but we have seen that animals can make this adjustment with great rapidity (figures 11.1-11.3).

4. What is the rule translating E into observed behavior? Is the translation absolute or stochastic? Does the subject always go to the patch with the strongest E (the strongest association with food), or does it apportion its time among patches in accord with the relative strengths of the Es. Under the experimental conditions reviewed above, the appropriate assumption here is that the allocation is stochastic and in accord with the relative strengths of the Es.

5. What is the initial value of E? Is it 0? Is it the value found in similar environments in the past? Is it the value as of the end of the previous session?

Lea and Dow describe the difficulties they have encountered in trying to make versions of this basic model explain the results of operant experiments they designed to simulate foraging situations. Before quoting conclusions, however, I want to bring out certain purely analytic problems that arise when one tries to use any equation of the form 11.9 as a model for the process that computes an index of recent rate of occurrence. It is worth spending some time on this question because the common model described by Lea and Dow tries to use the association-forming process to create a representation of a parameter of experienced reality: rate of reward occurrence. The difficulties that beset this approach help to make it clear why associations cannot readily serve as representatives of aspects of external reality. There are two problems inherent in all models of this kind. First, for any fixed set of parametric assumptions, they work only for a narrow range of rates. Second, they conflate four unrelated aspects of the problem: what the animal learns, how rapidly it learns it, how rapidly it forgets it, and its uncertainty regarding the correctness of what it has learned.

For E, the strength of the association between the patch and food, to be approximately proportionate to the number of food occurrences observed per unit time, its value must be updated at regular intervals independent of the occurrence or nonoccurrence of an event. That is, there must be an internal trial clock. The trial clock must have a period; that is, there must be an average trial duration. The average trial duration is a property of the animal (or of the relevant neural circuitry), not of the experienced world. The period of the trial clock together with the value of w determine the rapidity with which the value of E decays to 0 during periods when rewards do not occur. The rate of decay of E in turn determines the narrow range of rates for which the current value of E can be taken as an approximation to the recently observed rate of occurrence. During the barren stretches between rewards, $C = 0$ at every update, and E is therefore decremented by the factor w at every update. On the bth barren update, the value of E is reduced by the factor w^b from the value attained at the last rewarded update. For a given value of w, there is a value of b such that $w^b = .5$. Call this the halving value of b, or $b_{.5}$. (The halving value of b is: $b_{.5} = \log (.5)/\log (w)$.) For a given w, the halving value of b times the period, p, between updates (the trial duration) is the half-life of E, the time since the last reward required for E to lose half its value. For E to serve as a reasonably stable index of the rate of occurrence of rewards, the average interval between rewards, i_r, must be on the order of one-tenth the half-life of E, or: $i_r \leq .1pb_{.5}$. If i_r is much longer than this, then E is a gyrating index of a stable rate. It declines substantially between rewards, only to jump back up with each new reward. In other words, when the halflife of E is not at least tenfold longer than the expected interreward interval, E fluctuates widely when driven by a stable rate of reward occurrence; hence it is a poor index of that rate.

It is also essential to this model that there seldom be more than one occurrence of a reward within the period of an internally timed trial. If there are multiple occurrences of the reward within a single trial, the only way to make E reflect the rate of reward occurrence is to have the value of C at update be proportionate to the count of the number of rewards that have occurred during a trial. But the point of the model is to have a process that indexes rate without counting rewards. In order that there seldom be more than one reward in a given trial, the value of p must be much less than the expected interreward interval, or: $p \leq .1i_r$. (Poisson rate processes, which are the simplest kind of random average rate of occurrence processes, are bursty; it is common to have two or three occurrences within an interval less than the average interevent interval.) The only way to jointly satisfy the conditions $i_r \leq .1pb_{.5}$ and $p \leq .1i_r$ is to have $b_{.5}$ be large. Some algebra with these inequalities yields $b_{.5} \geq 100$, which means that $w \geq .993$ because $.993^{100} \cong .5$.

One might conclude from this that all one needs to do to make the model in equation 11.9 operate in such a way that E is an index of the rate of reward occurrence is to choose the value of w very close to 1 (e.g., $w = .9999$). However, in seeking to avoid the problems of multiple rewards per trial and the gyrating values of the index on one side of the strait, one has to beware of the problem of slow learning on the other side. When w gets very close to 1, the value of E approaches its asymptote very slowly, but E is an index of the recent rate of reward occurrence only when it is near its asymptote. The larger w is, the more slowly the animal learns the rate of occurrence. At the limit, when $w = 1$, the animal never learns: $(1-w) = 0$, hence $\Delta E = 0$ on every trial. Thus for E in equation 11.9 to be approximately proportionate to the recent rate of occurrence of the rewards after no more than thirty or so rewards, w must be chosen such that $b_5 \cong 100$, which is to say, $w \cong .993$.

The upshot of these constraints on the values of the parameters w and p is that any given instantiation of the model in equation 11.9 works only for a modest range of rates of reward occurrence, rates such that $1/r \cong 10p$, where p is the period of the internal trial clock. To make the model work for widely different rates—and the data show that the apportionment of foraging time is proportionate to relative rates of reward over several orders of magnitude variation in rates—one has to change the parameter p from situation to situation, which is odd, to say the least. It amounts to saying that the crucial parameter of the trial clock, which is part of the system that is to compute an index of rate, has to be adjusted a priori so that it is in approximately the correct proportion to the rate to be estimated. To make the a priori value of p situation specific and dependent on the rate to be estimated is to beg the question of how the system estimates rate.

Even for rates that are suited to the a priori value assigned to trial duration (p), one has the problem that the value that b must have to yield a stable value of E at asymptote requires that E approach that asymptote slowly, over many reward occurrences. E approaches its asymptote as w^b goes to zero. When $w \cong .993$, it takes more than 300 updates for E to climb to within 10 percent of its asymptotic value. Assuming an average interreward interval equal to ten update periods (ten trials), the animal must observe more than thirty rewards before E gives a reasonably accurate estimate of their rate of occurrence.

Suppose that there has been a long period with no rewards and then rewards begin to occur at a high rate, as was the case in the ideal free fish experiment (figure 11.1). During the period when E is climbing to its asymptotic value, it is not a good indicator of the current rate of reward. Its value during this period reflects the course of learning (the process of strengthening the association over trials), not the relevant parameter of the external world (the current rate of reward). From the standpoint of inferential statistics, the occurrence of the first few rewards provides sufficient evidence that there has been a change in the rate of reward. (The statistics of this are treated in chapter 13.) Given that the rate has changed, it does not make sense to average the period prior to the occurrence of the first reward with the period since that occurrence, but that is what this kind of model does.

If one estimates rate from the occurrence of the first reward in a frankly representational way—dividing the number of occurrences observed up to any moment by the time elapsed up to that moment—then the expected value of the estimate is constant, unlike the expected value of the estimate obtained from equation 11.9. The rate of reward estimated in this (the normal) way does not grow or shrink systematically with continued exposure to a constant rate of reward. In a frankly representational approach to dealing with rate, what ought to change systematically with continued exposure to a constant rate is not the rate estimate itself but rather the representation of the statistical uncertainty regarding the correct value of the estimate—the animal's representation of its uncertainty about the correct value of "what it knows." The statistical uncertainty of an estimate is a separate aspect of the representational problem. A representational model must deal with it separately, whereas nonrepresentational models conflate this problem with the problem of computing the estimate itself.

The conflating of the state of learning about rate with the rate that has been learned—the fact that E reflects both of these quite separate aspects of the situation—is a fundamental property of associative theories, including connectionist versions of associative theory. It is one reason that these theories are not and probably cannot be representational theories of learning (in the sense in which the term *representational* is employed in this book). The nodes in associative nets (or, in Lockean terms, the ideas between which associations form) may have a structure that enables them to represent aspects of the animal's experience, and there may be an interpretive system that processes the contents of these nodes in such a way as to make the system a richly representational one, but associative theories are not about the nodes or about the structure of systems that interpret the contents of nodes. They are about the process of association formation—the process that governs the evolution of connections among the nodes. These associations cannot themselves serve as satisfactory representations of any "objective" aspect of reality.

By an objective aspect of reality, I mean a property of the animal's experience that may be specified without reference to the characteristics of a learning process, an aspect like the rate of occurrence of rewards. Associative connections cannot correspond with regularity or fidelity to the objective properties of an animal's experience because their strength is assumed to vary as a function of the amount of exposure the animal has had to a given aspect of reality. The variation in associative strength as a function of the amount of exposure to a constant experience is a function of the form and parameters of the learning process. In the present instance, for example, the expected value of the strength of E after a given amount of exposure to a constant rate of reward occurrence is a function of the particular learning law we have assumed (the law given by equation 11.9), plus w (the associability parameter) and p (the period of the internal trial clock). The value of E is as much a function of these parameters as it is of the reality it is meant to index; hence it cannot be a faithful representative of that reality.

The fact that the strength of an association reflects the extent of an animal's exposure to a parameter of reality as well as the value of that parameter is often seen as an attraction of the associative view because the animal's behavior changes as a function of the extent of its exposure. It takes time and repeated experience before an animal's behavior conforms to the relative rates of reward. When the value of the world parameter (for example, rate of reward) changes, the behavior lags behind. It is tempting to conceptualize this lag as the time it takes for the associative strength to change.

As Lea and Dow point out, the representational hypothesis that the animal's estimate of rate is based on a count of the number of occurrences divided by the observation interval does not take account of the fact that the rate of reward is likely to change. A fairer way to put it is that any such account forces one to confront the problem of how the animal determines whether and when the rate has changed, which is separate from the problem of estimating the current rate. It is a separate problem because it requires the system to represent not only the rate itself but also the statistical uncertainty of that rate estimate. A decision as to whether the rate has changed must take account of the uncertainty as to the true value of the rate both before and after the putative change. The associative approach tries to deal with both problems with a single variable. The advantage of this is the economy of internal variables (intervening variables). The disadvantage is the inherent incapacity of any such system to distinguish between an estimate based on extensive and stable data and an estimate in transition. Does the association have this strength because a corresponding rate of occurrence has been observed for a long time, or does it have this strength because it is in transition from a much lower value to a much higher value, or vice-versa? It is not apparent how to make this distinction within the framework of an associative approach.

When animal behavior seems to reflect the hard-to-capture aspects of animal experience just mentioned, associative theorists generally try to accommodate the data by adjusting the parameters of the model. The predictions of associative models are often highly parameter dependent. One result of the complex assumptions about how the parameters of the model depend on various aspects of the situation is that "except in the simplest possible cases, the kind of model [produced] does not lend itself to analytic treatment. If we want to compare the predictions of any fully specified variant of the common model with observed behavioral data, we have to obtain our theoretical predictions by running computer simulations." (Lea and Dow 1984, p. 271) The inability to derive predictions analytically is a general feature of modern associative models, most notably connectionist models.

Lea and Dow describe their attempts to make a version of the basic model that will account for the results of the operant simulations of foraging situations. They discover that the value of w, the associability parameter, has to depend in complex ways on the situation. They have to make the value of w depend on session length and on whether patches deplete in the course of a session, and they find that they have to allow the value of w to be different for different patches. They take this last step with some reluctance because it introduces more free parameters into the model and because they conceive of w as the parameter that sets the width of the "memory window." They are reluctant to assume that the animal can "look into its past through two different memories at once."

Lea and Dow end on a note of skepticism about the viability of the common model:

> it would be wrong to leave the reader with the impression that we actually favor the common model, or that our pigeons' behavior is normally consistent with simulations based on it. The model is certainly imperfect. Using it, we have never been able to find simulation parameters that will get the number of changeovers between patches even approximately right, no matter what rule we use for translating estimated prey densities [values of E] into behavior. We suspect that ultimately a model that allows the subject to "know" ... "structural" properties of its environment will have to replace the common model, which only allows the subject to learn parameters. (p. 275)

Conclusions

There is extensive experimental evidence that animals allot their time among foraging patches and operant analogues thereof (keys and levers) in proportion to the relative rates of return in these patches. These rates of return are the product of the number of food encounters per unit time and the average amount of food observed or obtained per encounter. Attempts to model the underlying process with associative models have not been notably successful. It appears that a representational account is called for. The capacities to represent temporal intervals and number, which have been reviewed in the preceding two chapters, are the foundations on which the ability to represent the rate of return and other relevant statistics would presumably be built.

The use of representations of time and number in the computation of rates of return and associated statistics implies that the representations of time and number are rich representations, not simply nominal ones. Animals do more with their representations of number than make discriminations based on them. They manipulate these representations in computations whose validity depends on an isomorphism between internal relational and combinatorial operations and the external world. For example, they divide a representation of numerosity by a representation of temporal interval to obtain a representation of rate. Because the definition of representation as employed in this book requires this kind of rich isomorphism if representation is to be used in a nontrivial sense— because it requires that there be more than simply a mapping from states of the world to states of the nervous system—it is the assumed existence of these internal operations on the representatives of number and time that justifies calling this conception of the causation of behavior a representational one. Although a mapping from numerosity to numerons (representatives of numerosity) must be demonstrated if one is to claim that the nervous system of an animal represents number, the demonstration that such a mapping exists is not sufficient to establish the claim that the nervous system has a conception of number. For that claim to be supported, it must be shown that the system employs the representatives of numerosity in a manner consistent with what it is they are supposed be represent. Insofar as we are persuaded that the rather precise correspondence between the allocation of an animal's time and the relative rates of reward is evidence that the animal has computed a representation of those rates from representations of numerosity and time, in that measure are we persuaded that the animal has a representation of number in a rich sense of the term.

To go down this road is also to commit ourselves to the idea that the animal can represent the statistical uncertainty associated with an estimate of rate. Without such a representation, it is unclear how the system could determine whether the rate had changed, which it clearly must be able to do.

Chapter 12

Classical Conditioning: Modern Results and Theory

Events important to an animal occur at rates that often are conditioned by other events in a time-dependent manner. The density of angle worms in a field is conditioned by the magnitude of recent rainfall, by the time elapsed since the rainfall, and by proximity to sunrise. Sea gulls eat worms, among other things, and they prefer to forage for their food where and when the foraging is easy. It is to their advantage to be able to estimate the number of worms likely to be found in a minute's searching in a given field at a given interval after the sunrise that follows a rainy night, so that they may rationally choose between searching that field for worms, searching another field for worms, or scrapping with the other gulls in the local garbage dump (McFarland 1977; Sibly and McCleery 1983). In other words, it is to their advantage to be able to represent the temporal structure of the events in their behavioral space—to represent the expected number of worms to be found per unit time as a function of events that relate to this expectation in a time-dependent manner.

The study of conditioning has traditionally approached this problem from a nonrepresentational perspective. It has tried to show that the animal may adapt its behavior to the temporal dependencies in its environment without representing those dependencies, that is, without anything forming inside the organism isomorphic to the dependencies to which the animal's behavior becomes adapted. The presumed mechanism of adaptation is the formation of an association between the internal "representation" of the conditioning event (the conditioned stimulus, or CS) and the internal representation of the motivationally significant event (the unconditioned stimulus, or US). *Representation* is in quotation marks because theorists are not of one mind as to whether the internal entities corresponding to and evoked by stimuli should be conceived of in representational terms. Some theorists are inclined to think they should be. When conceiving of them in this way, they may refer to the internal representatives of external entities as "gnostic units" (Konorski 1948; Rescorla 1979) or some other such term connoting an entity that can, by virtue of its complex structure, code for some complex state of the world. More traditionally, however, the internal entities that become linked by associations have not been conceived of in representational terms. When theorists wish to treat these entities nonrepresentationally, they refer to them as stimulus traces or, more recently, as nodes in an associative net.

It does not matter for present purposes whether one conceives of the entities between which associations form in representational or nonrepresentational terms because contemporary animal learning theory is not about these entities. It is about the associations that are thought to form between them. Conditioning theory deals primarily with those aspects of learning that depend on the temporal relations among stimulus occurrences. These temporal relations determine associative strengths, and it is associative strengths that adapt the animal's behavior to the temporal structure of events.

At the conclusion of the preceding chapter, I reviewed the difficulties one confronts if one attempts to make the strength of an association represent a scalar parameter of the animal's experience, such as the density of food in a given patch. When more than one dimension is required to represent the relation between the CS and the US, as in the case of a time-lagged worm density, then the association between the internal representatives of the CS and US cannot in principle be isomorphic to the CS-US relationship. The CS-US association has only one dimension (only its strength varies), while the relation has two dimensions (a density and a time lag). One number cannot do the work of two.

Conditioning theorists are generally aware of the difficulty of having the strength of an association represent an aspect of external reality, which is why they would resist a representational interpretation of the strength of the association (see, however, Anderson and Bower 1973). Alternatively, in connectionist versions of associative theory, it may be argued that the representation of objectively specifiable properties of the animal's past experience, such as time-lagged worm density, is distributed across the strengths of a great many associations (Hinton, McClelland, and Rumelhart 1986). It is not yet clear if or how these distributed representations of discrete dimensions of experience permit these representations to enter into the kinds of computational processes that are at the heart of the mathematical definition of representation here employed. It is not clear, for example, how a distributed representation of the number of morsels thrown may be divided by a distributed representation of the temporal interval elapsed during the throwing to yield a distributed representation of the rate of throwing, or how this may be multiplied by a distributed representation of morsel magnitude to yield a distributed representation of net food density. The lack of any simple mapping between readily definable aspects of the to-be-represented reality and discrete elements of the representing system is one reason for calling the kinds of representations that arise in connectionist networks "subsymbolic representations" (Smolensky 1986). In symbolic representations, definable entities and parameters of the world map to specifiable entities and quantities in the representing system. In subsymbolic connectionist representations, there often is no such mapping; the representation of a specified entity or parameter of the world is distributed across many nodes or across many associative connections, many of which also participate in the representation of other entities.

The conviction behind most associationist analyses of animal conditioning is that it is possible to define a process of association formation in such a way that the strength of the association formed between the CS and the US is a variable whose value integrates the contribution of a number of different aspects of their relationship in such a way as to determine a reaction to the CS appropriate to the overall import of this relationship. The name of the game is to capture the effects of a number of variables at the expense of losing a unique representation of any one variable. Conditioning theorists believe that it is possible to specify rules for changing internal quantities—usually conceived of as the strengths of neural connections of some kind—in such a way that the strengths of these connections adapt the animal's behavior efficiently to external reality, even though the strengths of these connections are not isomorphic to any particular aspect of the reality to which behavior is adapted.

In the last twenty years, accumulating experimental data have necessitated a substantial change in the assumed complexity of the associative process. Associative theorists, working with both human and animal learning, have responded to similar sorts of empirical difficulties with a similar change in the assumptions. There have been two major and widely agreed on theoretical insights, insights that are valid whether one continues to work in the associative tradition or not.

First, and most important, it is now widely recognized that the memory state space relevant to the change in a given element of memory must be multidimensional. What this insight means within the context of associationist theory is that the change in the strength of an association on a trial depends not only on the pretrial strength of that association but also on the pretrial strengths of other associations. This conclusion is a major achievement. It has led to the introduction of a new class of associative learning theories. It is also a point of departure for the representational approach to conditional expectations.

The other widely agreed on conclusion is more mundane, but it represents nonetheless an important change from the thinking of thirty years ago, which was willfully naive in its assumptions about how the strengths of associations mapped into parameters of the observed behavior. It assumed that this mapping was a simple one (although the theorists of the time knew that this was unlikely to be true). The advantage of assuming a simple linear mapping between the underlying change (associative strength) and the resulting parameters of behavior (probability of response) was that mathematical models could deal directly with observed parameters of the learned behavior rather than with the less accessible (hence less clearly testable) underlying changes. In the last decades, however, this willful naiveté has been recognized to be untenable. It is now widely conceded that the relationship between what is learned and what the animal does is highly complex (see, for example, Wasserman 1981). It needs a theory of its own. This theory—the theory of how what is learned gets translated into what is done—will obviously depend on the theory of what is learned. Therefore we must try to work out a theory of what gets learned, working in situations where we feel secure about making certain (preferably very weak) assumptions about the relationship between the underlying change produced by learning and the observed change in behavior. Then we can turn to the theory of how this is translated into behavior.

Premodern Associative Learning Theory

Until well into the 1960s, formally specified associative learning theories generally assumed that changes in the strength of an association between a CS and a US on a trial (an occurrence of the CS) depended only on the pretrial strength of the association and on the occurrence or nonoccurrence of the US. This conception of association formation still dominates attempts to model the association-forming process as a process of change in synaptic connectivity in the nervous system. The fundamental law of association formation was—and for most neurophysiologically oriented theorists still is—that if the onset of the US followed the onset of the CS within a matter of a few seconds, there would be an increment in the strength of the association linking the representative of the CS to the representative of the US. If the onset of the CS was not followed within a few seconds by the onset of the US, there would be a decrease in the strength of the CS-US association.

In mathematical formulations of these theories, the magnitude of the increment or decrement was assumed to depend only on three quantities: the strength of the CS, the strength of the US, and the pretrial strength of the CS-US association. For example, in the Bush and Mosteller (1951) model, which derived in appreciable measure from Hull's (1943) theory, the increment on trial n in the probability of an appropriate response to the CS was given by:

$$\Delta p_n = \beta(US)(1 - p_n),$$

where Δp_n was the magnitude of the change in the probability of a conditioned response on trial n, $\beta(US)$ was a parameter whose value depended on the delivery or nondelivery of a reward (US), and p_n was the pretrial probability of a conditioned response to the CS. The pretrial probability of a conditioned response depended implicitly on the strength of the associative connection linking the representative of the CS to the representative of the US. The pretrial strength of this association was the only quantity in the animal's memory that entered into the determination of the size of the increment or decrement in its strength.

In algebra, a variable (such as the strength of an association) is said to be a dimension if it enters into a computational procedure that maps one set of variables into a new set with the same number of variables, and the new set can itself be an input to the computational procedure. Associative learning theories specify computations that map pretrial associative strengths into posttrial associative strengths. The number of posttrial associations is the same as the number of pretrial associations because associations of zero strength are nonetheless imagined to exist (unconnected stimulus representatives—nodes—are ones between which there is a connection of strength 0). Finally, the posttrial associations from trial n are the pretrial associations on trial $n + 1$. Thus from the mathematical point of view, associative strengths are variables in the "space" on which the learning process is said to "operate." The greater is the number of variables in the input entering into the determination of the value of any single variable in the output, the greater is the dimensionality of the space the procedure operates on. In the Bush and Mosteller model, which is representative of pre-1960 theories, only one memory variable plays a role in determining what the strength of a given posttrial association will be: the pretrial strength of that association. The computational procedure (the learning model) in this theory is such that from the standpoint of any one association, the other associations in memory might as well not exist. What happens to an association is not influenced in any way by the values of other associations. Each memory variable in this theory is a space unto itself. Thus memory spaces in this theory are one-dimensional and there are as many such spaces as there are memories (associations).

Another point to note about this earlier formulation is that p_n, the quantity that is changing in consequence of the experience of a given trial, is an observable behavioral quantity: the probability of a conditioned response to the CS rather than the unobservable underlying quantity, such as the strength of the association between the internal representatives of the CS and the US. This reflects the convenient assumption that the underlying change is directly mirrored in the observed change—an assumption now known to be unrealistic.

The final important point about Bush and Mosteller's formulation of the law of learning is that the temporal lag between CS and US onset is not explicitly dealt with. An explicit treatment of the effects of the temporal lag is also absent from the modern associative theories. This absence is noteworthy because the crucial role of some kind of temporal contiguity or near contiguity between CS and US occurrences has been a central tenet of associationist theories since their inception in the eighteenth century. A specification of the effects of the temporal lag between CS and US is absent because it has proved hard to formalize its effect in an empirically defensible manner.

It is not difficult to come up with a formal specification of what might be meant by temporal contiguity, but these formulations have always proved empirically indefensible. After reviewing experiments that varied the details of the temporal relation between the CS and the US, Rescorla (1972, pp. 39-40) states, "While some forms of conditioning may intimately involve precedence of the US by the CS, it is clear that such temporal relations cannot be used as a general description of Pavlovian conditioning." Rescorla goes on to conclude that "to be sure, both sequential and temporal variables are important in conditioning and will demand adequate theoretical treatment. But the present data...do not serve as a solid base for expansion of the theory [to include an explicit treatment of the effects of temporal variables]." This is as true now as it was seventeen years ago (cf. Rescorla 1988). Formal theories of classical conditioning still do not deal explicitly with the effects of time (see, however, Gibbon and Balsam 1981; Wagner 1981), although verbal statements of the laws of conditioning invariably refer to the importance of some kind of temporal contiguity between CS and US. The notion of temporal contiguity is an unresolved problem at the core of associative learning theories.

The Empirical Foundations for the Multidimensionality Assumption

The work of Kamin (1969), Rescorla (1968), and Wagner (Wagner et al. 1968) in the late 1960s convinced the field that the one-dimensionality assumption in the traditional theories could not be maintained. Information relevant to what is learned about a CS in a learning trial is not localized in either of the two ways assumed by previous theories. Previous theories assumed that the learning-relevant information in memory was localized to the strength of the particular association that was to be incremented or decremented (the unidimensionality of the memory space). These experiments showed, however, that what was learned about the relation between a CS and a US depended not only on what had already been learned about their relation but also on what had been learned about the relations between the US and other CSs present on a trial.

Previous theories had also assumed that the relevant information was localized in time. What mattered was the temporal relation on each trial: did the US occur concurrently with or slightly after the CS? Rescorla's experiments showed, however, that what was learned depended on the distribution in time of other occurrences of the US, occurrences that were not even approximately contiguous with an occurrence of the CS. I will review these findings under headings that indicate these two different kinds of nonlocalizability: associative multidimensionality and the effects of the global temporal distribution of the US. Modern associative theory treats the second kind of effect as an instance of the effects of associative strengths on one another (associative multidimensionality). The effects of USs remote in time from a CS are assumed to be mediated by the associations these USs create between the US and the background (the experimental situation). The background is treated as another CS, which is present on trials with other CSs. The association between the background and the US is an important variable in determining the increments in the CS-US associations for other CSs.

The Effects of Other CSs

Overshadowing. Both tones and lights are good CSs for most animals, at least with the most commonly used USs. They have been used in innumerable conditioning experiments. If the onset of a tone signals the imminent occurrence of a US such as food, shock to the feet, or a puff of air to the eyeball, this onset soon elicits a response appropriate to the US whose occurrence it signals. Kamin (1967, 1969) showed, however, that if these two CSs were presented together during training and then tested separately, it often emerged that the animal was responding almost entirely to one and not the other.[1] Thus presentation of a clearly audible 50-decibel tone alone for ten trials would lead to excellent conditioning, and so would the presentation of clearly visible light alone, but presentation of the two stimuli together resulted in excellent conditioning to the

1. Pavlov (1928) was the first to describe overshadowing, but it did not get much attention until the work of Kamin. For more recent experiments on overshadowing, see Mackintosh (1975).

light and no conditioning to the tone. In other animals, or for other intensities of the stimuli, the reverse was observed, conditioning to the tone but not the light. (For similar findings in operant conditioning experiments, see Reynolds 1961.)

These experimental findings showed that the increment in associative strength between a given CS and a given US depended not just on their characteristics and the characteristics of their observed temporal relationship but also on the characteristics of the other CSs presented concurrently. It is possible to conceive of this effect as depending on intrinsic properties of individual animals' perceptual reactions to the two stimuli. One can imagine some sort of perceptual interaction between the stimuli, perhaps mediated by an attentional process, which causes the associative process to operate primarily on the representative of one or the other CS (Mackintosh 1975). Whether this is an appropriate interpretation of what occurs in these experiments or not, such an effect has come to be called an overshadowing effect. Overshadowing occurs when the intrinsic properties of one CS prevent the associative process from operating normally on the association between the US and another concurrently presented CS.

Blocking.   In a blocking experiment, a tone or a light is presented by itself and followed quickly by a US for a number of trials, until the animal's behavior anticipates the US; then another CS is presented together with the first CS for many further trials. In tests of the reaction to the second CS alone, the animal does not respond as if it predicts the US, despite its many pairings with the US (Kamin 1969; Mackintosh 1975; Rescorla and Wagner 1972). Since it does not matter which CS is trained first, this cannot be due to an interaction based on the intrinsic properties of the animal's perceptual reaction to these stimuli. What the animal has learned about the predictive power of the initially trained CS prior to the introduction of the second CS blocks its learning an association between the second CS and the US. This blocking effect, which is robust and can be demonstrated in all of the traditional conditioning paradigms, forces the assumption that the dimensionality of the relevant memory space is greater than one. What happens to a given CS-US association on a trial clearly depends on what the animal already knows about other CSs. Within the associationist tradition, there are differing accounts of the mechanism by which the knowledge about other CSs affects what is learned (compare Rescorla and Wagner 1972 with Mackintosh 1975), but all assume that what gets learned about a given CS depends on what has already been learned about the other CSs presented along with it. Thus they all assume that the memory space governing the updating of the value of an associative connection is multidimensional. The multidimensionality assumption is also a central feature of connectionist models of human memory (Rumelhart and McClelland 1986).

Predictive sufficiency.   What is learned about one CS affects what is learned about the other CS even when learning about the first does not precede learning about the second. An experiment by Wagner et al. (1968) demonstrates this in an interesting and theoretically consequential manner. They used three conditioned stimuli: stimulus A, stimulus B and stimulus X. In both experimental conditions, X was presented together with A on half the trials and together with B on the other half of the trials. In both conditions, the US occurred on half the trials. For the first group (first condition), the trials on which the US occurred were those on which X was paired with A. Thus AX predicted that the US would occur, and BX predicted that it would not. Note that it is really A doing the predictive work, not X. A learning mechanism that took the predictive powers of A fully into account would attribute no predictive powers to X. In the other group, the US occurred on a random half of the AX trials and on a random half of the BX trials. For this group, all three stimuli were equally predictive of the US; however, X alone was a sufficient predictor. A procedure for estimating predictive power that keeps the number of predictive variables to a minimum would attribute all of the predictive power to X rather than to A or B.

When X is tested alone, one might expect animals in the first group—the group where A was doing the predictive work—to show little reaction to X. This is what was in fact found. Despite the fact that X was paired with the US on one of every two trials and despite the fact that the US never occurred except shortly after X, the rats in the first group did not react to X as if it predicted the US to any appreciable extent. By contrast, when X was tested alone on animals in the second group (the group where X alone was a sufficient predictor of the US) the animals showed robust conditioning to X—about as good conditioning as they would have shown had X been presented alone during training. Thus pairing X with other stimuli, even with other stimuli that predict the US as well as it does, does not necessarily interfere with the conditioning of X. It interferes only when the animal's experience with X does not allow it to assess how well the consideration of X alone would predict the US (as in overshadowing experiments, where the training conditions are such as to preclude separating out the predictive powers of the two CSs).

The results of Wagner et al. (1968) are not reconcilable with the assumption that the learning process acting on the representative of a given CS looks only at what is already known about the relation between that CS and the US. These results also make the learning process appear extraordinarily sophisticated. It picks out the sufficient or maximally efficient predictors and ignores the redundant predictors. We will see, however, that a generalization of the Bush and Mosteller learning law from a one-dimensional memory space to a multidimensional memory space can predict these results—with a judicious choice of parameter values. We will also see that in a representational model, a simple principle, uncertainty minimization, yields the same result.

Effects of USs Elsewhere in Time

In science, progress is often made when someone thinks to ask a simple question—in retrospect an obvious question—that no one else has thought to ask before. For close to one hundred years, it had been experimentally demonstrated that pairing a CS with a US leads an animal to respond to the CS in a manner that anticipates the occurrence of the US (leads the animal to give a conditioned response). Early on, people asked what happens when this pairing is not infallible. What happens if the US follows the CS on only some of the occasions on which the CS occurs (but never when the CS does not occur)? The answer has long been known to be that the animal gives a conditioned response to the CS even when the US only infrequently follows (or accompanies) the CS (Mackintosh 1983, p. 99). Rescorla (1967) asked about the other side of this coin: what happens if the US occurs in the absence of the CS? More interestingly, what if the US occurs sufficiently often in the absence of the CS so that the US is no more likely in the presence of the CS than in its absence?

Suppose, asked Rescorla, we set up a schedule of pairings between CS and US occurrences that would ordinarily lead to robust conditioning, and now we add US occurrences at other times, times remote from the occurrences of the CS. The temporal localization assumption in traditional associative learning theories predicts that these additional occurrences of the US will have no effect on the association between the CS and the US because this association depends in theory only on how many times the US does or does not occur in approximate temporal contiguity with the CS. The additional USs are to be added at times remote from the occurrence of the CS; hence, in traditional theory they should have no effect. In fact, however, when Rescorla did the experiment, he found that the additional USs had a profound effect. The more of the temporally remote additional USs he added, the less was the conditioning. When he added enough so that there was no longer any predictive relation between the CSs and the USs, the CS no longer elicited a conditioned response.

Rescorla ran several versions of this experiment, and there have been many others since—all yielding substantially the same result despite many differences in procedures, apparatus, and animals. One of the early ones will be recounted in detail because it figures prominently in subsequent theoretical treatments.

Rescorla (1968) used the conditioned emotional reaction paradigm, in which a rat is first taught to press a lever steadily for food and then exposed to stimuli that predict (or do not predict) foot shock. When the rat perceives a stimulus that signals an increased likelihood of its being shocked, it stops pressing the lever for the food and prepares for the jolt. The reduction in its rate of pressing (the suppression ratio) is the measure of its conditioned response to the previously neutral CS. When Rescorla's rats had learned to press steadily for food, he blocked off the lever and the food delivery bin and gave them five daily sessions of conditioning with a shock US. For one group of rats, 2-minute-long tones came on at random times during each session (twelve tones per session with a mean intertone interval of 8 minutes). In the course of each session, a rat also got twelve short shocks to its feet. In one group (group R-1), these were programmed to occur with a fixed probability per unit time throughout the session, so that there was no relation between the presence or absence of the tone and the probability of getting shocked within a given unit of time.

A comparison group (group G) got the same treatment, except that whenever a shock was programmed to occur in the absence of the CS, it was suppressed. This meant that the expected number of shocks per unit time while the CS was on was the same for both of these groups; hence both groups experienced an equal number of pairings between the CS and the US. What differed between the groups was the expected number of shocks per unit time when the CS was not on. Put another way, what differed was the number of USs that occurred at times other than those when the CS was on (temporally remote USs).

The suppression of the shocks during non-CS intervals for the second group meant that this group got only one-fifth as many shocks as did the rats in the first group. It was possible that the total number of shocks received might have an effect, so Rescorla included a third group (group R-2), which got the same number of shocks per session as the second group—2.4 shocks per session instead of the 12 per session received by the first group—but the rate of the occurrence of these shocks did not vary as a function of whether the CS was on. Thus the first R group equated for number of shocks received during the CS, while the second R group equated for the total number of shocks received. In both R groups, the distribution of shocks in time was unrelated to the distribution of the CS in time, while in the G group, the shocks occurred only when the CS was on.

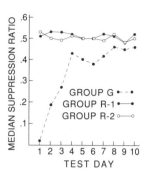

Figure 12.1
The median suppression ratios for Rescorla's three groups of rats as a function of the number of days of postconditioning (extinction) testing. The suppression ratio is the ratio of the number of presses (for food) during the CS to the sum of the numbers during the two periods of equivalent duration immediately before and after the CS. A ratio of .5 indicates no conditioned response to the CS (no diminishment in rate of pressing during the CS); a ratio of 0 indicates complete suppression of pressing. During this postconditioning testing, there was no shock, which is why group G, for which there was a differential rate of shock occurrence during CS and non-CS periods, shows less suppression from day to day. (Redrawn from Rescorla 1968, p. 2, by permission of author and publisher.)

   After five shock-conditioning sessions, the lever and the food delivery bin were unblocked, and the rats were allowed to resume pressing for food. When their rate of pressing had stabilized (that is, when they had overcome their fear of the box itself), Rescorla sounded the tone. The results could not have been clearer (figure 12.1). The two R groups showed no conditioned response to the tone: they went on pressing the lever as if the tone had never been paired with shock. The G group stopped pressing the lever altogether while the tone was on, though shock had been paired with tone the same number of times for the rats in this group as it had for the rats in the first R group.
   In a second version of this experiment, Rescorla (1968) varied the relative and absolute rates of delivery of shock during the CS and non-CS periods. Over the fourfold range in the absolute rate of delivery he used, absolute rate had no effect on the extent of the conditioned reaction to the CS. A fourfold change in the number of times that shock had been paired with the CS had no effect on the extent to which the rat gave a conditioned response to the CS, provided there was also a fourfold change in the number of shocks received in non-CS periods (figure 12.2). On the other hand, the relative rates of shock deliveries in CS and non-CS periods had a strong effect: the greater was the ratio between shocks per minute during the CS periods and the shocks per minute during the non-CS periods, the stronger was the conditioned response to the CS. When

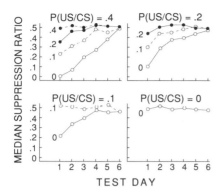

Figure 12.2
Median suppression ratios as a function of days of postconditioning (extinction) testing in groups that experienced various rates of shock occurrence during CS and non-CS periods. At the top of each panel is the probability of the US occurrence during the CS. (The rate of US occurrence is this probability divided by the 2-minute duration of the CS.) The number to the left of each curve is the probability of shock during any 2-minute interval of time in the absence of the CS (the background shock probability). (Redrawn from Rescorla 1968, p. 4, by permission of author and publisher.)

these two rates were equal, there was no conditioned response to the CS, no matter how often the shocks had occurred in the presence of the CS. When these two rates were unequal, there was a substantial conditioned response, even in the groups where the shock had occurred in the presence of the CS on only one-tenth of the CS presentations. The .1-0 group in figure 12.2, for which shocks occurred at the rate of 0.05 per minute during each 2-minute-long CS and at the rate of 0 per minute in the absence of the CS, showed a conditioned response to the CS during testing, though these animals experienced only six pairings between the tone and the shock (approximately one pairing in each 2-hour session). By contrast, the .4-.4 group, for which shocks occurred at the rate of 0.2 per minute in both the presence and the absence of the CS, showed no conditioned response, though they experienced twenty-four pairings of the CS and the US.

Pairing not Necessary for the Formation of an Association
The experiments on overshadowing, blocking, predictive sufficiency, and background conditioning lead to the conclusion that pairing of stimuli is not sufficient for the formation of an association because there are many training conditions in which two readily associable stimuli do not become associated despite repeated pairing. Findings now to be reviewed show that pairing is not necessary. The combined conclusion—

that, in Rescorla's (1987) words, "pairing is neither necessary nor sufficient for conditioning"—represents a fundamental change in thinking about the associative process. It is this change that distinguishes contemporary theories of associative conditioning from their predecessors.

Poison-avoidance conditioning.   The best-known results that raise doubts about the necessity for, and/or the meaning of temporal pairing in classical conditioning are from experiments on the ability of animals to learn to avoid nauseating poisons. Garcia and his collaborators (Garcia, Kimmeldorf, and Hunt 1961; Revusky and Garcia 1970) showed that animals readily associate nauseating illness with brief tastes experienced many hours earlier. While these results were initially greeted with incredulity because they appeared radically at variance with the long-established notion that close temporal contiguity was a sine qua non of associative conditioning, they have been repeatedly replicated and extended. Conditioning with taste CSs and nausea-producing USs behaves very much like more familiar kinds of conditioning, except that excellent conditioning is obtained in one to three trials even when there is an interval of 12 hours between the CS and the US. It is now sometimes maintained that the only difference between poison-avoidance conditioning and other instances of classical conditioning is a parametric one—the associability parameter for the taste CS and the illness US is unusually high and the parameter that determines the width of the "pairing window"—the interstimulus interval (ISI) function—is several orders of magnitude greater than with other CSs and USs (Domjan 1981; Logue 1979).

The accommodation of associative theory to the poisoning data by adjustments in parameter values, while it is a time-honored and readily defensible theoretical response to new data, does call attention to the fact that the notion of temporal pairing has no substance if one cannot specify when two stimuli may or may not be regarded as temporally paired. The ISI function in associative theory specifies for the pairing-produced increment in associative strength a scaling factor that is a function of the interval, τ, between the CS and the US. If this function is imagined to be flat from $\tau = -\infty$ to $\tau = +\infty$, the CS and US may be said to be paired no matter what their temporal relation, and the notion of temporal pairing is vacuous. The willingness of associative theorists to regard an illness that begins at 18:00 as paired with a taste that was experienced for a few minutes at 06:00 calls attention to the need to say what the ISI function in associative conditioning is. It also implies that there is no ISI characteristic of conditioning in general. Hence, we need a theory of the ISI function itself, a model that specifies what the form and parameters of this function will be from one case to the next.

The effect of the duty cycle (the ITI/ISI ratio). A finding in a variety of traditional conditioning paradigms, which has only begun to receive the theoretical attention it deserves, is that whatever the function may be that defines what constitutes temporal pairing in classical conditioning, it is not a function of the ISI alone; it is a function of the ISI and the intertrial interval (ITI). For a given ISI, the rate at which conditioning proceeds is a function of the ITI in a wide variety of conditioning paradigms. The longer the ITI, the more rapidly conditioning proceeds, that is, the fewer the trials required to attain some conditioning criterion. A strong effect of the ITI on the rate of conditioning is seen in paradigms as diverse as eyeblink conditioning and autoshaping.

It is widely asserted in the secondary literature (for example, Schwartz 1984, p. 71) that for the conditioning of simple reflexes like the eyeblink, a CS-US interval of about 0.5 second is optimal. In the literature on the cellular basis of conditioning, an ISI function that rises rapidly to a peak at 0.5 second and declines to negligible levels by 2 seconds is sometimes taken as a signature of the conditioning process (Hawkins and Kandel 1984). The results commonly cited to justify this assumption about the form and parameters of the ISI function in classical conditioning come from experiments by Gormezano and his collaborators on eyeblink conditioning in the rabbit (Gormezano 1972). The CS in these studies is a tone, and the US is a mild puff of air or mild electric shock to the eyeball, a stimulus just strong enough to elicit a blink of the nictitating membrane that protects and lubricates the eyeball in rabbits. In studies by Gormezano and his collaborators, there was a minimum of fifty trials per experimental session, so the ITI was short. It has since been shown that lengthening the ITI shifts the peak of this function to substantially longer intervals (Mis, Andrews, and Salafia 1970). When there is only one trial per daily conditioning session, eyeblink conditioning is significantly faster with an ISI of 1.1 or 2.2 seconds than with an ISI of 0.5 second (Levinthal et al. 1985). The values of the ISI at which the efficiency of eyeblink conditioning begins to decline when trials are widely spaced has yet to be determined; the efficiency at 2.2 seconds, the longest ISI so far tested, is not significantly below the peak of the function. Even in eyeblink conditioning, a 2.2 second ISI yields maximally efficient conditioning when the ITI is long.

Eyeblink conditioning with widely spaced trials is dramatically faster. With an ISI of 1 second and 70 trials per session, Schneiderman and Gormezano (1964) found that it took about 400 trials for their rabbits to attain a criterion of 80 percent anticipatory eyeblinks; with an ISI of 2 seconds, a 40 percent criterion was not attained in more than 550 trials. By contrast, Levinthal et al.'s subjects, which got only one trial per day or one trial every other day, reached the 80 percent criterion after 15 trials with ISIs of 1.1 or 2.2 seconds—an increase in rate of conditioning of one and one-half orders of magnitude. The measured effects of ITI on the rate of eyeblink conditioning in the rabbit are as big or bigger than the measured effects of ISI.

The most systematic investigations of the joint effects of the ITI and ISI have used the autoshaping paradigm in pigeons (Gibbon et al. 1977). In this paradigm, the CS is the illumination of a key,and the US is the delivery of food, which occurs some seconds after the key is illuminated. These contingencies—key illumination followed by food presentation— condition an association between key illumination and food, which is manifest in the pigeon's pecking of the key. The pecking is not instrumental in producing the food, which comes at the appointed time whether the pigeon pecks or not. As with experiments on the reactions of pigeons to rates of food presentation, it is not the relation between the pigeon's behavior and its consequences that is crucial in pigeon learning; it is statistical properties of observed events. The pigeon is so constructed that it pecks at any peckable stimulus that predicts food; hence its pecking serves as an index of its representation of the predictive relation between key illumination and food, or, in associative terms, of the association between key illumination and food. The interval between the onset of key illumination and the delivery of food is the CS-US interval (ISI). When food is delivered, the key light goes out. The interval to its next illumination is the ITI.

In experiments of this kind, it is essential that one arrange the conditions in such a way that the interval elapsed since the last occurrence of food does not itself predict the next occurrence, since we saw in chapter 10 that animals readily use elapsed intervals to anticipate food. From an associative perspective, this means that the elapsed interval may itself be regarded as a CS. One must take care that this temporal CS does not compete with the CS whose pairing with the US is intended to be the independent variable. To make the duration of the ITI of no use in predicting the next occurrence of food, the duration of this interval varied randomly about a mean value or expectation. It was the value of the mean ITI that changed from condition to condition. For example, when the ITI was nominally 96 seconds, the programming equipment was set to produce a variety of ITIs that approximated what one would observe from Poisson process with a rate parameter equal to 1/96. (Recall that the expected or mean interval between events in a Poisson process is the reciprocal of the rate parameter.) The Poisson process has the property that the likelihood of the next occurrence of an event—in this experiment the next occurrence of a trial—is independent of the time elapsed since the last occurrence. Thus the time elapsed since the last oc-

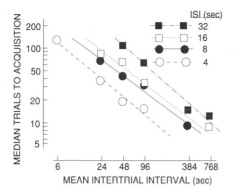

Figure 12.3.
Median trials to reach the acquisition criterion as a function of the intertrial interval (ITI) for various values of the ISI (= CS-US interval) on double logarithmic coordinates. The straight lines are the best-fitting regression lines. (Redrawn from Gibbon et al. 1977, p. 267, by permission of author and publisher.)

currence of food does not predict the next occurrence of food; only key illumination does.

For values of the CS-US interval (or ISI) of 4, 8, 16 and 32 seconds, Gibbon et al. varied the mean ITI from 6 to 768 seconds and plotted the number of trials to an acquisition criterion of at least one key peck on three out of four successive trials. Their data are given in figure 12.3, which plots the trials to acquisition as a function of the ITI for the four different values of the CS-US interval. At each CS-US interval, the longer the interval between trials, the fewer trials to acquisition. More important, when the functions for different ISIs are plotted against a logarithmic ITI axis, as in figure 12.3, they are parallel. This log parallelism means that the rate of conditioning is a function of the ratio between the CS-US interval and the average intertrial interval (the ISI/ITI ratio). In other words, the efficiency of conditioning is determined not by the interval between the onset of the CS and the onset of the US but rather by the ratio of this interval to the average interval between USs. For any given value of this ratio, conditioning progresses at a given rate regardless of the absolute values of the ISI and ITI. This important quantitative result, if it proves to be generally valid, must be the starting point for any attempt to specify the meaning of *temporal pairing* in associative conditioning.

The Gibbon et al. result has far-reaching implications for attempts to ground associative conditioning processes in processes of synaptic change induced by paired signals (Abrams and Kandel 1988; Crow 1988; Farley and Alkon 1985; Thompson 1988). These synaptic processes must depend not on temporal intervals per se but rather on the ratios between temporal intervals. How this might be accomplished within the framework of the kinds of processes currently thought to mediate changes in synaptic connectivity is unclear.

Conditioning with 0 or negative ISIs.   While it is widely recognized that there is no single ISI function in associative conditioning, there might be a parametrically related family of functions. It has long been thought that the rate of conditioning is a forwardly biased, nonmonotonic function of the temporal asynchrony between CS and US: conditioning appears to be nonexistent when US onset precedes CS onset (a negative ISI), poor when the onsets are simultaneous (ISI = 0), best when CS onset slightly precedes US onset, and poor again when there is a long interval between CS onset and US onset (see Rescorla 1988, figure 1). There are clear exceptions to this generalization, however. Recent well-controlled studies have shown substantial conditioning between stimuli with simultaneous onsets (Fudim 1978; Holman 1980). In some cases, the conditioning obtained with simultaneously presented stimuli is superior to that obtained with asynchronous presentation (Rescorla 1980; Rescorla and Cunningham 1978). Thus it is not generally true that conditioning is poor when the interstimulus interval is zero. Moreover, in one of their experiments, Heth and Rescorla (1973) obtained strong conditioning when US onset preceded CS onset by 1 to 2 seconds—backward conditioning or conditioning with a negative ISI.

Generally, the experiments that have demonstrated the classic forwardly biased nonmonotonic ISI function have employed a neutral CS (a tone or light) and a US with strong motivational significance for the animal (food or shock), whereas several of the experiments that show good conditioning with 0 or negative ISIs have studied the formation of associations between motivationally neutral stimuli (though not always—Heth and Rescorla 1973 used a tone CS and a shock US in their demonstrations of simultaneous and backward conditioning). The differences in the motivational significance of the traditionally employed CSs and USs raise the possibility that the forward bias in the ISI is a consequence not of the associative process itself but rather of the process that maps associations into behavior. Perhaps two stimuli are associated regardless of the temporal order in which they occur, but only a forward association from a neutral CS to a motivationally charged US is manifest in the usual behavioral tests. This possibility must be considered in the light of results recently reported by Matzel, Held, and Miller (1988). They combined what is called sensory preconditioning with a conditioned suppression paradigm similar to that employed by Rescorla (1968).

Sensory preconditioning is ordinary conditioning but with a motivationally neutral US. The tones and lights traditionally used only as CSs now appear also in the role of USs, so that, for example, a tone, called S1 and conceived of as a CS, is paired with a light, called S2 and conceived of as a US. Since S2, the US, is motivationally neutral, the association that forms as a result of the predictive relationship between S1 and S2 has no behavioral manifestations. To reveal the S1-S2 association, one must subsequently condition S2 to a motivationally potent US and see how this conditioning alters the animal's response to S1, whose only link to the motivationally potent US is by way of its association to S2, the stimulus that took part in both phases of the conditioning.

In the first phase of Matzel et al.'s experiments, the rats repeatedly experienced a clicking sound followed after five seconds by a tone. (There were four of these click-tone pairings in the course of a 60 minute session.) In other words, there was forward pairing of S1 (clicking) and S2 (the tone) in the first phase.[2] In the second phase of the experiment, S2 was paired with shock in one of three ways: In the forward pairing conditioning, S2 onset preceded shock onset by five seconds; in the simultaneous condition, S2 onset and shock onset coincided; in the backward pairing condition, shock onset preceded S2 onset by five seconds.

After the second phase of conditioning, the extent of the conditioning of shock to S2 was tested in two ways. Both ways measured the extent of the animal's fear reaction to the motivationally neutral S1 and S2 stimuli by determining the extent to which the presentation of these stimuli suppressed the rat's lever pressing for food. When the conditioning of S2 to shock was assessed in the usual way—by testing the animal's reaction to S2—the usual temporally asymmetric result was obtained: only the forward conditioning group reacted fearfully to S2. However, when the association of S2 to shock was probed by presenting S1, the temporal asymmetry disappeared. The group that had received backward pairing of the shock US and S2 reacted as strongly to S1 as the forward conditioning group. Appropriate control groups showed that in both cases the animals' fear of S1 was a consequence of an association between S2 and shock, not a general fearfulness brought on by exposure to shock (an artifact known as pseudo-conditioning or sensitization).

Informally, what the animals that received backward conditioning in phase 2 had been taught in the course of the two phases was that the tone follows the clicking with a delay of five seconds (phase 1 of training) and

2. This could equally as readily be viewed as backward pairing of S2 with S1. When the stimuli being paired are motivationally neutral, the CS-US distinction is arbitrary, and so is the direction of pairing.

the shock precedes the tone by five seconds (phase 2 of training). If we grant the animals the capacity to represent the signs and magnitudes of these temporal relations (as chapter 9 indicates we should) and if we grant them the capacity to perform elementary arithmetic operations on these representations of positive and negative temporal intervals (as, again, chapter 9 indicates we should), then we may not be surprised to discover that the rat can synthesize its experiences over the two phases of conditioning into a representation of the expected temporal relation between clicking and shock: that the onset of the shock may be expected to coincide with the onset of the tone. Nor should we be surprised that the rat responds appropriately to the resulting representation.

In essence, this is the explanation that Matzel and Miller suggested: "associations are not simple linkages, but contain information regarding the temporal relationship of the associates" (p. 317). In other words, associative bonds are to be endowed with representational significance. There are to be different kinds of associative bonds. One kind encodes the fact that A follows B; another kind encodes the fact that A precedes B. This move toward labeled associations, associations that represent specific kinds of stimulus relationships, does violence to the foundations of associative theory. For example, it would appear to be irreconcilable with the notion that it might be possible to specify the form of the ISI function. The temporal conditions on the formation of the kind of association that encodes temporal precedence must be the opposite of the temporal conditions on the formation of the kind of association that encodes temporal succession.

The introduction of associations that encode or represent different kinds of temporal order also forces one to ask how many kinds of associations one should expect to find and what kinds of stimulus relations an association may code. Can there be an association that encodes "to the right of" or "above" or "father of" or "prime divisor of"? One suddenly confronts the sorts of questions that representational theories of mind must confront but that associative theories of mind dismiss as irrelevant or unproductive. The positing of distinct kinds of associations that encode distinct kinds of information about the world is a radical one; it brings in its train changes in virtually every aspect of associative theory. Before moving in this direction, one ought to pause and reexamine the motivation for adopting the associative framework in the first place. It is unclear that any of those motives can still be satisfied once one permits labeled associations. Introducing labeled associations into associative theory is analogous to introducing into football the rule that the team with the ball may elect to advance toward either goal on any play. It is not the same game anymore.

Conditioning with undefinable ISIs.   In the background conditioning paradigm, which Rescorla (1968) used to demonstrate the importance of USs that are not paired with the CS, the CS-US interval is not readily definable. In most conditioning paradigms, there is a fixed interval of time between the onset of the CS and the onset of the US (an interval that takes on 0 or negative values in simultaneous or backward conditioning paradigms). In Rescorla's paradigm, however, the onsets and offsets of CSs—including the "onset" and "offset" of the background (the experimental chamber)—alter the value of a Poisson rate parameter governing the occurrence of the US. The USs are very short in relation to the CSs. US onset and offset occurs at unpredictable times during the CS. It is not linked to the onset or offset of the CS. In the case of the background CS, there are multiple onsets and offsets of the US during a single 2-hour-long occurrence of the CS. Thus in the background conditioning paradigm, the CS-US interval is undefined: the presence of the CS predicts a change in the rate at which the randomly programmed USs will occur, but it does not predict when a US will occur. Nonetheless, there is excellent conditioning.

Inhibitory conditioning.   The paradigms that produce inhibitory conditioning pose another problem for the hypothesis that temporal pairing is a sine qua non for associative conditioning. An inhibitory CS-US association is produced in one of three ways (Rescorla 1988). The first involves reversing the contingency that established an excitatory association: the US occurs only when the CS is not present. This is called the *explicitly unpaired condition*. It promotes the development of an inhibitory association between CS and US, which inhibits the behavior the animal would ordinarily show in anticipation of the US. The second procedure involves intermixing two kinds of trials. On some trials, only one CS, say, a tone, is presented, and the US occurs. On others, the tone is presented along with a second CS, say, a light, and the US does not occur. Under this condition—which again involves explicitly not pairing the light with the US—an inhibitory association grows up between the CS and the US. In the third procedure, one first establishes two excitatory CSs and then pairs both together with a third CS, without increasing the rate of US occurrence during CS presentations (so that the two excitatory CSs "overpredict" the US).

It is important to realize that simply presenting the CS in the absence of a US does not produce an inhibitory association. It is not clear how it could. An associative connection is by definition a connection between two stimulus representatives (or a stimulus representative and a response representative). When a CS is presented repeatedly in a context where no previous experience gives any reason to expect any particular

US, it is not clear what could occupy the position at the other end of the association from the CS. Gleitman, Nachmias, and Neisser (1954) pointed out this problem in their analysis of the Hullian theory of extinction. Under one reading of Hull's theory, extinction was the development of a conditioned "not-response." The trouble is that a "not-response" is nonspecific; it is the negation of every other response (not just the particular conditioned response whose frequency diminishes during extinction). If what the animal learned during extinction were a conditioned not-response, extinction would produce catatonia. For the same reason, one cannot imagine the presentation of a CS in the absence of a US as developing an association between the CS and a "not-US": the end result would be a kind of animal nirvana in which the representation of all motivationally significant stimuli was obliterated by the association of a CS with the not-US.

The phenomenon of conditioned inhibition must be treated in terms of the formation of an inhibitory association between CS and US representatives. It cannot be conceptualized in terms of a nonassociative process like habituation or reactive inhibition [see Gluck and Thompson's (1987) analysis of the difficulties with the Hawkins and Kandel (1984) habituation model and Gleitman et al.'s (1954) analysis of similar difficulties with Hull's (1943) reactive inhibition model]. Not pairing a CS with a US gives rise to an inhibitory association only if the occurrence of the US is predicted by the animal's previous experience or if the occurrence of the CS coincides with periods in which the rate of occurrence of the US is lower than usual. When a US is presented in such a way that there is no relation between the CS and the US—Rescorla's (1967) truly random presentation procedure—then neither an excitatory nor an inhibitory association forms (Kaplan and Hearst 1985). For either to form, there must be a nonrandom temporal relation between the two stimuli.

Two recent autoshaping experiments by Kaplan (1984) synthesize the difficulties with the pairing concept posed by the effects of the duty cycle and the phenomenon of inhibitory conditioning. Both experiments involved what is called trace conditioning because the CS terminates before the onset of the US, so only the fading trace of the CS representative may be imagined to be present when the US occurs. Kaplan's CS was the illumination for 12 seconds of either of two keys on the two sides of a pigeon chamber. His US was a 3-second access to a food hopper. There was a system for monitoring which side of the chamber the pigeon was on. In his first experiment, Kaplan fixed the interval from CS offset to US onset at 12 seconds and varied the mean ITI from 15 to 240 seconds. With the two longest mean ITIs (120 and 240 seconds), he got excitatory conditioning: when the key light came on, the birds moved to the side with the illuminated key and pecked at it. But when the average ITI was

15 seconds, he got inhibitory conditioning: the pigeons moved to the side away from the illuminated key and never pecked it. Thus the same ISI yields either excitatory or inhibitory conditioning depending on the ITI. The condition for the development of the inhibitory association is that the US reliably occur elsewhere in time, that is, that it be explicitly unpaired with the CS. This result is difficult to reconcile with the assumption that the development of an association depends on the pairing of the CS and the US as defined by some ISI function. For inhibitory associations, it depends on their being unpaired, and for both kinds of associations, what matters is not the ISI itself but the ISI-ITI relationship.

The groups trained with 30- and 60-second ITIs in Kaplan's first experiment did not show evidence of conditioning; they neither approached nor avoided the illuminated key. However, measuring the response to the CS is not the most sensitive or most unequivocally interpretable index of the sign or direction of an association. The best test from a methodological standpoint is the test for associative interference or negative transfer. Associations of opposite sign between the same CS and the same US may be expected to have antagonistic behavioral effects; thus the best test for a negative association between a CS and a US is to see whether the suspected association delays acquisition of an excitatory response to the CS. In his second experiment, Kaplan fixed the mean interval from one 3-second hopper access to the next at 87 seconds and varied the ISI from 6 to 72 seconds. With the longest ISI, the key illumination always came on immediately after hopper access. With shorter ISIs, there was a more variable delay between the end of hopper access and the onset of the CS because the complementary interval—from the offset of the 12 seconds of key illumination to the onset of hopper access— was the independent variable (the ISI). After a period of training with one or another ISI and the fixed interreward interval, Kaplan tested all those groups that did not learn to approach the illuminated key for the presence of negative associations to key illumination. He did this by switching them to the 6-second delay condition and comparing the course of their acquisition of an approach response with the course for birds not given the prior training. When the ISI was only 6 seconds, key illumination and hopper access were roughly co-localized in time in that the period from the onset of key illumination to the onset of food access was much less than the average period between hopper accesses. This co-localization of the key light and hopper access gave rise to excitatory associations; the birds learned to peck the key. However, for all other ISIs, the pigeons developed an inhibitory association between key illumination and food, which retarded the development of an excitatory association in subsequent training.

The importance of these results is that given any nonrandom temporal relation between CS and US, pigeons formed a CS-US association. The general import of such a finding is that the notion of pairing in associative conditioning ought to be redefined to mean any nonrandom temporal relation between stimuli. Thus what one should be looking for is a mechanism that detects nonrandom temporal relations—in other words, a mechanism based on a multivariate time-series analysis, not on the trial-by-trial "pairing" of CS and US. The multivariate time-series approach to classical conditioning is developed in chapter 13.

The Rescorla-Wagner Theory

In response to the findings on blocking and background conditioning, Rescorla and Wagner (1972) proposed a new multidimensional version of associationist learning theory. Their model has greatly influenced subsequent work and subsequent thinking. Recall that the Bush and Mosteller learning law was:

$$\Delta p_n = \beta \, (US)(1 - p_n):$$

the change on trial n in the probability of a conditioned response to the CS, Δp_n, is equal to a parameter, β, whose value varies as a function of reinforcement magnitude (US), times the difference between the maximum response probability and the current probability of the response, p_n. In interpreting this equation, it is understood that the value of p_n depends only on the strength of the underlying association between the representatives of the CS and the US.

The Rescorla-Wagner learning law is:

$$\Delta A_i = \beta \, (i, US) \, [\lambda \, (i, US) - \sum_{i=1}^{i=N} A_i]$$

This takes a little more saying. First, the theory no longer refers to a change in observable response probabilities; it refers to the change in A_i, the strength of the association between the US and a CS_i presented on trial n (the trial subscript, n, has been dropped to keep the notation simpler). Different CSs are indicated by different subscripts (different values of i), and so are the corresponding values of A_i, the association between the representatives of CS_i and the US. In the old model, one did not have to subscript the associations (or the response probabilities that depended on them) because each association was a world unto itself. The process governing its change took no account of other associations, so one did not need a notation for keeping track of the different associations. In the new model, other associations help determine what happens to any one association, so we must subscript them to keep track of which is which.

The change in an active association, A_i, on trial n is the product of a learning rate parameter, β (i,US), times a difference, $[\lambda \ (i,US) - \sum_{i=1}^{i=N} A_i]$, just as in the Bush and Mosteller law. But now the value of the learning rate parameter depends on both i (the CS in question) and the US. β has a different value on trials when the US occurs than on trials when it does not occur (trials when $US = 0$).

Turning now to the difference—the expression inside the brackets—we find the parameter, $\lambda(i,US)$, which is the strength at asymptote of the associative bond between CS_i and the US. In the original statement of the Rescorla model, this parameter was stated to be a function solely of the US. Insofar as one adheres to that assumption, one can drop i from the argument of $\lambda(i,US)$, because the value of λ is then independent of the CS being considered. However, in subsequent discussions of associative learning within the context of the Rescorla-Wagner model, it has sometimes been assumed (or implied) that λ may be a function of the CS as well as the US. It has been assumed that the asymptotic strength of an association to a given US (such as illness) may depend on which CS is used (taste versus tones and lights). If this is allowed to be a possibility, then one must include i among the arguments of $\lambda(\ )$, as I have done.

Finally we come to the quantity that is subtracted from this asymptote-determining parameter, which means that we come to the multidimensionality assumption. The sum of the strengths of all the active associations to the US on trial n, $\sum_{i=1}^{i=N} A_i$, is subtracted from λ (i,US). The active associations to the US on a given trial are those to the CSs present on that trial. Associations to CSs not present on a given trial are inactive. It is a fundamental tenet of associative theories that nothing happens to inactive associations, and they do not participate in determining what happens to active associations.

The explanation of overshadowing and blocking. Qualitative explanations of overshadowing and blocking follow directly from the multidimensionality assumption, that is, from the assumption that the increment in the strength of an active association A_i depends on the strength of the other active associations to the US. The stronger these other associations, the smaller the difference between the asymptotic associative strength parameter, $\lambda(i,US)$, and $\sum_{i=1}^{i=N} A_i$, the sum of the active associations; hence, the smaller the increment in the associative strength of A_i. Suppose, for example, that CS_i is always presented together with CS_b and that CS_b is a much stronger stimulus, so that $\beta(b,US)$ is much greater than β (i,US). The association A_b will approach the value of λ (b,US) within a few trials. If we assume that λ $(b,US) \geq \lambda$ (i,US) this will mean that the increments in A_i soon become very small. Asymptotically, instead of $A^*_i = \lambda$ (i,US) , we have $A^*_i = \lambda$ $(i,US) - A^*_b$, where an asterisk over an association indicates that it has its asymptotic value. Instead of coming over trials to equal the asymptotic-strength parameter, λ (i,US) , as in unidimensional models, the association to CS_i comes to equal this parameter minus A^*_b, the asymptotic strength of the association to CS_b. The association to the CS with the stronger associability parameter crowds out the association to the CS with the weaker parameter, which is what happens in overshadowing.

In blocking, the association to CS_b is built up to asymptotic or near asymptotic strength prior to the introduction of CS_i; hence the increments in A_i are small or negligible from the outset. The prior conditioning to CS_b prevents conditioning to CS_i. In short, simple overshadowing and simple blocking follow directly from the multidimensionality assumption—and the assumption that the asymptotic associations, $\lambda(i,US)$ and $\lambda(b,US)$ are approximately equal. The explanation of the effects of noncontiguous USs is more complex and requires the introduction of a radical new assumption, the assumption of an internal trial clock.

Associative theory has always been a discrete trials theory, which is part of the reason it has had difficulty introducing an empirically defensible formalization of the role of time, which is a continuous rather than a discrete variable. It has always been assumed that the trials were externally determined—by the events that drove conditioning. A trial occurred when a CS occurred. Then, and only then, did the learning process update the CS-US association. The discrete trials assumptions inherent in associative analyses are implied in the following quotation from Rescorla (1972, p. 10), which is the immediate preamble to a presentation of the theory he and Wagner elaborated: "We provide the animal with individual events, not correlations or information, and an adequate theory must detail how these events individually affect the animal. That is to say that we need a theory based on individual events." To explain the effects on learning of USs that did not occur in conjunction with CSs, Rescorla and Wagner (1972) suggested that the animal had a subjective trial clock. Each time its trial clock timed out, a trial had occurred. The stimuli present on that trial were those that were present during part or all of the interval marked off by the subjective trial clock.

Rescorla and Wagner did not specify how long a subjective trial was— nor has there been an attempt to determine this since. They pointed out that in considering any one experiment, the qualitative predictions (the orderings of associative strengths at asymptote or whether a given association was or was not zero at asymptote) did not depend on the assumed subjective trial duration over some range of conceivable durations (though by no means over the full range). They therefore felt justified in assuming, for purposes of illustration only, a subjective trial duration that was analytically convenient for whatever results they were attempting to analyze. Thus for example, in analyzing the experiments by Rescorla on the effects of presenting shocks at random moments during the period when the CS was not on, they assumed that the subjective trial clock carved the non-CS periods up into trials equal in duration to the 2-minute duration of the CS.

If we assume that the rat is internally generating trials with durations of the same order of magnitude as the CS Rescorla used, then the effects of the noncontiguous USs may be regarded as another instance of the blocking of conditioning to one CS by the conditioning to another CS that occurs together with it. The background stimuli, which are provided by the apparatus in which the experiment takes place, play the role of CS_b. During the periods when CS_i (the tone) is not on, trials nonetheless occur because trials are internally generated. The background, CS_b, is present on these trials. If shocks occur on some of these trials, an association between the shock and the background builds up. On trials when the tone is on, the background is also present. The association between it and the shock interferes with the growth of the association between the tone and the shock. The more frequently shocks occur during the no-tone periods, the stronger is the association between the background stimuli and the shocks; hence the weaker is the ultimate association between the tone and the shocks. In fact, if we assume that:

1. $\lambda(x,0) = 0$: the maximum possible associative strength when there is no US is 0;
2. $\lambda(i,US \neq 0) = \lambda(b,US \neq 0) = \lambda_{US} \neq 0$: the maximum possible associative strength on trials when the US is present is the same nonzero value for both CS_i and CS_b;
3. $\beta(i,US \neq 0) = \beta(b,US \neq 0) = \beta_{US}$: the conditioning parameters for CS_i and CS_b are the same on trials when the US is present;
4. $\beta(i,0) = \beta(b,0) = \beta_0$: the conditioning parameters for CS_i and CS_b are the same on trials when the US is absent;

then we get the expression:

$$A_i^* = \frac{p_{ib}\beta_{US}}{p_{ib}\beta_{US} + (1 - p_{ib})\beta_0} - \frac{p_b\beta_{US}}{p_b\beta_{us} + (1 - p_b)\beta_0} \tag{12.1}$$

where p_{ib} is the probability of the US on a trial where both CS_i (the tone) and CS_b (the background) are present and p_b is the probability of the US on a trial where just the background is present. Equation 12.1 asserts that the asymptotic strength of the association to the tone depends only on the two shock probabilities and on the βs.

If we make the further simplifying assumption that extinction occurs at the same rate as conditioning—$\beta_{us} = \beta_0$—then we see why the theory works. Under these maximally simple parametric assumptions, a scalar isomorphism emerges: the betas disappear from the equations for the asymptotic strengths of the associations, the denominators become equal to 1, and we have:

$$A^*_i = A^*_{ib} - A^*_b = p_{ib} - p_b = p_i.$$

The asymptotic strength of the association to the compound, A^*_{ib}, is equal to the probability of the US in the presence of the compound; the asymptotic strength of the association to the background, A^*_b, is equal to the probability of the US in the presence of the background; and the asymptotic strength of the association to the tone, A^*_i, is the probability of the US in the presence of background and tone minus the probability of the US in the presence of the background. In other words, the quantities formed inside the brain (the associative strengths) are isomorphic to the probability structure of the experienced external world.

In fact, Rescorla and Wagner do not assume that the rate of conditioning is equal to the rate of extinction. This assumption would not be consistent with the data showing good conditioning with partial reinforcement schedules less than 1:2 or with other results (for example, the results of Wagner et al. 1968 on predictive sufficiency). The assumption is made above only to bring out the isomorphism between the associative strengths in the Rescorla-Wagner model and the conditional probability structure of the animal's experience. When the conditioning and extinction βs are not equal, the isomorphism is no longer a scalar isomorphism, but the ordering of the corresponding probabilities is preserved in the ordering of the asymptotic strengths, which is why the theory works as well as it does.

The Importance of Ad Hoc Parametric Assumptions
The capacity of the Rescorla-Wagner model to explain various findings depends on the assumptions one makes about the values of the parameters that enter into its predictions. These assumptions have generally been ad hoc. It is not clear that a consistent set of parametric assumptions exists. It is probably fair to say that parametric assumptions fatal to any given prediction of the theory have been entertained in the context of a discussion of some other set of data. Some examples of this have already been obliquely alluded to. For example, the assumptions that

1. $\lambda\,(i, US \neq 0) = \lambda\,(b, US \neq 0),$

2. $\beta\ (i,US \neq 0) = \beta\ (b,US \neq 0)$,
3.   and $\beta\ (i,0) = \beta\ (b,0)$ were all employed in deriving the prediction that there will be no conditioning when the rate of shock occurrence in the presence of the background alone (CS_b) equals its rate of occurrence in the presence of the tone (CS_i). So was this assumption:
4. subjective trial duration $\ll 2$ hours.

Assumptions contrary to each of these have been made in other contexts. It has been assumed that the rate of association formation between the representatives of two stimuli may depend on how similar the stimuli are (Rescorla and Furrow 1977), in which case assumptions 2 and 3 may be violated, that is, the rates of conditioning and extinction may not be the same for CS_i as for CS_b. It has also been assumed that the asymptotic strength of the association between two stimuli may depend on some special relationship between the internal representatives of those two stimuli (Domjan 1985), in which case assumption 1 may be violated; that is, the maximum possible strengths at asymptote for the associations between CS_i and the US and CS_b and the US may not be the same. It has also been assumed that a trial may last as long as 12 hours (Logue 1979), in which case assumption 4 is violated.

One way to illustrate the tension between the parametric assumptions required in different cases is to put the explanation of the Rescorla (1968) background conditioning data alongside the explanation of the Wagner et al. (1968) data on predictive sufficiency. Recall that Wagner, et al. compared the conditioning produced to a stimulus X, which was paired with two other stimuli, A and B, and with the US in two different ways. In the first case |AX(+),BX(-)|, the pairing AX was invariably accompanied by the US, while the pairing BX was invariably not. There was negligible conditioning to X, despite the fact that X was paired with the US on half the trials. In the second case [AX(+1/2),BX(+1/2)], AX was accompanied by the US on half the trials, and so was BX. This produced strong conditioning to X, although X was paired with the US no more often here than in the first case. The questions are: What parametric assumptions must be made for the Rescorla-Wagner model to explain these two findings? How do these assumptions square with the assumptions that must be made to explain the effects of noncontiguous USs in Rescorla's background conditioning experiments?

In treating the data from the first group, the group for which AX predicted shock with probability 1 and BX predicted it with probability 0, Rescorla and Wagner begin by making the implicit assumption that the experienced probability of shock in the presence of AX was also 1. If the internal trial clock operates independently of the CSs, as it is assumed to do in explaining background conditioning, the experienced probability of shock in the presence of the CS will not be the same as its objective probability because there will be occasions on which an internally timed trial contains only the first part of the CS and not the US (which always came at the end of the CS in the Wagner et al. experiment). When an internally timed trial ends before the US occurs, the occurrence of the CS on that trial is not accompanied by the occurrence of the US; hence the experienced probability of shock in the presence of the CS is less than the objective probability. However, the effect of different assumptions about the subjective trial clock on the experienced probability of shock need not concern us because this probability appears as a scalar factor in the quantities that enter into predicting the difference between the groups. Assuming that $p_{AX} = 1$ and $p_{BX} = 0$, that the associations were all 0 at the beginning of the experiment (because the asymptotic values depend on the initial values), and, for the sake of simplicity, that the saliences of A, B, and X are equal, then the asymptotic value of the association between the representatives of X and the US is .33. (This value is computed from Rescorla and Wagner 1972, p. 84.)

Rescorla and Wagner go on to derive the formula for the asymptotic strength of the same association in the second condition, the pseudodiscrimination condition where the US is paired with AX on half the trials and with BX on half the trials. They then derive the expression for the difference in asymptotic associative strengths in the two conditions. Under the equal CS salience assumptions, this difference is (from Rescorla and Wagner 1972, p. 85):

$$\Delta A_x^* = .5\left(\frac{2\beta_{US}}{\beta_{US} + \beta_0} - 1\right) \tag{12.2}$$

Now the tension becomes apparent: The assumption $\beta_{US} = \beta_0$ makes the predictions for the Rescorla (1968) background conditioning data the prettiest because it makes the associative strengths equal to the occurrence probabilities. However, under this assumption, the factor within parentheses in equation 12.2 becomes equal to 0, which means that the Rescorla-Wagner theory predicts no difference between the two Wagner et al. conditions. To predict that the $AX(+1/2),BX(+1/2)$ group show a bigger conditioned response than the $AX(+),BX(-)$ group, one must assume "that [β_{US}] is considerably larger than [β_0] in the situations they employed." (Rescorla and Wagner 1972, p. 86).

The prediction that the rats in Rescorla's experiment will show no conditioning to CS_i when the background rate of US occurrence equals the rate when CS_i is present does not depend on the values for β_{US} and β_0 (provided these values are both nonzero). One need not—and Rescorla and Wagner do not—assume $\beta_{US} = \beta_0$. However, one is not free to assume whatever relative magnitudes of these parameters will best deal with the Wagner et al. data. If we look at equation 12.1, we see that as β_0 goes to 0 (with β_{US} fixed), the strength of the conditioning to CS_b, the background, goes to 1, the maximum possible value, which means that the strength of conditioning to CS_t, the tone, goes to 0. So we do not want to assume that β_{US} is much bigger than β_0 (though we may need to make this assumption when we come to deal with "thin" partial reinforcement schedules). The bigger the ratio between the rate of conditioning and the rate of extinction, the more conditioning occurs to the background at the expense of the tone in Rescorla's background conditioning experiments.

What Rescorla and Wagner assume in their illustrative calculations is that $\beta_{US} = .1$ and $\beta_0 = .05$, that is, that the rate of extinction is half as fast as the rate of acquisition. The parametric tensions that arise when one tries to use the model to account for different data sets become salient when one plugs these values into the Rescorla-Wagner equations, calculates the asymptotic associative strengths for both Wagner et al. conditions and the Rescorla conditions, and sets these calculated strengths alongside the observed suppression ratios, as I have done in table 12.1. In Rescorla's .4-0 and .2-0 Groups, the calculated asymptotic strengths of the associations to the tone CS are .57 and .33, respectively, and the tone produced complete suppression of responding. In his .1-0 group, the associations were probably not asymptotic, since these rats experienced only six pairings of the tone and the shock. Ignoring this, the calculated asymptotic association between the tone CS and the shock for this group is only .18, yet the tone produced strong but not complete suppression of responding. Now we turn to the Wagner et al. AX(+),BX(−) condition.

Table 12.1
Calculated asymptotic associative strengths and observed suppression ratios in the Rescorla (1968) and Wagner et al. (1968) CER experiments with rats

	Calculated asymptotic associative strength	Observed suppression ratio
Rescorla .4-0 group:	.57	.00 - .02[a]
Rescorla .2-0 group:	.33	.00 - .02[a]
Rescorla .1-0 group:	.18	.20[a]
Wagner et al. AX(+1/2),BX(+1/2):	.50	.045[b] (.06)[c]
Wagner et al. AX(+),BX(-):	.33	.50[b] (.42)[c]

Notes: a. Estimated from day 1 data point in figure 12.2
b. Calculated from the percentage suppression data in table 3 of Wagner et al. (1968, p. 175), using $SR = (1 - S\ \%)/2$
c. The figure obtained if carry-over effects due to the counterbalancing are averaged in.

Rescorla and Wagner (1972, p. 84) give the formula for calculating the asymptotic value of the association to X in this condition. Under the equal CS salience assumption, this value comes out to .33, the same value one gets for Rescorla's .2-0 group. But the suppression ratio in Rescorla's condition was essentially 0 (the maximum observable effect), whereas in the Wagner et al. AX(+),BX(–) condition, the suppression ratio was .42-.50, which means essentially no effect.

The Wagner et al. design was a counterbalanced one in which some of the rats were run first in the $AX(+),BX(-)$ condition, tested for conditioning to X, and then run in the $AX(+1/2),BX(+1/2)$ condition and again tested for conditioning to X, whereas other animals were run in the reverse sequence. The suppression ratio of .50—no suppression at all—was obtained from the rats run first in the $AX(+),BX(-)$ condition. This is the most appropriate value to compare with the Rescorla data because it is clear from examining table 3 in Wagner et al. (1968, p. 175) that there were carry-over effects from one condition to the next. The .42 suppression ratio, which is in any case a marginal effect, is obtained by ignoring the carry-over effects and averaging the suppression ratios observed following $AX(+),BX(-)$ training, whether that training occurred before or after $AX(+1/2),BX(+1/2)$ training. The same is true for the .045 and .06 figures in table 12.1. The .045 suppression ratio, the more appropriate value for comparison purposes, is for the rats trained first on $AX(+1/2),BX(+1/2)$.

If we now use the Rescorla and Wagner (1972, p. 85) equation to calculate how much greater the associative strength should be in the $AX(+1/2),BX(+1/2)$ condition, we get a difference of .17. Adding this to .33, we get an associative strength for this condition of .50. This produced nearly complete suppression, as one would expect given Rescorla's data. The problem, however, is this: from the Rescorla experiments, we conclude that associative strengths of .18 (or possibly less, since the association should not have been asymptotic) produce strong suppression and that strengths between .33 and .57 produce complete suppression. But from the Wagner et al. experiment, we conclude that an associative strength of .33 produces no suppression. To reconcile these findings, we would have to resort to radically different performance assumptions for the two situations. But both experiments used 2- to 3-minute tone or light CSs, shock USs, a CER paradigm, and rats as subjects, so there is little justification for assuming any appreciable difference in the read-out of associative strengths into observed behavior.

Comparisons of performance levels across conditioning experiments are often invalid because the minutiae of experimental design may have a big impact on the observed levels of performance. There may exist some set of performance assumptions that will extricate the model from the dilemma it encounters in trying to explain the Rescorla data on background conditioning and the Wagner et al. data on predictive sufficiency with a single set of parametric assumptions. The discussion does serve, however, to bring out the importance of parametric assumptions in most conditioning models. It also calls attention to the often overlooked fact that the assumptions made to explain one set of data may prove awkward when one considers another experiment. The experiments on background conditioning and predictive sufficiency were the core experimental results that Rescorla and Wagner sought to explain. Yet, for a single set of parametric assumptions (including a single set of assumptions about how associative strengths are translated into observed behavior in a CER paradigm in rats), the results of one experiment are difficult to reconcile with the results of the other within the confines of the proposed model. This suggests that more attention needs to be given to the empirical determination of the values of the various parameters and the manner in which these values depend on various aspects of learning paradigms. Until the values of these parameters are pinned down, it is not possible to say whether the models in fact account for the data they are designed to account for.

Conclusions

The experimental results of the last twenty years have led to a reconceptualization of the associative process, motivated by the discovery that temporal pairing is neither necessary nor sufficient for the formation of an associative connection. Modern theories of conditioning attempt to understand the insufficiency of pairing as a consequence of the newly posited multidimensionality of the associative process. The multidimensionality postulate is the postulate that the change in the associative connection between a CS and a US on a given trial depends on the pretrial strength of the associations between the US and all the active CSs, the other CSs present on a trial. This postulate has been invoked to explain overshadowing, blocking, background conditioning, and the effects of predictive sufficiency, all of which demonstrate that what an animal learns about a given CS-US relation depends on what it learns about the relation between that US and other CSs. The essence of these findings is that an association does not develop between a given CS and the US if other CSs suffice to predict the occurrence of the US. That is why pairing a CS with a US is not a sufficient condition for the formation of an association.

Pairing is not a necessary condition for the formation of an association because it has not been possible to define an empirically valid interstimulus interval function. Robust conditioning can be observed when the CS and US are separated in time by as much as 12 hours and in paradigms where the CS-US interval is 0, negative, or undefinable. It appears that the CS-US interval is not by itself an important determinant of conditioning. Excitatory conditioning depends on the ratio of the CS-US interval to the US-US interval (the duty cycle effect). It occurs when this ratio is small, so that the CS and US are, relatively speaking, co-localized in time. Inhibitory conditioning appears to occur for all those ratios that do not support excitatory conditioning. Thus an association of one kind or the other forms no matter what the temporal relation between the CS and the US, provided it is not a random one.

Wagner (1981) has attempted to revise the model of Rescorla and Wagner (1972) in such a way as to get rid of the internal trial clock, which they postulated to explain background conditioning. His revision deals with some of the findings that indicate that pairing is unnecessary in conditioning. How successfully and how consistently it deals with these data is unclear because it introduces a number of additional free parameters into a model in which there are already many. These new parameters determine how long the representatives of CSs and USs remain in two different discrete states of activity, which in turn determine whether they will contribute to the process of association formation on a given trial. For present purposes, it is sufficient to know that models of associative conditioning are getting much more complex as theorists attempt to come to grips with experimental findings that challenge the foundational assumptions of traditional theories of conditioning.

The computationally complex character of modern associative theories, the strong dependence of their predictions on the values assumed for a variety of free parameters, and the need to posit such things as internal trial clocks, or multiple states of activity for stimulus representations suggest that it may be time to rethink the theoretical and pretheoretical foundations of conditioning theory. One pretheoretical assumption is that learning must be explained in terms of the effects of "individual events," "not correlations or information." The assumption that learning is a process set in motion by the occurrence of particular events is what makes associative theories discrete trial theories. The discrete trials assumption in turn leads to the ubiquitous assumption that it is the probability of US occurrence (rather than the rate) that determines the strength of conditioning. The insistence on conceptualizing the crucial experiential variable in learning as the probability of the US occurring within an interval that constitutes a trial leads in turn to the postulation of internal trial clocks and other theoretical artifices.

Behind the assumption that learning is triggered by the occurrence of events is the still deeper assumption that animals do not have the records required by a learning process that is driven by the global correlation between CS occurrences and US occurrences, the assumption that animals cannot or do not represent the times of occurrence of individual events. To scan the global pattern of CS and US occurrences looking for a statistical dependency requires a mnemonic record analogous to that made by an event recorder, which preserves the time of occurrence of each instance of the CS and the US. In chapter 8, we reviewed experimental findings suggesting that the kinds of animals studied in learning experiments in fact record the times of occurrence of events. If we grant animals tape recorder-like records of what happened when, we need no longer conceptualize learning as an event-initiated process. We may think of it as an ongoing analysis of the event record, designed to extract the statistical dependencies in the record. In this view, what we present the animal with in a learning experiment is, indeed, correlations between events. The learning mechanism is driven by these correlations, not by the individual events, which are important only insofar as they contribute to the global correlation. The next chapter explores the kind of learning theory that we get if we take the import of recent experimental findings at face value: what an animal learns in conditioning experiments is the temporal correlation among stimuli.

Chapter 13

Classical Conditioning: A Representational Theory

The difficulties confronting associative models of conditioning are sufficient to warrant an attempt to reformulate our conception of the phenomena. The phenomena of conditioning have been taken to indicate the growth of an association between the representatives of stimuli co-localized in time. The conception of the associative process has become steadily more cognitive as theorists tried to capture the animals' sensitivity to subtle properties of the relationship between the CS and the US, properties that can be lumped together under the heading of the predictive relationship between the CS and the US. This empirically driven shift in the direction of a more cognitive theory of associative conditioning suggests that it might be instructive to discard our commitment to an associative framework and reconceptualize the phenomena of conditioning in frankly representational terms.

We must begin with the first question in a representational approach to learning phenomena: What property of its experience does the animal represent? What is the objective property of the experienced world that finds expression in an isomorphic system within the animal's nervous system? The model that follows rests on the assumption that conditioning phenomena reflect (1) an animal's representation of the time-lagged effect of variation in one stimulus on variation in the rate or prevalence of another stimulus (conditional rate or conditional prevalence) and (2) an animal's representation of the statistical uncertainty of its conditional rate and prevalence estimates.

The central problems the model deals with are two. First, there is the *multivariate problem:* the problem of ascribing the observed rates of occurrence or prevalence to the various stimuli and combinations of stimuli that may be imagined to condition those rates and prevalences in a time-dependent manner—the problem of determining what predicts what. This problem was brought into clear view by the experimental findings that led to the multidimensionality assumptions in contemporary associative theories of conditioning, the findings demonstrating that when experience indicated that a US was predicted by stimulus A, stimulus B did not get conditioned (did not get treated as a predictor of the US no matter how often it was paired with the US).

The second general problem is the *problem of time*. This is the area in which contemporary theories of conditioning are most deficient because there is no explicit representation of time and temporal relations in most associative models (the models of Wagner 1981 and Gibbon and Balsam 1981 to some extent excepted).

The Rate-Prevalence Distinction

The rate of occurrence of a temporally discrete US is the average number of instances of the stimulus per unit of time. If the probability of another occurrence within the next "instant" (very short interval) does not vary as a function of the time elapsed since the last occurrence, then the instances are said to occur at a random rate. The rate itself is not random; rather the average number of occurrences per unit time (the rate) is fixed but the intervals between occurrences vary randomly, which means that the length of the interval that has elapsed since the last occurrence is uncorrelated with the probability that there will be another occurrence in the next instant. The paradigmatic physical example of an event or stimulus with a random rate of occurrence is the rate of radioactive emissions. An atom of a radioactive substance emits an electron with a probability per unit time specific for that substance. The net rate of emissions is a function of the amount of the substance (the number of atoms). For a given amount of a given substance, the probability that one will observe an emission in any 1 millisecond is independent of the number of milliseconds that have elapsed since the last emission. Such processes are called Poisson processes. Their statistical properties are simple and well understood.

In the model to be elaborated, it is assumed that the brain represents rates of occurrence as the consequences of Poisson processes, even when they are not. In the statistics of rate, the assumption of a Poisson process is the default assumption, in much the way that the assumption of a normal distribution is the default assumption in the statistics of randomly varying scalar variables like height and weight. It is the assumption made when there is no a priori knowledge that would dictate a different assumption. It is the pattern of occurrences to which things tend when a large number of uncorrelated causes are operative, as is typically the case for the causes that determine the appearances of prey. The likelihood that one field mouse will emerge from hiding at a given moment is more or less independent of the likelihood that another will. Hence, the appearances of field mice in the area being scanned by a predator conform approximately to a random rate process—that is, to a Poisson process.

In treating the rate of occurrence of a US as a Poisson process, one assumes that the duration of an occurrence is negligible; hence the probability that two occurrences coincide or overlap in time is effectively zero. One also assumes that the USs are all or nothing; they do not vary in magnitude. For the USs most commonly used in conditioning experiments— brief noxious stimuli or small quickly consumed amounts of nutrients— both of these assumptions are approximately true. If, as is generally true in conditioning experiments, the amount of shock or the amount of food given in any one occurrence of the US is fixed, then two occurrences of the US never coincide and the USs are all or nothing. Thus, one can deal with most conditioning experiments by focusing only on the rate of occurrence of the US, which is what I will do in the first model to be presented.

However, if we move outside the context of the usual conditioning experiment to consider the world the experiments are meant to epitomize, limiting our vision to the representation of rate alone is inadequate for the general case. Motivationally significant stimuli routinely vary in magnitude and often last long periods of time. Nausea, for example, varies in both magnitude and duration, and so do periods of high or low environmental temperatures. These variables function very well as USs in conditioning experiments (Ollove 1980; Revusky and Garcia 1970). When the US is present during a substantial fraction of the observation interval and varies in its strength, then the behaviorally relevant aspects of that stimulus cannot be represented in terms of the random rate of occurrence of a temporally discrete all-or-nothing event. In such cases, what needs to be represented is the prevalence of the US.

The prevalence of a scalar variable (a stimulus that varies in its magnitude or intensity or amount) is its value per unit of time. The last part of this chapter sketches in the concepts and computations by which the model may be expanded to deal with prevalence as well as rate. Because the mathematics will be unfamiliar to most readers, this more ambitious form of the model is portrayed only in broad strokes. The intention is to make the reader familiar with the conceptual basis for the model and with the nature of the computations involved in realizing such a model rather than to make detailed derivations from the model. My purposes in formulating a model are to show what a frankly representational approach to the phenomena of conditioning might look like and to compare such a model with an associative model that also treats the US as a temporally discrete all-or-nothing variable (the Rescorla-Wagner model). Hence I consider in detail only the special case in which the relevant dimension of variation in the US is its rate of occurrence.

The Model

The model for conditioning with discrete USs builds directly on the conclusions of the preceding chapters on the representation of time of occurrence, temporal intervals, number, and rate. It assumes that the animal has a record of what occurred when, that it can segment this record into the temporal intervals over which a given CS was present, that it can sum these intervals, that it can count the number of occurrences of the US in each such interval, and that it can sum the number of occurrences of the US during different intervals of CS presence to obtain the total number of USs observed in the presence of a given CSs. The quantities thus obtained—representing the total time over which a given CS has been observed to be present and the total number of USs observed in that time—are the basic variables with which the computations to be described operate. The products of these computations are estimates of the rates of occurrence of the US to be expected in the presence of various CSs (conditional rates), together with representations of the statistical uncertainties regarding the true values of the conditional rate estimates.

Since many different CSs might condition (help determine) the rate of US occurrence, the central challenge is to constrain the estimation procedure in such a way that the process identifies the minimum number of conditioning stimuli required to account for the systematic variation in the observed rate of occurrence of the US and converges on the appropriate estimate of the extent to which each CS conditions the rate of occurrence of the US.

Constraining Principles

The computational system that estimates the predictive power of CSs is assumed to be so constructed that it operates in accord with certain principles that are the foundation of the model in that they guide its computational implementation. They are the heart of the theory.

The additivity principle. The system requires that the rates attributed to the influence of individual CSs sum (within the limits of statistical certainty) to the rates observed during periods when more than one CS is present. CSs are assumed to exercise independent and additive influence on observed rates unless no independent (additive) solution is possible. When no additive solution is possible, the system tries conjoint solutions, in which two or more CSs are assumed to influence the observed rates conjointly. When two or more CSs are treated as a conjoint CS, the conjunction of the CSs is treated as a single (compound) CS. A conjoint CS is present only so long as its constituents are all present. When forced by the data to try solutions involving conjointly acting CSs, the system always considers solutions involving minimal conjunctions first. Solutions involving only the conjunction of two CSs are sought before those involving the conjunction of three CSs.

The additivity assumption does much the same work in this model as the corresponding additivity assumption in the Rescorla-Wagner model—the assumption that the increment in associative strength on a given trial is the asymptote-determining parameter minus the sum of the associative strengths for the CSs present on a given trial. For example, in an overshadowing experiment, where two CSs are always presented together, the additivity constraint requires that the rates ascribed to the individual CSs sum to the rate of US occurrence actually observed during the periods of their joint presence. If the entire rate of US occurrence observed is ascribed to the influence of one of the two CSs, the rate ascribed to the other must be zero.

The inertia principle. The influence of a CS on the rate of occurrence of a US is taken as constant over all intervals in which the CS has been present unless the resulting solution predicts a rate of US occurrence during some period that is statistically irreconcilable with the rate observed during that period. This principle requires a computation designed to assess whether the rates predicted conform to the rates observed. This computation detects changes in the influence of a CS, such as occur in the extinction conditions of standard conditioning experiments, when the US ceases to occur in the presence of a CS. If, in accord with the inertia principle, the system obtains an estimate of the rate of US occurrence to be ascribed to a CS by averaging over the training and extinction periods, then the rate predicted for the training period will not be statistically reconcilable with the rate observed during that period (it will be too low) and similarly for the extinction period (the predicted rate will not be 0, but the observed rate will in fact have been 0). The computation associated with the inertia principle detects the cases in which the data are inconsistent with the assumption that the influence of a CS has been constant.

The first two principles may be summarized by saying that unless it has to, the system does not entertain solutions in which CSs act interactively (conjointly) or in which different rates are ascribed to a CS during different epochs. The system treats CSs as compounds (conjointly acting stimuli that have no independent effects) only when the observed pattern of US occurrences is statistically irreconcilable with an independent additive effects model, and it separates the periods of CS presence into different epochs only when the data are statistically irreconcilable with a model in which the effects of a given CS or combination of CSs have been constant across all the periods when those CSs were present.

Uncertainty minimization.   When the first two constraints do not yield a unique ascription of rate predictions to various CSs that might influence the rate, then the system adopts the ascription that minimizes the average statistical uncertainty factor associated with the nonzero rate predictors. The uncertainty factor associated with a rate prediction is the multiplicative confidence interval surrounding the estimate of the rate of US occurrence predicted by the presence of the CS. The uncertainty factor associated with a predicted rate is the confidence interval for the prediction. It represents the statistical uncertainty regarding the true value of the prediction. For a given total number of observed USs, the fewer the CSs predicting those occurrences, the narrower the confidence intervals surrounding their predictions, that is, the less the average uncertainty of the predictions. Hence this constraint serves to minimize the number of CSs to which a nonzero influence on rate is ascribed.

This constraint comes into play in situations in which there is more than one way (usually an infinite number of ways) to apportion the observed rates of US occurrence to the influence of different CSs in a manner consistent with the first two constraints. For example, in overshadowing experiments, any partitioning of the observed rate among the two CSs that are always present together is consistent with both rate additivity and rate inertia. Similarly, in the predictive sufficiency experiment of Wagner et al. (1968), there is an infinite number of rate ascriptions consistent with the experimentally arranged occurrences of the CSs and USs. In all such cases, the uncertainty minimization constraint drives the ascriptions to the solution that minimizes the number of CSs to which a nonzero influence on the rate is ascribed.

The Response Rule

The response to a conditioned CS is a function of the magnitude of the change in the rate of US occurrence predicted by the presence of the CS and the uncertainty regarding the magnitude of that change.

The uncertainty regarding the effect of a CS on the rate of US occurrence is greatest when the US is first experienced. The first few occurrences of the US in the presence of a CS give rise on average to a correct estimate of the rate predicted by that CS because rate estimates, unlike associative strengths, do not change systematically with continued experience of a constant CS-US relationship: the number of occurrences of a US divided by the interval of observation yields an unbiased estimate of the rate no matter how small the number of occurrences. What increases as the number of observed USs increases is the certainty of the estimate, not the estimate itself. Estimates based on a very few observations of the US are highly variable. As the number of observations on which estimates of rate are based increases, the variability in those estimates decreases. If we follow the evolution of rate estimates as more and more USs accumulate, we see that sometimes an estimate increases because the timing of the first few US occurrences produced an erroneously low initial estimate, and sometimes it decreases because the timing of the first few USs produced an erroneously high estimate. Thus the direction in which an estimate moves under the impact of further experience with a constant CS-US relationship (a constant random rate of US occurrence in the presence of the given CS) is unsystematic. However, as the number of observed USs increases, all estimates of its rate of occurrence move toward the correct value (the true rate) from whatever somewhat erroneous value the first few observations happen to produce. Thus the uncertainty associated with an estimated rate decreases as the number of US occurrences attributed to the CS increases. The decrease in this uncertainty accounts for the increasing strength of the animal's response to the CS in a conditioning experiment (figure 13.1).

The form of the learning curve is assumed to be a function solely of the probability, p, that the rate of US occurrence is different in the presence of the CS. This function, $f(p)$, is assumed to be monotonic but nonlinear; it increases very slowly until $1-p$, the probability that the CS makes no difference in the rate of US occurrence, approaches a critical value, α,

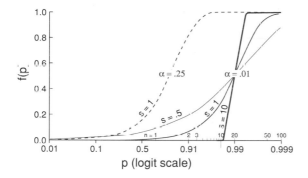

Figure 13.1
The function $f(p)$ for various values of its parameters, α and s. This function is the component of the performance function that changes in the course of learning, giving rise to the growth in the strength of responding. The increasing strength of responding is assumed to be a function of the increasing probability (p) that the CS makes a difference in the rate of US occurrence. The parameter α is equivalent to the critical value in a test of statistical significance. The parameter s determines how abruptly the strength of responding grows as $1-p$ approaches the critical value. The values of n just above the abscissa give the number of "trials" (reinforced CS occurrences) required to attain the corresponding value of p in an autoshaping experiment like that of Gibbon et al. (1977), with an ITI:ISI ratio of ten (for example, a 10 second CS and a 100 second intertrial interval).

then it rises rapidly to its asymptote as $1-p$ drops below the critical value. An example of a function with the requisite form is:

$$f(p) = 1 - 2^{-[(\alpha p/(1-p))^s]}$$

which is graphed in figure 13.1 for various values of α and s. Note that α plays the role of the critical level in hypothesis-testing statistics, the level of improbability that must be reached for the null or no-difference hypothesis to be rejected. The smaller the value of α, the more statistically conservative the animal is, that is, the more certain it must be that the CS makes a difference before it is inclined to respond. The s parameter determines the abruptness with which the learning curve rises as $1-p$ approaches the critical value α. The greater the value of s, the more abruptly the learning curve rises.

The rates of US occurrence in the presence (λ_{CS}) and absence (λ_B) of the CS do not affect the form of the learning curve, they only scale it. The scaling factor is $g(\lambda_{CS}, \lambda_B)$. The learning curve is the product of this scaling factor and $f(p)$. The form of the function for the scaling factor, $g(\lambda_{CS}, \lambda_B)$, must vary from one experimental paradigm to the next, because the values of the scaled learning function, $g(\lambda_{CS}, \lambda_B)f(p)$, must conform to experimentally recorded numbers, whose range is determined by the apparatus and the scoring procedure. In the case of the autoshaping paradigm, which Gibbon et al. (1977) used to demonstrate that the rate of conditioning depends on the ratio of CS intervals to nonCS (intertrial) intervals, an appropriate form might be:

$$g(\lambda_{CS}, \lambda_B) = A \frac{\lambda_{CS}}{\lambda_{CS} + \lambda_B + k}$$

where A is the maximum possible rate of responding and k is a threshold parameter, specifying what constitutes a negligibly low rate of US occurrence. Note that when λ_B (the rate of US occurrence in the absence of the CS) is an appreciable fraction of λ_{CS} (the rate in the presence of the CS), the asymptotic rate of responding to the CS will be reduced. Note also that when $\lambda_{CS} \gg \lambda_B + k$, $g(\lambda_{CS}, \lambda_B) \approx A$, in which case the observed learning function will be approximately $Af(p)$. That is, when the estimated rate of US occurrence in the presence of the CS is far from negligible and much greater than the estimated background rate, then the growth of responding over trials will be determined almost entirely by the increasing certainty that λ_{CS} differs from 0. Precisely these conditions obtain in experiments like those of Gibbon et al. (1977).

The Statistics of Poisson Processes
A Poisson process is the mathematical idealization of a random series of point events, a series entirely defined by a rate parameter, λ, which speci-

fies the average number of occurrences per unit time. When the rate parameter does not vary, the Poisson process has the following computationally convenient (and unique) properties:

1. The number of events observed in any given interval divided by that interval is an unbiased estimate of the rate of US occurrence, provided only that the choice of the starting point of the time interval over which USs are counted does not depend on a property of the series of USs. The proviso means that one cannot, for example, choose to start the interval over which USs are to be counted 1 second before the first US. If the starting point of the interval is chosen in this sort of post hoc and retrospective way, the estimate of the rate when the first US has just occurred is 1 per second no matter what the rate actually is. One forces the estimate to have this value at the moment when the first US has just occurred by choosing the starting point retrospectively on the basis of the time of occurrence of an event in the series of events whose rate is to be estimated. On the other hand, one can start the interval immediately after the first US is observed or at any latency thereafter (so that the first US is not counted). This is because in a Poisson process the amount of time one has to wait to observe the second US is independent of how long after the first event one waits before beginning one's observations. This property of random rate processes is counterintuitive. It means, for example, that if major earthquakes occur randomly at a certain rate in a given region, an observer who begins an earthquake watch the day after a major quake will on average have to wait just as long to observe the second quake as will an observer who begins his watch a half-century later. What changes as the latency to the onset of observation increases is not the expected amount of time between the beginning of the watch and the next ensuing occurrence of an event but rather the likelihood that the second occurrence will have taken place before the beginning of the watch. One can also determine the end of the interval on the basis of the occurrence of an event. Provided that the starting point of the interval is independently chosen, N/T is an unbiased estimate of rate when T is the time taken to observe N events. It follows that one also gets an unbiased estimate by additively combining the observed Ns (counts) and observed Ts (time intervals taken to achieve a given count) from nonoverlapping observation periods, provided again that the starting points of these nonoverlapping intervals are not chosen retrospectively on the basis of a time of US occurrence. In practice the total time a CS has been present divided by the number of USs that have occurred in its presence is an unbiased estimate of the rate of US occurrence.

2. When two or more independent Poisson processes operate concurrently, the numbers of events expected in a unit of time are additive. If one

expects to observe two events per unit time from the first process and five events per unit time from the second, the expected number of events per unit time when the processes operate concurrently is seven. More formally, the sum of two independent Poisson processes with rate parameters λ_1 and λ_2 is itself a Poisson process with rate parameter $\lambda_1 + \lambda_2$.

3. The upper and lower uncertainty factors for an estimate, λ, of a true rate of occurrence, Λ, are a function solely of N.[1] If an interval of observation, T, includes only one occurrence of the event, then $\lambda = 1/T$, and the chances are less than 10 percent that Λ is greater than $2.3(1/T)$ and the chances are less than 10 percent that Λ is less than $.1(1/T)$. The factors 2.3 and .1 are the uncertainty factors for an estimate based on a single occurrence of the event. The products of the estimate and these factors $(2.3\lambda$ and $.1\lambda)$ give the 80 percent confidence interval (the interval within which one can be 80 percent confident that Λ lies). Since these are multiplicative rather than additive factors, it is appropriate to measure the interval they delimit (the confidence interval) on a logarithmic scale. When an estimate of rate is based on a single occurrence of the event, the logarithmic confidence interval is $\log(2.3) - \log(.1) = 1.36$. If one observes 10 occurrences of the event in the interval T (rather than only one 1), the chances are less than 10 percent that the true value is greater than $1.4(10/T)$ and less than 10 percent that it is less than $.62(10/T)$. Thus, for a rate estimate based on 10 events, the logarithmic confidence interval is $\log(1.4) - \log(.62) = .41$, an interval more than three times narrower than the interval after a single observed occurrence. The logarithmic confidence interval, which specifies the inherent uncertainty about the true value of Λ after a limited number of observations, depends only on the number of events used in computing λ, not on the time intervals (see figures 13.2 and 13.3).

The processes that govern the rates of occurrence of events are frequently not in fact Poisson processes. However, because of the simplicity of the computational operations required in dealing with a Poisson process, I assume that the design of the relevant brain circuitry reflects the fact that other probabilistic occurrence processes can be usefully approximated by Poisson processes with time-dependent rate parameters.

Computational Realization
I now describe how the principles of the model are translated into computational procedures, algorithms that are meant to describe the brain processes that occur during classical conditioning experiments,

1. Formulae for computing the confidence limits for a given N are given on p. 30 of Cox and Lewis (1966).

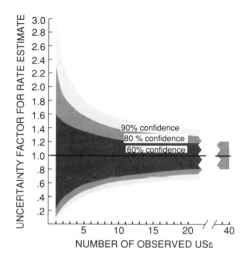

Figure 13.2
Uncertainty factors for the estimate of the Poisson rate of occurrence of a US as a function of the number of USs on which the estimate is based. Uncertainty factors, when multiplied times the rate estimate, give the limits beyond which the true rate is unlikely to lie; that is, they give the confidence interval.

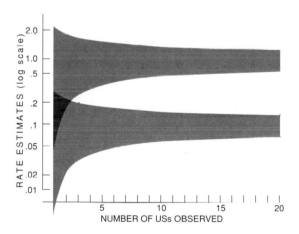

Figure 13.3
Another way to think about uncertainty is that an estimate of a rate is not a point but rather a vertical blur. What is represented here is the 90 percent confidence blurs for the estimates of two different rates differing by an order of magnitude—a rate of 0.1 per minute and a rate of 1 per minute. If the rate estimates are represented on a log scale, the vertical extent of the blur is the same for all estimates based on a given number of US occurrences.

and I deduce from this computational model the results of the various classical conditioning experiments described in the preceding chapter.

It is assumed that the system keeps a running total of (1) the amount of time that each CS has been present [T_1, T_2, etc.]; (2) the amount of time each pairwise combination of CSs has been present [$T_{1,2}$, $T_{1,3}$, $T_{2,3}$, etc.]; and (3) the number of USs in the presence of each CS [N_1, N_2, etc.]. The numerical totals ignore combinations of CSs; the total N for a given CS is accumulated without regard to whatever other CSs were present. The growth of the temporal and numerical totals over time during an initial segment of a background conditioning experiment like Rescorla (1968) is portrayed in figure 13.4. The rate ascribed to each CS at any point in time is computed from the totals accumulated up to that time.

An uncorrected estimate of the rate of US occurrence in the presence of a given CS is the total number of USs observed in the presence of that CS divided by the total amount of time that CS has been present. It is called the uncorrected rate estimate because it does not take into account the

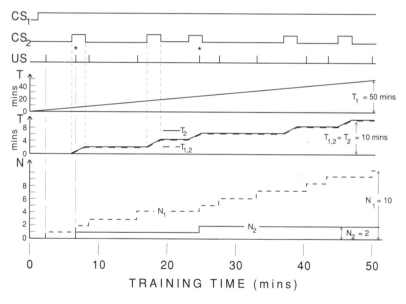

Figure 13.4
Schematic representation of the first 50 minutes of a background conditioning experiment like Rescorla (1968). The time lines at the top indicate the presence (up) or absence (down) of each CS and the US. CS_1 is the background (the experimental apparatus), which is present throughout the session. Asterisks mark those USs that occur in the presence of CS_2 (the tone). The three graphs portray the accumulation of the quantities that enter into the computation of the rates of US occurrence to be attributed to the influence of each CS.

presence of other CSs during part or all of the time the CS in question was present. This computation attributes all the occurrences of the USs in the presence of a given CS to the influence of that CS, regardless of what other CSs were present. For example, if two CSs were always present together, all the USs would be attributed to each CS; hence the sum of the uncorrected rate attributions would not match the rate of US occurrence actually observed (it would be twice that rate). Thus uncorrected rate estimates do not conform to the additivity principle.

To estimate the rate properly ascribed to any one CS, the system must correct the raw estimates of rate for the effects of other CSs. The making of these corrections is an exercise in solving systems of simultaneous equations. The unknowns are the corrected rate estimates, the rates of US occurrence properly ascribable to each CS. The coefficients of the unknowns are determined by the temporal intervals during which pairs of CSs have been present simultaneously. For example, in the case of an experiment with two CSs, the additivity constraint requires that:

$$\frac{N_1}{T_1} = \lambda_1 + \frac{T_{1,2}}{T_1}\lambda_2 \qquad\qquad (13.1)$$

and

$$\frac{N_2}{T_2} = \frac{T_{1,2}}{T_2}\lambda_1 + \lambda_2, \qquad\qquad (13.2)$$

where N_1 is the number of USs observed in the presence of CS_1; N_2, the number observed in the presence of CS_2; T_1, the total interval over which CS_1 has been observed to be present, T_2, the total interval for CS_2, $T_{1,2}$, the total interval over which CS_1 and CS_2 were present together, and λ_1 and λ_2, the unknowns, that is, the correct estimates of the rate of US occurrence in the presence of CS_1 alone and CS_2 alone. Equation 13.1 says that the uncorrected rate of US occurrence in the presence of CS_1, (N_1/T_1), is equal to the true rate (λ_1) plus an error term. The error term arises during intervals when CS_2 is present as well. The error term is equal to the rate properly ascribed to CS_2 (λ_2) multiplied by the proportion of CS_1 time that CS_2 was also present $(T_{1,2}/T_1)$. Equation 13.2 makes the corresponding assertion regarding the raw rate for CS_2. In finding the values of λ_1 and λ_2 that simultaneously satisfy these two equations, we find the corrected rate attributions. The corrected rates conform to the additivity principle: the observed rate of US occurrence during the presence of more than one CS is the sum of the corrected rates ascribed to each CS present.

The logic that led to these simultaneous equations applies to any conditioning experiment. The more CSs there are, the greater is the number of simultaneous equations. Each additional CS yields an additional unknown—the true rate of US occurrence predicted by that CS acting alone—and an additional equation. The additional equation has the form of equations 13.1 and 13.2. The uncorrected or raw rate estimate for a given CS appears on the left-hand side of the equation. The unknowns—the corrected rate estimates symbolized by subscripted λs—appear on the right-hand side of the equation. The coefficient of the unknown λ for the given CS is 1, and the coefficient for each other λ is the ratio between the interval when its CS and the given CS were present together (regardless of what other CSs may also have been present) and the total interval for the given CS.

Matrix algebra systematizes the solving of systems of simultaneous equations. The coefficients of the unknowns in a solvable system of simultaneous equations form a square matrix. The matrix is square because, for the system to be solvable, there must be as many equations as there are unknowns. Each unknown may be imagined to appear in each equation because the failure of an unknown to appear in an equation is equivalent to its having a coefficient of 0. Thus, if there are four equations, the coefficients that define the right-hand sides of the equations consist of four rows (one row for each equation) of four coefficients each (one coefficient for each unknown). The coefficients of the unknowns form a table (matrix) of four columns by four rows. The values of the coefficients in this matrix, together with the values of the "inhomogeneous" terms that appear on the left-hand sides of the equations, determine the values of the unknowns. The terms on the left-hand side are called inhomogeneous because, unlike the terms on the right-hand side, they do not involve the product of a coefficient (a variable whose value is known) and an unknown. The inhomogeneous terms are simply variables whose value is known. In the present case, they are the uncorrected estimates of rates, $N_1/T_1, N_2/T_2,$ and so on, whose values are known, because the values of $N_1, N_2, T_1, T_2,$ and so on are known (figure 13.4).

The solving of a system of simultaneous equations corresponds to computing the inverse of the coefficient matrix and multiplying this inverse matrix by the vector of inhomogeneous terms. The string of values constituting the corrected rates is called the corrected rate vector, and symbolized by λ_c. Thus $\lambda_c = <\lambda_1, \lambda_2...>$, where the λs in normal type face represent the corrected rates and the λ_c in bold typeface represents the whole set of corrected rates. Thus, solving the system of equations corresponds to computing the corrected rate vector. The left-hand sides of these equations (the inhomogeneous terms) are the uncorrected rate estimates, called the *uncorrected rate vector* and symbolize by λ_u:

$$\lambda_u = \left\langle \frac{N_1}{T_1}, \frac{N_2}{T_2} \right\rangle$$

The temporal totals form the temporal coefficient matrix, symbolized *T*. The temporal coefficient matrix for the case where four different CSs are present is:

$$
T_4 = \begin{vmatrix}
1 & \dfrac{T_{1,2}}{T_1} & \dfrac{T_{1,3}}{T_1} & \dfrac{T_{1,4}}{T_1} \\
\dfrac{T_{1,2}}{T_2} & 1 & \dfrac{T_{2,3}}{T_2} & \dfrac{T_{2,4}}{T_2} \\
\dfrac{T_{1,3}}{T_3} & \dfrac{T_{2,3}}{T_3} & 1 & \dfrac{T_{3,4}}{T_3} \\
\dfrac{T_{1,4}}{T_4} & \dfrac{T_{2,4}}{T_4} & \dfrac{T_{3,4}}{T_4} & 1
\end{vmatrix}
$$

The 4-CS temporal coefficient matrix is given because:

1. Few conditioning experiments employ more than four CSs, so the matrix given enables one to make the computational analysis for almost any experiment.
2. The matrix reveals the regular pairwise combinations of temporal totals that compose the coefficients. From this pattern, it is evident how to form still larger matrices.
3. In experiments with fewer than four CSs, one obtains the (smaller) temporal coefficient matrix by plugging in 0s for every coefficient that contains a *T* with a supernumerary subscript. For example, Rescorla's background conditioning experiment (figure 13.4) has only two CSs—the tone and the apparatus itself (the background CS). Thus, every coefficient with a *T* whose subscripts include a number larger than 2 is 0 and the temporal coefficient matrix collapses to:

$$
T_2 = \begin{vmatrix}
1 & \dfrac{T_{1,2}}{T_1} \\
\dfrac{T_{1,2}}{T_2} & 1
\end{vmatrix}
$$

The coefficients appearing in this matrix are the coefficients for the unknowns in equations 13.1 and 13.2, while the inhomogeneous terms in these equations, the terms on the left-hand side, are given by λ_u, the uncorrected rate vector. The system computes the corrected rate vector, λ_c, in multiplying the uncorrected rate vector, λ_u, by the inverse of the temporal coefficient matrix, T^{-1}. Thus, the essence of the computational model is contained in the matrix algebra formula:

$$\lambda_c = T^{-1}\lambda_u. \qquad \text{(M)}$$

Programs for inverting square matrices are part of math packages for microcomputers and scientifically oriented pocket calculators. The complete model is easily implemented on microcomputer spreadsheet programs that permit matrix (array) operations. To follow the discussion below, one needs to know that the computation of what is called the determinant of the matrix reveals whether the system of equations has a unique solution, which is often not apparent simply from examining the equations. If the determinant of the matrix is 0, the matrix does not have an inverse, and a unique solution to the corresponding system of equations does not exist.

In deriving the computational model given by equation M, I used both the additivity principle and the inertia principle. The system of simultaneous equations arises from the additivity principle, which stipulates that the corrected rates (those ascribed to each CS acting alone) must sum to the rates actually observed during intervals when more than one CS is present. In composing the coefficients in the temporal coefficient matrix from the temporal totals for the entire period of observation, I used the inertia principle, which says that in the absence of evidence to the contrary, the rate to be ascribed to a given CS is assumed to be the same during all intervals when the CS was present. Obviously this principle will not always be valid. The model requires a computation indicating when the inertia assumption is inconsistent with what has been observed. However, the model given by equation M, together with the uncertainty minimization principle, accounts for the salient results in the modern classical conditioning literature, the results that have necessitated far-reaching revisions in the assumptions of associative models of conditioning. It also accounts for several findings that revised (multidimensional) models of the association-forming process do not account for. The derivation of these results from the computation model given by equation M follows. The role of the uncertainty minimization principle will be made clear when it becomes relevant. These derivations have been verified by plugging the training regimes from the experiments cited into a spreadsheet realization of the model.

Background conditioning. In the background conditioning experiment (figure 13.4), CS_1 is the always present background (the experimental apparatus); hence $T_{1,2} = T_2$ and equations 13.1 and 13.2 become:

$$\frac{N_1}{T_1} = \lambda_1 + \frac{T_2}{T_1}\lambda_2 \qquad \text{(13.1')}$$

and

$$\frac{N_2}{T_2} = \lambda_1 + \lambda_2. \tag{13.2'}$$

Solving for λ_2 yields:

$$\lambda_2 = \frac{\dfrac{N_2}{T_2} - \dfrac{N_1}{T_1}}{1 - \dfrac{T_2}{T_1}}. \tag{13.3}$$

If the rate during CS_2 is the same as the background rate (as in figure 13.4), the numerator of equation 13.3 is equal to zero; hence the rate of US occurrence attributed to CS_2 is 0. The animal should not react to CS_2 as though it predicted any change in the rate of US occurrence, and this is just what Rescorla (1968) in fact found. On the other hand, if all the USs that fall during the background alone are suppressed, leaving only the USs marked with an asterisk in figure 13.4, then $N_1 = N_2 = N$ and equation 13.3 yields:

$$\lambda_2 = \frac{N}{T_2}.$$

The rate attributed to CS_2 is the number of shocks observed divided by the time that CS_2 was on. The animal should attribute all the observed shocks to the influence of CS_2 and react accordingly, which was what Rescorla found in the groups in which the background shocks were suppressed. Intermediate cases, where USs occur at a lower but nonzero rate in the absence of the CS, yield intermediate solutions; the rate ascribed to the CS is the rate observed during the CS minus the rate observed in the absence of the CS.

The explicitly unpaired case. The explicitly unpaired experiment is the complement of the case just considered. Rather than suppressing the shocks that occur when only the background (CS_1) is present, the experimenter suppresses the shocks scheduled to occur when the tone (CS_2) is present. In this case, $N_2 = 0$, $N_1 = N$ and equation 13.3 yields:

$$\lambda_2 = \frac{-\dfrac{N}{T_1}}{1 - \dfrac{T_2}{T_1}}.$$

The rate of US occurrence attributed to CS_2 is negative, that is, CS_2 reduces the rate of US occurrence. One would expect the animal to react accordingly and it does: if the US is motivationally positive, the animal avoids CS_2, if the US is aversive, the animal seeks CS_2.

The effect of having the *"background" USs predicted by another CS*　Giving USs at times other than when CS_2 is present does not reduce conditioning to CS_2 provided the other USs are signaled by a third CS_3, which does not co-occur with CS_2 (Goddard and Jenkins 1987; Rescorla 1984). This result is difficult for the model of Gibbon and Balsam (1981), which is akin to the present model in taking time explicitly into account. This result is, however, predicted by the present model. The simultaneous equations in the general 3-CS case may be written:

$$\lambda_1 = \frac{N_1}{T_1} - \frac{T_{1,2}}{T_1}\lambda_2 - \frac{T_{1,3}}{T_1}\lambda_3 \tag{13.4}$$

$$\lambda_2 = \frac{N_2}{T_2} - \frac{T_{1,2}}{T_2}\lambda_1 - \frac{T_{2,3}}{T_2}\lambda_3 \tag{13.5}$$

$$\lambda_3 = \frac{N_3}{T_3} - \frac{T_{1,3}}{T_3}\lambda_1 - \frac{T_{2,3}}{T_3}\lambda_2 \tag{13.6}$$

In the experiments in which a second, nonbackground CS (such as a flashing light) signals all the USs not signaled by the first nonbackground CS (such as a tone), let the background be designated CS_1, the tone CS_2, and the flashing light CS_3. The experimental conditions are such that:

$$N_1 = N_2 + N_3 \quad T_{1,2} = T_2 \quad T_{1,3} = T_3 \quad T_{2,3} = 0.$$

Substituting these equalities into equations 13.4 through 13.6 yields:

$$\lambda_1 = \frac{N_2 + N_3}{T_1} - \frac{T_2}{T_1}\lambda_2 - \frac{T_3}{T_1}\lambda_3$$

$$\lambda_2 = \frac{N_2}{T_2} - \lambda_1 - 0$$

$$\lambda_3 = \frac{N_3}{T_3} - \frac{T_{1,3}}{T_3}\lambda_1 - 0.$$

One may check that $\lambda_c = <\lambda_1,\lambda_2,\lambda_3> = \left\langle 0, \frac{N_2}{T_2}, \frac{N_3}{T_3}\right\rangle$ is the solution by plugging these values for the λs into the simplified equations.[2] In other words, when another CS signals the "background" USs, the present model predicts that these USs lose their capacity to block conditioning, which is in accord with the experimental findings.

---

2. The simplified determinant is $1 - \frac{T_2}{T_1} - \frac{T_3}{T_1}$ which is not 0, when $T_3 + T_2 \neq T_1$, so the solution is unique.

Blocking. As in the Rescorla-Wagner model, background conditioning and blocking are examples of the same thing. The explanation of the results of blocking experiments is basically the same as that of the background conditioning experiments, except that there are three CSs present: the two intermittent CSs (for example, the blocking tone and the blocked light, CS_2 and CS_3, respectively) and the background (the apparatus, CS_1). CS_2 is always present when CS_3 is present, and it is also present without CS_3, at which times USs occur at the same rate as they do when both CS_2 and CS_3 are present; hence, CS_2 functions as a "local" background. In a blocking experiment, the following equalities hold:

$$N_2 = N_1 \qquad N_3 = \frac{T_3}{T_2} N_2 \qquad T_{1,2} = T_2 \qquad T_{1,3} = T_{2,3} = T_3.$$

Substituting these into equations 13.4 through 13.6 yields:

$$\lambda_1 = \frac{N_2}{T_1} - \frac{T_2}{T_1}\lambda_2 - \frac{T_3}{T_1}\lambda_3$$

$$\lambda_2 = \frac{N_2}{T_2} - \lambda_1 - \frac{T_3}{T_2}\lambda_3$$

$$\lambda_3 = \frac{N_2}{T_2} - \lambda_1 - \lambda_2$$

One may check that $\lambda_c = \left\langle 0, \dfrac{N_2}{T_2}, 0 \right\rangle$ is the solution by plugging these values into the simplified equations.[3] Thus, all the US occurrences are attributed to CS_2. The solution specifies a rate of 0 for the background, not surprising since no USs occur in the presence of the background alone. To simplify the mathematical analysis (to reduce the number of simultaneous equations by one), the background will hereafter be ignored in the experiments in which USs never occur in the presence of the background alone. When the background is ignored, the mathematical analysis of blocking is identical to the analysis of the effects of background conditioning.

An important difference between the account of blocking in the Rescorla-Wagner model and this account is that conditioning with CS_2, the blocking CS, must precede conditioning with CS_2 and CS_3 together in the Rescorla-Wagner model, while in the present model, blocking should, on the simplest analysis, occur just as strongly when the experience with the blocking CS alone occurs after the experience with the blocked and blocking CSs together (retroactive blocking). The present model looks only at

---

3. The simplified determinant is $1 + \dfrac{T_3}{T_1} - \dfrac{T_2}{T_1}\dfrac{T_3}{T_2}$, which is not 0 when $T_3 < T_2 < T_1$, so the solution is unique.

the total Ts and total Ns and assumes that the rates of US occurrence to be attributed to each CS are constant over the period when the totals were gathered; hence it is indifferent to the order in which the intervals of various kinds are experienced.

However, the present analysis, in common with the Rescorla-Wagner analysis of ordinary blocking, neglects the second-order effects due to the conditioning of the blocking stimulus to the blocked stimulus. In comparing proactive and retroactive blocking, these second-order effects may become important. The question is discussed at greater length below.

Overshadowing and uncertainty minimization. The simplified equations for overshadowing are the same as for blocking because all the temporal equalities that obtain in the case of a blocking experiment also obtain in the case of an overshadowing. However, in the overshadowing case, there is a further temporal equality: $T_2 = T_3 = T_{2,3}$. The "blocking" stimulus and the "blocked" stimulus are always on together; neither occurs without the other (hence the additional equality given in roman). This makes the determinant of the temporal coefficient matrix $= 0$, which means there is an infinite number of solutions to the equations. When neither CS_2 nor CS_3 is ever on without the other, the experimental conditions no longer pose two independent constraints on the rates for CS_2 and CS_3 because the effects of one are never observed apart from the effects of the other. Thus, the additivity and inertia principles, which have done all the work so far, no longer determine a solution. Suppose that USs have occurred at the rate of 1 per minute during the intervals when CS_2 and CS_3 were on and that the sum of such intervals is 10 minutes; hence, the total number of USs from those intervals is also 10. One solution consistent with the additivity constraint is that the rate due to CS_2 was .5 per minute and likewise the rate for CS_3. Another equally good solution is that the rate due to CS_2 was 1 per minute and that for CS_3 was 0 per minute—or vice-versa—or any intermediate partitioning.

When the determinant of the temporal coefficient matrix is zero, the system seeks a solution that minimizes the average uncertainty factors associated with nonzero rate estimates. The uncertainty associated with a rate estimate is a function of the N on which the estimate is based: the greater is the N, the less is the uncertainty. The N on which a given rate ascription is based is the product of the rate ascribed to the influence of a CS and the total interval during which that CS was observed to be present. The solution that splits the rate fifty-fifty between the two CSs imputes an N of 5 (half the total of 10) to each of the CSs; hence the average uncertainty for these two nonzero rate estimates will be the uncertainty factor for an N of 5. The solutions that assign all the occurrences to one

CS create only one nonzero rate estimate, which is based on an N of 10, so its uncertainty factor is smaller than the uncertainty factors for solutions that split the rate up among the CSs (see figure 13.2). Because the uncertainty interval is nonlinear for small N, the average uncertainty is at its global minimum when all the USs are ascribed to only one of the CSs and at a local minimum when the USs are divided equally among the CSs. Thus the uncertainty minimization principle predicts that under overshadowing conditions, animals will tend to become conditioned to one or the other CS (thereby attaining a global minimization of uncertainty); but if they become conditioned to both, they should be equally strongly so (thereby attaining only the local minimum).

Predictive sufficiency and uncertainty minimization. In the predictive sufficiency experiments of Wagner et al. (1968), one group was trained under $AX(+)BX(-)$ contingencies. That is, there were three CSs (A,X,B). When X was present, either A or B was also present. USs occurred only when the AX combination was present. Although X was paired with the US on half the occasions on which it occurred, it did not get conditioned. Only A did. By contrast, in the $AX(1/2)BX(1/2)$ group, where USs occurred on half the AX presentations and also on half the BX presentations, X and only X became strongly conditioned, although here too it was paired with the US on only half the occasions on which it was present. This result, more than any other, emphasizes the fact that the system seeks the attributions that minimize the number of predictors (predictive sufficiency). For both groups, the determinant of the temporal coefficient matrix is 0, which means that additivity and inertia alone do not yield a solution. Neither condition allows the system to observe the effects of X alone: whenever X is present, either A or B is also. Thus the conditions do not provide three independent constraints on the values of the true rates (three independent equations).

For example, let the observed rate of occurrence during AX trials be 1 shock per 3 minutes or .33 shocks per minute (because Wagner et al. used a 3-minute CS with a shock at the end). The sum of the rate predicted by A and the rate predicted by X must equal .33. The observed rate of occurrence during BX trials is 0, so the sum of the rate predicted by B and the rate predicted by X must equal zero. It would be consistent with these observations to assume that A predicts .33 shocks per minute and that B and X each predict 0 shock. However, it would be equally as consistent to assume that A predicts .20 shocks per minute, X predicts .13 shocks per minute, and B predicts -.13 shocks per minute; or that A predicts 0 shocks per minute, B −.33, and X +.33, and so on. All of these values and an infinity of other values are solutions to the system of simultaneous equations under these conditions.

Because the determinant of the temporal coefficient matrix is zero, the system seeks a solution that minimizes the average uncertainty factors associated with nonzero rate estimates. Under the $AX(+)BX(-)$ conditions, uncertainty minimization dictates the ascription of 0 rates to X and B, and the ascription to A of the full rate of occurrence observed on AX trials, because this maximizes the average number of USs attributed to the nonzero rate predictors, thereby minimizing the average uncertainty factor. Under $AX(1/2)BX(1/2)$ conditions, the unique ascription that satisfies the constraints is the ascription of all the shocks to X.

The present theory correctly predicts the relative suppression ratios for the Wagner et al. groups and the Rescorla background conditioning groups, considered together. The Rescorla-Wagner model does not explain the difference between the results from Wagner et al.'s $AX(+)BX(-)$ group, which showed no suppression, and Rescorla's .2-0 group, which showed complete suppression. Under the parametric assumptions suggested by Rescorla and Wagner, these two groups should have comparable strengths of association between the CS and the shock, but they showed very different suppression ratios. The Rescorla group behaved as though it was strongly conditioned to the CS, while the Wagner et al. $AX(+)BX(-)$ group, with the same computed strength of conditioning, behaved as though it were completely unconditioned (see table 12.1). On the present analysis, the Rescorla group would have a veridical attribution of .2 USs per CS minute, while the Wagner et al. group would have a zero attribution. The prediction of the combined pattern of Rescorla's and Wagner et al.'s results, like the other predictions so far considered, is achieved by a model in which there are no parameters. These predictions depend only on the basic principles of the model: additivity, inertia, and uncertainty minimization.

Negative conditioning to a CS paired with an "overpredictive" combination of other CSs.   These constraints also generate the "counterintuitive" predictions of the Rescorla-Wagner model—the predictions that seem particularly bizarre from a more traditional (unidimensional) conditioning perspective. Consider, for example, an experiment by Kremer (1978)(see also Kamin and Gaioni 1974). He too used three CSs: A, B, and X. He first conditioned A and B separately to shock (thus, during this phase, the two CSs did not occur together). Then he presented the two already conditioned CSs and the novel CS, X, all together for several trials. Shock occurred on these compound (ABX) trials, just as it had on the earlier trials, when A and B were presented individually. When the rats were then tested with X alone, they reacted as though it predicted a reduction in the likelihood of shock. They reacted to X as though it predicted safety, even though every occurrence of X had been paired with shock.

This result follows from the additivity and inertia constraints. From the trials with A alone, the rat will have an estimate of the rate of occurrence of shock in the presence of A, let us say 1 per minute, and a similar estimate for B. When the two are presented together, the anticipated rate of shock must be 2 per minute (by the additivity principle), but the observed rate on these compound trials is only 1 per minute. The inertia constraint specifies that rather than change its estimates of the rates indicated by A and B, the rat will ascribe the discrepancy between the rate observed and the rate predicted to another predictor, *provided* that predictor first appears at the time when one would otherwise have to alter the estimates of the rates due to A and B. Thus, the rat ascribes to X a rate equal in magnitude to the rates ascribed to A or B but opposite in sign (a negative rate). (The reader may wish to plug the temporal equalities that obtain under these overprediction conditions into the temporal coefficient matrix to verify that the solution for λ_x must be negative.)

So far, I have shown that the theory accounts for the same phenomena that the Rescorla-Wagner model accounts for—those phenomena that force us to recognize the inherent multidimensionality of the memory space on which the learning process operates. The Rescorla-Wagner model takes the multidimensionality of learning into account by making the change in a given association on a given trial depend on the sum of the pretrial strengths of all the active CS-US associations. The representational theory takes the multidimensionality into account through the constraints on the process by which the observed rate of occurrence is parceled out among the possible predictors of that rate—the additivity, inertia, and uncertainty minimization constraints. The effect of these constraints is to make the rate attributed to one predictor depend on the rates attributed to other predictors, hence on the rat's experience with those predictors acting alone. So far, both theories account for the phenomena. The only reasons that might be advanced for preferring the computational-representational account is that it has no parameters (hence its predictions do not depend on ad hoc parametric assumptions) and that it reconciles the results of Wagner et al. (1968) with those of Rescorla (1968). We now consider two phenomena that are explained by the present model but not by the Rescorla-Wagner model: latent inhibition and the Gibbon et al. (1977) finding that the rate of conditioning is constant for CSs of widely different durations provided that the ITI:ISI ratio is constant (the effect of the duty cycle on the rate of conditioning). The explanation of this latter finding is one of the attractions of the Gibbon and Balsam (1981) model of conditioning.

Latent inhibition refers to the fact that presenting a CS by itself for a number of trials prior to the introduction of the US retards the development of a conditioned response to the CS. For example, Reiss and Wagner (1972), in a preconditioning phase of an eyeblink experiment with rabbits, presented one CS (A) almost 1400 times and another CS (B) only 12 times, so that A had been strongly "habituated" while B had not. Before pairing these two differentially habituated CSs with the US (a mild shock to the eye), they introduced a third CS (C), which was paired with the US on 60 trials (The reason for this intervening training with a third CS will be apparent when we come to the second Reis and Wagner experiment.) Finally, they introduced trials on which A, the thoroughly prehabituated CS was paired with the US and trials on which B, the weakly prehabituated CS, was paired with the US. These two kinds of trials were interspersed with additional trials on which C and the US were paired. The excitatory conditioning of the eyeblink to the thoroughly prehabituated CS proceeded more slowly than did the excitatory conditioning to the weakly prehabituated CS.

The retarding effect of habituating a CS prior to pairing it with a US was known to Pavlov, who ascribed it to conditioned inhibition. He argued that the presentation of a CS without any US led to a generalized inhibitory association, an inhibitory association to any US that might subsequently be introduced. (How this would be possible was always obscure. See the discussion in Chapter 12 of the difficulties with global inhibition postulates; they lead to catatonia and/or nirvana.) The behavioral effects of this inhibitory association were latent until a US was paired with the CS, at which point the effects of the inhibitory association became manifest in the slower-than-usual conditioning.

Reiss and Wagner tested this explanation with a second experiment, similar in design to the first. There was differential habituation of A and B in the first phase, conditioning to C, and then a final phase, which differed from their first experiment in that A and B were presented in compound with C. For some animals, the AC and BC compounds were reinforced (paired with the US), while in others these compounds were not reinforced. In both groups, C alone was reinforced on interspersed trials. Thus, in the first group, the animals eventually learned to blink in response to C alone and also to the compounds AC and BC, while in the second group, they eventually learned to blink in response to C alone but not to blink in response to AC or BC. In associative theory, this second group is imagined to have developed inhibitory associations between A and the US and between B and the US. In the first group, all the associations are excitatory.

If prehabituation induces the development of a latent inhibitory association between a CS and the to-be-introduced US, then initially, in both groups, the AC compound should produce a bigger reduction in the conditioned response than should the BC compound. The inhibitory associations developed during the prehabituation of A and B should counteract the excitatory association to C, with A counteracting more strongly than B because it had been more strongly habituated. For the same reason, the development of nonresponding to the compounds in the second group should proceed more rapidly for AC than for BC. The reverse should be seen in the first group, where the compound CSs are reinforced: the strengthening of the excitatory response to the BC compound should proceed more rapidly. What was in fact found, however, was the opposite of these predictions. A, the more strongly prehabituated CS ,produced less response decrement when paired with C than did B. Nonresponding to the BC compound developed faster than did nonresponding to the AC compound (in group 2), while blinking in response to the AC compound developed faster than did blinking to the BC compound (in group 1).

These results are not predicted by the Rescorla-Wagner theory. No association should develop between the CS and the US on trials when the US is not presented. Thus preexposure to the CS should not have an effect on subsequent conditioning.

The representational theory, by contrast, assumes that whenever a US occurs, the computation of the predictors for its rate of occurrence will be influenced by the animal's previously recorded experience with those predictors, because the inertia principle stipulates that the rate of US occurrence predicted by a CS is constant (unless such an assumption is statistically untenable). Preexposure to a CS means that when the first US occurs, the animal already has evidence relevant to estimating the rate of US occurrence predicted by that CS. In the Reiss and Wagner experiment, the appearance of the US was in fact the consequence of a change in the rate of US occurrence in the presence of the CS (a change in the influence of the CS), but, on the first few trials, there is in principle no way the animal could know this. Until data have accumulated from more trials, it is inherently ambiguous whether the CS has always predicted a low rate of US occurrence or whether there has in fact been a change in the rate it predicts.

In Rescorla's (1968) background conditioning experiment, there was for one of the groups a .1 probability of the shock's occurring during one of the 2-minute-long CSs. One may calculate that a rat in this group had a 35 percent chance of not experiencing a shock during the first 10 CSs. When such a rat experiences its first shock during the eleventh occurrence of the CS, it has no way of knowing whether it is in an experiment like Rescorla's, where the rate of shock occurrence during CS periods has held constant, or in a latent-inhibition experiment, where the first 10 trials were "habituation" trials and the CS is paired with the US from the eleventh trial onward. In short, if animals estimate the rates of US occurrence associated with various predictors, then preexposure to a predictor (a CS) must retard the development of an accurate estimate of the rate predicted by the tone in the period after the US is introduced.

To explain the effects of preexposure to the CS, various authors have suggested the introduction of an attentional process that reduces the value of the β parameter, which determines the rate of conditioning. This would increase the computational complexity of the Rescorla-Wagner theory or any other associative theory. Now, β would depend not only on which CS-US pair was being employed and whether the US was or was not present but also on the animal's past experience with the CS. By contrast, the prediction of the results of the Reiss and Wagner experiment follows directly from the starting assumption of the representational theory: that the system computes an estimate of the rate of US occurrence in the presence of various possible predictors. No matter what computational elaboration of this assumption might ultimately emerge, it must have the property that preexposure to the CS retards the emergence of a correct estimate of the rate to be ascribed to that CS when the experimenter introduces the US. Rate estimation procedures average over time; hence the estimate of the new rate following a step change in the true rate must initially reflect the smoothing effect of averaging.

These considerations make it clear why the temporal inertia constraint has the effect of assigning a change in the observed rate of US occurrence to a predictor that makes its appearance more or less coincident with the change in observed rate. Such a predictor has no track record to interfere with its being assigned the rate required to explain the change (it has no inertia). They also make clear the importance of distinguishing the problem of estimating the current rate of US occurrence from the problem of determining whether the rate of US occurrence has remained constant.

The effect of the duty cycle.   The representational theory takes rate of occurrence as its primitive, while the Rescorla-Wagner model takes probability of occurrence as its primitive. Because it takes rate of occurrence as its primitive, the present theory applies straightforwardly to the explanation of the important finding that rate of conditioning is approximately the same over two orders of magnitude difference in the duration of the CS, provided the ITI:ISI ratio is held constant (Gibbon et al. 1977). In the Gibbon et al. experiment, a US (food delivery) occurred at the end of each CS (the illumination of a key). When probability of a US occurring during a CS is fixed and independent of the duration of the CS, the longer is the duration of the CS, the lower is the rate of US occurrence during the CS (that is, the probability is "spread in time"; cf Gibbon and Balsam 1981) . If the ITI is also fixed, then the longer is the CS, the less is the difference between the rate of US occurrence during the CS and in the absence of the CS (the background rate of US occurrence), hence the greater is the statistical uncertainty regarding whether there is in fact a difference. If the observations indicating a difference in rates of US occurrence between CS and non-CS periods must attain a certain level of statistical significance for the animal to respond to the CS (the response rule), then the smaller the ITI:ISI ratio, the more total observations will be required to attain the requisite level of significance. Thus, the slower conditioning observed with greater duty cycles (smaller ITI:ISI ratios) follows directly from the assumption that conditioning reflects the formation of significantly different estimates of λ during CS and nonCS intervals. It follows, in other words, from the assumptions that rate of US occurrence is the primitive, not probability, and that the learning curve is driven by the increasing statistical certainty of an observed difference.

More formally, the probability, p, that the difference between two independent estimates of rate, λ_a and λ_b, based on observations of n_a and n_b occurrences during nonoverlapping intervals T_a and T_b, indicates a difference in the true rates of occurrence, Λ_a and Λ_b, is:

$$p\left\{ F(2n_a, 2n_b) < \frac{n_a\, T_b}{n_b\, T_a} \right\}. \qquad (13.7)$$

In the present instance, we have $T_a = T_{CS}$, the total time that the CS is present, $T_b = T_B - T_{CS}$, the total time that the background alone is present, $n_a = (\lambda_{CS} + \lambda_B)T_{CS} = n_{CS}$, the number of CSs that occur when the CS (and of course the background) is present, and $n_b = \lambda_B(T_B - T_{CS}) = n_B$, the number of USs that occur in the presence of the background alone. Plugging these values into expression 13.7 and simplifying yields:

$$p\left\{ F(2n_{CS}, 2n_B) < \frac{\lambda_{CS} + \lambda_B}{\lambda_B} \right\}, \qquad (13.8)$$

which means that the critical value of the F statistic (the term to the right of the inequality sign inside the braces in expression 13.8) is the ratio between the rate of US occurrence in the presence of the CS (and background) and the rate in the presence of the background alone, and the degrees of freedom for the numerator and the denominator of the F statistic are $2n_{CS}$ and $2n_B$, respectively. The probability that the rate of US occurrence in the presence of the CS differs from the rate in its absence is a function of these three quantities (the critical value and the two degrees of freedom).

If USs occur both in the presence of the CS and in the presence of the background alone, then the critical value for the F statistic (right side of inequality in expression 13.8) does not on average change over trials because the rate estimates do not change systematically over trials. When there is a genuine difference in the two rates of US occurrence, the certainty that the observed difference is genuine grows as the number of trials increases primarily because the degrees of freedom in the denominator ($2n_B$) increases. The effect of the degrees of freedom in the numerator ($2n_{CS}$) on the F distribution is generally small, and it becomes negligible when the degrees of freedom in the denominator is greater than 10.

In the experiment of Gibbon et al. (1977), there was one reward at the end of each CS; hence $\lambda_{CS} = 1/ISI$, where ISI is the CS duration, and $n_{CS} = n$, the number of trials. As in most experiments that have studied the effect of varying the ITI, there were no USs in the presence of the background alone, hence λ_B is undefined, and so therefore is the probability in expression 13.8. Although there can be no estimate of the true rate of US occurrence in the presence of the background alone when there has been no such occurrence, one can take $1/nITI$ (the reciprocal of the total intertrial time so far elapsed) as the upper limit of the possible estimates of λ_B because this assumes that the first US in the presence of the background alone occurs in the next instant of observation. The n for the upper limit on the background rate of occurrence is 1. Plugging these values into expression 13.8, we get:

$$p\left\{F(2n,2) < n\frac{ITI}{ISI} + 1\right\}. \qquad (13.9)$$

Under the conditions of the Gibbon et al. (1977) experiment, the value of p in expression 13.9 is determined only by n, the number of trials, and ITI/ISI, the ratio of the intertrial interval to the interval between CS onset and US delivery. When the estimated rate of US occurrence in the presence of the CS is far from negligible and much greater than the estimated background rate, then the growth of responding over trials is determined by $f(p)$, the "learning" function—see figure 13.1 and accompanying discussion. Thus the n required to reach a given strength of responding is determined by the ITI:ISI ratio, which is the Gibbon et al. (1977) result.

There is a further prediction from this explanation of the Gibbon et al. (1977) result: there should be little effect from deleting most of the trials prior to the trials on which responding begins to occur, *provided* the birds were left in the test apparatus an equivalent amount of time. What drives the increase in the value of p under the Gibbon et al. conditions is the decreasing upper limit on λ_B, which is a function only of the total amount of exposure to the background alone. This can be seen by examining expression 13.8 while bearing in mind that the degrees of freedom in the numerator ($2n_{CS}$) has little effect on p and that the degrees of freedom in the denominator is fixed at 2 under the Gibbon et al. conditions. Thus the only variable with a strong effect on p that changes systematically with n is λ_B, and λ_B undergoes the same decrease with increasing time in the apparatus whether or not exposure to the background alone is interrupted by CSs. The rate of US occurrence in the presence of the CS, λ_{CS}, will not change systematically with increasing n. The first few exposures to a CS followed by food should establish this rate estimate, and they should also render negligible the effect of further increases in the degrees of freedom for the numerator ($2n_{cs}$). Thus on this account, what really matters in the Gibbon et al. experiment and other experiments on the effects of the ITI is not the ITI:ISI ratio but the apparent rate of occurrence of the US in the presence of the CS and the amount of exposure to the background alone.

The Test for Rate Constancy
The inertia assumption—that the influence of a CS on the rate of US occurrence is constant over time—requires a computation that tests for its validity because the influence of a CS is not always constant over time. Rates of US occurrence change "for no reason," that is, in the absence of any new CS to whose influence the change in observed rate can be ascribed. The most common experimental example is extinction. When USs stop occurring in the presence of the CS, the animal stops responding to the CS. We saw other examples of animals adjusting to a change in rate in chapter 11. In the ideal free fish experiment, for example, no food dropped into the tank during the first 5 minutes (300 seconds) of each trial; then, it suddenly began to drop into one end of the tank at the rate of 1 per 6 seconds and into the other end at an equal or slower rate. The fish adjusted rapidly to this change (see figure 11.1). In the discussion of attempts to model the fishes' "representation" of rate associatively, it was pointed out that associative models conflate the representation of rate itself with the representation of change in rate. They do not distinguish between an associative strength in transition and one that represents a steady state. A representational theory treats the problem of representing the stability of a rate separately from the problem of representing its current value. There must therefore be a computation that detects a change in rate and indicates approximately where the change occurred.

In the illustrative model here elaborated, the detection of changes in the rate of US occurrence in the presence of a CS is mediated by a retrospective function, $D(T,\tau)$. This function looks backward by an amount τ through the total interval T during which a CS has been observed (the sum of all the different intervals when it has been present). For a given value of T, $D(T,\tau)$ is a function of τ, the length of the backward look. As τ increases, the function looks backward over a bigger and bigger portion of T. Intervals during which the CS is not on are ignored by this function; when $\tau = T$, the function is looking back over all the intervals that combine to yield T. The function $D(T,\tau)$ takes N_T/T as its estimate of the (presumed) constant rate of US occurrence and computes for each backward interval, τ, the probability that $\{n \leq n_{T,\tau} | \lambda = N_T/T\}$, where $n_{T,\tau}$ is the number of US observed in the portion of T from $T-\tau$ to T, then takes the logit of this conditional probability:

$$D(T,\tau) = \text{logit} \left[\sum_{i=0}^{n_{T,\tau}} \frac{(\lambda\tau)^i e^{-\lambda\tau}}{i!} \right],$$

where $\lambda = (N_T/T)$.

In computing this function, the minimum size of τ is set at $T/2N_T$, so that the "grain" of the backward scan is determined by the current estimate of Λ; the lower that estimate, the coarser the grain of the backward scan. $D(T,\tau)$ is computed for each CS to which a nonzero influence on the rate of US occurrence is attributed. Whenever two such CSs are present concurrently, the number of USs that occur are prorated among the CSs in proportion to their relative influence, that is, in proportion to their relative rate predictions: if one CS predicts twice the rate of another CS, it is "credited" with two-thirds of USs that occur when the two CSs are on together.

Figure 13.5 shows the evolution of $D(T,\tau)$ in two different cases. The first case (figure 13.5A) is that confronted by the fish in the ideal free fish experiment. The rate of US occurrence is 0 for 5 minutes, then changes to 1 per 6 seconds. The second case is the converse: the rate is 1 per 6 seconds for 5 minutes, then drops to 0. Notice that at $T = 310$, when only two pieces of food have dropped (one at $T = 300$ and one at $T = 306$), the value of $D(T,\tau)$ is already at a level that would be reached by chance with a probability of only about .01. By $T = 330$, when six morsels have dropped, the $D(T,\tau)$ function has already developed a peak at $T = 300$ and this peak is at the $p = .00001$ level of improbability. In short, the function quickly detects the kind of change in rate to which the fish were exposed.

The reaction to a change in rate.   The simplest assumption is that when there is a peak in the $D(T,\tau)$ for a given CS that exceeds a critical value, the system truncates the observations at the time indicated by the peak. Subsequent estimates for the current rate of US occurrence to be attributed to that CS are computed from the truncation point onward. The temporal intervals and USs prior to the truncation point are not used in computing the current rate for that CS. While something like this is assumed to be the case over the long run, it must be recognized that the transient reaction of animals to a change in rate, particularly their reaction to extinction conditions, is complex and poorly understood.

After simple conditioning (presentation of the US only during an intermittent CS) and simple extinction (cessation of all USs), reintroduc-

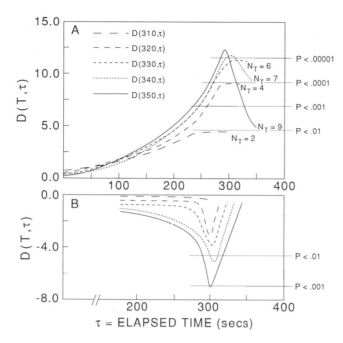

Figure 13.5
The evolution of the $D(T,\tau)$ function following the onset (A) or offset (B) of a constant US rate of 1/6 sec at $T = 300$. Each function is for a different value of T, which is the interval elapsed since the onset of the constant background CS (= the time of placement in the tank). $D(310,\tau)$ is the function as of $T = 310$ sec (10 seconds after the change in US rate); $D(320,\tau)$ the function as of $T = 320$, and so on. The p values indicate the likelihood of observing a value of $D(T,\tau)$ that discrepant from 0 when there has been no change in the rate of US occurrence.

ing the USs during non-CS periods causes a marked recovery of responding to the CS (Frey and Butler 1977; Rescorla and Heth 1975; Rescorla, and Skucy 1969). When extinction (cessation of responding to the intermittent CS) is produced by making the background rate of US occurrence equal to the rate during the CS, then when one switches these animals to traditional extinction (cessation of US occurrences), there is strong reinstatement of responding to the intermittent CS (Epstein and Skinner 1980; Linblom and Jenkins 1981). These findings imply that pigeons and rats preserve the records of past CS-US predictive relations and revert to the use of those records when confronted with a change that makes them uncertain as to the current CS-US relation. The well-known fact that repeated conditioning and extinction leads to much more rapid acquisition and elimination of responding to the CS (in the limit one-trial acquisition and one-trial extinction) suggests the same thing. While I believe that a representational model like the one being elaborated here can probably deal more readily with these phenomena than can associative models, I will not attempt to develop an account of these results here. The important point is that these are reactions to changes in the rate of US occurrence in the presence of the CS and/or in the presence of the background. The model assumes that when these changes are some while in the past—that is, when the CS-US relation has been stable for some while—the animal's behavior-determining representation of the current rate of US occurrence in the presence of the CS is based only on the observations made since the last significant peak in the $D(T,\tau)$ function for that CS.

Retroactive Blocking and Unblocking.
An assumption that contemporary associative theories of animal learning share with their predecessors is that nothing happens to the associations of inactive CSs. If a CS is not present on a trial, it is inactive, and the association between that CS and the US is not altered on that trial. This assumption rules out retroactive effects of subsequent experiences with other CSs on a previously conditioned CS-US association. The blocking effect of one CS-US association on another should be seen only if the blocking association is established prior to or coincident with experience with the blocked (or overshadowed) CS. There should be no effect of subsequent experience with the blocking or overshadowing CS alone— no retroactive blocking or unblocking. By contrast, in the model here suggested, it should not matter whether experience with the blocking CS alone occurs prior to or after the experience with the blocking and blocked CSs together. The present model assigns rate predictors solely on the basis of the total numbers of USs observed during periods when CSs are present alone or in combination. It takes no account of the order of these experiences—no account of whether experience with a CS alone precedes or follows experience of combined CSs. Thus experiments on retroactive blocking and unblocking are potentially important tests of the competing accounts.

Unfortunately the evidence from such experiments is inconclusive. Retroactive unblocking has been demonstrated but not retroactive blocking. However, so-called second-order conditioning is likely to have been an important factor in the failure to observe retroactive blocking. Second-order conditioning is the learning of a predictive relation between the two CSs and then between the second CS and a US. If CS_1 predicts CS_2 and CS_2 predicts the US, the animal will react to CS_1 as though it predicted the US, even though it has never experienced the co-occurrence of CS_1 and the US .

Matzel, Schachtman, and Miller (1985), using a suppression paradigm similar to that used by Rescorla in his background conditioning experiments, gave four initial trials in which a combination CS (a complex tone and a flashing light) was paired with shock. The tone and light had been chosen on the basis of previous work to be such that the tone reliably overshadowed the light; that is, the shock did not get conditioned to the light when the light was presented in the presence of the tone, but it did get conditioned if only the light was paired with the shock. Half the animals given the training with the tone-light combination were then tested with the light alone and did not respond to it, confirming that the tone had overshadowed the light. The other half of the animals were given eighteen extinction trials with the overshadowing tone—eighteen trials in which the tone was not paired with shock—and then tested with the light alone. These animals showed a strong reaction to the light, which is what the current model would predict. The experience with the tone alone, although it came after the experience with the tone and light together, requires that all the USs experienced during the training with the tone and light together be ascribed to the influence of the light. The temporal coefficient matrix and the uncorrected rate vector for this case are identical to the temporal coefficient matrix and uncorrected rate vector in the case where the experience with the tone alone precedes experience with the tone and light together, which, in conventional terms, forestalls the tone's overshadowing the light because the unreinforced experience with the tone alone is thought to induce inattention to the tone. Thus the rate ascriptions must be the same in the two cases and no appeal to attention is required in either case.

This result of Matzel et al. (1985) replicated an earlier report of a similar result by Kaufman and Bolles (1981). Matzel et al. added some important controls. For example, they showed that the appearance of responding to the light as a result of the extinction experience with the tone was specific to the extinction of the CS that had been paired with the light; it did not occur if some other previously conditioned CS was extinguished rather than the CS that had overshadowed the light. They also showed that if there were only a few extinction trials with the tone CS—not enough to degrade responding to this, the overshadowing CS—then responding to the overshadowed CS was not induced. For the animal to respond to the light as though it predicted shock, its subsequent (retroacting) experience with the tone alone had to be extensive enough to persuade it that the tone did not predict shock.

The present model predicts that one should see retroactive blocking as well as retroactive unblocking. If, subsequent to its experience with the light and tone together, the animal is shown that the light alone predicts the rate of shock it experienced with the light and tone together, then it should not react to the tone alone. The subsequent disambiguating experience with the light alone alters the initial conclusions regarding the predictive value of the tone, conclusions engendered by the uncertainty minimizing process. The temporal coefficient matrix for the case in which experience with the light alone follows experience of the light and tone together is identical to the matrix in the conventional blocking case, where the experience with the light alone precedes experience with the two CSs together, and so is the uncorrected rate vector; thus, in this model, the two training regimens must yield the same ascription to the tone (=0). Matzel, Shuster, and Miller (1987) did a follow-up study in which they also looked for retroactive blocking. After presenting an overshadowing tone and an overshadowed light together in initial training, they gave subsequent trials in which the light alone was paired with shock. This subsequent experience with the light alone failed to attenuate the animals' response to the tone alone; it failed to block the tone retroactively.

Unfortunately, in this follow-up experiment, the onset of the tone substantially preceded the onset of the light on trials in which they co-occurred. On each such trial, the light came on during the last half of the tone. If, as seems likely, the rats learned that the tone predicted the light and if they then learned that the light predicted shock, it is not surprising that they continued to react fearfully to the tone, even if they did not represent it as having a direct influence on the rate of shock occurrence. The present model predicts that the animals would represent the tone as having a conditioning effect on the rate of light occurrence and represent the light as having a conditioning effect of the rate of shock occurrence. Together the two representations might be expected to yield a fearful response to the tone, which was what was observed.

The problem of second-order conditioning complicates the design of an experiment to test for the equivalence of proactive and retroactive blocking, which is an important prediction of the present model, because even if the blocking CS and the blocked CS have coincident onsets, the second-order effects cannot be expected to be the same in the proactive and retroactive cases. In a conventional proactive blocking experiment, the initial experience with the blocking CS alone will lower its predictive value for the blocked CS (the "latent inhibition" effect already analyzed). In the retroactive case, where experience with the blocking stimulus alone follows experience with the two CSs together, the subsequent experience with the blocking CS alone constitutes a change in the rate at which the blocking CS occurs in the presence of the background alone. In initial training, when the two CSs co-occur, the rate of occurrence of the blocking CS in the presence of the background alone is 0 because this CS never occurs except when the other CS (the blocked CS) is present. During the subsequent training with the blocking CS alone, its rate of occurrence in the presence of the background alone is no longer 0. In the proactive case, there is no such change in the rate of occurrence of the blocking CS. The extent to which the background predicts the blocking CS is the same during training with the two CSs together as during the initial training with the blocking CS alone. It is, I believe, possible to design an experiment for comparing proactive and retroactive blocking in which the effects of direct conditioning between the two CSs and the US are not confounded with differing second-order effects; the design is complex, however, and the experiment has not been run.

Summary
This completes the presentation of the part of the representational model of classical conditioning that deals with the same experimental phenomena as contemporary associative models. Before considering how to incorporate temporal lags between the CS and the US into the model, let us take stock.

The representational model of the learning that occurs during classical conditioning takes the rate of US occurrence during the CS as the experiential primitive rather than the probability of its occurrence. Hence the representational model does not require a trial clock. The notion of a trial plays no role in the representational model, whereas it plays a central role in associative models because the probability of an event is defined only if one defines the trial duration. The probability of an event depends on the unit of time, whereas the rate of event occurrence does not. Hence associative models require a mechanism that defines a unit of time (the trial clock), whereas the representational model does not.

The representational model is computationally simpler than contemporary associative models because there are no parameters in the learning model itself. Its predictions depend directly on its basic assumptions, and these assumptions may be embodied in simple computational formulas. Thus the predictions may be derived analytically, without recourse to computer simulation. The three principles—the additivity of predicted rates, inertia (rate constancy), and uncertainty minimization—give analytically derived explanations of:

1. *Background conditioning*: The effects of USs that occur during non-CS periods on the conditioning of a US to an intermittent CS (such as a tone or light).

2. *Inhibitory conditioning in explicitly unpaired conditions*: If the US occurs only when an intermittent CS is not present, the animal reacts to the CS as if it predicted a diminishment in the rate of US occurrence.

3. *The effects of having 'background' USs signaled by other CSs*: If the USs presented in the absence of a given CS occur only when another CS is present, they do not interfere with conditioning to the first named CS.

4. *Blocking*: Conditioning with one CS alone blocks conditioning of the US to another CS that occurs only in the presence of the first-named CS. (On the present model, this should be true whether experience with the blocking CS alone precedes or follows experience with the two CSs together.)

5. *Overshadowing*: If two CSs are always presented together during training, conditioning to one CS tends to block conditioning to the other.

6. *Predictive sufficiency as shown in the Wagner et al. (1968) experiment*: If more than one ascription of rates is consistent with additivity and inertia, what gets conditioned is the CS that alone suffices to account for the observed rate of US occurrence.

7. *Inhibitory conditioning in overprediction experiments*: If two independently conditioned CSs are presented together with a third CS with no increase in the rate of US occurrence, the animal reacts to the third CS as if it predicted a decrease in the rate of US occurrence, although the US was paired with the third CS during every occurrence of that CS.

8. *Latent inhibition*: An initial period of experience with a CS unaccompanied by the US retards subsequent conditioning of the US to that CS.

None of the above predictions from the representational model requires assumptions about the values of learning parameters (there are none) or performance parameters. The only performance assumption they require is that the likelihood and strength of the animal's response to the CS is a monotonic function of the rate of US occurrence ascribed to the influence of that CS. The only prediction that requires stronger assumptions about the performance function is:

9. *The dependence of the rate of conditioning on the ITI:ISI ratio rather than on the ISI*. To derive this result, it is necessary to assume that in the Gibbon et al. experiment, the rate of US occurrence during the intermittent CS was great enough to saturate the effect of the size of the increment in rate predicted by the CS, so that the growth of a tendency to respond to the CS becomes a function solely of the statistical certainty that the rate of US occurrence in the presence of the CS is greater than its background rate (its rate in the absence of the CS). Given this assumption, the model predicts that the trials to criterion will be a function solely of the ITI:ISI ratio.

Prevalence

The fact that the USs in most conditioning experiments may reasonably be regarded as point events is a boon to the development of the model of classical conditioning. It permits the elaboration of a pivotal idea within a simple mathematical framework, the framework of Poisson processes. The key idea is that the gradual appearance of the conditioned response in the course of a conditioning experiment is the result of the animal's representation of an objective fact about its experience: the statistical uncertainty of rate estimates based on small numbers of occurrences. A fundamental idea (or hypothesis) in the elaborated model of conditioning is that the appearance of the conditioned response after some number of conditioning trials reflects the animal's representation of the increasing probability that the rate of US occurrence in the presence of the CS is different from its rate in the absence of the CS—the increasing probability that the CS does in fact condition the rate of US occurrence. The animal's behavior reflects the operation of neural circuitry whose computational properties have been shaped by the objective fact that a limited knowledge of the past reduces the certainty with which the future may be anticipated, even under the "semistationarity" assumption implicit in any attempt to use the past to anticipate the future, the assumption that the process one is observing has approximately constant properties over a behaviorally meaningful interval.

For a representational approach to the analysis of brain function to have substance, one must be able to give a formal (mathematical) description of the reality supposed to be represented. The claim that the brain represents an aspect of the world is the claim that processes inside the brain that adapt behavior to that aspect of reality have a formal description mirroring the formal description of the corresponding reality. There is no way to substantiate such a claim if one does not have a formal description of the reality that the brain is said to represent. It takes two systems to make an isomorphism: a represented system and a representing system. Both must be formally describable if one is to assert that they are isomorphic. The formal characterization of the rate of occurrence of point events by the statistics of Poisson processes provided the necessary formal description of the external reality.

The world of classical conditioning experiments, however, is rather far removed from the natural reality it is meant to epitomize. The changes in motivationally significant stimuli that animals in nature must learn to anticipate cannot, in general, be idealized as the occurrences of point events. Animals, for example, learn to anticipate prolonged changes in the temperature of the environment and take measures to defend themselves in advance against the predicted change (Ollove 1980). A more general theory must find some way to characterize the objective uncertainties that confront an animal that has made limited observations of the prevalence of a more or less continuously present stimulus—its value over time.

Suppose that an animal has observed that the temperature of the experimental environment has been 20°C over the 6 hours since it has been placed in that environment. In what sense can this sort of observation of the prevalence of the temperature variable be analogous to the observation of a number of point events? The occurrence of a number of point events serves to specify to within objectively computable limits of certainty the rate of event occurrence. On the assumption of stationarity, this computation permits the animal to anticipate the future with an appropriate degree of caution about the accuracy of its anticipations. As the number of occurrences increases, so does the accuracy of its anticipations (hence the learning curve). The caution evident in those aspects of behavior that reflect the representation of the statistical uncertainties inherent in limited observations is based not on the painful truth that the past may not predict the future—nothing can be done about that—but rather on the subtler truth that even when the past perfectly predicts the future, an imperfect knowledge of the past (a limited interval of observation) objectively limits the precision with which one may extrapolate into the future. When we turn to the analysis of the brain processes that use observations of past prevalence to predict future prevalence, we must ask in what sense the accumulation of observations on the prevalence of a stimulus permits an objectively specifiable increase in the degree of certainty about what the value of that variable may be expected to be at various times in the future.

To proceed, we need a general-purpose mathematical representation of patterns of variation in stimuli, permitting the extrapolation from past patterns of variation to future patterns of variation. The system must be capable of representing, at least approximately, all possible patterns of variation in any physical variable whose value (intensity, density, and so forth) is represented in the sensory input. It is also desirable that there be a computationally simple method of representing the manner in which variation in one variable (the US) depends on or may be predicted from variation in another (the CS). Finally, the method of representing patterns of variation and dependence must not be too strongly committed to stationarity because many environmental processes that animals adapt their behavior to are not stationary over long periods of time; they are only locally stationary.

The representation of temporal variation that seems best suited travels under the somewhat formidable name of complex demodulation (Bloomfield 1976; Redmond, Sing, and Hegge 1982; Sing, Thorne, and Hegge 1985). It is a temporally localized form of Fourier analysis. Perhaps the most generally familiar example of a limited form of complex demodulation is the representation of nonstationary sounds, like bird calls and speech sounds, by means of a spectrograph—a graph of the frequency content of the sound as a function of time.[4] Time is represented along the x-axis, frequency is represented along the y-axis, and the amount of power at any given frequency at any given moment in time is represented by ink density (the darkness of the plot at that point in the x-y frame). A sound spectrograph, unlike a simple Fourier analysis, assumes that the power in a signal at any given frequency changes over time; it does not assume that the frequency spectrum of a sound is stationary.

Like most other schemes for representing patterns of temporal variation, complex demodulation takes sinusoidal patterns of variation as the primitive or elementary pattern of variation. All patterns of temporal variation are represented as the sum of a number of elementary sinusoidal patterns, called the Fourier components of the pattern. What distinguishes one elementary pattern from another are the three parameters that uniquely specify a sine or cosine curve: frequency, amplitude, and phase. Representing patterns of variation by means of the sinusoidal elements of which the pattern may be imagined to be composed is called Fourier analysis. (For an elementary, heavily illustrated introduction to the mathematical description of sine curves and their use to construct complex nonsinusoidal patterns of variation , see chapter 4 of Gallistel 1980.) Complex demodulation, unlike ordinary Fourier analysis, assumes that the amplitudes and phases of the sinusoidal elements required to describe a pattern of variation will change over time. Therefore it is a temporally localized form of Fourier representation. Ordinary Fourier representation is temporally global; the sinusoidal components of a pattern are imagined to extend backward in time to minus infinity and forward to plus infinity.

The representation of variation by means of sinusoidal elements is particularly well suited to describing the manner in which variation in one variable may be predicted from variation in another, under the kind of additivity assumptions that were a cornerstone of the already elaborated model of classical conditioning. Predictive systems in which the isolated effects of different inputs combine additively to make up the

4. It is limited because it only gives information about the changes over time in the power of the frequency components of the sound; it does not represent the phases of these components.

output are called linear systems. For a linear system, the sinusoidal pattern of variation has the unique property that the output has the same form as the input. If the input is a sinusoid of a given frequency, the output is a sinusoid of the same frequency. Thus the predictive relation between the input and the output of a linear system has a uniquely simple description when variations in the predicting and predictor variables are represented by their Fourier components.

The predictive relation for a given Fourier component is completely characterized by two prediction coefficients. One coefficient gives the amplitude of the output variation (the size of the swings in the US) relative to the input variation (the size of the swings in the CS). The other gives the change in phase—the amount by which the up and down swings of the predicted variable are shifted in time relative to the up and down swings in the predicting variable. These two values (the gain coefficient and the phase-lag coefficient) are called the (complex) value of the prediction function (transfer function) at a given frequency.[5] The prediction function for two variables is the representation of the predictive relation between them. Computing the prediction function involves computing the values of the gain and phase coefficients over the range of sinusoidal frequencies required to give an acceptable representation of the patterns of variation encountered in the predicting and predicted variables (the CS and US).

The more general model of classical conditioning is that the animal computes CS–US prediction functions, which describe the systematic relations between observed variations in the US and observed variations in CSs. It then assigns predictive value to the CSs in accord with the constraints of the additivity, inertia, and uncertainty minimization principles.

Having settled on the device of representing patterns of variation by means of their temporally localized Fourier components, we can answer the question with which this section began. As an animal accumulates observations on the prevalence of a variable such as environmental temperature, there is an objectively specifiable increase in the certainty with which the frequency domain representation of the variation in temperature may be specified. For example, the constancy of the temperature

5. The value of the transfer function at a given frequency is a complex number (that is, a two-dimensional vector). The gain predictor is the absolute value (or modulus, or magnitude, or r) of the complex number, while the predictor of the phase shift is its angle (φ). Thus, the transfer function is a complex valued function of frequency: the gain and phase prediction coefficients are the magnitude and angle in the polar form of the complex values of this function.

over the first 6 hours means that the amplitudes of Fourier components (sinusoidal constituents) with frequencies greater than 2 cycles per day are unlikely to be large. The longer the temperature holds constant, the less likely it becomes that high frequency Fourier components have appreciable amplitudes. Less formally, this means that it is increasingly unlikely that the temperature variable, under the present regime, undergoes appreciable fluctuations in intervals measured in minutes. The onset of temperature fluctuations on such a time scale would imply a change in regime, just as the sudden onset of fish eggs coming at a 6-second intervals implied a change in the rate parameter. On the other hand, a gradual cooling or warming extending over several days would be consistent with the seeming steadiness of the temperature in the first 6 hours; it would not imply a change in regime. The Fourier description of the pattern of variation in a stimulus is like the Poisson representation of the rate of occurrence of a random point event in that the more observations one has (in this case, the longer the interval over which the value of the variable has been observed), the narrower are the confidence bands surrounding the estimated values of the Fourier descriptors (amplitudes and phases) by which one represents past and future values of the variable.

The Computational Realization of Univariate and Bivariate Time Series Analysis by Complex Demodulation
An attraction of complex demodulation as an approach to the problem of representing the predictive relation between time-dependent variables is that it builds naturally on the material we have already covered—on assumptions that have already been made for other reasons and with their own empirical support. In particular, it builds directly on the assumption that animals record the times at which observations are made by recording the values of the sine and cosine constituents of endogenous oscillators. The explanation of anticipatory feeding activity developed in chapter 8, which built on the assumption that animals record the times at which things happen by recording cosine-sine representations of the phases of endogenous oscillations, foreshadows the model now to be elaborated.

The principles behind the computational model are:

1. The nervous system uses the array of endogenous oscillations with which it keeps track of time to compute a frequency domain representation of the patterns of observed variation in environmental variables (CSs and USs).
2. It computes Laplace transforms of observed patterns of vari-

ation by cross-correlating the observed variable with the cosine and sine constituents of these endogenous oscillations.[6] A complete set of such cross-correlations, one pair of sine and cosine correlation coefficients for each endogenous oscillation, is a frequency domain representation of the pattern of variation.

3. The weight given to a recorded value of the variable in computing a cross-correlation with the sine or cosine constituent of an endogenous oscillation decays as an exponential function of the interval elapsed between the time the value was recorded and the present moment. Thus more recently recorded values are weighted more heavily than values recorded in the more distant past. The exponentially decreasing weighting of past observations makes the transformation of the time series a Laplace transform rather than a simple Fourier transform. The rate of exponential decay determines the length of the backward look—how big a chunk of the past is given nonnegligible weight in computing the current frequency domain representation of a variable. The faster the rate of exponential decay, the more strongly the current frequency domain representation of the variable is weighted in favor of the testimony of the very recent past.

4. The frequency domain representation of each variable (each CS and US) is computed for several different values of the exponential decay constant, thereby varying the length of the backward look.

5. From the frequency domain representations of CSs and USs, the system computes the prediction (transfer) functions. A prediction function gives the expected magnitude and timing (phase) of variations in US intensity as simple functions of the magnitude and timing of variations in a CS. The coefficient that predicts US magnitude from CS magnitude is the gain coefficient, and the coefficient that predicts the temporal lag between CS variation and US variation is the phase coefficient.

6. Changes in the patterns of CS or US variation and/or changes in the predictive relation between CS and US variations are recognized by comparing the results from representations computed using different exponential decay constants; that is, representations based on the recent past are compared to representations based on longer intervals of observation to detect "nonstationarity," nonconstancy over time in the patterns of variation and/or the predictive relation between them.

6. By Euler's identity, this is equivalent to multiplying the intensity function $I(t)$ by the complex exponential $e^{i\omega t}$, where ω is the frequency of the demodulating oscillation in radians per unit time.

The computation of the frequency domain representation of CSs and USs. The correlation coefficient for the cosine constituent of an oscillation is obtained by multiplying each observed value of the variable (for example, each observed value of temperature) by the contemporaneous value of the cosine fluctuation (see figure 13.6), then summing these products. Similarly for the correlation with the sine constituent: it is the sum of the cross-products of the observed values of the variable and the contemporaneous values of the sine constituent of the demodulating oscillation. If the observed values tend to be high when the cosine constituent of the demodulating oscillation is near its peak and low when the cosine constituent is near its minimum, then the sum of the cross-products with the cosine constituent of the demodulating oscillation will be large—for the same reason that the ordinary correlation coefficient gets large when the big values of *x* coincide with the big values of *y* and the small with the small. Similarly if peak values of the variable tend to

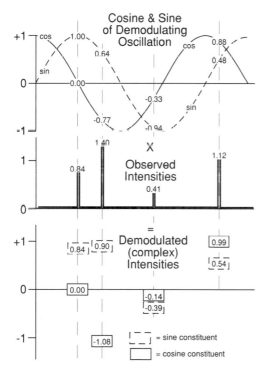

Figure 13.6
The cross-multiplication of the values of the cosine and sine constituents of an oscillator (first panel) with the temporally corresponding values of a time series (second panel) yields the complex time series (third panel).

coincide with peaks in the sine constituent and minimal values with valleys, then the sum of the cross-products with the sine constituent will be large. If peaks in the variable tend to coincide with valleys in one or the other constituent of the demodulating oscillation (and valleys with peaks), then the sum of the cross-products will be large and negative (a negative correlation). If the peaks and valleys in the observed variable tend to fall between the peaks and valleys of both the sine and cosine constituents of the demodulating oscillation, then both sums of cross-products will be intermediate in size. If there is no consistent pattern of correspondence between the maxima and minima of the observed variable and the maxima and minima of the cosine and sine constituents of a demodulating oscillation, then both sums of cross-products will be low, because cross-products with negative signs will on average be equal to (and therefore cancel) cross-products with positive signs.

A systematic pattern of coincidences or near-coincidences between the maxima and minima of the observed variable and the maxima and minima of a cosine or sine constituent can occur only if the observed variable is fluctuating with a period near the period of the demodulating oscillation. Whenever this is the case, the absolute values of one or both of the sums of cross-products will be large—appreciably different from zero in either a positive or negative direction. When this happens, the pattern of variation in the observed variable is said to have "power" at or near the frequency of the demodulating oscillation. The power in the pattern at the demodulating frequency is the sum of the squared average cosine and sine cross-products.

If the sum of cosine cross-products is large relative to the sum of sine cross-products, the phase of the fluctuation in the observed variable is close to the phase of the cosine constituent. Conversely, when the sine correlation is large relative to the cosine correlation, the phase of the fluctuation is approximately that of the sine constituent. More generally, the phase of the fluctuation in the observed variable is specified by the ratio between the sum of the sine cross-products and the sum of the cosine cross-products, with the signs of both the numerator and denominator taken into account.

Taking the sums of the cross-products between the values of the variable and the cosine and sine constituents of an oscillation is the process by which a Fourier component in a pattern of variation is computed. In an ordinary Fourier analysis, the sums of the cosine and sine cross-products at a given frequency of oscillation (for a given Fourier component) are computed over the entire interval of observation, giving equal weight to all observations, no matter how temporally remote. This creates problems when the pattern of variation is not stationary over the interval of observation. Suppose that the observed pattern fluctuates in phase with the cosine constituent of a Fourier component during the first half of the interval of observation but in antiphase (180° out of phase) with this cosine constituent during the second half of the observation interval. The sums of both the cosine and sine cross-products will be close to zero, and the analysis will report that there is no power in the variable at the frequency in question. This will be a serious misrepresentation of the observed pattern, arising from the fact that the ordinary Fourier analysis assumes stationarity; it assumes that the pattern of variation does not evolve or change over time.

Complex demodulation differs from ordinary Fourier analysis in that it employs a running or temporally weighted sum of the cross-products. Cross-products further back in time are given progressively less weight (figure 13.7). More formally, in the form of complex demodulation used in this model, the cosine cross-products and sine cross-products are convolved with exponentially relaxing retrospective temporal filters.[7] From these running sums—that is, from the demodulated (complex) intensity signal after it has been convolved with a temporal filter—the system may compute the local power and phase of a Fourier component—the characteristics of the pattern during its recent history. This is equivalent to determining the amount of power in a sound at a given frequency at a given moment in time, which is what is plotted in the sound spectrograph. How recent is recent depends on the decay constant (neper frequency) of the running sum (retrospective temporal filter). If

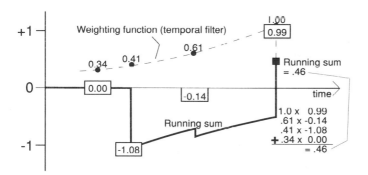

Figure 13.7
The computation of the retrospective exponentially weighted running sum of the cosine series from figure 13.6. The value of this running sum at a point in time is obtained by multiplying each value in the time series by the weight specified by the backward-decaying exponential function and summing the products. When this operation is applied to the complex representation of a time series, the resulting pair of sums (one for the cosine cross products and one for the sine cross products) is the (complex) value of the (retrospective) Laplace transform of the time series at the demodulating frequency, ω, and time, t.

the weights used in computing the running sums of cross-products fall off slowly as cross-products recede in time, then "recent" may extend over many cycles of the demodulating oscillation (many cycles of the Fourier component). If the weights fall off rapidly, "recent" may extend back only a fraction of a cycle.

Computing prediction functions. Figure 13.8 gives the computational model. The first stage (the stage of complex demodulation) is repre-sented by the two boxes for which the time series $US(t)$ serves as input. The expression $US(t)$ stands for the record of the occurrences of the US as a function of time, that is, the time line (or time series) for the US. The expression $£[US]$ stands for the demodulated time series (more formally, the representation of the US time series in the complex frequency domain). There are two such boxes (in actuality, probably several) because the system looks backward in time by varying amounts (varying numbers of cycles). The constant that determines how far back in time a given demodulating box looks is the complex constant s (a two-dimen-sional vector). The "real" part of s (the first of the two values in the vector, symbolized $R[s]$) determines the number of cycles that make a nonneg-ligible contribution to this backward look. If $R[s]$ is large, then the retro-spective look decays rapidly; if it is small, the look backward is longer. If the time series is stationary, the expected value of the ratio between two $£[US]$s computed with different values of $R[s]$ is 1.

The next stage of the computation, symbolized by the box with "$\varphi[\ ]$" inside, computes the phase vector for the current value of the complex representation of the US series. The phase vector represents where in the cycle the most recent US(s) occurred. The phase vector is defined only if there has in fact recently been a US. If not, the momentary power of the US time line at the demodulating frequency will be negligible. The momentary power of the US is symbolized by $|£[US]|^2$ (the square of the magnitude of the complex variable $£[US]$). Whenever the power be-comes negligible (whenever $|£[US]|^2 < T$, the threshold or criterion for

---

7. Taking the exponentially relaxing running (retrospective) sums of the cross-products between an intensity function, $I(\tau)$, and the cosine and sine components of an oscillation with radian frequency ω is equivalent to integrating the product of the intensity function and the complex exponential $e^{-s\omega(t-\tau)}$. The real part of the term $s\omega$, denoted $R[s\omega]$, is equal to the time constant of exponential relaxation (the neper frequency), scaled by the demodu-lating frequency, ω. The amplitudes of the sine and cosine fluctuations that are cross-multiplied with the intensity function decrease by -1 ln unit in $1/R[\omega s]$ time units. The imaginary part of the same term, denoted $I[\omega s]$, equals $i\omega$, the radian frequency of the de-modulating oscillation. The computation being described is equivalent to a retrospective running Laplace transform, $£(\omega,t)$, with the dummy variable, τ, used inside the integral. The value of this transform at time, t, is the retrospective Laplace integral from $-\infty$ to t.

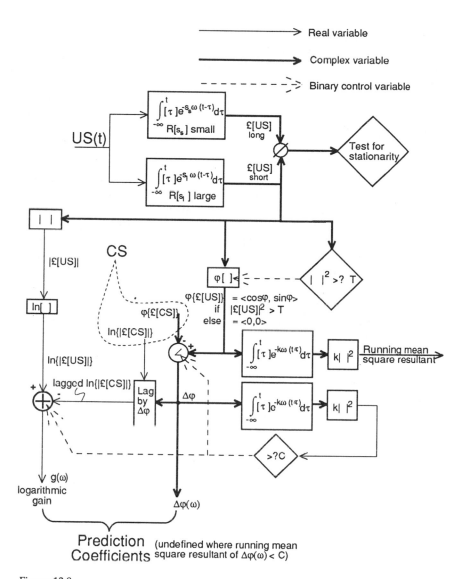

Figure 13.8
The computational model for the detection of a temporal dependence between the CS and
the US and the computation of the prediction coefficients. The prediction coefficients
(logarithmic gain and phase lag) permit the prediction of the time and magnitude of a US
fluctuation from the time and magnitude of a CS fluctuation.

significant power), the complex phase vector (which is the cosine-sine representation of the phase of occurrence of the US) becomes <0,0>. This means the phase is undefined because there is no phase angle whose cosine and sine are simultaneously 0.

Next, there is a process that takes an exponentially relaxing backward look at the values of the complex (cosine-sine) representation of the phases of US occurrence and computes the mean square resultant of the recent phase vectors (the two boxes leading to the arrow labeled "running mean square resultant"). The number of cycles over which this process looks back is determined by the value of a (real) constant k; the smaller k is, the further back the process looks. The computation of the mean square resultant of the phase vectors was postulated to explain the data on anticipatory feeding in chapter 8. If the US (feeding) occurs at approximately the same phase of the circadian cycle on several successive cycles, the output from this process will rise to statistically significant levels. The mean square resultant of several phase vectors is the statistic by which one assesses whether there is statistically significant clustering of phase vectors, or departure bearings, or anything else that can be represented as a point on the circumference of the unit circle. The likelihood of this variable's having a given value is almost independent of the number of phase vectors that enter into its computation. Hence its value can be used in tests that assess whether there is a statistically improbable clustering of phase vectors (for example, daily feeding times) over several cycles (days).

The CS is subject to a similar analysis, which is not shown in figure 13.8. The signal processing pathways for the CS appear at the stage where the analyses of the CS and US time series come together in a computation that tests for a statistically significant phase relationship between them. If a statistically significant phase relationship between CS fluctuations and US fluctuations is detected, the system computes the logarithmic gain, the coefficient that allows the amplitude of a US fluctuation to be predicted from the amplitude of a preceding CS fluctuation. When the CS appears in the diagram, its short-range complex representation, $£[CS]$, has already been analyzed into a representation of its very recent phase, $\varphi\{£[CS]\}$, and the natural logarithm of its very recent amplitude, $\ln\{|£[CS]|\}$. The complex (cosine-sine) representation of the phase of the CS is subtracted from the complex representation of the phase of the US (circle with an angle in it) to obtain the complex representation of the amount by which the most recent US lagged the most recent CS. This represents the time interval between the CS and the US, expressed as a fraction of the period of the demodulating cycle, hence as a phase angle, $\Delta\varphi$. If either the US or the CS phase is undefined because one or both has not recently occurred, $\Delta\varphi = <0,0>$, which means that $\Delta\varphi$ is momentarily undefined.

The complex representation of the phase angle between the CS and the US is also subject to an exponentially relaxing backward look, by a process that looks back over several cycles (the number being determined by a real-valued constant k). If the mean square resultant attains statistically significant levels (if phase angles separating CS and US occurrences tend to be the same, which means that the CS and US are "temporal paired"), then the logarithmic amplitude of the CS is lagged (shifted backward in time) by $\Delta\varphi$ and subtracted from the logarithmic amplitude of the US to yield the coefficient by which the magnitude of US fluctuations may be predicted from the magnitudes of the CS fluctuations that precede them.

By using the outputs from the short-range temporal filters, the system detects systematic phase differences between aperiodic variables. This is remarkable because aperiodic patterns of occurrence—of which Poisson processes are paradigmatic—do not have power localized in any range of the frequency spectrum; their power is spread across all the Fourier components. Worse, the Fourier components of a Poisson occurrence pattern have no consistent phase values; there is no predicting when during a cycle a Poisson event will occur. Nonetheless, given two dependent Poisson processes—two distinguishable kinds of randomly occurring events, in which one kind of event (the CS) reliably precedes the other (the US) by a certain interval—the temporal dependence between the two kinds of events can be detected by a computation based on the output of a temporal filter that decays to negligible values within the span of one cycle of the demodulating oscillation, provided that the period of the demodulating oscillation is of the same order of magnitude as the expected interval between two events of the same kind (the average ITI = intertrial interval).

The appendix to this chapter gives a short program in Systat™ Basic, which performs the computations diagrammed in figure 13.8. The computations are analytic; no simulations or iterative computations are required; and the only parameters are the periods of the demodulating frequencies (endogenous oscillators), the exponential time constants that determine the lengths of backward looks, and the thresholds used as decision criteria.

Conclusions

Chapters 7 through 12 review the experimental evidence that the nervous systems of many invertebrates and vertebrates record the times at which events happen, count events, and compute temporal intervals. On the assumption that these primitive variables are available to work with, one may elaborate nonassociative, representational models of classical conditioning. This chapter has sketched one such model. The model accounts for a broader range of results than do the standard associative models, with fewer free parameters; indeed, most of its predictions are parameter independent. It is computationally less complex than associative models, in the sense that it achieves its results with fewer elementary computational operations and with a simpler high-level program structure. Its computational simplicity is particularly striking in comparison to connectionist models, which are computationally complex and slow. They cannot be evaluated analytically; theoretical results (whether the model does or does not predict something) can only be obtained by simulations involving iterative computations (hence the slowness). The computer programs for these simulations are lengthy, and their execution requires orders of magnitude more elementary computational operations than does a spreadsheet realization of the matrix inversion model. The computations described in this chapter may be done by a computer that fits in a shirt pocket, so there is little reason to assume that they would be beyond the computational capabilities of the brain of, say, an ant. The ant's brain does the computations underlying sun-compass navigation, which are of the same order of complexity as the computations sketched in this chapter.

Appendix

Systat™ Basic program for analyzing a CS and US series to obtain prediction coefficients

```
USE ?
SAVE ?D
NOTE 'Demodulating {X} & {Y}; {X} = CS series; {Y} = US series.'
NOTE 'PERIOD = number of time bins in one day'
NOTE 'DMODFREQ = cycles/day.'
NOTE 'ω = radians/unit time = 2*3.14159*DMODFREQ/PERIOD'
HOLD
  LET PERIOD = 12
  LET DMODFREQ=1
  LET ZREX=X*COS(2*3.14159*DMODFREQ*(CASE-1)/PERIOD)
  LET ZIMX=X*SIN(2*3.14159*DMODFREQ*(CASE-1)/PERIOD)
  LET ZREY=Y*COS(2*3.14159*DMODFREQ*(CASE-1)/PERIOD)
  LET ZIMY=Y*SIN(2*3.14159*DMODFREQ*(CASE-1)/PERIOD)
NOTE 'Smoothing the complex series'
NOTE 'K1 = e-R[ωs] = the fraction remaining after one time interval'
  LET K1 = .61
  LET SMREX = K1*SMREX + ZREX
  LET SMIMX = K1*SMIMX + ZIMX
  LET SMREY = K1*SMREY + ZREY
  LET SMIMY = K1*SMIMY+ ZIMY
NOTE 'Computing cos-sin rep of phase angles of smoothed {ZX} & {ZY}'
NOTE 'THRESH1 = T in the flow diagram, Fig. 13.8.'
  LET THRESH1 = .01
  IF (SMREX^2 + SMIMX^2) > THRESH1 THEN FOR
  LET COSPHX = SQR(SMREX^2/(SMREX^2 + SMIMX^2))
  LET SINPHX = SQR(SMIMX^2/(SMREX^2 + SMIMX^2))
  NEXT
  ELSE FOR
      LET COSPHX = 0
      LET SINPHX = 0
  NEXT
  IF SMREX < 0 THEN LET COSPHX = -COSPHX
  IF SMIMX < 0 THEN LET SINPHX = -SINPHX
  IF (SMREY^2 + SMIMY^2) > THRESH THEN FOR
  LET COSPHY = SQR(SMREY^2/(SMREY^2 + SMIMY^2))
  LET SINPHY = SQR(SMIMY^2/(SMREY^2 + SMIMY^2))
  NEXT
  ELSE FOR
```

```
        LET COSPHY = 0
        LET SINPHY = 0
    NEXT
    IF SMREY < 0 THEN LET COSPHY= -COSPHY
    IF SMIMY < 0 THEN LET SINPHY = -SINPHY
    NOTE 'The cos-sin representation of delta phase'
      LET COSD = COSPHY*COSPHX + SINPHY*SINPHX
      LET SIND = SINPHY*COSPHX - COSPHY*SINPHX
    NOTE 'The running sum of delta phase'
      LET K2 = .98
      LET SMCOSD = K2*SMCOSD + COSD
      LET SMSIND = K2*SMSIND + SIND
    NOTE 'The normalized square resultant'
      LET SUMW = K2*SUMW + 1
      LET NSQRES = (SMCOSD^2 + SMSIND^2)/SUMW
    NOTE 'Lagging {ZX}=moving complex CS series forward in time.'
      DIM LAGREX(6)
      DIM LAGIMX(6)
      FOR I = 6 TO 2 STEP -1
          LET LAGREX(I) = LAGREX(I-1)
          LET LAGIMX(I) = LAGIMX(I-1)
      NEXT
      LET LAGREX(1) = LAGREX0
      LET LAGIMX(1) = LAGIMX0
      LET LAGREX0 = ZREX
      LET LAGIMX0 = ZIMX
      DROP LAGREX0 LAGIMX0
    NOTE 'Computing log power gain'
      IF INT(.5+PHDIFF*PERIOD/6.2832) > 0 THEN
          LET L = INT(.5+PHDIFF*PERIOD/6.2832)
      ELSE LET L = 0
      IF L > 0 THEN LET XPOW = (LAGREX(L)^2 + LAGIMX(L)^2)
      ELSE LET XPOW = (ZREX^2 + ZIMX^2)
      LET YPOW = (ZREY^2 + ZIMY^2)
      IF XPOW > THRESH AND YPOW > THRESH THEN LET LOGPGAIN
      = LOG(YPOW) -
      LOG(XPOW)
      ELSE LET LOGPGAIN = .
    NOTE 'Computing running average of log power gain'
      IF LOGPGAIN <>. THEN FOR
          LET SUMGAIN = K2*SUMGAIN + LOGPGAIN
          LET SUMWG = K2*SUMWG + 1
      NEXT
```

```
IF SUMWG > 0 THEN LET MEANGAIN = SUMGAIN/SUMWG
ELSE LET MEANGAIN = .
RUN
```

Chapter 14

Vector Spaces in the Nervous System

An animal's nervous system constructs representations of behavior-relevant aspects of the animal's environment as a means of adapting the animal's behavior to that environment. These constructions are representations in the mathematical sense of the term; there is a formal isomorphism between entities and processes within the nervous system and selected aspects of the external world. The isomorphism is not fortuitous; the entities and processes in the nervous system isomorphic to selected aspects of the external world play a causal role in generating behavior adapted to those same external aspects. The isomorphism between the internal and external systems is the key to the success of the internal system in carrying out its function.

The aspects of reality—space, time, probability— whose representation has so far been discussed lend themselves to vector representation, in the loose sense of a representation composed of a string of numbers or quantities, each specifying the value of a particular attribute. The relative position of a point in space is represented by a three-dimensional vector $<x, y, z>$. Each successive number (each dimension) specifies the distance of the point from an origin along one of three orthogonal axes. The time-of-occurrence vector has been assumed to be composed of pairs of numbers, each pair specifying the phase of an oscillation, with the period of oscillation differing from pair to pair. If we imagine that the system covers the range of conceivable times of occurrence with six different oscillation periods, differing one from the next by approximately an order of magnitude, then the dimensionality of the time-of-occurrence vector is twelve.

Aspects of nervous system structure and function also lend themselves to representation in terms of vectors. If we assign to each axon in a bundle the number that represents the number of action potentials in that axon in the past 1 second, the resulting string of numbers is a vector, the firing-frequency vector. This vector will be a function of time because the number in each position in the string will change from moment to moment. If we assign to each postsynaptic site on the soma and dendrites of a neuron the number that represents the transmembrane current at that site, we get a string of numbers that we might call the current vector. The numbers in the current vector, unlike those in the firing-frequency vector, may be either positive or negative, since the current may flow either inward (by convention a positive current flow) or outward (a negative flow).

Conversely a set of physical magnitudes of supposed functional relevance in the nervous system, such as firing frequency and current, may be said to be the physical embodiment of the abstraction that we call a vector in a computational analysis of the operation of the nervous system. When the computational theorist speaks of the visual input vector and one asks what that might be, one potentially appropriate answer is that it is the amounts of isomerized (light-activated) photopigment in each of the photoreceptors. This set of physical quantities is the physical realization of the computational abstraction called the input vector.

A vector, in the generalized sense in which I am using it here, is an ordered set of numbers or, equivalently an ordered set of magnitudes. In saying that a vector is ordered, we indicate that position in the string matters; the string <2, 7> is not equivalent to the string <7, 2>. Whether a set of numbers or physical quantities is a vector cannot be determined from an analysis of the set itself. This classification depends on the use made of the numbers. Loosely speaking, if the numbers enter into computational operations—for example, vector addition—that generate different outputs for different orderings of the numbers, then the input sets are vectors.[1] If the operations into which the numbers enter yield the same result when the order of the numbers within the set is arbitrarily scrambled, as does, for example, the operation of averaging the numbers, then the set is not a vector. Similarly to speak of a set of physical magnitudes as a vector indicates a belief that the outcomes of the physical processes in which these quantities play a role depend on which magnitudes are which. The set of all the photopigment molecules in a disk in the outer segment of a photoreceptor could be regarded as a binary vector, one in which a given position in the string had the value 1 if a given molecule was not isomerized and the value 0 if it was. However, so far as we know, the functionally relevant consequences of rhodopsin isomerization do not depend on which molecules are isomerized. The only thing that matters is how many are isomerized because the ensuing processes average their effects. Thus it would be inappropriate to treat the isomerization pattern in a disk membrane as a vector. By contrast, in

1. It is in this loose sense that one may call the string of numbers (or quantities) that specify a time of occurrence a vector. In the strict sense, a string of numbers is a vector only if it may be handled in accord with the rules of vector algebra. The string of numbers representing time of occurrence is not a vector in this strict sense.

an organism with pattern vision, it matters to the behavioral outcome which photoreceptors have which amounts of isomerized photopigment, so this set of quantities is appropriately treated as a vector in an analysis of visual function. In short, the decision whether to regard a set of physical magnitudes as a vector is like the decision whether to regard a set of physical variables as a representation; both decisions depend on our beliefs about how those variables determine the course of subsequent processes within the system being analyzed.

There is nothing remarkable about the appearance of vector representations in our formal descriptions of the representations that animals appear to have or in the reappearance of this same formal device in our descriptions of the physical state of the nervous system. Vector representation is a powerful, versatile, and ubiquitous form of mathematical representation. However, the formal convenience of our representing by means of vectors the representations that an animal appears to have gives no assurance that the physical realization of this representation within the nervous system of the animal has a vectorial form.

The purpose of this chapter is to review neurophysiological data supporting the hypothesis that the nervous system does in fact quite generally employ vectors to represent properties of both proximal and distal stimuli. The values of these representational vectors are physically expressed by the locations of neural activity in anatomical spaces whose dimensions correspond to descriptive dimensions of the stimulus. The term *vector space*, which refers to the space defined by a system of coordinates, has a surprisingly literal interpretation in the nervous system. The functional architecture of many structures that process higher-level sensory inputs is such that anatomical dimensions of the structure correspond to descriptive dimensions of the stimulus. There is reason to think that this correspondence is not fortuitous; rather, it is a foundation for the nervous system's capacity to adapt its output to the structure of the world that generates its inputs.

The data that illustrate this point most clearly come from studies of structures that compute from auditory inputs a representation of the spatial relationship between the animal and the sound source, most notably the superior colliculus of the barn owl and subdivisions of the auditory cortex of the mustache bat.

In what follows, the distinction between proximal and distal stimuli is fundamental, as it is in any discussion of higher order sensory processing. Proximal stimuli act directly on sensory receptors, for example, light falling on the retina or sound falling on the ear drum. Distal stimuli do not act directly on sensory receptors; they indirectly and partially determine one or more aspects of a proximal stimulus. Examples of distal stimuli are the reflectance characteristics of a surface from which light incident on the retina has been reflected, the size of the surface, its distance from the retina, its position in space, the size of a sound emitter or reflector, its distance, and so on. The task of perceptual mechanisms is to compute properties of distal stimuli from properties of proximal stimuli.

The Tectal Map of Angular Deviation

The tectum forms the roof of the midbrain, just as the cortex forms the roof of the forebrain. Like the cortex, the tectum is clearly layered, and its functional architecture is also analogous to that of the cortex. In short, the tectum is a sort of midbrain cortex. Classically the tectum has been subdivided on both anatomical and functional grounds into an anterior portion, the optic tectum (or, in mammals, the superior colliculus), and a posterior portion, the auditory tectum (inferior colliculus). These designations are misleading, however, at least for the optic tectum because the neuronal elements in the deeper layers of the optic tectum respond to auditory and somasthetic stimuli, as well as visual stimuli.

The superficial layers of the optic tectum receive fibers directly from the retina. Like most other visual projections, the retino-tectal projection is primarily crossed (most of the fibers coming from the right eye go to the left tectum and vice-versa), and it is retinotopically organized: neighboring points on the retina project to neighboring points in the optic tectum. This crossed retinotopic projection results in a correspondence between the location of an image on the retina and the location of the resulting neural activity in the superficial layers of the optic tectum. An image falling on the lateral (temporal) edge of the retina elicits activity at the anterior end of the contralateral tectum, while an image on the medial (nasal) edge elicits activity at the posterior end (figure 14.1A). An image falling on the dorsal (top) edge of the retina elicits activity at the ventro-lateral margin of the tectum, while an image on the ventral (bottom) edge elicits activity on the dorsomedial margin (figure 14.1B). Thus temporal-to-nasal on the retina corresponds to front-to-back on the tectum, while top-to-bottom on the retina corresponds to out from the midline and down around the circumference of the tectum, which has approximately the shape of a half-barrel.

So long as we consider only visual input to the tectum, the functional significance of this orderly projection is obscure. This organization may be an afunctional consequence of developmental mechanisms: fibers that start out together from the retina stay together all the way to the tectum. On the other hand, in an animal such as the barn owl, which cannot move its eyes relative to its head, an orderly mapping of the retina is an orderly mapping of the angular deviation of the image source from the angle of

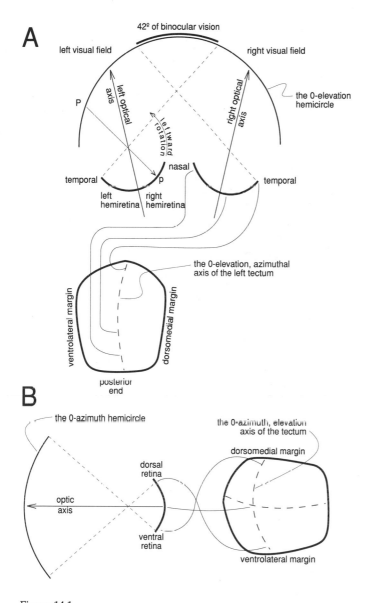

Figure 14.1
The geometry of the projection from the visual space to the retina and then to the optic tectum. In this illustration, the optic axes of the two eyes do not converge, which is characteristic of birds. In primates, the axes converge. Note that the image of the world is left-right reversed and inverted on the retina. The projection from the right retina crosses over to the left tectum, and vice-versa. The azimuthal dimension of the visual hemisphere is mapped to the anterior-posterior dimension of the optic tectum (A), while the elevational dimension is mapped to the dorsomedial-ventrolateral dimension (B).

gaze and hence from the caudo-rostro axis of the head. A source located at the leftward limit of the right eye's vision (about 21° to the left of the midline) will activate the anterior end of the left tectum, while a source at the rightward limit of vision (95° to the right of the midline) will activate the posterior end (figure 14.1A). A source at the dorsal edge of vision will activate the dorsomedial margin of the hemi-barrel, while a source at the ventral limit will activate the ventrolateral margin (figure 14.1B). Thus the central positional tendency in the tectal activity elicited by an image may represents either the retinal location of the image (an attribute of the proximal stimulus) or the azimuth and elevation of the source in a coordinate framework anchored to the eyes (an attribute of the distal stimulus). An anatomical vector with dimensions anterior-posterior and dorsomedial-ventrolateral is the physiological representive of either a retinal vector with dimensions of horizontal and vertical or a source-angle vector with dimensions of azimuth and elevation.

Data on the mapping of auditory inputs to the optic tectum and data on the effects of stimulating at different points in the tectum strongly suggest that it is the distal, spatial mapping rather than the proximal, retinal mapping of stimulus descriptors that is the functionally significant aspect of tectal architecture. When one makes a radial penetration of the deeper layers of the optic tectum of the barn owl with a recording microelectrode (a penetration perpendicular to the tectal surface), most of the neurons one encountered are driven by both visual and auditory inputs (Knudsen 1982). Since the visual projection to the tectum is retinotopic, it is no surprise that these neurons have circumscribed visual fields; they are excited only by images falling on a small part of the retina, which is to say, only by a source within a small cone of angles with respect to the owl's head. When one turns one's attention to the characteristics that an auditory stimulus must have to excite these same neurons, one finds no correspondence with dimensions of the proximal stimulus (the region of the basilar membrane stimulated by the emitted sound) but the same correspondence with the dimensions of the distal stimulus (the angular deviation of the sound source). Tones of different pitches—hence tones that stimulate different portions of the basilar membrane—are equally effective in exciting these neurons. What determines whether a sound excites one of these neurons is not its pitch but rather the angular deviation of the loudspeaker from which the sound emanates. Thus in the auditory domain, where the dimensions of the proximal stimulus (position on the basilar membrane) are not confounded with those of the distal stimulus (angular deviation from the optic axis), the tectal mapping accords with the latter, not the former.

Moreover, the mappings of visual and auditory inputs into the same anatomical region are, for the most part, in correspondence: the best deviation for a visual stimulus is the same as the best deviation for an auditory stimulus (Knudsen 1982). When, in the young bird, one distorts this correspondence by putting a sound-attenuating plug in one ear, the projection of the auditory stimulus onto the tectum gradually changes so as to bring the effect of a sound back in register with the effect of a visual stimulus originating at the same angular deviation (Knudsen 1983). It is the mapping of the aural angular deviation that changes not the mapping of the visual angular deviation, even when the discrepancy is produced by visual means. Angular deviation from the axis of gaze is primary.

Activity in these bimodally driven units in the deeper layers of the optic tectum cannot represent the position of an image on the retina because the activity may be excited by a sound rather than by a visual stimulus. Activity in the deeper layers represents an amodal property of the stimulus. By monitoring the location within the tectum of activity in these deep units, a readout system could not distinguish between seeing something and hearing it. What it could distinguish is the angular deviation of the distal stimulus. The sensitivity of these units to the angular deviation of sound sources does not reflect a topographic pattern of connections between the sheet of auditory receptors on the basilar membrane and the tectum; rather, it reflects a series of computational operations at successive stages of the multisynaptic auditory projection leading to the tectum (Knudsen and Konishi 1978). These operations extract a representation of azimuthal angle from small differences in the timing of the firings of auditory fibers originating at similar positions along the basilar membranes on opposite sides of the head. They extract a representation of elevation from differences in the intensities of the sounds received by the two ears, which are differentially oriented in the transverse vertical plane (Knudsen and Konishi 1979; Moiseff and Konishi 1981). The only readily apparent rationale for the orderly change in the best-deviation for exciting these neurons as one moves along the anterior-posterior or dorsomedial-ventrolateral dimensions of the tectum is that the arrangement is crucial to the behavioral function of the structure.

To say that the orderly mapping from the distal stimulus deviation to the position of activity in the tectum is crucial to the proper functioning of the tectum is to imply that the anatomical position of an active unit in the tectum is a determinant of the behavioral-computational effect of the unit's activity. Experiments on the behavioral effects of electrically stimulating the tectum support this conclusion. It has been shown in a variety of vertebrates that stimulating the tectum elicits a reflex (saccadic) orienting movement (a quick turn of the head and/or eyes) and that the direction and magnitude of the saccade varies systematically with the site of tectal stimulation (Ewert 1974; Robinson 1972).

Schiller and Stryker (1972) combined single unit recording and stimulation in the alert (unanesthetized) monkey. They found that in the superficial layers of the superior colliculus, cells responded only to visual inputs. (The same is true in the optic tectum of the owl in the superficial layers, where the direct retinal input terminates. The bimodal cells in the owl are found in deeper layers.) The cells lower in the same radial penetration often did not respond to visual input consistently. Rather, they fired an intense burst of impulses immediately (20 milliseconds) prior to the onset of a subset of the monkey's saccadic eye movements. These units have come to be called "saccade-related" units. The subset of saccadic movements whose occurrence was closely anticipated by activity in a given saccade-related unit could be predicted from the best receptive areas for stimulus-sensitive units at that position in the tectum. If units at that position were best excited by a visual stimulus 10° to the right of the fovea and 5° above the retinal horizonline, then the saccade-related units would fire most vigorously to a saccade in which the eye rotated 10° left and 5° down (figure 14.2). Since the image of the world is left-right reversed and inverted on the retina, the described movement would ordinarily bring the described image to the center of the fovea; that is, it would direct the gaze toward the distal stimulus.

Finally, electrical stimulation in the intermediate and deep layers of the superior colliculus yielded saccadic eye movements whose direction and amplitude were predicted by the recording data for that site. Thus stimulation at the site just used as an example would elicit a saccade that moved the eye 10° left and 5° down. The intensity, duration, and pulse frequency of the stimulation had little effect on the direction and amplitude of the saccade. Provided the stimulation was suprathreshold, the site of stimulation and nothing else—including eye position—determined the direction and magnitude of the orienting movement. When the stimulation was lengthy, the eye made repeated saccades of the same direction and amplitude (jump, pause, jump, pause, and so on). Thus outputs from a given position in the tectum produce a given change in angular position, irrespective of the current angular position of the eyes in their orbits.

At first glance, the Schiller and Stryker data for the alert, mobile-eyed monkey appear to contradict one important aspect of the conclusion about tectal function that we drew from Knudsen's recording data from anesthetized owls, whose eyes do not move in their head, even when they are alert. We concluded that the multimodal cells in the intermediate and deep layers must represent an aspect of the distal stimulus (the angular deviation of the source from the optic axis) rather than of the proximal stimulus (the retinal position of the image). Recording and stimulation data of the kind reported by Schiller and Stryker were initially taken to

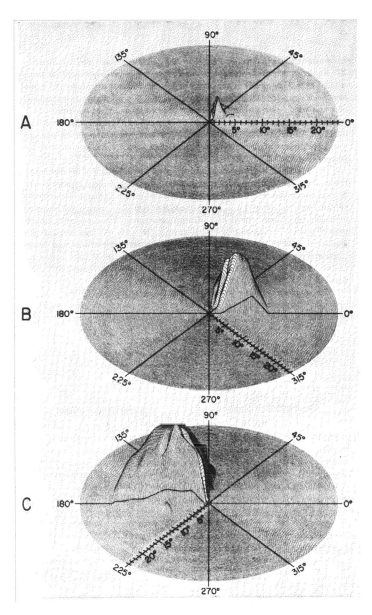

Figure 14.2
Magnitude of the presaccadic burst in three different tectal neurons as a function of the angular deviation of the ensuing saccade. This plot may be taken as a portrait of the spatial pattern of unit activity in this class of neurons prior to a saccade to the position represented by the tectal position of the peaks in these "mountains." (Redrawn from Sparks et al. 1976, p. 27, by permission of author and the publisher.)

imply a proximal model for the generation of saccades. It seemed natural to assume that the proximal error signal (the "error" in the site of retinal stimulation), which is represented by the site of neural activity in the superficial layers of the colliculus, caused the underlying saccade-related units to discharge, which caused the eyes to rotate by an amount calculated to correct the proximal error and bring the image onto the fovea. If this were a correct conception of the functioning of the deep layers of the monkey superior colliculus, then this functioning would be tied to proximal dimensions of the stimulus (where its image fell on the retina), not to distal dimensions (the angular deviation of the source from the direction of gaze). By contrast, the functioning of the multimodal units in deep layers of the owl optic tectum appear to relate to distal, not proximal, stimulus dimensions.

Recent further examination of activity in the superior colliculus in the alert monkey by Sparks and his collaborators has shown, however, that the representational function of the deep layers must be conceived in distal rather than proximal terms. These experiments, which combine behavioral training, single-unit recording, and electrical stimulation in ingenious ways, were inspired by the difficulty of reconciling the "proximal-error" model of collicular saccade generation with data on saccade generation from purely behavioral experiments. First, it was found that saccades may be triggered by nonvisual stimuli, for example, by auditory stimuli (Zahn, Abel, and Dell'Osso 1978). One might get round this by arguing that the superior colliculus was concerned only with visually triggered saccades. However, Schiller and Stryker (1972) had found that the burst of firing in a saccade-related neuron preceded a saccade of a given direction and magnitude even when that saccade had a nonvisual genesis.

More telling was the demonstration that accurate saccadic eye movements could be made to visual targets that were flashed before or during another saccade (Hallet and Lightstone 1976; Mays and Sparks 1980). These double-saccade experiments dissociate the experienced retinal position of the visual stimulus from the movement that must be made to orient the fovea toward the distal stimulus. By the time the second saccade is initiated, the position of the eye may be very different from the position it had when the image of the target fell on the retina. Thus the proximal error—the foveal deviation of the target's image when the image fell on the retina—is dissociated from the distal error—the present angular deviation of the target with respect to the retina. Suppose that the eye is induced to make a saccade by flashing an initial target stimulus for 50 milliseconds 15° to the right of the eye's momentary fixation point (creating an image that falls 15° to the left of the fovea). There is a latency of at least 150 milliseconds between the occurrence of a flash and the onset of the answering saccade. Suppose that 100 milliseconds after the first flash but 50 milliseconds before the eyes begin their 15° rightward jump, we flash a second 50 milliseconds stimulus directly at the fixation point, the image of which falls in the center of the fovea. An image that falls on the center of the fovea does not normally elicit a saccade; however, if there is no response to the second stimulus after the first saccade is completed, the eye will be incorrectly oriented with respect to the source of the second flash. The response to the first target creates a distal error—a misalignment between the second target and the direction of gaze—for which there has been no corresponding proximal error. For the eye to attain a correct orientation to the source of the second flash, it must make a 15° leftward jump after it has completed its response to the first stimulus. This is what the eye in fact does, which means that it makes a 15° leftward jump in response to a foveal stimulus.

Varying the positions of the first and second flashes elicits a saccade of almost any direction and magnitude by stimulating a given spot on the retina. Conversely a saccade of a given direction and magnitude may be elicited by stimulating almost any point on the retina. These results are irreconcilable with a proximal error model for the generation of visually elicited saccades (let along those nonvisually elicited). The direction and amplitude of a saccade is a function of the angular deviation of the stimulus source from the direction of gaze at the moment the saccade begins, not the position on the retina that may or may not have been stimulated by energy from that source. If we continue to assume that the superior colliculus plays a role in the genesis of saccades, we have to revise our conception of what the deep layers do.

When the double-saccade procedure is employed in conjunction with the recording of single unit activity in the deeper layers of the superior colliculus, it emerges that this activity reflects the angular deviation of the distal stimulus rather than the proximal position of the image on the retina (Mays and Sparks 1980). These experiments also reveal a new class of neurons, termed quasi-visual neurons, in the intermediate layers. The activity of these neurons, like that of the saccade-related neurons, is a function of the angular deviation of the distal stimulus. In these experiments, one makes a radial penetration at a point where, to continue using the previous illustration, the superficial (purely visual) units respond to a stimulus that falls 15° to the right of the fovea. The saccade-related units underlying this point in the tectum fire prior to a 15° leftward jump of the eyes. In the double-saccade paradigm, this jump may be elicited by a stimulus that falls almost anywhere on the retina, including the center of the fovea. Saccade-related units at this locus in the tectum fire prior to the 15° leftward jump, regardless of where the image of the target falls on the retina. These units fail to fire in response to a stimulus 15° to the right of the fovea unless that stimulus elicits a 15° leftward jump. If it is arranged by the double-saccade procedure that the stimulus elicit a different jump, there is no activity in the saccade-related units. Thus the tectal position of the saccade-related units that fire before a saccade represents the jump that the eye is about to make, regardless of the retinal position of the visual stimulus that elicits the jump.

The quasi-visual units in the intermediate layers do not show a prejump firing burst; their firing begins long before the jump and continues until shortly after the jump is completed. Only in the double-saccade paradigm does it become clear why these units cannot be called simply visual (retinal position) units. When a 15° leftward jump is elicited by a stimulus falling elsewhere on the fovea, purely visual units give no response. Quasi-visual units, however, do respond, as if a stimulus had fallen in their receptive fields after the completion of the first saccade, though there is no stimulus at this time, and though the second visual stimulus, when it did occur, did not fall in the supposed receptive field of the unit. Thus the quasi-visual units could signal the direction and amplitude that a saccade to the second stimulus must have. Put another way, they appear to signal the deviation of the second stimulus source relative to the axis of gaze after the eye has completed its first saccade.

One might suppose that on double-saccade trials, the two successive saccades are programmed in advance, with the program for the second saccade based on the position of the second stimulus relative to the first. The quasi-visual cells might form a buffer that expresses the direction and amplitude of a preprogrammed jump during the period immediately preceding and accompanying its execution. However, a subsequent stimulation experiment rules this model out (Sparks and Porter 1983). In these experiments, stimulation of the colliculus was used to divert the eye to new (and unforeseeable) positions after a flash had occurred but before the answering saccade. On such a trial, one might present a flash 5° to the left of the fovea, then use stimulation to drive the eye 20° to the right of its initial fixation. Although there has been only one visual stimulus, which fell 5° to the left of the fovea, a 15° leftward jump is required to orient the eye properly. This is what in fact occurs. Furthermore, the quasi-visual units and the saccade-related units that would usually fire in anticipation of such a jump also fire in this case.

Sparks and Porter's stimulation experiment demonstrates that the collicular position of the firing quasi-visual units represents the angular deviation of a stimulus source relative to the axis of gaze. This representation comes into existence whenever there is a stimulus toward which the monkey might wish to orient its eyes, whether or not it actually does do so. If this is so and if there is a homology of function between the optic tectum of the owl and the superior colliculus of the monkey, then the mapping of auditory sources into activity in the deep layers of the superior colliculus of the monkey should vary as a function of eye position. This is, indeed, what subsequent experiments have revealed (Jay and Sparks 1987).

In summary, data from the barn owl and the monkey suggest that in both of these evolutionarily very distant vertebrates, elements in the deeper layers of the optic tectum (or its homologue, the superior colliculus) transiently represent the angular deviation of a stimulus source toward which the animal may wish to orient. The angular deviation of the source is represented in a coordinate framework anchored to the optic axis of the eyes. This is shown by the fact that when the visual-auditory correspondence is disrupted by a unilateral earplug in the owl, the audiotectal mapping not the visuotectal mapping is adjusted, and by the fact that changes in eye position relative to the head alter the audiotectal mapping in the monkey. In both the monkey and the owl, the audiotectal mapping is not a mapping of the sensory surface (basilar membrane).

In the owl, where the head has a fixed position relative to the direction of gaze, the mapping results from a computation based on several different attributes of the proximal sound stimulus related in systematic, if complex, ways to the angular deviation of the source. In the monkey, where the head (and hence the ears) moves in a coordinate framework anchored to the eyes, the computation of the deviation of the sound source from the axis of gaze is based not only on several different aspects of the proximal sound stimulus but also on signals indicating the position of the head relative to the eyes. In the monkey, the computation of the positional representation from visual input also takes into account signals indicating the position of the head relative to the eyes, so that for a retinal stimulus that has come and gone, the site of the stimulus-initiated activity in the intermediate and deep layers of the superior colliculus shifts when the eyes move. In the owl, the head cannot move relative to the eyes. However, the deeper significance of the shift in the site of tectal activity during eye movements may be that the tectum is taking into account the movement of the source relative to the eyes. From this perspective, the eyes' moving with respect to the head is just a special case of the eyes' moving with respect to points of interest in the world. In that case, one might find that head (hence eye) rotations in the owl changed the tectal site of source-related activity.

The physiological embodiment of the tectal representation of angular deviation is the site of the active units in the intermediate and lower layers, relative to the anterior-posterior and dorsomedial-ventrolateral axes of the tectum. Thus anatomical dimensions of the tectal area corre-

spond to dimension of the vector space that describes the angular
deviation of the distal stimulus; the mapping carries units of angular
deviation from the axis of gaze monotonically, but nonlinearly into
micrometers of deviation from the orthogonal lines on the tectum that
represent the horizontal and vertical meridians of the eye (the anatomical
axes of the projection). The correspondence between the site of tectal
activity and the angular deviation of a stimulus source is a necessary but
not sufficient condition for concluding that the site of activity subserves
a representational function. One must also show that the readout system
treats this activity appropriately. The correspondence between the angular deviation of the distal stimulus required to excite a given position in
the deeper layers of the optic tectum and the orienting movements
produced by stimulating at that locus is the evidence that this second
criterion for representational function is satisfied. The movements produced by stimulating in the tectum vary with the site of stimulation in a
manner that suggests that the locus of tectal activity represents for the
rest of the system the angular deviation of an external point of interest
from the coordinate system established by the direction of gaze.

Reading the Map of Angular Deviation
The tuning of single units in the optic tectum to the angular deviation of
visual and auditory sources is less precise than the saccadic movements
whose direction is presumed to be determined by tectal activity. If all you
knew was that a specified saccade-related unit in the tectum was firing,
you would have an imperfect estimate of the angular deviation of the
next saccade (see figure 14.2). To put the same point in another way, prior
to the occurrence of a saccade of a given direction and magnitude, there
is activity over a considerable patch of the optic tectum. Clearly the
activity of a single tectal unit does not by itself determine the direction
and magnitude of a saccade under normal conditions. The question
naturally arises what the algorithm is for combining the outputs from the
many active units.

Two simple possibilities suggest themselves. The simplest is the peak-
detector hypothesis: the coordinates of the most active unit determine the
angular deviation of the saccade. This hypothesis requires a process
(neural circuit) that identifies the most active unit. An alternative hypothesis is the resultant-vector hypothesis. According to this, the currently favored hypothesis, the change in the angular position (Δp) of the
eyes signaled by the activity of a population of tectal units is the resultant
(vector sum) of the Δp vectors of the active units, with the contribution of
each unit weighted by the unit's firing rate (figure 14.3). In this algorithm,
the firing rate of a relevant tectal unit is treated as the length of a vector
that may be imagined to project outward from the center of a sphere. The

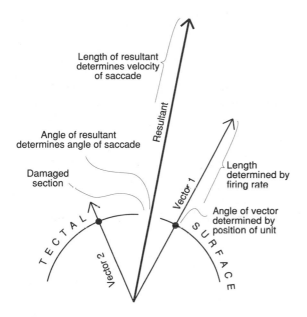

Figure 14.3
 Illustration of the resultant-vector hypothesis. Each tectal unit (each quasi-visual cell or each saccade-related unit) may be thought of as a finger (vector) pointing toward a certain angular deviation from the eye's current position, that is, to a particular Δp, which symbolizes the angular deviation of the target. The higher is the firing rate of the unit, the longer is the vector pointing toward that Δp. In this case, the unit for vector 1 is firing more vigorously than the unit for vector 2. The Δp indicated by one population of active cells is the angle of the resultant (sum) of the corresponding vectors. The length of the resultant (the magnitude of the vector sum) determines the velocity of the saccade. In this case, the angle of the resultant corresponds to a Δp for which there are no active units because the region of the tectum that represents that angular deviation is assumed to be damaged or anesthetized. Thus the position in the descriptive space indicated by the resultant of the population activity may not be indicated by any single unit in the population.

angle of the vector, which is the point at which it intersects the surface of the sphere, corresponds to the angular deviation of the target from the fovea. The angle of the vector for a given tectal unit is specified by the position of the unit within the orderly mapping of elevational and azimuthal deviations in the deeper layers of the optic tectum. The length of the vector (the firing rate of the unit) may be thought of as representing how vehemently the unit is pointing toward "its" direction. Units that point more vigorously have more influence over the angle of the resultant, which is the angle of the vector obtained by summing all the active vectors. Thus the resultant of the activity of a population of units is itself a vector, which may also be imagined to project outward from the center of the sphere. The point at which this resultant intersects the sphere specifies the angular deviation for the to-be-made saccade. The length of the resultant—how far beyond the surface of the sphere it projects— specifies the vigor or velocity of the saccade.

The resultant-vector hypothesis is interesting from several perspectives. One is that the angle of the resultant computed from the firing in undamaged tissue may correspond to a tectal locus where, because of tissue damage, there is no activity (see figure 14.3). Thus the hypothesized mode of operation may yield what appear to be examples of mass action or vicarious function. The tectum may signal a given saccade even when the tissue that one might naively take to be responsible for saccades in that particular direction has been destroyed or inactivated.

The hypothesis requires elaboration, however. Among other things, the elaboration will have to specify how activity corresponding to one source is distinguished from that corresponding to a second source, since summing across populations of units activated by two different sources would produce a saccade oriented toward neither source. The algorithm for determining what constitutes a cluster of active units remains to be specified.

Lee, Rohrer, and Sparks (1988) have recently reported an experiment confirming the predictions of the resultant-vector hypothesis. They injected minute amounts of local anesthetic into different areas within an active population of tectal units. The injections altered the directions of saccades in the manner predicted by the resultant vector hypothesis. Knocking out activity on one edge of the active population displaced the saccades away from the angular deviation represented by the inactivated units toward the deviation represented by the still-active units. Knocking out units in the center of the active population did not alter the angular angular deviation of a saccade, but it did reduce its velocity. This is what one would expect on the basis of the resultant-vector hypothesis. Knocking out units representing symmetrically opposed directions, as an injection of locally acting anesthetic into the center of an active population should do, would not alter the angle of the resultant vector but would reduce its length.

The relatively broad tuning of tectal units and the correspondingly broad area of the projection field active in representing a single value of the represented entity (such as, a single angular deviation) is characteristic of the other mappings that we now turn to. In all of these, the tuning of the individual units, while it is sometimes impressively sharp (particularly in the bat cortex), is never so sharp that it is reasonable to imagine that the value of the represented entity is specified by the activity of a single unit. In all cases, the value delivered by the representing area to circuits that employ that representation for various purposes must derive from the activity of a population of units in the projection area that represents that particular combination of descriptive parameters.

The fact that the functionally relevant output of a given projection area generally derives from the combined effect of many different units within that area should not be taken to imply that the activity of individual units considered in isolation has no functional meaning (an argument that reappears time and again in discussions of the relation between unit activity and brain function). If the resultant-vector hypothesis is correct, the activity of an individual unit is an "assertion," given with a "confidence" specified by the firing rate, that the stimulus has the value represented by the position of that unit within the projection field. In such a scheme, individual units have clear functional roles, which are specified by their position within the field. A unit at the 15°-left, 5°-down position in the field votes the 15°-left-5°-down "ticket" in proportion as it gets input consistent with such a conclusion. The upshot of the election (the resultant vector) is determined by the positions of the other voting units and how many ballots (impulses) each of them casts. In the unlikely event that only a single unit votes, its activity alone can, at least in principle, specify an angular deviation and saccade velocity. This is to be contrasted with the view of the functional meaning of activity in individual units sometimes argued by proponents of holographic schemes or, more recently, by the more extreme proponents of distributed processing schemes. In a truly holographic system, as in an undecoded holographic image, the activity of a single point cannot in principle convey a meaningful message. (In an undecoded holographic image, the darkness of a given point acquires meaning solely by virtue of its relation to the darkness of other points in the image.) In some connectionist schemes, the activity of a given unit has representational significance only by virtue of its relation to the activities of other units. Its activity considered in isolation has no significance.

Distance and Velocity Maps in the Auditory Cortex of the Bat

In most mobile animals, visual information plays an important role in the construction of a representation of the spatial relationship between the animal and its environment. Information about the relative spatial positions of surfaces and their reflectance characteristics is conveyed to the animal by the light that reflects off the surfaces. Reflected or emitted sound also contains a great deal of spatial information about the distal environment, which the animals extract.

The study of the neural mechanisms by which animals compute spatial representations from auditory inputs is greatly aided by the existence of a genus, the bats, in which the animals generate the sounds whose reflected echos convey information about surfaces in the environment. Since the bat is the source of the energy that gets reflected, it can choose the characteristics of the emitted energy so as to optimize the information content in the echo. The characteristics of the bat's cry in turn suggest what aspects of the echo it relies on to obtain different kinds of information. This knowledge of the structure of the bat's cry is a valuable guide to the scientific analysis of the computational processes by which the bat constructs its representations of the world. This in part explains the rather surprising fact that we have a more advanced understanding of the neural mechanisms that recover spatial information from auditory inputs than of the mechanisms that recover the same information from visual inputs.

The cry that a bat emits to obtain an echo varies from species to species and from one behavioral context to the next within a species, depending on which kind of information is sought in a given context. However, the cry almost always contains an FM sweep. The cry is composed of frequency formants—three or four narrow, harmonically related frequency bands where the energy of the cry is concentrated. In the FM sweep, these frequencies change rapidly but continuously, so that within a few milliseconds, the formants of the cry have between them covered a substantial portion of the spectrum. In the mustache bat, for example, there are four formants. During the initial steady portion of each cry (the CF, or constant frequency portion), the frequencies of these formants are 30.5, 61, 92, and 122 kilohertz. At the end of each cry, these frequencies drop by about 20 percent within less than 5 milliseconds. This rapid drop in the frequencies of the fundamental (30.5) and its first three harmonics is the FM sweep.

From basic principles, it may be deduced that the CF portion is designed to yield information about radial velocity (the rate at which the distance between the bat and a surface is changing), while the FM sweep at the end is designed to yield information about the distances of surfaces from the bat. Sound waves travel about 30,500 centimeters in one second, so at 61,000 Hz, the wavelength is 0.5 centimeter. If the surface off which the sound bounces moves toward the source of the sound at 100 centimeters per second (radial velocity = -100 centimeters per second), the distance between successive wave peaks is shortened in proportion to the ratio between the radial velocity and the sound velocity: 100/30,500 = 0.33 percent shortening. Since the frequency of a sound is the reciprocal of its wavelength, the 0.33 percent shortening of the wavelength "seen" by the moving surface translates into a 0.33 percent increase in the frequency of the sound that bounces off the surface and returns to the bat. Hence the frequency of the echo from the 61 kilohertz formant of the bats cry increases to 61,203 hertz when the echo-surface has a radial velocity of -100 centimeters per second. At 61 kilohertz, the bat can detect frequency changes much smaller than this (changes on the order of 10 hertz); hence it can determine the radial velocity with some precision from the Doppler shift (change in frequency) in the 61 kilohertz formant of the echo.

The Doppler shift is a function solely of the radial velocity of the echo-producing surface; it is the same regardless of the radial distance; hence, it cannot tell the bat anything about radial distance. What changes as a function of distance is the phase relationship between the cry and the echo. The phase relationship is the percentage remainder that one gets on dividing the distance the sound must travel from bat to echo surface and back by the wavelength of the sound. Put another way, the phase shift is the temporal displacement of the echo waveform relative to the cry waveform expressed in fractions of a wavelength. A shift in the phase relationship between the cry and the echo is formally equivalent to a shift in the position of the echo in time relative to the position of the cry. Figure 14.4 shows why, whenever the precise position of a signal in time must be determined, the signal should have energy spread across a wide range of frequencies, which the FM sweep does. The sweep spreads the energy of the cry across a wide range of frequencies so that the bat may extract from the temporal shift between cry and echo an unambiguous estimate of the distance to the echo surface.

One further aspect of the bat's cry-emitting behavior must be noted. When the bat is approaching a surface, it reduces the frequency of the formants in the CF portion of its cry so that the frequency of the second formant in the echo remains close to 61 kilohertz, the frequency around which the bat's auditory system can make the most precise determinations of small differences in frequency. This frequency is sometimes called the "acoustic fovea" by analogy to the high-resolution area of many retinas. The bat reduces the frequency of the formants in its cry to offset the Doppler shift in the echo, thereby keeping the second formant

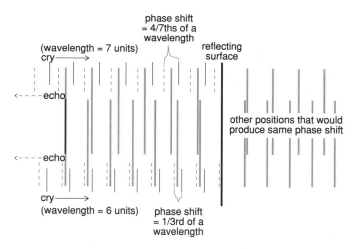

Figure 14.4
Accurate determination of distance from phase shifts in echoed sound requires a sound
with many frequencies. The phase shift at one frequency is consistent with many different
positions for the reflecting surface (gray copies of the reflecting surface located at fixed
distances behind the echo peaks for one or the other frequency). When there is more than
one frequency, only those positions consistent with the phase shifts at both frequencies are
acceptable—in this case, the position of the reflecting surface itself and the darkened position where the ghost positions for the two frequencies coincide. Adding more frequencies reduces the valid alternatives.

of the echo centered in the acoustic fovea. The term *acoustic fovea* is the
more apt in that the region of the basilar membrane that resonates to this
frequency is greatly enlarged, so there is specialization of the receptor
surface designed to promote high resolution in a restricted range. Because the bat changes the frequency of its cry to keep the echo centered
in the acoustic fovea, the velocity of the target cannot be computed from
the frequency of the echo alone; the frequency of the cry must be taken
into account in the computation.

Electrophysiology
Recordings of the activity of single units in the bat auditory cortex reveal
several distinct areas (figure 14.5). The units within each area are tuned
to (selectively excited by) different combinations of cry and/or echo
parameters.

The representation of proximal stimulus dimensions. The first such area is
the tonotopic area, found in all mammals. Units within this area are
tuned to selected auditory frequencies and arranged along the long axis
of the area in accord with their best frequencies. This is a mapping of the
sensory surface (the basilar membrane) analogous to retinotopic map-

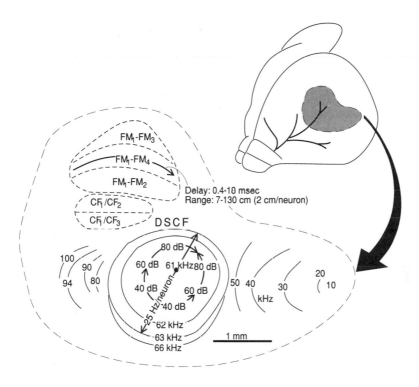

Figure 14.5
Vector spaces in the auditory cortex of the mustache bat. The DSCF area gives a representation in polar anatomical coordinates of the frequency and intensity of the second formant of the echo. The CF areas give representations in Cartesian anatomical coordinates of the velocity relationship between the bat and the target (and possibly other dimensions of the stimulus). The FM areas give representations in Cartesian anatomical coordinates of the distance between the bat and the target (and possibly other dimensions of the stimulus). (Based on Suga 1982.)

pings of the visual receptor surface. Thus it is a mapping of a proximal dimension of the stimulus. Within this area in the bat auditory cortex is a large and highly specialized subarea called the DSCF (Doppler-shifted constant frequency), in which all the units are tuned to frequencies within 61–66 kilohertz, the acoustic fovea (figure 14.5). Within the DSCF, units are arranged radially with respect to their best frequencies. The units at the center of the circle are tuned to 61 kHz. As one moves the electrode out along any radius, one encounters units tuned to progressively higher frequencies. This suggests that in this area, the nervous system has opted for a polar rather than a Cartesian mapping of the descriptive space onto the cortical surface.

The question naturally arises, What, if any, parameter of the stimulus is represented along the orthogonal dimension of the circle: the angular or circumferential dimension of the mapping? The answer is surprising. It suggests the nervous system's strong commitment to a place or anatomical vector representation of stimulus dimensions. The units in the circle are tuned to intensity (amplitude) as well as frequency, and they are arranged along the angular dimension with respect to their best intensities. The tuning to intensity means that the firing of these units is not a monotonic function of sound intensity; rather, when excited by the appropriate sound frequency, each unit has a best intensity. Intensities below and above the best intensity are less effective (figure 14.6). As one moves along any one radius of the circle, the best intensity of successively encountered units remains the same. When one shifts the radius (moves circumferentially), the best intensity changes systematically. In short, there is an amplitopic representation, as well as a tonotopic representation.

In the auditory system, differences in frequency translate into differences in the locus of neural firing at the transducer stage (the basilar membrane), but this is clearly not the case for differences in intensity. At the periphery, differences in intensity translate into differences in firing rate and number of active units. En route to the cortex, the nervous system converts from a rate coding of intensity to a place (locus of activity) coding. This suggests that locus of activity plays a fundamental role in the cortical representation of many different stimulus dimensions. The system appears to be committed to representing variations along descriptive dimensions of the stimulus by variations along anatomical dimensions of activity, even when the stimulus dimensions are in no way spatial.

The DSCF elaborates an amplitude-versus-frequency representation of the second formant of the continuous frequency segment of the echo. This is a representation of dimensions of the proximal stimulus, not the distal stimulus. While the frequency of the second formant of the echo is

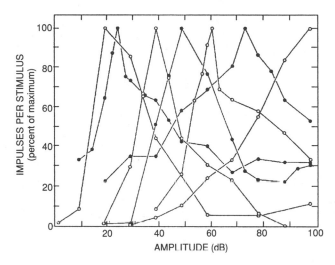

Figure 14.6
The responses elicited from seven different neurons at different locations within the DSCF
as a function of the intensity of a sound at the unit's best frequency. For each unit there is
a best intensity. (Redrawn from Suga 1977, p. 65, by permission of author and publisher).

a systematic function of the radial velocity between the bat and the
reflecting surface (a distal dimension), this velocity cannot be determined from the site of activity within the DSCF because the bat lowers the
frequency of its cry to hold the site of activity near the center of this area.
A tuning to the frequency of the echo is a tuning to radial velocity only
in units that are also tuned to the frequency of the cry, which these units
are not. Similarly, while sound intensity is a systematic function of target
distance, it is just as much a function of target size; hence neither distance
nor size is given by the locus of activity in DSCF. A tuning to intensity is
a tuning to target size only in units that are also tuned to target distance,
which units in this area are not.

Units in the DSCF area are also differentially sensitive to other parameters of the stimulus. Some are excited by very small (0.01 percent) high-
frequency (5–100 hertz) modulations in the frequency of the second
formant, such as would be produced by the fluttering of a moth's wings.
Others are insensitive to this modulation. Whether units have best flutter
frequencies has not been determined, nor has it been determined whether
flutter sensitivity is a columnar property, that is, whether all units
encountered in a penetration perpendicular to the cortical surface either
have flutter sensitivity or lack it. Units in this area also vary in their
sensitivity to the direction of the echo; some are highly directionally
sensitive, while others are directionally insensitive. The presence or lack

of directional sensitivity is a columnar property, but whether the best direction is constant in a column has not been determined. If, as seems likely, best direction is columnar, this suggests a third dimension to the descriptive space represented by the site of activity in the DSCF area. If best flutter frequency also proves to be columnar, this suggests a fourth dimension.

The question arises how a four-dimensional description of the stimulus can be represented by the site of activity in a two-dimensional anatomical space. This will be addressed at greater length when we come to consider areas in the visual cortex of primates where there is clear evidence for the orderly representation of three or more stimulus dimensions within a single cortical area. In general, it appears that the system projects the higher dimensions onto the base-plane to create complex anatomical layouts in which slabs, blobs, and wedges of tuning characteristics are interleaved in a repetitive way.

The representation of distal stimulus dimensions. The representation of radial distance and radial velocity takes place in separate areas of the bat auditory cortex. In both cases, the principle of representing the stimulus dimension by an anatomical dimension is adhered to. Radial velocity is represented in the CF_1/CF_2 and CF_1/CF_3 areas (figure 14.5). As indicated by the notation for these areas, the units here are sensitive to the nonharmonic frequency ratio between the first formant of the constant frequency segment of the cry (CF_1) and the second and/or third formant of the constant frequency segment of the echo (CF_2 and/or CF_3). The Doppler shift in the second and third formants of the echo makes the frequencies of these formants no longer harmonics (integer multiples) of the fundamental pitch of the cry. Each unit has a best frequency shift, that is, a best ratio between the frequency of the second and/or third formant of the echo and the fundamental frequency of the cry. To each such frequency ratio, there corresponds a radial velocity. When the best radial velocities (best frequency ratios) are mapped, it emerges that radial velocity is represented along the long axis of the CF/CF subareas. Large negative (approach) velocities are represented at the anterior-dorsal end of the subareas and moderate positive (retreat) velocities at the posterior-ventral end. These units are also amplitude (intensity tuned). Whether best amplitude is mapped in an orderly way onto an anatomical dimension of the subarea has not been determined. In any event, since these units are not tuned to distance, amplitude sensitivity does not correspond to target size sensitivity.

Units tuned to distance are found in the FM_1-FM_2, FM_1-FM_3, and FM_1-FM_4 areas. As the notation suggests, these units are sensitive only to the FM segments of the cry and echo. Each unit is sensitive to the delay (temporal shift) between the first formant of the cry and the second, third, and/or fourth formant of the echo, which is computed from the phase shifts at different frequencies, as indicated in figure 14.4. The best delay varies from unit to unit. To each delay, there corresponds a radial distance between the bat and the reflection surface. When the best distances (best delays) are mapped, it emerges that radial distance is represented along the long axis of the area, with the shortest distance represented at the anterior-dorsal end and the longest at the posterior-ventral. When the recording electrode moves parallel to the cortical surface along the axis of the subarea, the best delay for successively encountered neurons is a linear function of the distance the electrode has moved, with a slope of 5.8 milliseconds change in best delay per cortical millimeter, which corresponds to about 2 centimeters change in radial distance per neuron (figure 14.7).

The units in this area are also tuned to stimulus amplitude (intensity). Given their tuning to distance, this implies a tuning to distal target size (the cross-area of the reflecting surface). Whether best amplitudes (best sizes) map in an orderly way onto an anatomical dimension has not been determined. These units also appear to be tuned to radial velocity. The best response at a given delay and amplitude is often obtained by Doppler shifting the higher formants relative to the base formant. Again, whether there is an orderly mapping of this tuning characteristic has not been determined. In the light of available data, it is, however, reasonable

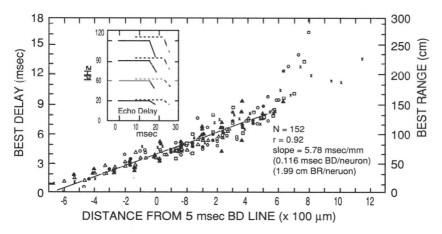

Figure 14.7
Best delays (best ranges) for units in the FM-FM area as a function of their position along the long axis of the field. (Redrawn from Suga 1982, p. 190, by permission of author and publisher.)

to imagine that the distance, cross-sectional size, and closing velocity of the reflecting surface are represented by the site of activity in this area.

Summary
 In the auditory cortex of the bat, we see three further examples of the brain's propensity to represent stimuli by means of anatomical vector spaces, cortical projection fields in which anatomical axes of the projection field correspond to axes of the vector space that describes a stimulus mathematically. A striking example of the brain's dedication to this functional architecture is the DSCF area, where the radial axis of the circular projection field represents frequency, while the angular or circumferential axis represents intensity. The use of an axis of this projection field to represent intensity makes it clear that the mapping of descriptive dimensions of the stimulus onto anatomical dimensions is not limited to spatial dimensions of the stimulus.
 While the DSCF area maps dimensions of the proximal stimulus (its frequency and intensity), the $CF_1/CF_2\text{-}CF_3$ area and the $FM_1\text{-}FM_2\text{-}FM4$ areas appear to map one or more distal dimensions. The CF/CF area maps radial velocity along the long axis of the projection field, while the FM-FM areas map distance along the long axis of the field. It seems likely that other dimensions of the stimulus are mapped along the orthogonal axes of these fields, but the data are still sparse.
 In all of these areas, individual units are tuned to (sensitive to variations in) additional descriptive dimensions of the stimulus, and this tuning varies from unit to unit within the area. Thus many units in the DSCF are sensitive to the echo direction as well as its frequency and amplitude, and many units are sensitive to the slight modulations in the carrier frequency, which would be produced by a fluttering surface. Units in the CF/CF area are differentially tuned to base frequency (as well as to the frequency discrepancy) and to amplitude. Units in the FM-FM areas are differentially tuned to amplitude (distal size?) and also to Doppler shift (radial velocity?). The fact that units are tuned to these additional dimensions and that the tuning varies from unit to unit raises the question of whether there is also an orderly mapping of these dimensions within these same areas. If so, this order will be hard to discern from single unit sampling studies. The spatial resolution obtainable from multiple penetrations is inherently poor, which makes the method ill suited to reveal complex anatomical orderliness. The orderliness in the mapping of these supernumerary stimulus dimensions, if it exists, must be complex because the system must project descriptive vector spaces of three or more dimensions onto a two dimensional surface. Anyone who has tried to construct easily digestible data tables for a multifactor ANOVA will recognize the problem the brain confronts.

The electrophysiological evidence for orderly mappings of stimulus dimensions that are not dimensions of the sensory surface itself suggests that the principle of place coding is preeminent in the cortex. The nervous system appears to be committed to a functional architecture in which the meaning of activity in a single unit is determined by the position of that unit relative to functionally specified anatomical axes. The brain uses a spatial scheme to represent combinations of stimulus properties, even when those properties are not spatial. The vectors by which the brain represents stimuli, like the vectors by which mathematicians represent them, are rooted in spatial considerations. In mathematics, these roots are historical; in the brain, they derive from a principle of functional architecture: what a unit represents is determined by where it is in a an anatomical vector space (projection field).

The Primary Visual Cortex of the Macaque Monkey

In the bat auditory cortex, we encountered principles that have become dominant themes in modern work on the functional anatomy of the cortex:

1. There are multiple functionally distinct projection areas within each sensory modality.
2. Within a given projection area, units are tuned to several different dimensions of the stimulus.
3. The best values along the various tuning dimensions vary from unit to unit.
4. The units are arranged along axes of the cortical surface in accord with the variations in best values.

The most intensively studied cortical region is area 17 of the visual cortex, also known as the striate cortex, and, more recently, as V1, in recognition of the fact that it is the terminal field for the largest projection from the lateral geniculate. V1 is only one of many different retinotopically organized areas in the visual cortex of most mammals. At last count, a dozen such areas have been identified in the cat (Rosenquist 1985) and between 11 and 20 in the macaque monkey, depending on the criteria used (Van Essen 1985). Within V1, there is evidence for units with differential sensitivity to twelve dimensions that describe the stimulus and one system parameter (for review, see Van Essen 1985). The descriptive dimensions are retinal position (two dimensions), retinal orientation, retinal spatial frequency, retinal length (of a line or grating), retinal speed of movement, retinal direction of movement, binocular disparity, motion in depth, luminosity, and color (three dimensions). The system parameter is ocular dominance, the relative strengths of the inputs to a unit from corresponding positions on the two retinas. No one cell is differentially sensitive to all of these dimensions and the extent to which individual cells are tuned to any given dimension—the selectivity index—appears to vary along a continuum (Van Essen 1985).

The evidence regarding the orderly arrangement of units along cortical axes with respect to the best values of their tuning curves is so diverse, complex, and subject to controversy as to defy summary (see Van Essen 1985 for a valiant and lucid attempt). It is, however, clear that within V1 there is an orderly arrangement along the surface with respect to at least five continua: retinal position (two dimensions), retinal orientation, ocular dominance, and color. It is unclear whether there is anatomical order with respect to the three dimensions that together constitute color, but there is anatomical order in the positioning of the color subspace relative to the other mapped continua. Thus V1 provides an unequivocal instance of the mapping of a descriptive space with supernumerary dimensions onto a two-dimensional cortical surface.

Not surprisingly, the concurrent mapping of retinal position, retinal orientation, color, and ocular dominance along the surface of V1 is complex. The axes of the different mappings cannot be and are not orthogonal. The mapping exhibits some of the features that one might expect to see when a multidimensional descriptive space is projected onto an anatomical space of smaller dimensionality (Ballard 1986). In particular, one sees the fine-scale repetition of a mapping of a given dimension.

Units in V1 differ systematically in the extent to which they are driven by one eye or the other. The dominance ratio, the relative effectiveness of the right eye versus the left eye, is columnar. In penetrations perpendicular to the cortical surface, the units encountered have the same dominance ratio—save in the input layer, IVc, where "eyedness" is categorical, entirely from one eye or the other. Since the two dimensions of retinal position exhaust the orthogonal dimensions available for mapping on the cortical surface, whether dominance is mapped in an orderly way is an interesting question, and, if so, how. In tangential penetrations (penetrations parallel to the cortical surface, which run across cortical columns rather than down them), the dominance ratio varies in small steps that form a cyclical progression. This is what one would expect if columns with the same dominance ratio were arranged next to each other along some local axis of the cortical surface to form narrow isodominance strips and if strips with adjacent dominance ratios were themselves adjacent. A complete cycle of ocular dominance ratios, from total dominance by the left eye to total dominance by the right, constitutes what I will call a dominance hyperstrip. The half of each hyperstrip in which a given eye dominates will be called a hemistrip (because hemihyperstrip is a mouthful). Dominance hyperstrips were originally inferred from electrophysiological recording data and have subsequently been confirmed by a variety of anatomical techniques (Hubel and Wiesel 1977). The width of a dominance hyperstrip is 600-800 micrometers. The hyperstrips snake across the cortex in a complex pattern (figure 14.8).

The functional significance of ocular dominance variation and ocular dominance hyperstrips is mysterious. Unlike the other mappings we have considered, this variation and the associated orderly mapping do not deal with a dimension of the stimulus but rather with a property of the visual system itself. The mystery surrounding the functional significance of ocular dominance is deepened by the fact that ocular dominance variation and the associated ocular dominance strips are not prominent in many other mammals, not even in some other primates. The ocular dominance selectivity of single units in the squirrel monkey is much less than in the macaque (Hubel and Wiesel 1978), and it has not been possible to demonstrate ocular dominance strips by anatomical methods in this New World monkey (Tigges, Tigges and Perachio 1977; Hendrickson and Wilson 1979). For whatever reason, however, it is clearly something that the cortex of Old World primates cares to map systematically. Its relevance to the present discussion is that it constitutes a third mapping dimension on the two-dimensional surface of V1.

The majority of units in V1 are also tuned to the retinal orientation of a grating stimulus, a stimulus composed of alternating light and dark bars. Orientation tuning is columnar; units in the same vertical column have the same orientation tuning, except, again, for units in IVc, the input layer, which have no orientation preference. When one makes tangential penetrations of the cortex, the best orientation of successively encountered units generally varies in small steps, which often form a linear progression of orientations. The best orientations may cycle repeatedly through the 180° of distinct orientations that a nonpolar stimulus like a grating may assume (figure 14.9). This is what one would expect if columns with the same best orientations were arranged next to each other along a local axis of the cortical surface to form narrow strips of columns with the same best orientation and if these iso-orientation strips were in turn arranged so that strips with adjacent best orientations were adjacent. A complete set of strips, covering the 180° range of possible orientations, would constitute a hyperstrip.

The concept of orientation hyperstrips derived from the patterns of orientations encountered during tangential penetrations of the cortex, patterns like that in figure 14.9. It was initially conjectured that these hyperstrips snaked across the cortical surface, intersecting the dominance hyperstrips at right angles. It is clear from the microelectrode data that the orientation hyperstrips are not aligned with the dominance hyperstrips because the sequence of best orientations commonly passes

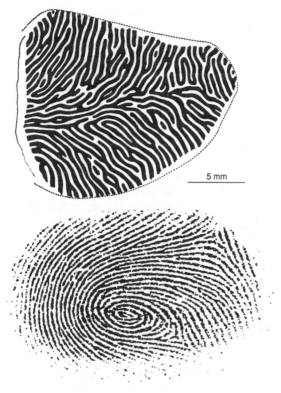

Figure 14. 8
Upper pattern. Reconstruction of the spatial pattern of ocular dominance over a portion of V1 in the macaque. The dark stripes cover the locations of units that are more responsive to one eye; the complementary white stripes cover the locations of units more responsive to the other eye. Lower pattern: Fingerprint (for scale). (Reproduced from Hubel and Wiesel 1977, p. 35, by permission of author and publisher.)

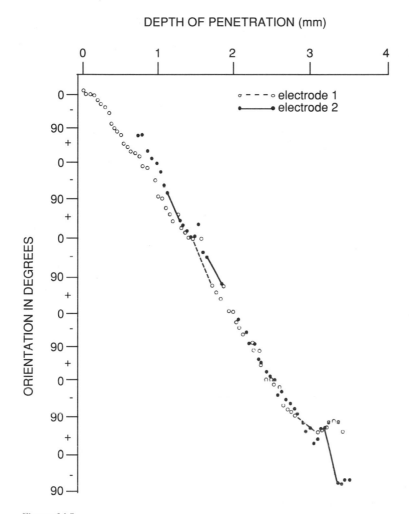

Figure 14.9
The best orientations for units along two parallel penetrations parallel to the surface of V1 in the macaque, as a function of the distance along the penetration. The lines connecting points indicate the passage of the electrode through a blob, where the units were not tuned to orientation. (Redrawn from Livingstone and Hubel 1984, p. 318, by permission of author and publisher.)

from one dominance hemistrip to the next without disruption. However, the task of building up an accurate picture of the two-dimensional arrangement of unit characteristics from sequences of microelectrode penetrations has been likened by its leading practitioners to cutting the back lawn with a pair of nail scissors (Hubel and Wiesel 1977, p.28). Hence, the establishment of this arrangement has had to await the emergence of suitable anatomical techniques.

One approach to establishing by anatomical methods the macroscopic arrangement of orientation sensitivity in V1 is to inject monkeys with a radioactive metabolic tracer, which is taken up by neurons in proportion to their activity. The injected monkey is stimulated with stripes of a single orientation during the period when the metabolic tracer is being taken up into cells. When tangential slices (slices parallel to the cortical surface) from the V1 area of monkeys thus treated are exposed to X-ray film, the pattern of activity seen in the resulting autoradiograph is not so orderly as one would expect from the hypothesis that there are orientation hyperstrips wending across the cortical surface orthogonal to the dominance hyperstrips. Rather, one sees a mixture of strips and splotches (Hubel, Wiesel, and Stryker 1977, 1978). Recently a more sophisticated technique, using activity sensitivity dyes to reveal the spatial distribution of activity in living cortex, as the orientation of the stimulus stripes is changed systematically, indicates that orientation hyperstrips might better be called striped splotches (Blasel and Salama 1986). Splotches of several successive iso-orientation strips are separated one from another by "fracture" lines, where there are abrupt discontinuities in the sequence of best orientations. (Discontinuities are also often seen in the single unit sequences. Figure 14.9 is unrepresentative in this regard.) Within a splotch, there are narrow iso-orientation strips. Strips with adjacent best orientations are adjacent, as the single unit data indicate. The fracture lines that delimit orientation splotches tend to run either down the center of eye-dominance bands or perpendicular to the boundaries of these bands. Within a splotch, the iso-orientation strips are not necessarily arranged parallel to the boundaries of the splotch. Figure 14.10 attempts to portray the latest conception of the macroscopic spatial relationship between the orientation splotches and the dominance hyperstrips.

The fourth aspect of the stimulus description known to be represented in an orderly way in V1 is color. In the centers of ocular dominance strips, with the fractures that delimit orientation splotches running through them, are small "blobs" of tissue that are revealed by stains for metabolic enzymes (Horton and Hubel 1981; Livingston and Hubel 1984). Blobs are found at about 550 micrometer intervals along dominance hemistrips, centered in the hemistrips (Livingston and Hubel 1984; Blasdel and

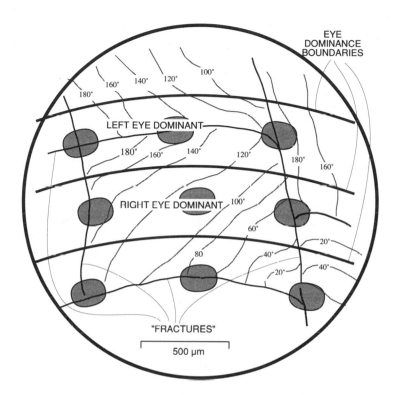

Figure 14.10
An attempt to represent the anatomical patterns in the arrangement of units in V1 on the
basis of their tuning characteristics. The heavy horizontal arches represent the boundaries
of ocular dominance strips like those portrayed in figure 14.8. Slanting across these are iso-
orientation contours (fuzzy lines), the loci of units having the same best orientation. The
orderly sequence of iso-orientation contours is interrupted by fractures, which tend to run
parallel or perpendicular to the ocular dominance contours and through the "blobs." The
blobs (shaded ovals) contain units that have weak or no tuning to orientation but a double-
opponent tuning to wavelength.

Salama 1986). Blobs are slightly elongated along the axis of the hemistrips, measuring about 150 x 200 micrometer. When investigated electrophysiologically, blobs turn out to contain units tuned to the "color" of the stimulus. *Color* is in quotation marks because it is not an objective property of either the distal or proximal stimulus, yet it is not entirely accurate to say that the units are tuned to spectral composition, which is an objective property of a proximal light stimulus, or to spectral reflectance, which is an objective property of distal stimuli.

Tuning to "color" is not unique to the units in blobs, but 60 to 70 percent of the units in blobs exhibit such tuning, while a considerably smaller proportion of units outside blobs do (Livingstone and Hubel 1984). Also, those units in blobs that are differentially sensitive to wavelength generally do not respond to white light, while many wavelength-sensitive units outside the blobs respond fairly well. Within each blob, there are cells with distinct tuning characteristics. These characteristics, which will be described below, make sense in terms of the theory of color representation first outlined by (Hering, 1878) and developed in recent times by Hurvich and Jameson (Hurvich and Jameson 1957; Jameson and Hurvich 1964; see Hurvich 1981 for overview). The essence of this theory is that color sensations are points in a space of three bipolar dimensions: white-black, red-green, and yellow-blue. The tuning characteristics of units in blobs are consonant with such a representation. It is not clear whether the units whose tuning characteristics vary along the three color dimensions are arranged in an orderly manner along corresponding anatomical axes within the blobs. There is no evidence that they are. However, the difficulty of determining from microelectrode recordings the spatial arrangement of tuning characteristics should be borne in mind. What is clear is that many different points within the three-axis color space of Hering and Hurvich-Jameson are represented by the tuning characteristics of different units within a single blob.

The blobs are portrayed by the stippled ovals in figure 14.10. The circle that encompasses figure 14.10 indicates the extent of the cortical area activated by stimulating a very small area on the retina (a retinal "point"). Within the cortical area activated by stimulating a retinal point, four different aspects of the stimulus are represented by the sites of active units within four overlaid representational modules. The general position of the active units within the V1 projection field (that is, the cortical locus of the circle) represents the retinal position of the stimulus. The activity engendered by a binocular point stimulus will be smeared out into a band running across a dominance hyperstrip within this circle. (Since dominance is a system property, not a stimulus property, the variations in locus activity due to this factor are independent of the characteristics of the stimulus.) The band of activity crossing a dominance hyperstrip will reach its peak in the orientation strip that represents the orientation of the curvature in the light intensity distribution at the point of stimulation. To quote Blasdel and Salama (1986), "The [best] orientation changes continuously within discrete domains, or modules [the splotches], and...these modules overlie ocular dominance borders in such a way that ocular dominance varies continuously within them" (p. 579). Finally, the spectral composition of the stimulus will be represented by the activity of the units in the blobs. Appropriate resultant-vector read out mechanisms would translate the activity in the overlayed modules into a point in a six-dimensional descriptive space: two devoted to retinal position, one to orientation and three to color.

The Color Space

The representation of the reflectance characteristics of surfaces by humans (and macaque monkeys—DeValois et al. 1974) is particularly interesting in that this representation is arranged in a three-dimensional vector space whose axes do not correspond to dimensions in a physical description of the stimulus or to the axes established by the system of three photopic light transducers (the three kinds of cones). Surfaces vary in the amount of light they reflect and in the spectral composition of this reflection, the relative amounts of energy at different wavelengths. The first property—net reflectance relative to other surfaces is roughly captured by the white-black dimension in color space; the other property—reflectance as a function of wavelength—is even more crudely captured by the blue-yellow and red-green dimensions. In what follows, these two aspects of a reflected light—its overall intensity relative to other contemporaneous light stimuli and its spectral composition—will be referred to as its reflectance spectrum.

If one adheres strictly to the definition of representation adopted in chapter 1, there is no representation of reflectance spectra in the brain because the color space into which spectra are mapped by color perception mechanisms is not isomorphic to the spectra themselves. Not even identity is preserved by the mapping of spectra into color sensations because this mapping is many-one. From the fact that two spectra produce the same color sensation, one emphatically cannot conclude that they are identical spectra. Metameric color matches are by definition distinct spectra that produce the same color sensation (map to the same point in color space). For any point in color space, there is an infinite number of metameric matches. The foundation of our understanding of color vision was the discovery that by varying the relative intensities of three superimposed monochromatic stimuli, it is possible to duplicate the color sensation aroused by any spectrum whatsoever, even spectra with no energy at any of the three base wavelengths.[2]

The vector space that represents spectra mathematically is a space of infinite dimensionality because the function that specifies the amount of energy a light contains at each wavelength may be thought of as an infinite string of numbers, each number specifying the energy at a wavelength infinitesimally shorter than the wavelength whose energy is specified by the preceding number in the string. The three-dimensionality of the space that the brain uses in its attempt to represent the reflectance spectra of surfaces is imposed by the photopic (bright light) transducer system, which is composed of only three kinds of transducers (cones). Each single kind of transducer is incapable of signaling anything about the spectrum of the light that excites it because it has a one-dimensional output. The output of a cone conveys only the net quanta absorbed by the cone's photopigment; it conveys nothing about the wavelength of those quanta. Because there are three kinds of cones, each with a different photopigment, they capture differences in spectra by differences in their absorptions. The use of only three spectrally distinct transducers results in a huge loss of information about spectra at the transducer stage. The infinitely dimensioned spectral space is collapsed to a space of three unipolar dimensions at the transducer level.

The dimensions of the receptor-level representation of reflectance spectra do not correspond to dimensions in the physical description of the stimulus. Nor do they correspond to dimensions in the psychological representation of the stimulus because these are bipolar: they depart from null in two opposed directions. The dimensions in the representation of spectra conveyed by cone signals are unipolar because there is no such thing as a negative absorption (just as there is no such thing as a negative amount of light). However, as soon as the neural signal emerges from the cones, it enters into a series of computational processes that perform the coordinate transformation by which the receptor representation of spectra is mapped into the representation on which performance in psychophysical tasks is based (the color space representation).

Hering (1920 [1964]) was the first to realize that psychophysical color judgments are based on a representation with bipolar dimensions. Helmholtz assumed that color judgments are based directly on cone outputs. Hering pointed out that this assumption failed to explain the psychological fact that certain pairs of color attributions are never

2. This is true if one imagines, for purposes of conceptual simplification, that it is possible to have a negative light intensity at a given wavelength. Those who will not allow this jeu d'esprit must give a more complex and confusing summary statement of this, the fundamental fact of color vision.

posited of the same point, whereas other pairs are. People speak of the relative amounts of red and blue in a purple. They also speak of the relative amounts of yellow and red in an orange and the relative amounts of blue and green in a blue-green. But if you show them a pure yellow and ask them if this green has a lot of red in it, they will have trouble making sense of your question. Similarly, if you show them a pure green and ask if this yellow has too much blue in it, they will be puzzled. Yellow-blue and red-green are pairs of mutually exclusive attributes; they cannot be perceived as attributes of the same point, whereas blue-red, yellow-red, blue-green and green-yellow are all pairs of attributes that can co-occur in the perception of a single point. The impossibility of the co-occurrence of red and green has nothing to do with physics; it is a fact about how human brains represent spectra, not a fact about spectra themselves. The attributions red and green (and yellow and blue) behave psychophysically as if they were the two poles of a single color dimension. Thus a point can no more be both red and green than a number can be both positive and negative.

Hering's insight was developed further by Jameson and Hurvich (Jameson and Hurvich 1955, 1959,1964; Hurvich and Jameson 1955), who devised psychophysical methods for measuring the distance of a color sensation from the null points (no-hue points) of the red-green and yellow-blue axes (the chromatic axes of the color space). They also developed quantitative models of the coordinate transformation by which the receptor representation is mapped into the color-space representation (Jameson 1972). It was clear from the outset that this coordinate transformation must involve subtracting some cone signals from other cone signals because subtraction is the only way to get numbers with negative values from numbers with positive values. Subtracting some cone signals from other cone signals is the only way to derive from physiological variables like absorption, which deviates only in one direction, physiological variables that deviate in two opposed directions from a null or resting state (as, for example, firing rates that increase or decrease from the spontaneous rate, in response to a stimulus). It was also clear from color contrast data that the visual system was tuned to spatial and temporal variations along the dimensions that it imposed on spectral reflectances. Surrounding a reddish spot with a green annulus makes it appear redder, just as surrounding a grey spot with a black annulus makes the spot appear whiter (spatial contrast). Preceding and following a reddish spot with a greenish spot also makes it appear redder (temporal contrast). Jameson and Hurvich developed quantitative models of these spatial and temporal interactions along chromatic dimensions (Jameson and Hurvich 1959, 1964; Varner, Jameson, and Hurvich 1984).

In summary, the color space on which psychophysical judgments are based has two bipolar chromatic axes (the red-green axis and the yellow-blue axis) and a bipolar achromatic axis (the white-black axis). These are not axes of the physical description of light or of the receptor representation of incident light. Between the representation of the spectrum at the level of the cone receptor and the representation on which psychophysical judgments are based, there intervenes a set of physiological processes isomorphic to a coordinate transformation in linear algebra.

The electrophysiological data are consonant with the conclusions drawn from the psychophysical data. They show that the signals from some cone types are subtracted from those of other cone types very early on in the visual system. By the time chromatic signals leave the retina, the individual signal pathways show bipolar tuning characteristics (De-Monasterio, Gouras, and Tolhurst 1975; DeMonasterio and Schein 1982). Some units are excited by long wavelength light and inhibited by mid-wavelength light, while complementary units are excited by the middle wavelengths and inhibited by long wavelengths. Together these are referred to as red-versus-green cells. Another class of cells is excited by short wavelength light and inhibited by middle wavelengths, or vice-versa. This class is called the blue-versus-yellow class. The red-versus-green and yellow-versus-blue terminology is unfortunate; it does not convey an accurate picture of the tuning characteristics, and it tends to imply that the activity of these cells is the basis for psychophysical color judgments, which a consideration of their tuning characteristics makes highly unlikely. These cells very likely carry signals that give rise eventually to psychophysical judgments, but their tuning characteristics do not explain the structure of those judgments. Although there is also some spatial tuning in these cells—they are sensitive to how light of different wavelengths is distributed within their receptive fields—the tuning is not such as to explain the psychophysical phenomena of color contrast.

In V1, there is clear chromatic opponency with a spatial aspect that is at least qualitatively similar to psychophysical color contrast judgments. About 70 percent of the cells in blobs are of the so-called double-opponent kind. A double opponent cell has a concentric receptive field. The effect of energy from a given part of the spectrum on the cell's activity depends on whether that energy falls in the center of the receptive field or on an annulus surrounding the center of the field. For example, in a double opponent cell with an R+G- center, long wavelength light falling in the center excites the cell, while middle wavelength light falling there inhibits it. By contrast, long wavelength light falling on the surrounding annulus inhibits the cell while middle wavelength light falling there excites it. Double opponent cells show some tendency to have spectral tuning curves that are complementary in ways consistent with the Hering-Hurvich-Jameson model. There are G+R- double opponent cells to complement the R+G- ones, and there are both B+Y- and Y+B- cells (figure 14.11).

The data in figure 14.11 suggest four well-defined classes of units with closely similar tuning curves, which correspond to yellow, blue, red, and green psychophysical judgments. This is not an accurate summary of the general findings. The tuning curves in the figure come from only 63 of the 130 cells whose spectral tuning was measured by Vautin and Dow (1985). The tuning curves for the other 67 cells did not cross-correlate strongly with any of the patterns portrayed in figure 14.11. Vautin and Dow measured the spectral tuning of cells in V1 using nineteen different color stimuli. For each stimulus, they found at least one cell for which that stimulus was the best one. Thus it is clearly not the case that the tuning curves of color opponent cells in V1 generally fall into one of four classes

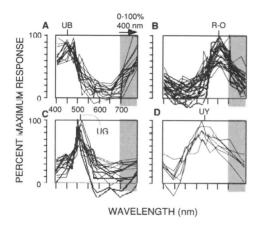

WAVELENGTH (nm)

Figure 14.11
Normalized wavelength-tuning curves of different "classes" of doubly opponent cells in V1 of the macaque. The vertical axes give the response to a light as a percentage of the maximum response. Responses less than 0 indicate decreases in the baseline firing rate. The gray areas to the right of 700 nanometers are the extraspectral hues from pure red to violet, which are produced by varying the mixture of 700 and 400 nanometer light. A mixture of100 percent 700 nanometer light is at the left edge of the gray and a mixture of 100 percent 400 nanometers is at the right edge. UB is the wavelength of unique (pure) blue for the average observer, UG the wavelength of unique green, and UY the wavelength of unique yellow. The units in classes A, C, and D peak at these wavelengths. R-O, where the units in B peak is the wavelength of a reddish orange. Unique red is an extraspectral color—it requires a mixture of long- and short-wavelength light. These data are not, however, representative—see text. (Based on Vautin and Dow 1985, p. 280.)

of curves, curves that would be predicted from the assumption that categories of psychophysical color judgments are determined by the tuning characteristics of the activated cells.

Nor do the tuning curves in figure 14.11 explain the mutual exclusivity of red-versus-green and yellow-versus-blue color judgments. It is true that the responding of the cells in figure 14.11A (the curves that peak near the psychophysical unique red) increases as the responding of the cells in B decreases (the curves that peak near unique green), and vice-versa. It is clearly not true, however, that the red and green cell groups are never simultaneously active. Energy at a wavelength of 577 nanometers, which maximally excites cells in the "yellow" group, excites both "red" and "green" cells to between 15 and 25 percent of their maximal response. If the activity of the cells in the "red" group led to 'red' judgments and activity in the "green" group to 'green' judgments and activity in the "yellow" group to 'yellow' judgments, then subjects ought to judge that a light at 577 nanometers is 'a strong yellow with a little green and a little red in it,' a judgment subjects never render.

What then should we conclude that the data on the chromatic tuning of cells in V1 tell us about the physiological mechanism underlying psychophysical color judgments? I suggest that we should conclude that the cortical mechanism for representing color adheres to the same principles as the cortical mechanisms for representing physical variables that are in fact bipolar, such as radial velocity and angular deviation. The tuning of tectal units to angular deviation is broad, just as is the tuning of cortical units to spectral composition. A tectal unit whose best deviation is to the left of the midline and above the horizontal plane nonetheless responds to stimuli to the right of the midline and below the horizontal plane. Thus units indicating a deviation to the right of center are active at the same time as units indicating a deviation to the left of center. "Left of center" and "right of center" are mutually exclusive categories of tectal output not because of the tuning characteristics of the individual tectal units but rather because of the manner in which the activity of the many active units is combined into a single tectal output.

Previously, I suggested that the tectal output is the resultant of tectal activity, the vector sum to which each active unit contributes in proportion to its rate of firing. The angle of the resultant vector specifies a position in anatomical space relative to two orthogonal axes of the orderly mapping of angular deviation, one corresponding to elevation and one to azimuth. The fact that left versus right and up versus down are mutually exclusive aspects of tectal output, while left and up, or right and down, or left and down, or right and up are not, derives from the geometric fact that a position in an anatomical space cannot be on both sides of a single axis of that space. Only deviations from orthogonal axes can occur in arbitrary combination. Left may combine with either up or down because the azimuthal and elevational axes of the tectal mapping are orthogonal. If chromatically tuned units in blobs are arranged according to the anatomical layout shown in figure 14.12 and if the output from this layout is a vector whose angle has the same dimensions as the layout itself, then it is clear why red-versus-green and yellow-versus-blue are mutually exclusive color judgments.

The scheme proposed in figure 14.12 generates mutually exclusive red-green and yellow-blue color judgments from activity in an area whose units have the wide and continuously varying spectrum of tuning characteristics revealed by the work of Vautin and Dow (1985). The mutual exclusivity within these pairs of judgments arises not from any tendency of these tuning characteristics to fall into groups, but rather from their orderly arrangement in a two-dimensional anatomical space (a blob) and the manner in which their activity is translated into an output from the blob. The blob is assumed to be a color-computing module, whose output, the resultant, is a vector with three bipolar dimensions. Each unit in the blob contributes a datum to the computation of the resultant. The contribution of a single chromatically tuned cell to this vector is jointly determined by its position with respect to the axes of the blob, which gives it the chromatic "angle" represented by the unit, and by its firing rate, which gives the length of that vector in the vector summing operation (see figure 14.3 for a graphic illustration of the envisaged vector summation).

In the case of the tectal output, the mutual exclusivity of deviations in opposing directions along a single axis is a necessary property of the observed behavioral output. It is physically impossible for an animal to turn both to the right and to the left or both up and down simultane-ously—a fact that has probably exerted a very decided selection pressure on the functional anatomy of the tectal projections. It is the lack of any physical necessity constraining color judgments that gives the brain's representation of color its interest in the present context. The distinctive properties of color judgments do not derive from the objective properties of the stimulus. The existence of energy at 475 nanometers (unique blue) does not exclude the existence of energy at 580 nanometers (unique yellow). Nor is there any physical constraint on the behavioral manifes-tations of color representations. It is not impossible to say something is reddish-green, it just is not said (not, I submit, because of semantic or social convention but because speakers never have the indicated per-cept).

Mutual exclusivities in color judgments and other properties of these judgments (such as the fact that a 425 nanometer stimulus is judged more

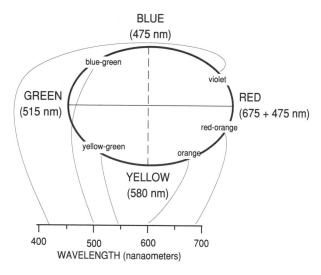

Figure 14.12.
Suggested arrangement of color tuned cells within the blobs in V1. Cells that respond best to 475 nanometer light (psychophysical unique blue) lie opposite cells that respond best to 580 nanometer light (unique yellow) along the short axis of the blob, while cells that respond best to 515 nanometer light (unique green) lie along one-half of the orthogonal (long) axis. Along the other half of this axis lie cells whose best response cannot be elicited by a monochromatic stimulus; they respond best to a mixture of light from the two ends of the spectrum. It is suggested that psychophysical hue judgments are determined by the mean firing vector, two of whose coordinates (the chromatic coordinates) specify positions with respect to these orthogonal bipolar anatomical axes. When the chromatic coordinates of this mean vector specify a position to the red side of the blob, the hue is judged to have red in it; when they specify a position to the green side, the hue is judged to have green in it. When they specify a position on the yellow-blue axis, which divides the red side from the green, the hue is judged to be either purely blue or purely yellow, depending on which side of the red-green axis the position is on. When the chromatic coordinates are <0,0>—the center of the blob—the stimulus is judged to have no hue. In addition to its two bipolar chromatic coordinates, the mean firing vector will have a bipolar achromatic coordinate whose value determines the extent to which the hue is perceived to be desaturated by white or black. It is suggested that position along this axis is computed from the firing of the "Broad Band Cells," which constitute about 30 percent of the cells found in blobs.

similar to a 675 nanometer stimulus than either is to a 580 nanometer stimulus) derive from the manner in which the brain represents spectral information. It represents the reflectance spectra of surfaces as vectors in a space of three bipolar dimensions. Since this form of representation is not dictated by the formal structure of reflectance spectra (indeed, it does violence to that structure) or by the requirements of the resulting behaviors, one is tempted to conclude that the form of this representation indicates what comes naturally to the brain; it may suggest the brain's general approach to representing things.

Another more general interest in the brain's representation of color is its illustration of the manner in which categorical judgments may derive from a continuous (noncategorical) representation of the stimulus. The red-green judgment is categorical: a hue may be either greenish or reddish but cannot be both (as a matter of psychological not physical fact). Yet in the scheme given in figure 14.12, this categorization is not reflected in the tuning curves of the individual units. All of the tuning curves spread across the category boundaries (see figure 14.11). Also, tuning curves peak at all possible spectral points and a great many extraspectral points (points corresponding to surfaces that reflect light from both ends of the spectrum, such as those perceived as purely red). Nor is this categorization reflected in the arrangement of the units in space. The arrangement is continuous (or finely graded) with respect to the governing parameter—the point at which the tuning curve peaks. The categorical character of red-versus-green and yellow-versus-blue judgments derives from the principle of judging on the basis of a computed position within an anatomical space and from the existence of privileged axes that partition that space into quadrants. It is a topographic property of position codes that a point cannot be on two sides of an axis (or of any boundary).

A third aspect of the proposed scheme is that the activity of a unit at the anatomical position specified by the output of the module (the angle of the resultant) is neither a necessary nor a sufficient condition for the module's rendering that output. It is not necessary because there need not be any activity at the position corresponding to the chromatic angle of the resultant (any more than a sample need contain a number equal to the sample's mean). It is not sufficient because we know from the broad tuning curves of the units that a stimulus must generate activity at many sites. The activity at one site is but one datum in the computation of the resultant vector. From knowledge of the activity of just one unit, there is no predicting the angle of the weighted sum of all the active vectors (units). Thus the scheme proposed is not one in which individual units function as detectors. There are no red detectors in this scheme, only red outputs from the blobs. However, it is a scheme in which the tuning curves of the units will be to some extent suggestive of a detector-like function. It is also a scheme in which the activity of a single unit within the blob, if it could be arranged that only one unit were active, would produce a meaningful output—a resultant whose angle was that represented by the active unit. Thus this not a distributed representation in the radical sense, a scheme in which the activity of a single unit cannot by itself have a significance (perform a representational function).

Finally, more comment is needed on the fact that the proposed representation of reflectance spectra by blobs does not satisfy the definition of a representation adopted in chapter 1. There are no isomorphisms to be specified between reflectance spectra and blob outputs. Not even the "equals" operator (the identity operator) can validly be applied to blob outputs because it is not true that two reflectance spectra are identical *iff* they generate the same blob output. Any given blob output may be generated by an infinite number of distinct reflectance spectra—the set of all spectra belonging to a given metameric category. That said, it may, however, be observed that the "not equals" operator (the nonidentity operator) is half valid. It is true that two reflectance spectra are not identical *if* they generate different blob outputs. The system is in fact extremely good at capturing small differences in reflectance spectra; it is estimated that humans can discriminate seven million shades. Furthermore, two distinct substances are unlikely to have identical reflectance spectra. Therefore the system may succeed in representing what it is the animal cares about—differences in the substances that reflect the light it receives. In practice, these two aspects of the representation—that distinct colors imply distinct substances and that distinct substances will more often than not yield distinguishable colors—may make the brain's representation of reflectance spectra useful to it. Nonetheless, it is well to bear in mind that if we adopt the definition of representation suggested in chapter 1, the brain does not, strictly speaking, represent reflectance spectra.

Summary
The facts about color vision suggest how deeply the nervous system may be committed to representing stimuli as points in descriptive spaces of modest dimensionality. It does this even for spectral composition, which does not lend itself to such a representation. The resulting lack of correspondence between the psychological representation of spectral composition and spectral composition itself is a source of confusion and misunderstanding in scientific discussions of color. Scientists persist in referring to the physical characteristics of the stimulus and to the tuning char-

acteristics of the transducers (the cones) as if psychological color terms like *red*, *green* and *blue* had some straightforward translation into physical reality, when in fact they do not.

Scientifically speaking, there is no such thing as green light. There is middle wavelength light, and there is light that produces a green sensation, but these are by no means the same. The sensation can be produced by an infinite number of different spectra, many of which have no energy at middle wavelengths. Conversely, a spectrum with a lot of energy at middle wavelengths can produce a color sensation with no green in it if the energy at other wavelengths is chosen appropriately. Similarly, the term *red cone*, which is often thought to refer to a cone sensitive to red light is doubly a misnomer: there is no such thing as red light (only short wavelength light) and the best wavelength for these cones, if presented alone, produces a yellow-green sensation in most people, a sensation with no red in it.

The lack of correspondence between the mathematical description of reflectance spectra and the brain's code for color has two sources, one retinal and one cortical. At the retina, the infinitely dimensioned spectral vector is collapsed into a three dimensional representation by the cones. The cone representation of spectra, while it grossly reduces the dimensionality of the stimulus, at least preserves the unipolarity of light. This unipolarity is lost, however, in the coordinate transformation that occurs between the cones and V1. By the time color signals appear in V1, they are bipolar variables. The bipolar tuning characteristics of double opponent color-sensitive cells in V1 do not, however, explain the mutually exclusive character of red-versus-green and yellow-versus-blue color judgments. The tuning curves are too broad; they spill across the red-green and yellow-blue boundaries. Also, one can find cells for which an arbitrarily chosen spectral or extraspectral stimulus is the best stimulus. Hence cells cannot be cleanly grouped on the basis of their tuning curves. The best values form a continuum.

From electrophysiological work, we know that color-sensitive cells tend to cluster in blobs. There is no evidence for the orderly arrangement of cells in blobs in accord with their best spectral or extraspectral stimulus, but there is no evidence inconsistent with the assumption of such an arrangement. The assumption that there is an orderly anatomical arrangement of color tuning characteristics within blobs, which mirrors the psychophysically derived color circle, and that judged color depends on the (angular) position of the vector sum of the active units yields an explanation of the first-order facts of color psychophysics. If this conjecture about the physiological basis of psychophysical color judgments is correct, the brain's representation of color may indicate its general approach to the problem of representation because this way of representing reflectance spectra is in no way dictated by the formal properties of these spectra or by constraints on the behavioral output.

General Summary

In describing animals' representations of relative spatial position, time (phase), time intervals (phase differences), and conditional probabilities, we repeatedly treated these representations in vector terms because that is the form their mathematical representation naturally takes. In this chapter, we have surveyed electrophysiological and psychophysical evidence to the effect that spatial representations have a vectorial form in the nervous system itself. The nervous system's commitment to representing stimulus properties in vector spaces of modest dimensionality extends beyond the representation of spatial properties to encompass other stimulus properties, such as sound intensity, radial velocity, and spectral composition. It appears that the nervous system is committed to representing diverse aspects of the experienced world by means of the positions of the activated neurons within modules in which neuronal units are arranged anatomically in accord with the best values of their tuning curves. It is this commitment to a positional code that makes vectorial representation a general feature of the nervous system's approach to representation. The mathematical term *vector space*, for a coordinate system in which objects may be described by their positions along orthogonal descriptive continua, has an anatomical significance in the nervous system's approach to representation: vector spaces in the nervous system are quite literally spaces, or rather overlaid or interspersed planar areas.

Brain representations are realized in a hierarchical system of modules. V1 is a higher-level module, one of twelve to twenty such modules in the visual cortex of higher mammals. V1 is itself composed of iterated assemblages of overlaid or interspersed position, dominance, orientation, and color modules. Position, orientation, dominance, and color modules are in turn assemblages of the most elementary and ubiquitous of cortical modules, the column (Mountcastle 1978).

It is suggested that the output of all higher order cortical modules is a vector that expresses the central positional tendency in the activities of units within that module—the angle of the resultant vector. Each unit within a module represents by virtue of its anatomical position an angular position in a vector space, which may be thought of as a position on the surface of a unit "sphere" of modest dimensionality. The dimensions of the vector space —the dimensions that specify where on the "sphere" a unit is—are those that are given an orderly mapping within the module in question. The firing rate of the unit determines the weight given to that position on the sphere in the vector summing operation that determines the module's output.

A system in which cells could store the magnitudes (coordinates) that define a resultant vector would be well suited to recording the sorts of representations that the cortex appears to elaborate. There appear to be many different cortical modules (many different retinotopic, somato-topic, tonotopic, and so on mappings), each corresponding to a description of the stimulus in a space with different axes. Spatial axes, however, are present in most if not all of these descriptive spaces. What varies are the other axes of the stimulus description.

If memory (recorded representations of stimuli) takes the form of recorded resultants from each of these anatomical spaces, then one and the same stimulus will be represented in many different records, each record giving a different description of the stimulus. The question arises, How does the system knit these records together?

Chapter 15
The Unity of Remembered Experience

A central tenet of this representational approach to learning is that the formal structure of the material to be represented more often than not shapes the formal structure of the representation. It also determines characteristics of the computational processes that derive a representation of a given (innately specified) form from sensory signals. A corollary is that learning must be modular because diverse aspects of reality will require diversely structured modules for their representation.

The different aspects of reality that are represented in the nervous system have different formal characteristics. Space is inherently three-dimensional, while time is one-dimensional. There is no natural polarity in the ordering of points along a spatial axis; no point is farther than another point except by reference to some third point. By contrast, there is a natural polarity in the ordering of points along the temporal axis. One moment is inherently later or earlier than another because time is unidirectional. Probabilistic aspects of reality introduce still different representational and computational requirements. There is no more reason to expect a single computational process in the nervous system equally suited to dealing with every aspect of reality than there is reason to expect a single branch of mathematics to deal equally felicitously with every aspect of reality or to expect a single sense organ to be adapted to the transduction of every kind of stimulus energy.

The results of modern cortical electrophysiology reinforce the expectation of modularity. The results reviewed in the preceding chapter imply that the brain divides in order to conquer; it breaks the task of representing diverse aspects of reality down and assigns different aspects of the task to different cortical modules. These modules may all make use of some basic principles, such as the principle of representing a stimulus as a point in descriptive spaces, but the descriptive spaces appear to be multiple and distinct, as do the computational processes that map stimuli into the different spaces. The evolution of distinct and specialized structures to deal with distinct problems is a process that has shaped the structure of the central nervous system just as much as the structure of the sensory organs.

If the world is represented through the activities of many distinct modules, the question arises how these diverse representations are put together. To make this question as stark as possible, let us assume that the cortical modules are the gateways to memory. Let us assume that the memory for an experience is captured by the storage of coordinates that specify the central tendency (and perhaps other distributional properties) of the activity the experience generates within each of the cortical modules—each of the projection fields in which several descriptive parameters receive an orderly mapping. Then the memory of single experiences will be fragmented. The experience will be recorded in as many memory fragments as there are active cortical modules. On the one hand, this fragmentation in the record of an experience might explain why the memory of an experience is on the whole surprisingly resistant to the effects of localized damage (Lashley 1950). On the other hand, it is obvious that most behaviors that depend on this recorded information require many of the fragments. The foraging animal with particular but transient nutritional requirements (such as a salt, water, or protein deficit) needs to remember the distinguishing sensory characteristics of possibly edible substances (color, taste, smell, feel, physiological effects of ingestion, and others), where the substance was encountered, with what frequency under which conditions, and at what time of day. On the modular hypothesis, these aspects of the animal's experience are separately computed and reside in different files. How can the fragments that go together—the fragments that derive from the same experience—be assembled? What accounts for the unity of remembered experience?

The problem of the unity of remembered experience is a general one, which will require for its solution insight into the deepest principles of brain function. It is probably ill advised to address so deep and central a problem at this early stage in our progress toward appreciating the mechanisms and principles by which the brain performs its function. There is so little relevant evidence from the brain itself at present. Nonetheless, the problem arises in such an obvious and pressing manner when one begins to elaborate modular representational theories of brain function that one cannot avoid the problem altogether (see Fodor 1983). In suggesting a solution to this problem, I hope only to get serious discussion and analysis of the problem started.

The solution I suggest is motivated primarily by considerations of what principle would be sufficiently general to work under almost all circumstances. Such a principle would have to reflect a very general truth about the world. It is a very general truth that two different objects cannot occupy the same region of space at the same time. Thus one principle that would make it possible to relate separately computed and stored memories deriving from the same stimulus is to require that spatial and temporal coordinates be an integral part of every record kept by the brain. On this hypothesis, the mechanisms by which memories are recorded must be such that every record contains quantities that specify the time at which the record was generated (or the temporal interval to which it applies) and the location of the stimulus (or stimuli) that generated the recorded activity. The hypothesis put forward in this chapter is that temporal and spatial coordinates are an obligatory component of every record kept by an animal brain because they play a pivotal role in interrelating the records.

On this hypothesis, the time and space coordinates that form part of every record are what enable search processes to move from record to record, assembling a coherent, unified representation of the experience, the kind required for intelligent behavior. Most of the rest of this chapter is devoted to reviewing experiments with humans that suggest that such an assembly operation is in fact at work and that the spatial and temporal locations of a stimulus appear to play a privileged role in conjoining separately recorded aspects of one stimulus or one experience. Before turning to the relevant literature, however, I give an illustration of the manner in which temporal and spatial coordinates may be used to interrelate records and generate intelligent behavior. This example also serves to illustrate the manner in which the motivation and performance systems may tap representational systems in the course of generating behavior that depends in part on acquired information.

Illustrative Example

Let us consider the foraging worker bees, whose command of the spatial and temporal facts regarding the location of nectar sources and the times of nectar availability has been an important part of the evidence that the representation of time and space plays a fundamental role, even in the learned behavior of invertebrates. A motivational process in the bee specifies that obtaining substances with the sensory characteristics of nectar is to be the goal of the bee's behavior. (For an account of the psychology and neurobiology of motivational states and the mechanisms by which they organize behavior, see Gallistel 1980). The emergence of the indicated motivational state into predominance (control of overall behavior) initiates a search of the file (memory module) where records are kept of those dimensions of experience that define nectar for the bee. The defining sensory characteristics of nectar are imagined to be principally sweetness (capacity to activate receptors tuned to sugars) and liquidity (capacity to activate receptors tuned to water). Thus the records in this memory module would be of the activation of points in an anatomical vector space, at least two of whose dimensions corresponded to sweetness and liquidity. I will term this memory module the chemical characteristics file.

Each record in the chemical characteristics file specifies the occurrence of a stimulus that activated a point or region in an anatomical space whose dimensions corresponded to those in the bee's description of the chemical characteristics of stimuli. The contents of a record in this module would consist of a specification of the central tendency of the activation (the resultant vector) and perhaps some quantities that further described the distribution of activity evoked in this vector space by a chemical stimulus. The hypothesis here advanced is that each record also contains quantities that specify the approximate position in time when the chemical stimulus was experienced and quantities that specify the approximate position where the stimulus was encountered—the position on the map the bee has made of its environment.

The motivational process, which coordinates behavior and determines the use made of acquired information, treats the chemical characteristics file (and all other files) as content addressable memories. It addresses records in files by setting the values of probe signals. These probe signals correspond to the descriptive dimensions that define a file and/or to specifications of temporal and spatial location. When the probing of files is controlled by the nectar-seeking motivational state, the system first probes for records at the extreme end of the sweetness and liquidity dimensions. It does this by setting these dimensions of the probe signal at their maximum values, then relaxing the sweetness and/or liquidity criteria (reducing the values on these dimensions of the probe vector) until the probe values for these dimensions match the value of a record, the sweetest and most liquid experience on file. When the values of the probe signal match those in a record, the response from the file is a signal specifying the spatial and temporal coordinates of the record addressed by the probe signals, the quantities that specify the time at which the record was laid down, and the spatial location of the distal source of the experience.

The spatial coordinates thus obtained may be used to probe the same file again. The purpose of reprobing with the location signal turned up by the initial sweetness probe is to retrieve subsequent records from that spatial location. The bee will not wish to return to that location if subsequent experience indicates that high sweetness and liquidity values are no longer experienced there. This is the first example of the use of spatial coordinates (the addresses of the distal sources) to link separate records. Here, the coordinates are used to link separate records within the same file. Although the records derive from repeated experience with the same source, there is nothing in the records themselves that links them a priori—no pointers or associative links from one record to another. The linking of records is accomplished a posteriori, at the time of their retrieval. Which records are linked to which depends on the purposes of the retrieval process not foresight in the storage process.

Assume that the probe with the location signal does not turn up another record from that point in the world; hence the record first turned up by the sweetness probe is the most recent from that location. The time of day component of the time signal from that record is compared to the current reading on the bee's internal clock to determine whether the current time of day corresponds approximately to the time at which the high-sweetness record was generated. If it does, the probability of the bee's setting a course for the location indicated by the location signal is enhanced.

Assume that the bee in fact sets its course for the indicated location. It thus uses the location signal to interrelate its records of chemical characteristics and its map—its record of the macroscopic shape of its environment. The hypothesis developed in chapter 6 was that the map file is a module of its own, which records the relative positions of surfaces and nothing else. By itself, the map does not contain the information necessary to specify a destination because the characteristics that make a point a suitable destination for a foraging bee are chemical, not spatial. It is the probing of the chemical characteristics file that yields the specification of a destination on the cognitive map. Given the map and a destination, the navigational system can compute how the bee must orient with respect to the surfaces it currently perceives in order to direct its flight toward a point it does not yet perceive.

To identify the target point when it comes in view, the bee needs information about the shape and reflectance characteristics of the nectar source. To retrieve this information, it uses the location and time signals generated by probing the chemical characteristics file to probe object-shape and reflectance-characteristics files. Probing these contacts the records generated by these characteristics of the nectar source and elicits signals indicating the values of the target along these dimensions. Thus, when the bee arrives in the vicinity of the target, the surface that generates corresponding values on these dimensions will control the direction of the bee's flight during the landing stage. The bee will land on the object whose shape and color correspond to those experienced at the same time and in the same place as the experience of high sweetness. The time and place coordinates of the high-sweetness record serve to link that record to the appropriate records of source shape and source reflectance.

In the present view, the process of probing one file to obtain time and space signals with which to probe other files plays a role traditionally assigned to associative bonds. It is the mechanism by which the record of one sensory-perceptual experience elicits the record of another experience, one associated with the first in time and space. There, however, all resemblance to the associative account of higher brain function ends. There is no bond linking the records of experiences that coincided in space and time. A fortiori, there is no link between records that can vary in strength. Each record contains its own time and space coordinates. These coordinates are not something that is shared between two records, whereas an associative bond is by definition something shared between two records (two sensory traces). Reexperiencing the same sweetness at an object with the same shape and color does not strengthen an associative bond between the records of sweetness, shape, and color. Rather it establishes additional records in the same files. These new records have the same spatial coordinates as the previous records but new temporal coordinates. The activation of a record (sensory trace) does not automatically evoke other records with the same time and space coordinates. Which other records are activated will depend on which other files are probed, which in turn depends on the behavioral purpose for which files are being probed.

The behavioral purpose is established by the bee's motivational state, which is conceived of as a set of signals that selectively potentiates a functionally cohesive set of acts (Gallistel 1980). In so doing, motivational signals potentiate whatever information retrieval processes are central to those acts. An act that orients the animal toward a location it does not currently perceive by reference to points it currently perceives depends on the retrieval of information about the position of the target relative to the positions of the points from which the animal gets its current bearings. This information is jointly contained in the chemical characteristics file (the coordinates of the destination) and the cognitive map (the record that gives meaning to destination coordinates). Thus probing the chemical characteristics file with a high-sweetness signal and then accessing the cognitive map to interpret the resulting spatial coordinates occur when the orienting act is potentiated.

This short example illustrates the hypothesis that time and place coordinates, which are a component of every record, are the medium by which separate records are knit together in the process of generating behavior. What follows is a review of evidence that memory consists of separate records, which require knitting together, and that time and place play a privileged role in the unifying process. Most of the evidence comes from the human literature, but the hypothesis is that humans operate in this regard by the same mechanisms and principles that govern the operation of other animal brains.

Behavioral Evidence for Separate Processing of Stimulus Attributes

The recent work of Anne Treisman and her collaborators provides much of the evidence that diverse attributes of a single stimulus are separately processed by different analyzing mechanisms operating in parallel across the visual field and that these separate aspects of the stimulus must then be combined by an operation in which location plays a privileged role (for recent reviews, see Treisman 1986a,b). This work was inspired in some measure by the evidence from cortical electrophysiology indicating that different retinotopically mapped cortical areas contain feature analyzers devoted to extracting different aspects of a visual stimulus (Zeki 1976 and chapter 14 of this book). It grows most directly out of a model of perception formulated by Treisman, Sykes, and Gelade (1977), which they call the feature integration theory of attention. The model assumes that elementary features of a stimulus are registered early and in parallel across the visual field. At this early stage, the visual scene is assumed to be coded along a number of separable dimensions, such as brightness, color, orientation, line endings, and closure. Objects—that is, percepts that combine information from several different processing dimensions—are identified later by a process that integrates the values registered along each of these separate dimensions into a unified percept. The unification process involves what they call focused attention, which they liken to a spotlight that illumines a selected region of the field, revealing the values registered for the different processing dimensions within that region.

The operation of the attention process may be seen in the contrast between the results obtained in two different search tasks. In these tasks, the subject must search a field of stimuli for targets defined by a single attribute or by a conjunction of attributes. For example, the field may consist of from one to thirty letters in different colors. Most of the letters are brown Ts or green Xs. These stimuli are called the distractor stimuli. Any given display may, however, contain a target letter that is anomalous in a prespecified way. The subject's task is to react as quickly as possible after the display appears, with a judgment as to whether an anomalous target letter is or is not present. In a disjunctive targets condition, the target, if present, will be anomalous in either color or shape: it may be blue (rather than brown or green) or it may be an S (rather than an X or a T). In the conjunctively anomalous condition, the target will be defined by an anomalous conjunction of shape and color: it will be a green T (rather than a brown T or a green X). In the disjunctive condition, the subject must be prepared to detect any of four different targets (a blue X, a blue T, a green S, or a brown S), whereas in the conjunctive condition, there is only one target (a green T).

Figure 15.1 shows the results of the illustrative experiment just described. Similar results have been obtained in a number of similar experiments. The error rates were low and comparable in the two conditions.

In the conjunctive condition, the reaction time for successful detections
of targets increases markedly as a function of the number of distractor
stimuli in the display. So does the reaction time for correct denial of target
presence. In figure 15.1, both of these increases appear to be linear, and
the slope of the curve for correct denials appears to be twice the slope for
successful detections. The apparent linearity of the increases in reaction
time with number of distractors and the slope ratio of 2:1 led Treisman
and Gelade to formulate a model of feature integration in which the
search for items defined solely by feature conjunctions was a serial self-
terminating process. In their "spotlight" model items were examined one
by one until an item with the sought-for conjunction was found or until
all the items had been examined. However, Pashler (1987) has recently
made a high-resolution determination of the function over the range

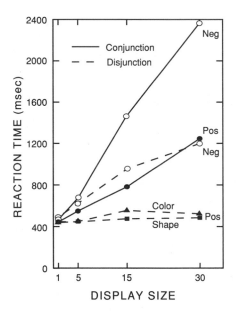

Figure 15.1
Reaction times in searches for conjunctively defined and disjunctively defined targets, as
a function of the number of distracting items in the search field. Negative functions (Neg)
are the latency to say that a target is not present; positive (Pos), the latency to say that a
target is present. Conjunctively defined targets have an anomalous conjunction of a shape
and a color that are present in distractor items as well but not conjoined, while disjunctively defined targets have a color or shape not present in any distractor item. (Redrawn
from Treisman and Gelade 1980, p. 104, by permission of author and publisher.)

from two to eight distractor items. (There is only one point within this range in figure 15.1.) Pashler's experiments show that the apparent linearity of the curves and the 2:1 slope ratio do not hold when the lower range is more finely sampled. In the range from two to eight display items, the slopes of the curves are one-half to one-quarter what they are over the range above eight items. In other words, the curves are positively accelerated somewhere around eight items. Also, the slopes for successful detections and correct denials do not differ at this low end of the curves.

On the basis of his more precise determinations of these reaction time functions plus his finding that the presence of more than one target substantially reduces the latency to detect a target, Pashler suggests that conjunction targets in arrays of modest numerosity are detected by means of a parallel self-terminating search process. The reaction time to detect a target or to deny the presence of a target increases because the time taken to determine whether any one item is the target increases with the number of items being processed—in such a way as to yield an approximately linear relation between target number and reaction time. (See Townsend and Ashby 1983 for a review of capacity-limited parallel search models that have this property.) This parallel search process is capacity-limited; it slows down as the number of items being processed simultaneously increases, and it can deal with only something like eight items at once. When the number of items to be processed substantially exceeds eight, clumps of roughly eight items are processed sequentially. The parallel search process is applied first to one clump, then to the next, and so on, until an item is found or until all clumps have been processed. Thus, for more numerous displays, a parallel search of small clumps is embedded within a serial self-terminating search of successive clumps. Pashler shows that such a model accurately accounts for the reaction time functions he obtained.

What is important for present purposes is not the search model that one is led to adopt but rather the contrast between the reaction time functions in the conjunctive target condition and in the disjunctive target condition. In the disjunctive condition, the reaction time for successful detection of a target was nearly the same regardless of the number of distractors. If an anomalous color (blue) or shape (S) was present, the subject could spot it in about the same amount of time no matter how many brown Ts and green Xs were also present. For successful detections, the slope of the reaction time function was only 3.1 milliseconds per additional distractor item present. There was also a significant deceleration of the curve, as opposed to the acceleration that Pashler found for conjunctive targets. Clearly the processing the perceptual representations of display items must be given to detect a conjunction of target features is distinct from the processing they must be given to detect the presence of either of two distinctive properties (blueness or S-ness).

The very different reaction time functions for the two kinds of searches are not what one would expect if color and shape were specified in separate fields of a single record, as they would be in familiar computerized data bases. Files in these data bases are organized by '"records." Different attributes (for examples, name, social security number, salary) are specified in distinct fields within each record. In these data bases, there is no reason why the time required to complete a disjunctive search of the records (blue in the color field *or* S in the shape field) should depend on the number of records searched in a completely different way than does the time required to complete a conjunctive search (green in the color field *and* T in the shape field). Yet that is what we find in the case of the perceptual "records" for visual stimuli: conjunction and disjunction are handled in very different ways. Why?

One answer may be that the perceptual files are not organized on the basis of stimulus records, with each record specifying the diverse properties of a single stimulus. It would be consistent with the data on cortical processing reviewed in the preceding chapter to suggest that perceptual "files" may be organized on the basis of the times and places of occurrence of different points within a single descriptive feature space (such as the three-dimensional color space). It is often implicitly assumed that a perceptual record suitable for storing in memory consists of the diverse attributes of a single stimulus item. I suggest instead that a perceptual datum destined for storage contains only the coordinates that specify the position of a given stimulus in a single kind of descriptive space (for example, the color space), along with the spatiotemporal coordinates that specify the time and place of origin of that record. Records from the same descriptive space are stored in the same file. Thus, one file (for example, the color file) contains the color values of different stimuli encountered at different times and places, while a different file contains the shape values of those same stimuli. I suggest that the perceptual search task is essentially the same as a memory search task, the only difference being that the records being searched in the perceptual task are "open," meaning that their spatial and temporal coordinates are in the process of being committed to memory. A closed record is one whose temporal probability density function (temporal position) has already been specified.

The search task is represented diagrammatically in figure 15.2. To search disjunctively for a shape value or a color value in this model, the system probes the open records in the shape file with the coordinates that specify the sought-for shape while simultaneously probing the open records in the color file with the coordinates that specify the sought-for

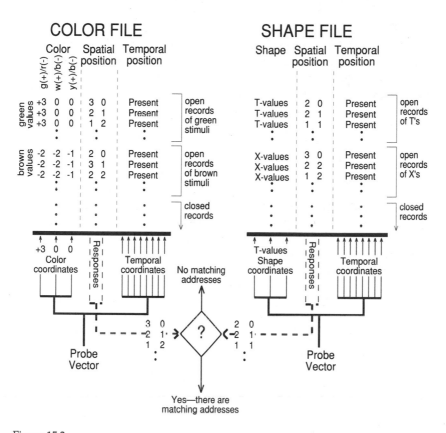

Figure 15.2

Diagram of the search and comparison processes in conjunctive search tasks. The color file is probed with a vector that specifies the sought-for color and the current moment (which specification means that only open records will respond). The responses to this probe give the spatial locations of stimuli with the requisite color. Simultaneously the shape file is probed with a vector that specifies the sought-for shape and the current moment. The responses to this probe give the spatial locations of stimuli with the requisite shape. Finally, the two sets of responses—one set from each file—are compared to see if there are any coincidences. Matching addresses imply a stimulus that has both the specified color and the specified shape. The check for matching addresses is unique to the conjunctive task.

color. (Recall that every color is a point in a three dimensional color space. I assume that every shape is represented as a point or points in one or more shape-description spaces of modest dimensionality.) The probes address records on the basis of their content: If an open record has the same coordinates as the probe, the response to the probe is the spatial address from that record. The temporal address is specified by the probe to be the present moment, limiting the search to the currently perceived stimuli. In the disjunctive search, if either the color probe or the shape probe yields an address, the system responds yes; if neither does, it responds no.

Like content-addressing search probes in general, the probes in the proposed model are assumed to operate in a parallel exhaustive fashion. The slight increase in reaction time for the successful detection of disjunctive targets as the number of records being probed increases has the negatively accelerated form that statistical considerations lead one to expect from an exhaustive parallel search process that is not capacity limited (that is, in which the time taken to probe one record does not increase as a function of the number of records being probed simultaneously; see Townsend and Ashby 1983).

To find a target defined by the conjunction of two sets of coordinates drawn from different descriptive spaces—one set specifying a point in the color space, the other a point in the shape space—the system must begin by probing the shape and color files simultaneously, just as in the disjunctive case. If both probes yield addresses, indicating that both the sought-for color and the sought-for shape are present in the currently open records, then the system must compare the two sets of addresses to see whether any of the addresses coincide (bottom of figure 15.2). It is this additional operation—determining whether any of the addresses generated by the probe of the color file coincide with any of the addresses generated by the probe of the shape file—that makes the reaction time function for conjunctive targets so different from that for disjunctive targets. The test for address coincidence is necessary because the model assumes that the color and shape attributes of the same stimulus item are stored in separate files and linked only by virtue of the fact that both records have the same spatiotemporal address. The test for address coincidence brings in Pashler's limited-capacity parallel search process.

On the hypothesis just outlined, the reaction time for correct denials of the presence of any of the disjunctively defined targets ought also to be almost independent of the number of distractors present. In fact, however, there is a systematic, nearly linear increase in this function. (In some variants of this experiment, this increase is not nearly so linear.) Treisman and Gelade conjecture that in the disjunction condition, the subjects tend to check several targets individually when the initial parallel probe fails to yield a detection. It seems reasonable that, to keep the rate of false negatives down, the system does some reprobing when an initial probe fails to return any addresses. This might account for the puzzling increase in this reaction time for the denial of disjunctively defined targets.

It is important to note that on trials where there was only one letter in the array, all the reaction times were the same. When only one stimulus is present, it takes no longer to spot (or deny the presence of) one of four possible disjunctive anomalies than it does to spot (or deny the presence of) a single conjunctive anomaly. This implies that probes for nonlocational attributes of stimuli may be made in parallel (simultaneously).

The Special Role of Spatial Position

Treisman's "spotlight of attention" is interpreted here as a spatially delimited probe of a file containing vectors that describe a stimulus property (shape, color, and so on) with some dimensions, while the spatial position of the source is represented along others. The vector space is the set of all possible such vectors—all possible combinations of color and spatial position. The vector space may also be viewed as giving the values that specify a stimulus property (such as the color coordinates) as a function of spatial coordinates (locations in the experienced world). The central claim of this chapter is that spatial and temporal coordinates play a privileged role in the operation of memory because everything else is stored as a function of these variables. To get from one stimulus property to another in the course of retrieving information about diverse aspects of a stimulus, the brain uses the spatiotemporal coordinates as index variables. Knowing one property of a sought-for stimulus enables it to retrieve the spatiotemporal coordinates of that stimulus. These coordinates in turn enable it to retrieve other properties of the stimulus and properties of other stimuli that have a specifiable spatial or temporal relation to the target stimulus.

This view may be contrasted with an associative net view of memory structure, in which there are no privileged variables. Color is as likely to be mapped as a function of shape as it is to be mapped as a function of position in space; that is, it is as likely to be associated with shape as with position in space. In most discussions of associative nets, associations to positions in space play little role and those to positions in time still less. Associations between properties like color and shape are taken to be paradigmatic.

The question raised by the Treisman spotlight hypothesis is whether position in space in fact plays a privileged role in linking separately processed stimulus properties together. To test this hypothesis, Treisman and Gelade did another experiment that contrasted searches for conjunctively defined targets with searches for disjunctively defined targets. Again, there were only two possible targets in the conjunctive condition (a pink X or a blue O), while there were four in the disjunctive condition (a pink or blue H or an X or O that was orange). In both the disjunctive and conjunctive conditions, one of the targets was present on every trial, in an array of twelve display items, eleven of which were false-conjunction distractors. The display of eleven distractors and one target was flashed on briefly in a tachistoscope. In the conjunctive condition, the subject's task was to spot the pink X or the blue O that was somewhere in an array of pink Os and blue Xs. In the disjunctive condition, the task was to spot the X or O that was orange (rather than pink or blue) or else the pink or blue letter that was an H (rather than an X or O). This experiment did not measure reaction time. Rather the subject had to report which target occurred (identify the target) and where in the array it occurred. In one version of the experiment, identification accuracy was equated across conditions by allowing more inspection time in the conjunctive than in the disjunctive condition. In the other version, inspection time was held constant across the two conditions, which meant that identification accuracy was much greater in the disjunction condition than in the conjunction condition.

Columns 1 to 3 of table 15.1 give the conditional probabilities of correct target identifications given an exactly correct ("Correct"), almost correct ("Adjacent") or substantially incorrect ("Distant") specification of target location. Column 4 gives the overall probability of a correct target identification, which was held constant in the first version of the experiment and allowed to vary in the second version (so that inspection time could be held constant). In both versions of the experiment, the probability of correctly specifying a target defined by an anomalous conjunction of the same feature values present in the distractor stimuli was at chance (.5) whenever the subject was substantially in error about the correct location of the anomalous conjunction (see entries in the cells where column = "Distant" and the row = "Conjunction"). To quote the authors' conclusion, "at least approximate perception of location appears to be a necessary condition for the identification of conjunction targets" (p. 130). On the other hand, the subjects can say whether they saw an orange letter in a sea of pink and blue ones or an H in a sea of Xs and Os at substantially above chance levels when they are grossly in error about the location of the anomalous color or shape feature (see entries in column = "Distant," row = "Feature").

These results suggest that the recognition of the conjunction of a shape and a color is not achieved by going directly from shape to color but rather by the intermediary of spatial position. It is as if Tinker, in the famous double-play trio of Tinker, Evers, and Chance, was not allowed

Table 15.1
Median probabilities of reporting target identity correctly given
different categories of location responses

Location response		Correct	Adjacent	Distant	Overall
Experiment VIII (hit	Conjunction	0.930	0.723	0.500	0.793
rate held constant)	Feature	0.897	0.821	0.678	0.786
Experiment IX (inspec-	Conjunction	0.840	0.582	0.453	0.587
tion time constant)	Feature	0.979	0.925	0.748	0.916

Source: Treisman and Gelade 1980, table 4.

to throw directly to Chance; he could get the ball to him only by way of Evers, even when there was no runner coming into second. In this case, spatial position is the obligatory intermediary. The brain cannot get from the color of a stimulus to its shape except by way of its position.

These results also suggest that the spatial position of a stimulus may be registered more or less well. Spatial position, like other variables, is not recorded with perfect precision or not at all but rather with variable precision. The "addresses" of stimuli (their recorded spatial positions) are not discrete variables but rather probability density functions defined over space—functions from which the brain may calculate by integration over a region of space the probability that the stimulus was in that region. One may think of the probability density functions that constitute the spatial addresses associated with records as spatial "receptive fields," on which the probe stimuli "fall." A probe stimulus specifies a region of the world and the spatial address associated with a given record is sensitive to probes falling in a certain region of the world. The response of a given record to a spatial probe is assumed to be the crossproduct of the probe and the spatial receptive field of the record, just as the response of a ganglion cell in the retina is the crossproduct of the light stimulus and the spatial tuning function ("receptive field") of the ganglion cell.

Nissen (1985) did a more refined test of the hypothesis that spatial position is an obligatory intermediary in relating one stimulus property to another. First she tested whether her subjects could link color to spatial position and spatial position to color with equal facility. She used tachistoscopic displays of four colored shapes. The colors were red, green, blue, and black. The shapes were circle, square, triangle, and diamond. The positions in which the four colored shapes appeared were above, below, to the left, and to the right of the fixation point. The conjunctions of shape, color and position were randomly determined from trial to trial. On some trials, subjects saw a positional cue word (*top*, *bottom*, *left*, *right*) after the stimulus array had been flashed, and they reported what color they thought had occurred at that position. On other trials, the cue word specified one of the colors, and the subject reported which position that color had occupied. The subjects were not asked to report the shape in this first experiment. In one condition, they had foreknowledge of which dimension (color or position) was to be the cue and which the report on a given trial. In another condition, they did not know which dimension was to be which until they saw the cue word.

In this first experiment, it did not matter which aspect of the stimulus functioned as cue and which had to be reported. Subjects reported color when given position as accurately as they reported position when given color, whether or not they had foreknowledge of which variable was to be the cue and which the report. In terms of the present model, the file that represents color as a function of position may be probed for color by position or for position by color with equal facility. Put another way, the file can be used with equal readiness as a mapping of color with respect to position or as a mapping of position as a function of color.

The next experiment contrasted two conditions, in both of which the subject was cued with one aspect of the stimulus and asked to report the values of the cued stimulus on the two uncued aspects. Shape was an uncued (to-be-reported) aspect in both conditions. In one condition, position was the cue; shape and color were to be reported. In the other condition, color was the cue; shape and position were to be reported. When shape and color were reported in response to a cue indicating the position of a stimulus, the reports were statistically independent; the probability of a correct shape report given a correct color report was the same as the probability of a correct shape report given an incorrect color report, and similarly for a correct color report. This is to be expected if the position cue given after the display has been flashed is used to probe two different memory files, one where color is recorded as a function of position and one where shape is recorded as a function of position. By contrast, when color was the cue, shape and position reports were not statistically independent; the probability of a correct shape report was significantly higher on trials when the position report was correct than on trials when it was not. In fact, the data were consistent with a model in which it was assumed that the probability of a subject's reporting shape correctly in response to a color cue is given by the product of the probability of his reporting location correctly given color and the probability of his reporting shape correctly given location. In sum, the data supported the hypothesis that the shape of a stimulus cannot be accessed directly from knowledge of its color; the brain must first obtain from the representation of stimulus color the representation of stimulus position, which then provides access to the representation of stimulus shape.

These conclusions are confirmed and extended by Isenberg, Nissen, and Case (MS).

Tsal and Lavie (1988), following up earlier work by Snyder (1972), showed that the location of a stimulus is accessed even it is irrelevant to the task, and this location has a strong effect on which other viewed items are then recalled. Subjects were shown a circular array of colored letters in a tachistoscopic presentation. They were instructed to recall first a letter of a certain color (or a certain shape) and then recall all the other letters that they could. The location of the first item recalled had a far stronger effect on which items were subsequently recalled than did the cue stimulus (color or shape) that specified a required property of the first letter to be recalled. If subjects saw a circle of three green, three brown, and three red letters, with the letters of a given color positioned ungrouped (randomly interspersed) around the circle, and were required to recall a red letter first, the letters they subsequently recalled were more likely to be the letters adjacent to the red letter first recalled than they were to be the other two red letters.

Separate in Memory or Only during Perceptual Processing?

In the experiments reviewed, there is no direct test of the hypothesis that the separate attributes of a stimulus reside in separate memory stores. The subjects were required to react to a stimulus display while they were still viewing it or immediately after they saw it (see, however, Nissen et al. MS). One could reasonably argue that these experiments demonstrate separate processing of stimulus attributes such as shape, size, and color but not separate storage. Perhaps the separately processed dimensions of stimulus experience are unified in the record kept of the stimulus. Is there any evidence that separate shape and color records are kept?

An experiment by Stefurak and Boynton (1986) demonstrates that independent records of shape and color are kept in short-term memory, if one takes measures to prevent the subject from covertly verbalizing what he sees. Their subjects inspected an array of five colored animal shapes for 5 seconds. The shapes presented were chosen at random from a set of ten shapes, with which the subject had been familiarized. The colors also were chosen from a set of ten with which the subject had been familiarized. Thus, on a given trial the subject saw a randomly conjoined selection of five colors and five shapes. Both the colors and the shapes were "categorically" distinct, in the sense that they were overlearned, never confused, and readily named. Three to 15 seconds after the array was removed, the subjects were shown a single probe item, which was also a colored animal shape. The subject's task was to press one (and only one) of three buttons. In pressing one button, he signified that the probe item had either a color or a shape that was not among the five colors and shapes in the array seen 3-15 seconds ago. In pressing the second button, the subject signified that the probe item was identical to one of the items in the array: the same in both color and shape. In pressing the third button, the subject signified that the probe item conjoined a color and shape that were present but not conjoined in the array.

In the experimental condition, the subjects had to perform this recognition task while simultaneously performing a rather arduous mental arithmetic task, designed to prevent their verbalizing to themselves what they saw during the inspection of the array. Beginning several seconds prior to the presentation of the array and continuing for several seconds after the subject's response to the recognition probe, the subject had to keep a running sum of randomly chosen positive and negative integers recited at 2-second intervals by a voice on a tape recorder. They had to report the final value of the running sum at the conclusion of the trial. The payoff system put a premium on correct reports of this sum.

Under these conditions, the subjects were able to recognize the presence of a "new" color or shape in the recognition probe at way above chance. Put another way, they could remember which colors and which shapes they had seen in the array and thereby distinguish between those and the ones they had not seen. However, their memory for which colors were conjoined with which shapes was nonexistent. The probability of their signifying a correct conjunction (a probe identical in color and shape to one item in the array) given a probe that was in fact a correct conjunction was no higher than their probability of so signifying when given a probe that was an incorrect conjunction (the F for this comparison was less than 1.00). Both aspects of the results—the ability to recognize which shapes and colors had been in the array and the inability to recognize which shapes went with which colors—were unaffected by the delay between array presentation and the recognition probe (3 versus 15 seconds). This experiment demonstrates the storage of shape and color records from the same stimuli in a completely unintegrated form, a form that does not permit the recovery of which shape went with which color.

In terms of the spatiotemporal coordinates hypothesis, one would assume that the specification of the spatial address for each experienced color and shape was so broad that colors could not be differentially linked to shapes on the basis of the addresses. In effect, the addresses recorded were only sufficiently precise to localize the records to the vicinity of the display area, not to specify where they originated from within that area. Put another way, the recorded probability density functions that specified the locations of individual color and shape records were so broad and their central points so close together that it was impossible for the system to discriminate one function from another (one address from another).

Stefurak and Boynton ran a control condition in which the subjects did not have to perform the mental arithmetic. Under these conditions, the subjects were well above chance at discriminating between correct and incorrect conjunctions of color and shape. However, even here they confused correct and incorrect conjunctions 13-20 percent of the time. Stefurak and Boynton suggest that it is verbal coding that enables subjects to distinguish correct and incorrect conjunctions in the control condition. Of course, the mental arithmetic may have interfered with any number of nonverbal processes as well, so the identity of the crucial process remains to be determined. Another possibility is that the mental arithmetic prevents the formation of more precise spatiotemporal addresses for the color and shape records laid down when the array is inspected.

In a second experiment, Stefurak and Boynton tested for mnemonic conjunctions between shape and color records by instructing the subjects to focus only on color (or only on shape). When the probe was presented, they were to indicate only whether its color (or only whether its shape) was one seen in the array. The experimenter measured the effect of the irrelevant (unrewarded) stimulus attribute on the accuracy of recognizing the relevant (rewarded) attribute. There was no effect. When the probe was a red camel, it did not matter, so far as the accuracy of the subject's recognition, whether a red camel or red whale had been seen in the array.

In sum, the Stefurak and Boynton results indicate that the separate processing of the shape and color of a stimulus carries through into short-term memory. So far as I am aware, no one has yet designed an experiment to test whether the independent coding of these and other stimulus attributes persists in long term memory. There are, however, some functional considerations that make it desirable that it should. If the attributes of experience are to be unified prior to being placed in permanent storage, the system must decide in advance what is to be united with what. It is undesirable to make any such commitment because there is no knowing in advance which aspects of an experience should be recalled in connection with which other aspects.

Disadvantages of A Priori Memory Linkages

It is a disadvantage of associative theories of memory that they presuppose an associative path (not necessarily direct) between a memory and any other memory capable of evoking it in some context or given some task. In a system with many memories to be accessed for many different purposes in many different contexts, this leads to an explosive proliferation of associative links. When there are only two memories, only one associative bond is required to link them directly. By the time there are ten memories, it requires forty-five associative bonds if each memory is to be directly linked to each other. By the time there are one-hundred memories, the required number of bonds has grown to almost five thousand. Even if we abandon the assumption that each memory is directly accessible from each other, it seems clear that in any large memory net, the preponderance of the system must be devoted to storing the links that unite the memories (the associative bonds) rather than the memories themselves. Most of memory must be given over to the linkages between records (the associative bonds) rather than to the records themselves.

The system may resort to some kind of hierarchical organization ("chunking of memories") to keep the required number of links within bounds, but it is not clear that this could overcome the dilemma inherent in a scheme that attempts to link records a priori—before a particular connection is required for some memory-dependent output. The dilemma is that any scheme to economize on linkages (on what is linked to what) limits the use that may subsequently be made of the recorded data, while any scheme that tries to overcome this by linking many records together in many different ways burdens memory with the resulting plethora of linkages, a burden that grows by increasing increments as the number of memories grows.

The advantage of the spatiotemporal address approach is that the growth in the number of stored addresses (the elements in memory that mediate the linking function) is proportionate to the number of records rather than increasing as an accelerating function of the number of records. And, the approach does not limit a priori which records may be accessed from which others. In moving from record to record by means of their spatiotemporal index variables, the system may do all sorts of computations on the retrieved index values and use the computed index values to probe any other kind of file. To take a fanciful example, if it wants to know what was smelled to the north of the point where a hot spot was observed 2 hours before the onset of the rise in ground temperature, the system can use the spatiotemporal address retrieved from the temperature record to compute an appropriate probe for the smell file (or for any other file). In laying down the records of smell and temperature, the system need not have foreseen the desirability of linking these two experiences over this remove in space and time. The richness of the use that may be made of the records is limited by the computational resources of the utilizing system, not by the foresight of the storing system.

The Special Role of Temporal Position

The proposed solution to the problem of linking records requires that both the place and the time of experience be recorded with every record of an experienced stimulus property because the scheme relies on the fact that more than one stimulus source cannot occupy the same place at the same time. Specifying the place alone would not be adequate to link the records of the diverse properties of a single experienced object because a different object may be experienced at that place on another occasion. Thus we should also expect to find evidence that the time of occurrence of a recorded experience is a fundamental variable in the ability to recall the diverse aspects of that experience, which is to say, of the ability to recall the experience as an integrated experience or episode. Such evidence is not far to seek. The literature on retrograde amnesias suggests that the ability to recall integrated experience is closely tied to time of the occurrence rather than to any other property of the experience, such as the content of the experience, its current importance to the subject, or its emotional impact on the subject.

Before examining the phenomenon of retrograde amnesia, however, we may ask whether there is nonpathological evidence that time plays a role similar to the role that spatial location appears to play in linking the distinct properties of a stimulus. Can we find a temporal equivalent of Nissen's findings regarding the role that a common place of occurrence plays in linking the recollections of different properties of the same stimulus? Does common time of occurrence link records of stimulus properties in the same way that common place appears to do?

The unidimensionality and unidirectionality of time makes it difficult to design a temporal analogue of Nissen's experiment. Ideally, one wants to present, for example, a red square at one time, a green triangle at another, a blue circle at a third, and a black diamond at a fourth, then either specify one of the presentation moments and ask the subject for the color and shape of the stimulus presented at that moment, or specify color and ask the subject for the shape and presentation moment of the stimulus with that color. However, it is difficult to deconfound time of presentation and serial position (first, second, third, fourth). Because time is unidimensional, difference in moment of presentation must covary with serial position. By contrast, there is no natural ordering of points in a two-dimensional space: real numbers are well ordered, complex numbers are not. Because time is unidirectional, one cannot use a probe that moves backward along the temporal axis to indicate which presentation moment the subject is to use in recalling stimulus properties. By contrast because spatial axes are bidirectional, one can move a probe to the spatial position previously occupied by a stimulus.

The Nissen experiment depends on the ability of both the experimenter and the subject to indicate spatial position directly, that is, independently of the stimuli presented. It is hard to see how to accomplish this in the temporal domain. When the experimenter or the subject refers to the first, second, or any other moment, they do not designate a temporal position (moment) defined independently of the stimuli presented. The moment indicated by any such phrase as *the first interval* could not be identified if there had been no sequence of experimental intervals. By contrast, when the experimenter or subject specifies the upper left portion of the tachistoscopic field, they refer to a position in space that is defined independently of the experimental trials, a position that could be found just as readily even if there had been no experimental trials. Because the subject can indicate recalled spatial position and color equally directly, Nissen's experiment can straightforwardly reveal whether the recollection of shape given color is contingent on the recollection of position given color. Things become more complicated if the suspected nodal variable (temporal position) cannot be directly (ostensively) indicated but must instead be indicated by the recall of another property of the stimulus (such as its position in the sequence of stimuli). The probability of recalling the indicator is the product of the probability of recalling the temporal position given the color and the probability of recalling the serial position given the temporal position. Failure to recall the serial position of the stimulus with a given color does not imply the failure to recall the presumed nodal variable, the temporal position of the stimulus; hence it is difficult to determine whether the recollection of shape given color is contingent on the recollection of temporal position given color.

It might be possible to tackle the problem directly by specifying the moment of presentation in relation to the time elapsed up to the present. The subject might be asked to say how long ago the red stimulus was presented and what the shape of that stimulus was. One would want to do this under conditions in which the magnitude of the subject's elapsed time estimate could be shown to distinguish one presentation from another. Since the recollection of how long ago the presentation was seems intuitively difficult, it would be remarkable if one obtained a result analogous to Nissen's: that the probability of recalling the shape given the color was both less than and conditional on the probability of recalling the presentation time given the color.

Short-Term Memory.
Since I am not aware of a temporal analogue to the Nissen experiment and since it may not be possible to construct one, we must look elsewhere for evidence that time plays a fundamental role in integrating the recollections of distinct stimulus properties under nonpathological

conditions. The findings from short-term memory experiments are at least consistent with such a view. The standard test of short-term memory (Brown 1958; Peterson and Peterson 1959) is to give the subject a list of three unrelated items (consonants, nonsense syllables, or unrelated words), then have the subject engage in a distracting task of some kind (such as counting backward by threes), until the moment when he is asked to recall the list. The longer the duration of the distracting task, the fewer the items correctly recalled, up to about 30 seconds, at which point normal subjects correctly recall about one item from a three-item list. The standard interpretation of this finding is that there is a volatile storage medium, with a decay constant on the order of 10 seconds. Items are thought to enter this volatile memory first. Unless they are transferred from this volatile short-term memory (sometimes called primary memory) to a nonvolatile long term memory (sometimes called secondary memory), they are lost from memory altogether (Atkinson and Shiffrin 1968; Waugh and Norman 1965).

One difficulty with the standard account is that the "decay" from the volatile memory is not usually observed in the first performance of the Brown-Peterson test. Recall on the first trial is generally nearly perfect no matter how long the retention interval. The decay of recall as a function of retention interval is only seen on later trials. The amount of decay seen at a given retention interval increases over the first six trials in a decelerating curve (Keppel and Underwood 1962). If the dependence of recall on the retention interval is taken to indicate the evaporation of un-refreshed records from a volatile memory, it is hard to explain why this evaporation should depend on the number of trials that have been made.

The dependence of the decay on trials implies that it is interference between the records from different trials that gives rise to the decay. The suggestion is reinforced by the repeated observation that many of the errors made at longer retention intervals involve the recollection of an item from an earlier list, particularly an item from the same serial position in an earlier list (Fuchs and Melton 1974). The evidence that it is interference between records is further strengthened by the release from proactive interference phenomenon (Wickens 1972). The subject is given four lists of three words each, all drawn from the same category, such as sports, followed by a fifth list of words drawn from a different category, such as the professions. The "decay" evident in the subject's recall of the third and fourth lists disappears from his recall of the fifth list. In short, as Keppel and Underwood (1962) pointed out long ago, there are reasons to think that the principal limitation on the ability to recall items from short-term memory is not the volatility of the records but rather interference: the inability to discriminate to-be-recalled records from not-to-be-recalled records. This is, of course, the same factor that limits recall from long-term memory.

Interference has traditionally been thought of in associative terms, although what was associated with what and how these associations operated to determine what the subject recalled has been much debated. I suggest a temporal account of interference: one record interferes with another either because its temporal address (temporal receptive field) is insufficiently differentiated from the temporal address of the other or because the temporal probe used to evoke the records is so broad as to have some likelihood of evoking the wrong record even though the addresses of the records are well differentiated (see figure 15.3). In the present account, it is not the records of a current stimulus that are volatile but rather the specification of the temporal address, the temporal probability density function that goes with each record. The decrease in the precision with which a temporal address is specified in the interval shortly after a record ceases to be current renders the temporal address for that record less distinguishable from the temporal addresses of other records from approximately the same time—for example, the records generated by earlier lists.

In this account, I distinguish between current ("open") records and past ("closed") records, rather than between short-term (primary) and long term (secondary) memory. A current record is the record of an experience that has just occurred and whose temporal address is in the process of being specified. The temporal address of a record may be thought of as a probability density function on the time axis, just as a spatial address may be thought of as a probability density function defined over three-dimensional space. An inchoate temporal address is one with a peak probability density only marginally different from 0. Such a distribution must be very broad because the area under the function (the integral) is always equal to 1. The integral of the probability density function that constitutes a temporal address must equal 1 because this integral gives the probability that the event occurred between the indefinite past and the present moment. Since the area under the probability density function is fixed, the lower the peak probability density, the wider the distribution must be. One may imagine the specification of a temporal address as the rise in the height of this probability density function and the commensurate decrease in its width. One may further imagine that this specification takes both time and limited processing resources. Hence the number of records for which temporal addresses may concurrently be specified is limited, and the rate at which specification occurs may also be reduced as the number of records receiving temporal specification increases. This would account for the limited capacity of short-term memory: the limit is set by the number of

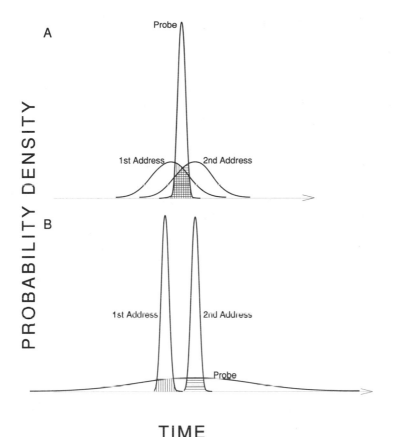

TIME

Figure 15.3
Schematic illustration of two different mechanisms of temporal interference in a temporally indexed system of records. Both the temporal addresses in memory records and the
temporal probe intended to elicit records from a given time may be thought of as
probability density functions. Alternatively, the temporal addresses associated with
records may be thought of as temporal receptive fields and the probes as temporal stimuli.
The response from a given record is proportionate to the cross-product of probe and
temporal address, here approximated by the vertically and horizontally lined areas that
the probe and an address function have in common. A. Although a precise (narrow)
probe is positioned near the center of the second address, the overlap in the temporal
addresses from two different records yields similar responses, hence the likelihood of
confusing the first record with the second. B. Although the addresses do not overlap, the
probe is imprecise (broad), so that it excites both records approximately equally.

records that may be "open", that is, undergoing spatiotemporal specification at any one time.

It may further be imagined that the distracting task (counting backward by threes) puts an end to the specification process ("closes the record") and that there is some subsidence of the temporal address in the first several seconds after a record is closed, a reduction in the peak probability density and commensurate broadening of the function. This subsidence in the temporal address (broadening of the temporal receptive field of a record) would account for the "decay" of short term memories in a manner consistent with the evidence that it is interlist interference rather than memory evanescence that accounts for the difficulty in correctly recalling items in the Brown-Peterson test of short-term memory. The broadening of their temporal receptive fields would render the temporal address of the items in the most recent list (the to-be-recalled items) less distinguishable from the temporal address of the items in previous lists (figure 15.3A). This would not be a problem when there were no previous lists because the broadened temporal receptive field would not overlap with the receptive fields of any other records in the same file. That is why the decay is not seen on the first trial of a Brown-Peterson test. The broadening of the temporal receptive field for a record would also not be a problem if the items on the most recent list differed in category from the items on previous lists because then a category probe would serve to restrict the records being probed to only those from the most recent list.

Another possibility is that the precision of the temporal probe used to elicit the records made on the most recent presentation of items decreases as a function of the length of the backward interval. In eliciting these items, the subject must set the value of the memory probe equal to the interval that has elapsed since the presentation. The error in setting the value of the probe may reasonably be expected to be an increasing function of the time elapsed: the further in the past the presentation, the broader the probability density function that specifies the estimated time at which the items were recorded, that is, the more imprecise the probe signal (the more blurred the memory stimulus). The more imprecise the probe, the greater the relative likelihood of its eliciting an item from an earlier presentation (figure 15.3B). Thus, even when a record from an earlier presentation has a narrowly specified temporal address, it may be elicited by mistake by an imprecise temporal probe.

This mechanism of temporal interference (increasingly imprecise probe signals), unlike the mechanism first discussed, might explain the tendency for intrusions to come from the same serial position in an earlier list. Assume that the property of being the second item is stored separately from the item itself. That is, "secondness" is treated just like redness or squareness. It is linked to the other recorded properties of a stimulus only by virtue of its having the same spatiotemporal address as these other properties. Assume further that both the record of the second item in an earlier list and the corresponding record of secondness have sharp temporal addresses. The blurry temporal probe intended to elicit the records from the most recent presentation may elicit by mistake the secondness record from an earlier list. This record, once elicited, provides the system with its own sharply delimited temporal address to use as a probe. When this is used, it will turn up the record of the item that has the same temporal address as the secondness record from which the probe value derives, namely, the second item in the earlier list. This explains two salient findings in research on short-term memory: the fact that intrusions from earlier lists fall off sharply as a function of how much earlier a given list was (Noyd 1965) and the fact that the intrusion tends to be an item occupying the same serial position in the earlier list (Fuchs and Melton 1974).

The suggested mechanisms of temporal interference in short-term memory tasks are not mutually exclusive. There may be both some degradation in the sharpness of at least some temporal addresses in the interval immediately after they are established and also a (scalar?) increase with elapsed interval in the error or uncertainty in the initial temporal probe used to elicit the most recent records (cf Bjork and Whitten 1974). In either case, one would predict that the "decay rate" in short-term memory testing would be a function of the interval between successive trials; the longer the intertrial interval, the less the decay over a given elapsed interval since the presentation of the list, which is in fact the case (Loess and Waugh 1967; Kincaid and Wickens 1970). One might expect to find a constant-ratio relation analogous to that observed when the effect of CS-US interval is determined as a function of intertrial interval: the postpresentation interval required to produce a given amount of "decay" may be a constant fraction of the intertest interval.

Retrograde Amnesia
The strongest evidence that memories of all kinds are linked together in recall by temporal indexes comes from clinical reports of retrograde amnesia. The temporal-index hypothesis explains two salient features of these reports. First, memories become unretrievable as a function of the time at which they were laid down, not as a function of their subject matter, their salience, their emotional significance, or any other property that current theories of learning and memory would lead one to think would control memory strength and accessibility. Second, most of the loss is more often than not temporary, indicating that the records became

unretrievable rather than obliterated. Both findings are explained by the assumption that a temporal index (time of occurrence) is used in the retrieval of memories and the further assumption that damage to the nervous system may transiently (and in some cases permanently) make it impossible for the system to generate or work with temporal probes that fall within certain past intervals. For all the records whose temporal addresses lie within the interval of unspecifiable times of occurrence, it will be impossible to get from one record to another; hence, it will be impossible to have any unified or integrated recollection of experience within that interval.

Before proceeding to a further discussion of the implications of this phenomenon, it will help to present a few of the many case reports in the literature, beginning with the often quite discrete temporal deletions of memory that are sometimes the most salient manifestations of transient neuropathologies of an unknown nature. For example, Barbizet (1970) reports two episodes of retroactive memory loss in a 44-year-old police-man who had suffered a cranial trauma and four days of coma a year earlier. In the first episode, he went to pay for his coffee in a restaurant and was startled to discover that his wallet, which had been full that morning, was now nearly empty. His astonishment stemmed from the fact that he had completely forgotten everything that had happened in the two previous hours, during which he had been shopping with his daughter, driven 10 kilometers to his favorite fishing ground, fished for an hour, and then driven to the restaurant. In this case, there appears to have been a deletion of two hours' worth of records. Whether these were ever recovered is not reported. Commonly, however, the records from the affected interval do become available again subsequently—the gen-erally observed phenomenon of recovery from retrograde amnesia. The following case illustrates this (Barbizet 1970, p. 109):

> On November 12, 1966, she woke up at about 7:15, and remained in bed for a few minutes speaking to her husband. She was perfectly normal. She got up and went to the kitchen to prepare the coffee. Having arrived there, she stopped in front of the table and called to her husband, who was still in bed, "What is this thermos bottle on the table for? Who put it there?" Her husband was very surprised, for his wife had put it there the evening before, and he told her so. She continued to ask the same questions several times, and finally said: "I feel very strange. What is the matter with me?" Her husband began to question her and realized that she could not remember what had happened during several weeks. He spoke of a close friend who had had a serious operation three weeks earlier and to whom she had shown great devotion, watching at the sickbed for several

nights. She was astonished and replied, "Oh, so they've operated on him?" and then gradually forgot what had been said to her. When her daughter and grandson arrived, however, she recognized them and called them by their names. Normally very active, she now remained seated the whole morning at her table, forgetting even to warm up the coffee, to which she was particularly partial. Although she recognized that some linen belonged to her grandson, she had forgotten that she had herself ironed and put it away the evening before. She saw the paper but no longer knew what the competition she had been trying to solve for several days meant. She recognized the doctor who arrived at about 11 o'clock, and from that time she began to recover her memory piecemeal. By noon she was in full possession of her memory. The whole process seems to have lasted for five or six hours, about which she can remember nothing. Except for fairly frequent headaches, no pathological antecedent was discovered; the neurological examination gave normal results, and so did the electroencephalograph.

Matilda's case is representative of the general course of retrograde amnesia, consistent accounts of which can be found in a number of books by clinical neurologists (Barbizet 1970; Russell 1959; Whitty and Zangwill 1977). She would appear to have suffered the onset of an unknown neuropathology on her way to the kitchen. This pathology had two mnemonic manifestations: it rendered her records for the last several weeks unretrievable (the retrograde amnesia), and it either blocked the establishment of new records or prevented their subsequent retrieval (the anterograde amnesia). The retrograde amnestic effect was transient. Six hours later, she could retrieve the records that had been unretrievable at breakfast time. Clearly there had not been a failure in the consolidation of these records, if consolidation is understood to mean a neurophysiological process by which records become steadily more permanent (less susceptible to destruction). The records of her watch at the sickbed of her friend and the records that rendered the newspaper competition comprehensible had not been obliterated; they had become temporarily unretrievable.

It is necessary to insist rather strenuously on the implications of recovery from retrograde amnesia because there is a persisting tendency to interpret it as evidence for the progressive consolidation of memories over time, despite the fact that recovery from most of the interval covered by a retrograde amnesia is the rule rather than the exception. Consolidation is imagined to be a process whereby the physical change that underlies the preservation of a record becomes "more resistant to disruption for years after learning occurs" (Squire and Schlapfer 1981, p. 332). If disruption is understood to mean the "loss of connections" in a "network of [learned] connections" (Squire and Schlapfer, p. 333), where the lost connections are the physical embodiment of the supposedly lost records, then the commonly observed recovery from retrograde amnesia (the reappearance in recollection of the supposedly lost records) is not readily reconcilable with any simple version of the consolidation hypothesis. Rather, it is evidence that the capacity to retrieve integrated collections of records is dependent on a temporal index of some kind.

Matilda's case is also representative in that the retrograde amnesia was accompanied by a period of anterograde amnesia, and the permanent records, if any, that were established during the 5-hour period of anterograde amnesia between breakfast and lunch never became recoverable. After lunch, Matilda could recollect the events from her recent past, but she could never recall events from the period between breakfast and lunch, the presumed period of neurophysiological malfunction. Similar episodes of transient retrograde amnesia together with enduring amnesia for the events of the period of malfunction are a fairly common occurrence in football games. The phenomenon is known among players as getting "dinged". The following case report is by a physician and a neuropsychologist who spent two seasons on the sidelines observing and testing players whose bell had been rung. It is one of several similar instances they observed (see also Fisher 1966):

> An 18 year old left-handed flanker back was gang tackled after catching a pass on a "91 curl pattern." He got up and started to run to the sidelines, pointing to his head, but was told to stay in the game. On the subsequent play he was confused regarding the signals, and had to ask for specific instructions. He then left the game. On immediate testing he had intact orientation and recent memory for the play and impact. Seven minutes later he began to have difficulty remembering the plays, and by 11 minutes after injury he was confused about any of the game events, including his finger dislocation of 90 minutes earlier. He appeared bewildered and continually repeated, "I can't remember, I can't remember; this has never happened to me before." However, he was able to do simple arithmetic, reverse spelling, and follow commands. He showed no focal neurologic deficit on screening examination that included ocular, speech and facial muscle function and gait, strength and coordination testing.
>
> The player remained confused for at least 30 minutes postinjury. He was not able to recall his locker combination to obtain his clothes. Beginning at this time, however, his memory started to return, and he could recall being admitted to the Student Health Service. By two

and one-half hours postinjury, he was bright and lucid. His memory then included the play and the impact on which he had gotten "his bell rung" and had wanted to leave the game and the following play with confusion regarding the signals; but he had only a vague, patch recollection of the one-half hour of bewilderment on the sidelines. He could not recall any of the memory testing examinations, only vaguely remembered speaking with the examiners, and did not recall his repeated statements, "I can't remember." (Yarnell and Lynch 1973, pp. 196-197)

The records laid down up to the time of the onset of malfunction eventually became recallable, but if records were laid down during the period of peak malfunction, they were never subsequently retrievable. Benson and Geschwind (1967) give a lengthy account of a man who had a similar but not nearly so transient episode of combined anterograde and retrograde amnesia. The patient was admitted to the hospital with a head injury of unknown origin, apparently incurred while he was on a drinking binge. The patient was married and had a family living in Washington, where he had worked as a bus driver, but he had separated from them two years ago and come to Boston, where he worked first as a messenger for a drugstore and then as a laborer in a mattress factory. He was stuporous for a week or so after admission to the hospital, but by the end of his first month in the hospital he was alert and free of any primary sensory or motor dysfunction. His most notable dysfunction was a combined anterograde and retrograde amnesia.

Because of the anterograde amnesia, he could not record in a subsequently retrievable form what was told to him; hence he did not understand why he was in the hospital, despite having been told repeatedly. Indeed he did not understand that he was in a hospital. When asked what type of building he was in, he could not say. When told that he was in a hospital, he did not argue that he was not, but when asked soon thereafter where he was, he again could not say. Nor could he remember what his problem was. When told that he was in a hospital and asked why he was there, he would guess that he was visiting or he would mention some problems with his eyes or feet or legs. (Benson and Geschwind interpret these responses as attempts to "fill a void in his knowledge of present occurrences with past knowledge.") He could not find his way around in the hospital, even after he had been an ambulatory patient there for more than a month. He had not learned which room or bed was his and would get in other people's beds in other rooms. In short, he was suffering a pronounced anterograde amnesia, similar in its essentials to the permanent anterograde amnesia suffered by H.M., the best known of all amnesia cases.

Concomitantly, he could not recall any records from the the past two years of his life. He behaved as if his knowledge of his current life and circumstances was based entirely on records laid down while he was still in Washington. When asked where he was, he always said Washington. When asked what he did, he said he was a bus driver.

The anterograde amnesia persisted for more than three months, then terminated abruptly within a day or two. He suddenly began to ask the nurses' names and remember them. (He had been told them repeatedly over the past months, to no effect.) He now understood that he was a patient in a Boston hospital; that is, he was able to store the fact in a retrievable form, so that it became capable of shaping his subsequent behavior, including his replies to questions about where he was and why. He now stated, however, that he had only recently been told of his head injury because , so far as his recollectable memories were concerned, this was the truth. (Until his abrupt recovery from the anterograde amnesia, he had repeatedly denied that he had a head injury, despite his having been told just as repeatedly that he did.) In short, he was now capable of remembering what he learned.

When first tested after his recovery from anterograde amnesia, the patient still had his retrograde amnesia. Over the remainder of his stay in the hospital, the interval covered by the retrograde amnesia shrank steadily, enabling the patient to recollect more and more of the events leading up to his hospitalization:

> During the remaining period in hospital, the retrograde amnesia consistently improved. Thus when he first returned to the Neurology Service he was unable to remember living in the Boston area. Three or four days later he spontaneously recalled separating from his wife and moving to Boston. Several days later he remembered the job that he held when he arrived in Boston and the name of his employer. He was unable to remember any other job in Boston. Within a few days, however, he recalled the second and last job but was still vague as to how long he had worked there. Before discharge the retrograde amnesia had cleared to the point that he remembered quitting work on the day before the injury, approximately 24 hours before admission to the University Hospital.

What did not recover was any recollection of his four months in the hospital prior to his recovery from anterograde amnesia, so once again one cannot know whether the pathological process in force during this period prevented the establishment of new records or merely established a permanent obstacle to the retrieval of the records that did get established. In the case of the retrograde amnesia, however, it is clear that what the pathological process did was not to disrupt the records (in the sense of removing the physical basis for their persistence) but rather it prevented their recollection. Once again, this interference with the retrieval process was temporally based, rather than being based on the content, importance, or any other property of the unretrievable records.

Cases of retrograde amnesia are by no means clinical rarities. Table 15.2 reproduces a table for 1029 consecutive cases of people that survived a head injury. Only 13 percent showed no retrograde amnesia. What is recorded in this table is the enduring or permanent retrograde amnesia that persists when recovery from the injury is judged to be complete, so the instances and durations of transient retrograde amnesia are underestimated in this table. This table also includes both concussive head injuries and penetrating or focal head injuries. Concussive head injuries produce amnesia more often than penetrating injuries (Russell 1959). In concussive head injuries, some degree of retrograde amnesia is the rule. In short, retrograde amnesia—and the recovery therefrom—is a routinely observable clinical phenomenon. It is often overlooked in discussions of memory mechanisms—and particularly the recovery aspect of the phenomenon, which is routinely ignored in the consolidation theories—perhaps because it is difficult to account for within the framework of any current model of memory, whether formulated at the psychological level or at the neurophysiological level. On the other hand, the phenomenon is readily explicable by a model in which temporal indexing is fundamental to the integrated recollection of separately stored records.

Retrograde amnesia typically extends backward from the time of injury over an unbroken interval, and the recovery of recollection once it begins typically proceeds from the more remote to the less remote.

Table 15.2
Duration of anterograde and retrograde amnesia in 1029 cases
of 'accidental' head injury

	Duration of the Anterograde Amnesia					
Duration of retrograde	Nil	< 1 hour	1-24 hours	1-7 days	>7 days	No record	Total
Nil	99	23	9	2	0	0	133
Under 30 minutes		178	274	174	80	1	707
Over 30 minutes		3	16	41	73	0	133
No record		4	14	14	15	9	56
Total	99	208	313	231	168	10	1029

Source: Russell 1959, p. 67.

However, islands of recollection are not uncommonly found. The recovery of an unbroken chain of recollection sometimes occurs by the gradual enlargement of these islands until they fuse. The following case from Russell (1959, pp. 72-73) is an example.

> CASE 15. Corporal G. W. was thrown from his horse on 20 July 1941. He came to himself twenty-four hours later, and his memory thereafter is quite clear. When examined on 22 August 1941 his memory of events before the injury was normal up to the morning of the day before the injury (19 July 1941). On this day, over twenty-four hours before the injury he remembers reporting sick at about 9 a.m. with synovitis of the knee. He was excused duties, but remembers little more of that day. His wife came to meet him that evening, but he has no memory at all of her visit, except that he remembers getting into a bus with her, to see her home, and later being at a station near where she was staying. For the day on which the accident occurred he has no memory except one island—he remembers tying up his horse at the gate where his wife was staying, going to the house and being told his wife was out. From 9 a.m. of the previous day, therefore, there was complete amnesia, except for three short islands. When he came to himself on 21 July 1941 his first memory was of tying his horse to the gate.

It is important to bear in mind that what the temporal-index hypothesis readily accounts for is only the loss of the ability to recollect records that were laid down at the same time regardless of their content or importance, not the retrograde nature of the loss. Islands of recollection are not a problem for the hypothesis. Indeed, a challenge that arises if one takes the model seriously is to specify what it is about the mechanism for setting the temporal probe that makes it more likely that the probe cannot be set to values within an interval that is less remote from the onset of mnemonic pathology. The hypothesis of temporal indexing does not in and of itself predict that less remote intervals should be any more or less susceptible than more remote intervals.

The hypothesis of temporal indexing becomes the more compelling insofar as there are cases of more or less complete loss of all recollection over an extensive period prior to the onset of pathology in combination with unimpaired recollection of memories that are remote but lie outside the amnestic interval. A recent case reported by Cohen, McCloskey, and Treadway (MS) is the most compelling case of this kind that I know. It is remarkable in many ways. A 39-year interval of total retrograde amnesia has persisted for four years since the precipitating incident, in the absence of any clinically significant anterograde amnesia.

The precipitating incident is not known. The 53-year-old patient was found on his kitchen floor clutching the heating element from an electric oven, but there were no other indications that he had suffered a severe electrical shock. The incident occurred in December 1984. A day after his admission to the hospital, it emerged that the patient believed the date was 1945 and that he was 14 years old and living in his hometown, more than a thousand miles away, where he had not lived since 1952. This 39-year amnestic interval has remained constant, which has made it possible for a team of investigators to establish and verify astonishingly sharp transitions between the amnestic interval, within which recollection is completely absent, and the preamnestic and postamnestic intervals, for which the subject has normal recollection.

The patient has intact memory of personal and world events up to the first few days of August 1945. He remembers his classmates and school experiences from the seventh grade (which he completed in June 1945) as well as or better than the classmates, several of whom have been found and interviewed. He remembers the progress of the fighting in World War II through the victory in Europe (May 1945). He remembers a family trip to Chicago taken in late July of 1945, and he remembers his 14th birthday in the first few days of August. But he does not remember the dropping of the atomic bombs (August 6 and 9, 1945) or Japan's surrender (August 14) or any other aspect of personal or world history since that time. He does not remember the assassination of John Kennedy, his later schooling, the jobs he has held, his marriage, the births of his children, or the emergence of television. He did not remember how to operate the television or any of the other everyday electronic appliances that have been developed since World War II. His recollection of his home town has been verified to reflect the town as it was in 1945, not as it was when he left it in 1952. In a test for recognition of public events, he scored 75 percent correct for events between 1940 and 1945 but at chance for events since 1945. At the other end of the amnestic interval, he could not recognize pictures of Walter Mondale, Geraldine Ferraro, or Olympic Star Mary Lou Retton, all of whom were constantly in the news in the months shortly before the precipitating incident, but he has no trouble recognizing less prominently featured individuals from the period subsequent to the incident—Madonna, Dr. Ruth Westheimer, "the Refrigerator (Perry), and "Rambo".

His behavior is consistent with that of someone who, when he consults his available memories for an indication of who and what he is, finds the records of a boy who has lived to the age of 14 in mid-America before and during World War II. He says "sir" or "ma'am" to people thirty years younger than he and complains of having no one to play with. He is shocked by his own appearance in the mirror because he looks forty years older than his chain of continuously available recollections tells him that he is. Because he has no anterograde amnesia, he has learned and "knows" that he is in fact a 53-year-old man, but the state of his memory makes him feel like a 14-year-old boy who has been put in the body and life circumstances of a middle-aged family man.

So far as the team of investigators studying his case have been able to determine, his amnesia covers every kind of memory, including his vocabulary and his skills (see table 15.3). When he left the hospital after the incident, his family discovered that he no longer knew how to shave or to drive. He had to relearn these basic adult skills. He also no longer knew how to deal with the sophisticated camera equipment in whose use he had acquired considerable proficiency. Before the incident, he took well composed, technically expert photographs, using appropriate filters for the sky conditions, and so on. After the incident, the photos he took—once the operation of his own camera had been explained to him—look like those one would expect from an inexperienced 14 year old.

The investigators have been sensitive to the possibility of malingering but argue convincingly that there is no evidence of it and much against it. In their report, the investigators pose the question, "How must normal memory be organized in order for there ever to occur a amnesia that is highly specific temporally, and cuts across *all* types of stored information?" They do not miss the answer that this case so powerfully suggests: that "temporal organization could be realized by associating each new item stored in memory with a temporal marker, or by storing items in such a way that their order of acquisition is preserved." They note that the chief objection to this view is that it "conflicts with current views of memory, which almost universally stress an organization based on explicitly *non*temporal dimensions, especially for world knowledge and skills."

Episodic versus Propositional Records

A modular representational theory of learning poses the question of how the representations computed by the distinct modules are linked together in episodic recollection. Associative theories of memory generally assume that representations are linked in recollection because they are linked in storage. According to the spatiotemporal index hypothesis, representations are not linked in memory, only in recollection. The recollective process is able to link one record to another because every record contains a spatiotemporal address or index, which specifies the time at which the record was laid down and the region of space (region on the cognitive map) that was the computed source of the input. In this hypothesis, the representation of time and space are the foundation of all

Table 15.3
Scope of J's memory loss

World knowledge	*Personal events and facts*
Vocabulary	Wife, children and home life
1945-84 public events and figures	Death of father
1945-84 products and inventions	Jobs and fellow employees
1945-84 advertising slogans	1945-1984 schooling and classmates
New customs and values	1945-1984 hometown landmarks
	Living in Arizona, California,Florida, and Maryland
Skills	
Accent	*Personality*
Handwriting	Behavior and affect
Shaving	Interests and pastimes
Tying a tie	Sexual desires
Driving	
Photography	*Personal identity*
Operating stereo, VCR, microwave	Sense of age
Swimming	Body image
Tennis	

Note: Evidence has been collected documenting the loss or modification of each of these examples of memory or knowledge
Source: Cohen et al. (MS)

higher mental activity, all activity that involves the integration of the records generated by previous experience in the guidance of present behavior.

In considering this hypothesis, it is important to bear in mind the hierarchical structure of memory. The contents of some records are computed from the contents of other records. The higher-level memories specify relationships present in a set of lower-level records. For example, the record an animal has of the central tendency (resultant phase vector) for the daily times of occurrence of an event like feeding is computed from the records of individual feedings. Similarly, the records specifying a CS-US prediction function are computed from the records of individual CS and US episodes.

The temporal address for a higher-level or propositional record is inherited from the individual records that entered into its computation. Whereas the address for the record of a feeding episode specifies a single interval on a single day, the record for the resultant phase vector has a temporal address that spans the period of days covered by the records of the feeding episodes from which it was computed. Similarly, the record of the CS-US prediction function is computed from records of CS and US episodes, each of which has a temporal address specifying the time of its occurrence. The record for the prediction function has a temporal address that spans the interval occupied by the temporal addresses of the episodic records from which it was computed.

The CS-US prediction function specifies an observed statistical relationship between the CS and the US. In this sense, it links the CS to the US and vice-versa. Thus the information about relationships observable between sets of records may itself be specified by a higher-level record. One must distinguish between the integration of memories effected through the use of spatiotemporal addresses at the time of recollection and the integration effected by means of higher-order records. The distinction is roughly analogous to the distinction between "episodic" memory and "propositional" or "semantic" memory (Tulving 1972). When two records are related to one another during recollection by virtue of their spatiotemporal addresses, one has an instance of episodic memory. When a relationship or property manifest across a set of records is captured by a higher-order record, one has an instance of propositional memory.

The evidence from retrograde amnesia is that both kinds of records—first-order records of individual experiences (episodes) and higher-order records of the relations extractable from multiple experiences (propositions)—are recollected by means of spatiotemporal addresses. Evidently temporal addresses may span intervals that differ by orders of magnitude. The address for an episodic record spans a short interval, while the address for a propositional record will generally span an interval orders of magnitude greater.

Just as temporal addresses may differ by orders of magnitude in the intervals they span, so may spatial addresses. A spatial address may be so extensive as to encompass the entire map. An all-encompassing spatial address may arise in two ways. In the case of the record of an individual experience, it would arise if the source of the experience was perceived as occupying the entire perceptible space. This would be the record of a property that was perceived as immanent in a given locale (for example, a pervasive odor). Alternatively, in the case of a higher-order record computed from many individual records, an all-encompassing address would arise if the addresses for the individual experiences varied from record to record over the entire map. Such a higher-order record would indicate a relationship that appeared to hold everywhere, a general truth.

Chapter 16
The Search for the Engram

The discovery of the material basis of memory is an important goal in behavioral neuroscience. The elucidation of the physiological and biochemical processes mediating the storage of information in the nervous system would be the most important addition to our conception of basic neural processes since the elucidation of the processes of axonal conduction and synaptic transmission. It would also be a triumph for the materialist theory of mind because memory is at the heart of every theory of mind. The case of retrograde amnesia with which the previous chapter concluded indicates how central memories are to a sense of conscious self, the phenomenological origin of the concept of mind.

The extraordinary progress of molecular biology in the second half of this century has led to the widespread conviction that all of the major problems of the life sciences can be most fruitfully addressed by the techniques and concepts of molecular biology. Every problem must succumb to the onslaught of this juggernaut if only the problem is addressed by those in command of the latest molecular methods. This faith is naive. It overlooks an important historical truth. The processes that have succumbed to molecular analysis are the processes for which one had a nonmolecular theory that was valid in its broad outlines and for which one had determined some basic quantitative properties of the crucial theoretical entities.

Classical genetic theory as of 1950 was valid in its broad outlines, and there was important quantitative information about the gene and well–established methods for determining quantitative facts about genes. Among the important formal-quantitative insights was the knowledge that changes in genes (mutations) were instantaneous rather than gradual, and they were extremely rare. Thus, the molecular embodiment of a gene had to be an extremely stable thermodynamic configuration, which was altered only by processing accidents or by high energy interactions.

Among the important quantitative methods was Morgan's method for measuring the relative distances separating two genes by determining the probability of separate assortment in the traits they controlled. Among the crucial pieces of knowledge generated by this measures of gene separation was that genes came in linear sets, and there were in any organism exactly as many such linear sets of genes as there were chromosomes. The crucial inference that the chromosomes contained the genes in a linear arrangement was the more or less inescapable conclusion from these quantitative determinations of gene separation.

Anyone who studies the history of molecular genetics will notice that progress depended at every turn on the conceptual framework of classical genetics (Judson 1980). Without Mendel and Morgan and the conceptual framework they did so much to establish, Watson and Crick could not have thought fruitfully about what the molecular basis for the storage and transmission of hereditary information might be. Prior to the development of classical genetics, it was more or less universally assumed that the hereditary information was modified by the life experiences of the bearer before being passed on to offspring. Even Darwin was inclined to believe this so-called Lamarckian fallacy. Anyone who set out to look for the molecular basis of heredity within this preclassical conceptual framework would have been barking up the wrong tree from the outset. In fact, DNA was isolated from salmon sperm in the nineteenth century, long before the conceptual framework existed that would one day make it possible to recognize this molecule as the carrier of genetic information.

Within neuroscience, the conceptual framework for understanding axonal conduction was developed through behavioral work on the nerve-muscle preparation by Helmholtz, Herman, Lilly, Lucas, Adrian, and Hill. Their behavioral work was followed up by the electrophysiological work of Hodgkin and Huxley on the giant squid axon. These behavioral and electrophysiological approaches established the conceptual foundation for modern attempts to identify the protein molecules that serve as voltage dependent ionic gates and to understand the biophysics of their action. Similarly, the behavioral work of Sherrington established the modern concept of the synapse, which was augmented by the electrophysiological work of his student Eccles, laying the foundation for modern molecular work on ionic channels whose conductance is altered by the binding of transmitter substances.

Sherrington's work also laid the foundation for the modern conception of learning as a change in synaptic conductivity. It is this deeply ingrained conception of what learning is fundamentally about at the neuronal level—a change in synaptic conductance—that is called into question by the analysis of learning here offered.

Just as the conceptual framework and experimental methods of classical genetics and classical neuroscience have played a fundamental role in the development of molecular genetics and molecular neuroscience, so too the conceptual framework and experimental methods of classic learning theory play a fundamental role in current attempts to determine the cellular and molecular basis of learning. Anyone concerned with the success of this effort must also be concerned with the validity of this conceptual framework and with its quantitative methods and conclusions.

The conceptual framework one adopts determines the kinds of model systems that one works with. With one exception, current model systems for studying the cellular and molecular basis of learning have been chosen in the belief that the associative theory of learning provides the correct framework. In this book, I have elaborated an alternative framework, in which there are no associations. Within the predominant framework, the unit of analysis in learning is the formation of an association. Within the framework I have suggested, the unit of analysis is the computation and storage of a quantity. In this concluding chapter, I summarize the conceptual framework that each approach offers to those interested in establishing the material basis of memory.

The Distinction between Computation and Storage

Associative learning theory is a theory about the computational process that generates the physical changes that underlie learning. One could imagine an effort to determine the chemical identity of the material out of which the engram is fashioned that ignored the computational process to focus on properties of the change itself. Such an approach would require some minimal information about the mutable variable—the physical variable or process that undergoes an enduring change of state in the course of learning.

To know what an appropriate material change in the nervous system would look like, such an approach would need answers to questions like the following: Is the mutable variable discrete or essentially continuous? That is, can it exist in only a few stable states (in the limit, only two) or in a very large number of states, differing one from the next by a very small amount (in the limit, an infinite number of states differing infinitesimally)? How stable are the states? When the mutable variable has been set to a given state, does it remain in that state indefinitely (for the life of the animal)? This would mean that there is no "forgetting" at the molecular level, only retrieval failures. Or does it lapse back through intermediate states to some null or resting state (molecular forgetting)? If the null state is the only truly stable state of the mutable variable, by what time course does it return to its null state from the other states to which it may be moved by the learning process (what is the law of molecular memory decay and what are its parameters)? Can the mutable variable be moved by the learning process from any state to any other state, or are the transitions irreversible (except possibly by the passage of time)? This last question relates to the long-standing controversy within learning theory about whether extinction decreases the strength of excitatory associations (reverses the effects of excitatory conditioning) or strengthens competing inhibitory associations.

Associative theories of classical conditioning do not provide answers to these questions. In the literature of the last twenty years, one can find opposite answers to each of the questions just posed, and no clear consensus has emerged. It is widely assumed that the strength of an associative change can vary continuously, but it has been argued on the basis of extensive experimental findings that the associative change is all-or-nothing, that is, that the associative bond is a discrete variable with only two stable states (Estes 1960).

It is widely assumed that the associative change lapses back to a null state over some period of time, thereby accounting for forgetting. On the other hand, if you ask many people who study vertebrate learning what the time course and rate of decay is for an associative bond, they may answer that an associative change lasts more or less indefinitely since the effects of a conditioning experience early in life are commonly demonstrable over the lifetime of the animal (Honig and James 1971). Indeed, many theories of forgetting stress interference from other associative changes as the principal engine of forgetting rather than the temporal instability of individual associations (Gleitman 1971; Underwood 1957). It is sometimes even argued that the strength of an association increases with time—the theory of consolidation (Squire and Schlapfer 1981).

It is commonly assumed that the strength of an associative bond may be incremented during conditioning and decremented during extinction. On the other hand, students of extinction, including Pavlov himself, have often suggested that extinction does not involve the decrementing of previously established excitatory associations but rather the incrementing of competing inhibitory associations (Rescorla 1979). A corollary of the view that extinction is the result of conditioned inhibition rather than the decrementing of an excitatory association is that the material change underlying the formation of an association is irreversible—or, at least, not reversible by conditioning (the learning process). The irreversibility of previously established associative bonds is sometimes invoked to explain why both conditioning and extinction occur more rapidly when the animal has been subject repeatedly to the same conditioning and extinction experiences (Bullock and Smith 1953; Davenport 1969; Gonzales et al. 1967; Mackintosh 1974, p. 442).

It is clear, then, why a search for the material basis of associative memory that rests on a consideration of the characteristics of the associative change itself rather than on a consideration of the computational process that produced the change has no clear basis on which to proceed.

In part for this reason, efforts to establish the material basis of conditioning have focused on simplified preparations that incorporate the conditioning process itself. Modern cellular research on associative learning aims at identifying the mutable substance—the material change underlying the formation of an association—by identifying the computational mechanism that produces the mutations (the changes in molecular state). However, these efforts have not taken full account of the fundamental changes in the conception of the conditioning process that have occurred in the last twenty years. In the section that follows, I argue that if one is going to continue to pursue the material basis of memory within an associative conceptual framework, then modern changes in that conceptual framework are not consistent with the reductionist approaches now being pursued.

The modern conception of the association forming process requires that the computation of the changes in an association be carried out within a network capable of taking into account many different variables. It cannot be done locally on the basis of the timing of events at any one synapse, as is currently generally assumed in neurophysiological models of conditioning. The computations performed by a network looking at many variables may result in a signal indicating what the strength of the association should now be. The material change underlying association formation could lie in the enduring molecular change that occurs in response to this signal. This view, however, divorces the computational problem from the problem of identifying the material change underlying an association, because one does not have to understand the origins of the signal indicating what the association strength should be in order to study the enduring cellular and molecular changes caused by this signal.

A representational approach to learning makes a similarly sharp distinction between the diverse computational processes that generate signals for to-be-stored magnitudes and the possibly simple and unitary cellular and molecular changes by which values are stored. One need not know how the memory-generating signals in a computer are computed nor what they represent in order to study the effects of these signals on the mnemonic elements (such as magnetic rings, bubbles, and capacitors).

If, however, we divorce the problem of the material change underlying memory from the problem of the computations that specify how much of this change is to occur, then we must have answers to the questions posed regarding the formal and quantitative characteristics of this change. Is it binary or continuous, transient or permanent, and so on? Otherwise there is no conceptual basis for the molecular analysis. We do not know what to look for at the cellular and molecular level.

*The Discordance between Current Neuronal Models of Association Formation
and the Modern Behaviorally Based Framework*

A powerful attraction of the premodern view of associative learning for
those concerned with establishing its physiological mechanism was the
central role played by the concept of pairing. In the traditional view, the
crucial condition for the occurrence of an associative change was the temporal pairing of two stimuli. The attraction of this view from a reductionist point of view is that the underlying mechanism would appear to be a
temporally asymmetric local coincidence detector, a physiological mechanism sensitive to the condition in which the activation of one of its inputs
slightly precedes the activation of another. It has never been difficult to
imagine a cellular mechanism with the appropriate sensitivity to the ISI,
which could be thought of as the interval between two signals arriving
at a single locus, for example, two presynaptic action potentials arriving
at the same postsynaptic neuron or an action potential and a local
hormone converging in the same presynaptic ending.

The fundamental role of temporal pairing in current cellularly oriented
work is emphasized by Gluck and Thompson (1987), who write, "In our
view, the effect of the interstimulus onset interval on conditionability is
perhaps the most fundamental property of basic associative learning" (p.
178). They proceed to spell this assumption out graphically (figure 16.1).
The importance of temporal pairing is also stressed by Hawkins and
Kandel (1984), who write, "Thus, conditioning in *Aplysia* resembles
conditioning in vertebrates in having a steep ISI function, with optimal
learning when the CS precedes the US by approximately 0.5 s." Hawkins
and Kandel then ask, "What cellular processes give classical condition-

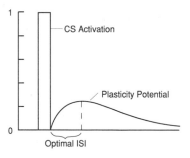

Figure 16.1
The ISI function assumed by Gluck and Thompson (1987). The function gives the assumed
sensitivity of the association-forming process to the interval between the offset of the CS
and the onset of the US. Hawkins and Kandel (1984) assume a similar function. A function
something like this is implicit in any approach to conditioning that assumes that temporal
pairing of the CS and US is a sine qua non of associative conditioning.

ing this characteristic temporal specificity?" (p. 379). They proceed to describe a pairing-sensitive mechanism in the gill-withdrawal circuitry of *Aplysia*. The discovery of a pairing-sensitive presynaptic process producing fairly long-lasting changes in synaptic conductivity within the gill-withdrawal circuitry is widely regarded as a milestone on the road to a reductionist account of associative learning (Hawkins et al 1983; Walters and Byrne 1983).

The trouble with focusing on a sensitivity to pairing as the sine qua non for the cellular mechanism of associative learning is the recent discovery that pairing is neither necessary nor sufficient for conditioning. Traditional notions about the role of temporal pairing in associative conditioning are untenable in the light of modern experimental findings, including findings on conditioning in *Aplysia* (Colwill, Asher, and Roberts 1988).

The experimental results demonstrating the unnecessariness and the insufficiency of temporal pairing in classical conditioning were reviewed at length in chapter 12. Following is a brief summary of those findings and an assessment of their implications for modern attempts to specify the cellular basis of association formation.

Pairing Undefinable or Not Necessary
That pairing is not necessary for conditioning and/or that pairing cannot be defined by an ISI function like that in Figure 16.1 is shown by many findings: poison-avoidance conditioning, simultaneous and backward conditioning, the effect of the ITI on the optimal value of the ISI, context conditioning, conditioning by negative correlation between the CS and the US, and the phenomenon of extinction.

Garcia and his collaborators (Garcia et al. 1961; Revusky and Garcia 1970) showed that animals readily associate nauseating illness with brief tastes experienced many hours earlier. This finding was initially greeted with incredulity, because it was so at variance with the long-held belief that "near" temporal coincidence of CS and US was the sine qua non of conditioning. Subsequently, there has been a tendency to assimilate these results to the general framework of associative conditioning by relaxing the definition of temporal coincidence to the point that, under some circumstances, or for some stimuli, an ISI of 12 hours is regarded as temporal pairing. The facile incorporation of Garcia's astonishing (and initially disbelieved) result emphasizes the important fact that in the absence of an ISI function whose mathematical form and parameters have been experimentally established, the notion of temporal pairing has no substance.

Hawkins and Kandel (1984) suggest that an ISI function of the form assumed by Gluck and Thompson (1987) is representative of classical conditioning in general. While Gluck and Thompson recognize that the units of the abscissa of such a function must be imagined to vary from fractions of a second to hours, Hawkins and Kandel suggest that a temporally narrow function is characteristic, a function that peaks at 0.5 seconds and subsides back to zero within about 2 seconds. Rescorla (1988, 1972) has pointed out, however, that this is clearly not the case. Good conditioning may be obtained with CSs that come on at the same time as or even after the onset of the US (Heth and Rescorla 1973).

The results from poison-avoidance experiments and the results showing good simultaneous or backward conditioning might be explained by positing an ISI function that varies depending on the nature of the US and the CS. Such an approach will not, however, deal with the important findings regarding the effect of the intertrial interval on the ISI function within a single conditioning experiment (Gibbon et al. 1977). The most important result from this line of research is that the determinant of the increment in associative strength on a given trial is the ratio of the ITI to the ISI, not the ISI itself.

The well-established phenomenon of conditioning by negative correlation between the CS and the US (see Miller and Spear 1985) is another demonstration that temporal pairing is not necessary for the development of an associative connection between the representation of the CS and the representation of the US. An inhibitory association between a CS and a US is produced by two procedures that involve explicitly not pairing the CS and the US (and by one that involves pairing them). The first of these reverses the contingency that establishes an excitatory association; the US occurs only when the CS is not present. The second (and most common) procedure involves intermixing two kinds of trials. On some trials, only one CS—say a tone—is presented and the US occurs. On others, the tone is presented along with a second CS—say a light— and the US does not occur. Under this condition—which again involves explicitly not pairing the light with the US—an inhibitory association grows between the CS and the US.

Presenting the CS in the absence of a US does not produce an inhibitory association. It is not clear how it could. An associative connection is a connection between two stimulus representations (or a stimulus representation and a response representation). When a CS is presented repeatedly in a context where no previous experience gives any reason to expect any particular US, it is not clear what could occupy the position at the other end of the association from the CS. The phenomenon of conditioned inhibition must be treated in terms of the formation of an inhibitory association between the CS and the US; it cannot be conceptualized in terms of a nonassociative process like habituation. Hull (1943) used a decremental process (reactive inhibition) similar to his incremental process in accounting for extinction, just as Hawkins and Kandel (1984) use habituation. A strong critique of this approach was given by Gleitman et al. (1954). The difficulties they describe have been rediscovered by Gluck and Thompson (1987) in their simulation of the model proposed by Hawkins and Kandel (1984).

Not pairing a CS with a US gives rise to an inhibitory association only if the occurrence of the US is predicted by the animal's experience with other stimuli. The same point can be made with regard to the phenomenon of extinction: the inhibitory associations that arise during extinction depend for their growth on the prior existence of excitatory associations. In inhibitory conditioning, as in excitatory conditioning, the development of an association between a CS representation and a US representation depends on the strength of other associations to the same US. Cellular models of conditioning must come to grips with this fundamental fact.

Insufficiency of Pairing
That the temporal coincidence of CS and US is not sufficient for conditioning is shown by the blocking, background conditioning, and correlated stimulus experiments, which led to the formulation of the Rescorla-Wagner model (see chapter 12). If a to-be-conditioned CS is presented along with an already-conditioned CS, any number of pairings of the new CS and the US do not suffice to establish an association (the blocking effect; Kamin 1969). The occurrence of any number of USs during CS presentations does not suffice to establish an association if the US occurs with equal frequency during intervals when the CS is not present (the effect of background conditioning; Rescorla 1968). Pairing the CS with the US any number of times does not suffice to establish an association if there is another CS with whose appearance the occurrence of the US is more highly correlated (Wagner et al. 1968). The appearance of these three experimental findings marked the beginning of the modern era in the study of classical conditioning. All three prove, each in a different way, that pairing is not sufficient for the establishment of an association.

The third and most recent experimental procedure for producing inhibitory associations makes this same point in a dramatic way. In the "overprediction" procedure, one establishes two excitatory CSs and then pairs them with a third CS, without increasing the rate of US occurrence during CS presentations, so that the two excitatory CSs "overpredict" the US. The result is the development of a conditioned inhibition between a CS and a US with which the CS has been paired on every one of its presentations (Kremer 1978).

Implications for the Reductionist Program

The findings just summarized have forced far-reaching revisions in the computational models of association formation, as Rescorla (1988) stresses in a recent review oriented to neuroscientists. First there is the multidimensionality assumption: the increment in a given association depends on the strengths of the associations between the US and other CSs. For an experience-dependent molecular change at a given synapse to be a good instance of association formation, the course of that change must depend on the course of similar alterations at other synapses. Only a system with access to the values of associative strengths at other points in the system can compute the increment in the strength of a given association on a given trial. The change cannot be determined by the timing of events at a single synaptic junction.

The cellular process that computes increments and decrements in the strengths of associations must also have input from a clock or time base. The need for a clock as a central constituent of the association-computing process first emerged in the Rescorla-Wagner theory. Rescorla and Wagner had to introduce an internal trial clock. The trial clock breaks up the continuously present background into many separate internal experiences of the background. Unless the internal experience of the continuously present background was broken up in this way by an internal clock, it was not possible to explain Rescorla's finding that conditioning to an intermittent CS occurred only if the frequency of US occurrence during that CS was higher than the frequency of US occurrence when only the background was present. Colwill et al. (1988) also call attention to the difficulties that background conditioning poses for current cellular models. The finding that the ratio between the ITI and the ISI determines the increment in associative strength also puts a time-keeping process at the heart of the association-computing process (see Gibbon and Balsam 1981).

In summary, modern models of associative conditioning incorporate a degree of computational complexity that no longer makes it reasonable to look for model systems in which the essential association-changing computation is carried out locally, at the site of association formation, by a molecular process whose product is the enduring change that constitutes the physical embodiment of the formed association (for example, the enduring change in the dynamics of a potassium channel in the presynaptic, membrane: Hawkins and Kandel 1984). The computational complexity of the association-changing process implied by modern findings appears to require that one break the problem of the physiological bases of learning up into two quite distinct subproblems: that of computing the change in associative strength and that of implementing the change (storing the association).

The problem of computation requires specifying the functional architecture of the neural circuits that compute a quantity to be stored. In an associative theory, the quantities to be stored are the new values of associative strength. The functional architecture of the circuit that computes these quantities must be complex enough to take into account the current strengths of the associations to other stimuli and the ITI:ISI ratio.

To solve the other aspect of the problem—the problem of storing the computed quantity—requires determining the molecular change by which associative strength is preserved and later read out. If we distinguish between the circuit that computes the new values of associations, on the one hand, and the process that stores these values, on the other, then we realize that the preparation in which the storage mechanism is studied need not include the computational circuitry that gives the conditioning process its distinctive characteristics. This may simplify the task but only if we can identify a neural pathway that carries a signal specifying the strength that an association is to have, or the magnitude of the change it is to undergo.

The Distinction between Computation and Storage within a Representational Framework

What tempts researchers to try to solve the storage problem and the computational problem simultaneously is the assumption of computational universality in associative learning theory: that many different learning phenomena reflect the same basic underlying computational process that associates the representation of one stimulus with the representation of another stimulus. The alternative framework I have proposed directly challenges the assumption of computational universality.

If learning is the construction of representations of behavior-relevant aspects of the animal's environment, the assumption of computational universality is not plausible. The computations required to extract diverse representations from diverse sense data must differ. They must differ as a function of the formal structure of the representation being computed and as a function of the kind of sensory data from which it is being computed. Algorithms suitable for computing spatial relationships in a vector space with three bidirectional axes will not be suitable for computing temporal relationships, which are arranged on a unidirectional "line," and vice-versa. Nor will algorithms suited to spatial or temporal computations be suitable for computing conditional rate estimates and the associated uncertainties.

Even when the representation being computed is the same, the computational processes will differ as a function of the kind of sensory input from which that representation is being computed. The architecture of the circuitry that computes the angular deviation of a distal stimulus from visual input is very unlikely to be the same as the architecture of the circuit that computes angular deviation from auditory input, although both circuits converge on a single representation of distal angular deviation in the tectum (chapter 14). In short, within the framework of a representational treatment of the phenomena of learning, it does not make sense to look for elementary learning mechanisms that constitute an "alphabet of learning" (Hawkins and Kandel 1984), although it may very well make sense to look for elementary computational mechanisms that constitute an alphabet of computation—biophysical mechanisms in the nervous system that implement basic computational operations such as addition, multiplication, differentiation, and integration.

If, however, the results of different computations are always vectors— ordered sets of quantities—then the problem of storing the representations computed by diverse circuits reduces to that of storing and retrieving the values of quantities. This problem may admit of a universal solution.

Within the conceptual framework provided by a representational analysis of learning, the problem of computation involves finding answers to four types of questions:

1. What representations does the system compute?
2. What is the functional architecture of the neural circuitry that computes a given kind of representation from a given kind of sensory data?
3. What computations are done in making use of each kind of representation in the genesis of behavior?
4. What is the functional architecture of the circuitry that makes use of the representations in behavior-generating computations?

The problem of storage is conceptually much less complex, although the uncovering of the molecular mechanism may well prove to be of more profound importance to neuroscience. The problem involves finding answers to two basic questions: (1) What is the physical change that mediates the storage of the results of computation? (2) How does the system read out the stored values?

Preparations Suitable for Tackling the Storage Problem

One may reasonably ask what more specific guidance the computational-representational framework offers for someone interested in an experimental approach to the cellular and molecular basis of learning. What sort of preparation would be suitable for the analysis of the storage process? What one wants is a nerve-memory preparation. Such a preparation would involve a nerve (one or more axons) carrying a signal that determines the magnitude of the change in a mutable variable and the site where this change is effected, the site of memory formation. It must be possible to activate this nerve under the kinds of conditions where cellular and molecular variables can be manipulated directly.

The Dead Reckoning Phenomenon

At the head of the list of behavioral phenomena that show promise of providing neuroscience with suitable preparations, I would place dead reckoning. A temporally stable integrator must reside at the heart of the neural circuit that performs the dead reckoning computations. This integrator must possess properties that make it ideal for the storage of quantitative data, that is, for storing the results of other computations. The dead reckoning process is ubiquitous in mobile organisms. Since some of the most compelling experimental demonstrations of dead reckoning have been done with invertebrates (chapter 4), there is every reason to think that this process may be found and isolated in the kind of animal whose nervous system lends itself to cellular analysis, an animal like *Aplysia*.

Necessary properties of the integrator.   The integration process in dead reckoning is the physical variable or process that undergoes enduring changes in state as the animal moves through the environment, changes of such a nature that the current state of the integration (current value of the integral) represents the animal's current position relative to its starting position. We can define this process by answering the same quantitative questions raised with regard to the physical embodiment of an associative change:

1. Is the change discrete or continuous?
2. Is it stable or does it decay slowly to a null state?
3. Can inputs either increase or decrease the value of the variable, or are its state changes irreversible?

Clearly the physical variable that represents the current value of the integral must be a continuous variable, which exists in a large number of states differing from one to the next by a very small amount. Clearly the state of this physical variable must be smoothly and easily varied by the input signal (the velocity signal being integrated), and yet the state must be extremely stable when the velocity signal is zero. Any tendency for the value of the integrator to decay back to a null state with time would be manifest in a very peculiar way in the behavior of an animal moving under dead reckoning control: it should behave as if the simple passage of time brought it closer to its starting position. There is no evidence of this and, indeed, any appreciable temporal instability in the integrator (any tendency of the integrator to "leak") would render it unsuitable for its purpose. Thus, one is looking for a physical variable that is labile in the face of signal input but highly stable in its absence, a variable with a large number of temporally stable states. Finally, the value of the integral in dead reckoning must increase and decrease with equal facility, in response to signals indicating positive or negative velocity, respectively. (Negative velocity arises whenever the direction of the animal's motion is such as to bring it nearer to its starting position.)

The representational approach yields clear answers to important questions about distinctive characteristics of the physical process that must underlie the mnemonic change.

The physical simplicity of the integration operation.   Because one does not generally learn the concept of an integral and how to compute one until college (if then), I have sometimes encountered students (and even an occasional neuroscientist or psychologist) who imagine that integration is a physically mysterious process unlikely to occur in the nervous system. Nothing could be further from the truth. The physical realization of integration is often extremely simple. A bucket fed by a small jet of water integrates the jet with respect to time. If the inflow to a cylindrical bucket were made proportionate to the animal's positive velocity (its rate of movement away from the starting position along one of the axes of integration) and the outflow (through a valve) proportionate to its negative velocity, then the height of the water in the bucket would represent the animal's distance from the starting point along the axis of integration. In other words, the height of the water in the bucket would represent the integral with respect to time of the animal's velocity along that axis. If the bucket were shielded from evaporation, its contents would have the requisite temporal stability, and it would be a good analogue of the integration process we are looking for in the nervous system of an organism capable of dead reckoning navigation.

Integration by transmitter-controlled gene transcription.   Lest this analogy be taken with the same literal-mindedness that Lorenz's hydraulic model of motivation has sometimes been taken, I hasten to supply an experimentally identified process in neurons that would have the requisite properties, namely, transmitter controlled gene transcription. The transcription of a gene is the process of synthesizing a protein with the amino acid sequence specified by that gene. The broad outlines of the regulation of this synthetic process within cells were first recognized by Jacob and Monod (1961).

The Jacob and Monod model of transcription has two essential features. First is a distinction between the "structural" genes, which code for proteins, and the regulator genes, which regulate the protein syntheses specified by functionally related groups of structural genes. The regulator genes are now called operators. The group of structural genes whose transcription is controlled by a given operator gene or complex of operator genes is called an operon. The other feature is the concept of repressor and promoter substances, proteins that bind to operators and, in so doing, determine the rate at which the structural genes in the corresponding operon will be transcribed.

In the model of neural integration I suggest, the physical embodiment of the value of one dimension of the dead reckoning integral is imagined to be the amount of a stable intracellular protein. This protein is the memory substance. The velocity signal in the nerve of the dead reckoning preparation is imagined to determine the rate of release of one of two interneuronal transmitter substances. These two transmitter substances, the "positive" substance and the "negative" substance, are released from pairs of mutually opposed axons that carry the velocity signal (two-neuron velocity channels). The positive substance is released in proportion to the positive value of the velocity signal (the rate of firing of the axon on the positive side of the channel), the negative substance in proportion to the negative value (the rate of firing of the axon on the negative side of the channel). The positive substance, when it binds to the postsynaptic membrane, increases the level of an intracellular substance (via a so-called second messenger). The intracellular second messenger acts as a promoter on the operator for the gene that specifies the memory substance. Thus memory substance is synthesized at a rate determined by the positive value of the velocity signal. The negative transmitter substance acts by way of a second intracellular messenger, which is a promoter for the gene specifying the enzyme that breaks down the memory substance. The greater is the amount of this promoter, the greater is the synthesis of the degradative enzyme. The greater is the synthesis of the degradative enzyme, the more memory substance is degraded. Thus memory substance builds up at a rate determined by the positive signal and is removed at a rate determined by the negative velocity signal. When the velocity signal is zero (when neither axon is active), memory substance is neither synthesized nor broken down. Whatever amount of the substance has accumulated in the cell remains there indefinitely. The amount of memory substance in the cell represents one coordinate of the animal's current position in a coordinate system anchored to the animal's starting position.

For this mechanism to work, a precise proportionality must hold at every stage of both the positive and negative processes because a given value of the negative velocity signal must degrade exactly as much protein in 1 second as is synthesized in 1 second in response to the equivalent level of the positive velocity signal. The simplest way to ensure this would be to have each molecule of the positive promoter promote the synthesis of one molecule of memory substance and each molecule of the negative promoter promote the synthesis of one molecule of the degradative enzyme, and, finally, have the enzyme itself break down (become inactive) in the process of catalyzing the breakdown of a molecule of the memory substance.

For the amount of memory substance to enter into computations that determine how the organism orients when it turns for home, there must be a mechanism for reading the value of the dead reckoning integral, a mechanism whereby the current amount of the memory substance determines the response of the cell to a read signal. It is not difficult to imagine various suitable memory reading processes, but it would be pointless to elaborate one here. The point of this excursion into the process of gene transcription and its control by neural signals is that transmitter-controlled gene transcription is an experimentally demonstrated phenomenon in the nervous system (Born and Rubel 1988; Comb, Hyman, and Goodman 1987; Greenberg, Ziff, and Greene 1986), and it is a biochemical process that could constitute the physical embodiment of integration in dead reckoning.

The form of transmitter-controlled gene transcription envisioned would be a suitable general-purpose information storage mechanism. It could be used to store the values generated by the many different computations described in this book, the computations by which the nervous systems of animals build up behaviorally useful representations of the animal's environment. This, then, is one conception of the cellular embodiment of a representation. It is an intracellular protein whose synthesis and degradation is controlled in such a way as to make it a representation of a behavior-relevant aspect of the environment in which the animal operates. The point of this example is to show that there is nothing remotely incompatible between a reductionist approach to the explanation of behavior and a representational theory of mind.

The principal advantages of the dead reckoning phenomenon from the standpoint of a reductionist approach to the problem of memory are these:

1. The phenomenon is likely to be found in very simple organisms, which lend themselves to cellular and molecular analysis. In principle, there is no reason it could not exist even in a motile bacterium.
2. One knows what the input signal must be—a velocity signal. When the pathway that carries this signal (the "nerve" in the nerve-

memory preparation) has been identified, it should be easy to induce this signal experimentally in in vitro preparations.

3. The relation between the input signal and the resulting magnitude of the change in the mutable variable is precisely specified: the change in the mutable variable must be the integral of the input signal.

4. The integrator process must possess the properties that would make it a good general-purpose process for the storage of quantitative information.

The disadvantage of the dead reckoning preparation is that no one has yet attempted to establish the neural circuit underlying dead reckoning in any animal.

The Self-stimulation Phenomenon

In vertebrates, a promising phenomenon is electrical self-stimulation of the brain. Running through the medial forebrain bundle in the basolateral parts of the diencephalon, and more medially and dorsally through the midbrain, is a system of small myelinated fibers. Electrically stimulating these fibers by means of chronically implanted electrodes produces the most potent form of goal-oriented behavioral control known to behavioral science. When a rat is given control of the electrical stimulation, it spends nearly every waking moment reexciting this system of axons, taking just enough time out to eat, drink, and nap enough to keep itself in good health (Yanovski, Adler, and Gallistel 1986). The interesting aspect of this phenomenon in the present context is that the stimulation generates an enduring record of its magnitude. The animal's future stimulation-directed behavior is a systematic function of the magnitude of the stimulation it has received in the indefinite past. The enduring, behavior-determining record of the magnitude of past stimulations is termed the rewarding effect of the stimulation (Gallistel, Stellar, and Bubis 1974). The reward-producing system of small myelinated axons excited by the stimulation is the nerve in a nerve-memory preparation.

The advantages of the self-stimulation phenomenon are these:

1. The signal indicating the magnitude of the rewarding stimulation the animal has received is generated by direct electrical stimulation of axons in the CNS. Thus, this same signal—the input signal for the storage process—may be generated in an anesthetized animal, or even in vitro, if the relevant circuitry is removed from the brain and kept alive in cell culture. The ability to generate the relevant input signal under conditions favorable for the analysis of cellular processes is an essential feature of a good preparation.

2. Self-stimulation behavior lends itself to psychophysical analysis because of its exceptional vigor and persistence and because it is directed toward a stimulus, electrical stimulation, whose parameters are readily and finely controlled by automated equipment. Psychophysical analysis establishes quantitative characteristics of the processes that underlie stimulus-controlled behaviors. It most commonly does so by studying the trade-offs between various parameters of the stimulus situation, that is, by determining the functions that describe how much of an adjustment in one parameter of the situation is required to neutralize the effect of a given change in another parameter.

The classic example of a trade-off function is the human scotopic spectral sensitivity function, which describes how much of a change is required in the intensity of a light flash to neutralize the effect of a change in the wavelength for the dark adapted human observer. This function is identical to the in situ absorption spectrum for rhodopsin, which is why rhodopsin is believed to be the photolabile substance in dark-adapted vision (rod vision).

The rich store of results from visual system psychophysics provides the conceptual framework for modern work on the molecular and cellular mechanisms of vision and describes important quantitative properties of the crucial molecular processes. Psychophysical work in vision has established, for example, the scotopic-photopic (rod-cone) distinction, the fact that there must be three photochemically distinct types of cones, the absorption spectra for the photolabile substance in rods, and the fact that the absorption of a single quantum suffices to generate a signal well above the noise level in a rod with more than ten million rhodopsin molecules. In short, psychophysical work in vision has established the conceptual and quantitative foundations for the molecular inquiry, just as the work of Morgan and other classical geneticists established the conceptual and quantitative foundations for modern molecular genetics. The self-stimulation phenomenon opens up the opportunity to apply this powerful quantitative form of analysis to a nerve-memory preparation.

3. The psychophysical analyses so far carried out on this preparation have defined a number of distinctive quantitative characteristics of the directly stimulated axons (the nerve; Gallistel, Shizgal, and Yeomans 1981; Shizgal, Bielajew, and Rompré 1988; Yeomans 1988). Also, recent findings suggest that the magnitude of the mnemonic effect of the rewarding signal (the recorded magnitude of the reward) depends in a simple way on simple parameters of the rewarding signal (Waraczynski, Stellar, and Gallistel 1987). This encourages the supposition that for this signal—unlike for most signals generated by sensory input—no complex computations intervene between the signal and the storage process, the

formation of the engram. In short, the identification of the directly stimulated axons, the nerve in this nerve-memory preparation, may lead quite
directly to the identification of the site of memory formation, the site
where the transient rewarding signal in these axons is converted to an
enduring record of the magnitude of the reward.

4. A sustained effort to identify the reward-relevant axons, using the
psychophysical results to indicate what kinds of axons to look for, and
where they are, is under way in several laboratories (Gallistel et al. 1985;
Glimcher 1989; Gratton and Wise 1985; Rompré and Miliaressis 1985;
Shizgal, Bielajew, and Rompré 1988; Stellar and Corbett, in press; Waraczynski 1988; Yeomans 1988).

Summary

The complexity of the computations underlying simple conditioning
suggests that the conditioning process cannot be mediated by a process
in which an enduring cellular change is produced by the temporal
coincidence of two inputs to one cellular site. It is not clear how this
conceptualization, which is taken for granted in most attempts to determine the cellular basis of learning, can be made to explain the manner in
which the changes that occur during conditioning depend on the values
of other variables (other "associations") and on temporal ratios rather
than temporal intervals. The concept of associative learning as a process
set in motion by the temporal pairing of neurohumoral signals ignores
the implications of the findings from the behavioral study of the conditioning process over the last twenty years: that temporal pairing is
neither necessary nor sufficient to produce an associative change.

We need to separate the problem of computation from the problem of
storage, whether we continue to search for the engram within the
conceptual framework provided by the associative analysis of learning
or shift to the kind of representational framework that I have argued for.
Within either framework, it is now clear that the cellular changes underlying memory must be the product of complex computational processes
requiring substantial neural networks for their realization. This does not
mean that we need to study these networks to understand the physical
basis of memory. We need to study them to understand the physical basis
of learning but not to understand the physical basis of memory. Regardless of the conceptual framework one adapts, it seems reasonable to
imagine that the upshot of the computations that mediate learning are
signals whose magnitudes control the magnitude of an enduring change
in a mutable variable, the memory substance. Understanding the physical basis of memory requires identifying the memory substance, the
processes by which transient neural signals make adjustments in the

form or amount of this substance, and the processes by which the form or amount of this substance may control the response to read signals, the signals that retrieve the contents of memory for use in current behavior.

The understanding of the cellular and molecular bases of memory may be achieved in the absence of an understanding of the computational processes that underlie learning. Biochemists have understood for more than thirty years that the sequence of base pairs in certain segments of the DNA helix controls biological form. They know how this sequence is translated into a sequence of amino acids to form a protein, but they do not yet understand the process that translates from these one dimensional linear sequences of nucleotides or amino acids to three dimensional molecular and organic form. By analogy, it may well be possible that we will come to know the molecular basis of memory without knowing how memories are computed from inputs or used in behavior.

What the rest of neuroscience needs from psychology are answers to questions about the formal and quantitative characteristics of the memory substance itself. Is it bistable or multistable? How stable? There is compelling behavioral evidence for integration processes that require for their realization a multistable mutable substance whose value (amount?) can be increased or decreased with equal facility but remains stable indefinitely in the absence of adjusting inputs. The mutable variable underlying these integration processes would be an excellent candidate for a general memory substance.

Another phenomenon that is yielding formal and quantitative characteristics of the memory-formation process itself (as opposed to the learning process) is electrical self-stimulation of the brain. This phenomenon provides the kind of nerve-memory preparation that we will need to determine the cellular and molecular bases of memory.

Chapter 17

Synthesis

The phenomena of learning reflect the nervous system's computation of representations of behavior-relevant aspects of its environment. The structure of the computational mechanisms is dictated by the formal structure of the representations to be computed and by the structure of the sensory or mnemonic data from which they are computed. Thus the analysis of learning mechanisms should be organized in accord with formally distinct representational domains, such as space, time, number, rate, and predictive uncertainty.

Associative models of learning assume a kernel learning process whose formal structure does not reflect the formal structure of the to-be-mastered facts about the world. The assumption of a universal learning process with no commitments to the a priori structure of the data has been challenged as abiological (Rozin and Kalat 1971; Seligman and Hager 1972) because it overlooks the biologically plausible role of natural selection in shaping learning mechanisms adapted to the solution of specialized problems in specialized animals. Nonetheless, theories of learning continue to reflect philosophical rather than biological antecedents. The continued resistance to viewing learning within an evolutionary framework hinges in part on the belief that such an approach is not consistent with the common scientific commitment to generality. If learning mechanisms are tailored to specific problems peculiar to specific animals, then the study of learning might become a purely descriptive kind of natural history, akin to eighteenth-century botanizing.

The focus on the formal structure of the representations whose construction underlies learning offers a new basis for the generality of learning mechanisms. On this view, learning mechanisms have the same kind of generality that one finds for other organic mechanisms, such as circulatory systems, gas-exchange systems, metabolic systems, and reproductive systems. There are several solutions to each of these basic problems in animal physiology, but the solutions to each kind of problem, for example, the gas-exchange problem, fall into a few broad categories. Large classes of organisms use the same basic mechanism, for example, lungs or gills because of the powerful adaptive and historical constraints inherent in the evolutionary process. Gills will not work for animals that live in air and lungs will not work for animals that live in water—an example of an adaptive constraint. Vertebrates increase the speed of axonal conduction by myelinating their axons, while invertebrates do not—an example of a historical constraint. Among the animals that use a particular mechanism, there are interesting differences (for instance, the flow-through lungs of birds versus the bellows lungs of mammals), but there are also large communalities, dictated by the adaptive and historical constraints. In no animal, however, is there a single kind of organ that copes with all the different problems confronting the animal. An organ like the liver, which copes with the conversion between different sources of chemical energy, is hopelessly ill suited to solving gas-exchange problems, and vice-versa. The structure of an organ reflects the nature of the problem it is designed to solve and its evolutionary antecedents.

Similarly, when it comes to learning, we must expect to find different organs of learning (different computational mechanisms) for such fundamentally different problems as the problem of representing the structure of three-dimensional space and the problem of representing time and temporal intervals. Within one problem domain, we may expect to find only a few basic types of learning mechanism, with interesting variations that adapt a common basic solution to the spectrum of demands peculiar to a given species. Thus we may expect to find in Sierra nutcrackers elaborations of the general location-learning mechanism that enable them to remember an unusually large number of cache locations, just as we find in desert rodents adaptations of the kidney that enable them to concentrate their urine to an unusual degree. The analysis of learning should be like the analysis of other aspects of animal physiology in that it should be organized around the basic types of problems that must be solved and the basic types of solutions to these problems. I have attempted to define some of the basic representational problems in animal behavior and sketch some basic solutions to them.

The mathematical conception of a representation is central to this approach. A representation is a correspondence between the formal structure of the *represented system* and the formal structure of the *representing system* that enables one to predict results in the represented system on the basis of operations conducted within the representing system. For example, the formal correspondence between geometry and algebra devised by Descartes and Fermat enables one to predict the intersection or nonintersection of lines on the basis of algebraic operations with their corresponding equations. To say the brain represents aspects of the world is to say there is a correspondence between the formal structure of processes in the nervous system and the formal structure of the represented aspects of the world that enables operations in the nervous system to anticipate relations in the environment and to predict the consequences of acting in specified ways on or within that environment.

The first of many examples of the postulated isomorphism between aspects of the world and aspects of neural functioning is the mechanism for dead reckoning. The temporal integration of geocentrically orthogonal velocity signals during an ant's foraging journey gives it a representation of its position relative to its starting point, which enables it to set a course back to that starting point. It is a formal fact about the world that an object's change in position over a temporal interval is the integral of its velocity vector over that interval. In the evolution of sensory-perceptual mechanisms that generate geocentrically orthogonal velocity signals and of a mechanism that integrates these signals with respect to time, natural selection has created a process within the nervous system whose mathematical description mirrors the mathematical description of the problem that must be solved. Natural selection creates functioning isomorphisms between processes in the nervous system and aspects of the world to which those mechanisms adapt the animal's behavior.

The integration of velocity to obtain changes in position yields the geocentric position signals necessary to construct a representation of the spatial relationship between the points visited by an animal in the course of its journeys. I hypothesize that the experimentally documented capacity of animals to reckon the spatial relationship between their current position and heading and a previous position and heading is a cornerstone of their ability to construct a map of their environment. The other cornerstone is the ability of sensory-perceptual mechanisms to compute a representation of the location of distal stimulus sources in an egocentric system of coordinates, a system anchored to the head. The computations sketched in figure 5.1 combine egocentric representations at different points of view with the geocentric reckoning of the relations between those points of view to yield a geocentric cognitive map, a metric representation of the relative positions of points and surfaces in the world in a system of coordinates anchored to the earth.

The geocentric metric map is the foundation of an animal's ability to orient its movements with respect to objects and points not currently perceived on the basis of its perception of the macroscopic shape of its current surroundings and its position within that shape. The nervous system updates its representation of the animal's position within the environment from moment to moment by dead reckoning (velocity integration) rather than by the taking of fixes, which is the determination of a position and heading on a map by reference to the bearings and distances of currently perceived and recognized features of the environment. Fixes are taken only intermittently, to correct the estimate of position derived from velocity integration.

The taking of a fix is hypothesized to be a process of computing a congruence between the macroscopic shape of the currently perceived surroundings and a portion of the cognitive map (the representation of environmental shape computed from earlier experiences of it). It is suggested that the computation of congruence is mediated by the computation of shape parameters, such as principal axes. The system takes a fix by computing the translation and rotation required to make its egocentric perception of the shape of its surroundings congruent with a portion of its geocentric cognitive map. The required translation is found by computing the principal axes (for example) of the perceived shape of its surroundings and aligning these axes with the principal axes of the corresponding portion of its geocentric map.

Shape parameters are determined solely by the relative positions of surfaces and points. Therefore, the fix-taking process is impenetrable by sense data giving nonpositional attributes of the perceivable points and surfaces, which, it is suggested, is why rats are 180° misoriented half the time in a rectangular environment, even when opposing ends and sides are distinguished by salient nonpositional attributes such as brightness, smell, visual pattern and tactile texture. The process by which the rat takes a fix is impenetrable by nongeometric data for computational reasons. The computation of shape parameters requires data with a formal structure that nongeometric data (data about smells, reflectances, and so on) do not have.

The representation of the relative positions of the points, lines and surfaces in the environment is taken to be both primitive and foundational: Primitive, because the capacity to construct an enduring representation of the shape of the environment is a basic, irreducible learning process; it cannot be conceptualized in terms of the formation of associations nor in terms of any other more primitive or basic learning process. Foundational, because the resulting cognitive map is the basis for the animal's ability to use the information gained from sensory inputs received in the indefinite past to orient its movements adaptively. Because it has elaborated the information contained in earlier sensory inputs into a representation of the shape of its environment, it can orient itself with respect to points it cannot presently discern by reference to the perceived shape of its surroundings and to its representation of the positions of itself and the goal within that shape.

It is suggested that the representation of the shape of the environment must be made at several different scales because on the one hand detailed representations are required for moving through certain parts of the environment (for example, a bat's home cave), while on the other hand the map must extend outward to encompass the broad territory with which the animal has some familiarity. If a bat represented its entire foraging territory with the degree of precision and detail required in its representation of its home cave, the demands on memory would be staggering. Hence, one is led to conclude that animal maps, like human maps, are constructed on several different scales, with each fine-scale map having a specified position and orientation on the global map, the map that covers the largest area with the least resolution.

It appears that in defining "places" and orientations, animals default to the most global perceivable spatial framework. If, for example, a rat is taught to find food at a certain "place" within a maze and the maze is then rotated so that the goal place defined with respect to the maze no longer coincides with the goal place defined with respect to the room, the rat resolves the conflict between frames of reference in favor of the larger frame (the room), unless it is shown by repeated experience that the "place" in question moves with the maze. The principle that places are defined with reference to the largest available frame of reference, together with the principle that the fix-taking process uses the shape of the frame of reference and not the salience of any one point within that frame, explains many seemingly contradictory findings within the experimental literature on "place-versus-response" learning. Small stimuli (such as light bulbs) have negligible impact on the fix-taking process, no matter how otherwise salient they may be (no matter what their wattage). Places are defined with respect to shapes (configurations of surfaces, lines, or points), not with respect to individually recognizable points. When a place defined by the more local shape of the environment no longer coincides with the place defined by the more global shape, the animal will go by the more global framework. Consequently, it will show what was called "place" responding; that is, it will go to a different place within the local framework (a different arm of the maze) in order to reach the same place within the more global framework (the same place in the room). On the other hand, if the more global framework is neutralized in some way, as it commonly was in experiments that favored the "response" hypothesis, the rats use the more local framework (the maze itself), going to the same locally defined place as before (the same arm as during training). Extramaze stimuli that do not appreciably alter the perceived macroscopic shape of the extramaze environment have little effect on behavior within the maze, no matter how salient they are.

The capacity to record the time of observation is taken to be another learning process that is both primitive and foundational. The mechanism by which temporal position is recorded is hypothesized to be the recording of the phases (momentary states) of endogenous physiological oscillations. A record of a time of occurrence is comprised of the recorded phases of several different endogenous oscillators, with periods ranging from a second or less to many years. Time, like space, is mapped at several different scales.

The capacities to record times of occurrence and to compute differences between times of occurrence are hypothesized to be the foundations of the capacity to represent temporal intervals. Thus the ability to learn temporal intervals is taken to be a derived or second-order learning capacity rather than a primitive capacity. Whether derived or primitive, the representation of temporal intervals in rats and pigeons appears to be a rich one, in the formal sense of rich. Successful computational models of timing behavior appear to require decision processes that employ operations isomorphic to the addition, subtraction, and division of represented intervals.

To explain the many findings indicating that the standard deviation in the representation of a temporal interval is proportionate to the interval (the scalar variance hypothesis of Gibbon 1977), it is assumed that the error in the recording of the phase of an endogenous oscillation is a fixed fraction of the period of the oscillation (for example, ± 10 percent); and the accuracy of the interval obtained by subtracting one phase from another is determined by the accuracy with which the phases are recorded from the oscillation whose period is just greater than the interval being computed. The recorded phases of oscillations with periods shorter than the interval being computed do not contribute to the precision with which intervals are computed, perhaps because the faster oscillations are not always strongly phase-locked to the slower oscillations. Thus the recording of phases from oscillations with shorter periods increases the resolving power of the interval-computing process—its power to differentiate short intervals—but not its precision. Longer intervals are computed from the recorded phases of slower oscillations (the phases recorded at the onset and offset of the interval), with a proportionate loss of absolute accuracy, which is why the representation of temporal intervals obeys Weber's law.

The ability to represent number is taken to be a third primitive form of learning. It is hypothesized that animals derive their representations of number from a process conforming to the formal characterization of counting processes given by Gelman and Gallistel (1978). The counting model given by Meck and Church (1983) to explain their data on counting and timing in rats and pigeons is an instance of a process that conforms to the analysis of Gelman and Gallistel. Capaldi and Miller (1988) have demonstrated the applicability of the Gelman and Gallistel analysis of counting to the counting of rewarded and unrewarded trials by the rat. Whatever the process is that maps from the numerosities of sequentially and simultaneously presented sets to numerons (representatives of numerosities), the numerical representation in rats and pigeons appears to be as rich, formally speaking, as is their representation of temporal interval: successful models of numerical behavior in laboratory animals appear to require decision processes that employ operations isomorphic to the addition, subtraction, and division of numerons.

The capacity to compute temporal intervals, including their sums and differences, and the capacity to count occurrences together provide the foundation for the capacity to represent rates of occurrence. It is argued that the well-documented tendency of a variety of animals to apportion their time among foraging locations in accord with the relative rates of food occurrence reflects their capacity to compute representations of those rates by dividing the number of food morsels observed in a given region by the interval of observation. The postulated capacity to compute and store representations of rates is a tertiary learning capacity: it depends on the capacity to represent temporal intervals, which is itself assumed to depend on the primitive capacity to record times (phases) of occurrence.

Myerson and Miezen (1980) have shown that operant data from "matching" and "maximizing" experiments are explained by a model in which a key assumption is that an animal's relative affinity for a given patch is equal to the observed prevalence of food in that patch divided by the sum of the prevalences observed in all accessible patches. For an animal to behave in accord with this principle, it would appear necessary for the animal to have a formally rich representation of the prevalences, a representation in which the prevalence computed for one patch may be divided by the sum of the prevalences computed for the other patches. The computations of the prevalences themselves would appear to require formally rich representations of number, time, and morsel magnitude because food prevalence is the number of morsels observed multiplied by the average size of a morsel and divided by the interval of observation. There is experimental evidence that these variables combine appropriately in determining the allocation of foraging time among foraging patches (see, for example, figures 11.3 and 11.6).

The assumptions that the common laboratory animals compute rates from the numbers of observed occurrences and temporal intervals is central to the theory of classical conditioning advanced in chapter 13. Also central to this theory is the assumption that the brains of rats and pigeons compute the uncertainty intervals surrounding estimates of rates. The learning curve—the growth in the strength of the conditioned response as a function of the extent of the animal's experience with the predictive relation between the CS and the US—is assumed to reflect the reduction in the statistical uncertainty of the conditional rate estimate. A conditional rate estimate is an estimate of the rate of US occurrence expected in the sole presence of a given CS. When the difference between the observed rates of US occurrence in the presence and in the absence of the CS is large, then the change in the strength of the conditioned response in the course of training is assumed to be a monotonic function of the unlikelihood that the observed difference arose by chance from independent observations of a single underlying Poisson process. The sensitivity of the animal's behavior to the statistical unlikelihood of observed differences in rate is assumed to reflect an underlying response (decision) process in which a representation of the statistical uncertainties inherent in limited observations plays a critical role. Thus the formal richness of the animal's representation of rate is assumed to encompass statistical computations.

In addition to the traditional challenge of explaining the negatively accelerated form of the learning curve, a central challenge for modern theories of conditioning is to explain the experimental data showing that the conditioning to one stimulus depends strongly on the conditioning to other stimuli. This challenge arose twenty years ago with the nearly simultaneous publication of findings on blocking and overshadowing (Kamin 1967), the effects of background conditioning (Rescorla 1968), and the effects of predictive sufficiency (Wagner et al. 1968).

The model published by Rescorla and Wagner (1972) is the best known attempt to deal with these findings within an associative framework. What distinguishes this model from its predecessors is the assumption that the change in the strength of a CS-US association on a trial depends on the sum of the strengths of the associations between the US and other CSs present on that trial (the multidimensionality assumption). The success of the Rescorla-Wagner model in explaining particular results depends on the values assumed for its numerous free parameters. There has been little effort to determine the values of these parameters experimentally, and it is not clear that the values assumed in explaining one set of findings may be reconciled with the values required to explain other findings. For example, it is not clear that the parameter values required to explain the background conditioning effects reported by Rescorla (1968) may be reconciled with the values required to explain the effects of predictive sufficiency reported by Wagner et al. (1968). (See table 12.1.)

The Rescorla-Wagner model also postulates an internal trial clock, which carves up time into discrete trials in the absence of external events. The trial clock is required because the formal model takes the probability of a US occurrence as a primitive. The probability of an event is only defined for a given interval.

A second challenge confronting modern theories of conditioning is to deal with data on the effects of varying the temporal relationship between the CS and the US. The traditional manner of dealing with this is by postulating an Interstimulus Interval (ISI) function, which gives the sensitivity of the association-forming process to the interval between the onset of the CS and the onset of the US. The narrow unimodal function often given in secondary sources (see figure 16.1, for example) is incapable of accounting for the extensive data on the effects of varying the CS-US interval. In particular, it is incapable of explaining the important finding that the rate of conditioning depends not on the CS-US interval per se but on the ratio between this interval and the intertrial or US-US interval (Gibbon et al. 1977). A distinguished authority in the field, after reviewing the data on ISI intervals, including experiments showing strong backward conditioning, has concluded that present experimental data do not serve as a solid basis for specifying the role of temporal variables in conditioning (Rescorla 1972, 1988), which means that the notion of temporal pairing is at present an ill defined notion in the theory of associative conditioning.

The special theory of conditional rate estimation advanced in chapter 13 deals with the first challenge. It specifies the process that apportions observed rates (not probabilities) of US occurrence among the CSs that might condition that rate. This model is restricted in the same way as modern associative theories: it treats USs as point events and it only recognizes a binary valued temporal relationship between the CS and US (coincidence/noncoincidence). The computational model for the apportionment problem rests on three principles:

1. *Additivity* — the rate observed over an interval must be equal to the sum of the rates ascribed to the influences of the CSs present during the interval, within the limits of statistical uncertainty.

2. *Inertia*—the rate of US occurrence ascribed to the influence of a CS is constant, unless the observed occurrences are statistically irreconcilable with this assumption.

3. *Uncertainty minimization* —when the rates to be ascribed to various CSs are underdetermined, the system gravitates to the solution that minimizes the average uncertainty surrounding the nonzero conditional rate estimates by minimizing the number of CSs assumed to have a nonzero influence (minimizing the number of predictors).

The additivity and inertia principles lead to a matrix-inversion model of the apportionment problem:

$$\lambda_c = T^{-1}\lambda_u,$$

where λ_c represents the rate estimates after correction for the influence of other CSs, λ_u represents the raw (uncorrected) rate estimates, and T^{-1} is the inverse of the temporal coefficient matrix. The temporal coefficient matrix is the matrix of the coefficients one gets when one sets up the system of simultaneous equations implied by the additivity and inertia principles. The coefficients in this matrix are all of the form $T_{i,j}/T_i$, where $T_{i,j}$ is the total interval over which CS_i and CS_j were present concurrently and T_i is the total interval over which CS_i was present.

The matrix-inversion model has no free parameters in the learning model itself, and it gives analytically derivable explanations of the major experimental findings relevant to the apportionment problem, the problem of which CSs predict what proportion of the observed US occurrences. It predicts (a) the effects of background USs, which occur in the absence of a given CS; (b) inhibitory conditioning when the US occurs only in the absence of the CS; (c) the negligible effects of background USs predicted by other CSs; (d) the blocking of conditioning when a new CS is presented along with an already conditioned CS; (e) the overshadowing that occurs when a CS is paired with a more salient CS during conditioning; (f) predictive sufficiency, wherein only that CS gets conditioned that could by itself have predicted the observed pattern of US occurrences; (g) inhibitory conditioning when a new CS is presented along with two separately conditioned CSs that 'overpredict' the US when presented together; (h) latent inhibition or the retardation of conditioning to a CS that is presented several times without a US, prior to the onset of CS-US pairing. Given one parametric assumption about the function that translates differences in estimated rates into probabilities of responding, the model also predicts the Gibbon et al (1977) finding that the number of trials required to reach a given probability of responding is a function of the ratio between the CS-US interval and the US-US interval. The requisite parametric assumption is that the differences in the rates of occurrence in the presence and absence of the CS are sufficiently large that the probability of responding is determined almost entirely by p, the probability that the observed difference is genuine.

Thus one of the fruits of a representational approach to the phenomena of animal learning is a simple but surprisingly successful model of the conditioning process, as it operates for USs that are point events and coincide in time with the CSs that predict them. The model has no free parameters, its predictions may be derived analytically rather than by numerical simulation, and it accounts for a broader range of findings than current associative models.

The concluding section of chapter 13 sketches a more general approach. The more general model of conditioning allows for long-duration, continuously varying USs, and it captures more or less arbitrary temporal relationships between CS and US. The suggested model rests on complex demodulation, which is a temporally restricted form of frequency-domain or transfer-function analysis. At the heart of complex demodulation is a process that cross-correlates the pattern of CS occurrence and the pattern of US occurrence with the endogenous oscillations that are the foundation of the nervous system's ability to represent time. The cross-correlation process gives more weight to recent history, by means of a weighting scheme in which the weight given to earlier crossproducts decreases exponentially as one looks backward in time from the present moment. This is equivalent to cross-correlation with an oscillation that decreases exponentially in amplitude as one looks backward in time. By cross-correlating the pattern of CS occurrence and the pattern of US occurrence with exponentially relaxing oscillations of different frequencies, the nervous system does a Laplace transformation of the time series for each stimulus. From the Laplace representation of any two time series, a simple computation yields the transfer (or prediction) function, which expresses the amplitude and phase of expected variations in a US as functions of the amplitude and phase of variations in a CS.

By varying the length of the backward look—the rate of retrospective exponential decay in the Laplace transformation—these analyses can deal with nonstationary time series and with temporally correlated but aperiodic patterns of CS and US occurrence. It is once again a matter of the nervous system analyzing a pattern at different scales simultaneously. A long backward look (slow rate of exponential decay) analyzes patterns of CS and US occurrence over a large-scale temporal framework, averaging over many cycles of an oscillation; a short backward look (rapid decay) looks over a small-scale framework, averaging over as little as one cycle.

In the proposed models of classical conditioning, the experimental phenomena do not reflect the operations of a primitive or foundational learning process. They reflect the operation of a higher-order process, which is dependent on the primitive mechanisms for recording the description of a stimulus, the temporal position of an observation, and number. They depend further on secondary or tertiary mechanisms for computing temporal intervals, rates, and statistical uncertainties. On this view, classical conditioning experiments are studies of the high-level mechanism that does a multivariate time-series analysis of the animal's recorded experiences.

A fourth primitive mechanism of learning is the mechanism that records descriptions of distal stimuli. Recordings from single neurons in the neocortex and tectum confirm the psychophysical conclusion that the nervous system divides in order to conquer: it describes stimuli as points in a variety of different descriptive spaces of modest dimensionality. The electrophysiological findings suggest that the dimensions that describe a stimulus are mapped into anatomical dimensions of cortical subregions, so that recording the description of a stimulus reduces to the problem of recording the resultant vectors (and perhaps a few other descriptors) for the activity the stimulus generates in a variety of different cortical regions with anatomical dimensions corresponding to descriptive dimensions of the stimulus.

The psychophysical and electrophysiological evidence that the recorded description of a distal stimulus consists of many quite separate descriptions poses the question of how these descriptions are unified when behavior requires that the system identify, for example, the recorded smell corresponding to a recorded shape or color—the longstanding problem of how the system remembers the smell (or taste, or weight, or feel) of the thing that looked like a rose. It is suggested that different descriptions of the same stimulus are linked by means of spatiotemporal coordinates stored with each description. This suggestion makes representations of spatial and temporal position the foundation of the nervous system's capacity to synthesize diverse descriptions of an experience into a unified recollection of that experience, the foundation of episodic memory.

The suggested process for linking recorded stimulus descriptions in episodic memory gives a new interpretation for the phenomena of short-term memory. On this account, short-term memory is not a separate, volatile memory process. The seeming volatility of short-term memory, as manifest in the Brown-Peterson test for the ability to recall a short list of items in tests that involve the presentation of many such lists, is an instance of interlist temporal interference. The temporal probe used to retrieve the items in the most recently presented list retrieves items from earlier lists, either because the probe is mispositioned, specifying a moment too far back in time, and/or because the temporal specification (address) of items from a previous list overlaps the temporal specification of items from the most recent list. The limit on the length of the list that may be committed to memory at one time is interpreted as a limit on the number of items whose temporal address may be recorded with precision at any one time, not as a limit on the capacity of a volatile memory process.

The proposed process for linking records suggests an explanation for the fact that in retrograde impairments of memory, recall of experience is lost on the basis of the time at which the experience was recorded, not on the basis of its subject matter nor its importance. According to this suggestion, what is impaired in retrograde amnesia is not the records themselves but the retrieval process. The global injury renders the retrieval process incapable of specifying a retrieval probe whose value falls within the amnestic interval, the interval of past time from which records cannot be retrieved. Since the malfunction lies in the retrieval process and not in the memories to be retrieved, recovery of function in the retrieval process leads to recovery of the previously unrecallable records, explaining the commonly observed recovery from amnesia. What this suggestion explains is not the retrograde character of the memory loss—the tendency of the deficit to extend backward in time from the moment of injury and for the more remote memories to become retrievable prior to more proximal memories—but rather the fact that the loss is governed by the time at which memories were laid down. It is, I believe, the only account of memory function that explains this puzzling but well established aspect of memory losses produced by global injuries, such as concussions.

The behaviorally based conceptual framework for the analysis of learning and memory has profound implications for attempts to determine the cellular and molecular basis of information storage in the nervous system because memory is a behaviorally defined process. The behaviorally derived conception of the process determines what is to be looked for at cellular and molecular levels of analysis.

Current attempts to discover the molecular basis of information storage take a premodern associative conception as their conceptual framework. In this framework, the mnemonic change is set in motion by the near temporal coincidence of two signals (temporal pairing). The behavioral study of learning within an associative framework has yet to establish formal and quantitative characteristics of the mutable variable in memory— how long the associative change endures, whether an association is a continuous or discrete variable, whether a change in associative strength is reversible, and so on. Since behavioral work has not supplied a consensus characterization of the associative change itself, attempts to identify the material change that mediates the formation of an association focus on the presumed properties of the process that produces the change, such as the presumed necessity for close temporal pairing of the to-be-associated signals. In focusing on temporal pairing, modern cellular and molecular work parts company with modern behavioral work because an important conclusion of modern behavioral work is that temporal pairing is neither necessary nor sufficient for the creation of an association.

Behavioral results imply that the associative process operates within a network capable of taking into account many different mnemonic variables because the change in one association on a given trial depends on the values of other associations. Modern findings also show that time enters into the process in a more complex manner than envisioned by premodern theories, in which temporal pairing was assumed to be defined by reference to an empirically determined interstimulus interval function. Recent findings show that the effect of the interval between the

CS signal and the US signal depends in a quantitatively simple fashion on the US-US interval: equal ratios between the CS-US and US-US intervals produce equal rates of conditioning. Further, the associative changes that occur during inhibitory conditioning and extinction cannot be seen as consequences of the temporal pairing of signals.

The computational complexity of the association-forming process implied by modern findings does not appear consistent with the assumption that the molecular change mediating association fromation is set in motion by the near temporal coincidence of two physiological signals arriving at a single presynaptic or postsynpatic site. Modern theories would appear to require that we separate the computational process in learning from the process by which the upshot of computation is stored. This leaves us with little conceptual guidance for efforts to find the molecular basis of storage because it means that the storage mechanism need not be found in physical proximity to the mechanisms that mediate the computation of associative strengths.

The concept of an association plays no role in the conceptual framework I have elaborated. Hence, the problem of finding the molecular basis for storage appears in a different light. Within this framework, learning is the computation and storage of quantities that represent diverse aspects of the animal's experience. Thus there is little reason to assume what is often taken as a truism: that at the cellular level learning must involve changes in synaptic strengths. There is no more reason to think of learning in brains as changes in the connectivity among neurons than there is to think of information storage and retrieval in conventional computers as changes in the strengths with which elements of the computer's memory are connected. What the representational conception of learning requires in the way of a storage mechanism is similar to what is required of the memory system in a conventional computer: a mechanism for converting into nonvolatile form the quantitative information contained in transient signals and a mechanism for reading the values of stored quantities.

The proposed framework suggests what the characteristics of the mutable variable must be. It must be a continuous variable or at least multistable because it must be capable of preserving any of the many different values a representational variable may assume. It must not decay back to some null state with time because the decayed values of the mnemonic variable would represent erroneous values of the stored variable, values that did not reflect the originally computed value but rather the time elapsed since the computed value was recorded. If, for example, the physical variables representing the position of a temporarily imprisoned ant forager relative to its nest were to decay toward <0,0>, which is the value for its position when at the nest, then the ant would represent itself as closer and closer to the nest the longer its imprisonment. We may conclude that the physical variable that preserves information in the nervous system has many indefinitely stable states, for example, many different levels of a stable intracellular substance. It also seems likely that its value may be adjusted upward or downward with equal readiness because new information may require a change in either direction. When the foraging ant moves closer to its nest, the physical variables that represent its distance from the nest must decrease in value.

It is not difficult to imagine cellular mechanisms with the requisite characteristics for the storage mechanism. The control by neurotransmitters of gene expression is one obvious candidate. It is known that transient events can trigger the synthesis of large amounts of a stable protein within bacterial cells, which protein acts as a memory of the trigger event and controls the process of cell division (bacterial replication).

It is less clear how the amount of such a memory substance within a neuron (the value of the stored variable) might be read, but suitable mechanisms may well be found if a search is made. Functionally important processes in cells—like the hypothesized reading process— are seldom found (or at least recognized for what they are) unless they are looked for. What determines what is looked for is the conceptual scheme that defines what the functionally important processes must look like. Within the conceptual scheme here elaborated, there must be a mechanism by which a signal to a cell may read the value of a memory variable laid down in that cell.

In reading the values recorded in cells, the nervous system retrieves the information required by currently operating behavior-generating mechanisms, for example, by the mechanisms that orient the animal toward a goal position in its environment, govern the time of day at which it goes there, or the interval it allows to elapse between visits, or the number of responses it makes in one location before going to another. The values of representational cellular variables are read out by the innumerable response processes whose innately programmed structure presupposes the availability of empirically acquired data about the inherently idiosyncratic aspects of any behavioral space.

References

Abrams, T. W., and Kandel, E. R. (1988). Is contiguity detection in classical conditioning a system or a cellular property? Learning in *Aplysia* suggests a possible molecular site. *Trends in Neurosciences*, 11, 128–135.

Adams, J. A. (1977). Feedback theory of how joint receptors regulate the timing and positioning of a limb. *Psychological Review*, 84, 504–523.

Ainslie, G. W. (1974). Impulse control in pigeons. *Journal of the Experimental Analysis of Behavior*, 21, 485–489.

Anderson, J. R., and Bower, G. H. (1973). *Human associative memory*. Washington, D.C.: V. H. Winston and Sons.

Aronson, L. R. (1951). Orientation and jumping behavior in the gobiid fish, *Bathygobiis soporator*. *American Museum Novitates*, No. 1486, 1–22.

Aronson, L. R. (1971). Further studies on orientation and jumping behavior in the gobiid fish, *Bathygobius soporator*. *Annals of the New York Academy of Sciences*, 188, 378–392.

Aschoff, J. (1981). *Biological rhythms*. New York: Plenum.

Aschoff, J. (1984). Circadian timing. In J. Gibbon and L. Allan (Eds.), *Timing and time perception* New York: New York Academy of Sciences. [*Annals of the New York Academy of Sciences* Vol. 423]

Aschoff, J., Goetz, C. v., and Honmah, K. I. (1983). Restricted feeding in rats: Effects of varying feeding cycle. *Zeitschrift für Tierpsychologie*, 63, 91–111.

Atkinson, R. C., and Shiffrin, R. M. (1968). Human memory: A proposed system and its control processes. In K. W. Spence and J. T. Spence (Eds.), *The psychology of learning and motivation*. *Vol*. 2 (pp. 89–105). New York: Academic.

Balda, R. P. (1980). Recovery of cached seeds by a captive *Nucifraga caryocatactes*. *Zeitschrift für Tierpsychologie*, 52, 331–346.

Balda, R. P., and Turek, R. J. (1984). The cache–memory system as an example of memory capabilities in Clark's nutcracker. In H. L. Roitblatt, T. G. Bever, and H. S. Terrace (Eds.), *Animal cognition* (pp. 513–532) Hillsdale, NJ: Erlbaum.

Ballard, D. H. (1986). Cortical connections and parallel processing: Structure and function. *Behavioral and Brain Sciences*, 9, 67–120.

Balsam, P. (1984). Relative time in trace conditioning. In J. Gibbon and L. Allan (Eds.), *Timing and time perception* New York: New York Academy of Sciences. [*Annals of the New York Academy of Sciences* Vol. 423]

Barbizet, J. (1970). *Human memory and its pathology*. San Francisco: Freeman.

Bardach, J. E. (1958). On the movements of certain Bermuda reef fishes. *Ecology*, 39, 139–146.

Batschelet, E. (1981). *Circular statistics in biology*. New York: Academic.

Baum, W. M., and Rachlin, H. C. (1969). Choice as time allocation. *Journal of the Experimental Analysis of Behavior*, 12, 861–74.

Beatty, W. W., and Shavalia, D. A. (1980). Rat spatial memory: Resistance to retroactive interference at long retention intervals. *Animal Learning and Behavior*, 8, 550–552

Beling, I. (1929). Über das Zeitgedächtnis der Bienen. *Zeitschrift für vergleichende Physiologie*, 9, 259–338.

Benson, D. F., and Geschwind, N. (1967). Shrinking retrograde amnesia. *Journal of Neurology, Neurosurgery, and Psychiatry*, 30, 539–544.

Beusekom, G. v. (1948). Some experiments on the optical orientation in Philanthus Triangulum Fabr. *Behaviour*, 1, 195–225.

Bitterman, M. E. (1965). Phyletic differences in learning. *American Psychologist*, 20, 396–410.

Bjork, R. A., and Whitten, W. B. (1974). Recency–sensitive retrieval processes in long–term free recall. *Cognitive Psychology*, 6, 173–189.

Blakemore, and Frankel, R. B. (1981). Magnetic navigation in bacteria. *Scientific American*, 245(6), 58–65.

Blanchteau, M., and Le Lorec, A. (1972). Raccourci et détour chez le rat: Durée, vitesse et longueur des parcours. *Année Psychologique*, 72, 8–16.

Blasdel, G. G., and Salama, G. (1986). Voltage–sensitive dyes reveal a modular organization in monkey striate cortex. *Nature*, 321, 579–585.

Bloomfield, P. (1976). *The Fourier analysis of time series: An introduction*. New York: Wiley.

Bolles, R. C., and de Lorge, J. (1962). The rat's adjustment to a–diurnal feeding cycles. *Journal of Comparative and Physiological Psychology*, 55, 760–762.

Bolles, R. C., and Moot, S. A. (1973). The rat's anticipation of two meals a day. *Journal of Comparative and Physiological Psychology*, 83, 510–514.

Bolles, R. C., and Stokes, L. W. (1965). Rat's anticipation of diurnal and a–diurnal feeding. *Journal of Comparative and Physiological Psychology*, 60, 290–294.

Born, D. E., and Rubel, E. W. (1988). Afferent influences on brain stem auditory nuclei of the chicken: Presynaptic action potentials regulate protein synthesis in nucleus magnocellularis neurons. *Journal of Neuroscience*, 8, 901–919.

Boulos, Z. A., Rossenwasser, A. M., and Terman, M. (1980). Feeding schedules and the circadian organization of behavior in the rat. *Behavioral Brain Research*, 1, 39–65.

Bowditch's. (1977). *American practical navigator*. Washington, DC: Defense Mapping Agency Hydrographic Center.

Bower, T. G. R. (1975). Infant perception of the third dimension and object concept development. In L. B. Chohen & P. Salapatek (Eds.) *Infant perception: From sensaton to cognition*. Vol. 2 *Perception of space speech and sound*. New York: Academic. pp. 33-50.

Boysen, S. T., and Berntson, G. G. (1989). Numerical comptetence in a chimpanzee (*Pan troglodytes*). *Journal of Comparative Psychology*, 103, 23–31.

Brines, M. L., and Gould, J. L. (1979). Bees have rules. *Science*, 206, 571–573.

Broekhuizen, S., and Maaskamp, F. (1980). Behavior of does and leverets of the European hare (Lepus europaeus) whilst nursing. Journal of Zoology (London), 191, 487–501.

Brown, J. (1958). Some tests of a decay theory of immediate memory. Quarterly Journal of Experimental Psychology, 10, 12–21.

Brown, T. G. (1914). On the nature of the fundamental activity of the nervous centres; together with an analysis of the conditioning of rhythmic activity in progression, and a theory of evolution of function in the nervous system. Journal of Physiology, 48, 18–46.

Brownell, P. H. (1984). Prey detection by the sand scorpion. Scientific American, 251(6), 86–97.

Brunswik, E. (1939). Probability as a determiner of rat behavior. Journal of Experimental Psychology, 25, 175–197.

Bullock, D. H., and Smith, W. C. (1953). An effect of repeated conditioning–extinction upon operant strength. Journal of Experimental Psychology, 46, 349–352.

Bünning, E. (1936). Die endonome Tagesperiodik als Grundlage der photoperiodischen Reaktion. Berichte deutsches botanisches Gesellschaft, 54, 590–607.

Bünning, E. (1958). Die Physiologische Uhr. Berlin: Springer. [Bünning, E. (1973). The physiological clock (3 ed.). New York: Springer.]

Burkhalter, A. (1972). Distance measuring as influenced by terrestial cues in Cataglyphis bicolor (Formicidae, Hymenoptera). In R. Wehner (Ed.), Information processing in the visual systems of arthropods (pp. 303–308). New York: Springer.

Bush, R. R., and Mosteller, F. (1951). A mathematical model for simple learning. Psychological Review, 68, 313–323.

Busnel, R. G., and Fish, J. F. (1980). Animal sonar systems. New York: Plenum.

Buttel Reepen, H. B. v. (1915). Leben und Wesen der Bienen. Braunschweig: Vieweg.

Cabot, R. C. (1981). A note on the application of Hilbert transform to time delay estimation. IEEE Transactions on Acoustics, Speech and Signal Processing, ASSP–29, 607–609.

Capaldi, E. J., and Miller, D. J. (1988). Counting in rats: Its functional significance and the independent cognitive processes which comprise it. Journal of Experimental Psychology: Animal Behavior Processes, 14, 3–17.

Carr, H. (1917). Maze studies with the white rat. Journal of Animal Behavior, 7, 259–306.

Carr, H., and Watson, J. B. (1908). Orientation of the white rat. Journal of Comparative Neurology and Psychology, 18, 27–44.

Cartwright, B. A., and Collett, T. S. (1983). Landmark learning in bees: Experiments and models. Journal of Comparative Physiology, 151, 521–543.

Cartwright, B. A., & Collett, T. S. (1979). How honey bees know their distance from a nearby visual landmark. Journal of Experimental Biology, 82, 367–372.

Caspers, H. (1961). Beobachtungen über Lebensraum und Schwärmperiodizität des Palolowurmes Eunice viridis. Internationale Revue der gesamte Hydrobiologie, 46, 175–183.

Catania, A. C., and Reynolds, G. S. (1968). A quantitative analysis of the responding maintained by interval schedules of reinforcement. *Journal of the Experimental Analysis of Behavior*, 11, 327–383.

Cheng, J. K., and Huang, T. S. (1982). Image registration by matching relational structures. *Proceedings of the 6th international conference on pattern recognition* (Munich) (pp. 354–356).

Cheng, K. (1984) *The primacy of metric properties in the rat's sense of place.* Ph.D. Thesis, University of Pennsylvania.

Cheng, K. (1986). A purely geometric module in the rat's spatial representation. *Cognition*, 23, 149–178.

Cheng, K., Collett, T. S., Pickhard, A., and Wehner, R. (1987). The use of visual landmarks by honey bees: Bees weight landmarks according to their distance from the goal. *Journal of Comparative Physiology*, 161, 469–475.

Cheng, K., and Gallistel, C. R. (1984). Testing the geometric power of an animal's spatial representation. In H. L. Roitblatt, T. G. Bever, and H. S. Terrace (Eds.), *Animal cognition* (pp. 409–423). Hillsdale, NJ: Erlbaum.

Church, R. M. (1984). Properties of the internal clock. In J. Gibbon and L. Allan (Eds.), *Timing and time perception* (pp. 567–582). New York: New York Academy of Sciences. [*Annals of the New York Academy of Sciences* Vol. 423]

Church, R. M., and Gibbon, J. (1982). Temporal generalization. *Journal of Experimental Psychology: Animal Behavior Processes*, 8, 165–186.

Church, R. M., and Meck, W. H. (1984). The numerical attribute of stimuli. In H. L. Roitblatt, T. G. Bever, and H. S. Terrace (Eds.), *Animal cognition* (pp. 445–464). Hillsdale, NJ: Erlbaum.

Cohen, N. J., McCloskey, M., and Treadway, M. (MS). Temporally–specific, informationally general retrograde amnesia: Implications for theory of memory.

Coleman, G. J., Harper, S., Clarke, J. D., and Armstrong, S. (1982). Evidence for a separate meal–associated oscillator in the rat. *Phsyiology and Behavior*, 29, 107–115.

Collett, T. S. (1978) Peering: A locust behavior for obtaining motion parallax information. *Journal of Experimental Biology*, 76, 237–241.

Collett, T. S., and Harkness, L. I. K. (1982). Depth vision in animals. In D. J. Ingle, M. A. Goodale, and R. J. W. Mansfield (Eds.), *Analysis of visual behavior* (pp. 111–176). Cambridge, MA: MIT Press.

Collett, T. S., and Land, M. F. (1975). Visual spatial memory in a hoverfly. *Journal of Comparative Physiology*, 100, 59–84.

Colwill, R. M., Absher, R. A., and Roberts, M. L. (1988). Context–US learning in *Aplysia californica*. *Journal of Neuroscience*, 8, 4434–4439.

Comb, M., Hyman, S. E., and Goodman, H. M. (1987). Mechanisms of trans–synaptic regulation of gene expression. *Trends in Neurosciences*, 10, 473–478.

Connor, J. A. (1985). Neural pacemakers and rhythmicity. *Annual Review of Physiology*, 47, 17–28.

Cowcroft, P. (1954). The daily cycle of activity in British shrews. *Proceedings of the Zoological Society* (London), 123, 715–729.

Cox, D. R., & Lewis, P. A. W. (1966). *The statistical analysis of series of events.* London: Methuen.

Crow, T. (1988). Cellular and molecular analyisis of associative learning and memory in *Hermissenda*. *Trends in Neurosciences*, 11, 136–141.

Daan, S., and Aschoff, J. (1981). Short–term rhythms in activity. In J. Aschoff (Ed.), *Biological rhythms* (pp. 491–499). New York: Plenum.

Daan, S., and Slopsema, S. (1978). Short term rhythms in foraging behavior of the common vole, *Microtus avarilis*. *Journal of Comparative Physiology*, 127, 215–227.

Darwin, C. (1845). *Journal of researches into the natural history and geology of the countries visted during the voyage of H.M.S. 'Beagle' round the world under the command of Capt. FitzRoy, R.N.*. New York: Appleton.

Darwin, C. (1881). *The formation of the vegetable mould, through the action of worms, with observations on their habits.* London: John Murray.

Dashiell, J. F. (1930). Direction orientation in maze running by the white rat. *Comparative Psychology Monographs*, 7(32),

Davenport, D. G. (1969). Successive acquisitions and extinctions of discrete bar–pressing in monkeys and rats. *Psychonomic Science*, 16, 242–244.

Davis, H. (1984). Discrimination of the number three by a raccoon (Procyon lotor). *Animal Learning and Behavior*, 12, 409-413.

Davis, H., and Albert, M. (1986). Numerical discrimination by rats using sequential auditory stimuli. *Animal Learning and Behavior*, 14, 57–59.

Davis, H., and Bradford, S. A. (1986). Counting behavior by rats in a simulated natural cnvironment. *Ethology*, 73, 265–280.

Davis, H., and Memmott, J. (1982). Counting behavior in animals: A critical evaluation. *Psychological Bulletin*, 92, 547–571.

Dember, W. N., and Fowler, H. (1979). Spontaneous alternation behavior. *Psychological Bulletin*, 55, 412–428.

DeMonasterio, F. M., Gouras, P., and Tolhurst, D. J. (1975). Trichromatic colour opponency in ganglion cells of the rhesus monkey retina. *Journal of Physiology* (London), 251, 197 216.

DeMonasterio, F. M., and Schein, S. J. (1982). Spectral bandwidths of color–opponent cells of geniculostriate pathway of macaque monkeys. *Journal of Neurophysiology*, 47, 214–224.

Dennis, W. (1932). Multiple visual discrimination in the block elevated maze. *Journal of comparative and Physiological Psychology*, 13, 391–396.

Deutsch, J. A. (1960). *The structural basis of behavior.* Chicago: University of Chicago Press.

DeValois, R. L., Morgan, H. C., Polson, M. C., Mead, W. R., and Hull, E. M. (1974). Psychophysical studies of monkey vision. I. Macaque luminosity and color vision tests. *Vision Research*, 14, 53–67.

Domjan, M. (1981). Ingestional aversion learning: Unique and general processes. In J. S. Rosenblatt, R. A. Hinde, C. Beer, and M. Busnel (Eds.), *Advances in the study of behavior* New York: Academic.

Domjan, M. (1985). Cue–consequence specificity and long–delay learning revisited. *Annals of the New York Academy of Sciences*, 443, 54–66.

Douglas, R. J. (1966). Cues for spontaneous alternation. *Journal of Comparative and Physiological Psychology*, 62, 171–183.

Dyer, F. C., and Gould, J. L. (1981). Honey bee orientation: A backup system for cloudy days. *Science*, 214, 1041–1042.

Dyer, F. C., and Gould, J. L. (1983). Honey bee navigation. *American Scientist*, 71, 587–597.

Edmonds, S. C., and Adler, N. T. (1977a). Food and light as entrainers of circadian running activity in the rat. *Physiology and Behavior*, 18, 915–919.

Edmonds, S. C., and Adler, N. T. (1977b). The multiplicity of biological oscillators in the control of circadian running activity in the rat. *Physiology and Behavior*, 18, 921–930.

Ellard, C. G., Goodale, M. A., and Timney, B. (1984). Distance estimation in the Mongolian Gerbil: The role of dynamic depth cues. *Behavioural Brain Research*, 14, 29–39.

Emlen, S. T. (1967). Migratory orientation in the Indigo Bunting, *Passerina cyanea*. Part I. Evidence for use of celesstial cues. *Auk*, 84, 309–342.

Emlen, S. T. (1969a). The development of migratory orientation in young Indigo Buntings. *Living Bird*, 8, 113–126.

Emlen, S. T. (1969b). Bird migration: Influence of physiological state upon celestial orientation. *Science*, 165, 716–718.

Emlen, S. T. (1972). The ontogenetic development of orientation capabilities. *Symposium of animal orientation: NASA special publications SP–262* (pp. 191–210). Washington, D.C.: National Aeronautics and Space Administration.

Emlen, S. T. (1975). Migration: Orientation and navigation. In D. S. Farner and J. R. King (Eds.), *Avian biology* (pp. 129–219). New York: Academic.

Enright, J. T. (1975). The circadian tape recorder and its entrainment. In F. J. Vernberg (Ed.), *Physiological adpatation to the environment* New York: Intext.

Epstein, R., and Skinner, B. F. (1980). Resurgence of responding after cessation of response–independent reinforcement. *Proceedings of the National Academy of Sciences*, 77, 6251–6253.

Erkinano, E. (1969). Der Phasenwechsel der lokomotorischen Activität bei *Microtus agrestis* (L.), *M. arvalis* (Pall.) und *M. oeconomous* (Pall.). *Aquilo, Series Zoologica*, 8, 1–31.

Estes, W. K. (1960). Learning theory and the new "mental chemistry". *Psychological Review*, 67, 207–223.

Estes, W. (1964). Probability learning. In A. W. Melton (Ed.), *Categories of human learning* New York: Academic.

Ewert, J. P. (1974). The neural basis of visually guided behavior. In R. Held (Ed.), *Recent progress in perception* (pp. 96–104). San Francisco: W.H. Freeman.

Farley, J., and Alkon, D. L. (1985). Cellular mechanisms of learning, memory, and information storage. *Annual Review of Psychology*, 36, 419–494.

Farner, D. S. (1985). Annual rhythms. *Annual Review of Physiology*, 47, 65–82.

Fernandes, D. M., and Church, R. M. (1982). Discrimination of the number of sequential events by rats. *Animal Learning and Behavior*, 10, 171–176.

Ferster, C. B., and Skinner, B. F. (1957). *Schedules of reinforcement*. New York: Appleton–Century–Crofts.

Fisher, C. M. (1966). Concussion amnesia. *Neurology* (Minneapolis), 16, 826–830.

Fitzgerald, R. E., Isler, R., Rosenberg, E., Oettinger, R., and Bättig, K. (1985). Maze patrolling by rats with and without food reward. *Animal Learning and Behavior*, 13, 451–462.

Fodor, J. A. (1983). *The modularity of mind*. Cambridge, MA: MIT Press.

Forder, H. G. (1927). *The foundations of Euclidean geometry.* London: Cambridge University Press.

Forel, A. (1910). *Das Sinnesleben der Insekten.* Munich: E. Reinhardt.

Frankel, R. B. (1984). Magnetic guidance of organisms. *Annual Review of Biophysics and Bioengineering*, 13, 85–103.

Fretwell, S. D. (1972). *Populations in seasonal environments.* Princeton, NJ: Princeton University Press.

Fretwell, S. D., and Lucas, H. L. J. (1970). On territorial behavior and other factors influencing habitat distribution in birds. I. Theoretical development. *Acta Biotheoretica*, 19, 16–36.

Frey, P. W., and Butler, C. S. (1977). Extinction after aversive conditioning: An associative or non–associative process? *Learning and Motivation*, 8, 1–17.

Fuchs, A. F., and Melton, A. W. (1974). Effects of frequency of presentation and stimulus length on retention in the Brown–Peterson paradigm. *Journal of Experimental Psychology*, 103, 629–637.

Fudim, O. K. (1978). Sensory preconditioning of flavors with a formalin–produced sodium need. *Journal of Experimental Psychology: Animal Behavior Processes*, 4, 276–285.

Gallistel, C. R. (1980). *The organization of action: A new synthesis.* Hilladale, NJ: Erlbaum.

Gallistel, C. R. (1985). Motivation, intention, and emotion: Goal directed behavior from a cognitive–neuroethological perspective. In M. Frese and J. Sabini (Eds.), *Goal directed behavior: The concept of action in psychology* (pp. 48–66). Hillsdale, NJ: Erlbaum.

Gallistel, C. R., Gomita, Y., Yadin, E., and Campbell, K. A. (1985). Forebrain origins and terminations of the medial forebrain bundle metabolically activated by rewarding stimulation or by reward– blocking doses of pimozide. *The Journal of Neuroscience*, 5, 1246–1261.

Gallistel, C. R., Shizgal, P., and Yeomans, J. (1981). A portrait of the substrate for self–stimulation. *Psychological Review*, 8, 228–273.

Gallistel, C. R., Stellar, J. R., and Bubis, E. (1974). Parametric analysis of brain stimulation reward in the rat. I. The transient process and the memory–containing process. *Journal of Comparative and Physiological Psychology*, 87, 848–860.

Garcia, J., Kimmeldorf, D. J., and Hunt, E. L. (1961). The use of ionizing radiation as a motivating stimulus. *Psychological Review*, 68, 383–385.

Gelman, R., and Gallistel, C. R. (1978). *The child's understanding of number.* Cambridge, MA.: Harvard University Press.

Gelman, R., and Tucker, M. F. (1975). Further investigations of the young child's conception of number. *Child Development*, 46, 167–175.

Gibbon, J. (1977). Scalar expectancy theory and Weber's Law in animal timing. *Psychological Review*, 84, 279–335.

Gibbon, J. (1981). On the form and location of the psychometric bisection function for time. *Journal of Mathematical Psychology*, 24, 58–87.

Gibbon, J., and Allan, L. (1984). *Timing and time perception.* New York: New York Academy of Sciences. [*Annals of the New York Academy of Sciences* Vol. 423]

Gibbon, J., Baldock, M. D., Locurto, C. M., Gold, L., and Terrace, H. S. (1977). Trial and intertrial durations in autoshaping. *Journal of Experimental Psychology: Animal Behavior Processes*, 3, 264–284.

Gibbon, J., and Balsam, P. (1981). Spreading associations in time. In C. M. Locurto, H. S. Terrace, and J. Gibbon (Eds.), *Autoshaping and conditioning theory* (pp. 219–253). New York: Academic.

Gibbon, J., and Church, R. M. (1981). Time left: Linear versus logarithmic subjective time. *Journal of Experimental Psychology: Animal Behavior Processes*, 7, 87–107.

Gibbon, J., Church, R. M., and Meck, W. H. (1984). Scalar timing in memory. In J. Gibbon and L. Allan (Eds.), *Timing and time perception* (pp. 52–77). New York: New York Academy of Sciences. [*Annals of the New York Academy of Sciences* Vol. 423]

Gibbs, F. P. (1979). Fixed interval feeding does not entrain the circadian pacemaker in blind rats. *American Journal of Physiology*, 236, R249–253.

Gibson, J. J. (1966). *The sense considered as perceptual systems*. Boston: Houghton Mifflin.

Gill, F. B. (1988). Trapline foraging by hermit hummingbirds: Competition for an undefended renewable resource. *Ecology*, 69, 1933–1942.

Gill, F. B., Mack, A. L., and Russell, T. R. (1982). Competition between hummingbirds *Phaethorinae* and insects for nectar in a Costa Rican rain forest. *Ibis*, 124, 44–49.

Gleitman, H. (1971). Forgetting of long term memories in animals. In W. K. Honig and P. H. R. James (Eds.), *Animal memory*. New York: Academic.

Gleitman, H., Nachmias, J., and Neisser, U. (1954). The S–R reinforcement theory of extinction. *Psychological Review*, 61, 23–33.

Glimcher, P. (1989). *The anatomical identification of the directly stimulated neurons in brain stimulation reward*. Ph.D., University of Pennsylvania.

Gluck, M. A., and Thompson, R. F. (1987). Modeling the neural substrates of associative learning and memory: A computational approach. *Psychological Review*, 94, 176–191.

Goddard, M. J., and Jenkins, H. M. (1987). Effect of signaling extra unconditioned stimuli on autoshaping. *Animal Learning and Behavior*, 15, 40–46.

Godin, J. J., and Keenleyside, M. H. A. (1984). Foraging on patchily distributed prey by a cichlid fish (Teleosti, Cichlidae): A test of the ideal free distribution theory. *Animal Behaviour*, 32, 120–131.

Gonzales, R. C., Holmes, N. K., and Bitterman, M. E. (1967). Asymptotic resistance to extinction in fish and rat as function of interpolated retraining. *Journal of Comparative and Physiological Psychology*, 63, 342–344.

Gormezano, I. (1972). The stimulus trace hypothesis and investigations of defense and reward conditioning in the rabbit. In A. Black and W. F. Prokasy (Eds.), *Classical conditioning II* (pp. 151–181). New York: Appleton–Century–Crofts.

Goshtasby, A., Gage, S. H., and Bartholic, J. F. (1984). A two–stage cross correlation approach to template matching. *IEEE Transactions on Pattern Analysis and Machine Intelligence*, 6, 374–378.

Gould, J. L. (1980). Sun compensation by bees. *Science*, 207, 545–547.

Gould, J. L. (1983). The map sense of pigeons. *Nature*, 296, 205–211.

Gould, J. L. (1984). Processing of sun–azimuth information by bees. *Animal Behaviour*, 32, 149–152.

Gould, J. L. (1985). How bees remember flower shapes. *Science*, 227, 1492–1494.

Gould, J. L. (1986a). The locale map of honey bees: Do insects have cognitive maps? *Science*, 232, 861–863.

Gould, J. L. (1986b). Pattern learning by honey bees. *Animal Behaviour*, 34, 990–997.

Gould, J. L. (1987). Landmark learning by honey bees. *Animal Behaviour*, 35, 26–34.

Gould, J., and Gould, C. G. (1988). *The honey bee.* New York: Freeman.

Graf, V., Bullock, D. H., and Bitterman, M. E. (1964). Further experiments on probability matching in the pigeon. *Journal of the Experimental Analysis of Behavior*, 7, 151–157.

Gratton, A., and Wise, R. A. (1985). Hypothalamic reward mechanism: Two first–stage fiber popoulations with a cholinergic component. *Science*, 227, 545–548.

Graue, L. C. (1963). The effects of phase shifts in the day–night cycle on pigeon homing at distances of less than one mile. *Ohio Journal of Science*, 63, 214–217.

Greenberg, M. E., Ziff, E. B., and Greene, L. A. (1986). Stimulation of neuronal acetylcholine receptors induces rapid gene transcription. *Science*, 234, 80–83.

Griffin, D. R. (1982). Ecology of migration: Is magnetic orientation a reality? *Quarterly Review of Biology*, 57, 293–295.

Grünwald, A. (1969). Untersuchungen zur Orientierung der Weisszahnspitzmäuse. *Zeitschrift für vergleichende Physiologie*, 65, 191–217.

Gunier, W. J., and Elder, W. H. (1971). Experimental homing of gray bats to a maternity colony in a Missouri barn. *American Midlands Naturalist*, 86, 502–506.

Gwinner, E. (1981). Circannual systems. In J. Aschoff (Ed.), *Biological rhythms* (pp. 391–410). New York: Plenum.

Hallet, P., and Lightstone, A. D. (1976). Saccadic eye movements to flashed targets. *Vision Research*, 16, 107–114.

Hamilton, P. V., and Russell, B. J. (1982). Celestial orientation by surface swimming *Aplysia braziliana* (Mollusca: Gastropoda). *Journal of Experimental Marine Biology and Ecology*, 56, 145–152.

Harper, D. G. C. (1982). Competitive foraging in mallards: Ideal free ducks. *Animal Behaviour*, 30, 575–584.

Harth, E. (1986). Does the brain compute? *Behavioral and Brain Sciences*, 9, 98–99.

Hauenschild, C., Fischer, A., and Hoffman, D. K. (1960). Untersuchungen am pazifischen Palolowurm *Eunice viridis* (Polychaete) in Samoa. *Helgoländer wissenschaftliche Meeresuntersuchungen*, 18, 254–295.

Hawkes, L., and Shimp, C. P. (1974). Choice between response rates. *Journal of the Experimental Analysis of Behavior*, 21, 109–115.

Hawkins, R. D., Abrams, T. W., Carew, T. J., and Kandel, E. R. (1983). A cellular mechansim of classical conditioning in *Aplysia*: Activity–dependent amplification of presynaptic facilitation. *Science*, 219, 400–404.

Hawkins, R. D., and Kandel, E. R. (1984). Is there a cell–biological alphabet for simple forms of learning? *Psychological Review*, 91, 375–391.

Hendrickson, A. E., and Wilson, J. R. (1979). A difference in [14C]deoxyglucose autoradiographic patterns in striate cortex beween *Macaca* and *Saimiri* monkeys following monocular stimulation. *Brain Research*, 170, 353–358.

Hering, E. (1878). *Zur Lehre vom Lichtsinn*. Vienna: Gerolds Sohn.

Hering, E. (1920 [1964]). *Grundzüge der Lehre vom Lichtsinn* [*Outlines of a theory of the light sense*]. Berlin [Cambridge, MA]: Springer [Harvard Univ. Press].

Herrnstein, R. J. (1961). Relative and absolute strength of response as a function of frequency of reinforcement. *Journal of the Experimental Analysis of Behavior*, 4, 267–272.

Herrnstein, R. J., and Loveland, D. H. (1975). Maximizing and matching on concurrent ratio schedules. *Journal of the Experimental Analysis of Behavior*, 24, 107–116.

Heth, C. D., and Rescorla, R. A. (1973). Simultaneous and backward fear conditioning in the rat. *Journal of Comparative and Physiological Psychology*, 82, 434–443.

Hilbert, D. (1921). *The foundations of geometry*. Chicago: Open Court.

Hinton, G. E., McClelland, J. L., and Rumelhart, D. E. (1986). Distributed representations. In D. E. Rumelhart and J. L. McClelland (Eds.), *Parallel distributed processing* (pp. 77–109). Cambridge, MA: MIT Press.

Hoin–Radovsky, I., Bleckman, H., and Schwartz, E. (1984). Determination of source distance in the surface feeding fish *Pantodon buchholzi* Pantodontidae. *Animal Behavior*, 32, 840–851.

Holloway, F. A., and Sturgis, R. D. (1976). Periodic decrements in retrieval of the memory of nonreinforcement as reflected in resistance to extinction. *Journal of Experimental Psychology: Animal Behavior Processes*, 2, 335–341.

Holloway, F. A., and Wansley, R. (1973). Multiphasic retention deficits at periodic intervals after passive avoidance learning. *Science*, 180, 208–210.

Holman, E. W. (1980). Irrelevant incentive learning with flavors in rats. *Journal of Experimental Psychology: Animal Behavior Processes*, 6, 126–136.

Holst, E. von. (1939). Die relative Koordination als Phänomen und als Methode zentralnervöser Funktionsanalyze. *Ergebnisse der Physiologie*, 42, 228–306.

Honig, W. K. (1978). Working memory in the pigeon. In S. H. Hulse, H. Fowler, and W. K. Honig (Eds.), *Cognitive processes in animal behavior* Hillsdale, NJ: Erlbaum.

Honig, W. K., and James, P. H. R. (1971). *Animal memory*. New York: Academic.

Honmah, K., Goetz, C. v., and Aschoff, J. (1983). Effects of restricted daily feeding on freerunning circadian rhythms in rats. *Physiology and Behavior*, 30, 905–913.

Honzik, C. H. (1936). The sensory basis of maze learning in rats. *Comparative Psychology Monographs*, 13, 1–113.

Horter, M. (1977). Der Anwendungszeitraum als lernbare Grösse. *Zeitschrift für Tierpsychologie*, 45, 256–287.

Horton, J. C., and Hubel, D. H. (1981). A regular patchy distribution of cytochrome oxidase staining in primary visual cortex of the macaque monkey. *Nature*, 292, 762–764.

Hu, M. K. (1962) Visual pattern recognition by moment invariants. *IRE Transactions on Information Theory*, IT8, 179–187.

Hubel, D. H., and Wiesel, T. N. (1977). Functional architecture of macaque monkey visual cortex. *Proceedings of the Royal Society* (London). *Series B*, 198, 1–59.

Hubel, D. H., and Wiesel, T. N. (1978). Distribution of input from the two eyes to striate cortex in squirrel monkeys. *Society for Neuroscience Abstracts*, 4, 632.

Hubel, D. H., Wiesel, T. N., and Stryker, M. P. (1978). Anatomical demonstration of orientation columns in macaque monkey. *Journal of Comparative Neurology*, 177, 361–380.

Hubel, D. H., Wiesel, T. N., and Stryker, M. P. (1977). Orientation columns in macaque monkey visual cortex demonstrated by the 2–deoxyglucose autoradiographic technique. *Nature*, 269, 328–330.

Hull, C. L. (1943). *Principles of behavior.* New York: Appleton–Century–Crofts.

Hulse, S. H., and O'Leary, D. K. (1982). Serial pattern learning: Teaching an alphabet to rats. *Journal of Experimental Psychology: Animal Behavior Processes*, 8, 260–273.

Hunsicker, J. P., and Melgren, R. L. (1977). Multiple deficits in the retention of an appetitively motivated behavior across a 24–h period in rats. *Animal Learning and Behavior*, 5, 14–26.

Hurvich, L. M. (1981). *Color vision.* Sunderland, MA: Sinauer.

Hurvich, L. M., and Jameson, D. (1955). Some quantitative aspects of an opponent–colors theory. II. Brightness, saturation, and hue in normal and dichromatic vision. *Journal of the Optical Society of America*, 45, 602–616.

Hurvich, L. M., and Jameson, D. (1957). An opponent–process theory of color vision. *Psychological Review*, 64, 384–404.

Huston, J. P. (1982). Searching for the neural mechanism of reinforcement (of "stamping in"). In B. Hoebel and D. Novin (Eds.), *The neural basis of feeding and reward* Brunswik, ME: Haer Co.

Isenberg, L., Nissen, M. J., & Case, L. (MS). Attentional processing and the independence of color and orientation.

Jacklet, J. W. (1985). Neurobiology of circadian rhythm generators. *Trends in Neurosciences*, 8, 69–73.

Jacob, F., and Monod, J. (1961). On the regulation of gene activity. *Cold Spring Harbor Symposia on Quantitative Biology*, 26, 193–211.

Jameson, D. (1972). Theoretical issues of color vision. In D. Jameson and L. M. Hurvich (Eds.), *Handbook of sensory physiology, Vol. VII/4.1, Visual psychophysics* Berlin: Springer.

Jameson, D., and Hurvich, L. M. (1955). Some quantitative aspects of an opponent–colors theory. I. Chromatic responses and spectral saturation. *Journal of the Optical Society of America*, 45, 546–552.

Jameson, D., and Hurvich, L. M. (1959). Perceived color and its dependence on focal, surrounding, and preceding stimulus variables. *Journal of the Optical Society of America*, 49, 890–898.

Jameson, D., and Hurvich, L. M. (1964). Theory of brightness and color contrast in human vision. *Vision Research*, 4, 135–154.

Jander, R. (1957). Die optische Richtungsorientierung der roten Waldameise (*Formica rufa L.*). *Zeitschrift für vergleichende Physiologie*, 40, 162-238.

Janzen, D. H. (1971). Euglossine bees as long–distance pollinators of tropical plants. *Science*, 171, 203–205.

Jarrard, L. E. (1983). Selective hippocampal lesions and behavior: Effects of kianic acid lesions on performance of a place and cue task. *Behavioral Neuroscience*, 97, 873–889.

Jay, M. F., and Sparks, D. L. (1987). Sensorimotor integration in the primate superior colliculus. II. Coordinates of auditory signals. *Journal of Neurophysiology*, 57, 35–55.

John, R. E. (1967). *Mechanisms of memory*. New York: Academic.

Judson, H. (1980). *The eighth day of creation*. New York: Simon and Schuster.

Kamil, A. C. (1978). Systematic foraging by a nectar–feeding bird, the Amakihi (*Loxops virens*). *Journal of Compartive and Physiological Psychology*, 92, 388–396.

Kamin, L. J. (1967). "Attention–like" processes in classical conditioning. In M. R. Jones (Ed.), *Miami symposium on the prediction of behavior: Aversive stimulation* Miami: Univ. Miami Press.

Kamin, L. J. (1969). Predictability, surprise, attention, and conditioning. In B. A. Campbell and R. M. Church (Eds.), *Punishment and aversive behavior* (pp. 276–296). New York: Appleton–Century–Crofts.

Kamin, L. J., and Gaioni, S. J. (1974). Compound conditioned emotional response conditioning with differentially salient elements in rats. *Journal of Comparative and Physiological Psychology*, 87, 591–597.

Kaplan, P. (1984). Importance of relative temporal parameters in trace autoshaping: From excitation to inhibition. *Journal of Experimental Psychology: Animal Behavior Processes*, 10, 113–126.

Kaplan, P., and Hearst, E. (1985). Contextual control and excitatory vs inhibitory learning: Studies of extinction, reinstatement, and interference. In P. D. Balsam and A. Tomie (Eds.), *Context and learning* Hillsdale, NJ: Erlbaum.

Kaufman, E. L., Lord, M. W., Reese, T. W., and Volkman, J. (1949). The discrimination of visual number. *American Journal of Psychology*, 62, 498–525.

Kaufman, M. A., and Bolles, R. C. (1981). A nonassociative aspect of overshadowing. *Bulletin of the Psychonomic Society*, 18, 318–320.

Kavanau, J. L. (1969). Behavior of captive white–footed mice. In E. R. Williams and H. L. Raush (Eds.), *Naturalistic viewpoints in psychology* New York: Holt, Rinehart, Winston.

Keeton, W. T. (1974). The orientational and navigational basis of homing in birds. *Recent advances in the study of behavior* New York: Academic.

Keppel, G., and Underwood, B. J. (1962). Proactive inhibition in short–term retintion of single items. *Journal of Verbal Learning and Verbal Behavior*, 1, 153–161.

Killeen, P. (1975). On the temporal control of behavior. *Psychological Review*, 82, 89–115.

Kincaid, J. P., and Wickens, D. D. (1970). Temporal gradient of release from proactive inhibition. *Journal of Experimental Psychology*, 86, 313–316.

Kirchner, W. H., & Srinivasan, M. V. (1989). Freely flying honey bees use image motion to estimate object distance. *Die Naturwissenschaften*, 76, 281-282.

Klahr, D., and Wallace, J. G. (1973). The role of quantification operators in the development of conservation. *Cognitive Psychology*, 4, 301–327.

Kleber, E. (1935). Hat das Zeitgedächtnis der Bienen biologische Bedeutung? *Zeitschrift für vergleichende Physiologie*, 22, 221–262.

Klein, F. (1939). *Elementary mathematics from an advanced standpoint. II. Geometry.* New York: MacMillan.

Knudsen, E. I. (1982). Auditory and visual maps of space in the optic tectum of the owl. *Journal of Neuroscience*, 2, 1177–1194.

Knudsen, E. (1983). Early auditory experience aligns the auditory map of space in the optic tectum of the barn owl. *Science*, 222, 939–942.

Knudsen, E. I. (1984). Synthesis of a neural map of auditory space in the owl. In G. M. Edelman, W. E. Gall, and W. M. Cowan (Eds.), *Dynamic aspects of neocortical function* (pp. 375–396). New York: Wiley.

Knudsen, E. I., and Konishi, M. (1978). Space and frequency are represented separately in auditory midbrain of the owl. *Journal of Neurophysiology*, 41, 870–884.

Knudsen, E. I., and Konishi, M. (1979). Mechanisms of sound localization by the barn owl. *Journal of Comparative Physiology*, 133, 13–21.

Koehler, O. (1950). The ability of birds to "count". *Bulletin of Animal Behavior*, 9, 41–50.

Koffka, K. (1935). *Principles of gestalt psychology.* New York: Harcourt and Brace.

Köhler, W. (1920). *Die physichen Gestalten in Rohe und im stationären Zustand.* Vieweg: Braunschweig.

Köhler, W. (1925). *The mentality of apes.* New York: Harcourt, Brace.

Köhler, W., and Wallach, H. (1944). Figural after–effects. *Proceedings of the American Philosophical Society*, 88, 269–357.

Koltermann, R. (1971). 24–Std–Periodik in der Langzeiterrinerung an Duft– und Farbsignale bei der Honigbiene. *Zeitschrift für vergleichende Physiologie*, 75, 49–68.

Koltermann, R. (1974). Periodicity in the activty and learning performance of the honey bee. In L. B. Browne (Ed.), *The experimental analyisis of insect behavior* (pp. 218–226). Berlin: Springer.

Konishi, M. (1986). Centrally synthesized maps of sensory space. *Trends in Neurosciences*, 9, 163–168.

Konorski, J. (1948). *Conditioned reflexes and neuron organization.* Cambridge: Cambridge Univ. Press.

Kramer, G. (1951). Eine neue Methode zur Erforschung der Zugorientierung und die bisher damit erzielten Ergebnisse. *Proceedings of the 10th international congress on ornithology* (Upsala), pp. 269–280.

Kramer, G. (1952). Die Sonnenorientierung der Vögel. *Verhandlungen der deutschen zoologishen Gesellschaft Freiburg*, 72–84.

Kramer, G. (1961). Long distance orientation. In A. J. Marshall (Ed.), *Biology and comparative physiology of birds* (pp. 341–371). New York: Academic.

Kreithern, M. L., and Quine, D. B. (1979). Infrasound detection by the homing pigeon: A behavioral audiogram. *Journal of Comparative Physiology*, 129.

Kremer, E. F. (1978). The Rescorla–Wagner model: Losses in associative strength in compound conditioned stimuli. *Journal of Experimental Psychology: Animal Behavior Processes*, 4, 22–36.

Landau, B., and Gleitman, L. R. (1985). *Language and experience Evidence from the blind child*. Cambridge, MA: Harvard University Press.

Landau, B., Spelke, E., and Gleitman, H. (1984). Spatial knowledge in a young blind child. *Cognition*, 16, 225–260.

Lashley, K. S. (1950). In search of the engram. *Symposium of the society of experimental biology. No. 4* (pp. 454–482). Cambridge: Cambridge University Press.

Lea, S. E. G., and Dow, S. M. (1984). The integration of reinforcements over time. In J. Gibbon and L. Allan (Eds.), *Timing and time perception* (pp. 269–277). New York: Annals of the New York Academy of Sciences. [*Annals of the New York Academy of Sciences* Vol. 423]

Lee, C., Rohrer, W. H., and Sparks, D. L. (1988). Population coding of saccadic eye movements by neurons in the superior colliculus. *Nature*, 332, 357–360.

Lee, D. N., and Thompson, J. A. I. (1982). Vision in action: The control of locomotion. In D. Ingle, M. A. Goodale, and R. J. W. Mansfield (Eds.), *Analysis of visual behavior* (pp. 411–436). Cambridge, MA: MIT Press.

Lehmann, U. (1976). Short-term and circadian rhythms in the behaviour of the vole, *Microtus agrestis* (L.). *Oecologia*, 23, 185–199.

Levine, M. (1959). A model of hypothesis behavior in discrimination learning in rats. *Psychological Review*, 66, 353–366.

Levinthal, C. F., Tartell, R. H., Margolin, C. M., and Fishman, H. (1985). The CS–US interval (ISI) function in rabbit nictitating membrane response conditioning with very long intertrial intervals. *Animal Learning and Behavior*, 13, 228–232.

Levitt, T., Lawton, D., Chelberg, D., and Nelson, P. (1987). Qualitative landmark–based path planning and following. *Proceedings of the AAAI National Conference on Artificial Intelligence*, Seatle

Lieblich, I., and Arbib, M. A. (1982). Multiple representations of space underlying behavior. *Behavioral and Brain Sciences*, 5, 627–659.

Linblom, L. L., and Jenkins, H. M. (1981). Responses eliminated by noncontingent or negatively contingent reinforcement recover in extinction. *Journal of Experimental Psychology: Animal Behavior Processes*, 7, 175–190.

Livingston, M. S., and Hubel, D. H. (1984). Anatomy and physiology of a color system in the primate visual cortex. *Journal of Neuroscience*, 4, 309–356.

Lock, A., and Collett, T. (1979). A toad's devious approach to its prey: A study of some complex uses of depth vision. *Journal of Comparative Physiology*, 131, 178–189.

Loess, H., and Waugh, N. C. (1967). Short–term memory and intertrial interval. *Journal of Verbal Learning and Verbal Behavior*, 6, 455–460.

Logue, A. W. (1979). Taste aversion and the generality of the laws of learning. *Psychological Bulletin*, 86, 276–296.

Lohmann, M. (1967). Zur Bedeutung der lokomotorischen Aktivität in circadianen Systemen. *Zeitschrift für Vergleichende Physiologie*, 55, 307–332.

Lucas, D. (1983). Moment techniques in picture analysis. *Proceedings of the IEEE conference on computer vision and pattern recognition. June 19–23, Washington, D.C.* (pp. 178–187). Silver Springs, MD: IEEE Computer Society Press.

Mackintosh, N. J. (1974). *The psychology of animal learning.* New York: Academic Press.

Mackintosh, N. J. (1975). A theory of attention. *Psychological Review, 82*, 276–298.

Mackintosh, N. J. (1983). *Conditioning and associative learning.* New York: Oxford University Press.

Maki, W. S., Brokofsky, S., and Berg, B. (1979). Spatial memory in rats: Resistance to retroactive interference. *Animal Learning and Behavior, 7*, 25–30.

Mandler, G., and Shebo, B. J. (1982). Subitizing: An analysis of its component processes. *Journal of Experimental Psychology: General, 11*, 1–22.

Margules, J., and Gallistel, C. R. (1988). Heading in the rat: Determination by environmental shape. *Animal Learning and Behavior, 16*, 404–410.

Mariscal, R. N. (1972). The behavior of symbiotic fish and anemones. In H. E. Wynn and B. L. Olla (Eds.), *The behavior of marine animals* (pp. p. 335–366). New York: Plenum.

Marlow, R. W., & Tollestrup, K. (1982). Mining and exploitation of natural deposits by the desert tortoise, *Gopherus agassizii. Animal Behaviour, 30*, 475–478.

Marr, D. (1982). *Vision.* San Francisco: W. H. Freeman.

Martin, D. D., and Meier, A. H. (1973). Temporal synergism of corticosterone and prolactin in regulating orientation in the migratory White–throated Sparrow (*Zonotrichia albicollis*). *Condor, 75*, 369–374.

Matsuzawa, T. (1985). Use of numbers by a chimpanzee. *Nature, 315*, 57–59.

Matthews, G. V. T. (1962). The astronomical basis of 'nonsense' orientation. *Proceedings of the Thirteenth International Ornithological Congress* (pp. 415–429).

Matthews, G. V. T. (1968). *Bird navigation* (2 ed.). Cambridge, England: Cambridge University Press.

Matzel, L. D., Held, F. P., and Miller, R. R. (1988). Information and expression of simultaneous and backward associations: Implications for contiguity theory. *Learning and Motivation, 19*, 317–344.

Matzel, L. D., Schachtman, T. R., and Miller, R. R. (1985). Recovery of overshadowed association achieved by extinction of the overshadowing stimulus. *Learning and Motivation, 16*, 398–412.

Matzel, L. D., Shuster, K., and Miller, R. R. (1987). Covariation in conditioned response strength between stimuli trained in compound. *Animal Learning and Behavior, 15*, 439–447.

Mays, L. E., and Sparks, D. L. (1980). Dissociation of visual and saccade–related responses in superior colliculus neurons. *Journal of Neurophysiology, 43*, 207–232.

Mazur, J. E., and Logue, A. W. (1978). Choice in a "self–control" paradigm: Effects of a fading procedure. *Journal of the Experimental Analysis of Behavior, 30*, 11–17.

McFarland, D. J. (1977). Decision making by animals. *Nature, 269*, 15–21.

Mechner, F. (1958). Probability relations within response sequences under ratio reinforcement. *Journal of the Experimental Analysis of Behavior, 1*, 109–122.

Mechner, F., and Guevrekian, L. (1962). Effects of deprivation upon counting and timing in rats. *Journal of the Experimental Analysis of Behavior*, 5, 463–466.

Meck, W. H. (1983). Selective adjustment of the speed of an internal clock and memory processes. *Journal of Experimental Psychology: Animal Behavior Processes*, 9, 171–201.

Meck, W. H., and Church, R. M. (1983). A mode control model of counting and timing processes. *Journal of Experimental Psychology: Animal Behavior Processes*, 9, 320–334.

Meck, W. H., and Church, R. M. (1984). Simultaneous temporal processing. *Journal of Experimental Psychology: Animal Behavior Processes*, 10, 1–29.

Meck, W. H., Church, R. M., and Gibbon, J. (1985). Temporal integration in duration and number discrimination. *Journal of Experimental Psychology: Animal Behavior Processes*, 11, 591–597.

Meck, W. H., Komeily–Zadeh, F. N., and Church, R. M. (1984). Two–step acquisition: Modification of an internal clock's criterion. *Journal of Experimental Psychology: Animal Behavior Processes*, 10, 297–306.

Medugorac, I., and Lindauer, M. (1967). Das Zeitgedächtnis der Bienen unter dem Einfluss von Narkose und sozialen Zeitgeber. *Zeitschrift für vergleichende Physiologie*, 55, 450–474.

Menzel, E. (1973). Chimpanzee spatial memory organization. *Science*, 182, 943–945.

Miller, R. R., and Spear, N. E. (1985). *Information processing in animals: Conditioned inhibition*. Hillsdale, N.J.: Erlbaum.

Mis, F. W., Andrews, J. G., and Salafia, W. R. (1970). Conditioning of the rabbit nictitating membrane response: ISI x ITI interaction. *Psychonomic Science*, 20, 57–58.

Mittelstaedt, H. (1962). Control systems of orientation in insects. *Annual Review of Entomology*, 7, 177–198.

Mittelstaedt, M. L., and Mittelstaedt, H. (1980). Homing by path integration in a mammal. *Naturwissenschaften*, 67, 566–567.

Modenov, P. S., and Parkhomenko, A. S. (1965). *Geometric transformations*. New York: Academic.

Moiseff, A., and Konishi, M. (1981). Neuronal and behavioral sensitivity to binaural time differences in the owl. *Journal of Neuroscience*, 1, 40–48.

Morris, R. G. M. (1981). Spatial localization does not require the presence of local cues. *Learning and Motivation*, 12, 239–260.

Mountcastle, V. B. (1978). An organizing principle for cerebral function. In G. M. Edelman and V. B. Mountcastle (Eds.), *The mindful brain* Cambridge, MA: MIT Press.

Müller, H. G. (1966). Homing and distance orientation in bats. *Zeitschrift für Tierpsychologie*, 23, 403–421.

Muller, R. A., Kubie, J. L., & Ranck, J. B. J. (1987). Spatial firing patterns of hippocampal complex-spike cells in a fixed environment. *Journal of Neuroscience*, 7, 1935-1950.

Munn, N. L. (1950). *Handbook of psychological research on the rat*. Boston: Houghton Mifflin.

Myers, C. W., and Daly, J. W. (1983). Dart–poison frogs. *Scientific American*, 249(2), 120–133.

Myerson, J., and Miezin, F. M. (1980). The kinetics of choice: An operant systems analysis. *Psychological Review*, 87, 160–174.

Neuringer, A. J. (1967). Effects of reinforcement magnitude on choice and rate of responding. *Journal of the Experimental Analysis of Behavior*, 10, 417–424.

Neuweiler, G., and Möhres, F. P. (1967). Die Rolle des Ortgedächtnisses bei der Orientierung der Grossblatt–Fledermaus *Megaderma lyra*. *Zeitschrift für vergleichende Physiologie*, 57, 147–171.

Nissen, M. J. (1985). Accessing features and objects: Is location special? In M. I. Posner and O. S. Marin (Eds.), *Attention and performance XI* (pp. 205–219). Hillsdale, NJ: Erlbaum.

Noyd, D. E. (1965). Proactive and intra–stimulus interference in short–term memory for two–, three–, and five–word stimuli. Paper presented at meeting of the Western Psychological Association, Honolulu, June.

O'Gorman, L., and Sanderson, A. C. (1984). The converging squares algorithm: An efficient method for locating peaks in multidimensions. *IEEE Transactions on Pattern Analysis and Machine Intelligence*, 6(3), 280–287.

O'Keefe, J., and Nadel, L. (1978). *The hippocampus as a cognitive map*. Oxford: Oxford University Press.

Ollove, M. (1980). *Anticipatory thermoregulation in the rat*. Ph.D. Thesis, University of Pennsylvania.

Olton, D. S., Becker, J. T., and Handelmann, G. E. (1979). Hippocampus, space, and memory. *Behavioral and Brain Sciences*, 2, 313–365.

Olton, D. S., and Collison, C. (1979). Intramaze cues and "odor trails" fail to direct choice behavior on an elevated maze. *Animal Learning and Behavior*, 7, 221–223.

Olton, D. S., Collison, C., and Werz, M. A. (1977). Spatial memory and radial arm maze performance in rats. *Learning and Motivation*, 8, 289–314.

Olton, D. S., and Feustle, W. A. (1981). Hippocampal function required for nonspatial working memory. *Experimental Brain Research*, 41, 380–389.

Olton, D. S., and Papas, B. C. (1979). Spatial memory and hippocampal function. *Neuropsychologia*, 17, 669–682.

Olton, D. S., and Samuelson, R. J. (1976). Remembrance of places passed: Spatial memory in rats. *Journal of Experimental Psychology: Animal Behavior Processes*, 2, 97–116.

Olton, D. S., Walker, J. A., Gage, F. H., and Johnson, C. (1977). Choice behavior of rats searching for food. *Learning and Motivation*, 8, 315–331.

Ornstein, R. E. (1969). *On the experience of time*. New York: Penguin.

Papi, F. (1982). Olfaction and homing in pigeons: Ten years of experiments. In F. Papi and H. G. Walraff (Eds.), *Avian navigation* (pp. 149–159). New York: Springer.

Papi, F., and Walraff, H. G. (1982). *Avian navigation*. New York: Springer.

Pashler, H. (1987). Detecting conjunctions of color and form: Reassessing the serial search hypothesis. *Perception and Psychophysics*, 41, 191–201.

Pavlov, I. (1928). *Lectures on conditioned reflexes: the higher nervous activity of animals*. London: Lawrence and Wishart.

Peterson, L. R., and Peterson, M. J. (1959). Short term retention of individual verbal items. *Journal of Experimental Psychology*, 58, 193–198.

Pittendrigh, C. S. (1980). Some functional aspects of circadian pacemakers. In M. Suda, O. Hayaishi, & H. Nakagawa (Ed.), *Biological rhythms and their central mechanism* (pp. 3-12). New York: Elsevier.

Platt, J. R., and Johnson, D. M. (1971). Localization of position within a homogeneous behavior chain: Effects of error contingencies. *Learning and Motivation*, 2, 386–414.

Pliskoff, S. S. (1971). Effects of symmetrical and asymmetrical changeover delays on concurrent performances. *Journal of the Experimental Analysis of Behavior*, 16, 249–256.

Poucet, B., Thinus–Blanc, C., and Chapuis, N. (1983). Route planning in cats in relation to the visibility of the goal. *Animal Behaviour*, 31, 594–599.

Pratt, K. (1974). Correlation techniques of image registration. *IEEE Transaction on Aerospace and Electronic Systems*, 10(3), 353–358.

Precht, W. (1978). *Neuronal operations in the vestibular system*. New York: Springer.

Quine, D. B., and Kreithen, M. L. (1981). Frequency shift discrimintation: Can homing pigoens locate infrasounds by Doppler shifts? *Journal of Comparative Physiology*, 141, 153–???

Quinn, T. P. (1982). Evidence for celestial and magnetic compass orientation in lake migratory sockeye salmon fry. *Journal of Comparative Physiology*, 137, 243.

Rachlin, H., and Green, L. (1972). Commitment, choice and self–control. *Journal of the Experimental Analysis of Behavior*, 17, 15–22.

Ranck, J. B. J. (1984). Head direction cells in the deep layer of dorsal presubiculum in freely moving rats. *Society of Neuroscience Abstracts*, 10(1), 599.

Redmond, D. P., Sing, H. C., and Hegge, F. W. (1982). Biological time series analysis using complex demodulation. In F. W. Brown and R. C. Graeber (Eds.), *Rhythmic aspects of behavior* Hillsdale, NJ: Erlbaum.

Reiss, S., and Wagner, A. R. (1972). CS habituation produces a "latent inhibition effect" but no active "conditioned inhibition". *Learning and Motivation*, 3, 237–245.

Renner, M. (1959). Über ein weiteres Versetzungs–Experiment zur Analyse des Zeitsinns und der Sonnenorientierung der Honigbiene. *Zeitschrift für vergleichende Physiologie*, 42, 449–483.

Renner, M. (1960). Contribution of the honey bee to the study of time sense and astronomical orientation. *Cold Spring Harbor Symposium on Quantiative Biology*, 25, 361–367.

Rescorla, R. A. (1967). Pavlovian conditioning and its proper control procedures. *Psychological Review*, 74, 71–80.

Rescorla, R. A. (1968). Probability of shock in the presence and absence of CS in fear conditioning. *Journal of Comparative and Physiological Psychology*, 66, 1–5.

Rescorla, R. A. (1972). Informational variables in Pavlovian conditioning. In G. H. Bower (Ed.), *The psychology of learning and motivation* (pp. 1–46). New York: Academic.

Rescorla, R. A. (1979). Conditioned inhibition and extinction. In A. Dickenson and R. A. Boakes (Eds.), *Mechanisms of learning and motivation* Hillsdale, NJ.: Erlbaum.

Rescorla, R. A. (1980). Simultaneous and successive associations in sensory preconditioning. *Journal of Experimental Psychology: Animal Behavior Processes*, 6, 207–216.

Rescorla, R. A. (1984). Signaling intertrial shocks attenuates their negative effect on conditioned suppression. *Bulletin of the Psychonomic Society*, 22, 225–228.

Rescorla, R. A. (1987). *Presidential Address to the Eastern Psychological Association, Baltimore*, April 10.

Rescorla, R. A. (1988). Behavioral studies of Pavlovian conditioning. *Annual Review of Neuroscience*, 11, 329–352.

Rescorla, R. A., and Cunningham, C. L. (1978). Within–compound flavor association. *Journal of Experimental Psychology: Animal Behavior Processes*, 4, 267–275.

Rescorla, R. A., and Furrow, D. R. (1977). Stimulus similarity as a determinant of Pavlovian conditioning. *Journal of Experimental Psychology: Animal Behavior Processes*, 3, 203–215.

Rescorla, R. A., and Heth, C. D. (1975). Reinstatement of fear to an extinguished conditioned stimulus. *Journal of Experimental Psychology: Animal Behavior Processes*, 104, 88–106.

Rescorla, R. A., and Skucy, J. C. (1969). Effect of response–independent reinforcers during extinction. *Journal of Comparative and Physiological Psychology*, 67, 381–389.

Rescorla, R. A., and Wagner, A. R. (1972). A theory of Pavlovian conditioning: Variations in the effectiveness of reinforcement and nonreinforcement. In A. H. Black and W. F. Prokasy (Eds.), *Classical conditioning II* New York: Appleton–Century–Crofts.

Revusky, S., and Garcia, J. (1970). Learned associations over long delays. In G. H. Bower and J. T. Spence (Eds.), *The psychology of learning and motivation* (pp. 1–89) New York: Academic.

Reynolds, G. S. (1961). Attention in the pigeon. *Journal of the Experimental Analysis of Behavior*, 4, 203–208.

Richelle, M., and Lejeune, H. (1984). Timing competence and timing performance: A cross–species approach. In J. Gibbon and L. Allan (Eds.), *Timing and time perception* (pp. 254–268). New York: New York Academy of Sciences. [*Annals of the New York Academy of Sciences* Vol. 423]

Richter, C. P. (1922). A behavioristic study of the activity of the rat. *Comparative Psychology Monographs*, 1.

Rijnstrop, A., Daan, S., and Dijkstra, C. (1981). Hunting in the kestrel, *Falco tinnunculus*, and the adaptive significance of daily habits. *Oecologia*, 50, 391–406.

Rilling, M. (1967). Number of responses as a stimulus in fixed interval and fixed ratio schedules. *Journal of Comparative and Physiological Psychology*, 63, 60–65.

Rilling, M., and McDiarmid, C. (1965). Signal detection in fixed ratio schedules. *Science*, 148, 526–527.

Ritchie, B. F. (1947). Studies in spatial learning III. Two paths to the same location and two paths to two different locations. *Journal of Experimental Psychology*, 37, 25–38.

Roberts, A., and Roberts, B. (1983). *Neural origin of rhythmic movements*. Cambridge: Cambridge University Press.

Roberts, S., and Church, R. M. (1978). Control of an internal clock. *Journal of Experimental Psychology: Animal Behavior Processes*, 4, 318–337.

Roberts, S. K. (1965). Photoreception and entrainment of cockroach activity rhythms. *Science*, 148, 958–960.

Roberts, W. A. (1979). Spatial memory in the rat on a hierarchical maze. *Learning and Motivation*, 10, 117–140.

Roberts, W. A. (1984). Some issues in animal spatial memory. In H. L. Roitblat, T. G. Bever, and H. S. Terrace (Eds.), *Animal cognition* (pp. 425–444). Hillsdale, NJ: Erlbaum.

Robinson, D. A. (1972). Eye movements evoked by collicular stimulation in the alert monkey. *Vision Research*, 12, 1795–1808.

Rompré, P. P., and Miliaressis, E. (1985). Pontine and mesencephalic substrates of self–stimulation. *Brain Research*, 359, 246–259.

Rongstad, O. J., and Tester, J. R. (1971). Behavior and maternal relations of young snowshoe hares. *Journal of Wildlife Management*, 35, 338–346.

Rosenquist, A. C. (1985). Connections of visual cortex areas in the cat. In A. Peters and A. G. Jones (Eds.), *Cerebral cortex. Vol 3. Visual cortex* (pp. 81–118). New York: Plenum.

Rosenwasser, A. M., Pelchat, R. J., and Adler, N. T. (1984). Memory for feeding time: Possible dependence on coupled circadian oscillators. *Physiology and Behavior*, 32, 25–30.

Rozin, P., and Kalat, J. W. (1971). Specific hungers and poison avoidance as adaptive specializations of learning. *Psychological Review*, 78, 459–486.

Rumbaugh, D. M., Savage–Rumbaugh, S., and Hegel, M. T. (1987). Summation in the chimpanzee *(Pan troglodytes)*. *Journal of Experimental Psychology: Animal Behavior Processes*, 13, 107–115.

Rumelhart, D. E., and McClelland, J. L. (1986). *Parallel distributed processing*. Cambridge, MA: MIT Press.

Russell, W. R. (1959). *Brain, memory, learning: A neurologist's view*. Oxford: Oxford University Press.

Saint Paul, U. v. (1982). Do geese use path integration for walking home? In F. Papi and H. G. Wallraff (Eds.), *Avian navigation* (pp. 298–307). New York: Springer.

Santchi, F. (1913). Comment s'orient les fourmis. *Revue Suisse de Zoologie*, 21, 347–426.

Scharlock, D. P. (1955). The role of extramaze cues in place and response learning. *Journal of Experimental Psychology*, 50, 249–254.

Schiller, P. H., and Stryker, M. (1972). Single–unit recording and stimulation in superior colliculus of the alert rhesus monkey. *Journal of Neurophysiology*, 35, 915–924.

Schlichte, H. J., and Schmidt–Koenig, K. (1971). Zum Heimfindevermögen der Brieftaube bei erschwerter optische Wahrnehmung. *Die Naturwissenschaften*, 58, 329–330.

Schmidt–Koenig, K. (1972). New experiments on the effect of clock shifts on homing in pigeons. *NASA special publication: SP–262* (pp. 275–282.). Washington, DC: NASA.

Schmidt–Koenig, K., and Schlichte, H. J. (1972). Homing in pigeons with impaired vision. *Proceedings of the National Academy of Sciences*, 69, 2446–2447.

Schmidt–Koenig, K., and Walcott, C. (1973). Flugwege und Verblieb von Brieftauben mit gertrübten Haftschalen. *Die Naturwissenschaften*, 60, 108–109.

Schneiderman, N., and Gormezano, I. (1964). Conditioning of the nictitating membrane of the rabbit as a function of CS–US interval. *Journal of Comparative and Physiological Psychology*, 57, 188–195.

Schwartz, B. (1984). *Psychology of learning and behavior* (2 ed.). New York: Norton.

Seligman, M. E. P., and Hager, J. L. (1972). *Biological boundaries of learning.* New York: Appleton–Century–Crofts.

Shepard, R. N. (1975). Form, formation and transformation of internal representations. In R. Solso (Ed.), *Information processing and cognition: The Loyola Symposium* Hillsdale, NJ: Lawrence Erlbaum.

Sherry, D. (1984). Food storage by black–capped chickadees: Memory for location and contents of caches. *Animal Behaviour*, 32, 451–464.

Shizgal, P., Bielajew, C., and Rompré, P.–P. (1988). Quantitative characteristics of the directly stimulated neurons subserving self–stimulation of the medial forebrain bundle: Psychophysical inference and electrophysiological measurement. In M. L. Commons, R. M. Church, J. R. Stellar, and A. R. Wagner (Eds.), *Quantitative analyses of behavior: Biological determinants of reinforcement* (pp. 59–88). Hillsdale, NJ: Erlbaum.

Sibly, R. M., and McCleery, R. H.(1983). The distribution between feeding sites of Herring Gulls breeding at Walney Island, UK. *Journal of animal Ecology*, 52, 51–68.

Sing, H. C., Thorne, D. R., and Hegge, F. W. (1985). Trend and rhythm analysis of time–series data using complex demodulation. *Behavior Research Methods, Instruments, and Computers*, 17, 623 629.

Skinner, B. F. (1981). Selection by consequences. *Science*, 213, 501–504

Slocum, J. (1900). *Sailing alone around the world*. New York: Century.

Smith, J. N. M., and Dawkins, R. (1971). The hunting behavior of individual Great Tits in relation to spatial variations in their food density. *Animal Behaviour*, 19, 695–706.

Smolensky, P. (1986). Information processing in dynamical systems: Foundations of harmony theory. In D. E. Rumelhart and J. L. McClelland (Eds.), *Parallel distributed processing: Vol. 1. Foundations* (pp. 194–281). Cambridge, MA: MIT Press.

Snyder, C. R. R. (1972). Selection, inspection, and naming in visual search. *Journal of Experimental Psychology*, 92, 428–431.

Sobel, E. (1989). *Characteristics of the mechanim that computes distance from motion parallax in the locust*. Ph.D. Thesis, University of Pennsylvania.

Sparks, D. L., Holland, R., and Guthrie, B. L. (1976). Size and distribution of movement fields in the monkey superior colliculus. *Brain Research*, 113, 21–34

Sparks, D. L., and Nelson, J. S. (1987). Sensory and motor maps in the mammalian superior colliculus. *Trends in Neuroscience*, 10, 312–317.

Sparks, D. L., and Porter, J. D. (1983). Spatial localization of saccade targets. II. Activity of superior colliculus neurons preceding compensatory saccades. *Journal of Neurophysiology*, 49, 64–74.

Squire, L. R., and Schlapfer, W. T. (1981). Memory and memory disorders: A biological and neurological perspective. In H. M. Van Prag, M. H. Lader, O. J. Rafaelsen, E. J. Sachar (Eds.), *Handbook of Biological Psychiatry. Part IV. Brain Mechanisms and Abnormal Behavior—Chemistry* (pp. 309–341). New York: Marcel Dekker.

Srinivasan, M. V., Lehrer, M., Zhang, S. W., & Horridge, G. A. (1989). How honey bees measure their distance from objects of unknown size. *Journal of Comparative Physiology. A.*, 165, 605-613.

Staddon, J. E. R. (1977). On Herrnstein's equations and related forms. *Journal of the Experimental Analysis of Behavior*, 28, 163–170.

Starkey, P., and Cooper, R. G. (1980). Perception of numbers by human infants. *Science*, 210, 1033–1035.

Starkey, P., Spelke, E. S., and Gelman, R. (1983). Detection of intermodal numerical correspondences by human infants. *Science*, 222, 179–181.

Stein, H. v. (1951). Untersuchungen über den Zeitsinn bei Vögeln. *Zeitschrift für vergleichende Physiologie*, 33, 387–403.

Stein–Beling, I. v. (1935). Über das Zeitgedächtnis bei Tieren. *Biological Reviews*, 10, 18–41.

Stellar, J. R., and Corbett, D. (in press). Regional neuroleptic microinjections indicate a role for nucleus accumbens in lateral hypothalamic self–stimulation reward. *Brain Research*.

Stewart, K., Rosenwasser, A. M., and Adler, N. T. (1985). Interactions between nocturnal feeding and wheel running patterns in the rat. *Physiology and Behavior*, 34, 601–608.

Stoltz, S. P., and Lott, D. F. (1964). Establishment in rats of a persistent response producing net loss of reinforcement. *Journal of Comparative and Physiological Psychology*, 57, 147–149.

Suga, N. (1977). Amplitude-spectrum representation in the Doppler-shifted-CF processing area of the auditory cortex of the mustache bat. *Science*, 196, 64–67.

Suga, N. (1982). Functional organization of the auditory cortex. In C. N. Woolsey (ed.), *Cortical sensory organization: Multiple auditory areas* (pp. 157–271). Clifton, NJ: Humana Press.

Sutherland, N. S., and Mackintosh, N. J. (1971). *Mechanisms of animal discrimination learning*. New York: Academic.

Suzuki, S., Augerinos, G., and Black, A. H. (1980). Stimulus control of spatial behavior on the eight–arm maze in rats. *Learning and Motivation*, 11, 1–18.

Szymanski, J. S. (1920). Activität und Ruhe bei Tieren und Menschen. *Zeitschrift der allgemeinen Physiologie*, 18, 105–162.

Terman, M., Gibbon, J., Fairhurst, S., and Waring, A. (1984). Daily meal anticipation: Interaction of circadian and interval timing. In J. Gibbon and L. Allan (Eds.), *Timing and time perception* (pp. 470–487). New York: New York Academy of Sciences.[*Annals of the New York Academy of Sciences* Vol. 423]

Thompson, R. F. (1988). The neural basis of basic associative learning of discrete behavioral responses. *Trends in Neurosciences*, 11, 152–155.

Thorpe, W. H. (1950). A note on detour behaviour with *Ammophil pubescens* Curt. *Behaviour*, 2, 257–264.

Tigges, J., Tigges, M., and Perachio, A. A. (1977). Complementary laminar terminations of afferents to area 17 originating in areas 18 and in the lateral geniculate nucleus in squirrel monkeys. *Journal of Comparative Neurology*, 176, 87–100.

Tinbergen, N., and Kruyt, W. (1938). Über die Orientierung des Bienenwolfes (*philanthus triangulum* Fabr.). III. Die Bevorzugung bestimmter Wegmarken. *Zeitschrift für vergleichende Physiologie*, 25, 292–334.

Tinkelpaugh, O. L. (1932). Multiple delayed reaction with chimpanzee and monkeys. *Journal of Comparative Psychology*, 13, 207–243.

Tolman, E. C. (1948). Cognitive maps in rats and men. *Psychological Review*, 55, 189–208.

Tolman, E. C., Ritchie, B. F., and Kalish, D. (1946a). Studies in spatial learning. I. Orientation and the short–cut. *Journal of Experimental Psychology*, 36, 13–24.

Tolman, E. C., Ritchie, B. F., and Kalish, D. (1946b). Studies in spatial learning. II. Place learning versus response learning. *Journal of Experimental Psychology*, 36, 221–229.

Tolman, E. C., Ritchie, B. F., and Kalish, D. (1947). Studies in spatial learning. V. Response learning vs. place learnng by the non–correction method. *Journal of Experimental Psychology*, 37, 285–292.

Tomback, D. F. (1978). Foraging strategies of Clark's nutcrackers. *Living Bird*, 16, 123–161.

Townsend, J. T., and Ashby, G. (1983). *Stochastic modeling of elementary psychological processes*. Cambridge: Cambridge University Press.

Treisman, A. (1986a). Features and objects in visual processing. *Scientific American*, 256(5), 114B–125.

Treisman, A. (1986b). Properties, parts, and objects. In K. R. Boff, L. Kaufman, and J. P. Thomas (Eds.), *Handbook of perception and human peformance. Vol II* (Chap. 35). New York: Wiley.

Treisman, A., and Gelade, G. (1980). A feature integration theory of attention. *Cognitive Psychology*, 12, 97–136.

Treisman, A., Sykes, M., and Gelade, G. (1977). Selective attention and stimulus integration. In S. Dornic (Ed.), *Attention and performance VI* (pp. 333–361). Hillsdale, NJ: Erlbaum.

Tsal, Y., and Lavie, N. (1988). Attending to color and shape: The special role of location in selective visual processing. *Perception and Psychophysics*, 44, 15–21.

Tulving, E. (1972). Episodic and semantic memory. In E. Tulving and W. Donaldson (Eds.), *Organization of memory* (pp. 381–403). New York: Academic.

Turek, F. W. (1985). Circadian neural rhythms in mammals. *Annual Review of Physiology*, 47, 49–64.

Underwood, B. J. (1957). Interference and forgetting. *Psychological Review*, 64, 49–60.

Uster, H. J., Bättig, K., and Nägeli, H. H. (1976). Effects of maze geometry and experience on exploratory behavior in the rat. *Animal Learning and Behavior*, 4, 84–88.

Van Essen, D. C. (1985). Functional organization of primate visual cortex. In A. Peters and A. G. Jones (Eds.), *Cerebral cortex. Vol. 3. Visual cortex* (pp. 259–329). New York: Plenum.

Vander Wall, S. B. (1982). An experimental analysis of seed recovery in Clark's nutcracker. *Animal Behaviour*, 30, 84–94.

Vander Wall, S. B., and Balda, R. P. (1977). Coadaptations of the Clark's nutcracker and the piñon pine for efficient seed harvest and dispersal. *Ecological Monographs*, 47, 89–111.

Vander Wall, S. B., and Balda, R. P. (1981). Ecoloy and evolution of food–storage behavior in conifer–seed–caching corvids. *Zeitschrift für Tierpsychologie*, 56, 217–242.

Varner, D., Jameson, D., and Hurvich, L. M. (1984). Temporal sensitivities related to color theory. *Journal of the Optical Society of America. A.*, 1, 474–481.

Vautin, R. G., and Dow, B. M. (1985). Color cell groups in foveal striate cortex of the behaving macaque. *Journal of Neurophysiology*, 54, 273–292.

Von Frisch, K. (1919). Über den Geruchssinn der Bienen und seine blütenbiologische Bedeutung. *Zoologisches Jahresbuch: Abteilung für allgemeine Zoologie und Physiologie*, 37, 1–238.

Von Frisch, K., and Lindauer, M. (1954). Himmel und Erde in Konkurrenz bei der Orientierung der Bienen. *Die Naturwissenschaften*, 41, 245–253.

Von Frisch, K., Lindauer, M., and Schmiedler. (1960). Wie erkennt die Biene den Sonnenstand bei geschlossener Wolkendecke? *Naturwissenschäftliche Rundschau*, 13, 169–172.

Wagner, A. R. (1981). SOP: A model of automatic memory processing in animal behavior. In N. E. Spear and R. R. Miller (Eds.), *Information processing in animals: Memory mechanisms* (pp. 5–47). Hillsdale, NJ: Erlbaum.

Wagner, A. R., Logan, F. A., Haberlandt, K., and Price, T. (1968). Stimulus selection in animal discrimination learning. *Journal of Experimental Psychology*, 76, 171–180.

Wahl, O. (1932). Neue Untersuchungen über das Zeitgedächtnis der Bienen. *Zeitschrift für vergleichende Physiologie*, 16, 529–589.

Wahl, O. (1933). Beitrag zur Frage der biologischen Bedeutung des Zeitgedächtnisses der Bienen. *Zeitschrift für vergleichende Physiologie*, 18, 709–717.

Wallace, G. K. (1959). Visual scanning in the desert locust *Schistocera gregaria* Foskål. *Journal of Experimental Biology*, 36, 512–525.

Walraff, H. G. (1983). Relevance of atmoshperic odours and geomagnetic field to pigeon navigation: What is the 'map' basis? *Comparative Biochemistry and Physiology*, 76A, 643–663.

Walters, E. T., and Byrne, J. H. (1983). Associative conditioning of single sensory neurons suggests a cellular mechanism for learning. *Science*, 219, 405–408.

Wansley, R. A., and Holloway, F. A. (1975). Multiple retention deficits following one–trial appetitive training. *Behavioral Biology*, 14, 135–149.

Waraczynski, M. A. (1988). Basal forebrain knife cuts and medial forebrain bundle self–stimulation. *Brain Research*, 438, 8–22.

Waraczynski, M., Stellar, J. R., and Gallistel, C. R. (1987). Reward saturation in medial forebrain bundle self–stimulation. *Physiology and Behavior*, 41, 585–593.

Wasserman, E. (1981). Response evocation in autoshaping: Contributions of cognitive and comparative–evolutionary analyses to an understanding of directed action. In C. M. Locurto, H. S. Terrace, and J. Gibbon (Eds.), *Autoshaping and conditioning theory* (pp. 21–54). New York: Academic.

Watson, A. B., and Robson, J. G. (1981). Discrimination at threshold: Labelled detectors in human vision. *Vision Research*, 21, 1115–1122.

Watson, J. B. (1907). Kinaesthetic and organic sensations: Their role in the reactions of the white rat. *Psychological Review, 8, Monograph Supplement* (100 pages).

Waugh, N. C., and Norman, D. A. (1965). Primary memory. *Psychological Review*, 72, 89–104.

Webb, W. B., and Dube, M. G. (1981). Temporal characteristics of sleep. In J. Aschoff (Ed.), *Biological rhythms* (pp. 499–517). New York: Plenum.

Wehner, R. (1981). Spatial vision in arthropods. In H. Autrum (Ed.), *Comparative physiology and evolution of vision in invertebrates* (pp. 287–617). New York: Springer.

Wehner, R., and Flatt, I. (1972). The visual orientation of desert ants, *Cataglyphis bicolor*, by means of territorial cues. In R. Wehner (Ed.), *Information processing in the visual system of arthropods* (pp. 295–302). New York: Springer.

Wehner, R., and Srinivasan, M. V. (1981). Searching behavior of desert ants, genus *Cataglyphis* (*Formicidae*, Hymenoptera). *Journal of Comparative Physiology*, 142, 315 338.

Whitty, C. W. M., and Zangwill, O. L. (1977). *Amnesia: Clinical, psychological and medicolegal aspects* (2nd ed.). Boston: Butterworths

Wickens, D. D. (1972). Characteristics of word encoding. In A. W. Melton and E. Martin (Eds.), *Coding processes in human memory* (pp. 191–215). Washington, D.C.: Winston.

Yanovski, J. A., Adler, N. T., and Gallistel, C. R. (1986). Does the perception of reward magnitude of self–administered electrical brain stimulation have a circadian rhythm? *Behavioral Neuroscience*, 100, 888–893.

Yarnell, P. R., and Lynch, S. (1973). The 'ding': Amnestic states in football trauma. *Neurology*, 23, 196–197.

Yeomans, J. S. (1988). Mechanisms of brain stimulation reward. In A. E. Epstein and A. R. Morrison (Eds.), *Progress in psychobiology and physiological psychology Vol. 13* (pp. 227–266). New York: Academic.

Yeomans, J. S., Kofman, O., and McFarlane, V. (1988). Cholinergic involvement in hypothalamic and midbrain rewarding brain stimulation. In M. L. Commons, R. M. Church, J. R. Stellar, and A. R. Wagner (Eds.), *Quantitative analyses of behavior: Biological determinants of reinforcement* (pp. 87–102). Hillsdale, NJ: Erlbaum.

Yerkes, R. M., and Yerkes, D. N. (1928). Concerning memory in the chimpanzee. *Journal of Comparative Psychology*, 8, 237–271.

Yonas, A., & Pick, H. L. (1975). An approach to the study of infant space perception. In L. B. Cohen, & P. Salapatek (Ed.), *Infant perception: From sensation to cognition, vol. 2, Perception of space, speech and sound.* (pp. 3-31). New York: Academic.

Zahn, J. R., Abel, L. A., and Dell'Osso, L. F. (1978). Audio–ocular response characteristics. *Sensory Processes*, 2, 32–37.

Zeki, S. (1976). The functional organization of projections from striate to prestriate visual cortex in the rhesus monkey. *Cold Spring Harbor Symposium on Quantitative Biology*, 15, 591–600.

Zoladek, L., and Roberts, W. A. (1978). The sensory basis of spatial memory in the rat. *Animal Learning and Motivation*, 6, 77–81.

Author Index

Abel, L.A., 484
Abrams, T.W., 401, 567
Absher, R.A., 567, 570
Adams, J.A., 222
Adler, N.T., 261, 263, 268, 269, 272, 273, 577
Ainslie, G.W., 291
Albert, M., 329
Alkon, D.L., 401
Allan, L., 240
Anderson, J.R., 386
Andrews, J.G., 399
Arbib, M.A., 135, 140, 174
Armstrong, S., 261, 268
Aronson, L.R., 141, 143
Aschoff, J., 222, 229, 230, 261, 266, 267, 272, 275, 276, 277, 279, 283
Ashby, G., 531, 534
Atkinson, R.C., 545
Augerinos, G., 162, 183

Balda, R.P., 155, 156
Baldock, M.D., 400, 401, 427, 428, 443, 446
Ballard, D.H., 502
Balsam, P., 294, 390, 422, 438, 443, 446, 570
Barbizet, J., 550, 551
Bardach, J.E., 142
Bartholic, J.F., 209
Batschelet, E., 274
Bättig, K., 162, 163
Baum, W.M., 359, 360
Beatty, W.W., 160, 162
Becker, J.T., 196, 217
Beling, I., 243, 253
Benson, D.F., 553
Berg, B., 160
Berntson, G.G., 349
Beusekom, G.V., 129, 158

Bielajew, C., 578, 579
Bitterman, M.E., 351, 352, 564
Bjork, R.A., 549
Black, A.H., 162, 183
Blakemore, 43
Blanchteau, M., 158, 160
Blasdel, G.G., 506-508, 509
Bleckman, H., 112
Bloomfield, P., 458-459
Bolles, R.C., 260, 261, 262, 268, 453
Born, D.E., 576
Boulos, Z.A., 261, 263, 266
Bowditch's, 41
Bower, G.H., 386
Bower, T.G.R., 174
Boysen, S.T., 349
Bradford, S.A., 334
Brines, M.L., 132
Broekhuizen, S., 292, 293
Brokofsky, S., 160
Brown, J., 545
Brown, T.G., 221
Brownell, P.H., 110, 111
Brunswik, E., 351
Bubis, E., 577
Bullock, D.H., 352, 564
Bünning, E., 222
Burkhalter, A., 91, 92
Bush, R.R., 376, 388
Busnel, R.G., 112
Butler, C.S., 451
Buttel-Reepen, H.B.V., 243
Byrne, J.H., 567

Cabot, R.C., 209
Campbell, K.A., 579
Capaldi, E.J., 334, 337, 341, 586
Carew, T.J., 567

Carr, H., 93, 94, 95, 97, 184
Cartwright, B.A., 113, 123, 124, 128, 130, 213
Case, L., 539
Caspers, H., 236
Catania, A.C., 297
Chapuis, N., 159
Chelberg, D., 104
Cheng, K., 113, 116, 125, 173, 174, 187, 209, 215
Church, R.M., 7, 299, 301, 302, 305, 306, 308, 309, 311, 312, 315, 318-319, 328, 329, 330, 337, 340, 341, 343, 344, 348, 349, 350, 586
Clarke, J.D., 261, 268
Cohen, N.J., 556, 559
Coleman, G.J., 261, 268
Collett, T.S., 112, 113, 116, 117, 118, 121, 123, 124, 125, 128, 130, 213
Collison, C., 160, 196, 217
Colwill, R.M., 567, 570
Comb, M., 576
Connor, J.A., 222
Cooper, R.G., 345
Corbett, D., 579
Cowcroft, P., 229
Cox, D.R., 430
Crow, T., 401
Cunningham, C.L., 402

Daan, S., 229, 230, 260
Daly, J.W., 158
Darwin, C., 144
Dashiell, J.F., 163, 165
Davenport, D.G., 564
Davis, H., 318, 319, 328, 329, 334
Dawkins, R., 352
de Lorge, J., 260, 261
Dell'Osso, L.F., 484
Dember, W.N., 162
DeMonasterio, F.M., 512
Dennis, W., 97
Deutsch, J.A., 135, 159, 174
DeValois, R.L., 509
Dijkstra, C., 260
Domjan, M., 398, 413
Douglas, R.J., 96, 162
Dow, B.M., 513, 515
Dow, S.M., 318, 374, 375, 382
Dube, M.G., 228
Dyer, F.C., 43, 77, 78, 80, 132, 133

Edmonds, S.C., 263, 272
Elder, W.H., 148
Ellard, C.G., 113, 114
Emlen, S.T., 66, 81, 82, 83, 84, 144, 145, 147
Enright, J.T., 243
Epstein, R., 451
Erkinano, E., 229
Estes, W.K., 564
Ewert, J.P., 481

Fairhurst, S., 294
Farley, J., 401
Farner, D.S., 222, 235
Fernandes, D.M., 328
Ferster, C.B., 294, 297
Feustle, W.A., 195, 218
Fischer, A., 236
Fish, J.F., 112
Fisher, C.M., 552
Fishman, H., 399
Fitzgerald, R.E., 162, 163
Flatt, I., 60
Fodor, J.A., 173, 208, 524
Forder, H.G., 181
Forel, A., 243
Fowler, H., 162
Frankel, R.B., 43
Fretwell, S.D., 353
Frey, P.W., 451
Fuchs, A.F., 545, 549
Fudim, O.K., 402
Furrow, D.R., 413

Gage, F.H., 161, 163
Gage, S.H., 209
Gaioni, S.J., 442
Gallistel, C.R., 7, 69, 73, 85, 174, 192, 201, 221, 317, 335, 338, 339, 345, 348, 459, 525, 528, 577, 578, 579, 586
Garcia, J., 398, 423, 567
Gelade, G., 529, 530, 537
Gelman, R., 7, 317, 335, 338, 339, 345, 346, 348, 586
Geschwind, N., 553
Gibbon, J., 7, 240, 288, 294, 297, 300, 301, 302, 305, 311, 315, 330, 340, 341, 343, 390, 400, 401, 422, 427, 428, 438, 443, 446, 570, 586
Gibbs, F.P., 261

Gibson, J.J., 174
Gill, F.B., 258, 288, 290
Gleitman, H., 99, 406, 564, 569
Gleitman, L.R., 99
Glimcher, P., 579
Gluck, M.A., 406, 566, 567, 569
Goddard, M.J., 438
Godin, J.J., 353, 354
Goetz, C.V., 261, 266, 267, 272, 275, 277, 279, 283
Gold, L., 400, 401, 427, 428, 443, 446
Gomita, Y., 579
Gonzales, R.C., 564
Goodale, M.A., 113, 114
Goodman, H.M., 576
Gormezano, I., 399
Goshtasby, A., 209
Gould, C.G., 79, 131
Gould, J.L., 43, 77, 78, 79, 80, 130, 131, 132, 133, 134, 145
Gouras, P., 512
Graf, V., 352
Gratton, A., 579
Graue, L.C., 90
Green, L., 291
Greenberg, M.E., 576
Greene, L.A., 576
Griffin, D.R., 147
Grünwald, A., 97
Guevrekian, L., 324
Gunier, W.J., 148
Guthrie, B.L., 483
Gwinner, E., 235

Haberlandt, K., 390, 393, 412, 413, 415, 416, 426
Hager, J.L., 581
Hallet, P., 484
Hamilton, P.V., 77
Handelmann, G.E., 196, 217
Harkness, L.I.K., 117, 118
Harper, D.G.C., 356, 357
Harper, S., 261, 268
Harth, E., 30
Hauenschild, C., 236
Hawkes, L., 297
Hawkins, R.D., 399, 406, 566, 567, 569, 570, 572
Hearst, E., 406
Hegel, M.T., 333, 344, 349
Hegge, F.W., 459

Held, F.P., 402
Hendrickson, A.E., 503
Hering, E., 508, 510
Herrnstein, R.J., 361, 362, 366, 367, 368
Heth, C.D., 402, 451, 568
Hilbert, D., 181
Hinton, G.E., 386
Hoffman, D.K., 236
Hoin-Radovsky, I., 112
Holland, R., 483
Holloway, F.A., 278, 279
Holman, E.W., 402
Holmes, N.K., 564
Holst, E. von, 221
Honig, W.K., 196, 564
Honmah, K.I., 261, 266, 267, 272, 275, 277, 279, 283
Honzik, C.H., 97
Horridge, G.A., 113
Horter, M., 283
Horton, J.C., 506
Hu, M.K., 210
Huang, T.S., 209
Hubel, D.H., 503, 504, 505, 506, 508
Hull, C.L., 86, 388, 406, 568
Hull, E.M., 509
Hulse, S.H., 186, 191
Hunsicker, J.P., 280
Hunt, E.L., 398, 567
Hurvich, L.M., 508, 511
Huston, J.P., 86
Hyman, S.E., 576

Isenberg, L., 539
Isler, R., 162, 163

Jacklet, J.W., 222
Jacob, F., 574
James, P.H.R., 564
Jameson, D., 508, 511
Jander, R., 78
Janzen, D.H., 139, 158, 288
Jarrard, L.E., 195, 218
Jay, M.F., 487
Jenkins, H.M., 438, 451
John, R.E., 246
Johnson, C., 161, 163
Johnson, D.M., 322, 348-349, 350
Judson, H., 562

Kalat, J.W., 83, 581

Kalish, D., 216
Kamil, A.C., 163, 292
Kamin, L.J., 390, 391, 392, 442, 569
Kandel, E.R., 399, 401, 406, 566, 567, 569, 570, 572
Kaplan, P., 406
Kaufman, E.L., 344, 345
Kaufman, M.A., 453
Kavanau, J.L., 162
Keenleyside, M.H.A., 353, 354
Keeton, W.T., 146, 147
Keppel, G., 545
Killeen, P., 288, 297, 300
Kimmeldorf, D.J., 398, 567
Kincaid, J.P., 549
Kirchner, W.H., 113
Klahr, D., 346
Kleber, E., 243
Klein, F., 177
Knudsen, E.I., 480, 481
Koehler, O., 317
Koffka, K., 29
Köhler, W., 29, 30
Koltermann, R., 248, 250, 251, 278
Komeily-Zadeh, F.N., 299, 312
Konishi, M., 112, 481
Konorski, J., 385
Kramer, G., 144
Kreithern, M.L., 146
Kremer, E.F., 442, 569
Kruyt, W., 104
Kubie, J.L., 3

Land, M.F., 121, 123
Landau, B., 99
Lashley, K.S., 524
Lavie, N., 539
Lawton, D., 104
Le Lorec, A., 158, 160
Lea, S.E.G., 318, 374, 375, 382
Lee, C., 490
Lee, D.N., 98
Lehmann, U., 230
Lehrer, M., 113
Lejeune, H., 292, 294
Levine, M., 163
Levinthal, C.F., 399
Levitt, T., 104
Lewis, P.A.W., 430
Lieblich, I., 135, 140, 174
Lightstone, A.D., 484

Linblom, L.L., 451
Lindauer, M., 132, 133, 256
Livingston, M.S., 505, 506, 508
Lock, A., 118
Locurto, C.M., 400, 401, 427, 428, 443, 446
Loess, H., 549
Logan, F.A., 390, 393, 412, 413, 415, 416, 426
Logue, A.W., 291, 398, 413
Lohmann, M., 231
Lord, M.W., 344, 345
Lott, D.F., 97
Loveland, D.H., 366, 367, 368
Lucas, D., 210
Lucas, H.L.J., 353
Lynch, S., 553

Maaskamp, F., 292, 293
Mack, A.L., 258
Mackintosh, N.J., 352, 391, 392, 394, 564
Maki, W.S., 160
Mandler, G., 345, 346, 347
Margolin, C.M., 399
Margules, J., 192, 201
Mariscal, R.N., 140
Marlow, R.W., 145
Marr, D., 214
Martin, D.D., 85
Matsuzawa, T., 332
Matthews, G.V.T., 83, 90
Matzel, L.D., 402, 453, 454
Mays, L.E., 484, 485
Mazur, J.E., 291
McCleery, R.H., 285
McClelland, J.L., 386, 393
McCloskey, M., 556, 559
McDiarmid, C., 324
McFarland, D.J., 385
Mead, W.R., 509
Mechner, F., 319, 320, 324, 350
Meck, W.H., 7, 299, 301, 302, 306, 308, 311, 312, 315, 318-319, 329, 330, 337, 340, 341, 343, 344, 348, 349, 350, 586
Medugorac, I., 256
Meier, A.H., 85
Melgren, R.L., 280
Melton, A.W., 545, 549
Memmott, J., 318, 319, 328
Menzel, E., 165, 167
Miezin, F.M., 369, 372, 587
Miliaressis, E., 579

Miller, D.J., 334, 337, 341, 586
Miller, R.R., 402, 453, 454, 568
Mis, F.W., 399
Mittelstaedt, H., 68, 71
Mittelstaedt, M.L., 68
Modenov, P.S., 177
Möhres, F.P., 150, 151
Moiseff, A., 481
Monod, J., 574
Moot, S.A., 260, 261, 262, 268
Morgan, H.C., 509
Morris, R.G.M., 152
Mosteller, F., 376, 388
Mountcastle, V.B., 520
Müller, H.G., 149
Muller, R.A., 3
Munn, N.L., 218
Myers, C.W., 158
Myerson, J., 369, 372, 587

Nachmias, J., 406, 569
Nadel, L., 174, 215
Nägeli, H.H., 162
Neisser, U., 406, 569
Nelson, J.S., 483
Nelson, P., 104
Neuringer, A.J., 363, 364
Neuweiler, G., 150, 151
Nissen, M.J., 537, 539
Norman, D.A., 545
Noyd, D.E., 549

Oettinger, R., 162, 163
O'Gorman, L., 209
O'Keefe, J., 174, 215
O'Leary, D.K., 186, 191
Ollove, M., 423, 457
Olton, D.S., 160, 161, 162, 163, 194, 195, 196, 217, 218
Ornstein, R.E., 222

Papas, B.C., 162, 194
Papi, F., 145, 146
Parkhomenko, A.S., 177
Pashler, H., 530
Pavlov, I., 391
Pelchat, R.J., 268, 269, 273
Perachio, A.A., 503
Peterson, L.R., 545
Peterson, M.J., 545
Pick, H.L., 174

Pickhard, A., 113, 116, 125
Pittendrigh, C.S., 227
Platt, J.R., 322, 348-349, 350
Pliskoff, S.S., 369
Polson, M.C., 509
Porter, J.D., 486
Poucet, B., 159
Pratt, K., 209
Precht, W., 69
Price, T., 390, 393, 412, 413, 415, 416, 426

Quine, D.B., 146
Quinn, T.P., 43

Rachlin, H., 291
Rachlin, H.C., 359, 360
Ranck, J.B.J., 3
Redmond, D.P., 459
Reese, T.W., 344, 345
Reiss, S., 444
Renner, M., 81, 255, 256
Rescorla, R.A., 385, 390, 392, 394, 395, 396, 398, 402, 405, 406, 408, 410, 413, 414, 415, 416, 418, 432, 437, 438, 443, 451, 468, 564, 568, 570, 588, 589
Revusky, S., 398, 423, 567
Reynolds, G.S., 297, 392
Richelle, M., 292, 294
Richter, C.P., 260
Rijnstrop, A., 260
Rilling, M., 324, 326, 329
Ritchie, B.F., 216, 217
Roberts, A., 222
Roberts, B., 222
Roberts, M.L., 567, 570
Roberts, S., 306
Roberts, S.K., 224
Roberts, W.A., 96, 160, 162, 169
Robinson, D.A., 481
Robson, J.G., 214
Rohrer, W.H., 490
Rompré, P.-P., 578, 579
Rongstad, O.J., 292, 293
Rosenberg, E., 162, 163
Rosenquist, A.C., 501
Rosenwasser, A.M., 261, 263, 266, 268, 269, 273
Rozin, P., 83, 581
Rubel, E.W., 576
Rumbaugh, D.M., 333, 344, 349
Rumelhart, D.E., 386, 393

Russell, B.J., 77
Russell, T.R., 258
Russell, W.R., 551, 555, 556

Saint Paul, U.V., 65, 66
Salafia, W.R., 399
Salama, G., 506-508, 509
Samuelson, R.J., 160, 161
Sanderson, A.C., 209
Santchi, F., 77
Savage-Rumbaugh, S., 333, 344, 349
Schachtman, T.R., 453
Scharlock, D.P., 217
Schein, S.J., 512
Schiller, P.H., 482, 484
Schlapfer, W.T., 551, 552, 564
Schlichte, H.J., 146
Schmidt-Koenig, K., 90, 146
Schmiedler, 132
Schneiderman, N., 399
Schwartz, B., 399
Schwartz, E., 112
Seligman, M.E.P., 581
Shavalia, D.A., 160, 162
Shebo, B.J., 345, 346, 347
Shepard, R.N., 54
Sherry, D., 157
Shiffrin, R.M., 545
Shizgal, P., 578, 579
Shuster, K., 454
Sibly, R.M., 285
Sing, H.C., 459
Skinner, B.F., 162, 294, 297, 451, 866
Skucy, J.C., 451
Slocum, J., 40, 41
Slopsema, S., 230
Smith, J.N.M., 352
Smith, W.C., 564
Smolensky, P., 359, 387
Snyder, C.R.R., 539
Sobel, E., 112
Sparks, D.L., 483, 484, 485, 486, 487, 490
Spear, N.E., 568
Spelke, E., 99, 345
Squire, L.R., 551, 552, 564
Srinivasan, M.V., 60, 61, 113
Staddon, J.E.R., 369
Starkey, P., 345
Stein, H.v., 240, 295, 296
Stein-Beling, I.v., 222
Stellar, J.R., 577, 578, 579

Stewart, K., 261
Stokes, L.W., 260, 261
Stoltz, S.P., 97
Stryker, M.P., 482, 484, 506
Sturgis, R.D., 278
Suga, N., 497
Sutherland, N.S., 352
Suzuki, S., 162, 183
Sykes, M., 529
Szymanski, J.S., 222

Tartell, R.H., 399
Terman, M., 261, 263, 266, 294
Terrace, H.S., 400, 401, 427, 428, 443, 446
Tester, J.R., 292, 293
Thinus-Blanc, C., 159
Thompson, J.A.I., 98
Thompson, R.F., 401, 406, 566, 567, 569
Thorne, D.R., 459
Thorpe, W.H., 139
Tigges, J., 503
Tigges, M., 503
Timney, B., 113, 114
Tinbergen, N., 104
Tinkelpaugh, O.L., 168, 170
Tolhurst, D.J., 512
Tollestrup, K., 145
Tolman, E.C., 174, 216
Tomback, D.F., 155
Townsend, J.T., 531, 534
Treadway, M., 556, 559
Treisman, A., 529, 530, 537
Tsal, Y., 539
Tucker, M.F., 346
Tulving, E., 560
Turek, F.W., 222
Turek, R.J., 155

Underwood, B.J., 545, 564
Uster, H.J., 162

Van Essen, D.C., 501, 502
Vander Wall, S.B., 155, 157
Varner, D., 511
Vautin, R.G., 513, 515
Volkman, J., 344, 345
Von Frisch, K., 132, 133, 247

Wagner, A.R., 390, 392, 393, 408, 410, 412,
    413, 414, 415, 416, 418, 422, 426, 444, 588
Wahl, O., 243, 244, 248, 249, 253, 254, 255

Walcott, C., 146
Walker, J.A., 161, 163
Wallace, G.K., 112
Wallace, J.G., 346
Wallach, H., 30
Walraff, H.G., 145, 146
Walters, E.T., 567
Wansley, R., 278, 279
Waraczynski, M., 578, 579
Waring, A., 294
Wasserman, E., 388
Watson, A.B., 214
Watson, J.B., 93, 94, 97, 184
Waugh, N.C., 545, 549
Webb, W.B., 228
Wehner, R., 60, 61, 113, 116, 125, 130, 135
Werz, M.A., 160
Whitten, W.B., 549
Whitty, C.W.M., 551
Wickens, D.D., 545, 549
Wiesel, T.N., 503, 504, 506
Wilson, J.R., 503
Wise, R.A., 579

Yadin, E., 579
Yanovski, J.A., 577
Yarnell, P.R., 553
Yeomans, J.S., 578, 579
Yerkes, D.N., 168, 170
Yerkes, R.M., 168, 170
Yonas, A., 174

Zahn, R.R., 484
Zangwill, O.L., 551
Zeki, S., 529
Zhang, S.W., 113
Ziff, E.B., 576
Zoladek, L., 96, 160

Subject Index

A priori memory linkages, disadvantages of, 541–542
Abstraction principle, of counting, 338–341
Acoustic fovea, 493–494
Ad hoc parametric assumptions, in associative modeling, 381, 412
Adaptive specializations, in learning, 83, 173
Addition
of numerons, 330, 348–350
of temporal intervals, 307
Additivity
in apportionment problem, 589
in classical conditioning, 9, 424
in representational theory of conditioning, 424–425
in Rescorla-Wagner model, 413
Affine geometry, 105, 128–129, 179
Affine transformations
bee navigation and, 128–129, 140
description of, 179–182
rat navigation and, 185, 188–189, 202–204
Amphiprion, homing in, 140–141
Amplitopic mapping, in bat DSCF, 496–498
Analogue computers, 29
Anemones, homing to, 140
Angle invariance in landmark recognition, 122
Angle worms, density of, 385
Angular deviation from optic axis, tectal mapping of, 478–488
Angular distance, animal perceptions of, 110, 125
Angular measurement, 21
Angular position of stimulus, 10
Animals. *See specific animals*

Ant(s)
dead reckoning in, 57, 59–65
foraging journey of, 583
spatial orientation of, 1
sun-compass orientation and, 77, 78
transition from dead reckoning to piloting, 91–93
Anticipation, of events recurring within periods, 287
Anticipation of daily feeding time
in bees, 243–252
in birds, 300
circadian phase and, 263
computational model of, 273–277
dusk-onset activity and, 266
entrainment and, 262–263
failure of occurrence, 253, 275, 300
in rats, 260–273
Aplysia
conditioning in, 566–567
dead reckoning of, 573
sun-compass orientation and, 77, 78
Apparent size, use in bee navigation, 124
Arcs of position, 49–50
Arthropods, cognitive map of, 171–172
Associations
between color and shape, 535
formation of, 570–571, 584
pairing and, 397–398
and temporal order, 404
Associative bonds
memory and, 527–528
strength of, 386–388, 409, 564, 570, 588
types of, 404
Associative conditioning models, 421, 570
Associative learning
cellular mechanism of, 566–567
models, kernel learning process of, 581
premodern view of, 566

Associative process, in classical conditioning, 8
Associative theories
a priori linkages in memory and, 541–542
associative strength and, 259
computationally complex character of, 418–419
distinction between computation and storage, 563–565
of memory, disadvantages of, 541–542
memory and, 387
multidimensional, 390–391, 417
poison-avoidance conditioning and, 398
premodern, 388–390
reconceptualization of, 417–419
representational character of, 387
temporal localization in, 394
unidimensional, 387
Attention process, 529
Auditory cortex, functional anatomy of, 501
Auditory inputs, 477
Auditory mechanisms, 116
Auditory source angle, tectal mapping of, 480–481
Auditory stimuli, triggering of saccades, 484
Autoshaping, 400, 406–408
Axonal conduction, conceptual framework for, 562
Azimuth
definition of, 44
geographic, 44
optical, 10
solar, 45–46, 57, 72, 75, 79–80, 86
of star, 83
Azimuth-time function. See Ephemeris function
Azimuthal velocity of sun, 78–80

Background conditioning. See also Blocking
habituation trials and, 445–446
indefinability of temporal pairing and, 405
representational theory of conditioning and, 436–438, 455
Rescorla-Wagner theory and, 408, 410, 413–418, 454, 569
US not paired with CS and, 394–397, 405
Backward conditioning. See Interstimulus interval (ISI)
Barn owl, 477, 478
Basilar membrane, 480
Bat(s)
auditory cortex of, 10, 492–495
avoidance of hard-to-perceive obstacles by, 150–152, 153
cry-emitting behavior of, 492–494
distal stimulus dimensions, representation of, 498–500
DSCF (Doppler-shifted constant frequency), 496–498, 500
electrophysiological evidence of vector space, 494, 495, 501
homing from unfamiliar release site, 148–150
proximal stimulus dimensions, representation of, 494–498, 500
vector spaces of, 500–501
Beacon homing
definition of, 59, 120, 149
in desert ants, 59–65
Bearing. See also Compass bearings
computation of, in dead reckoning, 74
of landmark, 44
Bearing line, 51
Bee(s)
additional landmarks for food search flight, 124–127
anticipation of daily feedings, 245, 260–261
calibration of solar ephemeris function in, 79–80
capture-and-release experiments, 139–140
concentration of food, memory for, 248–249
contour vs. point-by-point correspondence, 129–130
contour parsing in, 130
cues for, 247
daily events, distinction of, 235
daily habits of, 260
dance of, 132, 133–134, 139
dead reckoning by, 57
displacement experiment, 135–140
estimation of parallax distance, 113
foraging activities of, 59
foraging map, range of, 137–139
importance of compass bearings,

127–128
infradian periods, learning of, 287
internal time sense of, 81, 255–256, 258
landmark bearing and size, 126
large-scale map in, 131–140
local map in, 123
memory module of, records in, 525–528
metric spatial representation and, 123
periodic recurrences and, 6
phase shifting and, 255
sun-compass orientation and, 77, 78
temporal orientation of, 1
time-dependent food-seeking behavior, 259
time of occurrence and, 243–252
time-of-training effects in, 278
Bezier curve, 103–104
Bezier spline, 103
Bicoordinate navigation, 146–147
Big Dipper, 48, 84, 85
Bigons, 175
Biological clocks, 5–6
Biological oscillators. *See* Endogenous oscillators
Biological rhythms, 221–231
Bird(s). *See also* Migratory bird(s); *specific types of birds*
anticipation of daily feedings, 260–261, 300
computation of source angle and distance, 116
course holding and setting, process of, 89–91
daily events, distinction of, 235
daily habits of, 260
discrimination of number, 324–328
infradian periods, 284–286, 287
learning of cycles longer than 24 hours, 295
localization of multiple seed caches, 155–158
migratory, 40, 49
representation of elapsed intervals, 288–292
representation of experimental cycles, 295–300
short-term estimate of compass bearings and, 148
time-of-training effects in, 278
Bisection procedure, temporal, 304–305
Blobs, in primary visual cortex, 506–509
Blocking

background conditioning and, 411
in classical conditioning, 392–393
representational theory of conditioning and, 438–439
Rescorla-Wagner theory and, 408–412
retroactive, 439, 452–455
temporal pairing insufficiency and, 397, 417, 569
Boxing the compass, 90
Brain
cortical modules of, 523–524
electrical self-stimulation of, 577–579
modular representational theories of, 524
nonspatial stimulus representations, 10
Bunting, 87
Bush and Mosteller model, 376, 388–390

Calcium mining, by tortoise, 142, 144–145
Calendar-clock system, 22–23
Canaries, and experimental cycles, 295–300
Cardinal principle, of counting process, 338
Cartesian coordinates, 5, 15, 178–179
Cartesian model of dead reckoning, 57, 71–73, 74, 76
Cartesian representation, 234
Cataglyphis bicolor, dead reckoning in, 59–65
Caudo-rostro axis of head, 480
Celestial fixing of position, 55–56
Celestial pole and sphere, 46, 47, 48
Center of rotation of sky, 86, 87
Centroid of image, 54–55
CF/CF areas of bat auditory cortex, 492–493
Chameleon, route choices of, 116–118, 158
Change-over delay, 359
Chemical characteristics file, in memory module, 526
Chickadees, localization of seed caches, 157–158
Chimpanzee
counting process in, 332–333, 344
metacognition and, 171
multiple delayed choice experiment, 168–171
numerosity labeling and addition in, 332–333
radial maze analogue, behavior in, 168–171

route choosing, 165–168
Choice, as time allocation, 359–361
Chromatic opponency, 512–513
Chronometer, marine, 56
Chunking of memories, 542
Cichlids, ideal free distributions of, 353–356
Circadian oscillations
  endogenous, 261
  entrainment to day-night cycle, 45, 226–229
Circadian oscillators. *See also* Oscillators
  effect of phase shifts on, 81
  emphermis function and, 72, 75, 81
  entrainment of, 223
  food-entrainable, 273
  history of their recognition, 222
  phase of, 6, 238
  time-of-day learning and, 254–256
  timing signals and, 264
Circadian phase. *See* Time of occurrence
Circadian rhythm, 6
Circannual oscillations, 235–236
Circles of position, 49–50
Circuitry, in coding relative spatial position, 176
Circular vs. sine-cosine measure of angular position, 72
Circumpolar sky, 48, 84
Classical conditioning
  additivity principle in, 9
  associative theories of, 564
  dependence on other associations, 8, 390–391, 588
  models of, 164
  nonassociative analysis of, 8–9
  pathway independence assumption of, 164
  rate computation and, 587–588
  reductionist analysis, implications for, 570, 593
  representational theory of, 421–475
  temporal pairing in, 8, 397–398
  vs. naturalistic approach to learning, 7–8
Clock-shifting experiments, 81–83, 147
Clocks, internal. *See* Oscillators
Cockroach, entrainment of, 223–225, 231
Code-mediated isomorphisms, 28–29
Cognitive map(s)
  affine transformations, 128–129
  apparent size and, 124–125
  of arthropods, 171–172

in avoiding obstacles, 150–152, 153
in chameleon route choices, 116–118
comparative primatology in analogue of radial maze, 168–171
compass bearings and, 123–124, 127–128
construction of, 106–109, 583
contour vs. point-by-point correspondence, 129–130
dead reckoning and, 88–89
definition of, 5, 103–104
differing geometric powers of, 5, 105, 176–177
estimation of egocentric distance and angle in, 110–112
evidence of, in animals, 121–123
in honey bee, 123, 131–140
landmarks, and, 125–127
metric nature of, 121, 133, 140
nonegocentric estimates of distance in toad, 118–120
in orientation to multiple goal sites, 154–158
piloting and, 4, 120–123
remembrance of places passed and, 159–165
in route choosing, 158–159, 165–168
scales for, multiplicity of, 213–214, 584
shape of environment and, 174
spatial relationships and, 583
of stars, 84
strength of geometric representation in, 104–106
use for, other than homing, 141–142, 143
of vertebrates, 171–172
Collinearity operator, 18, 20
Color
  bee memory for, 251–252
  mapping of, 535
  primary visual cortex and, 506, 508–509
  time of occurrence and, 248, 250, 251–253
Color judgements, 10
Color space, psychophysical, 509–518
Color vision, 518–520
Columnar organization, 497–498, 502–503
Compass bearings
  in bee food search flight, 123–124, 127–128
  crossed, 126
  and dead reckoning, in maze running rat, 93–96
  definition of, 44
  determination from map, 89

as metric relation, 140
Compass orientation. *See also* Heading
  in dead reckoning, 76–77
  hormonal conditions and, 85–86
  maze performance and, 94–96
  neural sensitivity to, 3
  sense of, 90, 94–95, 184, 192, 200, 212
  from stars, 85
Compass sense, 200–202
Complex demodulation, 459
Computation
  definition of, 30–31
  with temporal interruptions, 306
  vs. storage, 563–565
Computational model
  of anticipatory circadian activity,
    273–277
  of cognitive map construction, 106–109
  of dead reckoning, 71–76
  of elapsed intervals, 307–311
  of frequency-domain, for classical
    conditioning, 461–466
  of rate matching, 369–373
Computational vs. storage processes,
  30–32
Computational-representational theories
  of brain function, 3, 10–12, 38
Conditional learning, 2
Conditional rate estimation theory, 589
Conditioned emotional reaction paradigm
  (CER paradigm), 395–397, 402, 415, 452
Conditioned inhibition, 406
Conditioned stimulus (CS)
  association with US, 588
  blocking, 392–393
  in classical conditioning, 164
  insufficient pairing with US, 569
  in multidimensional associative learning
    theory, 390–391
  overshadowing of, 391–392
  predictive sufficiency, 393–394
  preexposure to, 446
  in premodern associative learning
    theory, 388–390
  rate of ocurrence and, 9
  relationship with US, 386
Conditioning, classical
  conditional rate or prevalence and, 421
  with discrete US, model for, 424
  duty cycle effects, 399–402
  extinction and, 564

multidimensionality of, 588
poison-avoidance, 398
representational theory of. *See* Represen-
  tational theory of conditioning
temporal dependencies of, 385–386
with undefinable ISIs, 405
underlying computations in, 579–580
with zero or negative ITIs, 402–405
Conditioning theories, 164, 386, 588–589
Conjunction targets, 530–531
Conjunctive search tasks, 532–534
Connectionist models of human memory,
  393
Conscious access, 332
Consolidation, theory of, 564
Constellations, 46–47, 84
Constraining principles, of representa-
  tional model, 424
Content-addressable records, 526, 534
Contour parsing, 130
Contour vs. point-by-point correspon-
  dence, 129–130. *See also* Cognitive
  map(s); Bee(s)
Control transformations, 184
Coordinate-transformation computations,
  109
Coordinates
  Cartesian, 178–179
  systems of, 42–43
Corrected rate vector, 434
Correspondence problem, in image
  matching, 129–130
Cortical fields, multiplicity of, 10
Cortical neurons, 10–11
Counting
  abstraction principle of, 338–339
  adaptive nature of, 318–319
  cardinal principle of, 338
  different kinds of rewards in rat and,
    334–338
  formal analysis of, 338–343
  in mapping process, 338–339, 586
  Meck and Church model of, 340–343
  number representations and, 318
  one-one principle of, 338
  order-irrelevance principle of, 338
  process of, 237
  in rate estimation, 374
  stable-order principle of, 338
  stimuli, 328–330
  subitizing, 343–348

Course, setting vs. holding of, 89–91
"Course made good," 36–37
Crossbearings, 50–52
Cross-fixes, 50–52
Cross-validation, in isomorphisms, 21
CS-US prediction function, 560
Cues
  for bees, 247
  in dead reckoning, 96
  for homing, 98
  for gerbils, 115
Culmination, 46
Current vector, 476

Dashiell maze, 163
Dead reckoning
  accuracy of, 39–41
  as animal behavioral phenomenon, 573
  in animal navigation, 37–38
  in desert ant (Cataglyphis bicolor), 59–65
  calibration of ephermis function, 79–80
  Cartesian model of, 57, 71–73, 74, 76
  cognitive map and, 58, 88–89, 96, 99, 101,
    106–107, 583
  and compass bearings, in maze running
    rat, 93–96
  computational models of, 70–76
  cue in, 96
  definition of, 4
  experimental evidence of, 57
  in familiar terrain, 91
  in geese, 65–68
  in humans, 98–101
  inertial, 68–69, 95, 146–147
  integration process in, 573–574
  interplay with piloting, 58, 88–89
  maintenance of compass orientation in,
    76–77
  in map construction, 58
  maze behavior and, 96–98
  moving through familiar space and,
    93–94
  multimodal inputs in, 69
  in navigation, 35–41
  polar coordinates and, 57
  polar model of, 73, 75–76
  semi-inertial, in gerbil, 68–70
  setting vs. holding a course, 89–91
  stellar orientation and, 83–88
  transition to piloting, 91–93
Decay or accumulation processes, 237
Delimitation, of rewards, 335–336

Desert tortoise, 142, 144, 145
Digger wasp, survey flight of, 104–105
Direct isomorphisms, 28–29
Discrete trials theory, 410
Discriminative stimulus, numerosity as,
  319–328
Disjunctive targets, search for, 529–535
Displacement
  ant experiments, 61
  bat experiments, 148–150
  computation of, 57
  geese experiments, 65
  geometric view of, 179
  pigeon experiments, 66, 81, 89, 144–148
Displacement transformations, 179, 180,
  183
Distal stimulus
  dimensions, vector representation of,
    498–500
  vs. proximal stimulus, 477–478
Distance
  comparisons, in chameleon, 116
  egocentric, estimation by sand scorpion,
    110–112
  nonegocentric estimation by toad,
    118–120
  parallax, estimation of, 112–116
Distance and velocity maps, in bat,
  492–494
Distance-comparing operator, 21
Distance perception, 110–111, 125
Distance triangulation. See Parallax
  distance
Distractor stimuli, 529–530
Domain of numerosity, 338–339
Dominance hyperstrips, 506, 507
Doppler-shifted-constant-frequency field
  (DSCF), 496–498
Double-opponent cells, 513
Double-saccade procedure, 485–486
DRL schedules (differential reinforcement
  of low rates), 291–292
Duck(s)
  foraging strategy of, 2
  ideal free distributions of, 356–359
  matching on basis of reward rates and
    magnitude, 363–366
Duty cycle. See ITI/ISI ratio

Earth, center of rotation, 47, 48
Effect, law of, 162

Efference copy, 73
Egocentric angle estimates, in sand
    scorpion, 110–112
Egocentric distance estimates
  in locust, 112
  in sand scorpion, 112
Egocentric north, 43
Egocentric representations, 41, 43, 54,
    106–109
Electromagnetically propagating waves,
    116
Endogenous oscillators, 5, 221–225
Engram, search for
  associative theory and, 566–567
  dead reckoning and, 573
  electrical self-stimulation and, 577–579
Entrainment
  anticipatory feeding behavior and,
    261–264, 272–273
  of bees' endogenous oscillations, 255–256
  in daily activity of cockroach, 223–225
  definition of, 223
  model of, 276
  in temporal interval determination,
    239–241
  underlying principle of, 225
Environment, anticipated image of, 53
Ephemeris angle, 72
Ephemeris function
  bee navigation and, 57, 131
  calibration of, 79–80, 134
  phase shifiting and, 81
  stellar, 83
  in sun-compass orienting, 72, 75, 77, 134
Ephemeris tables, 45, 46
Episodic memory, vs. propositional,
    558–560
Erlangen program, 177, 183
Euclidean geometry, 176
Euclidean representations, 5
Eukaryotic organisms, magnetic compass
    sense of, 43
Euler's identity, 462
Eunis viridis, 236
Evolution, probability learning and, 352
Experience, remembered, unity of, 11
Explicitly unpaired condition, 405–406,
    437
Extinction, 412, 450–451, 564, 567
Eyeblink conditioning, duty cycle and,
    399–400

Fall migration, 85
Family get-togethers, scheduling of,
    292–295
Feature integration theory of attention,
    529
Feeding cycles, 48-hour, 295
FI scallop, 297, 306
Finches, experimental cycles of, 295–300
Fish. See also specific fish
    Amphiprion, homing in, 140–141
  homing of, 140
  ideal free distribution of, 353–356
  puddle jumping, 141–143
  use of map for purposes other than
    homing, 141–142, 143
Fix-taking process, 122, 584
Fixed-interval scallop (FI scallop), 297, 306
Fixed-interval schedule (FI schedule), 297
Fixed-time schedule (FT schedule), 297,
    299–300
Fixes. See also Position
  celestial, 55
  global, 54
  intermittent taking of, 97
  running, 52–53, 88
  stationary, 50–52
Fixing position, by sightings, 49–55
Flow diagrams, 71, 315
Flowers, artificial, 290–292
FM/FM areas of bat auditory cortex,
    498–500
FM sweep, 492
Focused attention, 529
Food-caching, 154–158
Food-seeking behavior
  intensity of, 250–251, 254, 259
  time-dependent preferences, 259
  time of occurrence and, 243–252
Foraging behavior
  of ant, 583
  of bee, 59, 137–139
  choice as time allocation and, 359–361
  rate of success, matching law and,
    361–363
  rates of return and, 382–383
  of sea gulls, 385
Forgetting, theories of, 564
Frame of reference, 585
Frequency-domain representation, of CS

and US occurrence, 463–466
Frogs, orientation, 158
Functional specificity, of individual
  neurons, 491
Functional structures
  for classical conditioning, 467
  for dead reckoning, 74–75
  for interval timing behavior, 311–315

Geese, dead reckoning in, 65–68
Gene separation, measurement of,
  561–562
Gene transcription, transmitter-con-
  trolled, 574–577
Generalization procedure, for remember-
  ing and comparing elapsed intervals,
  304
Genetic theory, classical, 561
Geocentric coordinates, 43, 106–107
Geocentric heading, 70
Geocentric maps, 106–107, 124, 583–584
Geocentric representations, 106–109
Geocentric system, origin of, 106–109
Geographical position of sun, 45
Geometric module in rat
  affine transformations and, 202–204
  for coding metric relations and sense,
    199–200
  compass sense, importance of, 200–202
  global congruence and, 205–207
  and nongeometric stimuli, 204–205
  purpose of, 173
Geometric properties of surfaces,
  definition of, 212
Geometric spatial relationships
  heuristic principles of, 174–177
  metric assumptions, 174
Geometry
  analytic, 178–179
  definition of, 174
  Euclidean, 176
  hierarchial structure of, 105, 113, 177–182
  projective, 105
  types of, 174
Gerbil(s)
  estimation of parallax distance, 113–116
  homing in, 57
  semi-inertial dead reckoning in, 68–70
Gestalt theory of isomorphism, 29–30
Global determination, of position and
  heading, 53–55
Global fixes, 54

Gobiid fish, 141–142, 143
Grid north, 43, 44
Grids, navigational, 42
Gull(s), foraging behavior of, 2, 385

Hampton Court Maze, Postscript
  encoding of, 109
Hamster(s), circadian cycle entrainment,
  226–229
Hare(s), nursing of, 292–294
Harmonic oscillation, 234
Heading
  compass, maintenance of, 76–77
  definition of, 35
  determination by astronomical reference,
    44–45
  determination by global rotation, 53,
    190–191
  determination by reference to terrain,
    134
  determination of, 5, 43–44, 48–49, 89–90,
    98
  sense of, maintenance of, 90, 94–96, 184
  from stars, 46, 85
  sun-compass, 77, 78
Heart muscle, rhythmic contractions of,
  221
Herrnstein's matching law, 361–363, 369
Hippocampus, 3
Holographic schemes, 491
Homing
  in *Amphiprion*, 140–141
  in ant, 61
  in bat, 148–150
  beacon. *See* Beacon homing
  cues for, 98
  in desert ants, 59–65
  failures of motivation, 149
  by geese, 65–68
  in gerbil, 57
  in hoverfly, 121–122
  in pigeons, 66, 81–83, 144–148
  from unfamiliar release sites, 144–150
Honey bee. *See* Bee(s)
Humans
  dead reckoning in, 98–101
  multiple delayed choice experiment,
    168–171
Hummingbird(s)
  conditional learning of, 1–2
  traplining by, 288–290
  win-shift strategy of, 163

Ideal free distribution
definition of, 353
of ducks, 356–359
of fish, 353–356
Identity transformation, 183, 184
Image alignment, algorithms for, 209–211
Impenetrability
computational reasons for, 207–211, 584
evolutionary reasons for, 211–212
Incentive theories, 87
Indigo buntings, 84–85
Indirect isomorphisms, 28–29
Inertia, 443, 589
Inertia assumption, 449
Inertia of rate estimates in classical conditioning, 9, 425
Inertial dead reckoning, by pigeons, 146–147
Information-processing models, 311
Infradian oscillations, 222, 284–286
Infradian periods, learning of, 287
Inhibitory association, between CS and US, 406
Inhibitory conditioning, 405–408, 437, 455, 568
Insect(s). See also specific insects
maintenance of compass orientation in, 77
memory for time of day in, 261
parallax distance estimation in, 115–116
time-of-training effects and, 278
Integration
of angular velocity with respect to time, 57, 95
cellular basis of, 574
in dead reckoning, 573–574
of linear velocity with respect to time, 37, 57, 73–76
physical simplicity of, 38, 574
by transmitter-controlled gene transcription, 574–577
Integrator, temporally stable
in dead reckoning, 573
necessary properties of, 573–574
Interference, temporal, 545–548
Internal circadian oscillation, 283–284
Internal clocks. See Oscillators
Interruptions, effect on timing intervals, 306
Interstimulus interval (ISI). See also ITI/ISI ratio

associative process and, 566–567
classical conditioning and, 399–402, 589
inhibitory vs. excitatory conditioning and, 407
undefinable, conditioning with, 405
zero or negative, 402
Intertrial interval (ITI). See also ITI/ISI ratio
conditioning and, 399–402
negative or zero, conditioning with, 402–404
Interval sense, vs. phase sense, 240–241
Interval and phase timing, in hares, 293–294
Intervals, elapsed
animal representation of, 288
changes in, 299–300
computational model of, 309–311
definition of, 288
remembering and comparing, 300–309
representation of, 288–294, 317
Isomorphisms
between objective temporal intervals and brain processes, 315
between points in time, 22–23
cross-validation in, 21
defined between systems, 24
definition of, 15–16
direct vs. indirect or code-mediated, 28–29
Gestalt theory of, 29–30
natural selection and, 27–28
numerical representation of mass, 16–17
simple-to-simple and complex-to-complex, 18–20
theory of measurement and, 16
ITI/ISI ratio
associative strength and, 568
conditioning and, 399–402
inhibitory conditioning and, 406–408
representational model and, 456, 466, 590

Kestrels, 260
Kinesthetic stimulus, for maze behavior, 97, 98

Labeled associations, 404
Lamarckian fallacy, 562
Landmarks
recognition by hoverfly, 122
use of, by bee, 125–128

vs. signs, 218–219
Laplace transforms of time series,
    461–462
Latent inhibition, 443–446, 454
Latitude, 37–38
Law of effect. *See* Selection by conse-
    quences
Learning
    adaptive specialization in, 83, 173
    animal, zoological tradition of, 7–8
    animal behavior and, 2–3
    computational-representational
        approach to, 315
    early, of stellar orientation, 83–88
    first-order, 87
    incentive theories of, 87
    as information accumulation, 33
    as neuronal phenomenon, 24
    rate of, 259
    representational analysis vs. physiologi-
        cal basis, 12
    representational approach to, 88, 565, 590
    second-order, 87
    by selection of consequences, 162
    Skinnerian analysis of, 364
    synaptic conductivity and, 562
Learning curve, 426–427, 587, 590
Learning law
    of Bush and Mosteller, 408
    of Rescorla-Wagner, 408–409
Learning-performance distinction, 86, 87
Learning theory, basis of generality in,
    581–582
Light, effect on circadian rhythm of
    cockroach, 223–225, 231
Light-dark cycle, 85, 273
Limit-cycle oscillations, 232
Linear distance, animal perceptions of,
    110
Linear measurement, 21
Lines of position, 49–50
Little Dipper, 47
Local magnetic north, 43
Locust(s) estimation of parallax distance,
    112–113, 115, 116
Long-term memory, 545
Longitude, 37–38
Looming, as distance cue, 115
Lubber line, 43–44

Macaque monkey, primary visual cortex

of, 501–509
Magnetic bicoordinate navigation, 147
Magnetic compass error, 89–90
Magnetic compass sense, 43, 80, 131, 133,
    147, 149, 202
Magnetic directional sense, of bats,
    149–150
Mammals, 116
Mapping process, in representation of
    numerosity, 338–340
Maps. *See also* Cognitive map(s)
    geometric relationships in, 5
    metric, 105–106, 121, 133, 135
    nonmetric, 135
Mass, numerical representation of, 16–17,
    18
Mass action, 490
Matching, on basis of reward rates and
    magnitude, 363–366
Matching addresses, 533, 534
Matching and maximizing experiments,
    587
Matching law, 361–363, 369–373
Materialist theory of mind, 561
Matrix-inversion model, 589–590
Maze behavior
    control of, in dead reckoning, 96–98
    extramaze environment and, 585
    kinesthetic stimulus for, 97
Mazes
    hexagonal, 162, 163
    radial or multi-armed, 159–162
    X-maze, 184–195
Mean, computation of, 318
Mean phase vector for recurring events,
    318
Mean reward latency computation, 318
Measurement
    theory of, 16
    of time and numerosity, 341
Megaderma lucfugus, 149
Megaderma lyra, 150–153
Memory
    a priori linkages, 541–542
    associative bonds and, 527–528
    associative learning theories and, 387
    in behavioral timing, 282
    episodic vs. propositional, 558–560
    in localization of multiple seed caches,
        156–157
    long-term or secondary, 545

material basis of, 561, 564–565
phase-dependent, 247
reference interval in, 315
retrograde amnesia and, 549–559
separate processing of stimulus
    attributes, 529–535
short-term or primary, 544–549
space and time coordinates for, 525
spatial position and, 535–539
spatiotemporal addresses and, 542, 560
state-dependent, 247
temporal position and, 543–544
time-dependent, 246–247, 282
for time vs. time-dependent memory,
    245–247, 282
Memory spaces, unidimensional vs.
    multidimensional, 389–390
Mental numbers. See Numerons
Metacognition, 171
Methamphetamine, effect on internal
    clock, 307–308
Metric geometry, 105, 128
Metric maps, 105–106, 121, 133, 135
Mice, maze running, 162
Migratory bird(s)
  behavior-production mechanisms of,
    85–86
  learning underlying compass heading
    orientation, 88
  stellar orientation of, 83–88
Minkowski metrics, 175
Missouri cave bats, homing in, 148–150
Models of learning, 164
Modular representational theory of
    learning, 558–560
Modularity, computational reasons for,
    207–211, 523
Modules, in nervous system, 32, 209,
    523–524
Monkey(s)
  in analogue of radical maze, 171
  ocular dominance variation, 501–504
  saccadic eye movements of, 482–484
  superior colliculus of, 482, 484, 487
  tectal representation of angular
    deviation, 487–488
Morris water maze, 152, 154
Motivational processes, memory and, 526,
    528
Motivational state
  as determinant of compass orientation,
    86

role in organizing behavior and memory
    utilization, 528
Multidimensionality assumption, 390–391
Multimodal basis for sense of position,
    69, 98
Mustache bat, 477
Mutations, 561
Myotis lucfugus, 149

Natural selection, 581–582, 583
Navigation
  bicoordinate, 146–147
  course setting and holding, 89–91
  by dead reckoning. See Dead reckoning
  definition of, 4, 35
  fixing position by sightings, 49–55
  heading, determination of, 43–49
  interplay between dead reckoning and
    piloting, 58
  north, types of, 43
  piloting, 41
  systems of coordinates in, 42
Nervous systems
  code for spatial position, 176–177
  modules in, 32, 209, 523–524
  quantities computed by, 31–33
  time of occurrence, recording of, 469–470
  vector representations of, 9–10, 475, 477
  vector spaces in, 475–521
Neural integration model, 575
Neuronal models of association forma-
    tion, 566–567
Nominal representations, 26–28
Noncircadian long intervals
  bee learning and, 253
  bird learning and, 300
  rat learning and, 275
Nonegocentric estimates in distance, in
    toad, 118–120
Nongeometric features
  definition of, 212
  detectability of, 204–205
  geometric module impenetrable to, 208
  global congruence of, 205–206
  location choice of rat and, 194
  rejection of shape congruences and,
    193–194, 219
Nonmetric maps, 135
Nonorthogonal system, 43
Nonoscillatory decay, 231
Normal equation, 107

North, types of, 43
"Not-response," 406
Number discrimination
  immediate transfer of, 329, 332, 337, 341
  techniques for, 319–328
  vs. discrimination of temporal interval,
    324–325
Number representations
  in computation of rate, 383
  counting model and, 586–587
  counting process and, 318
  direct testing of, 317–318
  of mass, 16–17, 18
  of rates of random occurrence, 24–26
  of space, 17–22
  of time, 22–23
Number system, 17
Numerons
  addition of, 348–350
  counting and, 338–339
  definition of, 317
  mental number and, 317
  mental operations with, 318, 322, 330,
    348
  primitive learning and, 586–587
  in statistical computations, 318
  subtraction of, 348–350
Numerosity
  discrimination of, 328–330, 333–334
  labeling and addition of, 332–333
  mapping process in representation of,
    338–340
  measurement processes for, 344. See also
    Counting
  representation of, 7
  of stimuli, 330–331
Nutcrackers, localization of seed caches,
  155–157
Nutritional factors, ultradian activity
  rhythm and, 230–231

Ocular dominance hyperstrips, 502–503
Ocular dominance variation, 501–504
Odor, time of occurrence and, 248, 250,
  251–253
One-one principle, 338
Operant conditioning, 367–368
Operators, 575
Operons, 575
Optic tectum
  auditory inputs to, mapping of, 480
  of barn owl, 480

mapping of angular deviation and, 10,
    478–479
  superficial layers of, 478
  tuning to angular deviation, 488
Order-irrelevance principle, 338–341
Orientation. See Heading
Orientation hyperstrips, 503, 506
Orientation-tuning, 503
Orthogonal system, 42
Oscillations, endogenous
  recording phases of, 586
  timing signals and, 228
Oscillators
  accuracy of, in bee, 258
  circadian, 295
  drug effects on, 307–309
  in classical conditioning, 461, 591
  effect on sun-compass navigation, 81–83
  endogenous, 5, 221–225
  free running, 225
  with measured periods, 313
  migratory bird orientation and, 83
  multiple periods of, 236
  phase locked, 313
  phase response curve for hamster, 227
  phase-setting, 223
  synchronization with external clock,
    222–223
Oscillatory processes
  definition of, 232
  in time recordings methods, 232–236
  variables in, 233–234
Outcomes, 351–352
Overprediction, 405, 442, 569
Overshadowing
  description of, 391–392
  representational theory of conditioning
    and, 425, 439–441, 455
  in Rescorla-Wagner theory, 409–412
  retroactive blocking and, 452–453
  uncertainty minimization and, 426,
    440–441
Owl(s)
  optic tectum of, 486–487
  tectal representation of angular
    deviation, 487–488

Pairing, temporal
  association and, 8, 397–398, 417–418
  in association formation, 566–567
  associative conditioning and, 401

cellular approaches to conditioning and, 566–567
implications for reductionist program, 570, 593
inhibitory conditioning and, 405–408
insufficiency of, 397, 417, 567–569
Palolo worm (*Eunis viridis*), 236
Parallax distance, estimation of
in bee, 113
formulas for, 52
in gerbil, 113–116
in locust, 112–113
in polar model of dead reckoning, 76
in wasp, 113
Parallel search process, 531–534
Parameter vectors, 103, 107
Parsing of contours, by bees, 130
Pavlovian conditioning. *See* Classical conditioning
Peak procedure, 301–304
Peak-detector hypothesis, 488–489
Perceptions, of distance, 110
Perceptual processing, 539–541
Period(s), 287, 288
Period of oscillation, 232
Periodic clocks, vs. interval clocks, 240
Phase, and interval timing, in hares, 293–294
Phase angle of oscillation, 234
Phase-dependent response, 225
Phase drift, 224–225
Phase-plane representation, 233–234
Phase-response function, 228
Phase sense, vs. interval sense, 240–241
Phase shifting, 255
Phases, 288
Photic oscillator, 273
Pigeon(s)
autoshaping paradigm in, 400
bicoordinate navigation of, 146–147
choice as time allocation, 359–361
clock-shifted, 90–91
dead reckoning by, 57–58
discrimination of number, 324–328
FI scallops and, 297–298
homing from unfamiliar release sites, 144–148
internal clock shifting, 81–83
matching on basis of reward rate and magnitude, 363–366
orientation toward home and, 65–66

phase shifting and, 255
relevant numerical operations of, 318
setting and holding of course, 89–90
time-left procedure, 305–306
Piloting
cognitive map and, 120–123
definition of, 4, 41
interplay with dead reckoning, 88–89
transition from dead reckoning, 91–93
Place
coordinates of, in memory, 528
definition of, 215, 585
vs. response, 215–216, 585
Point-by-point vs. contour correspondence, 129–130
Poison-avoidance conditioning, 398, 567
Poisson processes
aperiodic occurrences and, 468–469
in background conditioning, 405
burstiness, 378
in classical conditioning, 422–423, 457
computational properties of, 429–430
confidence intervals for rate estimates, 20, 25–26, 430–431
expected interevent interval and, 371, 400
hypothesis testing statistics and, 372
intertrial intervals and, 400
numerical representation of, 20
patch transition rates of, 369–370
statistics of, 428–430
training effects and, 588
Poisson rate processes, 25–26
Poisson transition parameter, 369
Polar system, 42
Polaris, 47, 48, 85, 90
Position. *See also* Fixes
arcs of, 49–50
celestial fixing of, 55–56
circles of, 49–50
determination of, 5
global determination of, 53–55
lines of, 49–50
Position vector, 103
Positioning
by apparent size, 130
in celestial sphere, 48–49
piloting and, 41
Precession of the axis, 47
Predicting stimulus, 9
Prediction function, 462, 466–467

Predictive sufficiency
  classical conditioning and, 393–394
Predictive sufficiency *Cont'd*
  insufficiency of pairing and, 397, 417
  representational theory of conditioning
    and, 441–442, 455
  Rescorla-Wagner theory and, 413–414
  uncertainty minimization and, 440–441,
    426
Prevalence, 421–422, 457
Primary memory, 544–549
Primary visual cortex, 501–502
Primitive learning mechanisms, 584, 585
Principal axes, 54–55, 210
Probability learning, 351–352
Projective geometry, 105
Promotor substances, 575
Propositional memory, vs. episodic,
    558–560
Proximal-error model, 484
Proximal stimulus, 477, 480, 494–498
Pseudodiscrimination. *See* Predictive
  sufficiency
Psychological level, 309
Puddle jumping, 141–142, 143

Quasi-visual neurons, 485–486

Racoon, numerosity discrimination, 334
Radial maze, 159–163
Range, 338
Range lines, 50, 51, 104
Rat(s)
  adding numerosities of stimuli, 330–331
  addition and subtraction of numerons,
    348–350
  anticipation of daily feedings, 260–261
  auditory discrimination of numerosity of
    time, 342–343
  choosing routes, 158–159
  comparisons of elapsed intervals by,
    306–309
  conditioned emotional reaction para-
    digm and, 395–397
  content of reward, effect on discrimina-
    tion, 336–337
  counting process in, 344
  counting stimuli, 328–330
  delimitation of rewards, 335–336
  discrimination of number, 319–324
  endogenous circadian clock, 265, 266
  fix-taking process for, 584

geometric module in. *See* Geometric
  module in rat
geometric power of spacial representation, 5
geometric power of spatial code, 183–184
maze behavior of, 58, 93–98
numerosity discrimination, 334
probability and, 351
relevant numerical operations of, 318
remembrance of places passed, 159–165
rewarded trials, 334–338
time-left procedure, 305–306
time-of-training effects in, 278
use of cognitive maps, 152, 154
win-shift strategy of, 163
working memory experiments, 196–199
X-maze experiment, 184–195
Rate
  computational model of, 369–373
  concurrent variable ratios and, 366–369
  of conditioning, 402
  group experiments, 353–359
  ideal free distributions, 353–359
  matching on basis of reward rate and
    magnitude, 363–366
  operant experiments with individual
    subjects, 359–369
Rate computation, 587–588
Rate constancy test, 449–450
Rate of conditioning, and ITI:ISI ratio, 456
Rate of occurrence, 351, 422–423
Rate predictions, 9
Rate-prevalence distinction, 422–423
Rates of random occurrence, 24–26
Rayleigh wave, 112
Reaction time function, slope of, 346
Recall, 544, 545
Reciprocal suppression phenomena, 266,
    268
Recognition, 121
Reference memory, 196, 312
Reflectance spectra, 509–510, 519
Reflection transformation, 188, 189
Reinforcement
  concept of, 162, 163
  over time, integration of, 318
  probability of, 367–369
Relative metric position, 103
Remembered experience. *See* Memory
Replenishment intervals, 24–26, 288–292
Representation, mathematical, 582
Representational theory of conditioning

additivity of predicted rates and,
  455–456
additivity principle of, 424–425
background conditioning and, 432,
  436–437, 455
"background" USs and, 456
blocking and, 438–439, 452–455, 456
computational realization of, 430–436,
  461–462
computing prediction functions, 466–469
constraining principles, 424
CS and US frequency domain, 463–466
duty cycle, effect of, 446–449
explicitly unpaired case, 437–438
inertia principle of, 425, 455–456
inhibitory conditioning, 455, 456
latent inhibition and, 456
model of, 424
multivariate problem of, 421–422
negative conditioning, 442–443
overshadowing and, 440–441, 456
performance assumptions, 456
Poisson processes and, 428–430
predictive sufficiency and, 441–442, 456
prevalence and, 457–461
rate constancy and, 449–450
rate-prevalence distinction, 422–423
reaction to change in rate, 450–452
response rule and, 426–428
time problem of, 422
uncertainty minimization and, 426,
  440–442, 455–456
Representations, nominal, 26–28
Repressor substances, 575
Rescorla-Wagner theory
ad hoc parametric assumptions in,
  408–417,
additivity assumption in, 425
blocking and, 409–412, 439–440
counterintuitive predictions of, 442
internal trial clock in, 570, 588
multidimensionality of learning and, 443
overshadowing in, 409–412
Response allocations, 366–369
Response rule, 426–427
Resultant-vector hypothesis, 488–491,
  514–515
Retina, 501
Retinal mapping, 480
Retinal orientation, 503, 505
Retino–tectal projection, 478–479
Retinotopic organization, 478

Retroactive blocking and unblocking,
  452–455
Retrograde amnesia
causes of, 12
memory linkages and, 549–559
recall and, 543
recovery from, implications of, 551
temporal index and, 550, 556
Rhodopsin isomerization, 476–477
Rhythms. See Oscillations, endogenous
Rotation transformation, 184
Route choice
between multiple goals, 165
and remembered relative distance, 116,
  158
Running activity, 260–262, 265, 267,
  268–273
Running fix, 52–53, 88

Saccade-related units, 482–484, 486, 489
Saccades
direction and amplitude of, 485
elicited by tectal stimulation, 481
Saccadic eye movements, 484–485
Saccadic reflex, 481–482
Sand scorpion, estimation of distance,
  110–112, 115, 116
Scalar timing theory, 301
Scalar variable, prevalence of, 423
Scalar variance hypothesis, 586
Scales of representation, 213–214
Sea anemones, homing in, 140–141
Sea gulls, foraging behavior of, 2, 385
Second messenger, 575
Second-order conditioning, 452–455
Secondary memory, 545
Selection by consequences, 86, 162
Self-stimulation of brain, 577–579
Semicircular canals, 68–69
Sensory-perceptual processes, 110
Sensory preconditioning, 402–403
Serial vs. parallel search models, 531
Shape
constancy of, in hoverfly, 122
definition of, 42, 178
of environment, 106, 172–174
memory and, 538, 539
parameters, 209
representations of, scale for, 584–585
of star patterns, 45, 84
Shipcentric north, 44
Short-period cycles, 295–296

Short-term memory, 544–549
Sighting, 131
Sine-cosine representation of angular
    position, 72, 107, 233, 238
Slit sensillium, in scorpion, 112
Songbirds, 84, 86
South American arrow poison frog, 158
South, uniqueness of, 45
Sparrows, 295–300
Spatial coordinates, memory and,
    526–527
Spatial learning, 116
Spatial position, in memory, 535–536
Spatial relationships
  hierarchy of, 178
  nervous system and, 3–4
Spatial representation
  acquisition of, in congenitally blind
    humans, 99–101
  in animal environment, 3
  dead reckoning and, 58
  numerical, 17–22
  vector, 523
Spatially oriented animal behavior, 174.
    See also Geometric module in rat
Spatiotemporal hypothesis, 540
Spatiotemporal relationship, 11
Species differences, in learning, 287
Spectra, representation of, 10
Spectral tuning curves, 513–514
Speed, in dead reckoning process, 35–41
Speed signal, origin of in dead
    reckoning, 73
Spontaneous alteration, 162–163
"Spotlight of attention" hypothesis,
    535–539
Spring migration, 85
Stable-order principle of counting
    process, 338
Stationary fixes, 50–52
Statistical representations, 25–26
Stellar orientation, 83–88
Stimulus. See also Conditioned stimulus;
    Distal stimulus; Proximal stimulus;
    Unconditioned stimulus
  attributes of, 529–535
  motivationally neutral, 402
  separate attributes of, 539–541
Storage of association
  associative conditioning models and,
    570–571

vs. computation, 563–565, 571–572
Storage problem, nerve-memory
    preparation for, 572–573, 577
Strength of association, 386–388, 409, 564,
    570, 588
Striate visual cortex. See Primary visual
    cortex
Striped splotches, 506–508
Subitizing, 344, 345
Subjective time, 261–262, 273–275
Subsymbolic representations, 387
Subtraction of numerons, 318, 323,
    348–349
Suchintensität (search intensity), 250–251,
    254, 259
Summation skills, acquisition by
    chimpanzee, 332–333
Sun
  azimuth of, 45–46
  geographical position of, 45
Sun-compass orientation, 46, 57, 77–78,
    81–83
Superior colliculus. See Optic tectum
Suppression ratio, 395, 396, 442
Symbolic representations, 387
Synthesis, 581–595
Systat Basic program, 469–473
Systems of coordinates, 42–43

Tectum
  anterior portion. See Optic tectum
  map of angular deviation, 478–488
  posterior portion (inferior colliculus), 478
Temporal address, 534
Temporal coefficient matrix, 435, 589
Temporal coordinates, 22
Temporal interference, memory and,
    544–549, 592
Temporal intervals
  addition of, 307
  computational model of, 7, 309–311
  computed from time of occurrence,
    237–238
  determination by entrainment, 239–241
  deviation in representation of, 586
  drug effects on measuring, 307–308
  in hummingbird foraging, 288–289
  interrupted, 306
  multiple simultaneous, 306–307
  natural conditions requiring memory for,
    288–289
  in representation of cycles, 298–300

representations, generation of, 6, 237–238
vs. temporal position, 22
vs. time of occurrence, 241
Temporal pairing. *See* Pairing, temporal
Temporal position
memory and, 543–544
recording of, 585–586
vs. temporal interval, 22
Temporal variables, in conditioning, 588–589
Temporal vectors, 22
Terrain features, as reference for bees, 131–132
Tertiary learning capacity, 587
Theory of conditioning, 26
Theory of measurement, 16
Time
allocation of, in pigeon, 359–360
elapsed intervals of. *See* Intervals, elapsed
memory and, 527, 528
numerical representation of, 22–23
in rate computation, 383
recording moments in, 231
representation by animals, 3, 222
vector representation of, 523
Time allocation, 359–361
Time-dependent memory, vs. memory for time, 246–247, 282
Time-left procedure, 305–306
Time memory (Zeitgedächtnis), 240, 245–247
Time of day, 6
Time of occurrence
anticipation of daily feedings, 260–273
circadian oscillators and, 6–7, 254–255
color and, 248, 250–253
in computation of temporal intervals, 237–239
computational model for anticipatory circadian activity and, 273–277
computations with, 257–259
infradian oscillations recordings, 284–286
insect recording of, 243
memory and, 245–247
noncircadian intervals, 253–254
odor and, 248, 250, 251–253
precision of recorded circadian phase and, 283–284

recording of, 586
representation of by animal, 295
time of day vs. periodicity, 253
time of training effects and, 277–283
vector representation of, 475, 476
vs. temporal intervals, 241, 253
win-shift behavior and, 164
Time-of-training effects, 280–283
Time recording methods
decay or accumulation processes, 237
oscillatory processes, 232–236
Time sense (Zeitsinn), 240
Toad(s)
nonegocentric estimates in distance, 118–120
route choosing, 158
Topological transformations, 181
Tortoises, 142, 144, 145
Trace conditioning, 406–408
Transformations
affine, 179–180
displacement, 179, 180
in Erlangen program, 177
Transposition, 184
Traplining, 288–290
Trial clock, 377, 410–411, 418, 454, 570
Triangulation, 50, 51, 124–126
True north, 43
24-hour cycle, phase of, 287

Ultradian activity rhythm
nutritional factors and, 230–231
of rodents, 228–230
Ultradian oscillators, 313
Uncertainty minimization
apportionment problem and, 589
definition of, 9
representational theory of conditioning and, 440–442
Unconditioned stimulus (US)
"background" prediction by CSs, 438
in classical conditioning, 9, 11
infrequent, CS and, 394–397
in multidimensional associative learning theory, 390–391
in premodern associative learning theory, 388–390
temporal distribution of, 164

Variable-interval schedules, 359–361, 366, 368

Variable-ratio schedules, 366–367
Variable response schedules, 368
Vasopressin, 308–309
Vector, definition of, 17
Vector representations
  of animals, 477, 520–521
  dimensionality of, 9–10
  distance and velocity maps, in bat,
    492–494
  of nervous system, 475–476
  ordered, 476
  reading maps of angular deviation,
    478–491
Vector spaces
  in associative models of memory,
    387–388
  definition of, 477
  in nervous system, 509–518
Vertebrates. *See also specific vertebrates*
  cognitive map of, 171–172
  nervous system of, 3–4
Visual cortex (striate cortex), 501
Visual inputs
  in homing of birds, 146–148
  mapping of, 480–481
Visual language, in congenitally blind
  humans, 99–101
Visual mechanisms, 116
Visual stimuli, 484
Vole(s), 228–230, 260

Wasp(s)
  capture-and-release experiments of,
    139–140
  estimation of parallax distance, 113
  foraging, 59
  parallax distance estimation in, 115
  survey flight of, 104–105
Weber's law, 586
Win-shift strategy, 163
Wirkungsgefüge, 311
Working memory, 196–199, 340, 341

X-maze experiment
  choosing by feature associations only,
    194–196
  conceptions of, 185–193

Zeitgedächtnis (time memory), 240
Zeitsinn (time sense), 240